Human Relations for Career and Personal Success

Human Relations for Career and Personal Success

Concepts, Applications, and Skills

Andrew J. DuBrin
Rochester Institute of Technology

Eleventh Edition

PEARSON

Boston   Columbus   Indianapolis   New York   San Francisco   Amsterdam
Cape Town   Dubai   London   Madrid   Milan   Munich   Paris   Montréal   Toronto   Delhi
Mexico City   São Paulo   Sydney   Hong Kong   Seoul   Singapore   Taipei   Tokyo

Vice President, Business Publishing: Donna Battista
Editor-in-Chief: Stephanie Wall
Senior Sponsoring Editor: Neeraj Bhalla
Editorial Assistant: Linda Albelli
Vice President, Product Marketing: Maggie Moylan
Director of Marketing, Digital Services and Products: Jeanette Koskinas
Executive Field Marketing Manager: Adam Goldstein
Field Marketing Manager: Lenny Ann Raper
Product Marketing Assistant: Jessica Quazza
Team Lead, Program Management: Ashley Santora

Team Lead, Project Management: Jeff Holcomb
Project Manager: Ilene Kahn
Operations Specialist: Diane Peirano
Creative Director: Blair Brown
Art Director: Janet Slowik
Vice President, Director of Digital Strategy and Assessment: Paul Gentile
Manager of Learning Applications: Paul DeLuca
Full-Service Project Management and Composition: iEnergizer Aptara®, Ltd.
Interior Designer: iEnergizer Aptara®, Ltd.
Cover Designer: iEnergizer Aptara®, Ltd.
Cover Art: Spectrum Studio/Shutterstock
Printer/Binder: RR Donnelley/Menasha
Cover Printer: Phoenix Color/Hagerstown.

Library of Congress Cataloging-in-Publication Data

Names: DuBrin, Andrew J., author.
Title: Human relations for career and personal success : concepts, applications, and skills / Andrew J. DuBrin, Rochester Institute of Technology.
Description: Eleventh edition. | Boston : Pearson, [2017] | Includes index.
Identifiers: LCCN 2015042287 | ISBN 9780134130408 | ISBN 0134130405
Subjects: LCSH: Success in business. | Organizational behavior. | Psychology, Industrial. | Interpersonal relations.
Classification: LCC HF5386 .D768 2017 | DDC 650.1 / 3—dc23 LC record available at http://lccn.loc.gov/2015042287

10 9 8 7 6 5 4 3 2 1

PEARSON

ISBN 10:   0-13-413040-5
ISBN 13: 978-0-13-413040-8

Brief Contents

Contents

New to This Edition

In addition to thoroughly updating material throughout the text, I have also made other key changes, which include the following:

- Many of the introductory cases, Human Relations in Practice inserts, and case studies have been replaced with new material.
- Sixteen chapter-introduction cases are new, and one has been updated. Seventeen new cases have been included to replace existing cases. Five Human Relations in Practice inserts have been replaced with new inserts, and two have been updated.
- The text has been streamlined in the form of deleting many concepts that cover the same idea as other concepts, and of reducing duplicate mention of some ideas. Part of the streamlining is to not include a human-relations-in-practice insert in every chapter.
- In many places within the text, I have removed some material to reduce complexity, as well as to make room for new material
- Many new self-assessments and class activities have been added to this edition including four new skill-building exercises, five new self-assessment quizzes, and two new class activities. Three Internet skill-building exercises have been replaced with new exercises.
- Eighteen new role-playing exercises (all of them linked to the case studies), and two new class activities.
- Many more examples throughout the text and case problems include job titles that refer to interesting positions that our readers now hold or aspire to including sports club manager, emergency room office manager, support center supervisor, building inspector, and construction supervisor.

Chapter 1: Human Relations and You

- Addition of the Internet and social media era as part of the history of human relations
- Factors related to the external environment, including the weather, that can influence job performance and behavior

Chapter 2: Self-Esteem and Self-Confidence

- Information about practicing public speaking to help develop self-confidence
- New and shortened self-discipline model

Chapter 3: Self-Motivation and Goal Setting

- Conscientiousness as a motive driving behavior
- Discussion of self-determination as part of employee engagement
- Self-Assessment Quiz 3-1, The Conscientiousness Quiz
- Self-Assessment Quiz 3-4, My Self-Discipline Tendencies, replaces the original version

Chapter 4: Emotional Intelligence, Attitudes, and Happiness

- New listing of several of the 100 Best Companies to Work For
- Self-Assessment Quiz 4-3, Your Decision-Making Style and Happiness

Chapter 5: Values and Ethics

- New survey about the extent of ethical problems in business
- Blowing the whistle on highly unethical and illegal conduct
- Applying Human Relations Exercise 5-2, The Ethics of Whistle-Blowing

Chapter 6: Problem Solving and Creativity

- Human Relations Self-Assessment Quiz 6-1, The Concentration and Focus Checklist, replaces the original from the previous edition.
- Engaging in creative problem solving when not at one's best in order to enhance creativity
- Applying Human Relations Exercise 6-2, Helping the Alliance Rubber Company Prosper
- Human Relations Class Activity, Creative Problem Solving and Potholes

Chapter 7: Personal Communication Effectiveness

- Section on interpersonal communication and relationship building has been deleted
- In Figure 7-3, a section on being more persuasive by speaking with a big-picture perspective instead of small details

Chapter 8: Communication in the Workplace

- Open workspaces and informal communication

Chapter 9: Specialized Tactics for Getting Along with Others in the Workplace

- Exerting emotional effort to please customers
- Providing the Wow Experience, a new component to Applying Human Relations Exercise 9-1

Chapter 10: Managing Conflict

- Brief information about racial harassment as a source of workplace conflict
- The destructive hero as a type of difficult person

Chapter 11: Becoming an Effective Leader

- Proactivity as a key leadership trait
- Engaging in face time as a behavior of effective leaders
- Leader political support as a method of attaining good relationships with subordinates

Chapter 12: Motivating Others and Developing Teamwork

- The two-factor theory of work motivation is now placed under the category of job design, rather than as a separate topic
- Self-managed work groups as a form of empowerment

Chapter 13: Diversity and Cross-Cultural Competence

- New objective data from McKinsey & Company about the organizational advantages stemming from cultural diversity
- The metacognitive (higher-order intelligence) as a new dimension of cultural intelligence

Chapter 14: Getting Ahead in Your Career

- Launching a job search with a positive attitude
- Importance of job search engines for job finding
- Helping others as a method of career advancement
- Being a star performer as a method of career advancement
- Appearing intelligent as a tactic of impression management

Chapter 15: Learning Strategies, Perception, and Life Span Changes

- MOOCs as part of e-learning
- Updated information about the teenage brain
- How knowledge sharing contributes to group learning

Chapter 16: Developing Good Work Habits

- Section on making good use of digital technology, including productivity tools (replaces section on making good use of office technology)

- The role of self-discipline in improving concentration on one key task at a time
- Human Relations Self-Assessment Quiz 16-1, A Checklist of Potential Distractions Stemming from Coworkers or Boss

Chapter 17: Managing Stress and Personal Problems

- More information about the role of wellness programs in managing job stress
- Use of www.ChooseMyPlate.gov for selecting a healthy diet, including Figure 17-7, which presents the related graphic
- New Internet Skill Builder, Stress Management Component of Wellness Programs

Welcome to the eleventh edition of *Human Relations for Career and Personal Success: Concepts, Applications, and Skills*. This new edition continues the emphasis of the tenth edition on developing effective human relations skills for the workplace, including material on teamwork and motivating and influencing others. The purpose of this text is to show how you can become more effective in your work and personal life through knowledge of and skill in human relations. A major theme of this text is that career and personal success are related. Success on the job often enhances personal success, and success in personal life can enhance job success. Dealing effectively with people is an enormous asset in both work and personal life.

This text is written to help students deal with human relations problems in the workplace and in personal life. It is designed to be appropriate for human relations courses taught in colleges, career schools, vocational–technical schools, and other postsecondary schools. Managerial, professional, and technical workers who are forging ahead in their careers will also find this text immediately useful in improving workplace and personal relationships.

The relevance of studying human relations and interpersonal skills is underscored by a survey of business leaders conducted by the New York Fed in 2015: 48 percent of the leaders indicated they had difficulty finding workers with interpersonal skills, and 42 percent had trouble finding punctual workers.* Most likely, employers in other regions are also looking for workers at all levels with good human relations and interpersonal skills.

Organization of the Book

The text is divided into four parts, reflecting the major issues in human relations.

Part I covers four aspects of understanding and managing yourself. Chapter 1 focuses on the meaning of human relations, self-understanding, and the interrelationship of career and personal success. Chapter 2 explains how self-esteem and self-confidence are important parts of human functioning. Chapter 3 explains how to use self-motivation and goal setting to improve your chances for success. Chapter 4 deals with the importance of emotional intelligence and attitudes and factors associated with being happy. Chapter 5 explains the contribution of values and ethics to effective human relations. Chapter 6 explains the basics of solving problems and making decisions, with an emphasis on creativity.

Part II examines the heart of human relations: dealing effectively with other people. The topics in Chapters 7 through 13 are, respectively, personal communication effectiveness; communication in the workplace; specialized techniques for getting along with others in the workplace; managing conflict; becoming an effective leader; motivating others and developing teamwork; and developing cross-cultural competence.

Part III provides information to help career-minded people capitalize on their education, experiences, talents, and ambitions. The topics of Chapters 14 through 16 are getting ahead in your career; learning strategies, perception, and life span changes; and developing good work habits.

Part IV deals with staying emotionally healthy; Chapter 17 covers managing stress and personal problems.

---

*Myles Udland, "Companies Can't Find Workers Who Can Hold a Conversation or Show Up on Time," *Business Insider*, http://finance.yahoo.com, April 17, 2015, p. 1.

About the Author

Stefanie Donaldson

An accomplished author, Andrew J. DuBrin, PhD, brings to his work years of research experience in human relations and business psychology. He has published numerous articles, textbooks, and professional books on such subjects as impression management and proactive behavior in the workplace. Dr. DuBrin received his PhD from Michigan State University and is Professor Emeritus at the Saunders College of Business, Rochester Institute of Technology, where he has taught organizational behavior, leadership, and career management.

Experience the DuBrin Total Learning System

Human Relations for Career and Personal Success is not simply a textbook. The eleventh edition contains a wealth of experiential exercises, including new cases and self-assessment quizzes that can be completed in class or as homework.

Chapter-Opening Cases Set the Stage

Chapter-opening cases introduce students to the topic and set the stage for the chapter narrative.

Pedagogical Features Relate Concepts to What's Happening Today, Personally and in the Workplace

- **Self-assessment quizzes** give students the opportunity to explore their own opinions, feelings, and behavior patterns as related to chapter topics. All chapters include one or more self-assessment quizzes.
- **Human Relations in Practice** boxes in all chapters illustrate real human relations business practices in today's business world.

Expanded Assignment Material

End-of-chapter assignment material is organized into two sections:

Concept Review and Reinforcement, featuring exercises that focus on concept retention and developing critical thinking skills, and **Developing Your Human Relations Skills**, focusing on developing skills that can be used immediately in life and on the job.

Concept Review and Reinforcement	**Key Terms** **Chapter Summary and Review** provides an excellent detailed review of key chapter concepts. **Questions for Discussion and Review** provide questions and stimulate thinking about the issues. **Web Corner** provides informational websites and asks students to use the power of the web in researching outside resources. Three of the Internet Skill Builder exercises have been replaced by new exercises.

Developing Your Human Relations Skills	**Skills Exercises** tie together chapter topics and allow students to apply what they have just learned. **Role-Playing and Class Projects** allow students to practice and model human relations situations in the classroom. **Two Human Relations Case Studies** put students into a realistic scenario so they can practice making decisions in tough situations.

Supplements for Teaching and Learning

Instructor Resources

At the Instructor Resource Center, www.pearsonhighered.com/irc, instructors can easily register to gain access to a variety of instructor resources available with this text in downloadable format. If assistance is needed, our dedicated technical support team is ready to help with the media supplements that accompany this text. Visit http://247.pearsoned.com for answers to frequently asked questions and toll-free user support phone numbers.

The following supplements are available with this text:

- Instructor's Resource Manual
- Test Bank
- TestGen® Computerized Test Bank
- PowerPoint Presentation

Acknowledgments

A book of this nature cannot be written and published without the cooperation of many people. Many outside reviewers of this and the previous editions provided constructive suggestions for improving the book. The following reviewers provided detailed feedback that drove the refocusing of previous editions:

Verl Anderson, Dixie State College

Mary D. Aun, DeVry Technical Institute

Chet Eric Barney, New Mexico State University

Daniel Bialis, Muskegon Community College

Donna Ana Branch and H. Ralph Todd Jr., American River College

Hollis Chaleau Brown, Oakton Community College

Sheri Bryant, DeKalb Technical Institute

Jewel Cherry, Forsyth Technical Community College

Win Chesney, St. Louis Community College

Claudia Cochran, El Paso Community College

Joy Colwell, Purdue University

Tommy Gilbreath, The University of Texas

Dorothy Hetmer-Hinds, Trinity Valley Community College

Heidi Hilbert, Eastern Iowa Community College

Norma Johansen, Scottsdale Community College

Ruth Keller, Indiana Vo-Tech College

Jessica Li, University of North Texas

Darlean McClure, College of the Sequoias

Michelle Meyer, Joliet Junior College

Alvin Motley, Metropolitan Community College

Therese Nemec, Fox Valley Technical College

Marcia Polanis, Forsyth Technical Community College

Steve Quinn, Olympic College

Debra Rowe, Oakland Community College

Daniell Scane, Orange Coast College

Tom Shaughnessy, Illinois Central College

Nora Jo Sherman, Houston Community College

Bernice Rose Computer Learning Center

Pamela Simon, Baker College

Rudy Soliz, Houston Community College

Reginald St. Clair, Mountain Empire Community College

Carol Thole, Shasta College

James Van Arsdall, Metropolitan Community College

Susan Verhulst, Des Moines Area Community College

Jim Wilhelm, South Plains College

Special thanks go to Therese Nemec and Kath Lich from Fox Valley Technical College and Sharon Chacon-Mineau from Northeast Wisconsin Technical College for their assistance in revising and expanding the supplementary materials that accompany this textbook.

Thanks also to my family members, whose emotional support and encouragement assist my writing: Melanie, Will, Carson, Owen, Douglas, Gizella, Camila, Sofia, Eliana, Julian, Drew, Rosie, and Clare. My thanks also extend to Stefanie, the woman in my life, and her daughter Sofia.

Andrew J. DuBrin

Rochester, New York

Human Relations for Career and Personal Success

Fotolia

CHAPTER **1**

Human Relations and You

Outline

Beverly is the manager of building inspection in a metropolitan area with a population of approximately two million people. She has a staff of seven building inspectors and five support workers. Because the city has a strict building code in terms of safety, her staff is quite active. In addition to inspecting new buildings, the staff professionals also make periodic inspections of existing buildings. Beverly has a reputation of managing a department with exceptional productivity and high morale. Nevertheless, her unit was included in a 360-degree-feedback program in which every manager participates.

The feedback survey includes everybody who reports to the manager, along with a few people who use the output of the department. Survey participants rate the manager on ten different dimensions and are also requested to insert a few written comments. The 360-degree survey is done online, and anonymously. Beverly's manager, Beverly, and the survey administrator get to examine the feedback. The survey is designed to provide useful suggestions for improvement, but in Beverly's case there was not much room for improvement. She scored in the top 10 percent on all ten dimensions, and three of the written comments were as follows:

Beverly has got it as a manager. She is a great role model, and she helps us believe in the importance of inspecting buildings. But what I like best about Beverly is that she cares so much about my welfare. She always compliments me when I do something right, and gives me a gentle nudge when I do something wrong. She takes such great interest in my studying to obtain advanced certification in building inspection.

I've been a building inspector for fifteen years, and Beverly is no doubt the best supervisor I have ever had. Bev can be a little too motherly at times, like telling me to dress extra warm on one horribly cold day when I had to inspect a dilapidated factory. But it's great having a manager who really worries about me as a person.

Thanks for giving me the chance to write something about Beverly. I admire her talent and skills, but most of all I admire the way she cares about the entire staff. If you want me to criticize Beverly, okay. She should sometimes think more about her own good and not worry so much about us. If the building were burning down, she wouldn't leave until everyone else had escaped.

The comments made about this public-sector executive focus on the importance of effective human relations. Treating people with kindness helps Beverly deal effectively with her employees. This text presents a wide variety of suggestions and guidelines for improving your personal relationships both on and off the job. Most of them are based on systematic knowledge about human behavior.

We begin our study of human relations by inviting you to take Human Relations Self-Assessment Quiz 1-1, which will give you an opportunity to think through your attitudes about this field of study and practice.

Learning Objectives ▸

After studying the information and doing the exercises in this chapter, you should be able to:

1.1 Understand how studying human relations will help you.

1.2 Pinpoint how work and personal life influence each other.

1.3 Understand how effective human relations begins with self-understanding.

1.4 Understand the timeline and development of the human relations movement.

1.5 Understand the major factors influencing job performance and behavior.

Human Relations Self-Assessment Quiz 1-1

My Attitudes toward Studying Human Relations

Indicate whether you think the following statements are mostly true or mostly false.

No.	Statement about Human Relations	Mostly True	Mostly False
1.	High-paying jobs are based on technical skills, so studying human relations will hold you back financially.	_____	_____
2.	Leadership positions usually require both human relations and intellectual skills.	_____	_____
3.	Having good people skills is mostly common sense.	_____	_____
4.	The best-known business schools now emphasize human relations skills in addition to analytical skills.	_____	_____
5.	Because everybody in business has a smartphone these days, you never really have to worry about dealing with people face to face.	_____	_____
6.	A lot of self-made millionaires are rude and mean, so studying human relations won't get you very far.	_____	_____
7.	Should I encounter any difficulties in dealing with someone on the job, I will simply find the right app on my smartphone and solve the problem.	_____	_____
8.	With the right emoticons, such as a smiley face, I will be able to solve almost all my problems involving people.☺	_____	_____
9.	Taking a course in human relations is mostly a waste of time if it is not in your major.	_____	_____
10.	Good human relations skills help you hold onto a job, even in highly technical fields.	_____	_____

Scoring and Interpretation:

The more questions you answered "incorrectly" as suggested by the scoring key, the more you are likely to benefit from studying human relations. The fewer questions you answered "correctly," the more you need to study human relations.

1. **Mostly False.** It is definitely true that technical specialties pay much better to start than nontechnical specialties. Yet in the long run, those people who combine their technical skills with human relations skills generally get more promotions and earn more money than those people who rely exclusively on technical skills. (An exception here is that a great inventor can often get by almost exclusively on technical skill.)

2. **Mostly True.** Few people are promoted to leadership positions who do not combine interpersonal (or human relations) skills with intellectual skills. The highest level leaders in most fields are able to inspire other people and solve difficult business-related problems.

3. **Mostly False.** It would seem that having good human relations skills is common sense, but sadly this is not true. Relatively few people have good human relations skills. Also common sense is not so common, as indicated by all the problems people experience, including drunk driving, spending more than they earn, and not reading directions for the safe use of equipment.

4. **Mostly True.** During the past twenty years, the best-known business schools, such as those at Harvard, MIT, and the University of Pennsylvania, have recognized that they went too far in emphasizing analytical, technical, and financial skills. So now these schools place a heavier emphasis on soft skills such as leadership, motivation, and ethics.

5. **Mostly False.** Successful people in all types of organizations still take time to meet face to face with employees and customers and communicate with them. Even technology companies like Dell and IBM still maintain a large sales force that calls on customers.

6. **Mostly False.** It may be true that many self-made millionaires are rude and mean, but they are the exception. Mark Zuckerberg founded Facebook in his early twenties and is now one of world's best-known CEOs. He continues to refine his human relations skills by meeting regularly with his team to discuss ways in which he can improve his effectiveness with people.

7. **Mostly False.** Dealing with complex human relations problems takes more than a quick access to an app on your smartphone. Even if the app would point you in the right direction, such as an app for dealing with difficult people, you still need to have studied and practiced your skill before an immediate need arises, much like having practiced a maneuver in a sport before it is needed in a big game.

8. **Mostly False.** Emoticons may be cool and a form of nonverbal communication, but they cannot solve many human relations problems. Much more knowledge than sending an emoticon is needed to deal effectively with people when the issue is complex.

9. **Mostly False.** A course in human relations is rarely part of a student's major, but it is designed to supplement a major. The results from a course in human relations are never guaranteed, but anybody in any field can benefit from knowledge that might help him or her interact more effectively with others in the workplace.

10. **Mostly True.** During the past twenty-five years, large numbers of jobs have been outsourced to other companies, often located in other countries. To the extent that your job involves established relationships with people, the less likely it is to be outsourced. For example, a sales rep with good contacts in the industry is less likely to have his or her job outsourced to a firm that does sales and marketing for other companies.

Source: "My Attitudes Toward Studying Human Relations" by Andrew J. DuBrin.

How Studying Human Relations Can Help You

◀ Learning Objective 1.1 ◀

In the context used here, **human relations** is the art of using systematic knowledge about human behavior to improve personal, job, and career effectiveness. The field studies individuals and groups in organizations. Human relations is far more than "being nice to people," because it applies systematic knowledge to treating people in such a way that they feel better and are more productive—such as providing a more relaxed work atmosphere to enhance worker creativity.

Human relations
the art of using systematic knowledge about human behavior to improve personal, job, and career effectiveness

From the standpoint of management, human relations is quite important because it contributes to **organizational effectiveness**, that is, the extent to which an organization is productive and satisfies the demands of interested parties, such as employees, customers, and investors. Steve Kent, an equities analyst (not a human relations specialist), made extensive observations about the importance of treating employees well (using principles of human relations). He found that treating employees with respect and paying them fairly contribute to developing an efficient and creative organization. Business firms that go the extra mile to treat employees well often derive tangible benefits, such as a high quality of customer service.[1]

Organizational effectiveness
the extent to which an organization is productive and satisfies the demands of interested parties, such as employees, customers, and investors

Human relations knowledge and skills are also potentially beneficial for the individual as well as the organization. The following case history illustrates how a career-minded person made effective use of human relations principles to resolve a difficult situation that seemed to be blocking her career. You might be able to use the same approach if you face a similar problem.

Ashley worked as a business analyst at a large hospital. Her responsibilities included searching for ways to improve work processes at the hospital, such as developing better forms for collecting information about patients and reducing the time outpatients spent in the waiting room. Ashley enjoyed her work and believed that she was gaining valuable experience toward her goal of becoming a hospital administrator.

Another contributor to Ashley's job satisfaction was her relationship with Paul, her boss. Ashley perceived her work relationship with him to be ideal. Paul kept feeding Ashley interesting assignments, gave her useful suggestions from time to time, and frequently praised her work. On her most recent performance evaluation, Ashley was described as "an ideal hospital business analyst with great potential."

Ashley's smooth working relationship with her manager quickly changed one January. Paul informed the group that the hospital had offered him a promotion to a much bigger role at the hospital and that although he enjoyed his present position, he felt obliged to accept the promotion. In Paul's place, the hospital appointed Jody, an experienced supervisor in another department within the hospital.

Within the first three weeks, Jody began criticizing Ashley's work. Jody told Ashley that her approach to improving business processes was not up to date, and that it lacked the kind of depth the hospital needed. Ashley then worked diligently on her next project to make the kind of improvements Jody suggested. Jody then found something else to criticize, this time telling Ashley that her PowerPoint presentations supporting her report were too complex, making them difficult for hospital administrators to follow.

Soon Jody found ways to criticize Ashley personally, in addition to the work she was performing. She suggested that Ashley should be careful to never wear heels higher than one and one-half inches to the office and that the tattoo on her neck was unprofessional. Jody also suggested to Ashley twice that she should make sure to use the Internet only for job-related purposes during working hours.

After five months of regular criticism from her boss, Ashley decided to talk over the strained relationship with David, a close friend. Ashley explained to David that the negative chemistry between her and her boss was giving her chest pains and interrupted sleep. Ashley also emphasized that she was worried about receiving such a poor evaluation that it would damage her career.

David advised Ashley to "do what she had to do," by confronting her boss about the unjustified criticisms. If that didn't work, Ashley should communicate directly with Jody's manager to get the problem resolved. David explained that "in the modern organization, you are expected to bring problems right out on the table."

Ashley thanked David for his advice and then did some careful reflection. On the surface, David's advice made sense, but with her career potentially at stake, Ashley did not want to operate on common sense alone. She remembered studying about attitude change somewhere in human relations or social psychology. A point that stuck in her mind was that favorable interactions lead to attitude change.

Ashley developed a game plan to look for ways to have positive interactions with Jody whenever possible. One day she thanked Jody for the suggestions she made about preparing less complicated PowerPoint slides. She also incorporated ideas from a recent article about business process reengineering into her next suggestion for improving the workflow in the hospital laundry. Another day Ashley complimented Jody about a business suit she was wearing. At a luncheon meeting with Jody and several other department members, Ashley wore a blouse that covered the tattoo on her neck.

Ashley's game plan of applying a little-known principle of human relations to improving her relationship with her boss soon started to pay off. Jody actually complimented Ashley's report and stated that she was a strong contributor to the hospital. The most concrete evidence of an improved relationship was that Jody rated Ashley as "exceeding expectations" the first time she formally evaluated her performance.

As the case history just presented indicates, another way of understanding the importance of human relations is to examine its personal benefits. A person who carefully studies human relations and incorporates its suggestions into his or her work and personal life should derive the five benefits discussed next. Knowledge itself, however, is no guarantee of success. Because people differ greatly in learning ability, personality, and life circumstances, some will get more out of studying human relations than will others. You may, for example, be getting along well with coworkers or customers, so studying this topic might seem unnecessary from your viewpoint. Or you may be so shy at this stage of your life that you are unable to capitalize on some of the suggestions for being assertive with people. You might have to work doubly hard to benefit from studying that topic. The major benefits from studying human relations are the following:

1. Acquiring valid information about human behavior. To feel comfortable with people and to make a favorable impression both on and off the job, you need to understand how people think and act. Studying human relations will provide you with some basic knowledge about interpersonal relationships, such as the meaning of self-esteem, why goals work, and win–win conflict resolution. You will even learn such things as effective methods of dealing with difficult people.

2. Developing skills in dealing with people. People who aspire to high-level positions or enriched social lives need to be able to communicate with others, work well on a team, manage stress, and behave confidently. Relating well to diverse cultural groups is also an asset. Studying information about such topics, coupled with practicing what you learn, should help you develop such interpersonal skills.

3. Coping with job problems. Almost everyone who holds a job inevitably runs into human relations problems. Reading about these problems and suggestions for coping with them could save you considerable inner turmoil. Among the job survival skills that you will learn about in the study of human relations are how to deal with difficult people and how to overcome what seems to be an overwhelming workload.

4. Coping with personal problems. We all have problems. An important difference between the effective and the ineffective person is that the effective person knows how to manage them. Among the problems studying human relations will help you cope with are self-defeating behavior, dealing with a difficult coworker, overcoming low self-confidence, and working your way out of heavy job stress.

5. Capitalizing on opportunities. Many readers of this text will some day spend part of their working time taking advantage of opportunities rather than solving daily problems. Every career-minded person needs a few breakthrough experiences to make life more rewarding. Toward this end, studying human relations gives you ideas for developing your career, becoming a leader, and becoming more creative.

6. Demonstrating potential for advancement. As implied in the point just made, workers with skill and knowledge about human relations are more likely to be perceived as having advancement potential than workers who lack such skill and knowledge. Supervisors, managers, and other categories of leaders are typically selected from among those individual workers who have good human relations skills in addition to their technical skills and other types of job knowledge.

The Human Relations in Practice box on page 8 illustrates how human relations skill and understanding can be important in organized activity involving people. You are invited to take the Human Relations Self-Assessment Quiz 1-2 on page 9 to think through your current level of human relations effectiveness.

How Work and Personal Life Influence Each Other

◀ **Learning Objective 1.2** ◀

Most people reading this text will be doing so to improve their job effectiveness and careers. Therefore, the text centers on relationships with people in a job setting. Keep in mind that human relationships in work and personal life have much in common. Several studies have supported the close relationship between job satisfaction and life satisfaction. One such study conducted by Timothy A. Judge, psychology professor at Notre Dame University, and Remus Ilies, psychology professor at Michigan State University, involved seventy-four university employees with administrative support positions, such as secretaries or office managers. The researchers collected reports of mood and job satisfaction at work, mood away from work, and job satisfaction. Data were collected using questionnaires posted on a website.

The major findings of the study were that mood influences job satisfaction, with a positive mood increasing satisfaction. The effect decreases rapidly because moods pass quickly. The researchers also found that employees' satisfaction with their jobs, measured at work, influences the mood at home. Workers who are more emotional by nature are more likely to experience these connections, such as joy or anger on the job spilling over into home life. A related finding was that a mood developed on the job spilled over to the home later in the day.[2] In short, this study confirmed the old cartoons about a worker who is chewed out by the boss coming home and swearing at his or her dog or kicking the furniture!

Human Relations in Practice

Kansas State Football Coach Bill Snyder
Emphasizes the Human Touch

Bill Snyder is a successful major college football coach. Before the start of the 2015 season, he had won 187 games over twenty-three seasons as the head coach at Kansas State. His teams have won 66 percent of their games during Snyder's tenure. At age seventy-five, Snyder was inducted into the College Football Hall of Fame. He began his coaching at Kansas State by taking over one of the worst football teams in the country and has turned it into a team that regularly appears in bowl games (a postseason event open to about sixty-six teams from across the country).

Many factors have contributed to the success of Snyder's football teams, but two stand out: his unconditional support for his players and how he truly cares about them. Snyder is recognized for his ability to build a relationship of mutual trust and respect with team members. Snyder regularly works long hours and invests time in the lives of his players.

A symbol of Snyder's caring for members of his own team, and also members of competing teams, has been the letters he writes them, using a purple felt-tip pen and sending by postal mail. Each letter is individualized and sent to a player who had a great game or was injured. The letters arrive within a few days after the game, offering encouragement and expressing Snyder's admiration—whether or not the team has won. He sends these letters to players he believes have the right approach, as well as the right attitude about their lives and college football.

One of Snyder's touching letters received a lot of publicity because its recipient attached a photo of the letter to a tweet. The recipient was Clint Trickett, the quarterback of the West Virginia team who had to leave the game against Kansas State when he received a concussion. Part of Snyder's letter said, "I hope the symptoms are gone by now. That you will be back soon. Always appreciate you as a young man of great values, as well as being an excellent quarterback."

Part of Trickett's tweet said, "Coach Snyder is the epitome of college football coaches!"

Questions:

1. Who cares what a football coach does? This isn't a course in sports management. What relevance would his approach have to business and related fields?

2. In what way does Coach Snyder demonstrate good human relations skills?

3. In what way might writing notes by hand be considered a human touch?

Sources: The original story presented above was created based on facts presented in the following: Ian A. Boyd, "Demystifying Kansas State: When, Why, and How Are the Wildcats Good?" *Football Study Hall* (www.footballstudyhall.com), August 5, 2014, pp. 1–6; Pete Grathoff, "West Virginia Quarterback Touched by Letter He Received from K-State's Bill Snyder," *Kansas City Star* (www.kansascity.com), December 4, 2014, pp. 1–6; Chip Rouse, "K-State's Bill Snyder Adds Personal Touch to His Coaching," (http:talking12.com), January 8, 2015, pp. 1–3; David Skretta, "Snyder Puts Pen to Paper," Associated Press, December 26, 2014.

Human Relations Self-Assessment Quiz   1-2

Human Relations Skills

For each of the following statements about human relations skills, indicate how strong you think you are right now. Attempt to be as objective as possible, even though most of us tend to exaggerate our skills in dealing with people. To help obtain a more objective evaluation of your capabilities, ask some-one who knows you well (family member, friend, or work associate) to also rate you on these factors. Use the following scale: (1) very weak, (2) weak, (3) average, (4) strong, (5) very strong.

Person	Self-Rating	Rating by Other
1. Listen carefully when in conversation with another person.		
2. Smile frequently.		
3. Am tactful when criticizing others.		
4. Am comfortable in dealing with people from a different generation than myself.		
5. Am comfortable in dealing with a person from a different ethnic group than myself.		
6. Am comfortable in dealing with a person from a different race than myself.		
7. Let my feelings be known when I disagree with another person.		
8. Let my feelings be known when I am joyful about something.		
9. Have a neat, well-groomed appearance.		
10. Congratulate the winner when I lose an athletic or any other type of contest.		
11. Concentrate on another person when in conversation instead of accepting a call on my cell phone, making use of call waiting, or responding to e-mail.		
12. Compliment others when a compliment is merited.		
13. Have a good sense of humor.		
14. Am patient with people who do not understand what I am saying.		
15. Cooperate with others in a team effort.		
16. Have a controllable temper.		
17. Am respected for being honest and dependable.		
18. Hug people when the situation is appropriate.		
19. Am trusted by other people.		
20. Motivate others to do something they hadn't thought of doing.		
21. Am willing to talk to another person to resolve a problem rather than relying exclusively on text messaging.		
Total Score		
Combined Score (self plus other)		

Scoring and Interpretation:

1. **Self-ratings:** If your self-rating is 85 or more, and your scoring is accurate, you have exceptional human relations skills. Scores between 60 and 84 suggest moderate, or average, human relations skills. Scores of 59 and below suggest below-average human relations skills in the areas covered in this quiz.
2. **Rating by other person:** Because people tend to judge us a little more critically than we judge ourselves in human relations skills, use the following scale: 80 or more suggests exceptional human relations skills; 55 to 79 suggests moderate, or average, human relations skills; 54 and below suggests below-average human relations skills.
3. **Combined ratings:** 165 or more suggests exceptional human relations skills; 115 to 163 suggests moderate, or average, human relations skills; 114 or below suggests below-average human relations skills.

Action plan: Whether you scored high, low, or medium on this quiz, there is always room for improvement, just as athletes, actors, and musicians are always looking to improve their art. Scores in the bottom category suggest a more urgent need for improvement in human relations skill.

Source: "Human Relations Skills" by Andrew J. DuBrin.

FIGURE 1-1

HOW WORK AND PERSONAL LIFE INFLUENCE EACH OTHER

Source: "HOW WORK AND PERSONAL LIFE INFLUENCE EACH OTHER" by Andrew J. DuBrin.

1. Job satisfaction enhances life satisfaction.
2. An unsatisfying job can damage physical health.
3. Relationships with people on and off the job influence each other.
4. Certain skills contribute to success in both work and personal life.
5. Workers who achieve a good balance between the demands of work and family life are likely to be more productive and satisfied.

Work and personal life influence each other in a number of specific ways, as outlined in Figure 1-1 and described next.

1. *The satisfaction you achieve on the job contributes to your general life satisfaction.* Conversely, if you suffer from chronic job dissatisfaction, your life satisfaction will begin to decline. Career disappointments have been shown to cause marital relationships to suffer. Frustrated on the job, many people start feuding with their partners and other family members.

2. *An unsatisfying job can affect physical health, primarily by creating stress and burnout. Intense job dissatisfaction may even lead to heart disease, ulcers, intestinal disorders, and skin problems.* People who have high job satisfaction even tend to live longer than those who suffer from prolonged job dissatisfaction. These benefits may be attributed to better physical health and passion for life. Finding the right type of job may thus add years to a person's life.

3. *The quality of your relationships with people at work and in personal life influence each other.* If you experience intense conflict in your family, you might be so upset that you will be unable to form good relationships with coworkers. Conversely, if you have a healthy, rewarding personal life, it will be easier for you to form good relationships on the job. People you meet on the job will find it pleasant to relate to a seemingly positive and untroubled person.

Another way of explaining the third point is that how we behave at work is closely related to how we behave at home. Psychologist John M. Gottman, executive director of the Relationship Research Institute, has been studying married couples for over thirty-five years. He and his colleagues have used devices such as camcorders, along with heart monitors and other biofeedback equipment, to measure what takes place when couples experience moments of conflict or closeness. The research results indicate that successful couples look for ways to emphasize the positive and attempt to say yes as often as possible. Successful couples use conflict as a way of working through personality differences rather than to attack each other.

A useful inference from research at the Relationship Research Institute is that the way people manage their relationships in the workplace is closely linked to the way they manage their personal ones. People who frequently use the word *yes* in communications at home are likely to do the same on the job. Also, people who are abusive on the job are likely to be abusive at home.[3]

Personal relationships on the job also influence personal relationships off the job. Interacting harmoniously with coworkers can put you in a better mood for dealing with family and friends after hours. Crossing swords with employees and customers during working hours can make it difficult for you to feel comfortable and relaxed with people off the job.

4. *Certain skills contribute to success in both work and personal life.* For example, people who know how to deal effectively with others and get things accomplished on the job can use the same skills to enhance their personal lives. Similarly, people who are effective in dealing with friends and family members and who can organize things are likely to be effective supervisors.

5. *Workers who achieve a good balance between the demands of work and family life are likely to be more productive and have more job satisfaction.*[4] A repeated research finding related to this idea is that work can interfere with family life, and family life can interfere with work. The person who cannot attend a social event with friends and family because of work demands is likely to be frustrated. At the same time, a person who cannot work late into the night to meet a work deadline because of an event with friends and family is likely to be frustrated. When a person experiences conflict between work and family life, in the short run, the person will have a decrease in subjective (feelings of) well-being. However, many people seem to adjust to work–family conflict over time and experience fewer problems with subjective well-being.[5]

Another impact of the fit between work and family life is that when employees believe that they have a harmonious relationship between their work and personal responsibilities, they are more likely to stay with their employer. An American Psychological Association (APA) survey found that 67 percent of workers said they choose to stay with their employer because their job fits well with other aspects of their life.[6]

The discussion of balance between work and family will be discussed in Chapter 10. Can you think of other ways in which success in work and success in personal life are related to each other?

Human Relations Begins with Self-Understanding

◀ Learning Objective 1.3 ◀

Before you can understand other people very well and therefore practice effective human relations, you must understand yourself. You already know something about yourself. An important starting point in learning more about yourself is self-examination. Suppose that instead of being about human relations, this text were about dancing. The reader would obviously need to know what other dancers do right and wrong. But the basic principles of dancing cannot be fully grasped unless they are seen in relation to your own style of dancing. Watching a video of you dancing, for example, would be helpful. You might also ask other people for comments and suggestions about your dance movements.

Similarly, to achieve **self-understanding**, you must gather valid information about yourself. (Self-understanding refers to your knowledge about yourself, particularly with respect to mental and emotional aspects.) Every time you read a self-help book, take a personality quiz, or receive an evaluation of your work from a manager or instructor, you are gaining some self-knowledge.

In achieving self-understanding, it is helpful to recognize that the **self** is a complex idea. It generally refers to a person's total being or individuality. To help clarify the meaning of the self, a distinction is sometimes made between the self a person projects to the outside world and the inner self. The **public self** is what the person is communicating about himself or herself and what others actually perceive about the person. The **private self** is the actual person you may be.[7] A similar distinction is made between the real self and the ideal self. Many people think of themselves in terms of an ideal version of what they are really like. To avoid making continuous distinctions between the two selves throughout this text, we will use the term *self* to refer to an accurate representation of the individual.

A current addition to knowledge about the self is that we are also influenced by what could have happened to us or who we could have been. "I could have been a contender" is a famous line from a movie about prize fighting that illustrates the idea of how we think about what our lives might have been. The **alternative self** is an understanding of the self, based on *what could have been* if something in the past had happened differently.[8]

Imagining what could have been can be a positive force. Tanya might think, "If I had studied math more carefully in the past I could now perform much better in a

Self-understanding
gathering valid information about oneself; self-understanding refers to knowledge about oneself, particularly with respect to mental and emotional aspects

Self
a complex idea generally referring to a person's total being or individuality

Public self
what a person communicates about himself or herself and what others actually perceive about the person

Private self
the actual person an individual is

Alternative self
an understanding of the self based on what could have been if something in the past had happened differently

FIGURE 1-2

SIX SOURCES OF INFORMATION THAT CONTRIBUTE TO SELF-UNDERSTANDING

Source: "Six Sources Of Information That Contribute To Self-Understanding" by Andrew J. DuBrin.

1. General information about human behavior
2. Informal feedback from people
3. Feedback from superiors
4. Feedback from coworkers
5. Feedback from self-assessment quizzes
6. The Johari Window

manufacturing job." Tanya therefore begins to study basic math to serve as a foundation for new learning in manufacturing technologies. The alternative self might also be a negative force if it leads to discouragement. Brad might think, "If I hadn't married and had a family so early in life, I could have taken more risks in my career. Now instead of having started my own business, I'm stuck in a dead-end job."

Some scientific evidence suggests that the self is based on structures within the brain. According to the research of Joseph LeDoux at New York University, the self is the sum of the brain's individual components, or subsystems. Each subsystem has its own form of memory, along with its interactions with other subsystems.[9] Two examples of subsystems in the brain are the centers for speech and hearing. The implication to recognize here is that the self could be an entity that is both psychological and biological.

While we discuss the self in depth in the first chapter, the chapters that follow also deal with the self. Most of this text is geared toward using human relations knowledge for self-development and self-improvement. Throughout the text, you will find questionnaires designed to improve your insight. The self-knowledge emphasized here deals with psychological characteristics (such as personality traits and thinking style) rather than physical characteristics (such as height and blood pressure). As outlined in Figure 1-2, we discuss six types of information that contribute to self-understanding, along with potential problems in self-evaluation.

GENERAL INFORMATION ABOUT HUMAN BEHAVIOR

As you learn about people in general, you should also be gaining knowledge about yourself. Therefore, most of the information in this text is presented in a form that should be useful to you personally. Whenever general information is presented, it is your responsibility to relate such information to your particular situation, such as in studying sources of conflict. One such general cause is limited resources; that is, not everyone can have what he or she wants. See how this general principle applies to you. Here is an example involving others: "That's why I've been so angry with Melissa lately. She was the one given the promotion, whereas I'm stuck in the same old job."

In relating facts and observations about people in general to yourself, be careful not to misapply the information. Feedback from other people will help you avoid the pitfalls of introspection (looking into yourself).

INFORMAL FEEDBACK FROM PEOPLE

Feedback
information that tells one how well he or she has performed

As just implied, **feedback** is information that tells you how well you have performed. You can sometimes obtain feedback from the spontaneous comments of others or by asking them for feedback. An auto-insurance claims investigator grew one notch in self-confidence when coworkers began to call him "Super Sleuth." He was given this name because of his ability to quickly detect accident fraud. His experience illustrates that a valuable source of information for self-understanding is what the significant people in your life think of you. Although feedback of this type might make you feel uncomfortable, when it is consistent, it accurately reflects how others perceive you.

With some ingenuity you can create informal feedback. (In this sense, the term *informal* refers to not being part of a company-sponsored program.) For example, you might send an email or social media post to ten people in your social network asking them for a candid evaluation of your strengths and weaknesses. Make the promise that you will not retaliate if you don't like what you hear.

A few skeptics will argue that friends never give you a true picture of yourself; rather, they say flattering things about you because they value your friendship. Experience has shown, however, that if you emphasize the importance of their opinions, most people will give you a few constructive suggestions. You also have to appear sincere. Because not everyone's comments will be helpful, you may have to sample many people.

FEEDBACK FROM SUPERIORS

Virtually all employers provide employees with formal or informal feedback on their performances. A formal method of feedback is called a *performance evaluation*. During a performance evaluation (or appraisal), your superior will convey to you what he or she thinks you are doing well and not so well. These observations become a permanent part of your human resources record. Informal feedback occurs when a superior discusses your job performance with you but does not record these observations.

Many companies have moved toward supplementing annual performance evaluations with frequent informal feedback. Part of the reason for the shift to more frequent feedback is the growing number of Millennials (the latest generation) entering the workforce, many of whom prefer immediate and frequent feedback. Sussane Bond, director of professional services for Halogen Software Inc., says, "It's no longer a sit-down once a year. Performance reviews mean timely feedback face to face with employees."[10]

A recent tendency is for managers in many companies to soften negative feedback to avoid eroding the self-confidence of employees, and therefore hurting performance. "Accentuating the positive" has become the new mantra at many firms concerned about human relationships. Managers in these firms give frequent praise, encourage employees to celebrate small victories, and focus performance reviews on a worker's strengths.[11] As a result of this positive emphasis, feedback from employee reviews might not be so accurate in terms of pointing to areas for improvement.

When feedback obtained from superiors is reasonably candid, it can help you learn about yourself. For instance, if two different bosses say that you are a creative problem solver, you might conclude that you are creative. If several bosses tell you that you are too impatient with other people, you might conclude that you are impatient.

FEEDBACK FROM COWORKERS

A sometimes-used practice in organizations is **peer evaluations**, a system in which teammates contribute to an evaluation of a person's job performance. Although coworkers under this system do not have total responsibility for evaluating each other, their input is taken seriously. The amount of a worker's salary increase could thus be affected by peer judgments about his or her performance. The results of peer evaluations can also be used as feedback for learning about yourself. Assume that coworkers agree on several of your strengths and needs for improvement. You can conclude that others who work closely with you generally perceive you that way.

Teammates might rate each other on performance dimensions such as cooperation with other members of the team, customer service attitude, productivity, and contributions

Peer evaluations
system in which teammates contribute to an evaluation of a person's job performance

Developmental opportunity
area for growth or of weakness

to meetings. If several teammates rate you low in one of these dimensions, the ratings could indicate a **developmental opportunity**, an area for growth, or of weakness.

FEEDBACK FROM SELF-ASSESSMENT QUIZZES

Many self-help books, including this one, contain questionnaires that you fill out by yourself, for yourself. The information that you pick up from these questionnaires often provides valuable clues to your preferences, values, and personal traits. Such self-examination questionnaires should not be confused with the scientifically researched test you might take in a counseling center or guidance department or when applying for a job. Another source of useful self-assessment quizzes is www.queendom.com, which offers a variety of tests that contribute to self-understanding, including the classical intelligence quotient (IQ), mental toughness, risk-taking, and self-esteem tests, among many others.

The amount of useful information gained from self-examination questionnaires depends on your candor. Because no outside judge is involved in these self-help quizzes, candor usually is not a problem. An exception is that we all have certain blind spots. Most people, for example, believe that they have considerably above-average skills in dealing with people.

As a starting point in conducting self-examination exercises, you already completed Human Relations Self-Assessment Quiz 1-1. Quiz 1-3 gives you an opportunity to write some things down about yourself.

A general point about all forms of feedback is that it takes mental toughness to benefit from the negative type. Yet according to writer Karen Wright, without negative feedback we would be stuck in the Stone Age, unable to learn or improve our chances for attaining success. Negative feedback is useful for negotiating life and interpersonal relations. Much of our growth and development depends on interactions and other experiences that feel bad.[12] For example, suppose that early in his career, an information technology (IT) specialist keeps telling his coworkers how badly he is overloaded with work. Soon a few coworkers tell him essentially to shut up and stop complaining. The IT specialist might profit from the negative feedback and come to understand that he should spend much less time complaining to his coworkers about his heavy workload.

LOOKING AT THE SELF THROUGH THE JOHARI WINDOW

Johari Window
a grid showing how much information you know about yourself as well as how much other people know about you

A systematic approach to looking at yourself is through a model of communication called the Johari Window, which focuses on self-disclosure. The **Johari Window** is a grid showing how much information you know about yourself as well as how much other people know about you. (The term *Johari* came about because the method was created by Joseph Luft and Harry Ingram.)

The basics of the model are outlined in Figure 1-3. One axis of the grid is the degree to which information about you is known to or understood by you. The other axis is the degree to which information about you is known to others. The horizontal dimension involves soliciting, or obtaining, feedback from others about you; the vertical dimension involves feedback about you to others, or self-disclosure.[13]

The basic premise of the model, as well as the lesson it teaches, is that we can improve our personal and professional relationships through understanding ourselves in depth. But you also have to take the next step of selecting those aspects of the self that are appropriate to share with others. A packaging specialist might want to reveal to coworkers that he does his best creative thinking when jogging alone. However, he might not want to reveal that he finds coworkers to be an annoying distraction while he is attempting to think creatively.

Human Relations Self-Assessment Quiz   1-3

The Written Self-Portrait

A good starting point in acquiring serious self-knowledge is to prepare a written self-portrait in the major life spheres (or aspects). In each of the following spheres, describe yourself in about twenty-five to fifty words. For example, for the interpersonal sphere, a person might write, "I'm a little timid on the surface. But those people who get to know me well understand that I'm filled with enthusiasm and joy. My relationships with people last a long time. I'm on excellent terms with all members of my family. And my significant other and I have been together for five years. We are very close emotionally and should be together for a lifetime."

1. Occupational and school: _____
_____
_____
_____

2. Interpersonal (interactions with people): _____
_____
_____
_____

3. Beliefs, values, and attitudes: _____
_____
_____
_____

4. Physical description (body type, appearance, grooming): _____
_____
_____
_____

Source: "The Written Self-Portrait" by Andrew J. DuBrin.

FIGURE 1-3

THE JOHARI WINDOW

Source: "The Johari Window" by Andrew J. DuBrin.

Solicit Feedback →

Give Feedback ↓

		Known to Self	Unknown to Self
	Known to Others	**Open Area:** known to self and others	**Blind Area:** blind to self, seen by others
	Unknown to Others	**Hidden Area:** open to self, hidden from others	**Unknown Area:** unknown to self and others

Another premise of the model is that the more we share of ourselves with others, the higher the probability of developing high-quality relationships. To develop these positive relationships, we need to be aware of the four areas (or four panes of the window) indicating what is known about us and what is hidden. Observe that the four areas, or panes, of the window are the basics of the communication model.

Open area

pane of Johari Window consisting of information that is known to us and others

■ The **open area** consists of information that is known to us and others. Among these readily observable aspects would be hair color, skin color, physical appearance, and spoken communication skills. As a relationship builds we enlarge the open area by revealing more about ourselves. As the open area expands, relationships with others improve—unless you annoy others with too many details about your work and personal life.

Hidden area

pane of Johari Window that contains information known to us about ourselves but is hidden from others

■ The **hidden area** contains information known to us about ourselves but is hidden from others. Frequent hidden areas are ambitions and dislikes of specific individuals. Over the long term, fewer hidden areas lead to more openness and closeness in relationships with others. Yet it is prudent to keep some areas hidden, such as describing a strong physical attraction toward your coworker's or manager's spouse.

Blind area

pane of Johari Window that contains information that others are aware of but we cannot see in ourselves in reference to both positive and negative qualities

■ The **blind area** contains information that others are aware of but we cannot see in ourselves in reference to both positive and negative qualities. Many people suffer from thinking that they are not physically attractive, yet others in general have an opposite perception. In the opposite direction, many people perceive themselves to be highly skilled in getting along with other people, yet most people might have an opposite point of view. Feedback from others, if not blocked by defensiveness, will help reduce the blind area. As your blind area decreases, you are likely to enlarge your open area because you will have more accurate data to work with.

Unknown area

pane of Johari Window that contains information that you and others do not know about you

■ The **unknown area** contains information that you and others do not know about you. It sometimes takes an unusual situation to bring out this unknown information, such as emerging as a leader when a crisis, such as a hurricane, hits your unit of the company.

The Johari Window is useful in reminding you of the importance of self-disclosure, such as in enlarging your open area. As you disclose more about yourself, others will reciprocate and disclose more about themselves. The mutual disclosures lead to enhanced positive feelings among people in both work and personal life.

TWO SELF-EVALUATION TRAPS

The theme of this section of the chapter is that self-awareness is a positive force in our lives. Yet self-awareness also has two negative extremes or traps. One of these extremes is that focusing on the self can highlight shortcomings the way staring into a mirror can dramatize every blemish and wrinkle on a face. Certain situations predictably force us to engage in self-reflection and become the object of our own attention. When we talk about ourselves, answer self-quizzes, stand before an audience or camera, or watch ourselves on a video, we become more self-aware and make comparisons to some arbitrary standard of behavior. The comparison often results in negative self-evaluation in comparison to the standard and a decrease in self-esteem as we discover that we fall short of standards.[14] Keeping the self-awareness trap in mind will help you minimize needless underevaluation, thereby benefiting from gathering feedback about yourself.

In contrast to underevaluation, it is also true that many people tend to overestimate their competence, such as thinking they deserve a bigger raise or an A in every course. A particular area in which people overestimate their competence is in the moral domain. Many people suffer from a "holier than thou" syndrome. A study with college students, for example, found that they consistently overrated the likelihood that they would act in generous or selfless ways. On one test, 84 percent of the students initially predicted that they would cooperate with their partner, but in reality, only 61 percent did.[15]

Cultural differences help explain at least some of the differences in underevaluation versus overevaluation. Several studies have shown, for example, that East Asians tend to underestimate their abilities, with an aim toward improving the self and getting along with others. North Americans are more likely to overestimate their abilities and not to be so prone to look for areas of self-improvement.[16] Cultural differences reflect stereotypes that apply to the average individual from a culture.

The antidote to the twin self-evaluation traps is to search for honest and objective feedback from others to help you supplement your self-evaluation. Competing against peers, such as in school, sports, and contests on the job (for example, a sales contest or creative suggestion contest), can help you evaluate yourself more realistically. Next, we look more at human relations from the standpoint of the workplace rather than the individual.

How the Human Relations Movement Developed

◀ Learning Objective 1.4 ◀

The **human relations movement** began as a concentrated effort by some managers and their advisers to become more sensitive to the needs of employees or to treat them in a more humanistic manner. In other words, employees were to be treated as human beings rather than as parts of the productive process. As diagrammed in Figure 1-4, the human relations movement was supported directly by four different historic influences: the Hawthorne studies, the threat of unionization, and industrial humanism.[17] Scientific Theory X and Theory Y management, which predated the growth of human relations in industry, contributed indirectly to the movement.

Human relations movement
movement that began as a concentrated effort by some managers and their advisers to become more sensitive to the needs of employees or to treat them in a more humanistic manner

SCIENTIFIC MANAGEMENT

The study of management became more systematized and formal as a byproduct of the Industrial Revolution, which took place from the 1700s through the 1900s. Approaches to managing work and people needed to be developed to manage all the new factories that

FIGURE 1-4

INFLUENCES SUPPORTING THE HUMAN RELATIONS MOVEMENT

Source: "Influences Supporting the Human Relations Movement" by Andrew J. DuBrin.

Scientific management

theory that focuses on the application of scientific methods to increase individual workers' productivity

were a central part of the Industrial Revolution. The focus of **scientific management** was on the application of scientific methods to increase individual workers' productivity. Frederick W. Taylor, considered the father of scientific management, was an engineer by background. He used scientific analysis and experiments to increase worker output. Taylor's goal was to remove human variability so each worker could become essentially an interchangeable part. His model for human behavior was a machine, with inexpensive parts, each of which has a specific function. Using the principles of scientific management, a worker might assemble a washing machine with the least number of wasted motions and steps. United Parcel Service (UPS) relies heavily on the principles of scientific management to get the most productivity from carriers and shipping personnel, including tightly timing their deliveries.

With scientific management sounding so dehumanizing, how could the movement have contributed to good human relations? Taylor also studied problems such as fatigue and safety. He urged management to study the relationship between work breaks and the length of the workday and productivity. He convinced some managers that work breaks and shorter workdays could increase productivity. Furthermore, scientific management proposed that workers who produced more be paid more.

Scientific management also contributed to the human relations movement by creating a backlash against what many people thought was mistreatment of workers. The industrial engineer with his or her stopwatch and clipboard, hovering over a worker measuring each tiny part of the job and the worker's movements, became a hated figure.[18] The objection to this approach called for a better way to treat people, which came to be known as the human relations movement.

THE HAWTHORNE STUDIES

The human relations school of management is generally said to have begun in 1927 with a group of studies conducted at the Chicago-area Hawthorne plant of an AT&T subsidiary. These studies were prompted by an experiment carried out by the company's engineers between 1924 and 1927. Following the tradition of scientific management, these engineers were applying research methods to investigate problems of employee productivity.

Two groups were studied to determine the effects of different levels of light on worker performance. As prescribed by the scientific method, one group received increased illumination, whereas the other did not. A preliminary finding was that when illumination was increased, the level of performance also increased. Surprisingly to the engineers, productivity also increased when the level of light was decreased almost to moonlight levels. One interpretation of these findings was that the workers involved in the experiment enjoyed being the center of attention. In other words, they reacted positively because management cared about them. Such a phenomenon taking place in any work or research setting is now called the **Hawthorne effect**.[19]

Hawthorne effect

applying research methods to investigate problems of employee productivity using the scientific method; in the study, employees reacted positively because management cared about them

As a result of these preliminary investigations, a team of researchers headed by Harvard professors Elton Mayo and Fritz J. Roethlisberger conducted a series of experiments extending over a six-year period. The conclusions they reached served as the foundations for later developments in the human relations approach to management. It was found that economic incentives are less important than generally believed in influencing workers to achieve high levels of output. Also, leadership practices and work group pressures profoundly influence employee satisfaction and performance. An example of an effective leadership practice would be coaching and encouraging workers to higher performance. The researchers noted that any factor influencing employee behavior is embedded in a social system. For instance, to understand the impact of pay on performance, you have to understand the atmosphere that exists in the work group and how the leader approaches his or her job.

A major implication of the Hawthorne studies was that the old concept of an economic person motivated primarily by money had to be replaced by a more valid idea. The replacement concept was a social person, motivated by social needs, desiring rewarding on-the-job relationships and being more responsive to pressures from coworkers than to control by the boss.[20] Do you believe that workers are more concerned with social relationships than with money?

THE THREAT OF UNIONIZATION

Labor union officials and their advocates contend that the benefits of unionization extend to many workers who themselves do not belong to unions. Management in nonunion firms will sometimes pay employees union wages to offset the potential advantages of unionization. A similar set of circumstances contributed to the growth of the human relations movement. Labor unions began to grow rapidly in the United States during the late 1930s. Many employers feared that the presence of a labor union would have negative consequences for their companies. Consequently, management looked aggressively for ways to stem the tide of unionization, such as using human relations techniques to satisfy workers.[21]

Today the threat of unionization is primarily in the public sector. Although unionization has declined considerably in manufacturing, about 35.7 percent of government workers, including those in education, are union members, compared with about 6.6 percent of workers in private-sector industries. In 1945, about 36 percent of the U.S. workforce was unionized, versus about 12.3 percent today.[22] The decline of manufacturing jobs has contributed to the decline of union membership. Much of the decline can be attributed to the outsourcing of manufacturing jobs to other countries and the use of information technology to replace workers.

THE PHILOSOPHY OF INDUSTRIAL HUMANISM

Partly as a byproduct of the Hawthorne studies, a new philosophy of human relations arose in the workplace. Elton Mayo was one of the two key figures in developing this philosophy of industrial humanism. He cautioned managers that emotional factors (such as a desire for recognition) were a more important contributor to productivity than physical and logical factors. Mayo argued vigorously that work should lead to personal satisfaction for employees.

Mary Parker Follett was another key figure in advancing the cause of industrial humanism. Her experience as a management consultant led her to believe that the key to increased productivity was to motivate employees, rather than simply ordering better job performance. The keys to both productivity and democracy, according to Follett, were cooperation, a spirit of unity, and a coordination of effort.[23]

THEORY X AND THEORY Y OF DOUGLAS McGREGOR

The importance of managing people through more effective methods of human relations was advanced by the writings of social psychologist Douglas McGregor. His famous position was that managers should challenge their assumptions about the nature of people. McGregor believed that too many managers assumed that people were lazy and indifferent toward work. He urged managers to be open to the possibility that under the right circumstances people are eager to perform well. If a supervisor accepts one of these extreme sets of beliefs about people, the supervisor will act differently toward them than if he or she believes the opposite. These famous assumptions that propelled the human relations movement are summarized as follows:

Theory X Assumptions

1. The average person dislikes work and therefore will avoid it if he or she can.

2. Because of this dislike of work, most people must be coerced, controlled, directed, or threatened with punishment to get them to put forth enough effort to achieve organizational goals.

3. The average employee prefers to be directed, wishes to shirk responsibility, has relatively little ambition, and highly values job security.

Theory Y Assumptions

1. The expenditure of physical and mental effort in work is as natural as play or rest.

2. External control and the threat of punishment are not the only means for bringing about effort toward reaching company objectives. Employees will exercise self-direction and self-control in the service of objectives to which they attach high valence.

3. Commitment to objectives is related to the rewards associated with their achievement.

4. The average person learns, under proper conditions, not only to accept but also to seek responsibility.

5. Many employees have the capacity to exercise a high degree of imagination, ingenuity, and creativity in the solution of organizational problems.

6. Under the present conditions of industrial life, the intellectual potentialities of the average person are only partially utilized.[24]

The distinction between Theory X and Theory Y has often been misinterpreted. McGregor was humanistic, but he did not mean to imply that being directive and demanding with workers is always the wrong tactic. Some people are undermotivated and dislike work. In these situations, the manager has to behave sternly toward group members to motivate them. If you are a Theory Y manager, you size up your group members to understand their attitudes toward work.

THE INTERNET AND SOCIAL MEDIA ERA

As with every other field, human relations in organizations has been affected by the Internet, including social networks. Rather than being a new approach to human relations, these modern developments in information technology are incorporated into the work activities of the vast majority of workers at all levels in the organization. Rare exceptions do exist with respect to workers who do not have to use the Internet to accomplish their tasks. Among them are clam diggers, street food vendors, hotel housekeepers, and circus clowns. Following are three of hundreds of possible examples of how the Internet and social media influence human relations on the job:

- Workers communicate and collaborate with each other through company social media networks, as well as public networks such as Facebook, Twitter, and Instagram.

- Team leaders motivate subordinates by sending them electronic messages in place of face-to-face meetings.

- Job applicants do online most of the work preceding a face-to-face interview and also research their prospective employers online.

The focus of our approach in this text as to how the Internet and social media affect human relations will be in Chapter 8.

RELEVANCE OF THE HISTORY OF HUMAN RELATIONS TO TODAY'S WORKPLACE

Many of the pioneering ideas described in the history of human relations are still relevant, partly because human nature has not undergone major changes. Most of the core ideas in the history of the human relations movement are still part of the human relations and organizational behavior curriculum today, even though they have more research substantiation and new labels. A good example is the push toward creativity and innovation based on the involvement of many different workers, not only specialists from one department. The link to history is that Theory Y encourages empowering employees to use their ingenuity and creativity to solve organizational problems. Next is a bulleted summary of ideas from the human relations movement that still influence the practice of human relations today:

■ Many principles of scientific management are useful in making workers more productive so business firms can compete better in a global economy.

■ Ideas from the Hawthorne studies have helped managers focus on the importance of providing both congenial work surroundings and adequate compensation to motivate and retain workers.

■ Industrial humanism is widely practiced today in the form of looking for ways to keep workers satisfied through such methods as flexible work arrangements, family leave, and dependent-care benefits.

■ Theory Y has prompted managers to think through which style of leadership works best with which employees. Specifically, a modern manager is likely to grant more freedom to employees who are well motivated and talented. Spurred partially by Theory X, few managers today believe that being the "bull of the woods" is the best way to supervise all workers.

Major Factors Influencing Job Performance and Behavior

◀ **Learning Objective 1.5** ◀

Part of understanding human relations is recognizing the factors or forces that influence job performance and behavior. In overview, the performance and behavior of workers is influenced by factors related to the employee, manager, job, and organization plus the external environment, as discussed next and outlined in Figure 1-5. Here we present a sampling of these many factors, because a comprehensive understanding of them encompasses the study of human relations, organizational behavior, and management.

1. **Factors related to the employee.** The major influence on how a worker performs and behaves, or acts, on the job stems from his or her personal attributes. The worker's mental ability influences how quickly and accurately he or she can solve problems. Physical ability would influence some types of performance, such as the ability to stand up for long periods of time as a store manager or lift boxes as a warehouse attendant. Job knowledge is obviously important, such as a financial consultant being knowledgeable about a variety of investments. Employees who are well motivated and interested in the work are likely to perform better and behave in a more professional manner. Workers who receive encouragement from friends and family are likely to perform better. Being distracted, such as frequently accessing Facebook and Twitter during the workday or experiencing heavy personal problems, can influence

FIGURE 1-5

FACTORS CONTRIBUTING TO PERFORMANCE AND BEHAVIOR IN THE WORKPLACE

Source: "FACTORS CONTRIBUTING TO PERFORMANCE AND BEHAVIOR IN THE WORKPLACE" by Andrew J. DuBrin.

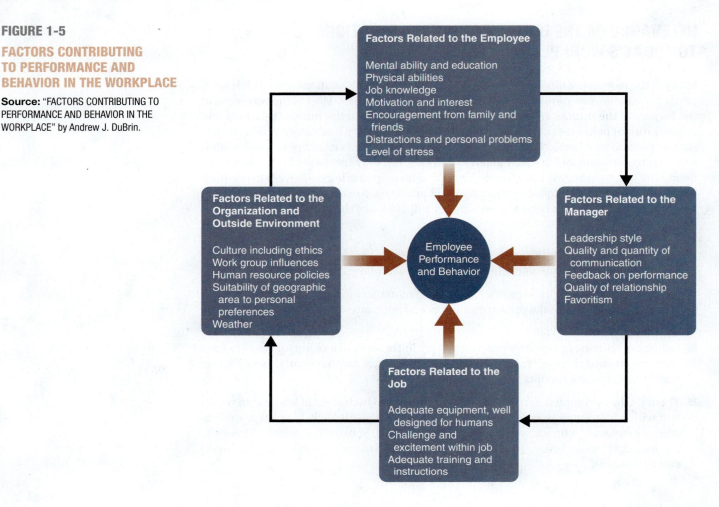

performance negatively. Having the right amount of stress can boost performance, whereas being overstressed can lower performance and lead to distracting behavior, such as being confused.

2. **Factors related to the manager.** The manager, or supervisor, is another major influence on work behavior. A manager whose style or approach is warm and supportive is likely to bring out the best in many employees. But some workers require a more directive and demanding supervisor to perform at their best. Ample communication among the manager and group members is likely to enhance performance and guide employees toward doing what is expected of them. Most workers need considerable feedback from their supervisor to stay on track and be highly motivated. A high-quality relationship between the manager and group members leads to high performance, more loyalty, and lower absenteeism. Favoritism is another key factor related to the manager. A manager who plays favorites is less likely to gain the cooperation of the entire group.

3. **Factors related to the job.** The job itself influences how well the worker might perform and behave. Given the right equipment, designed well for human use, a worker is likely to perform better, such as being less likely to have aches, pains, and wrist injuries as a result of many hours of keyboarding. A proven strategy for improving worker motivation is to give the employee an exciting, challenging job, such as the opportunity to make presentations to management about a project. Adequate training and instructions can also be a big boost to job performance. Information technology also has a major potential impact on the job. A good example is that when an organization

relies on one cohesive suite of productivity tools instead of workers using a wide range of devices of their own choosing, productivity will increase.[25]

4. **Factors related to the organization and the external environment.** The organization as a whole can have a profound influence on the individual worker's performance and behavior. The *culture*, or atmosphere and values of a company, establishes an unwritten standard for how employees perform and behave. At Google, for example, employees are placed in an atmosphere where being creative and making suggestions are expected. And all Zappos.com employees know that having fun is supposed to be part of the job. The culture of the organization also influences the ethical behavior of employees, with some companies expecting honest treatment of workers and employees. Other companies are much less ethical and encourage tactics such as deceiving customers. The work group, as part of the organization, can influence the employee by encouraging teamwork and high productivity, among other approaches. Human resource policies are another notable influence on the individual. If your company offers you generous medical and dental benefits and allows time off for family emergencies, it becomes easier to concentrate on the job.

It is also possible for the external, or outside, environment to influence job performance and behavior. A positive example would be living in a geographic location so enjoyable that the setting tips your mood in a positive direction on many days. A negative example would be the necessity of a long and difficult commute to work when you dislike commuting.

A series of found studies conducted by a team of researchers supports the idea that the external environment influences individual productivity. The studies found that on days of inclement weather, productivity increased rather than decreased as common sense might predict. Rainy weather, according to the interpretation of the findings, creates fewer cognitive distractions and thus facilitates concentrating on work.[26] You have probably asked yourself at least once in your life, "Why am I working inside on this beautiful day?" Your distracting thought might have lowered your productivity for that day.

The four factors just listed often have a combined influence on the worker. Let us take an extreme example: Jack, a well-motivated and talented assistant hotel manager, reports to a manager with whom he has a great relationship, which includes giving Jack ample feedback on his performance. Jack finds his job challenging, and his hotel has the advanced equipment necessary for success. The hotel has a friendly climate, along with generous benefits. Jack also thinks the geographic setting of the hotel is superb. As a result of this combination of factors, Jack is an outstanding performer who approaches his job with a high degree of professionalism.

Concept Review and Reinforcement

Summary and Review

Human relations is the art and practice of using systematic knowledge about human behavior to improve personal, job, and career effectiveness.

From the standpoint of management, human relations is important because it contributes to organizational effectiveness. Treating employees with respect and paying them fairly contributes to developing an efficient and creative organization. Major benefits of studying human relations include the following:

- Acquiring information about human behavior
- Developing skills in dealing with people
- Coping with job problems
- Coping with personal problems
- Capitalizing on opportunities
- Demonstrating potential for advancement

Work and personal life often influence each other in several ways, as follows:

- Mood influences job satisfaction, but the effect passes quickly.
- Job satisfaction influences the mood at home, with more emotional employees more likely to experience this relationship.
- A high level of job satisfaction tends to spill over to your personal life. Conversely, an unsatisfactory personal life could lead to negative job attitudes.
- Your job can affect physical and mental health. Severely negative job conditions may lead to a serious stress disorder, such as heart disease.
- The quality of relationships with people at work and in one's personal life influence each other.

- Certain skills (such as the ability to listen) contribute to success at work and in one's personal life.
- How we behave at work is closely related to how we behave at home.
- Workers who achieve a good balance between the demands of work and family life are likely to be more productive and satisfied.

To be effective in human relationships, you must first understand yourself. Six sources of information that contribute to self-understanding are as follows:

1. General information about human behavior
2. Informal feedback from people
3. Feedback from superiors
4. Feedback from coworkers
5. Feedback from self-examination exercises
6. Looking at the self through the Johari Window

Be aware of the self-evaluation traps of highlighting your shortcomings and unrealistically overevaluating your competence. Cultural differences help explain some of the differences in underevaluation versus overevaluation.

The human relations movement was a concentrated effort to become more sensitive to the needs of employees and to treat them in a more humanistic manner. Along with the indirect influence of scientific management, the movement was supported directly by five historic influences, and a new influence has emerged:

1. Scientific management applied scientific methods to increase worker productivity.

2. The Hawthorne studies showed that concern for workers can increase their performance as much as or more than improving physical working conditions.
3. Employers used the threat of unionization, in which management employed human relations techniques to deter workers from joining a labor union.
4. The philosophy of industrial humanism, in which motivation and emotional factors are important.
5. Theory X and Theory Y of Douglas McGregor.
6. The Internet and social media have influenced heavily how people communicate and relate to each other in the workplace.

Many of the pioneering ideas described in the history of human relations are still relevant, partly because human nature has not undergone major changes. An example of a pioneering idea in use is that Theory Y has prompted managers to think through which leadership style works best with which employees.

Part of understanding human relations is recognizing the factors that influence job performance and behavior, as follows: factors related to the employee, manager, job, and the organization and external environment.

Discussion and Review Questions

1.1 Why do you think good human relations skills are so important for supervisors who direct the work activities of entry-level workers?

1.2 How might participation in team sports enhance an individual's human relations skills? How might such participation encourage a person to develop poor human relations skills?

1.3 Give an example from your own experience of how work life influences personal life and vice versa.

1.4 How might a person improve his or her personal life to the extent that the improvement would also enhance his or her job performance?

1.5 How might a person improve his or her job or career to the extent that the improvement would actually enhance his or her personal life?

1.6 Describe a situation in which making Theory X assumptions about employees might be accurate.

1.7 How do you think having good human relations skills and knowledge might add to your job security in a competitive workplace?

1.8 Identify a person in public life, including a television show character, who you think has outstanding human relations skills, and explain the basis for your conclusion.

1.9 Identify a person in public life, including a television show character, who you think has terrible human relations skills, and explain the basis for your conclusion.

1.10 Based on what you have studied so far, in what way does human relations involve more than "being nice to people"?

Web Corner

The Dale Carnegie organization has long been associated with teaching human relations effectiveness. The company stemmed from the work of Dale Carnegie, who many years ago popularized the idea of "winning friends and influencing people." Visit www.dalecarnegie.com to understand what type of skills Dale Carnegie Training teaches. Compare the course listing to subjects listed in the table of contents in this text. What similarities do you see?

INTERNET SKILL BUILDER

The Importance of Human Relations Skills in Business

One of the themes of this entire text is that human relations skills are important for success in business. But what do employers really think? To find out, visit the websites of five of your favorite companies, such as www.wellsfargo.com. Go to the employment section and search for a job that you might qualify for now or in the future. Investigate which human relations or interpersonal skills the employer mentions as a requirement, such as "Must have superior spoken communication skills." Make up a list of the human relations or interpersonal skills you find mentioned. What conclusions do you reach from this exercise?

Developing Your Human Relations Skills

Applying Human Relations Exercise 1-1

Learning about Each Other's Human Relations Skills

A constructive way of broadening your insights about human relations skills is to find out what other people perceive as their strengths in dealing with others. Toward this end, class members come to the front of the class, one by one, to make a two-minute presentation on his or her best ability in dealing with people. To help standardize the presentations, each student completes the following sentence: "What I do best with people is _____."

In this exercise, and all other class presentation exercises contained in the text, students are asked to share only those ideas they would be comfortable in sharing with the class. Here, for example, you might be very good at doing something with people about which you would be embarrassed to let others know.

As the other students are presenting, attempt to concentrate on them and not be so preoccupied with your presentation that you cannot listen. Make note when somebody says something out of the ordinary. When the presentation is over, the class will discuss answers to the following questions:

1. What was the most frequent human relations capability mentioned?
2. To what extent do classmates appear to be exaggerating their human relations skills?
3. What omissions did you find? For example, were there any important human relations skills you thought a few students should have mentioned but did not?

Applying Human Relations Exercise 1-2

My Human Relations Journal

A potentially important aid in your development as a person with effective human relations skills is to maintain a journal or diary of your experiences. Make a journal entry within 24 hours of carrying out a significant human relations action or failing to do so when the opportunity arose. You will have entries dealing with human relations opportunities both capitalized on and missed. Here is an example: "A few of my neighbors were complaining about all the vandalism in the neighborhood. Cars were getting dented and scratched, and streetlights were being smashed. A few bricks were thrown into home windows. I volunteered to organize a neighborhood patrol. The patrol actually helped cut back on the vandalism." Or in contrast, given the same scenario: "I thought that someone else should take care of the problem. My time is too valuable." (In the first example, the key human relations skill the person exercised was leadership.)

Also include in your journal such entries as feedback you receive on your human relations ability, good interpersonal traits you appear to be developing, and key human relations ideas about which you read.

Review your journal monthly, and make note of any progress you think you have made in developing your human relations skills. Also consider preparing a graph of your human relations skill development. The vertical axis can represent skill level on a scale of 1 to 100, and the horizontal axis might be divided into time internals, such as calendar quarters.

Human Relations Case Study 1–1

Amanda, the Rejected Job Candidate

Amanda had several years of experience in website development at one company. She also had studied website development at college and had five years of experience in developing websites for friends and family as a hobby. The company she worked for was acquired by a larger firm that had a website development staff of its own, so Amanda's position was eliminated.

Although she received two months of severance pay and would soon be eligible for unemployment insurance, Amanda began a job search immediately. She concentrated her online job search for website developer positions within fifty miles of the apartment that she shared with her sister. After sending twenty-one inquiries and job résumés, Amanda landed a job interview with Noble Properties, a large regional real-estate sales company.

The interview began with a discussion of Amanda's technical qualifications for the job. Amanda described her experience in website development and also accessed, on the interviewer's desktop computer and her smartphone, two different websites she had developed. During her presentation, Amanda noticed that she had a text message waiting from a friend. She motioned to the interviewer with her index finger and a nod that she would take a brief pause from the interview to read the message and respond. Amanda said to the interviewer, "My friends won't stop texting me."

Later in the interview, Amanda was asked how well she got along with other workers in her past employment. Amanda replied, "I'm kind of a lone wolf, but who cares? I'm not applying for a job in sales. I work best alone. When coworkers ask me questions, it breaks my concentration."

At approximately twenty-five minutes into the interview, the manager explained to Amanda that after a ten-minute break, she would have a group interview with several other Noble Properties staff members.

Amanda was called into a small conference room where four Noble staffers and the interviewing manager were waiting. At first, Amanda said nothing while she sat staring at her hands. She then said, "What do you want from me?"

The CEO said to Amanda, "One thing I would like from you is to remove your sports cap. It interferes with seeing your facial expressions." Amanda replied, "I would hate to take off my cap because my hair is awful today, but I'll do it anyway. But I don't see how facial expressions are important for a website developer."

The interviewing manager concluded the interview by asking Amanda if she had any questions or comments. Amanda responded, "Please text me with your decision. I really prefer text messages to talking on the phone."

After Amanda left the conference room, the interviewing manager said, "So what if this woman is an effective website developer? Her people skills are unsuited for Noble Properties. I recommend that we do not make her a job offer."

Questions

1.11 What evidence do you see from the information presented that Amanda has poor people (human relations) skills?

1.12 Why should the interviewing manager at Noble Properties care if a website developer has good human relations skills?

1.13 What advice might you offer Amanda to increase her chances of being more successful during an interview for the position of a website developer?

Human Relations Case Study 1–2

Calvin Struggles to Balance His Life

Calvin, age twenty-nine, is a physical therapist working at a sports medicine clinic. Most of his work is helping people who have suffered sports-related or automobile-accident-related injuries to rehabilitate and get back to normal functioning. Many of the patients he treats have torn knee ligaments or broken ankles. Calvin derives a lot of satisfaction from his work, but at times he feels overwhelmed.

"I want to help every patient get back on track," he says. "Yet my work can be so frustrating because progress can be so slow. Emily, a fourteen-year-old girl, is a good example. The poor kid badly tore the ACL on her left knee during a soccer match. Emily and her parents want her walking great and playing soccer as soon as possible. I have been working with her for ten months, and the progress is so slow. Sure Emily can walk, but her left knee is still far too weak. And she is in no shape to play soccer. The orthopedist on the case agrees."

Asked how the highs and lows of his work as a physical therapist affect his life outside of work, Calvin replied with heavy emotion: "What you hint at is the biggest struggle in my life right now. My wife Ashley has a demanding career as an executive assistant, and she does a better job of keeping work and home life separate. We are also parents to Carter, who attends kindergarten.

"When I have a great day at the clinic, such as seeing a patient regain almost full strength, I feel like Superman. I come home to Ashley and Carter filled with love and warmth. I am ready to take my turn cooking for dinner and reading a bedtime story to Carter. But on days when the patients I work with have made no progress or feel frustrated and hopeless, I feel frustrated and hopeless. The problem is that when I arrive home in that down condition, I'm kind of a washout as a husband and father.

"What I would like to do is to be on more of an even keel and not let my work as a physical therapist have such an impact on my home life."

Questions

1.14 What does this case illustrate about the relationship between work and personal life?

1.15 What might Calvin do to soften the impact his professional life has on his personal life?

1.16 What role might Ashley play in helping Calvin with his struggle?

Human Relations Role-Playing Exercise

Here, as in all chapters, a role-playing (or role-assuming) exercise will be presented to provide practice in implementing a specific human relations skill or technique. The role-plays will typically be presented in front of others for about five to ten minutes. A natural and easy way of carrying out most of these role-plays is for you to get a general idea of the role and then spontaneously say and do what you think a person in that role might do and say. For many of the role-plays, it will be helpful for you to read the relevant text material to assist you in refining your skill. For these two introductory role-plays, just rely on whatever knowledge and skills you already have.

Scenario 1: Kindness at the Building Inspection Office

Getting back to the chapter-opening story, one person plays the role of Beverly, who is presented with what appears to be a way-off-base suggestion from a staff member. The staff member suggests that instead of making in-person visits to inspect buildings, robots should be programmed to make the inspections. Some of the inspections could be made late at night or early in the morning so as not to disturb workers in the buildings. One person plays the role of the staff member

who makes the suggestion. Another person plays the role of Beverly, who will reject the suggestion with kindness. Run the conversation for about six minutes.

Scenario 2: Having a Conversation about Work and Family Life

Getting back to Case Study 1-2, one person plays the role of Calvin, the physical therapist. Another person plays the role of Ashley, his wife. It is nine at night, and Carter is finally asleep. Calvin introduces the topic of not wanting to arrive home so frustrated and sullen when he falls short of meeting his expectations as a physical therapist that day. Ashley, who has become a little frustrated with Calvin's mood swings, is eager to have this conversation. One student plays the role of Calvin, and one student plays the role of Ashley.

For both scenarios, observers rate the role-players on two dimensions, using a scale of 1 to 5 from "very poor" to "very good." One dimension is "effective use of human relations techniques." The second dimension is "acting ability." A few observers might voluntarily provide feedback to the role-players in terms of sharing their ratings and observations. The course instructor might also provide feedback.

Human Relations Class Activity

The Unique People

Most of the self-assessment quizzes and human relations exercises presented throughout this text are performed by students working individually or in small groups. At the end of each chapter, we present an additional activity geared toward enhanced human relations knowledge or skill that is to be performed by the entire class, often interacting with each other. The unit of contribution might be you working alone, but at some point the contributions become collective.

Our first class activity is geared toward reinforcing the idea that part of effective human relations is to recognize that people are different in many ways, stemming from their group characteristics, culture, personality, problem-solving ability, experiences, and interests, among many other factors. Students in the class, or only those who volunteer, come up to the front of the class one at a time to make a

one-minute presentation about any way in which they are unique. Here are three statements of uniqueness among an infinite number of possibilities: "I graduated number one in my high school class of fifty-seven students"; "I was born and raised in China, but I don't like to eat in Chinese restaurants. I prefer Applebee's and Outback Steakhouse"; "I rigged up my house to be smart. I can use my Galaxy to start the air-conditioning or the oven in my house from miles away."

After the unique aspects of each class member are presented, volunteers might offer feedback to participants by completing the following statements:

1. "What really surprised me was _____."
2. "What made me really think positively about _____ was the fact that he (or she) _____."
3. "I really learned something about human relations today. Now I know that _____."

REFERENCES

1. Steven Kent, "Happy Workers Are the Best Workers," *The Wall Street Journal*, September 6, 2005, p. A20.

2. Timothy A. Judge and Remus Iles, "Affect and Job Satisfaction: A Study of Their Relationship at Work and Home," *Journal of Applied Psychology*, August 2004, pp. 661–673.

3. "Making Relationships Work: A Conversation with Psychologist John M. Gottman," *Harvard Business Review*, December 2007, pp. 45–50.

4. Kathy Gurchiek, "Not a 'Mommy' Issue," *HR Magazine*, April 2011, pp. 40–41

5. Russell A. Matthews, Julie Holliday Wayne, and Michael T. Ford, "A Work/Family Conflict/Subjective Well-Being Process Model: A Test of Competing Theories of Longitudinal Effects," *Journal of Applied Psychology*, November 2014, pp. 1173–1187.

6. Cited in Norman Anderson, "Psychologists' Role in Work–Life Fit Is More Important than Ever," *Monitor on Psychology*, November 2012, p. 9.

7. C. R. Snyder, "So Many Selves," *Contemporary Psychology*, January 1988, p. 77.

8. Otila Obodaru, "The Self Not Taken: How Alternative Selves Develop and How They Influence Our Professional Lives," *Academy of Management Review*, January 2012, p. 36.

9. Cited in Etienne Benson, "The Synaptic Self," *Monitor on Psychology*, November 2002, p. 40.

10. Rita Pyrillis, "The Reviews Are In," *Workforce Management*, May 2011, p. 21.

11. Rachel Feintzeig, "You're Awesome! Firms Scrap Negative Feedback," *The Wall Street Journal*, February 11, 2015, p. B1.

12. Karen Wright, "A Chic Critique," *Psychology Today*, March–April 2011, p. 55.

13. Joseph Luft, *Group Process: An Introduction to Group Dynamics* (New York: Mayfield Publishing Company/McGraw-Hill, 1984); Luft, *Of Human Interaction* (Palo Alto, CA: National Press, 1969); Suzanne C. De Janasz, Karen O. Dowd, and Beth Z. Schneider, *Interpersonal Skills in Organizations* (New York: McGraw-Hill, 2002), pp. 31–32.

14. Saul Kassin, *Psychology*, 3rd ed. (Upper Saddle River, NJ: Prentice Hall, 2001), p. 74.

15. Research summarized in Tori DeAngelis, "Why We Overestimate Our Competence," *Monitor on Psychology*, February 2003, p. 61.

16. Ibid.

17. Robert Kreitner, *Management*, 5th ed. (Boston: Houghton Mifflin, 1992), pp. 51–52.

18. Edward G. Wertheim, "Historical Background of Organizational Behavior," http://web.cba.neu.edu/~Wertheim/introd/history.htm, accessed March 15, 2006.

19. Elton Mayo, *The Human Problems of Industrial Civilization* (New York: Viking Press, 1960).

20. James A. F. Stoner and R. Edward Freeman, *Management*, 4th ed. (Upper Saddle River, NJ: Prentice Hall, 1989), p. 49.

21. Kreitner, *Management*, p. 50.

22. "Union Members Summary," *Economic News Release: Union Member Summary*, www.bls.gov/news, p. 1, accessed January 23, 2015.

23. Kreitner, *Management*, p. 62.

24. Douglas McGregor, *The Human Side of Enterprise* (New York: McGraw-Hill, 1960), pp. 33–48.

25. Sarah Fister Gale, "HR, Your Input Is Needed," *Workforce*, October 2012, pp. 24–26.

26. Joosa Julia Lee, Francesca Gino, and Bradley R. Staats, "Rainmaker: Why Bad Weather Means Good Productivity," *Journal of Applied Psychology*, May 2014, pp. 504–513.

Fotolia

CHAPTER **2**

Self-Esteem and Self-Confidence

Outline

Emilio Romano, an experienced media and aviation executive, was hired in 2014 by the giant Bank of America Corporation as the chief executive for Mexico. Upon his hiring, the Bank of America president and CEO for Latin America said, "Emilio is a natural and charismatic leader as well as a strong team player who will work to capture market opportunities to take our franchise in Mexico to the next level." Prior to joining Bank of America, Romano was the president of Telemundo, the second largest Spanish-language television network in the United States. When Romano departed Telemundo, Joe Uva, the chairman of NBC Universal's Hispanic enterprise and content, publicly thanked him for his contributions to the company. A specific contribution noted was that Romano had laid the foundation for growth with the rapidly growing millennial population. Uva also noted that Romano was a good business partner.

A proud and confident man, Romano said in a press release when he joined Telemundo that he was honored to be joining this team of professionals. He also expressed excitement about being part of the transformation taking place within the Hispanic/Latino media market in the United States.

Throughout his career, Romano has been confident enough to occupy a variety of roles. For three years he was CEO of Mexicana de Aviacion airline. He has also served as the president and chief executive officer of Grupo Puerta Alamedi (GPA), a real estate and investment company with operations in the United States and Mexico. An attorney by profession, he served as a professor in the doctoral program in tax law at the Escuela Libre de Derecho. He was well liked as a professor because of his passion for his work and the high standards he set for students.

Romano typically assumes a positive attitude toward any new challenge he faces, and his pride in taking on the challenge impresses his colleagues and subordinates. His typical business attire includes a fashionable suit and tie. He is an accomplished executive who keeps his ego in check.

The story just presented illustrates how self-confidence, such as being willing to take risks and try something new, helps a person succeed in a competitive field. Romano also has to have high self-esteem to think that his analytical skills are so good that he can compete in the worlds of aviation, real estate, Spanish-language broadcasting, and banking. Many other people you will meet in this text score high in self-esteem and self-confidence; otherwise they would never have been so successful. In this chapter the focus is on two of the biggest building blocks for more effective human relations: the nature and development of self-esteem and self-confidence.

Learning Objectives ▶

After studying the information and doing the exercises in this chapter, you should be able to:

2.1 Describe the nature, development, and consequences of self-esteem.

2.2 Explain how to enhance self-esteem.

2.3 Describe the importance of self-confidence and self-efficacy.

2.4 Pinpoint methods of strengthening and developing your self-confidence.

2.5 Describe the problem of codependence and how it is linked to low self-esteem and self-confidence.

▶ **Learning Objective 2.1** ▶

The Nature of Self-Esteem, Its Development, and Its Consequences

Self-esteem
the experience of feeling competent to cope with the basic challenges in life and of being worthy of happiness

Understanding the self from various perspectives is important because who you are and what you think of yourself influence many facets of your life, both on and off the job. A particularly important role is played by **self-esteem**, the experience of feeling competent to cope with the basic challenges in life and being worthy of happiness.[1] In more general terms, self-esteem refers to a positive overall evaluation of oneself.

A useful distinction is that our self-concept refers to what we *think* about ourselves, whereas self-esteem is what we *feel* about ourselves.[2] People with positive self-esteem have a deep-down, inside-the-self feeling of their own worth. Consequently, they develop positive self-concepts. Before reading further, you are invited to measure your current level of self-esteem by taking the Human Relations Self-Assessment Quiz 2-1. Next, the nature of self-esteem and many of its consequences are examined.

THE DEVELOPMENT OF SELF-ESTEEM

Part of understanding the nature of self-esteem is to know how it develops. Self-esteem comes about from a variety of early life experiences. People who were encouraged to feel good about themselves and their accomplishments by family members, friends, and teachers are more likely to enjoy high self-esteem. The basis for a healthy level of self-esteem grows out of a secure attachment to a parent. Self-esteem later in life can be weak if a parent is inconsistently supportive or lacks empathy and concern for the child. Self-esteem is enhanced if the parent is emotionally supportive toward the child even when the child does something wrong, such as spilling a glass of diet soda on a beige carpet.[3]

As just implied, early life experiences play a key role in the development of both healthy self-esteem and low self-esteem, according to research synthesized at the Counseling and Mental Health Center of the University of Texas.[4] Childhood experiences that lead to healthy self-esteem include the following:

- Being praised
- Being listened to
- Being spoken to respectfully
- Getting attention and hugs
- Experiencing success in sports or school

In contrast, childhood experiences that lead to low self-esteem include the following:

- Being harshly criticized
- Being yelled at or beaten
- Being ignored, ridiculed, or teased
- Being expected to be "perfect" all the time
- Experiencing failures in sports or school
- Often being given messages that failed experiences (losing a game, getting a poor grade, and so forth) were failures of one's whole self

An outdated explanation of self-esteem development is that compliments, praise, and hugs alone build self-esteem. Many developmental psychologists seriously question this

Human Relations Self-Assessment Quiz   2-1

The Self-Esteem Checklist

Indicate whether each of the following statements is mostly true or mostly false as it applies to you.

	Mostly True	Mostly False
1. I love me.	_____	_____
2. Most of any progress I have made in my work or school can be attributed to luck.	_____	_____
3. I often ask myself, "Why can't I be more successful?"	_____	_____
4. When my manager or team leader gives me a challenging assignment, I usually dive in with confidence.	_____	_____
5. I believe that I am truly a person of high value.	_____	_____
6. I am able to set limits to what I will do for others without feeling anxious.	_____	_____
7. I regularly make excuses for my mistakes.	_____	_____
8. Negative feedback crushes me.	_____	_____
9. I care very much how much money other people make, especially when they are working in my field.	_____	_____
10. I feel like a failure when I do not achieve my goals.	_____	_____
11. Hard work gives me an emotional lift.	_____	_____
12. When others compliment me, I doubt their sincerity.	_____	_____
13. Complimenting others makes me feel uncomfortable.	_____	_____
14. I find it comfortable to say, "I'm sorry."	_____	_____
15. It is difficult for me to face up to my mistakes.	_____	_____
16. My coworkers think I am not worthy of promotion.	_____	_____
17. People who want to become my friends usually do not have much to offer.	_____	_____
18. If my manager praised me, I would have a difficult time believing the praise was deserved.	_____	_____
19. I'm just an ordinary person.	_____	_____
20. Having to face change really disturbs me.	_____	_____

Scoring and Interpretation:

The answers in the high self-esteem direction are as follows:

1. Mostly True	8. Mostly False	15. Mostly False
2. Mostly False	9. Mostly False	16. Mostly False
3. Mostly False	10. Mostly False	17. Mostly False
4. Mostly True	11. Mostly True	18. Mostly False
5. Mostly True	12. Mostly False	19. Mostly False
6. Mostly True	13. Mostly False	20. Mostly False
7. Mostly False	14. Mostly True	

17–20 You have very high self-esteem. Yet if your score is 20, it could be that you are denying any self-doubts.

11–16 Your self-esteem is in the average range. It would probably be worthwhile for you to implement strategies to boost your self-esteem (described in this chapter) so that you can develop a greater feeling of well-being.

0–10 Your self-esteem needs bolstering. Discuss your feelings about yourself with a trusted friend or with a mental health professional. At the same time, attempt to implement several of the tactics for boosting self-esteem described in this chapter.

Questions: 1. How does your score on this quiz match your evaluation of your self-esteem?
2. What would it be like to be married to somebody who scored 0 on this quiz?

Source: "The Self-Esteem Checklist" by Andrew J. DuBrin.

"Even the most accomplished, beautiful, and celebrated human beings don't get a steady stream of compliments and positive feedback."
—*Harriet Brown*
Assistant professor of magazine journalism at the S. I. Newhouse School of Public Administration, Syracuse University. *Psychology Today,* January/February 2012, p. 69.

perspective. Instead, they believe that self-esteem results from accomplishing worthwhile activities and then feeling proud of these accomplishments.[5] Receiving encouragement, however, can help the person accomplish activities that build self-esteem.

The current view about self-esteem development in early life is that it should be done in moderation. Children should be praised but not with disregard for the outside world. For example, a child might be praised for improving his or her reading ability, but still using some outside standard such as the reading ability of his or her age-mates. Children who have a realistic—not exaggerated—perspective on how they are evaluated by others tend to be more resilient in dealing with setbacks. Occasional dips in self-esteem are also important for children, explains Mark Leary, professor of psychology and neuroscience at Duke University. Children feeling bad about themselves for having mistreated others will serve as a guide for relationships later in life.[6]

Although early life experiences have the major impact on the development of self-esteem, experiences in adult life also affect self-esteem. David De Cremer, of the Tilburg University (Netherlands), and his associates conducted two studies with Dutch college students about how the behavior of leaders and fair procedures influence self-esteem. The study found that self-esteem was related to procedural fairness and leadership that encourages self-rewards. The interpretation given of the findings is that a leader/supervisor can facilitate self-esteem when he or she encourages self-rewards and uses fair procedures.[7] A takeaway from this study would be that rewarding yourself for a job well done, even in adult life, can boost your self-esteem a little.

THE CONSEQUENCES OF SELF-ESTEEM

No single factor is as important to career success as self-esteem, as observed by psychologist Eugene Raudsepp. People with positive self-esteem understand their own competence and worth and have positive perceptions of their abilities to cope with problems and adversity.[8] Here we look at the major positive and negative consequences of self-esteem, as outlined in Figure 2-1.

POSITIVE CONSEQUENCES

The right amount of self-esteem can have many positive consequences, as described next.

Career Success

A major consequence of having high self-esteem is that you have a better chance of attaining career success, as mentioned at the beginning of this section, and supported by long-term research. The study in question was known as the National Longitudinal Survey of Youth, involving over 12,000 young men and women. The group was studied over a twenty-five-year period beginning in 1979. Human Relations Self-Assessment Quiz 2-2 gives you the opportunity to take the same survey used in the study to measure core self-evaluations.

The components of core self-evaluation include high self-esteem, self-efficacy (an aspect of self-confidence described later in this chapter), beliefs in personal control over events, and

FIGURE 2-1

CONSEQUENCES OF SELF-ESTEEM

Source: "CONSEQUENCES OF SELF-ESTEEM" by Andrew J. DuBrin.

1. Career success
2. Organizational prosperity
3. Good mental health
4. Profiting from negative feedback
5. Serves as a guide for regulating social relationships
6. Negative consequences: narcissism, envying too many other people, romance problems

emotional stability. Individuals with high core self-evaluations are better motivated, perform better on the job, tend to hold more challenging jobs, and have higher job satisfaction.

Among the many results of the study were that people with higher core self-evaluations performed better in their first jobs. Furthermore, over time those people with high core self-evaluations increase their career success at a faster pace than those with below-average core self-evaluations. Over a twenty-five-year span, the career success they have over others doubles. Success was measured in terms of job satisfaction, pay, and holding a higher-status position.[9] A practical conclusion to take away from this study is that if you have a high core self-evaluation, it will pay impressive career dividends.

Another aspect of career success related to the core self-evaluation is profiting from training. Performing well in training contributes to career success because of workplace emphasis on continuous learning. Evidence about the link between profiting from training and the core self-evaluation comes from a study of 638 military personnel who participated in job-required foreign language training. Training lasted eighteen to twenty-four weeks, depending on the difficulty of the language. Foreign language proficiency was considered necessary for the jobs of the study participants. A key finding of the study was that a positive core self-evaluation facilitates success in acquiring language skills partially because it contributes to the motivation to learn.[10]

People with core high core self-evaluations are more likely to have high job performance when they combine positive attitudes toward the self with a concern for the welfare of others. (Consistently good job performance enhances career success.) For example, call-center employees with positive core self-evaluations tended to perform better when they worried about letting other people down. The call-center work involved telemarketing to generate funds to support new jobs at a university.[11]

ORGANIZATIONAL PROSPERITY

The combined effect of workers having high self-esteem helps a company prosper. Self-esteem is a critical source of competitive advantage in an information society. Companies gain the edge when, in addition to having an educated workforce, employees have high self-esteem, as shown by such behaviors as the following:

- Being creative and innovative
- Taking personal responsibility for problems
- Feeling independent (yet still wanting to work cooperatively with others)
- Trusting one's own capabilities
- Taking the initiative to solve problems[12]

Behaviors such as these help you cope with the challenge of a rapidly changing workplace where products and ideas become obsolete quickly. Workers with high self-esteem are more likely to be able to cope with new challenges regularly because they are confident that they can master their environment.

Good Mental Health

One of the major consequences of high self-esteem is good mental health. People with high self-esteem feel good about themselves and have positive outlooks on life. One of the links between good mental health and self-esteem is that high self-esteem helps prevent many situations from being stressful. Few negative comments from others are likely to bother you when your self-esteem is high. A person with low self-esteem might crumble if somebody insulted his or her appearance. If you have high self-esteem, you might shrug off the insult as simply being the other person's point of view. If faced with an everyday setback, such as losing keys, if you have high self-esteem you might think, "I have so much going for me, why fall apart over this incident?"

Human Relations Self-Assessment Quiz   2-2

National Longitudinal Survey of Youth Measure of Core Self-Evaluations

	True	False
1. I have little control over the things that happen to me.	_____	_____
2. There is little I can do to change many of the important things in my life.	_____	_____
3. I feel that I am a person of worth, on an equal basis with others.	_____	_____
4. I feel that I have a number of good qualities.	_____	_____
5. All in all, I am inclined to feel that I am a failure.	_____	_____
6. I feel I do not have much to be proud of.	_____	_____
7. I wish I could have more respect for myself.	_____	_____
8. I've been depressed.	_____	_____
9. I've felt hopeful about the future.	_____	_____
10. What happens to me in the future depends on me.	_____	_____
11. What happens to me is of my own doing.	_____	_____
12. When I make plans, I am almost certain to make them work.	_____	_____

Scoring and Interpretation:

The answers in the high core self-evaluations direction are as follows:

1. False	5. False	9. True
2. False	6. False	10. True
3. True	7. False	11. True
4. True	8. False	12. True

Although there are no specific categories for scores, the more statements you answered in the direction of high core self-evaluations, the more likely it is that you have the type of core self-evaluations that will facilitate career success.

Questions: 1. How does your score on this quiz match your evaluation of your core self-evaluations?

2. How does your score on this quiz compare to your score on Self-Assessment Quiz 2-1?

3. How can you explain the fact that responses to the above statements were found to be related to long-term career success?

Source: "National Longitudinal Survey of Youth Measure of Core Self-Evaluations" by Timothy A. Judge and Charlice Hurst.

PROFITING FROM NEGATIVE FEEDBACK

Although people with high self-esteem can readily shrug off undeserved insults, they still profit well from negative feedback. Because they are secure, they can profit from the developmental opportunities suggested by negative feedback. Workers with high self-esteem develop and maintain favorable work attitudes and perform at high levels. These positive consequences take place because such attitudes and behaviors are consistent with the personal belief that they are competent individuals. The late Mary Kay Ash, the legendary founder of a beauty products company, put it this way: "It never occurred to me I couldn't do it. I always knew that if I worked hard enough, I could." Furthermore, research has shown that high-self-esteem individuals value reaching work goals more than do low-self-esteem individuals.[13]

SERVES AS A GUIDE FOR REGULATING SOCIAL RELATIONSHIPS

Another consequence of self-esteem is that you can use it as a guide in regulating social relationships. According to Mark Leary, self-esteem provides a gauge of performance during social interactions: "Self-esteem rises and falls, acting as an internal barometer of how well you're faring, telling you to fix this problem here, and helping you understand that you don't have to worry about it there."[14]

Following this reasoning, fluctuations in self-esteem provide information that is useful in working your way through social relationships. For example, if you are talking and the person you are talking to yawns, your self-esteem drops, signaling you to change the topic. When you tell a joke, and people laugh, your self-esteem climbs rapidly. If we did not feel bad when we bored or offended others or felt satisfied when we delighted them, we would not be inclined to change course.[15]

POTENTIAL NEGATIVE CONSEQUENCES

High and low extremes in self-esteem can create problems for individuals, as described next.

1. **Exaggerated levels of self-esteem can lead to narcissism.** Self-esteem can elevate to the level where the individual becomes self-absorbed to the point of having little concern for others, leading to narcissistic attitudes and behaviors. **Narcissism** is an extremely positive view of the self, combined with limited empathy for others. Quite often, extreme narcissism can hamper success because the narcissist irritates and alienates others in the workplace. A frequent human relations problem with office narcissists is that they are poor listeners because they attempt to dominate conversations by talking about themselves. Yet the right amount and type of narcissism can at times facilitate success because the narcissist appears to be self-confident and charismatic.[16]

2. **Envying too many people.** A potential negative consequence of low self-esteem is envying too many people. If you perceive that many individuals have much more of what you want and are more worthwhile than you, you will suffer from enormous envy. To decrease pangs of envy, it is best to develop realistic standards of comparison between you and other people in the world. If you want to evaluate your level of career success, a bad idea would be to compare yourself to a magazine listing of the forty must successful people under forty who have all amassed millions of dollars. A more realistic approach would be to track down some of your former classmates on the Internet and see what kind of career success they have achieved.

   Kristin Neff, a professor of educational psychology at the University of Texas at Austin, supports the idea that making social comparisons can lead to problems with self-esteem. She explains that in American culture, people tend to acquire a sense of self-worth from feeling special. A musician who compares herself to a musician of less talent will feel superior and will even have a boost in self-esteem. But if she compares herself to a more talented musician, she will feel a decrease in self-esteem even if her talent and skills have not diminished.[17]

3. **Poor romantic relationships when self-esteem is low.** Low self-esteem can have negative consequences for romantic relationships because people with self-doubts consistently underestimate their partners' feelings for them. People with low **self-respect** distance themselves from the relationship—often devaluing their partner—to prepare themselves for what they think will be an inevitable breakup. John G. Holmes, a psychologist at the University of Waterloo in Ontario, Canada, says, "If people think negatively about themselves, they think their partner must think negatively about them—and they're wrong."[18]

Narcissism
extremely positive view of the self, combined with little empathy for others

Self-respect
how you think and feel about yourself

▶ **Learning Objective 2.2** ▶

The Enhancement of Self-Esteem

Improving self-esteem is a lifelong process because self-esteem is related to the success of your activities and interactions with people. Following are approaches to enhancing self-esteem that are related to how self-esteem develops.

ATTAIN LEGITIMATE ACCOMPLISHMENTS

To emphasize again, accomplishing worthwhile activities is a major contributor to self-esteem in both children and adults. Self-esteem therefore stems from accomplishment. Giving people large trophies for mundane accomplishments is unlikely to raise self-esteem. More likely, the person will see through the transparent attempt to build his or her self-esteem and develop negative feelings about the self. The general-information point of view is the opposite: Accomplishment stems from a boost in self-esteem. The two different viewpoints are diagrammed in Figure 2-2.

What about you? Would your self-esteem receive a bigger boost by (a) receiving an A in a course in which 10 percent of the class received an A or by (b) receiving an A in a class in which everybody received the same grade?

Another way of framing the attainment of legitimate accomplishments is that to boost your self-esteem, you must engage in behaviors and make choices that are worthy of esteem. To implement this strategy, you must first size up what your reference group regards as esteemed. For most reference groups, or the people whose opinion matters to you, esteem-worthy behavior would include the following:

- Successfully completing a program of studies

- Occupying a high-status job and staying long enough to accomplish something worthwhile

- Investing time and money in charitable activities

- Taking pride in your physical appearance and condition

- Having a social networking page that is filled with honorable and sensible content

As you have probably observed, all these esteem-worthy accomplishments reflect values about what is important. For example, a person might have criminals and swindlers in his or her reference group. Self-esteem for this person based on the acclamation of others would therefore stem from such activities as defrauding others of money and not paying taxes.

A potential difficulty in assessing whether you have attained a legitimate accomplishment is the motivation of the person giving you feedback on performance. An extensive

FIGURE 2-2

GOAL ACCOMPLISHMENT AND SELF-ESTEEM

Source: "GOAL ACCOMPLISHMENT AND SELF-ESTEEM" by Andrew J. DuBrin.

The Social Science Perspective

Person establishes goal. → Person pursues goal. → Person achieves goal. → Person develops esteem-like feelings.

The General Information Perspective

Person develops esteem-like feelings. → Person establishes a goal. → Person pursues the goal. → Person achieves the goal.

analysis of the subject suggests that managers often give subordinates overly-positive performance reviews because high performers enhance the self-image of the manager.[19] The preconscious thinking might be "If the members of my team are all performing well, that means I am a very effective manager."

Closely related to attaining legitimate accomplishments is to have constructive goals that can make a difference for others. When a person's self-esteem is low, helping others can take the attention away from oneself thereby taking away some of the discomfort associated with low self-esteem. In this sense, a person's self-esteem would feel elevated. Jennifer Crocker, a psychology professor at the University of Michigan, explains that by taking your ego out of the situation—and focusing on helping others—your self-esteem will gain a legitimate boost.[20] An example of a constructive goal that would be to develop a plan to directly help others is to distribute donated food to families in dire need.

BE AWARE OF PERSONAL STRENGTHS

Another method of improving your self-esteem is to develop an appreciation of your strengths and accomplishments. Appreciating your strengths and accomplishments requires that you engage in **introspection**, the act of looking within oneself. Although introspection may sound easy, it requires considerable discipline and concentration to actually observe what you are doing. A simple example is that we are often not even aware of some of our basic habits, such as biting the lip when nervous or blinking when attempting to answer a difficult question. A good starting point is to list your strengths and accomplishments on paper. This list is likely to be more impressive than you expected.

The late Leo Buscaglia (aka Dr. Hug) was a major contributor to emphasizing the importance of people appreciating their strengths to boost their self-esteem. Part of his program for enhancing human relationships was for people to love others as well as themselves. He wanted people to understand that they were unique.[21]

Introspection
the act of looking within yourself

MINIMIZE SETTINGS AND INTERACTIONS THAT DETRACT FROM YOUR FEELINGS OF COMPETENCE

Most of us have situations in work and personal life that make us feel less than our best. If you can minimize exposure to those situations, you will have fewer feelings of incompetence. The problem with feeling incompetent is that it lowers your self-esteem. An office supervisor said she detests company picnics, most of all because she is forced to play softball. At her own admission, she had less aptitude for athletics than any able-bodied person she knew. In addition, she felt uncomfortable with the small-talk characteristic of picnics. To minimize discomfort, the woman attended only those picnics she thought were absolutely necessary. Instead of playing on the softball team, she volunteered to be the equipment manager.

A problem with avoiding all situations in which you feel incompetent is that it might prevent you from acquiring needed skills. Also, it boosts your self-confidence and self-esteem to become comfortable in a previously uncomfortable situation.

TALK AND SOCIALIZE FREQUENTLY WITH PEOPLE WHO BOOST YOUR SELF-ESTEEM

Psychologist Barbara Ilardie says that the people who can raise your self-esteem are usually those with high self-esteem themselves. They are the people who give honest feedback because they respect others and themselves. Such high-self-esteem individuals should not be confused with yes-people who agree with others simply to be liked. The point is that you typically receive more from strong people than weak ones. Weak people will flatter you but will not give you the honest feedback you need to build self-esteem.[22]

A related approach to boosting self-esteem is to create a webpage blog in which you enter positive comments, still photos, and videos about you. You invite others to respond with positive comments about you, thereby boosting your good feelings about yourself. A downside here, however, is that some people respond to warm invitations with negative and hurtful commentary. An underlying problem here is that many people are quite uninhibited when responding to a social media site. Have you ever noticed how nasty and uninhibited people can be on the Internet?

MODEL THE BEHAVIOR OF PEOPLE WITH HIGH SELF-ESTEEM

Observe the way people who are believed to have high self-esteem stand, walk, speak, and act. Even if you are not feeling so secure inside, you will project a high-self-esteem image if you act assured. Eugene Raudsepp recommends, "Stand tall, speak clearly and with confidence, shake hands firmly, look people in the eye and smile frequently. Your self-esteem will increase as you notice encouraging reactions from others."[23] (Notice here that self-esteem is considered to be about the same idea as self-confidence.)

Choose your models of high self-esteem from people you know personally as well as celebrities you might watch on television news and interview shows. Observing actors on the large or small screen is a little less useful because they are guaranteed to be playing a role. Identifying a teacher or professor as a self-esteem model is widely practiced, as is observing successful family members and friends.

▶ **Learning Objective 2.3** ▶

The Importance of Self-Confidence, and Its Sources

Although self-confidence can be considered part of self-esteem, it is important enough to study separately.

THE IMPORTANCE OF SELF-CONFIDENCE AND SELF-EFFICACY

Self-efficacy
confidence in your ability to carry out a specific task in contrast to generalized self-confidence

Self-confidence has also long been recognized as a trait of effective leaders. **Self-efficacy** is confidence in your ability to carry out a specific task in contrast to generalized self-confidence. When self-efficacy is high, you believe you have the ability to do what is necessary to complete a task successfully. If you have self-efficacy in relation to many tasks, you are likely to be self-confident. A current analysis of many studies about self-efficacy is that past performance has a major influence: The more successes you had in the past with the same or similar tasks, the stronger will be your self-efficacy. Conversely, if you performed poorly in the past, your self-efficacy will be relatively weak.[24]

A straightforward implication of self-efficacy is that people who think they can perform well on a task do better than those who think they will do poorly. Various studies have shown that people with a high sense of self-efficacy tend to have good job performance, so being self-confident is important for your career. They also set relatively high goals for themselves.[25] Self-efficacy contributes to goal setting because the higher your level of self-efficacy, the more likely you are to think that a goal is realistic. A person with high self-efficacy for learning German might say, "I think learning two German words per day is realistic."

The importance of self-confidence for your career can be illustrated by the tactics of Jack Welch, the former CEO of General Electric (GE), who is regarded by many business writers as one of the most influential leaders of all time. Welch has become a well-known business author and columnist, in addition to remaining active in directing several companies. Welch once said that his most important responsibility at GE was building the self-confidence of managers throughout the company. Although an intimidating and demanding boss, Welch would help managers develop their self-confidence by giving them lots of opportunities to succeed on major assignments.

THE SOURCES OF SELF-CONFIDENCE

Research by college professors and psychological consultants George P. Hollenbeck and Douglas T. Hall suggests that our feelings of self-confidence stem from five sources of information.[26] The first source is the *actual experience,* or *things we have done.* Having done something before and having succeeded is the most powerful way for you to build

---

Human Relations Self-Assessment Quiz   2-3

How Self-Confident Are You?

Indicate the extent to which you agree with each of the following statements. Use a 1 to 5 scale:
(1) disagree strongly, (2) disagree, (3) neutral, (4) agree, and (5) agree strongly.

	DS	D	N	A	AS
1. I frequently say to people, "I'm not sure."	5	4	3	2	1
2. I perform well in most situations in life.	1	2	3	4	5
3. I willingly offer advice to others.	1	2	3	4	5
4. Before making even a minor decision, I usually consult with several people.	5	4	3	2	1
5. I am generally willing to attempt new activities for which I have very little related skill or experience.	1	2	3	4	5
6. Speaking in front of the class or other group is a frightening experience for me.	5	4	3	2	1
7. I experience stress when people challenge me or put me on the spot.	5	4	3	2	1
8. I feel comfortable attending a social event by myself.	1	2	3	4	5
9. I'm much more of a winner than a loser.	1	2	3	4	5
10. I am cautious about making any substantial change in my life.	5	4	3	2	1

Total score: _____

Scoring and Interpretation:

Calculate your total score by adding the numbers circled. A tentative interpretation of the scoring is as follows:

45–50 Very high self-confidence with perhaps a tendency toward arrogance

38–44 A high, desirable level of self-confidence

30–37 Moderate, or average, self-confidence

10–29 Self-confidence needs strengthening

Questions: 1. How does your score on this test fit with your evaluation of your self-confidence?

2. What would it be like working for a manager who scored 10 on this quiz?

Source: "How Self-Confident Are You?" by Andrew J. DuBrin.

self-confidence. If you successfully inserted a replacement battery in your watch without destroying the watch, you will be confident in making another replacement.

The second source of self-confidence is the *experiences of others,* or *modeling.* You can gain some self-confidence if you have carefully observed others perform a task, such as resolving conflict with a customer. You might say to yourself, "I've seen Tracy calm down the customer by listening and showing sympathy, and I'm confident I can do the same thing."

The third source of self-confidence is *social comparison,* or *comparing yourself to others.* If you see other people with capabilities similar to your own perform a task well, you will gain in confidence. A person might say, "If that person can learn how to work with enterprise software, I can do it also. I'm just as smart."

The fourth source of self-confidence is *social persuasion,* or *the process of convincing another person.* If a credible person convinces you that you can accomplish a particular task, you will often receive a boost in self-confidence large enough to give the task a try. If the encouragement is coupled with guidance on how to perform the task, your self-confidence gain will be higher. So the boss or teacher who says, "I know you can do it, and I'm here to help you," knows how to build self-confidence.

The fifth source of self-confidence is *emotional arousal,* or *how you feel about events around you and manage your emotions.* People rely somewhat on inner feelings to know if they are self-confident enough to perform the task. Imagine a person standing on top of a high mountain ready to ski down. However, he or she is trembling and nauseous with fear. Contrast this beginner to another person who simply feels mildly excited and challenged. Skier number one has a self-confidence problem, whereas skier number two has enough confidence to start the descent. (Have your emotional sensations ever influenced your self-confidence?)

The more of these five sources of self-confidence are positive for you, the more likely your self-confidence will be positive. Human Relations Self-Assessment Quiz 2-3 provides some insight into your level of self-confidence.

▶ **Learning Objective 2.4** ▶

Developing and Strengthening Your Self-Confidence

Strengthening your confidence often facilitates success. As explained by motivational speaker and author Valorie Burton, a lack of authentic confidence holds most people from attaining their goals. People who are more successful are not necessarily better equipped than others, but they are bolder in their belief in themselves.[27] Career specialist Anthony Balderrama explains that workers at all levels should speak to work associates in a confident, self-assured manner.[28]

Self-confidence is generally achieved by succeeding in a variety of situations. A confident civil engineering technician may not be generally self-confident unless he or she also achieves success in activities such as forming good personal relationships, navigating complex software, writing a letter, learning a second language, and displaying athletic skills.

Although this general approach to building self-confidence makes sense, it does not work for everyone. Some people who seem to succeed at everything still have lingering self-doubt. Low self-confidence is so deeply ingrained in this type of personality that success in later life is not sufficient to change things. Following are ten specific strategies and tactics for building and elevating self-confidence. They will generally work unless the person has deep-rooted feelings of inferiority. The tactics and strategies described here and outlined in Figure 2-3 are arranged approximately in the order in which they should be tried to achieve best results.

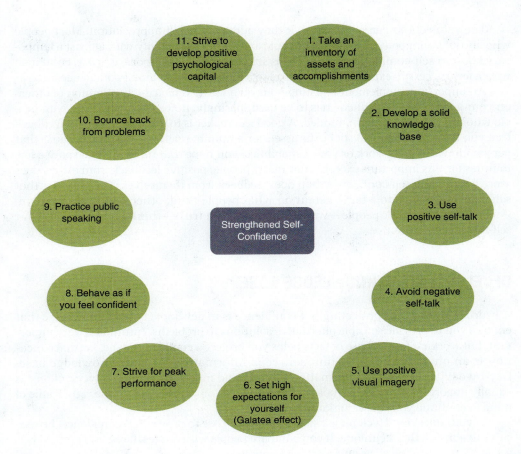

FIGURE 2-3

TECHNIQUES FOR STRENGTHENING YOUR SELF-CONFIDENCE

Source: "Techniques for Strengthening Your Self-Confidence" by Andrew J. DuBrin.

TAKE AN INVENTORY OF PERSONAL ASSETS AND ACCOMPLISHMENTS

Many people suffer from low self-confidence because they do not appreciate their own good points. Therefore, a starting point in increasing your self-confidence is to take an inventory of personal assets and accomplishments. A slight variation of this activity was offered previously as a method of developing self-esteem. Personal assets should be related to characteristics and behaviors rather than tangible assets, such as an inheritance or an antique car.

Accomplishments can be anything significant in which you played a key role in achieving the results. Try not to be modest in preparing your list of assets and accomplishments. You are looking for any confidence booster you can find. Two lists prepared by different people will suffice to give you an idea of the kinds of assets and accomplishments that might be included.

Danielle

Good listener; easy to get along with; good technology skills; good posture; inquisitive mind; good at solving problems; drug and tobacco free; good sense of humor; patient with people who make mistakes; skilled at refinishing furniture and woodwork; better-than-average appearance. Organized successful fund drive that raised $50,000 for a battered-person shelter; graduated tenth in high school class of 500; ran a complete marathon; daughter is happy and healthy.

Michael

Good mechanical and technology skills, including motorcycle repair and computer repair; can work long hours under pressure; good dancer; friendly with strangers; great physical health (drug and disease free); good housekeeper; can laugh at my own mistakes; positive personal appearance; respectful of authority. Made award-winning suggestion that saved company $45,000; scored winning goal in college basketball tournament; rescued drowning senior out of lake; large online following.

The value of these asset lists is that they add to your self-appreciation. Most people who lay out their good points on paper come away from the activity with at least a temporary boost in self-confidence, and perhaps self-esteem. The temporary boost, combined with a few successful experiences, may lead to a long-term gain in self-confidence.

An important supplement to listing your own assets is hearing the opinion of others on your good points. This tactic has to be used sparingly, however, and mainly with people who are personal-growth minded. A good icebreaker is to tell your source of feedback that you have to prepare a list of your assets for a human relations exercise. Because that person knows of your work or your capabilities, you hope that he or she can spare a few minutes for this important exercise. For many people, positive feedback from others does more for building self-confidence than does feedback from themselves. The reason is that self-esteem depends to a large extent on what people think others think about them. Consequently, if other people—whose judgment you trust—think highly of you, your self-image will be positive.

DEVELOP A SOLID KNOWLEDGE BASE

A bedrock strategy for projecting self-confidence is to develop a base of knowledge that enables you to provide sensible alternative solutions to problems. Intuition is very important, but working from a base of facts helps you project a confident image. Formal education is an obvious and important source of information for your knowledge base. Day-by-day absorption of information directly and indirectly related to your career is equally important. A major purpose of formal education is to get you in the right frame of mind to continue your quest for knowledge.

In your quest for developing a solid knowledge base to project self-confidence, be sensitive to abusing this technique. If you bombard people with quotes, facts, and figures, you are likely to be perceived as an annoying know-it-all.

USE POSITIVE SELF-TALK

Positive self-talk

saying positive things about yourself to yourself

A basic method of building self-confidence is to engage in **positive self-talk**, saying positive things about you to yourself. The first step in using positive self-talk is to objectively state the incident that is casting doubt about your self-worth.[29] The key word here is *objectively*. Terry, who is fearful of poorly executing a report-writing assignment, might say, "I've been asked to write a report for the company, and I'm not a good writer."

The next step is to objectively interpret what the incident *does not* mean. Terry might say, "Not being a skilled writer doesn't mean that I can't figure out a way to write a good report or that I'm an ineffective employee."

Next, you should objectively state what the incident *does* mean. In doing this, you should avoid put-down labels such as *incompetent, stupid, dumb, jerk,* or *airhead*. These terms are forms of negative self-talk. Terry should state what the incident does mean: "I have a problem with one small aspect of this job."

The fourth step is to objectively account for the cause of the incident. Terry would say, "I'm really worried about writing a good report because I have very little experience in writing along these lines."

The fifth step is to identify some positive ways to prevent the incident from happening again. Terry might say, "I'll get out my textbook on business communications and review the chapter on report writing" or "I'll enroll in a course or seminar on business report writing" or "I will look for some information online to help me write reports."

The final step is to use positive self-talk. Terry imagines his boss saying, "This report is really good. I'm proud of my decision to select you to prepare this important report."

Positive self-talk builds self-confidence and self-esteem because it programs the mind with positive messages. Making frequent positive statements or affirmations about the self creates a more confident person. An example would be "I know I can learn this new equipment rapidly enough to increase my productivity within five days."

Business coach Gary Lockwood emphasizes that positive self-talk is also useful for giving you the confidence to get people past difficult times. He explains that you are in charge of your feelings, as well as your attitude. He says, "Instead of berating yourself after making a mistake, learn from the experience and move on. Say to yourself something of the nature, 'Everyone makes mistakes,' or 'What can I learn from this?'"[30]

AVOID NEGATIVE SELF-TALK

In addition to making positive statements, you should minimize negative statements about yourself to bolster self-confidence. A lack of self-confidence is reflected in statements such as, "I may be stupid, but . . .," "Nobody asked my opinion," "I know I'm usually wrong, but . . .," "I know I don't have as much education as some people, but. . . ." Self-effacing statements such as these serve to reinforce low self-confidence.

It is also important not to attribute to yourself negative, irreversible traits, such as "idiotic," "ugly," "dull," "loser-type," "hopeless," "nerdy," and "dorky." Instead, look on your weak points as areas for possible self-improvement. Negative self-labeling can do long-term damage to your confidence. If a person stops that practice today, his or her self-confidence may begin to increase.

USE POSITIVE VISUAL IMAGERY

Assume you have a situation in mind in which you would like to appear confident and in control. An example would be a meeting with a major customer who has told you by e-mail that he is considering switching suppliers. Your intuitive reaction is that if you cannot handle his concerns without fumbling or appearing desperate, you will lose the account. An important technique in this situation is **positive visual imagery**, or picturing a positive outcome in your mind. To apply this technique in this situation, imagine yourself engaging in a convincing argument about why your customer should retain your company as the primary supplier. Imagine yourself talking in positive terms about the good service your company offers and how you can rectify any problems.

Positive visual imagery
picturing a positive outcome in your mind

Visualize yourself listening patiently to your customer's concerns and then talking confidently about how your company can handle these concerns. As you rehearse this moment of truth, create a mental picture of you and the customer shaking hands over the fact that the account is still yours.

Positive visual imagery helps you appear confident because your mental rehearsal of the situation has helped you prepare for battle. If imagery works for you once, you will be even more effective in subsequent uses of the technique.

SET HIGH EXPECTATIONS FOR YOURSELF (THE GALATEA EFFECT)

If you set high expectations for yourself, and you succeed, you are likely to experience a temporary or permanent boost in self-confidence. The **Galatea effect** is a type of self-fulfilling prophecy in which high self-expectations lead to high performance. The term *Galatea effect* stems from Greek mythology. Galatea was a maiden who was originally a statue carved by Pygmalion. She was later brought to life by Aphrodite in response to the sculptor's pleas. Similar to positive self-talk, if you believe in yourself, you are more likely

Galatea effect
a type of self-fulfilling prophecy in which high expectations lead to high performance

to succeed. You expect to win, so you do. The Galatea effect does not work all the time, but it does work some of the time for many people.

Workplace behavior researchers D. Brian McNatt and Timothy A. Judge studied the Galatea effect with seventy-two auditors within three offices of a major accounting firm for a three-month period. The auditors were given letters of encouragement to strengthen their feelings of self-efficacy. Information in the letters was based on facts about the auditors, such as information derived from their résumés and company records. The results of the experiment showed that creating a Galatea effect bolstered self-efficacy, motivation, and performance. However, the performance improvement was temporary, suggesting that self-expectations need to be boosted regularly.[31]

STRIVE FOR PEAK PERFORMANCE

Peak performance
exceptional accomplishment in a given task

A key strategy for projecting confidence is to display **peak performance**, or exceptional accomplishment in a given task. The experience is transient but exceptionally meaningful. Peak performance refers to much more than attempting to do your best. Experiencing peak performance in various tasks over a long time period would move a person toward self-actualization (full use of potential).[32] To achieve peak performance, you must be totally focused on what you are doing. When you are in the state of peak performance, you are mentally calm and physically at ease. Intense concentration is required to achieve this state. You are so focused on the task at hand that you are not distracted by extraneous events or thoughts. To use an athletic analogy, you are *in the zone* while you are performing the task. In fact, many sports psychologists and other sports trainers work with athletes to help them attain peak performance.

The mental state achieved during peak performance is akin to a person's sense of deep concentration when immersed in a sport or hobby. On days when tennis players perform way above their usual game, they typically comment, "The ball looked so large today. I could read the label as I hit it." On the job, focus and concentration allow the person to sense and respond to relevant information coming both from within the mind and from outside stimuli. When you are at your peak, you impress others by responding intelligently to their input. While turning in peak performance, you are experiencing a mental state referred to as *flow*.

Although you are concentrating on an object or sometimes on another person during peak performance, you still have an awareness of the self. You develop a strong sense of the self, similar to self-confidence and self-efficacy, while you are concentrating on the task. Peak performance is related to self-confidence in another important way. Achieving peak performance in many situations helps you develop confidence. The peak performance is related to the task itself, rather than the external reward that might be associated with peak performance. For example, a machine shop technician might be totally involved in restoring a machine part whether or not it would result in a compliment from the boss or a bonus.

BEHAVE AS IF YOU FEEL CONFIDENT

A principle of psychology developed over 100 years ago states that your behavior leads to attitudes. As you change your behavior, your attitudes will begin to change. This same idea can be used to project confidence. A useful example is the often-feared situation of making a presentation. Executive coach Gail Golden says that you should enter the room purposefully, holding your back straight. Look up and out at the audience instead of looking down at your notes or at the screen of your computer graphic presentation. Speak in a loud, clear voice, and look the audience in the eye or on their foreheads.[33] Behaving in this manner will often make you feel more confident within several minutes.

PRACTICE PUBLIC SPEAKING

Dale Carnegie, the original popularizer of human relations, built his empire on the foundation of the importance of public speaking in building self-confidence.[34] In the age of communication technology, this basic technique holds true. If you can stand in front of an audience, even a small meeting, and deliver your thoughts effectively you will gain in self-confidence. However, just reading PowerPoint slides to the group is not enough. You have to look at the facial expressions of the audience and speak directly to them. Making a successful presentation to the class has been a self-confidence builder for millions of students. Presentations in the workplace, to community groups, religious groups, and sports groups can also be self-confidence builders.

BOUNCE BACK FROM SETBACKS AND EMBARRASSMENTS

Resilience is a major contributor to personal effectiveness. Overcoming setbacks also builds self-confidence. An effective self-confidence builder is convincing yourself that you can conquer adversity, such as setbacks and embarrassments, thus being resilient. The vast majority of successful leaders have dealt successfully with at least one significant setback in their careers, such as being fired or demoted. In contrast, crumbling after a setback or series of setbacks will usually lower self-confidence.

Overcoming some adversity not only builds self-confidence but also contributes to a person's long-term well-being. A study involving 2,398 participants surveyed over a three-year period found that people who had experienced a few adverse events reported better mental health and well-being than people with a frequent history of adversity and people with no reports of misfortune. Mark Seery, a researcher in the Department of Psychology at the University of Buffalo, and his colleagues concluded "that a history of some lifetime adversity—relative to no adversity or high adversity—predicted lower global distress, lower functional impairment, lower PTS (posttraumatic stress) symptoms and higher life satisfaction."[35]

Three key suggestions for bouncing back from setbacks and embarrassments are presented next.

GET PAST THE EMOTIONAL TURMOIL

Adversity has enormous emotional consequences. The emotional impact of severe job adversity can rival the loss of a personal relationship. The stress from adversity leads to a cycle of adversity followed by stress, followed by more adversity. A starting point in dealing with the emotional aspects of adversity is to *accept the reality of your problem.* Admit that your problems are real and that you are hurting inside. The next step is *not to take the setback personally.* Remember that setbacks are inevitable as long as you are taking some risks in your career. Not personalizing setbacks helps reduce some of the emotional sting. If possible, *do not panic.* Recognize that you are in difficult circumstances under which many others panic. Convince yourself to remain calm enough to deal with the severe problem or crisis. Also, *get help from your support network.* Getting emotional support from family members and friends helps overcome the emotional turmoil associated with adversity.

A type of emotional turmoil that faces many people at some point in their careers is to be fired for what the company thinks is poor performance. Being fired hurts most people deeply, but if you follow the steps previously described, the impact can be softened and can ultimately lead to heightened self-confidence. A surprisingly large number of successful entrepreneurs were at one time fired from a corporate job, often because they were seen as mavericks who would not follow rules well.

FIND A CREATIVE SOLUTION TO YOUR PROBLEM

An inescapable part of planning a comeback is to solve your problem. You often need to search for creative solutions. Jason, a business student in Chicago, ran a sub shop to earn a living and support himself through college. Layoffs at nearby companies had driven his sales way down below the point at which it paid to keep the sub shop open. In the process of exploring all the possibilities of what he could do in a hurry to earn a living, Jason observed that loads of old buildings in downtown Chicago were being rebuilt and turned into apartments and retail space. Jason then thought of starting an "interior demolition" company, combining efforts with two relatives in the home repair business. Jason's creative solution accomplished what needed to be done to regain his financial equilibrium. His self-confidence continues to surge as his interior demolition business has prospered. If the preceding steps work for you and you bring your level of self-confidence to where you want it to be, you will have achieved a major milestone in applying human relations to yourself.

REGAIN CONFIDENCE BY RELAXING A LITTLE

Even the most successful businesspeople face a slump from time to time. The performance of sales representatives is highly measurable, so they are likely to be more aware of and pained by a slump. When the slump occurs, workers tend to lose self-confidence, obsess about past mistakes, and become anxious about performing tasks they once enjoyed. The loss of self-confidence tends to deteriorate performance further.

As recommended by some sports psychologists, an effective way to regain self-confidence when in a slump is to stop overworking and allow yourself to relax. A case in point is Dan Di Cio, a Pittsburgh account executive who was hoping for an excellent season selling high-tech equipment, but the big sales were not forthcoming. He became discouraged and self-doubting as he watched other sales professionals win awards. Di Cio contacted sports psychologist Gregg Sternberg after hearing him speak. The psychologist told the account executive that he was working so hard that he risked driving his sales results even lower. Di Cio's outlook improved so much that he doubled his sales over the previous year.[36]

STRIVE TO DEVELOP POSITIVE PSYCHOLOGICAL CAPITAL

Positive psychological capital
a positive psychological state of development in which you have a storehouse of hope, self-efficacy, optimism, and resilience

A comprehensive way of becoming more self-confident is to develop **positive psychological capital,** a positive psychological state of development in which you have hope, self-efficacy, optimism, and resilience. Note that self-efficacy and resilience have already been included in our study of self-confidence. In more detail, the components of positive psychological capital are as follows:

- *Hope* refers to persevering toward goals and, when necessary, redirecting paths to a goal in order to succeed. In everyday language, don't give up when pursuing your goals.

- *Self-efficacy* refers to having the confidence to take on and invest the necessary effort to succeed at challenging tasks. Experience is a big help here, because if you have successfully completed the same task, or a similar one, previously, you will be more confident that you can succeed.

- *Optimism* refers to making a positive attribution about succeeding now and in the future. If you are a natural pessimist you will have to work harder at looking for the positive aspects of a given situation.

- *Resiliency* refers to dealing with problems and adversity by sustaining effort and bouncing back to attain success. Conquering a major setback would be an enormous contributor to your self-confidence.

An encouraging note about positive psychological capital is that people can develop it. An experiment conducted with 187 working adults found that a web-based, highly focused two-hour training program raised the average level of psychological capital. The increase in psychological capital was measured by more positive responses after training to such statements as "If I should find myself in a jam at work, I could think of many ways to get out of it" (hope).[37] Should the participants in the study really do a better job of getting out of jams in the future, they could be even more confident about how much training improves psychological capital.

AVOID OVERCONFIDENCE

As with most human qualities, self-confidence can be a negative factor if carried to the extreme. The overly self-confident individual might become intimidating and unwilling to listen to the advice of others. During a group meeting, the highly self-confident person might typically make a comment before giving others their fair turn to speak. Overconfident individuals are so self-centered that they do not even notice eyes rolling when they hog the meeting.

The potential disadvantages of extremely high self-confidence also apply to too much concern about the self in general, including self-esteem. Too much attention to the self can lead a person to be self-centered, self-conscious, and uninterested in other people and the outside world. The highly self-confident person also runs the risk of being perceived as a narcissist and can therefore be annoying. You have probably met people who include in almost every conversation a statement about their health or an activity of theirs, indicating their self-centeredness.

The right balance is to be concerned about yourself, your self-esteem and self-confidence, and your personal growth yet still focus on the outside world. Focusing on the outside world can ultimately strengthen you because you develop skills and interests that will enhance your self-esteem and self-confidence.

Codependency and Its Link to Low Self-Esteem and Low Self-Confidence

◀ Learning Objective 2.5 ◀

A substantial negative consequence of having low self-esteem and low self-confidence is that it can lead people to look for something outside of the inner self to make them feel better. Some try to feel better through alcohol, drugs, or nicotine and become addicted. Another way people with low self-esteem attempt to take care of the problem is to play a martyr role and become the benefactor of someone else.

In personal life, as well as on the job, codependence can create unhealthy, dysfunctional relationships. Here we take a quick overview of the meaning, symptoms, and control and overcoming of codependence. Recognize, however, that codependency is a vast, complicated problem with millions of articles, books, and websites about the topic.[38] The topic of codependence could also fit into the section in Chapter 17 about personal problems. Yet codependence can also affect other topics in human relations such as coworker relationships and leadership.

MEANING OF CODEPENDENCY

Codependency is a state of being psychologically influenced or controlled by, reliant on, or needing another person who is addicted to substances such as alcohol and drugs, or to behavior such as gambling or Internet use. The codependent is mutually dependent because he or she relies on the other person's dependence. The codependent has a

Codependency
a state of being psychologically influenced or controlled by, reliant on, or needing another person who is addicted to substances, such as alcohol and drugs, or behavior, such as gambling or Internet use.

FIGURE 2-4

A KEY ASPECT OF A CODEPENDENT RELATIONSHIP

Source: "A key aspect of a codependent relationship" by Andrew J. DuBrin.

The two people in a codependent relationship rely on each other.

tendency to place the needs and wants of others first, to the exclusion of acknowledging his or her own needs. Such behavior is closely tied to low self-esteem. Codependency is also regarded as an emotional and behavioral condition that affects an individual's ability to have a healthy, mutually satisfying relationship.

Codependency is also referred to as *relationship addiction* because codependent people often form or maintain relationships that are one-sided, emotionally destructive, and abusive. Codependent behavior is usually learned by watching and imitating other family members who display this type of behavior. Yet it is possible for a person to drift into codependent behavior later in life in attempting to meet the needs of a partner or boss with intense personal problems.

Figure 2-4 illustrates the major transaction that takes place in a codependent relationship, whether or not the two people explicitly understand what is happening.

SYMPTOMS AND DESCRIPTION OF THE PROBLEM

1. The codependent feels responsible for the dependent by covering up the other person's addiction, such as excessive alcohol use, for fear of discovery. (For example, Jim is drunk today, so when his boss calls, Jim's wife, Jane, says, "I am sorry but Jim is terribly ill today. He seems to have caught a wicked virus.") The problem with the cover-up is that the addicted person's behavior becomes sustained.

2. The codependent will often feel good only when the dependent person feels good, so the codependent tries hard to please the dependent person. As a result the codependent person is extremely dependent, eager to please, and easily yields to the wishes of others.

3. A higher percentage of women than men are codependent, perhaps because some cultures emphasize the nurturing and supportive role of women, with men being more indifferent to the problems of others. (This is a broad gender stereotype that might apply to a small majority of men and women.)

4. The codependent will have difficulty leading a satisfying and productive life because he or she invests so much energy in taking care of a person with a dependency. Quite

often the codependent invests considerable time in keeping the other person addicted so as to feel useful.

5. The codependent has a strong need to be needed, so he or she gains some satisfaction from the partner having problems and needing to be rescued. As a result, the codependent's helping behavior goes beyond a healthy limit, such as arranging a loan for the gambling addict who spent his entire paycheck on online sports betting.

6. The codependent often believes that he or she is a victim of being trapped by a person who requires help. An example would be an administrative assistant who feels victimized because her boss spends a couple of hours per day accessing pornography on a company computer. She feels it is unfair that she is subject continually to this form of environmental sexual harassment.

7. The codependent has a strong need to rescue or fix another person—even though an unconscious motive might be present to keep the other person addicted and helpless.

8. The codependent may feel resentful for reasons such as the other person not appreciating the help, or because that person will not change.

9. Codependents have an unhealthy dependence on relationships and will do anything to hang onto a relationship to avoid feeling abandoned.

HOW TO CONTROL AND OVERCOME CODEPENDENCY

1. Codependency often stems from growing up in a dysfunctional family, so psychotherapy and counseling may be required to overcome the behavior pattern and attitudes of a codependent.

2. With or without therapy, the codependent must become aware of the problem and carefully process information about codependency. The codependent must examine thoroughly his or her caretaking. Good questions to ask the self are "Is my behavior preventing this person from functioning independently?" "Do I really want him (or her) to get better?" "Am I making it easier for him (or her) to stay addicted?"

3. The codependent person must learn to say "No," perhaps in small steps. For example, "No, I am not going to bring you a meal into the den so you can sit up for a few more hours and work the Internet"; "No, I am not going to bring you back a twelve-pack of beer from the convenience store"; "No, you call in sick to the office yourself or write your own e-mail explaining why you can't work today."

4. The codependent person must recognize that it is often not in his or her power to change the behavior of another person. That other person must first want to become independent and healthy.

Concept Review and Reinforcement

Key Terms

Self-esteem, 32
Narcissism, 37
Self-respect, 37
Introspection, 39

Self-efficacy, 40
Positive self-talk, 44
Positive visual imagery, 45
Galatea effect, 45

Peak performance, 46
Positive psychological capital, 48
Codependency, 49

Summary and Review

- *Self-esteem* refers to feeling competent and being worthy of happiness. People with high self-esteem develop positive self-concepts.
- Self-esteem develops from a variety of early-life experiences. People who were encouraged to feel good about themselves and their accomplishments by key people in their lives are more likely to enjoy high self-esteem.
- Of major significance, self-esteem also results from accomplishing worthwhile activities and then feeling proud of these accomplishments. Praise and recognition for accomplishments also help develop self-esteem.
- Self-esteem is important for career success. Workers with high self-esteem develop and maintain favorable work attitudes and perform at a high level. A company with high-self-esteem workers has a competitive advantage.
- High self-esteem is associated with long-term career success, including job satisfaction, higher pay, occupying high-status positions, and performing better in training. Companies also prosper when workers have high self-esteem. Good mental health is another major consequence of high self-esteem. One of the links between good mental health and self-esteem is that high self-esteem helps prevent many situations from being stressful. High self-esteem helps you profit from negative feedback.
- Self-esteem can be useful in guiding social relationships because you can adjust your behavior as your esteem feelings fluctuate.
- Potential negative consequences of excessively high or low self-esteem include becoming narcissistic, envying too many people, and having relationship problems. One's own reference group has the biggest impact on self-esteem.

You enhance your self-esteem when you do the following:

- Attain legitimate accomplishments, including engaging in behaviors and making choices that are esteem-worthy. Setting constructive goals is also helpful.
- Become aware of your personal strengths.
- Minimize settings and interactions that detract from your feelings of competence.
- Talk and socialize frequently with people who boost your self-esteem.
- Model the behavior of people with high self-esteem.

Various studies have shown that people with a high sense of self-confidence tend to have good job performance, so self-confidence is important for your career. Our feelings of self-confidence stem from five sources of information:

- Actual experiences, or things that you have done
- Experiences of others, or modeling
- Social comparison, or comparing yourself to others
- Social persuasion, the process of convincing another person
- Emotional arousal, or how people feel about events around them and managing their emotions

A general principle of boosting your self-confidence is to experience success (goal accomplishment) in a variety of situations. The specific strategies for building self-confidence described here are as follows:

- Take an inventory of your personal assets and accomplishments.
- Develop a solid knowledge base.
- Use positive self-talk.

- Avoid negative self-talk.
- Use positive visual imagery.
- Set high expectations for yourself (the Galatea effect).
- Strive for peak performance.
- Behave as if you feel self-confident.
- Practice public speaking.
- Bounce back from setbacks and embarrassments. (Get past the emotional turmoil; find a creative solution to your problem; regain confidence by relaxing a little.)
- Strive to develop psychological capital (hope, self-efficacy, optimism, and resiliency).

Avoiding overconfidence will help you make more effective use of your self-confidence. To achieve the right level of self-confidence and self-esteem, maintain a focus on others also.

A substantial negative consequence of low self-esteem and self-confidence is that it can prompt the person to develop a codependent relationship. The codependent is psychologically controlled by or reliant upon another person who is addicted to a negative substance or behavior. The codependent person must learn to say no to the other person, perhaps in small steps.

Questions for Discussion and Review

2.1 Imagine an accountant being told by a client, "I think that you are really stupid, and I am going to report you to your boss." Give one example of how a high-self-esteem accountant might respond, and one of how a low-self-esteem accountant might respond.

2.2 Identify a public figure, such as a business executive, professional athlete, or politician whose self-esteem is so extreme that he or she is a narcissist. Give a couple of examples of his or her narcissistic behavior.

2.3 In what way has a teacher, instructor, or professor ever raised your self-esteem? How long-lasting was the effect?

2.4 How might you improve your self-efficacy for a specific job that you are performing?

2.5 When you meet another person, on what basis do you conclude that he or she has high (or low) self-esteem?

2.6 The criticism is often made in the media that we have become a nation of superficial approaches to building

self-esteem, such as giving children and adults trophies for very small accomplishments. What is your opinion of this criticism?

2.7 In what way does your program of studies contribute to building your self-esteem and self-confidence?

2.8 Self-confidence has been identified as the personality trait most frequently associated with leadership (see Chapter 11). If you aspire to be a leader or already occupy a leadership position, what steps do you think you will take to further strengthen your self-confidence?

2.9 Visualize yourself applying for your dream job, and because you want the job so badly you do not feel highly self-confident. What steps can you take to appear self-confident?

2.10 Interview a person whom you perceive to have a successful career. Ask that person to describe how he or she developed high self-esteem. Be prepared to discuss your findings in class.

Web Corner

Integrating self-esteem into the fabric of society
www.self-esteem-nase.org

Building your self-confidence
www.mindtools.com/selfconf.html (includes video). Enter "building self-confidence" in the search box.

INTERNET SKILL BUILDER 2-1

Building Your Self-Esteem

An article published by *Psychology Today*—"Building Confidence and Self-Esteem," written by Neel Burton and found at www.psychologytoday.com/blog/hide-and-seek/201205/building-confidence-and-self-esteem—is designed to help you build your self-esteem. Many of the suggestions in the article reinforce what you have studied in this chapter. The help offered is mostly from the perspective of people who

have low self-esteem and are working to improve it. All the suggestions are easy to implement, such as "Dress in clothes that make you feel good about yourself."

INTERNET SKILL BUILDER 2-2

Developing Your Self-Confidence Online

As described in this chapter, self-confidence is a major contributor to leadership effectiveness in a variety of situations. The website www.self-confidence.co.uk offers a free self-confidence course online. After you sign up for the course, you will receive your first installment immediately. After that, you will receive one tutorial a week for six weeks. The lessons include self-confidence-boosting stories, information and quotes, and skill development exercises. Sponsors of the site will invite you to take related courses for a fee.

Developing Your Human Relations Skills

Applying Human Relations Exercise 2-1

Boosting the Self-Esteem of Another Person

Your assignment is for three consecutive weeks to help build the self-esteem of one person. Before embarking on the exercise, review the information about self-esteem development in the chapter. One of the most effective tactics would be to find somebody who has a legitimate accomplishment and give that person a reward or thank-you. Record carefully what the person did, what you did, and any behavioral reactions of the person whose self-esteem you attempted to build. The incident could become part of your human relations journal.

An example of this type of self-esteem building took place between a small business owner and a freelance tech support person. The business owner's desktop computer had become so infected by computer viruses that it was almost useless. The owner tried two different antivirus programs in addition to the one already installed on his computer. Finally, the owner hired an information technology technician to work on the virus problem. The technician restored the computer to normal functioning in two hours. The business owner then gave the IT technician updates on how well his computer was performing and also posted a detailed comment on the technician's Facebook page about her outstanding accomplishment.

Applying Human Relations Exercise 2-2

Building Your Self-Confidence and Self-Efficacy

Most people can use a boost to their self-confidence. Even if you are a highly confident individual, perhaps there is room for building your feelings of self-efficacy in a particular area, for example, as a proud and successful business owner learning a new skill such as editing digital photos or speaking a foreign language. For this skill-building exercise, enhance your self-confidence or self-efficacy in the next two weeks by trying out one of the many suggestions for self-confidence building described in the text.

As part of planning the implementation of this exercise, think about any area in which your self-confidence could use a boost. A candid human relations student who was also a confident cheerleader said, "Face it, I suck at PowerPoint presentations. I put up so many details on my slides that the audience is trying to read my slides instead of looking at me. I have to admit that my PowerPoint presentation consists mostly of my reading my slides to the audience. I'm much better at cheerleading." So this student studied information in her human relations text about making better graphic presentations. She revamped her PowerPoint approach to using her slides as headlines and talking points. She tried out one presentation in class and one at her church. She received so many compliments on her presentations that she now has much higher self-efficacy with respect to PowerPoint presentations.

The Self-Esteem and Self-Confidence Survey

Here is an opportunity to engage in data collection about a vital human relations topic. Each class member is required to obtain survey data from five people (survey anybody convenient, including yourself), asking each person four questions, as follows:

1. What is your sex (gender)?
2. What is your age?
3. How would you rate your self-esteem from 1 (low) to 10 (high)?
4. How would you rate your self-confidence from 1 (low) to 10 (high)?

Use any method of data collection you would like, including face-to-face interviews, e-mail, chat, instant messaging, a social networking site, or the phone. The results of the survey are entered into a class database run by one or two volunteers. After all data have been collected, one of the volunteers analyzes the data in terms of the following results:

1. Percentage of respondents who are male and percentage female
2. Average age
3. Average self-esteem rating
4. Average self-confidence rating
5. Average self-esteem and self-confidence ratings of men and women

6. Average self-esteem and self-confidence ratings of respondents of (a) those twenty-five and younger and (b) those twenty-six and older

Class discussion might include any conclusions drawn from the results and how the results fit expectations. For example, a few students might comment about what they predicted would be the average score on self-esteem and self-confidence or any sex or age differences they might have predicted. What about you? How do your self-esteem and self-confidence ratings compare to the survey average?

Human Relations Case Study 2–1

High-Self-Esteem Brandy

As Brandy Barclay navigated the challenging highways toward her job interview in Los Angeles, she rehearsed in her mind the importance of communicating that she is a unique brand. (A brand is a basket of strengths that sets you apart from others.) "I have to get across the idea that I am special, even if my brand is not as well established as Godiva Chocolates or Dr Pepper. This administrative assistant position at the hotel and resort company will be a good way to launch my career and brand. After all, I am a very special person."

An excerpt of her job interview with the hiring manager, Gloria, follows:

Gloria: Welcome Brandy, I am pleased that you made it through the online job application and the telephone screening interview. Tell me again why you would like to join our hotel company as an administrative assistant.

Brandy: Oh, I really don't want to join you as an administrative assistant. I would prefer a vice president job, but I have to start somewhere. (*Smiling.*) Seriously, I like the hotel field. It fits my brand, called Brandy. I am a great support person and a great people person. I'm so unique because I'm great with details and great with people. Many people have told me that I am a very special person."

Gloria: Tell me specifically, what key strengths would you bring to this job?

Brandy: As found in my brand called Brandy, I am high-info tech and high touch. I'm a whiz at Microsoft Office Suite, and I'm sweet with people. Kind of catchy, don't you think? Come to think of it, have you seen my business card? It contains loads of details about my skills and strengths on the back. The card is laminated so it will last, and it contains my photo. It even is like a hologram with a 3-D look.

Gloria: Yes, Brandy, I do have your card. You gave one to the receptionist, and she gave it to me. And why do you keep referring to yourself as a brand? Is this just a gimmick to get you noticed?

Brandy: Being a brand is the modern way to tell you that Brandy Barclay is one of a kind. I've got a skill set that is hard to beat. Besides, I want to build a reputation fast that will propel me to the top as an executive in the hotel field. I am quite proud of who I am.

Gloria: On your trip to the top, what do you plan to do for us as an administrative assistant?

Brandy: I will live up to the brand called Brandy by getting the job done big-time. Just ask me to do something, and it will be done. Don't forget I will be building my brand image while in this beginning assignment.

Gloria: Now let's talk about details like the job assignment, salary, and benefits.

Brandy: Fine with me. We have to deal with the mundane at some point.

Case Questions

2.11 How effectively is Brandy presenting herself as a brand (or a unique individual)?

2.12 What suggestions can you offer Brandy for presenting herself as a strong individual more effectively?

2.13 To what extent do you think that Brandy's high self-esteem has reached the point of narcissism?

Human Relations Role-Playing Exercise 2–1

Brandy Becomes More Humble

Assume that Brandy receives an e-mail that Gloria is not going to extend her a job offer because she appeared to be more interested in boosting her career than helping the company. Brandy decides that she will appear a little more humble in her next job interview, yet still present a positive self-picture. She lands an interview with another company for an administrative position. Her interviewing manager is Gus, who likes positive people but dislikes arrogance.

One student plays the role of Brandy, who wants to impress, yet plans to tone down her self-admiration. Another student plays the role of Gus, who is unaware of Brandy's recent rejection as a job candidate. Observers rate the role-players on two dimensions, using a scale of 1 to 5, from very poor to very good. One dimension is "effective use of human relations techniques." The second dimension is "acting ability." A few observers might voluntarily provide feedback to the role-players in terms of sharing their ratings and observations. The course instructor might also provide feedback.

Human Relations Case Study 2–2

Anthony Needs a Boost

"I'm losing my mojo," said Anthony, a salesman who sells cargo space on ocean liners to companies all over the world who want to ship goods to or from the United States. After five consecutive years of being one of the top sales reps in his company, Anthony's sales have plunged 25 percent. Quincy, his manager, is sympathetic, but he wants to see Anthony sell more cargo space. A ship crossing the ocean with too much empty cargo space usually loses money for the shipper. Anthony explains to Quincy that he, too, wants to boost sales, but you cannot force a company to ship goods it has not sold. Part of Anthony's problem is that many manufacturers in the United States are now doing more of their manufacturing in the United States, resulting in less demand for shipments of manufactured goods from other countries.

"My personal life is in a bigger slump than my sales performance," explains Anthony. Two months ago, Anthony totaled his car when he slipped off the road and hit a tree while driving ten miles per hour beyond the speed limit. In addition to his getting a speeding ticket, his insurance company has raised his auto insurance premium by 25 percent.

Another discouraging problem Anthony has faced is that his fiancée broke off their engagement two months ago. She claimed that she suddenly felt trapped by the prospects of a committed relationship as well as marriage.

Anthony's golf game life has also suffered recently. "Maybe I'm bringing too much of my outside life onto the golf course. I've been shooting about six strokes higher than my average game recently. A big part of my problem is that it is difficult for me to concentrate on golf, particularly the putting. I keep thinking about my work and personal problems when I line up the ball.

"I want to get my life back on track, but I don't know here to begin. I'm losing faith in my abilities."

Case Questions

2.14 To what extent is Anthony facing a self-confidence problem?

2.15 What do you recommend that Anthony do to regain his self-confidence?

2.16 How might Anthony's manager be able to help Anthony boost his self-confidence?

Human Relations Role-Playing Exercise 2–2

Quincy Attempts to Boost Anthony's Self-Confidence

Quincy is worried about the loss in self-confidence that Anthony appears to be experiencing and believes that as Anthony's manager he should attempt to be helpful. Quincy decides to conduct a one-on-one session with Anthony to do whatever he can to help the sales representative regain some of his self-confidence. Quincy believes that his knowledge of human relations should be useful in helping Anthony. Although Anthony is surprised about the meeting, he is eager to listen to any advice that could possibly help him regain his confidence.

Conduct this role-play for about seven minutes. Observers rate the role players on two dimensions, using a scale of 1 to 5 from very poor to very good. One dimension is "effective use of human relations techniques." Focus on the technique Quincy uses to attempt to boost Anthony's self-confidence. The second dimension is "acting ability." A few observers might voluntarily provide feedback to the role players in terms of sharing their ratings and observations. The course instructor might also provide feedback.

REFERENCES

1. Original story was created from facts presented in the following sources: "BofA Hires Romano as Mexican Chief in Latin America Push," *Bloomberg Business*, www.bloomberg.com/news/articles/2014-09-bofa-hires-romano-as-mexican-chief-inlatin-american-push, September 25, 2014, pp. 1–3; Justino Aguila, "Emilio Romano, President of Telemundo, Resigns," http://www.billboard.com/biz/articles/news/5748047/emilio-romano-president-of-telemundo-resigns; "Telemundo Gets New Boss," *Latin American Herald Tribune*, December 29, 2011, pp. 1–3.

2. Nathaniel Branden, *Self-Esteem at Work: How Confident People Make Powerful Companies* (San Francisco: Jossey-Bass, 1998).

3. April O'Connell, Vincent O'Connell, and Lois-Ann Kuntz, *Choice and Change: The Psychology of Personal Growth and Interpersonal Relationships*, 7th ed. (Upper Saddle River, NJ: Pearson/Prentice Hall, 2005), p. 3.

4. Harriet Brown, "The Boom and Bust Ego," *Psychology Today*, February 2012, p. 70.

5. "Better Self-Esteem," www.utexas.edu/student/cmhc/booklets/selfesteem/selfest.html accessed February 1, 2006.

6. A review of the scholarly research on this topic is contained in Mark R. Leary and Ray F. Baumeister, "The Nature and Function of Self-Esteem: Sociometer Theory," in *Advances in Experimental Social Psychology*, Vol. 32 (New York: Academic Press, 2000), pp. 1–49.

7. Research of Leary cited in Sue Shellenbarger, "Finding the Just-Right Level of Self-Esteem for a Child," *The Wall Street Journal*, February 27, 2013, pp. D1, D3.

8. David De Cremer et al., "Rewarding Leadership and Fair Procedures as Determinants of Self-Esteem," *Journal of Applied Psychology*, January 2005, pp. 3–12.

9. Eugene Raudsepp, "Strong Self-Esteem Can Help You Advance," *The Wall Street Journal*, August 10, 2004.

10. Timothy A. Judge and Charlice Hurst, "How the Rich (and Happy) Get Richer (and Happier): Relationship of Core Self-Evaluations to Trajectories in Attaining Work Success," *Journal of Applied Psychology*, July 2008, pp. 849–863.

11. Daniel S. Stanhope, Samuel B. Pond III, and Eric A. Surface, "Core Self-Evaluations and Training Effectiveness: Prediction through Motivational Intervening Mechanisms," *Journal of Applied Psychology*, September 2013, pp. 820–831.

12. Adam M. Grant and Amy Wrzenesniewki, "I Won't Let You Down . . . or Will I? Core Self-Evaluations, Other-Orientation, Anticipated Guilt and Gratitude, and Job Performance," *Journal of Applied Psychology*, January 2010, pp. 10–121.

13. Nathaniel Branden, *Self-Esteem at Work: How Confident People Make Powerful Companies* (San Francisco: Jossey-Bass, 1998); Timothy A. Judge and Joyce E. Bono, "Relationship of Core Self-Evaluations Traits—Self-Esteem, Generalized Self-Efficacy, Locus of Control, and Emotional Stability—with Job Satisfaction and Job Performance: A Meta-Analysis," *Journal of Applied Psychology*, February 2001, pp. 80–92.

14. Quoted in Jon L. Pierce, Donald G. Gardner, Larry L. Cummings, and Randall B. Dunman, "Organization-Based Self-Esteem: Construct Definition, Measurement, and Validation," *Academy of Management Journal*, September 1989, p. 623.

15. As quoted in Erika Casriel, "Stepping Out," *Psychology Today*, March–April 2007, p. 73.

16. Ibid.

17. Andrew J. DuBrin, *Narcissism in the Workplace: Research, Opinion, and Practice* (Cheltenham, UK: Edward Elgar, 2012), p. 1.

18. Cited in Brown, "The Boom and Bust Ego," p. 73.

19. Cited in Julia M. Klein, "The Illusion of Rejection," *Psychology Today*, January–February 2005, p. 30.

20. Alexander H. Jordan and Pino G. Audia, "Self-Enhancement and Learning from Performance Feedback," *Academy of Management Review*, April 2012, pp. 211–231.

21. Cited in Brown, "The Boom and Bust Ego," p. 73.

22. A good sampling of his thinking is Leo Buscaglia, *Living, Loving, and Learning* (New York: Ballantine Books, 1985).

23. Cited in "Self-Esteem: You'll Need It to Succeed," *Executive Strategies*, September 1993, p. 12.

24. Raudsepp, "Strong Self-Esteem."

25. Traci Sitzmann and Gillian Yeo, "A Meta-Analytic Investigation of the Within-Person Self-Efficacy Domain: Is Self-Efficacy a Product of Past Performance or a Driver of Future Performance?" *Personnel Psychology*, No. 3, 2013, pp. 531–568.

26. Marilyn E. Gist and Terence R. Mitchell, "Self-Efficacy: A Theoretical Analysis of Its Determinants and Malleability," *Academy of Management Review*, April 1992, pp. 183–211; Sitzmann and Yeo, "A Meta-Analytic Investigation," pp. 531–568.

27. George P. Hollenbeck and Douglas T. Hall, "Self-Confidence and Leader Performance," *Organizational Dynamics*, Issue 3, 2004, pp. 261–264.

28. Cited in Ayana Dixon, "The Center of Success: Author Explains How Confidence Can Get You Further," *Black Enterprise*, March 2008, p. 123.

29. Anthony Balderrama, "Soft Skills Job Seekers Needed," *Democrat and Chronicle*, August 7, 2011, p. 2F.

30. Jay T. Knippen and Thad B. Green, "Building Self-Confidence," *Supervisory Management*, August 1989, pp. 22–27.

31. Quoted from "Entrepreneurs Need Attitude: Power of Being Positive Can Help You to Succeed in Spite of Setbacks," Knight Ridder, September 16, 2002.

32. D. Brian McNatt and Timothy A. Judge, "Boundary Conditions of the Galatea Effect: A Field Experiment and Constructive Replication," *Academy of Management Journal*, August 2004, pp. 550–565.

33. Frances Thornton, Gayle Privette, and Charles M. Bundrick, "Peak Performance of Business Leaders: An Experience Parallel to Self-Actualization Theory," *Journal of Business and Psychology*, Winter 1999, pp. 253–264.

34. Cited in "Present with Panache," *Manager's Edge*, June 2007, p. 8.

35. Cited in Daniel Okrent. "The Best Salesman in Business," *Fortune*, May 3, 2010, p. 204.

36. Quoted in Mark Seery, Alison E. Holman, and Roxanne Cohen Silver, "Whatever Does Not Kill Us: Cumulative Lifetime Adversity, Vulnerability, and Resilience," *Journal of Personality and Social Psychology*, December 2010, pp. 1025–1041.

37. Sue Shellenbarger, "Slumping at Work? What Would Jack Do?" *The Wall Street Journal*, October 13, 2010, p. D1.

38. Fred Luthans, James R. Avey, and Jaime L. Patera, "Experimental Analysis of a Web-Based Training Intervention to Develop Positive Psychological Capital," *Academy of Management Learning and Education*, June 2008, pp. 209–221.

39. Much of the discussion here about codependency is based on "Co-dependency," *Mental Health America*, pp. 1–3, © 2012 Mental Health America; "Codependency," www.AllAboutCounseling.com/codependency.htm, pp. 1–2.

Fotolia

CHAPTER **3**

Self-Motivation and Goal Setting

Outline

In a PowerPoint presentation to its editorial staff a few years ago, owners of *The Oregonian* newspaper in Portland, Oregon, announced a new policy that links journalists' performance to the size of their paychecks. According to internal documents obtained by *Williamette Weekly,* a local alternative magazine, a quota system has been put into place that demands big increases in posting to www.Oregonlive.com, the newspaper's website. Furthermore, the newspaper pledges higher pay for reporters who post most frequently.

Beat reporters are expected to post a minimum of three times a day. All other reporters are required to raise their average number of posts by 40 percent by the end of the year. Reporters have also been told to solicit ideas from readers and stimulate online conversation and debate, according to the documents. The news-paper plans to give out bonuses—if the finances of the company allow it—to reporters who exceed these goals.

In response to the Internet posts demanded by newspaper, Matthew Bidwell, a professor of management at the Wharton School of the University of Pennsylvania, had some concerns. He said, "In the case of The Oregonian, *employers want a greater quantity of journalism. They will get it, but the quality will likely go down. You get what you pay for."[1]*

Learning Objectives ▶

After studying the information and doing the exercises in this chapter, you should be able to:

3.1 Explain how needs and motives influence motivation.

3.2 Identify several needs and motives that could propel you into action.

3.3 Explain how engagement relates to self-motivation.

3.4 Explain why and how goals contribute to self-motivation.

3.5 Describe how to set effective goals and identify the problems sometimes created by goals.

3.6 Describe several specific techniques of self-motivation.

3.7 Apply the self-discipline model to achieving your goals.

The story about the newspaper in Oregon illustrates two topics covered in this chapter. Establishing goals, such as Internet posts, can drive you and your employer toward better performance. Yet, at the same time, goals can backfire when quantity is pursued more rigorously than quality. Knowledge about motivation and goal setting is also important when attempting to influence others to get things accomplished. Motivating others, for example, is a major requirement of the manager's job.

Being well motivated is also important simply to meet the demands of employers. Most organizations insist on high productivity from workers at all levels. Assuming that you have the necessary skills, training, and equipment, being well motivated will enable you to achieve high productivity.

The general purpose of this chapter is to present information that can help you sustain a high level of motivation, centering on the importance of needs and goals. Chapter 12 contains information that you will find useful for moti-vating other people. Here is an example that might apply to you personally:

Assume that similar to many readers of this text, you are ambitious. You have many interesting career goals. You want to finish your formal education, you want to obtain professional certification in your field, you want to attain a high level of responsibility in your career, and you want to be among the top 10 percent of income earners. Your plate is also filled with personal goals: You want to im-prove substantially in your favorite sport, become fluent in your second language, network all your electronic devices together, and double your network of friends.

Despite all your exciting goals, you are not making much progress in attaining them. Could the problem be that your level of self-discipline is not quite high enough to propel you toward accomplishing these goals one by one? Not having sufficient self-discipline is the major reason most people fall short of reaching their goals. Later in the chapter, we describe a well-developed system for developing enough self-discipline for getting things done that are important to you.

▶ **Learning Objective 3.1** ▶

How Needs and Motives Influence Motivation

Need
an internal striving or urge to do something, such as a need to drink when thirsty

According to a widely accepted explanation of human behavior, people have needs and motives that propel them toward achieving certain goals. Needs and motives are closely related. A **need** is an internal striving or urge to do something, such as a need to drink when thirsty. It can be regarded as a biological or a psychological requirement. A person who is deprived in some way (such as not having enough fluid in the body) is motivated to take action toward a goal. In this case, the goal might be simply getting something to drink.

A discussion of needs often triggers a discussion of the difference between *needs* and *wants*. A need is essentially a craving or urge that must be satisfied to maintain your equilibrium. In contrast, a want refers to more of a luxury—something you would like to have but is not necessary to keep your system balanced. A need is a more technical concept than is a want. Here is an example of the difference between a need and a want:

> Visualize yourself jogging in 90-degree weather. Suddenly your need for water surfaces, so any old fountain water will satisfy your physiological craving. But at the same time, you want a prestige brand of flavored bottled water to drink. You don't need the bottled water, you want it.

Motive
an inner drive that moves a person to do something

A **motive** is an inner drive that moves you to do something. The motive is usually based on a need or desire and results in the intention to attain an appropriate goal. Because needs and motives are so closely related, the two terms are often used interchangeably. For example, "recognition need" and "recognition motive" refer to the same thing.

THE NEED THEORY OF MOTIVATION

The central idea behind need theory is that unsatisfied needs motivate us until they become satisfied. When people are dissatisfied or anxious about their present status or performance, they will try to reduce this anxiety. This need cycle is shown in Figure 3-1. Assume that you have a strong need or motive to achieve recognition. As a result, you experience tension that drives you to find some way of being recognized on the job. The action you take is to apply for a position as the team leader of your group: Being appointed as team leader would provide ample recognition, particularly if the team performs well. You are appointed to the position, and for now, your need for recognition is at least partially satisfied as you receive compliments from your coworkers and friends. Once you

FIGURE 3-1

THE NEED CYCLE

Source: "THE NEED CYCLE" by Andrew J. DuBrin.

receive this partial satisfaction, two things typically happen. Either you will soon require a stronger dose of recognition, or you will begin to concentrate on another need or motive, such as achievement. In either case, the need cycle will repeat itself. You might seek another form of recognition or satisfaction of your need for power. For example, you might apply for a position as department manager or open your own business. Ideally, in this former situation, your boss would give you more responsibility, which could lead to more satisfaction of your recognition need and to some satisfaction of your need for achievement. (The needs mentioned so far, and others, are defined next.)

The need theory suggests that self-interest plays a key role in motivation.[2] People ask, "What's in it for me?" (or "WIIFM," pronounced *wiff'em*), before engaging in any form of behavior. In one way or another, people act to serve their self-interest. Even when people act in a way that helps others, they are doing so because helping others helps them. For example, you may give money to poor people because this act of kindness makes you feel wanted and powerful.

IMPORTANT NEEDS AND MOTIVES PEOPLE ATTEMPT TO SATISFY

◀ Learning Objective 3.2 ◀

Work and personal life offer the opportunity to satisfy dozens of needs and motives. In this and the following section, important needs that propel people into action are described. As you read about these needs and motives, relate them to yourself. For example, ask yourself, "Am I a power-seeking person?"

Achievement   The **need for achievement** is the desire to accomplish something difficult for its own sake. People with a strong need for achievement frequently think of how to do a job better. Responsibility seeking is another characteristic of people with a high need for achievement. They are also concerned about how to progress in their careers. Workers with a high need for achievement are interested in monetary rewards primarily as feedback about how well they are achieving. They also set realistic yet moderately difficult goals, take calculated risks, and desire feedback on performance. (A moderately difficult goal challenges a person but is not so difficult as to most likely lead to failure and frustration.) In general, those who enjoy building businesses, activities, and programs from scratch have a strong need for achievement. Figure 3-2 outlines the preferences of workers with strong achievement needs.

Need for achievement
the desire to accomplish something difficult for its own sake

Power   People with a high power need feel compelled to control resources, such as other people and money. Successful executives typically have a high power motive and exhibit three dominant characteristics: (1) They act with vigor and determination to exert their power, (2) they invest much time in thinking about ways to alter the behavior and thinking of others, and (3) they care about their personal standing with those around them.[3] The power need can be satisfied through occupying a high-level position or by becoming a highly influential person. Or you can name skyscrapers, hotels, golf courses, and a line of clothing after yourself, following the lead of Donald Trump.

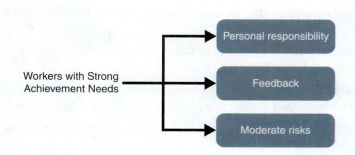

FIGURE 3-2

PREFERENCES OF WORKERS WITH STRONG ACHIEVEMENT NEEDS

Source: "PREFERENCES OF WORKERS WITH STRONG ACHIEVEMENT NEEDS" by Andrew J. DuBrin.

Affiliation People with a strong affiliation need seek out close relationships with others and tend to be loyal as friends or employees. The affiliation motive is met directly through belonging to the "office gang," a term of endearment implying that your coworkers are an important part of your life. Many people prefer working in groups to individual effort because of the opportunity the former provides for socializing with others.

Recognition People with a strong need for recognition want to be acknowledged for their contribution and efforts. The need for recognition is so pervasive that many companies have formal recognition programs in which outstanding or long-time employees receive gifts, plaques, and jewelry inscribed with the company logo. The recognition motive can be satisfied through means such as winning contests, receiving awards, and seeing your name online or in print. A major reason the need for recognition is such a useful motivator is that most people think they are underappreciated (and overworked).

Order People with a strong need for order want to achieve arrangement, balance, neatness, and precision. The order motive can be quickly satisfied by cleaning and organizing your work or living space. Occupations offering the opportunity to satisfy the order motive almost every day include accountant, computer programmer, and paralegal.

Risk Taking and Thrill Seeking Some people crave constant excitement on the job and are willing to risk their lives to achieve thrills. The need to take risks and pursue thrills has grown in importance in the high-technology era. Many people work for employers, start businesses, and purchase stocks with uncertain futures. The search for both giant payoffs and daily thrills motivates these individuals.[4] A strong craving for thrills may have some positive consequences for the organization, including willingness to perform such dangerous feats as setting explosives, capping an oil well, controlling a radiation leak, and introducing a product in a highly competitive environment. However, extreme risk takers and thrill seekers can create such problems as being involved in a disproportionate number of vehicular accidents and making imprudent investments.

Conscientiousness Although technically classified as a personality trait, the desire to be dependable, responsible, and persevering can also be regarded as a psychological need. People with the need to be conscientious also tend to have a strong need for achievement. Conscientiousness is the personality trait most consistently related to job performance in a wide variety of occupations, from the food-delivery person to the vice president of finance. Take Human Relations Self-Assessment Quiz 3-1 to measure your tendency toward being conscientious.

MASLOW'S HIERARCHY OF NEEDS

Maslow's hierarchy of needs
according to psychologist Abraham H. Maslow, people strive to satisfy the following groups of needs in step-by-step order: physiological needs, safety needs, social needs, esteem needs, and self-actualizing needs

The best-known categorization of needs is **Maslow's hierarchy of needs**. At the same time, it is the most widely used explanation of human motivation. According to psychologist Abraham H. Maslow, people strive to satisfy the following groups of needs in step-by-step order:

1. *Physiological needs* are bodily needs, such as the requirements for food, water, shelter, and sleep.

2. *Safety needs* refer to actual physical safety and to a feeling of being safe from both physical and emotional injury.

3. *Social needs* are essentially love, affection, and belonging needs. Unlike the two previous levels of needs, they center on a person's interaction with other people.

4. *Esteem needs* represent an individual's demand to be seen as a person of worth by others—and by himself or herself.

Human Relations Self-Assessment Quiz   3-1

The Conscientiousness Quiz

Indicate the extent to which each of the following statements describes your behavior or attitude by circling one number. The numbers refer to very inaccurate (VI), moderately inaccurate (MI), neither accurate nor inaccurate (N), moderately accurate (MA), and very accurate (VA). Consider enlisting the help of someone who knows your behavior and attitudes well to help you respond accurately to the statements.

Statement Related to Conscientiousness	VI	MI	N	MA	VA
1. I follow almost all rules on the job.	1	2	3	4	5
2. People who know me consider me to be quite dependable.	1	2	3	4	5
3. I frequently cut corners.	5	4	3	2	1
4. I am very involved in my work.	1	2	3	4	5
5. I go about my work methodically.	1	2	3	4	5
6. If somebody doesn't like the work I perform, it's that person's problem, not mine.	5	4	3	2	1
7. I typically plan my workday.	1	2	3	4	5
8. I attempt to avoid working too hard, so I have energy left over for life outside of work.	5	4	3	2	1
9. I go about my work with a sense of urgency.	1	2	3	4	5
10. I would strive for excellent performance only if I thought it would lead to a salary increase or bonus.	5	4	3	2	1
11. While at work, I regularly check personal e-mails, text messages, or my favorite websites.	5	4	3	2	1
12. I think I am much better organized than most of my coworkers.	1	2	3	4	5
13. I strive hard to reach the goals my supervisor has established for me.	1	2	3	4	5
14. I strive hard to reach the goals I have established for myself.	1	2	3	4	5
15. I lose patience easily when I am attempting to solve a difficult problem.	5	4	3	2	1

Scoring and Interpretation:

Calculate your score by adding up the numbers circled:

60–75: You are a highly conscientious person who is probably also self-disciplined.

45–59: You have an average degree of conscientiousness, including dependability.

15–44: You are below average in conscientiousness, dependability, and self-discipline. Solicit feedback from others to see if this low score is warranted. If the score is accurate, strive to become more conscientious in order to do well in your career.

Source: "The Conscientiousness Quiz" by Andrew J. DuBrin.

5. *Self-actualizing needs* are the highest level of needs, including the needs for self-fulfillment and personal development.

Maslow recognized that the five classes of needs in the hierarchy are only a partial description of human needs. Three other classes of needs are also important: *cognitive needs, aesthetic needs,* and *transcendence needs* (or *B-values*).

■ *Aesthetic needs* relate to the needs for symmetry, order, and beauty. This class of needs fits below the self-actualization needs on the hierarchy.

■ *Cognitive needs* relate to the needs to know, understand, and explore. This class of needs fits above the esteem needs—and just below the aesthetic needs—on the hierarchy.

■ *Transcendence needs,* or *B-values,* refer to needs to contribute to human welfare and to find higher meanings in life. This class of needs is an extension of self-actualization needs and fits above those needs on the hierarchy.[5]

A diagram of the needs hierarchy is presented in Figure 3-3. Notice the distinction between higher-level and lower-level needs. With few exceptions, higher-level needs are more difficult to satisfy. A person's needs for affiliation might be satisfied by being a member of a friendly work group. Yet, to satisfy self-actualization needs such as self-fulfillment, a person might have to develop an outstanding reputation in his or her company.

The needs hierarchy implies that most people think of finding a job as a way of obtaining the necessities of life. Once these are obtained, a person may think of achieving friendship, self-esteem, and self-fulfillment on the job. When a person is generally satisfied at one level, he or she looks for satisfaction at a higher level. As Maslow described it, a person is a "perpetually wanting animal." Very few people are totally satisfied with their lot in life, even the rich and famous.

The extent of need satisfaction is influenced by a person's job. Some construction jobs, for example, involve dangerous work in severe climates, thus frustrating both physiological and safety needs. Ordinarily there is much more opportunity for approaching self-actualization when a person occupies a prominent position, such as being a top executive or famous performer. However, a person with low potential could approach self-actualization by occupying a lesser position. In the current era, workers at all levels are threatened with the frustration of security needs because so many companies reduce the number of employees to save money.

How do Maslow's needs and the other needs described in this chapter relate to self-motivation? First, you have to ask yourself, "Which needs do I really want to satisfy?" After answering the question honestly, concentrate your efforts on an activity that will most likely satisfy that need. For instance, if you are hungry for power, strive to become a high-level manager or a business owner. If you crave self-esteem, focus your efforts on work and social activities that are well regarded by others. The point is that you will put forth substantial effort if you think the goal you will attain will satisfy an important need.

To learn more about how the needs hierarchy fits your need makeup, take Human Relations Self-Assessment Quiz 3-2. The class activity presented toward the end of the chapter will also enlarge your understanding of the need hierarchy.

FIGURE 3-3

MASLOW'S HIERARCHY OF NEEDS

Source: "MASLOW'S HIERARCHY OF NEEDS" by Andrew J. DuBrin. Based on "*A Theory of Human Motivation*" by Abraham H. Maslow.

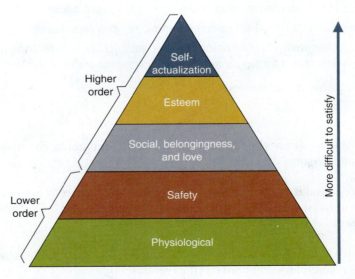

Note: Modern additions to the need hierarchy are (1) cognitive needs, (2) aesthetic needs, and (3) transcendent needs. The cognitive and aesthetic needs fit above the esteem needs, and the transcendent needs would fit above the self-actualization needs.

Human Relations Self-Assessment Quiz   3-2

My Standing on the Need Hierarchy

Respond to each of the following statements in terms of its importance to you, as follows: (1) not important, (2) a little bit important, (3) average importance, (4) important, and (5) very important.

Statement Number	Statement	Importance (1 to 5)
1.	Having a good reputation	_____
2.	Loving another person	_____
3.	Having a high evaluation of myself	_____
4.	Being somebody special and important	_____
5.	Having coworkers who are not physically abusive	_____
6.	Being respected by others	_____
7.	Feeling emotionally close to another person	_____
8.	Becoming much more than I am now	_____
9.	Avoiding big surprises in my work routine	_____
10.	Feeling useful and necessary in the world	_____
11.	Being a member of a group I care about	_____
12.	Feeling well rested	_____
13.	Feeling that I have the right balance of nutrients and chemicals in my body	_____
14.	Having a workplace that is relatively free of harmful germs	_____
15.	Being confident that I will achieve my full potential	_____
16.	Having an affectionate relationship with another person	_____
17.	Feeling completely self-fulfilled	_____
18.	Feeling comfortable rather than too hot or too cold	_____
19.	Not having to commute during hazardous road conditions	_____
20.	Eating food that has a pleasant taste	_____
21.	Being loved by another person	_____
22.	Becoming who I am capable of becoming	_____
23.	Having self-respect	_____
24.	Having enough food to eat	_____
25.	Avoiding loud, irritating noises	_____

Source: The ideas for the statements in the quiz stem from Abraham H. Maslow, "A Theory of Human Motivation," *Psychological Review*, July 1943, pp. 370–396.

Scoring and Interpretation:

The scoring key follows the five categories in the Maslow needs hierarchy. Enter your rating (1–5) for each statement, and compute your total for each of the five categories of needs.

Ranking

Physiological

12 _____   13 _____   18 _____   20 _____   24 _____   Physiological total _____   _____

Safety

5 _____   9 _____   14 _____   19 _____   25 _____   Safety total _____   _____

Love

2 _____   7 _____   11 _____   16 _____   21 _____   Love total _____   _____

Esteem

1 _____   3 _____   6 _____   10 _____   23 _____   Esteem total _____   _____

Self-actualization

4 _____   8 _____   15 _____   17 _____   22 _____   Self-actualization total _____   _____

The total for each of the five needs will be somewhere between 1 and 25. The highest score receives a rank of 1, and the lowest score receives a rank of 5. A tentative interpretation here is that your most important need category is the one with the highest rank, whereas the least important need category receives the lowest rank. A high-importance ranking might suggest that you are actively attempting to satisfy the need category in question. A low-importance ranking would suggest that you are not currently attempting to satisfy that need category because that category is already satisfied. It is also possible that you just don't care about the need category, such as not worrying about becoming self-actualized.

Questions: **1.** What importance ranking of these needs categories might a person give who is unemployed and currently living in his or her SUV or minivan? Why?

2. What importance rankings might one of your favorite celebrities give to these needs categories? Why?

Source: "My Standing on the Need Hierarchy" by Andrew J. DuBrin.

▶ **Learning Objective 3.3** ▶

ENGAGEMENT AS PART OF SELF-MOTIVATION

Another way of looking at self-motivation is that if you are strongly motivated you are engaged in your work or committed to the job and the company. Employees engaged in their work are more willing to help supervisors and coworkers and to voluntarily promote the company outside of work. An engaged employee also feels connected to the organization. An analysis of many studies indicates that **work engagement** refers to high levels of personal investment in the work tasks performed in a job.[6] As a result, the self is injected into the job. The engaged worker would therefore feel personally responsible for good and poor job performance and would take pride in accomplishment. An inventor would be likely to experience engagement, but so might a bookkeeper. Worker engagement shows some variation from time to time. Research conducted in a variety of industries suggests that work engagement fluctuates day by day around an average level of engagement.[7] As a result, on some days, you might feel more engaged than on others.

Work engagement

high levels of personal investment in the work tasks performed in a job

The engaged worker stands out because, according to research conducted with thousands of organizations, only 30 percent of employees are committed to doing a good job. Approximately 50 percent of employees do just enough work to get by. About 20 percent of employees act out their discontent in counterproductive ways, such as spreading negative attitudes to coworkers, staying home from work, and driving away customers through poor service.[8]

An engaged worker contributes to the prosperity of the organization. As the organization prospers, so does the individual in terms of compensation and opportunities for advancement. Productivity trainer Joe Robinson observes that engaged workers are more energized, dedicated, and committed to their task and the company than their less engaged counterparts. The "oomph" they provide enhances job performance and profits.[9]

Among the many initiatives companies take to enhance engagement are (a) opportunities for career advancement, (b) celebration of job successes, (c) encouragement of workers to bring forth problems to managers, and (d) giving employees breathing room in how they should complete their tasks.

The link between employee engagement and self-motivation is that self-motivated workers are more likely to be engaged with or committed to their companies. "Breathing room" is particularly helpful because people who have control over the method of solving a problem tend to feel that they are acting independently. An example would be a manager telling a worker, "See if you can find a way to decrease shipping costs by 5 percent. I won't give you any hints." A theory relating to self-motivation and engagement is presented next.

SELF-DETERMINATION AND ENGAGEMENT

Why and how employees become engaged in their work can be explained to some extent by **self-determination theory**. The theory contends that we are most deeply engaged, and that we do our most creative work, when we feel that we are acting according to our own will and pursing goals we find meaningful. Self-determination theory closely relates to self-motivation because it explains that motivation develops internally, grounded in three basic human needs. The *competency* need refers to wanting to develop our skills; the *autonomy* need refers to acing of our own accord; and *relatedness* refers to connecting with others in our environment.

An important focus of self-determination theory is that doing exciting work that meets our needs is more important than external rewards in staying motivated. Although external rewards, such as money and prizes, can influence motivation, the truly engaged worker focuses mostly on working somewhat independently on exciting tasks and connecting with coworkers.[10] (No wonder social media are so popular!)

Human Relations Self-Assessment Quiz 3-3 will help you think through job factors that are likely to engage you in your work. The accompanying Human Relations in Practice illustrates what a company might do to foster engagement.

Self-determination theory
the motivation theory contending that we are most deeply engaged, and do our most creative work, when we feel that we are acting according to our own will and pursuing goals we find meaningful

Human Relations Self-Assessment Quiz   3-3

My Engagement Drivers

A checklist follows of ten factors that have been observed to get many professional-level workers engaged in (or committed to) their employer. Check off the five factors that would be most likely to bring about your engagement.

1. An opportunity to learn new skills almost every month ☐
2. Receiving frequent coaching from my manager ☐
3. Free lunches served in the company cafeteria ☐
4. Well-above-average pay and benefits ☐
5. The opportunity to make use of the latest high-tech gadgets related to my work ☐
6. Company leaders who are inspiring and warm ☐
7. A manager who really listens to my concerns and problems ☐
8. A beautiful physical facility, including an onsite gym and showers ☐
9. An opportunity to be promoted if I am an outstanding performer ☐
10. Interesting, friendly, well-motivated, and intelligent coworkers ☐
11. Work that challenges me almost every day ☐
12. Good professional and social networking opportunities at the company ☐

As you review the five factors most likely to bring about your commitment, what pattern do you notice? For example, would the work itself be the most important for you? Or are you more likely to feel engaged with respect to factors not directly related to the job, such as free lunches?

Source: "My Engagement Drivers" by Andrew J. DuBrin.

Human Relations in Practice

Employee Engagement at Coca Cola

Coca-Cola Company leadership aims to create environments where employees are fully engaged, and where the company is viewed both internally and externally as the employer of choice. The Coca-Cola Company is the world's largest beverage company, offering more than 500 carbonated and still beverages to the public. Some of the company's best-known brands include Coca-Cola, Diet Coke, Powerade, and Minute Maid. Consumers in more than 200 countries drink Coca-Cola beverages. Together with bottling partners, Coca-Cola ranks among the world's top ten private employers with more than 700,000 system associates across the world

A major concern of Coca-Cola leadership is to keep this far-flung group of employees engaged and involved in their work. The lofty goal is to get employees to enjoy their work as much as they enjoy Coca-Cola beverages. Top-level management says that the company's success depends on motivated and committed employees who feel that they play a vital part in the business's meeting its goals. A challenge in keeping employees engaged in their work is that carbonated beverages have come under attack by some people as not being nutritious, and as facilitating obesity.

Although approaches to employee engagement vary within different regions of the world, several approaches are common practice. Coca-Cola Refreshments, the North American bottler, employs Robin Gee, as Director of Employee Engagement, who provides direction to employee engagement approaches and programs. The major thrust to attaining engagement is constructive dialogue with employee representative groups about working conditions. Employee surveys are another method for measuring engagement. Every year Coca-Cola distributes the Employee Insights Survey, seeking employee input on how the company is run and any suggestions for improvement. The survey has found in recent years that employee engagement is about 84 percent.

Training and mentoring are also aimed at engagement, with the company offering a number of development programs to encourage and motivate employees. Peak Performance offers continual opportunities to reward employees for good performance. Employee performance reviews give employees an opportunity to receive merit raises. Developmental forums offer teaching opportunities, and Coca-Cola University provides online training.

One large Coca-Cola bottling unit, Coca-Cola Hellenic (CCH), identified five key factors in employee engagement and used them in a survey. The factors are listed next with one survey item in parentheses to illustrate how the factor is measured:

- *Part of a Winning Team* ("We work together well across departments.")
- *Making a Difference* ("The work I do makes an impact.")
- *Realizing Your Full Potential* ("I am given ample opportunity to grow professionally.")
- *An Enjoyment Business* ("CCH is a fun place to work.")

Questions:

1. Does it seem too good to be true that approximately 84 percent of Coca-Cola employees throughout the world are engaged?

2. Imagine yourself as a supervisor at a Coca-Cola distributor. How would you help a Coca-Cola truck driver feel that he or she is making a positive impact on the world?

Source: Original story created from facts and observations in the following sources: "Keeping Our Employees Healthy and Happy Is Part of Coca-Cola's Ethos," *Coca-Cola Ireland* (www.coca-cola:ie/about-us/), February 17, 2015, pp. 1–3; "Aligning Employer Brand Management with Employee Engagement," www.employerbrand.com), © 2014, pp. 1–2; Rica Bhattacharyya and Shreya Roy, "Engaging Gen Y at Workplace: Coca Cola, Accenture, Mindtree and Others Create Career Progression Model," *Economic Times* (http://articles.economictimes.com), March 13, 2014, pp. 1–3; "Our Company" (www.coca-colacompany.com), © 2015 THE COCA-COLA COMPANY.

How Goals Contribute to Self-Motivation

◀ **Learning Objective 3.4** ◀

At some point in their lives, almost all successful people have established goals, attesting to the importance of goals. A **goal** is an event, circumstance, object, or condition a person strives to attain. A goal thus reflects your desire or intention to regulate your actions. Here we look at seven topics to help you understand the nature of goals: (1) the advantages of goals, (2) the learning and performing orientations toward goals, (3) goal setting on the job, (4) personal goal setting, (5) action plans to support goals, (6) guidelines for goal setting, and (7) problems sometimes created by goals.

Goal
an event, circumstance, object, or condition a person strives to attain

ADVANTAGES OF GOALS

Goals and goal setting have become embedded into our society both on and off the job. Sales quotas and New Year's resolutions are examples of goal setting. Five of the potential advantages of goals are outlined in Figure 3-4. Setting specific, reasonably difficult goals improves performance. A real estate agent might say, "Next month I will obtain five new listings." (Listings are the best way for a real estate agent to earn high commissions, but obtaining a listing requires a lot of work.)

Another advantage of goals is that when we guide our lives with goals, we tend to focus our efforts in a consistent direction. Our conscious goals affect what we achieve. Without goals, our efforts may become scattered in many directions. We may keep trying, but we will go nowhere unless we happen to receive more than our share of luck.

Goal setting increases our chances for success, particularly because success can be defined as the achievement of a goal. The goals you set for accomplishing a task can serve as a standard to indicate when you have done a satisfactory job. A sales representative might set a goal of selling $400,000 worth of merchandise for the year. By November, she might close a deal that places her total sales at $410,000. With a sigh of relief she can then say, "I've done well this year."

Goals serve as self-motivators and energizers. People who set goals tend to be motivated because they are confident that their energy is being invested in something

1. Reasonably difficult goals improve performance.
2. Goals can instill purpose, challenge, and meaning into ordinary tasks.
3. Goals focus our efforts in a specific direction.
4. Goals increase our chances for success because they serve as a standard for measuring success.
5. Goals serve as self-motivators and energizers.

FIGURE 3-4

ADVANTAGES OF GOALS

Source: "ADVANTAGES OF GOALS" by Andrew J. DuBrin.

worthwhile. Aside from helping them become more motivated and productive, setting goals can help them achieve personal satisfaction. Most people derive a sense of satisfaction from attaining a goal that is meaningful to them. Breakthrough goals are particularly good at generating excitement and inspiration because they stretch the imagination of people. Workers at Apple Inc. and Google Inc. have for years been pursuing the goal of "changing the world."

THE LEARNING AND PERFORMING ORIENTATIONS TOWARD GOALS

Another useful perspective on understanding how goals influence motivation is that goals can be aimed at either learning or hoping to perform well.[11] A learning-goal orientation means that an individual is focused on acquiring new skills and mastering new situations. For example, you might establish the goal of learning how to develop skill in using social media to market a product. You say to yourself, "My goal is to learn how to use social media so I know even more about how to apply communication technology."

A performing-goal orientation is different. It is aimed at wanting to demonstrate and validate the adequacy of your competence by seeking favorable judgments about your competence. At the same time, you want to avoid seeking negative judgments. For example, your goal might be to make Facebook posts that would highly impress whoever watched them. Your focus is on looking good and avoiding negative evaluations of your postings.

Desire for Feedback   A person's goal orientation usually affects his or her desire for feedback. People with a learning-goal orientation are more likely to seek feedback on how well they are performing. In contrast, people with a performing-goal orientation are less likely to seek feedback. If you focus too much on setting performance goals, you might have a tendency to overlook the value of feedback. Yet the feedback could help you improve your performance in the long run.

Impact on Work Performance   Goal orientation is also important because it can affect work performance. Attempting to master skills often leads to better results than does attempting to impress others. A study of the effects of the two different goal orientations was conducted with 167 salespeople working for a medical supplies distributor. The salespeople were paid mostly on the commission of the gross profits they generated. The researchers found that a learning-goal orientation was associated with higher sales performance. In contrast, a performing-goal orientation was unrelated to sales performance. An important implication of the study is that even if you are an experienced worker, a focus on skill development is likely to lead you to higher performance.[12]

Better Relationships with Supervisors   Another positive consequence of a mastery (or learning-goal) orientation is that it often prompts workers to develop better relationships with their supervisors. Workers with a mastery orientation are likely to have stronger job performance and job satisfaction than those workers with a performance orientation. The positive outcomes of stronger job performance and satisfaction appear to take place because the workers develop better relationships with their supervisors.[13]

A good reason exists for why a learning-goal (or mastery) orientation is so important in today's business world. The purpose of a learning goal is to stimulate a person's imagination, to engage in discovery, and to think imaginatively. A performance goal focuses more on exerting effort to attain an objective using the knowledge one already possesses. When an effective strategy requires innovation that has yet to emerge—as is often the case—specific, high-learning goals should be set.[14] An example of a learning goal of high importance would be figuring out how to dispose of debris after a hurricane.

GOAL SETTING ON THE JOB

Virtually all organizations have come to accept the value of goal setting in producing the results they want to achieve. Dennis Zeleny, an HR consultant, states that "goals are the most important tools that companies use to get things done."[15] Goals contribute to employee engagement because employees know what is expected of them every day.

Goal-setting programs designed to boost performance or personal development are in frequent use. The personal aspects of goal setting are described in the following section. In most goal-setting programs, executives at the top of the organization are supposed to plan for the future by setting goals such as "Improve profits 10 percent this year." Employees at the bottom of the organization are supposed to go along with such broad goals by setting more specific goals. An example is "I will decrease damaged merchandise by 10 percent this year. I will accomplish this by making sure that our shelving is adequate for our needs."

You participate in the goal-setting process by designing goals to fit into the overall mission of the firm. A bank teller might set a personal goal of this nature: "During rush periods, and when I feel fatigued, I will double-count all the money that I handle." In some goal-setting programs, employees are requested to set goals that will lead to their personal improvement. An auditor for the state government set this goal for herself: "Within the next twelve months, I will enroll in and complete a supervisory training course in a local college." This woman aspired toward becoming a supervisor.

The points made in the two previous paragraphs merit repetition because of their importance. In a well-designed organization, the goals the individual sets contribute to the company's organizational goals. The construction supervisor who establishes a goal to regularly consult a checklist to make sure that safety procedures are being followed is contributing to the company goal of reducing accidents on the construction site.

A key factor in the success of a goal-setting program is a basic human relations principle: Managers and employees have to communicate frequently about goals or the goals are soon forgotten. A recommendation is to have daily, ten-sentence conversations about progress toward the goals.[16] An example would be "You established the goal of developing a way to repurpose our obsolete lines of clothing. How is that project going?"

A sample set of work goals is shown in Figure 3-5. The service and repair department supervisor who set these objectives took into account the requirements of his boss and the automobile dealership. Even if you set goals by yourself, they must still take into account the needs of your employer.

JOB TITLE AND BRIEF JOB DESCRIPTION

Manager, Service Department:
Responsible for supervision of service department of automobile dealership. Responsible for staffing service department with appropriate personnel and for quality of service to customers. Work closely with owner of dealership to discuss unusual customer problems. Handle customer complaints about mechanical problems of cars purchased at dealership.

Objectives for Scott Gilley
1. By December 31 of this year, decrease by 10 percent customer demands for rework.
2. Hire two general mechanics within forty-five days.
3. Hire two body specialists within forty-five days.
4. Decrease by 30 percent the number of repairs returned by customers for rework.
5. Reduce by 10 percent the discrepancy between estimates and actual bills to customers.
6. Schedule at least 35 percent of our service appointments through our website by January 15 of next year.

FIGURE 3-5

FORM USED IN AUTOMOBILE DEALERSHIP FOR STATEMENT OF GOALS

Source: "Form Used in Automobile Dealership for Statement of Goals" Andrew J. DuBrin.

PERSONAL GOAL SETTING

If you want to lead a rewarding personal life, your chances of attaining your desire increase if you make plans that include goal setting. Personal goals heavily influence the formulation of career goals as well. For this reason, it is worthwhile to set personal goals in conjunction with career goals. Ideally, they should be integrated to help achieve a balance between the demands of work and personal life. For example, if your preferred lifestyle would be to live in a rural area, a career in manufacturing or food processing would be more sensible than a career in advertising. This is true because manufacturing and food processing within North America have moved mostly to rural areas, whereas advertising remains mostly in large cities.

Types of Personal Goals   Personal goals can be subdivided into those relating to social and family life, hobbies and interests, physical and mental health, career, and finances. An example of each type follows:

Social and family life.   "Have a spouse and two children by age thirty."

Hobbies and interests.   "Become a black belt in karate by age twenty-eight."

Physical and mental health.   "Be able to run four miles without stopping or panting for breath by April 15 of next year."

Career.   "Become a department manager by age twenty-eight."

Finances.   "Within the next four years, be earning $70,000 per year, adjusted for inflation."

Other categories of personal goals are possible, yet the list presented represents convenient categories for most people.

ACTION PLANS TO SUPPORT GOALS

Ideally, reading this chapter and doing the exercises in it will start you on a lifelong process of using goals to help you plan your life. But before you can capitalize on the benefits of goal setting, you need a method for translating goals into action. An **action plan** describes how you are going to reach your goal. The major reason you need an action plan for most goals is that without a method for achieving what you want, the goal is likely to slip by. If your goal were to build your own log cabin, part of your action plan would be to learn how to operate a buzz saw, to read a handbook on log cabin building, to learn how to operate a tractor, and so forth. Some goals are so difficult to reach that your action plan might encompass hundreds of separate activities. You would then have to develop separate action plans for each step of the way.

Action plan
describes how you are going to reach your goal

Some immediate goals do not really require an action plan. A mere statement of the goal may point to an obvious action plan. If your goal were to replace a set of worn tires on your vehicle, you would know which steps to take.

▶ Learning Objective 3.5 ▶

GUIDELINES FOR GOAL SETTING

Goal setting is an art in the sense that some people do a better job of goal setting than others. Following are suggestions on setting effective goals—those that lead to achieving what you hoped to achieve, as outlined in Figure 3-6.

Express Each Goal as a Positive Statement   Expressing your goals in positive statements is likely to be more energizing than focusing on the negative.[17] An example of a

1. Express each goal as a positive statement.
2. Formulate specific goals.
3. Formulate concise goals.
4. Set realistic as well as stretch goals.
5. Set goals for different time periods.
6. Strive for synergy among goals.

FIGURE 3-6

GUIDELINES FOR GOAL SETTING

Source: "GUIDELINES FOR GOAL SETTING" by Andrew J. DuBrin.

positive statement would be "During the next year when I am attending networking events, I will create a positive, professional impression on everybody I meet." The negative counterpart would be "During the next year, I will avoid making a fool of myself when I am attending networking events." Despite this suggestion, there are times when a negative goal is useful, such as in reducing errors.

Formulate Specific Goals A goal such as "attaining success" is too vague to serve as a guide to daily action. A more useful goal would be to state specifically what you mean by "success" and when you expect to achieve it. For example, "I want to be the manager of customer service at a telecommunications company by January 1, 2022, and receive above-average performance reviews."

Formulate Concise Goals A useful goal can usually be expressed in a short, punchy statement, for example, "Decrease input errors in credit-card statements so that customer complaints are decreased by 25 percent by September 30 of this year." People new to goal setting typically commit the error of formulating lengthy, rambling goal statements. These lengthy goals involve so many different activities that they fail to serve as specific guides to action.

Set Realistic as Well as Stretch Goals A realistic goal is one that represents the right amount of challenge for the person pursuing the goal. On the one hand, easy goals are not very motivational; they may not spring you into action. On the other hand, goals that are too far beyond your capabilities may lead to frustration and despair because there is a good chance you will fail to reach them. The extent to which a goal is realistic depends on a person's capabilities. An easy goal for an experienced person might be a realistic goal for a beginner. Self-efficacy is also a factor in deciding whether a goal is realistic. The higher your self-efficacy, the more likely you are to think that a particular goal is realistic. A person with high self-efficacy for learning Chinese might say, "I think that learning two new Chinese words a day is realistic."

Several goals that stretch your capability might be included in your list of goals. An extreme stretch goal might be for a store manager trainee to become the vice president of merchandising for Target Corp. within four years. Another type of stretch goal is striving for a noble cause. A logging supervisor may not get excited about having the crew load a certain number of felled trees on a flatbed truck, but she might get excited about the trees being used to build homes, schools, and hospitals.

A useful perspective on stretch goals is that if you are attaining all your goals, you are not stretching your capabilities. An example would be a recreational tennis player who establishes a goal of winning every match and then never loses. If playing against an occasional stronger player were in the list of goals, the person could not win every time.

Set Goals for Different Time Periods Goals are best set for different time periods, such as daily, short range, medium range, and long range. Daily goals are essentially a to-do list. Short-range goals cover the period from approximately one week to one year into the future. Finding a new job, for example, is typically a short-range goal. Medium-range goals relate to events that will take place within approximately two to five years. They concern such things as the type of education or training you plan to undertake and the next step in your career.

Long-range goals refer to events taking place five years into the future and beyond. They relate to the overall lifestyle you wish to achieve, including the type of work and family situation you hope to have. Although every person should have a general idea of a desirable lifestyle, long-range goals should be flexible. You might, for example, plan to stay single until age forty. But while on vacation next summer, you might just happen to meet the right partner for you.

Short-range goals make an important contribution to attaining goals of longer duration. If a one-year work goal is to reduce mailing and shipping costs by 12 percent for the year, a good way to motivate workers is to look for a 1 percent saving per month. Progress toward a larger goal is self-rewarding.

Strive for Synergy among Your Goals   A powerful approach to goal setting is to make your goals synergistic, to fit together in a way that makes them work together. Executive coach Joelle K. Jay explains that synergy takes place when one idea advances another.[18] Goals that are not synergistic run the risk of becoming a group of unrelated chores. Smaller, short-term goals fitting a long-range purpose (vision) bring about synergy. Assume that business student Tony has established the major goal of "helping hundreds of people have financially secure retirements." Two synergistic goals for Tony would be "Get an A in my personal finance course," and "Start preparing for Chartered Financial Analyst certification two years after graduation." (Do you think we are putting too much pressure on Tony?)

PROBLEMS SOMETIMES CREATED BY GOALS

Despite the many advantages of goals, they can create problems.

1. **Inflexibility.**   A major problem is that *goals can create inflexibility*. People can become so focused on reaching particular goals that they fail to react to emergencies, such as neglecting a much-needed machine repair in order to achieve a quota. Goals can also make a person inflexible with respect to missing out on opportunities. You develop tunnel vision and ignore important events not directly related to your goal. Sales representatives sometimes neglect to invest time in cultivating a prospective customer because of the pressure to make quota. Instead, the sales rep goes for the quick sale with an established customer. A person on a diet might establish the goal of avoiding networking events in restaurants because fattening foods and beverages are served. The person might lose weight but at the same time miss out on the development of useful professional contacts.

   A problem related to inflexibility is that goals can sometimes become obsessions, leading you to neglect other phases of work or life. A worker might become so obsessed with accomplishing work by the end of a quarter that he or she refuses to take the time to help a coworker in need.

   A recommended approach to combating the potential inflexibility and obsessive nature of goals is to recognize and admit when you might be pursuing the wrong goal. Imagine that you decide to start a vineyard so you can create and market wine that retails for less than $15 per bottle. Among the hurdles you encounter are that (a) nobody wants to finance such a venture and (b) the world already has far too many brands of wine. You finally surrender your wine-venture idea and look for a business activity with a greater chance of success. Life coach Pamela Mitchell explains the problem of pursuing wrong goals. She observes that when we make the strategic decision to stop investing in actions that offer little return or negative outcomes, we capture the power of positive quitting: "It is important to discontinue activities that steal our time, drain our energy, waste our money, or diminish self-esteem and respect."[19]

2. **Loss of interest in the task.**   Another problem is that *performing goals can sometimes detract from an interest in the task.* People with a performing-goal orientation (focusing on being judged as competent) will sometimes lose interest in the task. The loss of interest is most likely to occur when the task is difficult. Assume that your primary reason for working as an information technology specialist is to perform well enough so that you can earn a high income. If carrying out your responsibilities encounters some hurdles, you may readily become discouraged with information technology as a field. But if your orientation is primarily to advance your knowledge about a dynamic field, you will not be readily frustrated when you encounter problems. You might even look on a problem as a learning opportunity.

3. **Engaging in unethical behavior.**   A tight focus on goals can also encourage unethical behavior and a disregard for *how* the goals are attained. A sales representative might give kickbacks simply to gain a sale, and a CEO might lay off needed workers and neglect investing in new-product research simply to make certain profit figures. Too much emphasis on goals can also contribute to cheating in the form of people falsely reporting that they met a performance level.[20] An example would be a meat inspector claiming to have visited more meat packers than she actually did.

4. **Slacking off after the goal is reached.**   Goals can sometimes backfire because the worker who has attained the goal then slacks off. The worker might think, even below the level of full awareness, "Okay, I've done what is expected of me, I can therefore relax until the next goal-setting period." This problem is particularly acute with workers paid on commission who receive no additional compensation for exceeding quota. Matthew Bidwell, quoted in the opening case, puts it this way: "We work hard to achieve the goal and less hard once we achieved it."[21]

Despite the problems that can arise in goal setting, goals are valuable tools for managing your work and personal life. Used with common sense and according to the ideas presented in this chapter, they could have a major, positive impact on your life.

Self-Motivation Techniques

◀ Learning Objective 3.6 ◀

Many people never achieve satisfying careers and never realize their potential because of low motivation. They believe they could perform better but admit that "I'm simply not a high-initiative type" or "I'm simply not that motivated." Earlier we described how identifying your most important needs could enhance motivation. Here we describe six additional techniques for self-motivation.

1. **Set goals for yourself.**   As shown throughout this chapter, goal setting is one of the most important techniques for self-motivation. If you set long-range goals and support them with a series of smaller goals set for shorter time spans, your motivation will increase.

2. **Find intrinsically motivating work.**   A major factor in self-motivation is to find work in which performing the task can be its own reward.[22] **Intrinsic motivation** refers to the natural tendency to seek out novelty and challenges, to extend and use one's capacities, to explore, and to learn.[23] The intrinsically motivated person is involved in the task at hand, such as a technology enthusiast surfing the Internet for hours at a time. Finding a job that offers you motivators in ample supply will help enhance your intrinsic motivation. For example, you might have good evidence from your past experience that the opportunity for close contact with people is a personal motivator. Find a job that involves working in a small, friendly department or team.

Intrinsic motivation
the natural tendency to seek out novelty and challenges, to extend and use one's capacities, to explore, and to learn

Intrinsically motivating work often takes the form of *meaningful work,* or work that has personal meaning to you based on your values and interests. One person might think that working as a store manager for the Salvation Army is meaningful. Another person might think that working as an electronics technician at a missile defense systems company is meaningful.

Based on circumstances, you may have to take whatever job you can find, or you may not be in a position to change jobs. In such a situation, try to arrange your work so you have more opportunity to experience the reward(s) that you are seeking. Assume that solving difficult problems excites you but that your job is 85 percent routine. Develop better work habits so that you can take care of the routine aspects of your job more quickly. This approach will give you more time to enjoy the creative aspects of your job.

3. **Get feedback on your performance.** Few people can sustain a high level of motivation without receiving information about how well they are doing. Even if you find your work challenging and exciting, you will need feedback. One reason positive feedback is valuable is that it acts as a reward. If you learn that your efforts achieved a worthwhile purpose, you will feel encouraged. For example, if a graphics display you designed was well received by company officials, you would probably want to prepare another graphics display.

A study conducted with management students demonstrated that participants adjusted their goals upward after receiving positive feedback and downward after negative feedback. It was also found that when the students were more emotional about the feedback, the positive and negative results were more pronounced.[24] The link here to self-motivation is that when goals are higher, motivation will be higher.

4. **Apply behavior modification to yourself.** **Behavior modification** is a system of motivation that emphasizes rewarding people for doing the right things and punishing them for doing the wrong things. Many people have used behavior modification to change their own behavior. Specific purposes include overcoming eating disorders, tobacco addiction, Internet abuse, nail biting, and procrastination. To boost your own motivation through behavior modification, you would have to first decide what specific motivated actions you want to increase (such as working thirty minutes longer each day). Second, you would have to decide on a suitable set of rewards and punishments. You may choose to use rewards only because rewards are generally better motivators than punishments.

5. **Improve your skills relevant to your goals.** The **expectancy theory of motivation** states that people will be motivated if they believe that their efforts will lead to desired outcomes. According to this theory, people hold back effort when they are not confident that their efforts will lead to accomplishments. You should therefore seek adequate training to ensure that you have the right abilities and skills to perform your work. The training might be provided by the employer or on your own through a course or self-study. Appropriate training gives you more confidence that you can perform the work. The training also increases your feelings of self-efficacy.[25] By recognizing your ability to mobilize your own resources to succeed, your self-confidence for the task will be elevated. Another motivational advantage of self-efficacy is that you are likely to commit more resources, such as time and money, to attaining a goal when you feel confident that you can perform the task.[26] For example, if you had confidence in your skills to develop an eBay business, you might be willing to spend a lot of time in designing the business and money in buying products to sell on the site.

6. **Raise your level of self-expectation.** Another strategy for increasing your level of motivation is to simply expect more of yourself. If you raise your level of self-expectation, you are likely to achieve more. Because you expect to succeed, you do succeed. The net effect is the same as if you had increased your level of motivation. The technical term for improving your performance through raising your own expectations is the *Galatea effect.*

Behavior modification
system of motivation that emphasizes rewarding people for doing the right things and punishing them for doing the wrong things

Expectancy theory of motivation
people will be motivated if they believe that their efforts will lead to desired outcomes

High self-expectations and a positive mental attitude take a long time to develop, but they are critically important for becoming a well-motivated person in a variety of situations.

7. **Develop a strong work ethic.**   A highly effective strategy for self-motivation is to develop a strong work ethic. If you are committed to the idea that most work is valuable and that it is joyful to work hard, you will automatically become strongly motivated. A person with a weak work ethic cannot readily develop a strong one because the change requires a profound value shift. Yet, if a person gives a lot of serious thought to the importance of work and follows the right role models, a work ethic can be strengthened. The shift to a strong work ethic is much like a person who has a casual attitude toward doing fine work becoming more prideful.

> "Remind yourself that you have personal power, and that you can make things happen. Erase those negative mental tapes that say 'No, I can't.'"
>
> —E. Carol Webster, clinical psychologist, quoted in *Black Enterprise,* September 2005, p. 157.

How to Develop the Self-Discipline to Achieve Goals and Stay Motivated

◀ Learning Objective 3.7 ◀

Self-discipline
the ability to work systematically and progressively toward a goal until it is achieved

Another perspective on achieving goals and staying motivated is that they require **self-discipline,** the ability to work systematically and progressively toward a goal until it is achieved. If you are self-disciplined, you work toward achieving your goals without being derailed by the many distractions faced each day. Self-discipline incorporates self-motivation because it enables you to motivate yourself to achieve your goals without being nagged or prodded with deadlines. Self-discipline also has an element of faith in the sense that you keep moving forward in the hope of reaching your goal even when the outcome is uncertain. Demaurice Smith, the executive director of the National Football League Players Association (NFLPA), says that his grandfather taught him that having faith "is the courage to take steps forward even when you don't know how the story is going to end."[27] In this sense, self-discipline is the driving force that keeps you focused on your goal even with a low probability of reaching your goal.

Our discussion of how to develop self-discipline follows the model shown in Figure 3-7. You will observe that the model incorporates several of the ideas about goals already

FIGURE 3-7 THE SELF-DISCIPLINE MODEL

FOUR KEY COMPONENTS OF SELF-DISCIPLINE

Source: "THE SELF-DISCIPLINE MODEL" by Andrew J. DuBrin.

discussed in this chapter. Without realizing it, you have already invested mental energy in learning the self-discipline model. To think through your own tendencies toward being self-disciplined, you are invited to take Human Relations Self-Assessment Quiz 3-4. The components of self-discipline are described next.

Human Relations Self-Assessment Quiz 3-4

My Self-Discipline Tendencies

Indicate the extent to which each of the following statements describes your behavior or attitude by circling one number. The numbers refer to disagree strongly (DS), disagree (D), neither agree nor disagree (N), agree (A), and agree strongly (AS). Consider enlisting the help of someone who knows your behavior and attitudes well to help you respond accurately to the statements.

Statement Related to Self-Discipline	DS	D	N	A	AS
1. I usually stay focused on whatever goal I am pursuing.	1	2	3	4	5
2. I have a mission or purpose in life.	1	2	3	4	5
3. Saving or investing for the future makes little sense when you can have fun with the money in the present.	5	4	3	2	1
4. If a person is highly talented he or she does not have to invest much time in practicing the skill related to that talent.	5	4	3	2	1
5. I am able to work on my job for an entire hour without checking to see if I have a phone message, text message, or e-mail message.	1	2	3	4	5
6. I have developed a new skill in the last twelve months without being forced to by my employer or an instructor.	1	2	3	4	5
7. I almost never bother retaining facts any longer because I can find whatever facts I need on the Internet.	5	4	3	2	1
8. My days rarely turn out the way I hope.	5	4	3	2	1
9. Given a choice between receiving a gift of $1,000 today versus receiving a gift of $3,000 three months from today, I would wait for the $3,000.	1	2	3	4	5
10. I would be willing to devote fifteen minutes per day for two years to learning another language.	1	2	3	4	5
11. Working sixty hours per week for even a short period of time is something that I would never do.	5	4	3	2	1
12. I tend to daydream a lot even on the job or during quiet moments with family and friends.	5	4	3	2	1
13. I usually read the owner's manual before I spend much time operating a new vehicle or complicated piece of electronic equipment.	1	2	3	4	5
14. When I'm involved in an important work project, I can enjoy myself fully at a recreational event after hours.	1	2	3	4	5
15. I feel that I'm moving forward a little bit every day toward achieving my goals.	1	2	3	4	5
16. I accomplish very little unless I am closely supervised.	5	4	3	2	1
17. Several people have described me as being conscientious.	1	2	3	4	5
18. My work area is neat, clean, and well organized.	1	2	3	4	5
19. I become bored easily.	5	4	3	2	1
20. I am willing to work hard and long at a task even if the payoff is uncertain.	1	2	3	4	5
21. It makes sense for a marathon runner to keep going even when it appears that he or she has almost no chance of being among the top group of finishers.	1	2	3	4	5

22.	I frequently misplace or lose items such as my keys, wallet, smartphone, or glasses.	5	4	3	2	1
23.	Planning is difficult because life is so unpredictable.	5	4	3	2	1
24.	I am able to concentrate on an entire news story if the subject interests me.	1	2	3	4	5
25.	I'm terrible at remembering names of people I meet only once or twice.	5	4	3	2	1

Scoring and Interpretation:

Calculate your score by adding up the numbers circled:

110 – 125: You are a highly self-disciplined person who should be able to capitalize on your skills and talents. Continue reading for your enjoyment, and look for ways to enhance your self-discipline even further. Similar to most self-disciplined people, you will probably achieve additional insight into things you already do well.

61 – 109: You have an average degree of self-discipline. By reading and studying the self-discipline model, you are likely to acquire new ideas for improving your self-discipline.

1 – 60: You appear to have a below-average degree of self-discipline that could be interfering with your accomplishing goals and achieving satisfaction. Study carefully the ideas in this section of the chapter, as well as information about work habits and time management in Chapter 16.

Source: "My Self-Discipline Tendencies" by Andrew J. DuBrin.

Given that self-discipline is an ability including a collection of habits, it can be learned and strengthened. Although the topic has been researched and written about in many ways, much of this information suggests that self-discipline has the four key components shown in Figure 3-7.

Component 1: *Commitment to mission and goals.* What are you trying to accomplish in life, both now and in the future? When you know your mission or purpose, it is much easier to be self-disciplined because most of your actions in life can support your mission. We have all heard of young athletes or musicians who get up early every day to practice their talent because they are committed to becoming outstanding in their field. The same principle of commitment to a purpose applies to people in other fields, including business. Take the example of a person who early in her career decides she wants to become a certified financial planner, thereby helping lead a more secure life. With this mission as a driving force, it will be easier for her to exercise the self-discipline of regularly developing her professional network. (Without potential clients, a financial planner will not be able to earn a good income.)

With a mission, activities that may appear mundane become vital stepping-stones for you. An example would be for the person who wants to become an international businessperson to read the owner's manual for a television receiver in both English and Spanish. Each gram of knowledge of a second language helps the person become more fluent in the language. To help formulate a personal mission statement, answer three questions:

■ What are my five biggest wishes or hopes?

■ What do I want to accomplish in my career during the next five years?

■ What do I want to accomplish in my personal life during the next five years?

Adrienne Lofton, the chief marketing officer (CMO) at Dockers, used a mission statement to help power her career. She regarded every job she had ever taken as getting closer to becoming CMO. She said, "From the beginning of my career I would write five-year plans for myself and talk about them with my key mentors, identifying areas I needed to strengthen where I wanted to be."[28]

Mission statements usually have to be supported by goals that will help guide activity toward attaining a mission. The series of goals you establish will collectively enable you to achieve your mission. Successfully attaining goals eventually leads to fulfilling a mission. Each small goal achieved is a building block toward larger achievements. Referring back to the woman who aspires to become a certified financial planner, a few of her goals might be as follows:

■ Read at least three articles in the money and investing section of a business journal five times a week.

■ Reach out to build two new network members each month, either in person or on social media.

■ Spend less money than I earn each month, and invest the remainder, so I can be a positive role model for my potential clients.

■ Begin a self-funded retirement plan by age twenty-eight so I can experience what it is like to have a disciplined financial life.

After goals are established, they must be followed by action plans. As described previously in this chapter, action plans specify the steps that need to be taken to achieve the goals.

Component 2: *Intense concentration and focus.*   Intense concentration and focus lie at the heart of self-discipline. Limited ability to concentrate and focus has many negative side effects, including lost keys, wallets, and handbags; forgotten appointments; and vehicular accidents. It is precisely because of the intense concentration and focus component of self-discipline that becoming a more disciplined person is so difficult. We are often told that people have very short attention spans, perhaps less than ten seconds. As a result, it is difficult to learn to concentrate. This argument is naive because the vast majority of people can concentrate on some things but not others. Many people who cannot concentrate intensely on a demanding task at work can concentrate for hours watching television or playing video games. In contrast, many people who can concentrate superbly on their work cannot concentrate enough to read a newspaper editorial or to parallel-park accurately.

Component 3: *Minimization of excuse making.*   Self-disciplined people concentrate their energies on goal accomplishment rather than making excuses for why work is not accomplished. The person low in self-discipline relies on standard excuses, such as "I'll get started as soon as the weather improves"; "No sense beginning a job search during the holidays. Nobody hires then"; "I think I will wait until the new budget cycle begins before I get started on my proposal."

Instead of trying to justify why they have been diverted from attaining a goal, high-achieving, self-disciplined people circumvent potential barriers. The self-disciplined real estate agent might say, "I know that the holiday season is slow for selling a house. Yet I will hold an open house this Sunday afternoon anyway, because I am more likely to attract serious buyers."

The highly self-disciplined person not only minimizes excuse making but also creates circumstances that will require less excuse making. A relevant example is traveling by air for an important meeting, especially flying in the morning to make an afternoon meeting. If the flight is delayed by a couple of hours, the person with an ordinary level of self-discipline will have to phone colleagues and say, "I can't make the meeting because I'm stuck in the airport." Having a greater sense of planning, the self-disciplined person will leave the night before for a key meeting to avoid having to make excuses and being embarrassed.

Component 4: *Delay of gratification.*   Self-disciplined people are willing to put aside immediate pleasure to achieve a goal that goes beyond the present moment. Quite often, delay of gratification entails trading a lesser reward now for a bigger reward later. For example, a disciplined industrial sales representative will forgo a couple of quick sales now in order to cultivate a customer with the potential for a much bigger sale. (Yes, despite the overwhelming amount of business-to-business sales on the Internet, most large companies still have sales representatives calling on customers.)

The decision to delay gratification is often difficult. During a job search, the less-self-disciplined person will accept the first job offer that comes along, even if it pays less than what he or she needs and does not contribute to career growth. In urgent need of money and feeling anxious and insecure about being unemployed, the person's actions are understandable. Yet, looking at the long range, taking a job that does not pay enough to meet expenses could well mean that a new job search will have to begin soon.

Delay of gratification is part of self-control. Meghan Clyne, managing editor of *National Affairs*, points out that self-control means valuing the future more than the present.[29] For many people, this aspect of self-discipline could mean forgoing income now to complete a degree and eventually earn more money. The ability to delay gratification begins early in life, such as learning to complete a homework assignment first before being permitted to play games on a smartphone.

The belief that self-discipline contributes to goal attainment and success is about as strong as the belief that a healthy diet and exercise contribute to physical health. Nonetheless, a study conducted with 325 working adults provides reassurance about the benefits of self-discipline. The study participants completed the self-discipline questionnaire previously presented, and they also answered questions about their age, education, and salary and how they felt about their career success and goal accomplishment. As shown in Figure 3-8, positive relationships were found between being self-disciplined and education, salary, career success, and goal attainment. Self-ratings of career success and goal accomplishment were the most strongly related. In conclusion, self-discipline pays.[30] Why do you think it was found that self-discipline was positively associated with years of formal education?

> "Nothing in the world can take the place of persistence. Persistence and determination alone are omnipotent. The slogan 'press on' has solved, and always will solve, the problems of the human race."
>
> —*Calvin Coolidge*
> *Thirtieth President of the*
> *United States*

Key Factor	Average Score on Factor for 325 Adults	Relationship to Self-Discipline Score
1. Age	34.7 years	Almost zero
2. Years of formal education	15.9	Slightly positive
3. Salary in U.S. dollars	$45,899	Slightly positive
4. Self-rating of career on scale of 1 to 7	4.9	Quite positive
5. Self-rating of goal accomplishment on scale of 1 to 7	5.6	Quite positive
6. Self-discipline score on scale of 20 to 100	76.9	

Source: Table derived from data presented in Andrew J. DuBrin, "Career-Related Correlates of Self-Discipline," *Psychological Reports,* 2001, Vol. 89, p. 109.

FIGURE 3-8

RELATIONSHIP BETWEEN SELF-DISCIPLINE SCORE AND KEY FACTORS

Concept Review and Reinforcement

Need, 60
Motive, 60
Need for achievement, 61
Maslow's hierarchy of needs, 62

Work engagement, 66
Self-determination theory, 67
Goal, 69
Action plan, 72

Intrinsic motivation, 75
Behavior modification, 76
Expectancy theory of motivation, 76
Self-discipline, 77

Summary and Review

Self-motivation is important for achieving success in work and personal life. A well-accepted explanation of human behavior is that people have needs and motives propelling them toward achieving certain goals.

- The central idea behind need theory is that unsatisfied needs motivate us until they become satisfied.
- After satisfaction of one need, the person usually pursues satisfaction of another, higher need.

Work and personal life offer the opportunity to satisfy many different needs and motives. Among the more important needs and motives are achievement, power, affiliation, recognition, and order. The need for risk taking and thrill seeking is also important for some people. The personality trait of conscientiousness might also be considered a need. According to Maslow's hierarchy of needs, people have an internal need pushing them toward self-actualization:

- Needs are arranged in a five-step ladder. Before higher-level needs are activated, certain lower-level needs must be satisfied.
- In ascending order, the groups of needs are physiological, safety, social, esteem, and self-actualization (such as self-fulfillment).
- Additional classes of needs for the hierarchy are cognitive needs, aesthetic needs, and transcendent (or B-value) needs.

Another way of looking at self-motivation is that if you are strongly motivated you are engaged in your work, or committed to the job and company. *Work engagement* refers to high levels of personal investment in the work tasks performed in a job. Research conducted in thousands of organizations has found that American workers are not fully engaged in their work.

Substantial research indicates that setting specific, reasonably difficult goals improves performance. Goals are valuable because they

- Will improve performance if reasonably difficult
- Can instill purpose, challenge, and meaning into ordinary work
- Focus our efforts in a specific direction
- Increase our chances for success
- Serve as self-motivators and energizers

Goals can be aimed at either learning or performing. A learning-goal orientation means that an individual is focused on acquiring new skills and mastering new situations. A performing-goal orientation is aimed at wanting to demonstrate and validate the adequacy of one's competence by seeking favorable judgments of competence. People with learning-goal orientations are more likely to

- Seek feedback on how well they are performing
- Focus on skill development that will lead to higher job performance
- Develop better relationships with their supervisors
- Be innovative in solutions to problems

Goal setting is widely used on the job. Goals set for employees at lower levels in an organization are supposed to contribute to goals set at the top.

Goal setting in personal life can contribute to life satisfaction. For maximum advantage, personal goals should be integrated with career goals. Areas of life in which personal goals may be set include

- Social and family
- Hobbies and interests
- Physical and mental health

- Career
- Financial

To increase their effectiveness, goals should be supported with action plans. Effective goals are

- Expressed as a positive statement
- Specific and concise
- Realistically challenging, yet also include stretch goals
- Set for different time periods
- Synergistic with other goals you set

Goals have some problems associated with them. They can create inflexibility or become an obsession. Performing goals can detract from an interest in the task. Goals can also encourage unethical behavior and encourage people to slack off after the goal is reached. To combat the potential inflexibility and obsessive nature of goals, recognize and admit when you are pursuing the wrong goal.

Key techniques of self-motivation include the following:

- Setting goals for yourself
- Finding intrinsically motivating work

- Getting feedback on your performance
- Applying behavior modification to yourself
- Improving your skills relevant to your job
- Raising your level of self-expectation
- Developing a strong work ethic

Achieving goals and staying motivated require self-discipline. A model presented here for developing self-discipline consists of four components:

- Commitment to mission and goals
- Intense concentration and focus
- Minimization of excuse making
- Delay of gratification

A study found positive relationships between self-discipline scores and education, salary, satisfaction with career success, and satisfaction with goal attainment. Also, self-disciplined people are able to delay self-gratification.

Questions for Discussion and Review

3.1 Instead of worrying about self-motivation, why not just wait for your manager or employer to motivate you toward superior performance?

3.2 One of the biggest concerns of workers is that they want employers to pay more of their health-care insurance. What does this issue tell us about the importance of satisfying the lower-level needs of workers?

3.3 Identify two business-related jobs for which a high need for risk taking and thrill seeking would be an advantage. Also, identify two business-related jobs for which a high need for risk taking and thrill seeking would be a *disadvantage*.

3.4 At last report, a 102-year-old man was working in the lawn and garden department of a Wal-Mart store, and at another Wal-Mart, a 100-year-old woman was working as a greeter. (Both appear to be popular with customers.) What do you think keeps this man and woman motivated to stay members of the workforce?

3.5 Identify any self-actualized person you know or have heard of and explain why you think that person is self-actualized.

3.6 Which aspects or factors related to any job you have held made you feel work-engaged? Explain your reasoning.

3.7 Why does a learning-goal orientation often contribute to more peace of mind than a performing-goal orientation?

3.8 Many students have observed that it is easier to be self-motivated after you have decided on a major. Why might this be true?

3.9 Explain how you might be able to use the Galatea effect to improve the success you achieve in your career and personal life.

3.10 Ask a person who has achieved career success how much self-discipline contributed to his or her success.

Web Corner

Self-motivation

www.secretsofmotivation.com (Proceed to click on "personal motivation.")

Self-discipline

www.eruptingmind.com (Proceed to "self-improvement" and then "Increase Your Level of Self-Discipline." The section includes a video.)

INTERNET SKILL BUILDER

Personal Goal Setting

At www.mindtools.com, enter "personal goal setting" into the search box, and then click on "Personal Goal Setting."

You will find a program for personal goal setting useful for both career and personal success. The program includes a brief, thoughtful video. An important feature of the personal goal-setting plan is that it urges you to set goals in nine areas of life: artistic, attitude, career, education, family, financial, physical, pleasure (really recreation), and public service. After reviewing the program, give your opinion of the usefulness of SMART goals. Also, how does the use of SMART goals compare to the suggestions for goal setting presented in this chapter?

Developing Your Human Relations Skills

Human Relations Application Exercises

Applying Human Relations Exercise 3-1

Goal-Setting and Action Plan Worksheet

Goal setting, along with developing action plans to support the goals, is a basic success strategy. Here you are being asked to refine a process you may have already begun. Consider entering more than one goal and its accompanying action plan in each category. To clarify the meaning of the following entries, we provide examples in italics of a recent graduate entering the retail field. Before writing down your goals, consult the section "Guidelines for Goal Setting." If you are not currently employed, set up hypothetical goals and action plans for a future job.

Long-Range Goals (beyond Five Years)

Work: *Ultimately become CEO of a major division of a retail company, perhaps the CEO of Bloomingdale's.*

(Place your entry here.)

Action plan: *Work my way up, position by position, starting as assistant merchandising manager.*

(Place your entry here.)

Personal: *Married, with children, home ownership.*

(Place your entry here.)

Action plan: *Continue to develop relationship with my boyfriend as life partner. We will both save and invest at least 10 percent of our incomes each year.*

(Place your entry here.)

Medium-Range Goals (Two to Five Years)

Work: *Become merchandising manager for one store in a large retail chain.*

(Place your entry here.)

Action plan: *Will work hard as assistant merchandising manager, listen to and act on feedback from my supervisors, take courses in human relations and merchandising management.*

(Place your entry here.)

Personal: *Continue to develop relationship with my boyfriend and marry him within three years.*

(Place your entry here.)

Action plan: *Communicate in depth with each other regularly to build relationship. We will work on not criticizing each other so often. After he proposes marriage, we will use our business skills to plan the wedding.*

(Place your entry here.)

Short-Range Goals (within One Year)

Work: *Do an outstanding job as assistant merchandising manager this month.*

(Place your entry here.)

Action plan: *Will take care of more e-mail and other routine work when not in the store. In this way, I can put more time and energy into merchandising. I will ask my supervisor for feedback from time to time so I can make adjustments to my performance.*

(Place your entry here.)

Personal: *Get further into digital photography, particularly learning how to take action shots. Will go beyond the "point-and-click" approach to photography.*

(Place your entry here.)

Action plan: *I will study the camera manual more carefully and attend one of the digital photography workshops given at my former community college.*

(Place your entry here.)

Applying Human Relations Exercise 3-2

Setback in Goal Setting and Developing Action Plans

Goal setting does not always go as well as planned because barriers to goal attainment might arise, such as running out of money or motivational energy. In these cases, you may need to develop contingency plans, or backup goals, to avoid not accomplishing something important or feeling totally frustrated. In this exercise, reflect on what you would do (or have done) in response to a goal you did not attain. Sometimes that backup plan is referred to as "Plan B."

Important goal that I might not attain (or did not attain):

_____

Backup goal (or contingency goal): _____

_____

Action plan to attain backup goal (or Plan B): _____

_____

Human Relations Class Activity

How Important Is Need Satisfaction to People?

Here is an opportunity to engage in data collection about a major human relations topic. Each class member agrees to obtain survey data about need satisfaction by having five people complete Human Relations Self-Assessment Quiz 3-2. Perhaps a student will volunteer to make an electronic copy of the test. Obtain the sex and age of each participant. (Survey anybody convenient, including yourself.)

For each completed self-assessment quiz, record the importance ratings for each of the five need categories: physiological, safety, love, esteem, and self-actualization. To quantify the fact that people may differ in the strength of certain needs, choose participants who appear to be in quite different life situations. For example, you might look for a full-time student, an unemployed person, a professional worker, an entry-level worker, and a retired person. (The research lesson here is that you obtain more interesting results when your sample is diverse.)

A couple of class volunteers will then compile the data for all the completed self-assessment quizzes. Average importance ratings will be calculated for each of the five needs. An example result might be "For the total group, the average importance rating for safety needs is 3.24." Also calculate average importance ratings by sex and age group, such as above and below age twenty-five.

Among the questions for class discussion are these:

1. Does our sample appear to show much variation in the importance ratings attached to needs?
2. Which need appears to be the most frustrated among the participants in our sample?
3. Which need appears to be the most satisfied among the participants in our sample?

You might also compare your pattern of importance ratings to the averages obtained for the sample. If your need-importance profile seems to be quite different, you might explain to yourself why this fact is most likely true.

Human Relations Case Study 3–1

Charlotte Struggles to Get Involved

Charlotte dreams of becoming a marketing executive at a major company some day. She feels she is on the right track because she is working as a marketing analyst for Atlantic Steel Structures Inc. The company is a large manufacturer and distributor of storage buildings, including small steel warehouses, garden sheds, and storage lockers. Top-level management at her company believes that the future for the company and industry is bright. Many potential commercial and residential consumers have need for more space, yet do not want to invest in expanding their present buildings or home.

Charlotte's primary job responsibility is to study the market for steel structures, with the intent of finding possible new customers, and to search for new uses for steel structures. Charlotte reports to the director of marketing and sales, Jordan. During a recent luncheon, Jordan asked Charlotte if she was experiencing any passion for her work at the company. Charlotte responded, "Some days are a little more fun than others. I recently dug up some information that people with large families are running out of space to store all the bicycles, skateboards, and scooters. As a result, they welcome having a steel shed in the backyard that could store a lot of the sports equipment. Assuming that zoning laws permit a steel shed in the backyard, these people are potential consumers."

Jordan then commented, "But what about most days, Charlotte? Do you have fire in your belly for advancing the future of Atlantic? After all, you are our eyes to the outside world."

Charlotte replied, "Quite frankly, I like the company. I like having you as my manager, and I like the marketing research experience I am getting. Yet the basic work is a little dull. I mean, it's not easy for me to get excited about whether farmers are looking for more space to store their tractors or keep their pigs warm. If city people are looking for more ways to store junk they don't need, that's not as exciting as exploring outer space."

Jordan responded, "Charlotte, you are doing an okay job as a market analyst, but I would like to see you more involved in your job. Maybe you don't get yet how important Atlantic Steel Structures is to the world."

Questions

3.11 What do you recommend that Charlotte do to become more engaged in her work, and at the same time have stronger self-motivation?

3.12 What do you recommend Jordan do to help Charlotte become more engaged in her work and become more committed to the welfare of Atlantic Steel Structures?

Human Relations Role-Playing Exercise

Getting Charlotte More Engaged

The scenario presented in Case 3-1 hints at a major challenge facing many managers: how to get a staff member more excited about (engaged in) the work. Jordan requests that Charlotte meet with him in a conference room to discuss her work involvement. One student plays the role of Jordan, who is concerned that Charlotte is not as excited about the work and the company as a marketing analyst should be. Jordan does not want to fire Charlotte, but he wants to know what is blocking her from being more involved in her work.

Another student plays the role of Charlotte, who wonders if it is necessary to be thrilled about her work in order to perform well as a marketing analyst.

Observers rate the role-players on two dimensions, using a scale of 1 to 5 from very poor to very good. One dimension is "effective use of human relations techniques." The second dimension is "acting ability." A few observers might voluntarily provide feedback to the role-players in terms of sharing their ratings and observations. The course instructor might also provide feedback.

Human Relations Case Study 3–2

Trevor Aims for the Top

Trevor is employed as a sales representative for a company that sells storage space to individuals and small companies. The storage space consists of garagelike compartments placed at four locations in and around Phoenix, Arizona. The storage space as a concept has been growing rapidly for several groups of customers. One group is small enterprises that lack the space to keep all their supplies but do not want to invest in a larger office or manufacturing facility. The major group of retail customers is home owners who have excess furniture and other belongings they do not need urgently but still want to keep. Another group of retail

customers is people who have sold their houses yet are not sure whether they want to get rid of all their belongings that do not fit in their new reduced-size living quarters.

Trevor's boss, Mike, the owner of the storage company, has recently established a goal-setting program for every company employee as a way of expanding the business and improving operating efficiencies. Mike gave Trevor some general guidelines about goal setting and told him to also consult articles online that might help him with establishing goals for the new fiscal year. Four days later, Trevor sent Mike an e-mail, as follows:

Hi Mike,

As you requested, I've put together a bunch of goals for the upcoming year that I think will help me boost sales for the year and win that big prize of a company-paid trip to Las Vegas.

- ■ Be the best storage-space sales rep in the greater Phoenix area.
- ■ Strive to do my best every day.
- ■ Improve my sales by 30 percent by trying extra hard.
- ■ Network like crazy to increase my potential customer base.
- ■ Talk up the company whenever I have the chance.

Yours truly,
   Trevor

Mike thought to himself, "I like the sincerity that Trevor has shown, but I think he needs some more guidance about goal setting in business."

Questions

3.13 What is your evaluation of the effectiveness of the goals set by Trevor?

3.14 What specific suggestions can you offer Trevor to make his goals more likely to be attained?

3.15 How relevant is a program of goal setting for Mike's company?

REFERENCES

1. Excerpted and adapted slightly from "Productivity Quotas: 'You Get What You Pay For,'" *Knowledge @ Wharton*, http://knowledge.wharton.upenn.edu, April 17, 2014, pp. 1–2.

2. For a theoretical explanation of the principle of self-interest, see Dale T. Miller, "The Norm of Self-Interest," *American Psychologist*, December 1999, pp. 1053–1060.

3. David C. McClelland and Richard Boyatzis, "Leadership Motive Pattern and Long-Term Success in Management," *Journal of Applied Psychology*, December 1982, p. 737.

4. Marvin Zuckerman, "Are You a Risk Taker?" *Psychology Today*, November–December 2000, p. 53.

5. The original statement is in Abraham H. Maslow, "A Theory of Human Motivation," *Psychological Review*, July 1943, pp. 370–396. See also Maslow, *Motivation and Personality* (New York: Harper & Row, 1954); *Motivation and Personality*, 2nd ed. (New York: Harper & Row, 1970).

6. Michael S. Christian, Adela S. Garza, and Jerel E. Slaughter, "Work Engagement: A Quantitative Review and Test of Its Relations with Task and Contextual Performance," *Personnel Psychology*, No. 1, 2011, p. 89.

7. Ibid., p. 94.

8. Susan Sorenson, "How Employee Engagement Drives Growth," *Gallup Business Journal*, http://businessjournal.gallup.com, June 20, 2013, p. 2.

9. Joe Robinson, "The X-Factor: The Key to Developing Employees with Oomph Is Communication," *Entrepreneur*, May 2013, p. 64.

10. Edward L. Deci, James P. Connell, and Richard M. Ryan, "Self-Determination in a Work Organization," *Journal of Applied Psychology*, August 1989, p. 580; Karen McCally, "Self-Determined," *Rochester Review*, July–August 2010, p. 18.

11. Don VandeWalle and Larry L. Cummings, "A Test of the Influence of Goal Orientation on the Feedback-Seeking Process," *Journal of Applied Psychology*, June 1997, pp. 390–400; VandeWalle, William L. Cron, and John W. Slocum, Jr., "The Role of Goal Orientation Following Performance Feedback," *Journal of Applied Psychology*, August 2001, pp. 629–640.

12. Don VandeWalle, Steven P. Brown, William L. Cron, and John W. Slocum, Jr., "The Influence of Goal Orientation and Self-Regulation Tactics on Sales Performance: A Longitudinal Field Test," *Journal of Applied Psychology*, April 1999, pp. 249–259.

13. Onne Janssen and Nico W. Van Yperen, "Employee Goal Orientations, the Quality of Leader-Member Exchange, and the Outcomes of Job Performance and Job Satisfaction," *Academy of Management Journal*, June 2004, pp. 368–384.

14. Gerard H. Seijts and Gary P. Latham, "Learning versus Performance Goals: When Should Each Be Used?" *Academy of Management Executive*, February 2005, p. 130.

15. Quoted in Adrienne Fox, "Put Plans into Action: Tie Employee Goals to Business Objectives," *HR Magazine*, April 2013, p. 27.

16. Ibid., p. 28.

17. Susan B. Wilson and Michael S. Dobson, *Goal Setting: How to Create an Action Plan and Achieve Your Goals*, 2nd ed. (New York: American Management Association, 2008).

18. Joelle K. Jay, "Make Your SMART Goals WISE Goals," *Communication Briefings*, No. 2, December 2011, pp. 2–3.

19. Quoted in "Too Obsessed with Personal Goals?" *Executive Leadership*, June 2008, p. 5. Adapted from "Are You Too Obsessed with Your Goals?" www.HarvardBusiness.org

20. Lisa D. Ordóñez, Maurice E. Schweitzer, Adam D. Galinsky, and Max H. Bazerman, "Goals Gone Wild: The Systematic Side Effects of Overprescribing Goal Setting," *Academy of Management Perspectives*, February 2009, p. 10.

21. Quoted in "Productivity Quotas," p. 3.

22. Comment from Daniel H. Pink, as quoted in Jennifer Wang, "The Best Motivators in Business," *Entrepreneur*, October 2013, p. 37.

23. Richard M. Ryan and Edward L. Deci, "Self-Determination Theory and the Facilitation of Intrinsic Motivation, Social Development, and Well-Being," *American Psychologist*, January 2000, p. 70.

24. Remus Ilies and Timothy A. Judge, "Goal Regulation across Time: The Effects of Feedback and Affect," *Journal of Applied Psychology*, May 2005, pp. 453–467.

25. P. Christopher Earley and Terri R. Lituchy, "Delineating Goals and Efficacy: A Test of Three Models," *Journal of Applied Psychology*, February 1992, p. 96.

26. Jeffrey B. Vancouver, Kristen M. More, and Ryan J. Yoder, "Self-Efficacy and Resource Allocation: Support for a Nonmonotonic, Discontinuous Model," *Journal of Applied Psychology*, January 2008, pp. 35–47.

27. Quoted in interview by Ellen Florian, "The Best Advice I Ever Got: Demaurice Smith," *Fortune*, November 21, 2011, p. 28.

28. Quoted in Christopher Atwell, "See It. Plan It. Do It: How a Young Marketing Professional Strategized Her Way to CMO," *Black Enterprise*, February 2014, p. 41.

29. "Saying Yes to Saying No" (book review), *The Wall Street Journal*, January 5, 2011, p. A13.

30. Andrew J. DuBrin, "Career-Related Correlates of Self-Discipline," *Psychological Reports*, 2001, Vol. 89, pp. 107–110.

CHAPTER **4**

Emotional Intelligence, Attitudes, and Happiness

Fotolia

Outline

M any readers have heard of Aflac (American Family Life Assurance Company), or at least have seen the company's advertisements featuring a quacking, cartoon duck. The key business of the company is providing supplemental insurance to individuals and groups. Aflac believes strongly that a good package of benefits contributes heavily to job satisfaction and happiness, and that satisfied employees are more likely to be more productive and more committed to their employer. Company management has found that keeping employees happy improves positive consequences in its own company, as well as in surveys conducted in other companies.

Audrey Boone Tillman, the executive vice president for corporate services at company headquarters in Columbus, Georgia, believes strongly in the company focus on keeping employees happy. She reports that Aflac has the largest onsite day-care facility in Georgia. Tillman points out that the Aflac employee turnover rate is 8.9 percent in contrast to the industry rate of 20.3 percent. She observes that many company employees are working mothers. When a mother responds to a telephone call from a policyholder, and she knows her children are well taken care of, or she has seen her child during lunch, the interaction with the policyholder is likely to be constructive and helpful.

Tillman notes that another company benefit is providing seed money for employees to purchase a home, which contributes to the mutual allegiance between the employee and Aflac. Another company initiative to keep employees satisfied and happy is an employee competition called Just Stop It. Employees have the opportunity to identify outdated or inefficient work processes and systems they think should be eliminated, with senior executives judging the submissions. One thousand employees submitted ideas, with two top prizes of $5,000 each being awarded. One winner was a technology analyst who suggested that if Aflac eliminated postage-paid reply envelopes, the company would save $186,744 a year in mailing costs.

The Aflac Workforces Report has gathered considerable data from benefits decision makers and employees indicating that a strong benefits package contributes to employ satisfaction. Satisfaction, in turn, translates into stronger commitment to the company and high job productivity. A major finding is that workers who are extremely or very satisfied with their benefits program are nearly three times more likely to stay with their employer than employees who are dissatisfied with their benefits package. Furthermore, close to two-thirds of survey participants said that an overall benefits package is extremely or very important to work productivity.[1]

The insurance company experience and survey illustrate the important role played by employee attitudes, including job satisfaction and happiness in contributing to the success of the company. Employee attitudes and happiness are two of the topics in this chapter. We also feature the related topic of emotional intelligence.

Learning Objectives ▶

After studying the information and doing the exercises in this chapter, you should be able to:

4.1 Explain how emotional intelligence contributes to effective human relations.

4.2 Understand the components of attitudes and how they are acquired and changed.

4.3 Appreciate the importance of job satisfaction and positive attitudes.

4.4 Pinpoint why organizational citizenship behavior is so highly valued in the workplace.

4.5 Understand the nature of happiness and how it can be acquired and enhanced.

▶ **Learning Objective 4.1** ▶

Emotional Intelligence

How effectively people use their emotions has a major impact on their success. The term *emotional intelligence* has gathered different meanings, all relating to how effectively a person makes constructive use of his or her emotions. John D. Mayer, a professor of psychology at the University of New Hampshire, along with Yale psychology professor Peter Saloey, originated the concept of emotional intelligence. Mayer explained that from a scientific (rather than a popular) viewpoint, **emotional intelligence** is the "ability to accurately perceive your own and others' emotions; to understand the signals that emotions send about relationships; and to manage our own and others' emotions."[2]

Expressed more simply, emotional intelligence is the ability to perform emotional tasks. An example of an emotional task would be informing a homeowner whose house was destroyed in a flood that she did not have flood insurance. A person with high emotional intelligence would be able to engage in such behaviors as sizing up people, pleasing others, and influencing them. Jamie Dimon, CEO of the banking giant J. P. Morgan Chase, once told a group of graduating seniors that most of them had IQs high enough to be successful. However, most people fall short on emotional intelligence because it requires time to develop. Dimon also said that management skills deal heavily with emotional intelligence because management is all about how people function.[3]

Emotional intelligence
the ability to accurately perceive emotions, to understand the signals that emotions send about relationships, and to manage emotions

KEY COMPONENTS OF EMOTIONAL INTELLIGENCE

Four key factors included in emotional intelligence are as follows:[4]

1. Self-awareness. The ability to understand your moods, emotions, and needs as well as their impact on others. Self-awareness also includes using intuition to make decisions you can live with happily. (A person with good self-awareness knows whether he or she is pushing other people too far.)

2. Self-management. The ability to control one's emotions and act with honesty and integrity in a consistent and acceptable manner. The right degree of self-management helps prevent a person from throwing temper tantrums when activities do not go as planned. Effective workers do not let their occasional bad moods ruin their day. If they cannot overcome the bad mood, they let coworkers know of their problem and how long it might last. (A person with low self-management would suddenly decide to drop a project because the work was frustrating.)

3. Social awareness. Includes having empathy for others and having intuition about work problems. A team leader with social awareness, or empathy, would be able to assess whether a team member has enough enthusiasm for a project to assign him or her to that project. Another facet of social skill is the ability to interpret nonverbal communication, such as frowns and types of smiles.[5] (A supervisor with social awareness, or empathy, would take into account the most likely reaction of group members before making a decision affecting them.)

4. Relationship management. Includes the interpersonal skills of being able to communicate clearly and convincingly, disarm conflicts, and build strong personal bonds. Effective workers use relationship management skills to spread their enthusiasm and solve disagreements, often with kindness and humor. (A worker with relationship management skill would use a method of persuasion that is likely to work well with a particular group or individual.)

Emotional intelligence thus incorporates many of the skills and attitudes necessary to achieve effective interpersonal relations in organizations. Many topics in human relations, such as resolving conflict and helping others develop, and positive political skills would be included in emotional intelligence.

Self-awareness
the ability to understand one's own moods, emotions, and needs as well as their impact on others; self-awareness also includes using intuition to make decisions you can live with happily

Self-management
the ability to control one's emotions and act with honesty and integrity in a consistent and acceptable manner

Social awareness
having empathy for others and having intuition about work problems

Relationship management
the interpersonal skills of being able to communicate clearly and convincingly, disarm conflicts, and build strong personal bonds

Tests of emotional intelligence typically ask you to respond to questions on a scale of 1 to 5 (never, rarely, sometimes, often, consistently). For example, indicate how frequently you demonstrate the following behaviors:

I can laugh at myself.	1 2 3 4 5
I help others grow and develop.	1 2 3 4 5
I watch carefully the nonverbal communication of others.	1 2 3 4 5

CONSEQUENCES OF HIGH AND LOW EMOTIONAL INTELLIGENCE

Demonstrating good emotional intelligence is impressive because it contributes to performing well in the difficult arena of dealing with feelings. A worker with good emotional intelligence would engage in such behaviors as (a) recognizing when a coworker needs help but is too embarrassed to ask for help, (b) dealing with the anger of a dissatisfied customer, (c) recognizing that the boss is facing considerable pressure also, and (d) being able to tell whether a customer's "maybe" means "yes" or "no."

A synthesis of a large number of studies indicated that for high-emotional-labor jobs (those that require positive emotional displays), emotional intelligence contributes to good performance. Also of note, emotional intelligence makes a contribution beyond cognitive intelligence and personality traits when the job calls for emotional display. A sales manager who had the responsibility of firing up the sales force would therefore benefit from having good emotional intelligence. For jobs with low emotional content, such as an accounts payable specialist, emotional intelligence would typically make a very small contribution to job performance. Recent research suggests that emotional intelligence is associated with good job performance because emotional intelligence includes conscientiousness, self-efficacy, and extraversion.[6]

Another positive consequence of emotional intelligence is that if you know how to project positive emotion you will spread that positive feeling to others in your immediate workplace. **Emotional contagion** is the automatic and unconscious transfer of emotions between individuals based on cues the other person observes. The contagion takes place because people have a tendency to mimic and synchronize the facial expressions, sounds, postures, and movements of another person. As a result of the mimicking, the second person experiences the emotion of the first person.[7] Here is how you might use emotional contagion to solve a human relations problem: You are the team leader of a group of discouraged, disgruntled, and downtrodden people working in a distribution center of a large online retailer. You hear regular complaints such as "We get treated like prison labor in a third-world country," "The computer system keeps going down so we can't get our work done on time," "Even the Rollerblades that management gives us to scoot around the center are in drastic need of repair." From time to time, you tell the group to cheer up, but your words are not taken seriously.

Being skilled at emotional intelligence, you give emotional contagion a try. You enlist the help of the most cheerful member of the group, Willy, to duplicate your act so the effects of emotional contagion will be doubled. You and your confederate, Willy, come to work smiling, expressing positive thoughts, standing up straight, and making fist-bump contact with anybody who says something positive. Soon the positive mood and actions of you and Willy begin to rub off a little on other teammates. The mood becomes positive enough to start working on problems instead of simply moaning and complaining.

A review of many studies concluded that employees with low emotional intelligence are more likely than their high-emotional-intelligence counterparts to experience negative emotional reactions to job insecurity, such as high tension. Furthermore, workers with low emotional intelligence are more likely to engage in negative coping behaviors, such as expressing anger and verbally abusing an immediate supervisor for the organization's failing to provide job security.[8]

Emotional contagion
the automatic and unconscious transfer of emotions between individuals based on cues that one person observes in another

ACQUIRING AND DEVELOPING EMOTIONAL INTELLIGENCE

Many people believe that emotional intelligence can be acquired and developed, much as a person can learn to become more extraverted or learn to control his or her temper. Many consultants offer training programs for helping employees develop emotional intelligence, and school systems throughout North America provide students some training in emotional intelligence. Elkhonon Goldberg, a clinical professor of neurology at New York University School of Medicine, explains that emotional intelligence can be learned to a degree, much as musical talent or numerical ability can be developed. Having the right natural talent, however, is an important starting point. The combination of biological endowment (such as being aware of your emotions) and training will enable most people to enhance their emotional intelligence.[9]

Given that emotional intelligence has different components, to acquire and develop such ability would usually require working on one component at a time. For example, if a person had difficulty in self-management, he or she would study and be coached in an aspect of self-management, such as anger control. Training in anger management is widespread today because so many people have difficulty in managing their anger. Skill-Building Exercise 4-1 presented later in the chapter provides a step-by-step approach to the development of emotional intelligence.

CONCERNS AND CROSS-CULTURAL CONSIDERATIONS

A criticism of the idea of emotional intelligence is that it might simply be part of analytical (or traditional) intelligence. For example, if you can read the feelings of other people, aren't you just being smart? Another concern is that the popularized concept of emotional intelligence has become so broad it encompasses almost the entire study of personality. Emotional intelligence has become an all-inclusive term for many ideas about human behavior that were studied before and since the popularization of the term. Yet, when emotional intelligence is regarded as a series of skills that can be developed, it has more scientific backing.[10]

A useful concern about, or criticism of, the idea of emotional intelligence is that it should take into account both the motivation of the individual and the setting, or context. (The context has already been described in terms of the type of work influencing how much emotional intelligence is required.) In reference to motivation, if a worker dislikes a coworker or customer, he or she might not be motivated to act in an emotionally intelligent way. In contrast, in dealing with the boss, the worker might have more motivation to display emotional intelligence.[11]

As with all dimensions of human relations, in some situations it will be helpful to be aware of possible cross-cultural differences in what constitutes effective emotional intelligence. For example, an overt display of emotion might be more effective in a meeting conducted in Mexico City than in London, because the typical Mexican businessperson is more open in expressing emotion than his or her typical British counterpart.

▶ **Learning Objective 4.2** ▶

The Components of Attitudes and How They Are Acquired and Changed

Attitude
a predisposition to respond that exerts an influence on a person's response to a person, a thing, an idea, or a situation

"You've got an attitude," said the supervisor to the store associate, thus emphasizing the importance of attitude to job performance. For mysterious reasons, the term *attitude* in colloquial language often connotes a *negative* attitude. More accurately, an **attitude** is a predisposition to respond that exerts an influence on a person's response to a person, a thing, an idea, or a situation.

Attitudes are an important part of human relations because they are linked with perception and motivation. For example, your attitude toward a coworker influences your perception of how favorably you evaluate his or her work, and you will be better motivated if you have a positive attitude toward your work. Having and displaying positive attitudes will also help you build better relationships with coworkers, managers, and customers. In contrast, negative attitudes can be costly to a person's career, as implied from the statement by the supervisor. A study by Leadership IQ found that 46 percent of new hires are either fired or disciplined within the first eighteen months of their employment. In 89 percent of the cases, the reason is not inability to perform the technical aspect of the job, but a poor attitude, including low motivation, bad temperament, or emotional issues.[12]

Our study of attitudes includes the components of attitudes, how attitudes are acquired, the importance of positive attitudes, how attitudes are changed, how companies attempt to enhance positive attitudes and job satisfaction, and organizational citizenship behavior.

COMPONENTS OF ATTITUDES

Attitudes are complex, having three components, as shown in Figure 4-1. The **cognitive component** refers to the knowledge or intellectual beliefs an individual might have about an object (an idea, a person, a thing, or a situation). A market researcher might have accumulated considerable factual information about statistics (such as sampling procedures) and software for running data. The researcher might therefore have a positive attitude toward statistics.

The feeling or **affective component** refers to the emotion connected with an object or a task. The market researcher mentioned might basically like statistical analysis because of some pleasant experiences in college associated with statistics. The **behavioral component** refers to how a person acts. The market researcher might make positive statements about statistical methods or emphasize them in his or her reports.

The cognitive, affective, and behavioral aspects of attitudes are interrelated. A change in one of the components will set in motion a change in one or both of the others. If you have more facts about an object or process (cognitive), you form the basis for a more positive emotional response to the object (affective). In turn, your behavior toward that object would probably become more favorable. For example, if you have considerable information about the contribution of feedback to personal development,

Cognitive component
knowledge or intellectual beliefs an individual might have about an object (an idea, a person, a thing, or a situation)

Affective component
(of attitude) the emotion connected with an object or a task

Behavioral component
(of attitude) how a person acts

FIGURE 4-1

THE THREE COMPONENTS OF ATTITUDES

Observe that the three components of attitudes influence each other and that the attitude toward a subject, person, object, or thing is the combined effect of the cognitive, affective, and behavioral components.

Source: "THE THREE COMPONENTS OF ATTITUDES" by Andrew J. DuBrin.

you might have a positive feeling toward feedback. When receiving feedback, therefore, you would act favorably.

Moods are similar to the affective component of an attitude, yet are not the same thing. A mood is a short-term response associated with one stimulus, such as being in a bad mood because your vehicle was dented while in the company parking lot.[13] An attitude is a longer-term disposition or inner tendency such as having a favorable attitude about the work ethic of Mexicans.

At times, people do not experience the type of consistency previously described and feel compelled to search for consistency. **Cognitive dissonance** is the situation in which the pieces of knowledge, information, attitudes, or beliefs held by an individual are contradictory. When a person experiences cognitive dissonance, the relationship between attitudes and behaviors is altered. People search for ways to reduce internal conflicts when they experience a clash between the information they receive and their actions or attitudes. The same process is used when a person has to resolve two inconsistent sets of information.

A typical example of cognitive dissonance on the job might occur when a worker believes that the report she submits to team members is of high quality; her teammates, however, tell her the report is flawed and requires substantial revisions. To reduce the dissonance, the worker might conveniently ignore the criticism. Or the worker might reason that she is the resident expert on the topic of the report, and her teammates, therefore, are not qualified to judge the merits of her report.

Cognitive dissonance
situation in which the pieces of knowledge, information, attitudes, or beliefs held by an individual are contradictory

HOW ATTITUDES ARE FORMED

Attitudes usually are based on experience. Assume that you visited a convenience store, and you left your wallet on the counter without realizing it. Your wallet contained your credit cards, debit cards, driver's license, $150 in cash, and personal items. On your way home, you receive a phone call from the clerk, informing you that he is holding your wallet for you. You most likely develop an immediate positive attitude toward the convenience store, the clerk, and perhaps toward other people of his ethnic group. Next we look more closely at the processes underlying attitude formation.[14]

A starting point in developing attitudes is to receive direct instruction from another individual. A friend whose opinion you respect tells you that e-filing of income tax is fast, efficient, and modern. You might quickly have a positive attitude toward e-filing. Similarly, you might develop a positive attitude through modeling the behavior of another person. You have seen that your trusted friend e-files her income tax, so you develop a positive attitude toward e-filing.

Conditioning, or making associations, also contributes to attitude formation, as in the example of the convenience store. The attitudes that we develop based on conditioning or associations usually develop after at least several exposures. You might develop a favorable attitude toward the human resources (HR) department if you asked for help several times, and each time you received useful advice. In contrast, you might have developed negative attitudes toward HR if a department representative was unhelpful at each visit.

The way we think about things, or our *cognitions,* can influence attitude formation. You might be quite content with your salary and benefits provided by your employer. You then visit www.salary.com and discover that you make much less than other workers in your city performing the same work. As a result, your attitude toward your salary and benefits plunges.

The deepest contributor to attitude formation could be a person's standing on the personality trait of optimism. People with a high degree of optimism are predisposed toward viewing events, persons, places, and things as positive, which in turn leads to a positive attitude. In contrast, people who have a high standing on pessimism will harbor many negative attitudes. Many workers who have chronically low job satisfaction are pessimistic at the core.[15]

THE IMPORTANCE OF JOB SATISFACTION AND POSITIVE ATTITUDES

◀ Learning Objective 4.3 ◀

Positive attitudes have always been the foundation of effective human relations, as reflected in the writings of Dale Carnegie, the pioneer of the popular (rather than scientific) approach to human relations. He emphasized such truisms as "Don't criticize, condemn, or complain," and "Talk in terms of the other person's interests."

In recent years, positive attitudes have also become of interest to human relations specialists, as reflected in the fields called *positive psychology* and *positive organizational studies*. A major thrust of these fields is to enhance our experiences of enjoyment of work, as well as of love and play. The assumption is that when employees are in a positive mood, they are typically more creative, better motivated to perform well, and more helpful toward coworkers.[16] The discussion of job satisfaction presented later in this chapter focuses also on the contribution of positive employee attitudes.

A worker who consistently maintains a *genuine* positive attitude will accrue many benefits. Being genuine is important because people with good emotional intelligence can readily detect a phony smile used as a cover-up for anger. Assuming the worker with a positive attitude backs it up with good performance, he or she is more likely to (a) be liked by customers, (b) close more sales, (c) receive good performance reviews, (d) receive favorable work assignments, and (e) be promoted. Another potential benefit of having a positive attitude is that it makes you a more desirable coworker because you are perceived as comfortable to deal with.

Positive moods also make a positive impact on job performance and company productivity. A study with customer service representatives at a large company found that reps who were happy at the start of the day usually stayed that way as the day progressed. The reps in a good mood generally felt more positive after talking with customers. As a result, they provided better service on subsequent calls. One of the conclusions drawn in the study was that reinforcing good moods, such as offering cookies in the break room, may lead to improvement in work quality.[17]

A mild note of caution is that there is a negative side to workers being too positive. As analyzed by Timothy A. Judge and Remus Ilies, putting on a happy face can lead to stress, burnout, and job dissatisfaction. Workers who have an unrealistically positive self-concept might become self-centered and manipulative and think they deserve more attention and rewards than other workers.[18] Also a little negativity and cynicism is helpful in jobs such as auditor, budget analyst, tax accountant, store detective, and cyber security specialist. Sometimes being suspicious and negative contributes to a job role. Pessimism about a potential outcome can help mobilize us to act quickly to avoid future problems, such as the person who purchases an offsite backup service for valuable computer files.[19]

HOW ATTITUDES ARE CHANGED

In general, attitudes can be changed by reversing the processes by which they were formed. Yet we can look at the process of attitude change more specifically. First, we might receive information from a source we trust. A manager might have negative attitudes toward the value of employee training but then reads in a reliable business magazine that IBM spends more than $5,000 per employee annually on training. As a consequence, the manager develops a more favorable attitude toward training. A person might also be reconditioned to bring about attitude change. A small-business owner might have a negative attitude toward e-filing income taxes because of the need to learn new skills combined with a fear of lack of security. After trying e-filing for two consecutive years because of being almost forced to by the law, the business owner receives refunds promptly and finds the process not really so complicated. So her attitude toward e-filing becomes reconditioned in a positive direction.

Another way to change attitudes is to learn to look at the positive or negative aspect of situations, if you are a pessimist or optimist, respectively. A pessimistic person should concentrate on searching for the positive elements of a situation, such as a supervisor saying to himself or herself, "Okay, this employee is a pill, but maybe there is something good about him."

In contrast, a naturally optimistic person might learn to say, "I tend to fall in love with the credentials of most job candidates. So maybe I should scrutinize this candidate more carefully."

Looking at the positive aspects of a situation to change your attitude is often a question of where you choose to focus your attention. What we see tends to shape how we feel. Suppose you dislike your job. The way to change your attitude is to write down every single thing you like about your job, even something small, like the free espresso. It is also helpful to maintain a list of anything positive that happens to you during the workday. An example might be "Today Laura showed me how to position my mouse over a false e-mail address to uncover the true address. I found that interesting." Keep in mind also that you are being paid, and that without paid work, a person cannot live independently.[20]

HOW COMPANIES ENCOURAGE POSITIVE ATTITUDES AND JOB SATISFACTION

From the standpoint of management, it is beneficial for employees to have positive attitudes and job satisfaction. These two emotional states contribute to better customer service, less absenteeism and tardiness, less turnover, and often higher productivity. The logic is that satisfied employees will lead to satisfied customers, resulting in a more profitable business. Much of the effort of human resource professionals is aimed at making employees more content.

A recent Society for Human Resource Management survey indicates that the major drivers of job satisfaction include adequate compensation, opportunity to use skills, job security, and a positive relationship with the immediate superior.[21] Perhaps the most fundamental contributor to job satisfaction is workers having fun and happiness on the job.[22] (Contributors to happiness are covered later in this chapter.)

Following are three specific examples of companies voted among the 100 Best Companies to Work For (as evaluated by *Fortune* magazine) that take initiatives to enhance employee attitudes and satisfaction.[23]

SAS Institute, Cary, North Carolina (enterprise software for organizations, 6,647 employees). Voted in the top 100 for eighteen years, this software giant is known for its employee perks, including subsidized meals, onsite health care, summer camp for children, car cleaning, intramural sports leagues, and a full-size gym. The health-care facility has fifty-three medical and support staff including physicians, nurse practitioners, and physical therapists.

Carmax, Richmond, Virginia (retail used-car chain, 19,914 employees). The company survived a two-year recession in the used-car business and then rebounded by hiring 1,200 new employees and awarding the largest bonuses in its history. Each used-car location is sparkling clean and is staffed by well-mannered, pleasant workers. The company has a "time away" policy that permits associates to take off as much time as they need without any restrictions. The generous relocation package includes paying for new-home closing costs.

Hilcorp, Houston, Texas (oil and gas exploration, 1,170 employees). The company has an incentive program called Dream 2015 that promises to award $100,000 to every employee if goals are met. Children of employees can receive college scholarships of a maximum of $8,000 per year.

Although companies invest considerable money in satisfying employees, a good deal of job satisfaction stems from positive interpersonal relationships in the work environment. A comprehensive study about job satisfaction was conducted with 540 people in a variety of positions, including teachers, physicians, and construction workers. The nature of the work, such as having a variety of interesting tasks to perform, contributed to job satisfaction. A bigger impact on job satisfaction, however, stemmed from frequent interaction with others, office friendships, and receiving emotional support from supervisors and coworkers.[24]

Another important contributor to satisfaction is the extent to which the employee perceives a good fit with the job and the organization. A study conducted with 142 administrative assistants in a midwestern university substantiated this well-accepted observation.[25] If you think that your talents are being well utilized in your job and that the organization fits your values, your job satisfaction will increase. An example of an organization fitting a person's values would be a kind and generous person working for a company that donated heavily to charity.

Meaningful work was mentioned in Chapter 3 as a contributor to self-motivation. The same holds true for job satisfaction. Workers who perceive their work to be meaningful experience high levels of job satisfaction and work engagement. Researchers have found that workers who feel that their job is almost a calling are among the most satisfied. If you are an animal lover, you will not be surprised that zookeepers, although paid modestly and having little room for advancement, are passionate about their jobs. Many have volunteered for years until a paid position became available.[26]

ORGANIZATIONAL CITIZENSHIP BEHAVIOR

◀ Learning Objective 4.4 ◀

An employee attitude highly valued by employers is **organizational citizenship behavior (OCB)**, the willingness to go beyond one's job description to help the company, even if such an act does not lead to an immediate reward. Being a good organizational citizen is also tied in with values, because the person who goes beyond the job description to help others most likely has a strong work ethic and also values helping others. Recent research suggests that another contributor to organizational citizenship behavior is feeling grateful—perhaps about having a fine job or congenial coworkers. Feelings of gratitude vary from day to day, and on the days these employees feel the most grateful, they are most likely to engage in citizenship behavior.[27]

Organizational citizenship behavior (OCB)
the willingness to go beyond one's job description to help the company, even if such an act does not lead to an immediate reward

Human Relations Self-Assessment Quiz 4-1 offers you an opportunity to think through your actual or potential tendencies toward organizational citizenship behavior. Two examples of good organizational citizenship follow:

- Joshua, a business intern, observes that the office in which he works seems glum. So he goes out of his way to be cheerful to others and offers compliments for work well done.

- Penelope, a gifted information technology person is walking down the aisle toward her cubicle. She notices a worker from another department with a panicked look on his face as he stares into his computer screen. Penelope asks if there is anything she can do to help and proceeds to transfer valuable data from a corrupted document to a new document for the employee in panic.

Organizational citizenship behavior is so important to organizations that this set of attitudes has been the subject of many studies. A general finding has been that as a result of many workers being good organizational citizens, the organization functions more effectively in such ways as improved productivity, reduced costs, customer satisfaction, and reduced turnover. Employees who are good organizational citizens also benefit because they are more likely to perform better, and as a result they obtain better performance reviews and salary increases.[28]

The personal support dimension of OCB will help you understand how citizenship behavior contributes directly to effective human relations in the workplace. **Personal support** refers to assisting others in the workplace through the use of interpersonal skills.

Personal support
assisting others in the workplace through the use of interpersonal skills

Human Relations Self-Assessment Quiz 4-1

My Tendencies Toward Organizational Citizenship Behavior

Describe whether each of the statements in the quiz below is mostly true or mostly false about you. If you have not experienced the situation, estimate whether it would be most likely true or most likely false about you.

Number	Statement about Organizational Citizenship Behavior	Mostly True	Mostly False
1.	I have helped a coworker with a work problem without being asked.	❏	❏
2.	I pick up litter in the company parking lot or outside of the building and then dispose of the litter properly.	❏	❏
3.	Helping others is an important part of my job even if I am not a manager.	❏	❏
4.	I make a special effort to say thank you and smile when somebody helps me in any way on the job.	❏	❏
5.	I volunteer to do a nonglamorous task when nobody in particular has responsibility for the task.	❏	❏
6.	If I found an apparently intoxicated person sleeping on the ground outside my workplace, I would call for help rather than leaving him or her lying there.	❏	❏
7.	I am pretty good at putting myself in another worker's place and understanding his or her perspective.	❏	❏
8.	I do my best to give effective comforting messages to other workers in distress.	❏	❏
9.	I am able to initiate, maintain, and terminate casual conversations with coworkers.	❏	❏
10.	During group meetings, I listen carefully to whoever is speaking to the group without performing another task, such as looking at a smartphone placed on my lap.	❏	❏
11.	If my company faced an emergency such as a flood or hurricane, I would tell my supervisor that I will be on call twenty-four hours per day to help out.	❏	❏
12.	I have covered for workers who were absent or out on a break.	❏	❏
13.	I check with others before doing something that would affect their work.	❏	❏
14.	Even if I disliked a coworker, I would help him or her with a difficult problem.	❏	❏
15.	I help people outside my workgroup when I have the right knowledge or skill.	❏	❏
16.	I am willing to do work not in my job description even if the effort means that I will have to work a couple of extra hours.	❏	❏
17.	I am willing to point to things the workgroup might be doing wrong, even if others disagree with me.	❏	❏
18.	I am willing to risk disapproval in order to do what is best for the company.	❏	❏
19.	I challenge work procedures and rules that seem to be nonproductive.	❏	❏
20.	I have tried to resolve person-to-person conflicts between workers in my department or unit.	❏	❏
21.	I do what I can to raise the spirits of coworkers having problems on the job.	❏	❏
22.	If I pick up some new job-related knowledge, I will share it with team members for whom the knowledge is useful.	❏	❏
23.	When I think of something that will help the entire company, I will share that knowledge with my manager and/or company leadership.	❏	❏
24.	I have politely voiced my concerns about something I think the company is doing wrong.	❏	❏
25.	If I see a social media comment about our company that seems significant, I will forward that comment to the right person in my company.	❏	❏

Scoring and Interpretation:

Count the number of statements that you indicated are mostly true.

18–25 points   You have strong tendencies toward displaying positive organizational citizenship behavior. Your initiative and other proactive behavior will probably be an asset in your career.

7–17 points   You have about average tendencies with respect to engaging in positive organizational citizenship behavior. It would be helpful for you in your career to seek out ways to help coworkers and the company besides performing well in your own job.

0–7 points   You take very little initiative to work outside the limits of your job description. You run the risk of being perceived by the company as not caring about the welfare of coworkers. Such a negative perception could be a negative in terms of you being regarded as eligible for promotion.

Source: "My Tendencies Toward Organizational Citizenship Behavior" by Andrew J. DuBrin.

As outlined in Figure 4-2, and presented next, the personal support dimension has four components, or subdimensions.[29] The example of Penelope presented above involves a mixture of personal support and task-related assistance. She is providing personal support when she helps the frustrated computer user to calm down. She provides task-related assistance when she transfers the data to a new document.

1. **Helping.**   Person-focused helping includes self-esteem maintenance and other more personal problem-solving behaviors. Penelope would be engaged in self-esteem maintenance if she said to the man she was helping, "Don't feel bad; even IT support staff have trouble with corrupted documents." Helping behavior contributes to organizational effectiveness when the help is of high technical quality. If Penelope calms down the man she is trying to help but does not help him with the corrupted document, not much has been accomplished for the organization.

2. **Courtesy.**   In general, courtesy involves showing consideration and tact in interpersonal relationships. Although courtesy might be regarded as expected behavior on the job, many workers are rude and discourteous toward each other. Being courteous therefore stands out as part of organizational citizenship behavior. An example of courteous behavior during a department meeting would be to listen intently to the presenter without engaging in other activities, even if the person bored you.

3. **Cooperating.**   A person who cooperates on the job willfully contributes time, effort, and resources to accomplish joint tasks. As a member of a team, you are expected to cooperate. In terms of citizenship behavior, cooperating includes accepting the suggestions of work associates, following their lead, and placing team objectives over

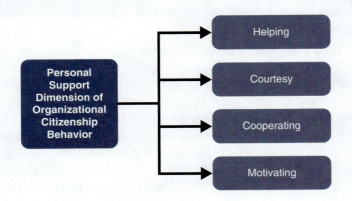

FIGURE 4-2

THE FOUR COMPONENTS OF THE PERSONAL SUPPORT DIMENSION OF ORGANIZATIONAL CITIZENSHIP BEHAVIOR

Source: "THE FOUR COMPONENTS OF THE PERSONAL SUPPORT DIMENSION OF ORGANIZATIONAL CITIZENSHIP BEHAVIOR" by Andrew J. DuBrin.

personal interests. Included also in cooperation is informing others of events or requirements that may affect them. Cooperation is most clearly part of organizational citizenship behavior when you go out of your way to cooperate with people outside of your immediate work unit. An example would be sending a job-relevant web link to someone in another department.

4. **Motivating.**   As related to organizational citizenship behavior, motivating behaviors include applauding the achievements and successes of coworkers, encouraging them when they face adversity, and helping them overcome setbacks. Expressing confidence in coworkers, and perhaps supervisors, is also part of the motivating component of personal support. In sum, you are a good organizational citizen if you are helpful, courteous, cooperative, and motivational, even if these behaviors are not part of your job description.

Although organizational citizenship behavior is desirable from the standpoint of the individual and the organization, some caution should be exercised. Too much time invested in organizational citizenship behavior can result in lowered task performance because one's own work is neglected. It has also been observed that spending too much time helping others can create work stress in the form of *citizenship fatigue*.[30] However, workers with good time management skills can often be outstanding organizational citizens and still perform their regular work assignments well.[31] An example of good time management would be not to invest so much time in helping others that a work deadline is missed.

◢ Learning Objective 4.5 ◢

Happiness and How It Can Be Acquired and Enhanced

Happiness is the ultimate goal of virtually all decisions we make, as observed by Daniel Gilbert, professor of psychology at Harvard. The measure of a good decision is whether it leads to well-being, pleasure, happiness, joy, or contentment. Research and opinion on the topic indicate that people can take concrete steps to achieve happiness.[32] Happier people have better physical health, live longer, achieve more career success, work harder, and are more caring and socially engaged. Misery can lead to self-obsession and inactivity.[33] Companies have developed an interest in developing specific ways of elevating employee happiness. The reason is particularly that workers who are happy, as measured by both satisfaction and engagement, tend to have higher productivity, obtain higher customer loyalty, and contribute more to company profitability.[34] The accompanying Human Relations in Practice illustrates company initiatives toward bringing about workplace happiness.

Human Relations in Practice

Companies Hire Happiness Coach Shawn Achor

Shawn Achor almost always has a positive expression on his face—never a scowl. Little wonder because he is one of the world's best known happiness coaches. Achor holds a master's degree from the Harvard Divinity School. He is hired by business firms to help get the workforce to think positively and be happy in order to be more productive and to experience less sick time.

One of Achor's client successes took place with tax managers at KPGM, the large accounting and professional services firm. A group of managers in the New York and New Jersey offices received Achor's training for changing your lens (or perspective) to a more positive one. Four months later, the trained group had significantly higher optimism, life satisfaction, and job satisfaction than the comparison group. The tax professionals receiving Achor's message reported a 24 percent improvement in job and life satisfaction.

At client firms, Achor urges employees to meditate, send regular e-mail messages thanking coworkers for their help, and help others without expecting something in return. Employees are also encouraged to keep a journal of happenings they are grateful for. These "gratitudes" focus on three moments in the past day for which the person is grateful. Engaging for three weeks in the activities that Achor urges is supposed to create lasting changes in happiness levels.

Achor provides research evidence that workers with more positive attitudes have higher job performance, get stronger performance reviews, and are more creative and better team players. He also makes the case that the single greatest advantage in the modern economy is a happy and engaged workforce. According to Achor, happiness increases nearly every business and educational outcome. Sales increase by 37 percent, productivity by 31 percent, and task accuracy by 19 percent, as well as numerous health and quality-of-life improvements.

Question:

Some critics of Achor and other happiness coaches say that pushing positive thinking is simply a way for management to improve morale while managers burden employees with threats of job loss and heavy workloads. What is your opinion of this criticism?

Source: This original story is based on facts from the following: Ed Frauenheim, "The Power of Positive Tinkering," *Workforce*, September 2013, pp. 44–47; Shawn Achor, "Positive Intelligence," *Harvard Business Review*, January–February 2012, pp. 100–102; Sue Shellenbarger, "Thinking Happy Thoughts at Work," *The Wall Street Journal*, January 27, 2010, p. D2; Achor, "Make Stress Work for You," http://blogs.hbr.org, February 15, 2011, pp. 1–2; "Workplace Blues? Call a 'Happiness Coach,'" http://blogs.wsj.com/juggle, January 27, 2010, pp. 1–2.

Our approach to the unlimited topic of understanding how to achieve happiness involves a model of happiness and a summary description of keys to happiness. To start thinking of happiness as it applies to you, take Human Relations Self-Assessment Quiz 4-2.

THE SPHERES OF LIFE AND HAPPINESS

Happiness can be considered a byproduct of having the various components of life working in harmony and synchrony. To understand this approach, visualize about six gears with teeth, spinning in unison. As long as all gears are moving properly, a state of equilibrium and fluid motion is achieved. Similarly, imagine that life has six major components. The exact components will differ among people. For most people, the components would be approximately as follows:

1. Work and career

2. Interpersonal life, including loved ones and romantic life

3. Physical and mental health

4. Financial health

5. Interests and pastimes, including reading, surfing the Internet, and sports

6. A spiritual life or belief system, including religion, science, or astrology

When you have ample satisfactions in all six spheres, you achieve happiness. However, when a deficiency occurs in any of these six factors, your spheres are no longer in harmony, and dissatisfaction or unhappiness occurs. Yet sometimes, if you are having

Human Relations Self-Assessment Quiz 4-2

The Happiness Checklist

Indicate whether you agree (A) or disagree (D) with the following statements.

Number	Statement about Happiness	A	D
1.	I look forward to almost every day.	_____	_____
2.	I love at least two other persons, including family members.	_____	_____
3.	I have no interests outside of work or school	_____	_____
4.	It bothers me when I learn that somebody else earns more money than I do now or will earn in the future.	_____	_____
5.	It disturbs me when I recognize that so many people are better looking than I am.	_____	_____
6.	I like my body.	_____	_____
7.	I am passionate about at least one interest outside of work or school.	_____	_____
8.	Thinking about how happy or unhappy I am makes me anxious.	_____	_____
9.	It makes me happy to see other people happy.	_____	_____
10.	Some things that are free or cost very little make me happy.	_____	_____

Scoring and Interpretation:

Happiness is difficult to measure on a scale, but the more the number of items you scored in the direction of happiness, the happier you probably are. "Agree" in response to the following items suggests happiness: 1, 2, 4, 6, 7, 9, and 10. "Disagree" in response to the following items suggests happiness: 3, 4, and 8.

problems in one sphere, satisfaction in the other spheres can compensate temporarily for a deficiency in one. For the long range, a state of happiness depends on all six spheres working in harmony. In short, the theme of this text surfaces again: Work and personal life are mutually supportive. Figure 4-3 presents the spheres-of-life model of happiness.

FIGURE 4-3

THE SPHERES-OF-LIFE MODEL OF HAPPINESS

Source: "THE SPHERES-OF-LIFE MODEL OF HAPPINESS" by Andrew J. DuBrin.

People vary as to how much importance they attach to each sphere of life. A person with intense career ambitions, for example, might place less weight on the interests sphere than would a more leisure-oriented person. However, if any of these spheres are grossly deficient, total happiness will not be forthcoming. Another source of variation is that the importance people attach to each sphere may vary according to the stage of life. If you are a full-time student, for example, you might need just enough money to avoid worrying about finances. However, after about ten years of full-time career experience, your expenses might peak. You would then attach more importance to the financial sphere.

THE KEYS TO HAPPINESS

If you are aware of known contributors to happiness, you might be able to enhance your happiness. Fortunately there is some consistency in information about what makes people happy. Here we summarize and synthesize a wide range of research and opinion on the keys to happiness.[35]

Give High Priority to the Pursuit of Happiness

Having the intention or goal of being happy will enhance your chances of being happy. Discover what makes you happy and make the time to pursue those activities, as spending time doing what you enjoy contributes directly to happiness. You need to put intentional effort into becoming happier. If people think about happy life events every day for three days, within four weeks they are happier than they were before they started this routine.[36] If you are going through a particularly unhappy period, you may have to stretch to think of a few happy life events. For example, did anybody pay you a compliment about anything you said or did recently?

Seek Satisfactory Outcomes from Decisions Rather than Looking to Maximize Gain

If you hope for reasonable outcomes from your decisions, rather than attempting to typically want the best possible outcome, you will be happier. Experimenters, led by psychology professor Barry Schwartz, have found that satisficers tend to be happier than maximizers. A maximizer is much like a perfectionist who is never satisfied with a decision outcome. In contrast, a satisficer is happier with his or her decision and does not worry about the possibility of not having made the ideal choice.[37] A maximizer might invest substantial amounts of time searching for the best possible smartphone and, after the purchase, continue to worry if he or she had made the best possible choice. A satisficer might look at a few models of smartphones, purchase a model with a reasonable number of features, then never look back. Quiz 4-3 presents a quiz to help you determine your decision-making style. A quiz measuring the same tendencies was used in the research just mentioned to reach the conclusion about happiness and decision making.

Develop and Maintain Friendships with Happy People

Positive interactions with people facilitate being happy. To quote Daniel Gilbert, "If I had to summarize all the scientific literature on the causes of human happiness in one word, that would be 'social.'"[38] (*Social* in this context means interaction with people, not exclusively social media on the Internet.) Evidence indicates that getting connected to happy people is especially important for improving a person's own happiness. Furthermore, people with the most social connections, including friends, spouses, neighbors, and relatives, were also the happiest. Each additional person in your network makes you happier.[39]

Human Relations Self-Assessment Quiz 4-3

My Decision Outcomes and Happiness

To analyze the nature of your desired decision outcomes (maximum versus sufficient gains) take the following quiz. A sufficient gain is equivalent to a satisficing solution. Answer each question on a scale of 1 (strongly agree) to 5 (strongly disagree).

Statement about Behavior and Attitudes	1	2	3	4	5
1. I will shop online for a long time to get the lowest price on a product or service.					
2. I think that in social life you should get involved only with someone who is close to being an ideal partner for you.					
3. I will often return merchandise to the store if I find a small flaw.					
4. I often ask the restaurant server which item on the menu is the highest quality or best tasting.					
5. When I make a decision about almost anything, I frequently think back about whether I made the best decision.					
6. After I finish reading a book, I often wonder if I should have read another book instead.					
7. Almost any time I have negotiated a price, I kept trying until I get the best possible price for myself.					
8. When I shop for a gift for somebody else, it takes me a long time to decide if I have made the right choice.					
9. If I gambled at a casino (or when I do) I wouldn't be happy unless I won at least $500.					
10. If I participated in a sports tournament (or when I have) success would mean reaching the finals or winning.					
11. If your life partner isn't perfect for you, you will never be happy.					
12. If I entered a lottery and won only $25 it would make me angry.					
13. Unless a person is among the top one percent of wage earners in his or her country, the person would not be happy.					
14. The secret to a good personal life is to find Prince Charming or Princess Charming as your partner.					
15. If I don't receive an A in this course I will not be happy.					

Interpretation:

The higher your score, the stronger your tendency is seek satisfactory or sufficient gains or outcomes when making a decision. The lower your score the stronger your tendency to seek a maximum outcome when making a decision. A higher score is usually associated with happiness about decision outcomes. However, a very high score, such as 70 or higher, could be associated with minimum decision outcomes that do not bring about happiness.

Source: "My Decision Outcomes and Happiness" by Andrew J. DuBrin.

Develop a Sense of Self-Esteem

High self-esteem enables one to love and be loved. Developing a good self-image leads to the self-esteem required for loving relationships. An early contributor to the importance of thinking positively about oneself was Émile Coué, a French psychologist. In the twentieth century he taught that mental health could be achieved by repeating the sentence, "Every day and in every way I'm becoming better and better."[40] An important part of developing self-esteem is to not want financial success more than other things. Insecure people seek society's approval in the form of purchasing consumer goods and accumulating investments. (In this way, the person might be admired by others.)

Appreciate the Joys of Day-to-Day Living

A major obstacle to happiness is **hedonic adaptation**, the tendency to adapt to exciting new aspects of life as routine after a while.[41] Imagine that a person who wants a luxurious lifestyle finally purchases a fiftieth-story condominium penthouse overlooking a harbor. At first, the view is breathtaking, yet after a while, looking at the harbor becomes routine. To overcome the hedonic adaptation, you therefore have to learn to appreciate the joys of day-to-day living. The essence of being a happy person is to savor what you have right now. Part of the same key to happiness is the ability to live in the present without undue worry about the future or dwelling on past mistakes. Be on guard against becoming so preoccupied with planning your life that you neglect to enjoy the happiness of the moment.

Hedonic adaptation
the tendency to adapt to exciting new aspects of life as routine after a while

Be Fair, Kind, and Helpful, and Trust Others

The Golden Rule is a true contributor to happiness. It is also important to practice charity and forgiveness. Helping others brings personal happiness. Knowing that you are able to make a contribution to the welfare of others gives you a continuing sense of satisfaction and happiness. Related to fairness and kindness is trust of others. Happy people have open, warm, and friendly attitudes.

Learn to Cope with Grief, Disappointment, Setbacks, and Stress

To be happy, you must learn how to face problems that occur in life without being overwhelmed or running away. It is also important to persevere in attempting to overcome problems rather than to whine or engage in self-pity. Once you have had to cope with problems, you will be more able to appreciate the day-to-day joys of life. An example of an everyday problem that ranks high on the misery list is lengthy commutes to work, by private or public transportation. If you cannot change the length of the commute for now, find ways to make commuting more enjoyable, such as finding a radio station that provides information useful for your professional growth or that is simply enjoyable.

Energize Yourself through Physical Fitness

Engage in regular physical activity, such as dancing or sports that make you aerobically fit. Whether it is the endorphins released by exercise, dopamine released by the excitement, or simply the relaxed muscles, physical fitness fosters happiness. Physical fitness also contributes to happiness because it helps us minimize the unhappiness linked to physical and mental illness. Another important part of energizing yourself is to attain adequate rest. Happy people invest time in revitalizing sleep and solitude.

Satisfy Your Most Important Values

Based on a survey of more than 6,000 individuals, social psychologist Steven Reiss concluded that people cannot find lasting happiness by aiming to have more fun or seeking pleasure. Instead, you have to satisfy your basic values or desires and take happiness in passing. To increase your value-based happiness, you have to first identify your most important desires and then gear your life toward satisfying these values. Among these key values are curiosity, physical activity, honor, power, family, status, and romance.[42] For example, if power and romance are two of your basic values, you can achieve happiness only if your life is amply provided with power and romance. Religion also fits into the realm of values, and religious people tend to be happier than nonreligious people, particularly societies under stress, such as those facing a lack of adequate foods, jobs, or health care.[43] (The topic of values will be explored in Chapter 5.)

Earn Enough Money to Do Meaningful Things and Avoid Misery

The role of money as a contributor to happiness is the subject of endless debate. Money cannot buy happiness, but having enough money to purchase the things and have the experiences that make you happy is important. Whether owning a tablet computer or a high-performance sports car would make you happy, they both require money—even though the amounts differ. It is widely acknowledged that helping less fortunate people contributes to a person's happiness. A person who decides to purchase a holiday meal for 100 residents of a mission for the homeless would need discretionary money to execute this act of generosity. Feeding the homeless would in turn contribute to his or her happiness. However, the pursuit of money for its own sake is less likely to contribute to happiness.

As implied above, substantial research by psychologists and economists shows that wealth alone does not bring happiness. The most important link to happiness is what is done with the money. For example, giving money to others brings more happiness than self-indulgent expenditures. Another finding is that spending money on experiences, such as travel or participation in sports, brings more happiness than purchasing material possessions.[44]

Research suggests that earning more than $75,000 per year does not yield additional happiness.[44] Yet large incomes do contribute to an overall feeling of well-being even if the money does not place the person in a happy mood every day. Even more important than a specific income level is which group we use for comparison. If your comparison group has elevated income, such as big-company CEOs or successful investment bankers, your cutoff point for contentment will be higher.

Another consideration is that not being able to pay for what you consider a necessity may lead to low self-esteem and unhappiness. Even if a person does not equate money with happiness, having a car repossessed or a house mortgage foreclosed contributes to at least a temporary state of unhappiness. Even a necessity such as replacing a roof requires a substantial amount of money, and a collapsed or leaking roof would make most people miserable. As long as you have enough money to pay for what you consider to be necessities, money is not a factor in your happiness.

Lead a Meaningful Life

Most of the principles previously stated, as well as the spheres-of-life happiness model, all point toward the conclusion that having a meaningful life is a major contributor to happiness. For example, if you are a greeting card designer and you perceive that you are contributing to improved personal relationships, you are likely to be happy. Meaningful work is a major contributor toward leading a meaningful life, as described in relation to self-motivation in Chapter 3 and job satisfaction in this chapter.

A major conclusion about attaining happiness is that it is the byproduct of working toward meaningful goals. For most people, the maximum positive feelings are generated, and negative feelings avoided, when they attain a goal that stretches their capabilities, but that is still within reach.[45] A meaning or an important purpose helps a person get through periodic annoyances that temporarily lower happiness.

Concept Review and Reinforcement

Emotional intelligence, 92
Self-awareness, 92
Self-management, 92
Social awareness, 92
Relationship management, 92

Emotional contagion, 93
Attitude, 94
Cognitive component, 95
Affective component (of attitude), 95
Behavioral component (of attitude), 95

Cognitive dissonance, 96
Organizational citizenship
behavior (OCB), 99
Personal support, 99
Hedonic adaptation, 107

Summary and Review

Emotional intelligence generally refers to how effectively a person makes constructive use of his or her emotions. The four key components of emotional intelligence are

1. Self-awareness (understanding the self)
2. Self-management (emotional control)
3. Social awareness (includes empathy and intuition)
4. Relationship management (includes interpersonal skills)

Demonstrating good emotional intelligence is impressive because it contributes to performing well in the difficult area of dealing with feelings. Another positive consequence of emotional intelligence is that if you know how to project positive emotion, you will spread those positive feelings to others in the workplace. In some situations, it will be helpful to be aware of possible cross-cultural differences in what constitutes effective emotional intelligence.

The combination of biological endowment and training will enable most people to enhance their emotional intelligence.

Attitudes are complex, having three components:

1. Cognitive (knowledge or beliefs)
2. Affective (emotional)
3. Behavioral (how a person acts)

Cognitive dissonance occurs when the three components are not consistent with each other.

Attitudes are formed based on experience, including receiving instruction from another person, conditioning, and cognitions (the way we think about something). The trait of optimism versus pessimism influences attitudes strongly. A worker who maintains a genuine positive attitude will accrue many benefits, yet being too positive can have disadvantages.

Attitudes can be changed by reversing the process by which they were formed. Looking at the positive or negative aspect of a situation can also lead to attitude change. From the standpoint of management, it is beneficial for employees to have positive attitudes and job satisfaction. Much of job satisfaction stems from good interpersonal relationships in the workplace. Workers who perceive their work to be meaningful experience high levels of job satisfaction and work engagement.

Organizational citizenship behavior is highly valued by employers because such attitudes can lead to improved product quality and quantity. Personal support is one aspect of organizational citizenship behavior and includes helping, courtesy, cooperating, and motivating. Too much time invested in organizational citizenship behavior can result in lowered task performance and stress.

A practical way of understanding happiness is that it is a byproduct of having the spheres of life working in harmony and synchrony. For most people these spheres would be the following:

- Work and career
- Interpersonal life, including romance
- Physical and mental health
- Financial health
- Interests and pastimes
- Spiritual life or belief system

Contributors or keys to happiness include the following:

- Giving priority to happiness
- Seek satisfactory outcomes from a decision rather than looking to maximize gain
- Developing and maintaining friendships with happy people

- Self-esteem
- Appreciation of the joys of day-to-day living
- Fairness, kindness, helpfulness, and trust
- Coping with grief, disappointment, setbacks, and stress
- Energizing yourself through physical fitness
- Satisfying your most important values
- Earning enough money to accomplish meaningful things and avoid feeling miserable

Questions for Discussion and Review

4.1 What has one of your professors or instructors done recently to demonstrate good emotional intelligence in dealing with students?

4.2 Describe what a business executive, an entertainer, or a well-known athlete has done recently to demonstrate low emotional intelligence. Explain your reasoning.

4.3 Imagine yourself as a manager or team leader. What could you do to make positive use of emotional contagion with the people in your group?

4.4 Imagine that a marketing specialist believes that his marketing vice president is an ideal boss, as well as an honorable and ethical person. He finds out one morning that the boss has been arrested for drunk driving and the possession of illegal drugs. How might the marketing specialist reduce this situation of cognitive dissonance?

4.5 How is a person supposed to maintain a positive attitude when major things in life are going wrong, such as a job loss, a personal bankruptcy, a broken relationship, or the premature death of a loved one?

4.6 Why do people often feel better when working with coworkers and a supervisor who have positive attitudes?

4.7 Not every human relations specialist is convinced that high job satisfaction leads to high productivity. What is your personal experience about the relationship between enjoying your job and your personal productivity?

4.8 Visualize yourself in your present or future job. How might you demonstrate organizational citizenship behavior in such a way as not to appear too obvious that you want to receive credit for being a good organizational citizen?

4.9 Assume that you are a business owner who is granted $20,000 to improve company productivity, and you are given two alternatives: software to improve operating efficiency or happiness training for employees. Make a choice and explain your reasoning.

4.10 Happiness researchers agree that having a high income is not necessarily associated with happiness. Yet, at the same time, activities that bring happiness, such as dining in restaurants or taking vacations with friends and family, require considerable money. How does a person resolve this conflict?

Web Corner

Emotional intelligence:

www.psychology.about.com (Enter "emotional intelligence" in the search box to find information about emotional intelligence that supports and reinforces the ideas presented in this chapter.)

The happiness test:

www.pathwaytohappiness.com (On the left side of the page, look for the category, "More Articles," and then click on "Happiness Test.")

Positive attitudes:

www.wikihow.com (Enter into the search box "Develop a positive attitude toward life," and you will find several valuable articles, including videos.)

Positive psychology center:

www.ppc.sas.upenn.edu

INTERNET SKILL BUILDER

Taking Daily Risks to Enhance Happiness

Visit www.PsychCentral.com and enter "15 Tips to Boost Your Well-Being and Happiness" into the search box. Tip 2 suggests that you take daily risks and gives you a couple of brief suggestions that would not consume much time. After trying out this approach to happiness for about ten days, you be the judge. Have you made strides toward becoming happier? Do you feel any better emotionally?

Developing Your Human Relations Skills

Applying Human Relations Exercise 4-1

Enhancing Your Emotional Intelligence

A realistic starting point in improving your emotional intelligence is to work with one of its four components at a time, such as the empathy aspect of social awareness. A complex behavior pattern or trait such as emotional intelligence takes considerable time to improve, but the time will most likely be a good investment. Follow these steps:

1. Begin by obtaining as much feedback as you can from people who know you. Ask them if they think you understand their emotional reactions and how well they think you understand them. It is helpful to ask someone from another culture or someone who has a severe disability how well you communicate with him or her. (A higher level of empathy is required to communicate well with somebody much different from you.) If you work with customers, ask them how well you appear to understand their position.
2. If you find any area of deficiency, work on that deficiency steadily. For example, perhaps you are not perceived as taking the time to understand a point of view quite different from your own. Attempt to understand other points of view. Suppose you believe strongly that only people with lots of money can be happy. Speak to a person with a different opinion, and listen carefully until you understand that person's perspective.
3. At a minimum of a few weeks later, obtain more feedback about your ability to empathize. If you are making progress, continue to practice.
4. Prepare a document about your skill development. Describe the steps you took to enhance your empathy, the progress you made, and how people react differently to you now. For example, you might find that people talk more openly and freely with you now that you are more empathetic.
5. Then repeat these steps for another facet of emotional intelligence. As a result you will have developed another valuable interpersonal skill.

Applying Human Relations Exercise 4-2

Achieving Happiness

The following exercises will help you develop attitudes that contribute mightily to happiness.

1. **Start the day off right.** Begin each day with five minutes of positive thought and visualization. Commit to this for one week. When and how do you plan to fit this into your schedule?

   _____
   _____
   _____

2. **Make a list of five virtues in which you believe.** Examples would include patience, compassion, and helping the less fortunate.

   _____
   _____
   _____

3. **Each week, for the next five weeks, incorporate a different virtue into your life.** On a simple index card, write this week's virtue in bold letters, such as "helping the less fortunate." Post the card in a prominent place. After you have completed one incident of helping the less fortunate, describe in about ten to twenty-five words what you did. Also record the date and time.

   _____
   _____
   _____

4. **Look for good things about new acquaintances.** List three students, customers, or coworkers you have just met. List three *positive* qualities about each.

   _____
   _____
   _____

5. **List the positive qualities of fellow students or coworkers you dislike or have trouble working with.** Remember, keep looking for the good.

   _____
   _____
   _____

6. **Think of school assignments or job tasks you dislike, and write down the merits of these tasks.** Identify the benefits they bring you.

   _____
   _____
   _____

7. **Look at problems as opportunities.** What challenges are you now facing? In what way might you view them that would inspire and motivate you?

   _____
   _____
   _____

Human Relations Class Activity

The World's Happiest Person

Hundreds of thousands of articles and websites have been devoted to the subject of the world's happiest man, woman, or person. Class time and resources most likely prohibit you from searching the globe for that person, but you and your classmates can search for that person in your classroom. If you are taking this course online, the work can be accomplished by e-mail or course website.

After about five minutes of reflection, each class member should decide whether he or she is totally happy, or almost totally happy. Several class members who feel that they might qualify for the title of World's Happiest Person (at least who comes closest within this classroom) volunteer to explain why to the rest of the class. Candidates for the Happiest Person category will make about a three-minute presentation of precisely why they feel so happy. As you listen to these presentations, attempt to identify any of the principles of happiness covered in this chapter.

After the presentations are completed, spend a few minutes looking for trends to arrive at a few conclusions. For discussion points, you might complete these sentences:

1. All the happy people seem to think that _____.
2. I notice that each candidate for the World's Happiest Person seemed to _____.
3. A difference I noticed between me and the volunteers (or between me and the rest of the volunteers) is that _____.
4. In terms of the candidates smiling, I noticed that _____.

The conclusions you reach can become information for class discussion. Look to see if many class members arrived at similar conclusions—perhaps in response to the four questions.

Human Relations Case Study 4–1

Miguel, the Hard-Hitting Organizational Citizen

Miguel is a petroleum engineering technician, working for a booming energy company in North Dakota. He enjoys his work and the fact that he earns much higher pay than he anticipated when he graduated from a technical college in El Paso, Texas. Based on his study of workplace relationships, and his personal values, Miguel thinks it is important to help coworkers even if it means taking a little time from his regular job responsibilities. Miguel describes what he did this past week to help coworkers:

On Monday, I noticed that our office assistant Sophia was looking sad and haggard. I asked her what her problem was. She told me that her father was diagnosed with a brain tumor. I took Sophia out for a long lunch and shared my experiences with an aunt of mine who survived a brain tumor.

On Wednesday, Karl, another petroleum engineering technician assigned to our project, came to me with a technical problem. He needed to understand a mathematical equation that dealt with making hydrofracking more efficient. I admit the equation was complex, but I'm pretty good with math. We spent two hours together figuring out how to apply the equation. The result was just what Karl needed to know.

On Friday, Priscilla one of the supervising engineers from another project wrote an e-mail saying that one of the drills was working too slowly, and that so far nobody had found a solution. I know that mechanical engineering is outside of my professional specialty, but mechanics are my hobby. I took two hours off from my regular job to visit the mine and see what I could add to solving the drill problem. I didn't exactly solve the problem myself, but the questions I asked helped get the problem solved.

A week later, Miguel's supervisor, Brett, said to him, "I notice that you have fallen a little behind on your project. I have also noticed that you are kind of a busybody who runs around the work site looking to help other people. Do you think you have a problem?"

Questions

4.11 How should Miguel respond to the comments from Bart?

4.12 What is your evaluation of Miguel's efforts to be a good organizational citizen?

4.13 What do you recommend that Miguel do to balance the demands of his job with his desire to be a good organizational citizen?

Human Relations Role-Playing Exercise

Miguel Attempts to Defend His Organizational Citizenship Behavior

This role-play continues where the above case ends. One student plays the role of Miguel, who decides to strongly defend his approaches to helping others in the workplace. Another student plays the role of Bart, who thinks that being helpful to others is important, but that taking care of one's own job responsibilities comes first.

Observers rate the role-players on two dimensions, using a scale of 1 to 5 from "very poor" to "very good." One dimension is "effective use of human relations techniques." The second dimension is "acting ability." A few observers might voluntarily provide feedback to the role-players in terms of sharing their ratings and observations. The course instructor might also provide feedback.

Human Relations Case Study 4–2

Margot Pursues Happiness

Margot is a vehicle claims adjuster for a regional branch of the property and casualty division of a large insurance company. She is responsible for preparing field reports on cars and small trucks that have been involved in an accident. In addition to making written observations, Margot photographs the vehicles that have been damaged.

Although Margot enjoys her work, she is not totally satisfied or happy. She says, "My personal life, including my relationship with my husband, daughter, parents, and relatives is fine. I also love playing in a woman's softball league. But something is missing. My job is okay, but something is missing. I'm not joyful every day."

After reading a couple of articles and two books about happiness, Margot develops a plan for being happier on the job. Her plan centers on a bulleted list of activities to make her work life happier and more joyful, as follows:

- Look at each vehicle wreck as a chance to give some much-needed funds to a person in trouble.

- Walk out my door each morning with a smile on my face, even if I have to force it a little.
- Place a few smiley face decals in my cubicle and on the windshield of my car.
- Read the comic strips in my local newspaper at least five times per week.
- Visit a website devoted to humor at least once a day.
- Watch at least one good comedy on television each night.
- Each month, think through all the good a property and casualty insurance company does for society.
- Find a different unfortunate person each week to hug.

Questions

4.14 What is your evaluation of Margot's plan for attaining happiness on the job?

4.15 Give Margot two more suggestions for attaining happiness through her work.

REFERENCES

1. Original story created from facts and observations in the following sources: Sonia Alleyne, "Getting to the Heart of Business," *Black Enterprise*, May 2012, pp. 62–63; "Satisfaction with Benefits a Factor in Job Turnover, Says Aflac Study," *BLR: HR and Employment News*, http://hr.blr.com, August 11, 2014, pp. 1–2: Warren S. Hersch, "Aflac Survey Links Job Satisfaction with Company Benefit Offerings," www.lifehealthpro.com, August 21, 2012, pp. 1–2; "View Point: Benefits Matter," www.aflac.com/aflac_workforces_report, April 2013, pp. 1–8.
2. Quoted in "Leading by Feel: Be Realistic," *Harvard Business Review*, January 2004, p. 28.
3. Cited in Al Lewis, "Lewis: Jamie Dimon's Theory of Self-Deception," *Denver Post*, www.denverpost.com, May 16, 2012, p. 1.
4. Daniel Goleman, Richard Boyatzis, and Annie McKee, "Primal Leadership: The Hidden Driver of Great Performance," *Harvard Business Review*, December 2001, pp. 42–51.
5. David A. Morand, "The Emotional Intelligence of Managers: Assessing the Construct Validity of a Nonverbal Measure of 'People Skills,'" *Journal of Business and Psychology*, Fall 2001, pp. 21–23.
6. Dana L. Joseph et al, "Why Does Self-Reported Emotional Intelligence Predict Job Performance?" *Journal of Applied Psychology*, March 2015, pp. 298–342.
7. Stefanie K. Johnson, "I Second That Emotion: Effects of Emotional Contagion and Affect at Work on Leader and Follower Outcomes," *Leadership Quarterly*, February 2008, p. 2.
8. Peter J. Jordan, Neal M. Ashkanasy, and Charmine E. J. Hartel, "Emotional Intelligence as a Moderator of Emotional and Behavioral Reactions to Job Insecurity," *Academy of Management Review*, July 2002, pp. 361–372.
9. Cited in "Leading by Feel: Train the Gifted," *Harvard Business Review*, January 2004, p. 31.
10. This is one of the major themes from Kevin R. Murphy, ed., *A Critique of Emotional Intelligence: What Are the Problems and How Can They Be Fixed?* (Mahwah, NJ: Lawrence Erlbaum, 2006).
11. Oscar Ybarra, Ethen Kross, and Jeffrey Sanchez-Burke, "The 'Big Idea' That Is Yet to Be: Toward a More Motivated, Contextual, and Dynamic Model of Emotional Intelligence," *Academy of Management Perspectives*, May 2014, p. 101.
12. Study cited in Mark Murphy, "Hiring for Attitude," *Business Management Daily* supplement, March 2015, p. 1.
13. Nancy P. Rothbard and Steffanie L. Wilk, "Waking Up on the Right or Wrong Side of the Bed: State-of-Workday Mood, Work Events, Employee Affect, and Performance," *Academy of Management Journal*, October 2011, p. 959.
14. Based to some extent on information synthesized in Dodge Fernald, *Psychology* (Upper Saddle River, NJ: Prentice Hall, 1997), pp. 562–563.
15. L. A. Burke and L. A. Witt, "Personality and High-Maintenance Employee Behavior," *Journal of Business and Psychology*, Spring 2004, pp. 349–363.
16. Timothy A. Judge and Remus Ilies, "Is Positiveness in Organizations Always Desirable?" *Academy of Management Executive*, November 2004, p. 152.
17. Nancy Rothbard, "Put On a Happy Face. Seriously," *The Wall Street Journal*, October 24, 2011, p. R2. Report based on Rothbard and Wilk, "Waking Up on the Right Side," pp. 959–980.
18. Judge and Ilies, "Is Positiveness in Organizations Always Desirable?" pp. 153–155.
19. Anne Murphy Paul, "The Uses and Abuses of Optimism (and Pessimism)," *Psychology Today*, November–December 2011, p. 61.
20. Judith Sills, "Take This Job and Love It," *Psychology Today*, November–December 2008, pp. 58–59.
21. Jennifer Schramm, "Happy Workers," *HR Magazine*, April 2014, p. 96.
22. Nancy Hatch Woodward, "Come On, Get Happy," *HR Magazine*, October 2014, pp. 46–52.
23. Milton Moskowitz and Robert Levering, "The 100 Best Companies to Work For," *Fortune*, March 15, 2015, pp. 140–154.
24. Frederick P. Morgeson and Stephen E. Humphrey, "The Work Design Questionnaire (WDQ): Developing and Validating a Comprehensive Measure for Assessing Job Design and the Nature of Work," *Journal of Applied Psychology*, November 2006, pp. 1321–1339.
25. Allison Gabriel et al., "The Dynamic Relationships of Work Affect and Job Satisfaction with Perceptions of Fit," *Personnel Psychology*, No. 2, 2014, pp. 389–420.
26. Kirsten Weir, "More than Job Satisfaction," *Monitor on Psychology*, December 2013, pp. 42–43.
27. Jeffrey R. Spence et al., "Helpful Today, but Not Tomorrow? Feeling Grateful as a Predictor of Daily Organizational Citizenship Behaviors," *Personnel Psychology*, No. 3, 2014, pp. 705–738.
28. Nathan P. Podaskoff, Steven W. Whiting, Philip M. Podaskoff, and Brian D. Blume, "Individual- and Organizational-Level Consequences of Organizational Citizenship Behavior: A Meta-Analysis," *Journal of Applied Psychology*, January 2009, pp. 122–141; Scott B. MacKenzie, Philip M. Podaskoff, and Nathan P. Podaskoff, "Challenge-Oriented Organizational Citizenship Behaviors and Organizational Effectiveness: Do Challenge-Oriented Behaviors Really Have an Impact on the Organization's Bottom Line?" *Personnel Psychology*, No. 3, 2011, pp. 559–592.
29. Nicole M. Dudley and Jose M. Cortina, "Knowledge and Skills That Facilitate the Personal Support Dimension of Citizenship," *Journal of Applied Psychology*, November 2008, pp. 1249–1270.
30. Mark C. Bolino et al., "'Well, I'm Tired of Tryin'! Organizational Citizenship Behavior and Citizenship Fatigue," *Journal of Applied Psychology*, January 2015, pp. 56–74.
31. Adam A. Rapp, Daniel G. Bachrach, and Tammy L. Rapp, "The Influence of Time Management Skill on the Curvilinear Relationship between Organizational Citizenship Behavior and Task Performance," *Journal of Applied Psychology*, July 2013, pp. 668–677.
32. Cited in Rebecca A. Clay, "Stumbling on Happiness," *Monitor on Psychology*, May 2010, p. 29.
33. Research reported in Hara Estroff Marano, "Clues to Character," *Psychology Today*, May–June 2011, pp. 59–60; Amy Novotney, "The Happiness Diet: Sonjya Lyubomirsky Argues That Limiting Overthinking Can Improve Our Emotional Well-Being," *Monitor on Psychology*, April 2008, pp. 24–25.

34. Evidence presented in Woodward, "Come On, Get Happy," p. 50.

35. The major sources of information for this list are Mihaly Csikzentmihalyi, "Finding Flow," *Psychology Today*, July–August 1997, pp. 46–48, 70–71; Carlin Flora, "The Pursuit of Happiness," *Psychology Today*, January–February 2009, pp. 60–69; interview with Daniel Gilbert, "The Science behind the Smile," *Harvard Business* Review, January/February 2012, pp. 85–90.

36. Cited in Novotney, "The Happiness Diet," p. 24.

37. Elizabeth Bernstein, "Decide to Be Happy: The Way You Make Decisions Says a Lot about How Happy You Are," *The Wall Street Journal*, October 7, 2014, pp. D1, D2; Barry Schwartz et al., "Maximizing versus Satisficing: Happiness Is a Matter of Choice," *Journal of Personality and Social Psychology*, No. 5, 2002, pp. 1178–1197.

38. Gilbert, "The Science behind the Smile," p. 88.

39. Study cited in Alice Park, "The Happiness Effect: How Emotions and Even Behaviors Can Spread like an Epidemic," *Time*, December 22, 2008; Maggie Fox, "Happiness Is Contagious, Study Finds," *Scientific American*, www.sciam.com, accessed December 5, 2008.

40. Quoted in George Melloan, "The Rich Are Getting Richer, but So Are Others," *Wall Street Journal*, December 23, 2003, p. A15.

41. Jonathan Clements, "The Pursuit of Happiness: Six Experts Tell What They've Done to Achieve It," *Wall Street Journal*, December 6, 2006, p. D1.

42. Steven Reiss, "Secrets of Happiness," *Psychology Today*, January–February 2001, pp. 50–52, 55–56.

43. Andrew Blackman, "Can Money Buy Happiness?" *The Wall Street Journal*, November 10, 2014, pp. R1, R2.

44. Tim Worstall, "The Importance of Rejecting the Easterlin Paradox," *Forbes*, www.forbes.com, May 4, 2013, p. 1; Farnoosh Torabi, "5 Ways Money Makes You Happy," *Yahoo! Finance*, http://finance.yahoo.com, 2013, pp. 1–2.

45. Richard Corliss, "Is There a Formula for Joy?" *Time*, January 20, 2003, p. 74.

Fotolia

CHAPTER 5

Values and Ethics

Outline

Juniper Networks Inc. is a well-known industrial company that designs and develops products and services that make network infrastructures possible, including switches, routers, and software. The company has headquarters in Sunnyvale, California, and operations in forty-six countries. An outstanding feature of how the company operates is a strong emphasis on establishing values, and making a deliberate effort to translate these values into the behavior of employees at all levels, from the custodial staff to the executive suite.

The Juniper Way, a commitment to every worker that the culture and company will inspire their best work, is based on five values:

- *We are authentic*—We are a company of honest individuals who can achieve extraordinary outcomes.
- *We are about trust*—We act with integrity, fairness, respect, and reliability.
- *We deliver excellence*—We are driven by our craft to produce results beyond expectation.
- *We pursue bold aspirations*—We believe that the networked world has unlimited possibilities.
- *We make a meaningful difference*—We operate as responsible corporate citizen as we drive toward a positive purpose.

An example of how Juniper applies its values internally was to accept in 2014 the resignation of its CEO, who had been involved in an improper customer negotiation (details not made public). Juniper extends its values beyond the confines of the corporation. A few years ago, company leadership embraced the goal of helping to end worldwide slavery. One way this value was put into action was to support the nonprofit organization Not for Sale. The organization's mission is to abolish slavery and human trafficking, partially by using social networking to attain its goals.

The focus on converting values into action has helped Juniper win an award from the Ethisphere Institutes as one of the World's Most Ethical Companies. Juniper earned the award by implementing highly ethical business practices and initiatives that facilitate the company's success, benefit the community, and elevate the standards within the industry.[1]

In this chapter, we study values, an important force contributing to a person's level of ethical behavior, as well as ethics. Values and ethics are foundation topics in human relations because our values and ethics influence how we treat others and how we are treated in return.

Learning Objectives ▶

After studying the information and doing the exercises in this chapter, you should be able to:

5.1 Understand the nature of values and how they are learned.

5.2 Be able to classify and clarify values.

5.3 Understand the importance of business ethics, the difficulty of being ethical, and the extent of ethical problems in business.

5.4 Identify workplace situations that often present ethical dilemmas.

5.5 Identify workplace situations that often lead to problems and mistakes.

▶ **Learning Objective 5.1** ▶

Values as a Part of Understanding Human Relations

Value
the importance a person attaches to something; values are also tied to the enduring belief that one mode of conduct is better than another mode of conduct

Ethics
the moral choices a person makes

Morals
an individual's or a society's determination of what is right and wrong

One group of factors influencing how a person behaves on the job is that person's values and beliefs. A **value** refers to the importance a person attaches to something. Values are also tied to the enduring belief that one's mode of conduct is better than another mode of conduct. If you believe that good interpersonal relations are the most important part of your life, your humanistic values are strong. Similarly, you may think that people who are not highly concerned about interpersonal relations have poor values.

Values are closely tied in with **ethics**, the moral choices a person makes. A person's values influence which kinds of behaviors he or she believes are ethical. Ethics converts values into action. A business owner who highly values money and profits might not find it unethical to raise prices higher than needed to cover additional costs. A corporate executive who strongly values family life might suggest that the company invest company funds in an on-premises dependent-care center. Another concept that ties in closely with values and ethics is **morals**, which are an individual's or a society's determination of what is right or wrong. Your morals are influenced by your values. If you value truth telling, for example, you would consider it immoral to lie to a coworker.

According to the late Stephen Covey, values play an important role in our work life. You should understand what is important in your life, and what gives your life meaning and fulfillment. Knowing the answer to these issues will help you cope with the inevitable ups and downs in most work roles.[2] A supervisor at a customer care center might be having a bad day because of equipment failure and two people quitting. Yet, focusing on her values, she thinks, "Our purpose is to make life more satisfying for our customers, and we are doing that. Today might be tough, but in the long run our group is helping customers."

HOW VALUES ARE LEARNED

People are not born with a particular set of values. Instead, people acquire values in the process of growing up, and many values are learned by the age of four. One important way we acquire values is through observing others, or modeling. Models can be teachers, friends, brothers, sisters, and even public figures. If we identify with a particular person, the probability is high that we will develop some of his or her major values, such as those of a parent, an instructor, or a coach.

Given that values are acquired in the process of growing up, your culture influences your values, as will be explained more in detail in Chapter 13. For now, consider this illustration. People growing up in a Malaysian culture, as well as other Far East cultures, learn to value age, hierarchy, and wisdom. When meeting the seventy-year-old CEO of his company, the young Malaysian customer service rep might say, "Sir, I am honored to have the opportunity to speak with you and benefit from your wisdom." In contrast, a young American worker might say, "Hi, Joe. How's it going?" (Of course, we are exaggerating a stereotype.)

Another major way values are learned is through the communication of attitudes. The attitudes that we hear expressed directly or indirectly help shape our values. Assume that using credit to purchase goods and services was considered an evil practice among your family and friends. You might therefore hold negative values about installment purchases.

Unstated but implied attitudes may also shape your values. If key people in your life showed a lack of enthusiasm when you talked about work accomplishments, you might not place such a high value on achieving outstanding results. If, however, your family and friends centered their lives on their careers, you might develop similar values. (Or you might rebel against such a value because it interfered with a more relaxed lifestyle.) Many key values are also learned through religion and thus become the basis for society's morals. For example, most religions emphasize treating other people fairly and kindly. To "knife somebody in the back" is considered immoral both on and off the job.

Later Life Influences on Values

Although many core values are learned early in life, our values continue to be shaped by events late in life. The media, including dissemination of information about popular culture, influence the values of many people throughout their lives. The aftermath of Hurricane Katrina intensified a belief in the value of helping less fortunate people. Volunteers from throughout the United States invested time, money, and energy in helping rebuild New Orleans and several other Gulf Coast cities. Influential people, such as NBA players, were seen on television building houses for Katrina victims. Such publicity sent a message that helping people in need is a value worth considering.

The publicity given to building a sustainable environment, or "being green," has shaped the values of countless thousands of people throughout the world. Many people regard being green as an important value and are attracted to business firms, such as Google Inc. and Wal-Mart, that have a green agenda.

The media, particularly advertisements, can also encourage the development of values that are harmful to a person intent on developing a professional career. People featured in advertisements for consumer products, including snack food, beer, and vehicles, often flaunt rudeness and sloppy grammar. The message comes across to many people that such behavior is associated with success.

Changes in technology can also change our values. As the world has become enormously digitized, more and more people come to value a *digital lifestyle* as the normal way of life. The changes in values lead to curious changes in the behavior of people. Antonio Perez, the former top executive at Eastman Kodak Co., commented years ago on how people have shifted away from storing prints of photos in shoeboxes, thereby being in danger of losing many important memories. Perez said, "As much as we complain about the old shoebox, it was brilliant. Because it was just a matter of going through the attic. This is going to be a lot more difficult in digital, as you all know. Formats are going to change. Hard drives will crash."[3] Of course, people who truly value stored memories can make prints.

The Influence of Company Values

Values can sometimes be learned later in life when we are introduced to values that did not capture our attention earlier. It is possible that the teaching and demands of an employer will help us acquire new values. A relevant example is the effort and time Juniper invests in teaching company values to employees (as described above). For example, company leadership insists that Juniper workers should emphasize being trusted. A sales representative when meeting a customer might say to himself or herself, "What Juniper product or service might help this company be more successful?" rather than "What Juniper product or service can I sell this company so I can meet my sales quota?" Three other examples of important company values are presented next.

Kindness and Compassion. Most people would probably think of kindness and compassion as individual rather than corporate values, yet some companies do promote kindness and compassion as a corporate value. For example, several companies, including the clothier Genesco Inc. and Whole Foods Market Inc., provide funds to families facing emergencies. At Genesco, circumstances that may qualify for a grant include a natural disaster, life-threatening or serious illness or injury, death of an employee or a dependent, and catastrophic or extreme circumstances.

A head physician who perceives kindness as a basic staff development strategy made this statement: "It's my job to make the people who work for me happy; if they're happy, they'll work harder."[4]

Being kind to employees may benefit the company because kindness contributes to job satisfaction, which in turn can lead to less turnover and higher productivity.

Sustainability. As mentioned above, sustainability, or protecting the environment, has surged in importance as a corporate value. Sustainability has also been perceived as a business megatrend, like electrification, mass production, and information technology, and will profoundly affect the competiveness and survival of business firms.[5]

A survey about business social responsibility found that approximately 75 percent of companies engage in sustainable practices. Among these practices are recycling, eco-efficient waste management practices, and the use of alternative energy sources such as wind turbines. Among the benefits to employers from emphasizing sustainability are improved employee morale, stronger public image, and increased employee loyalty. Green initiatives can also save a company directly, such as lowered energy costs.[6]

Corporate Spiritualism. Another value that individuals may acquire as a result of being part of an organization is *corporate spiritualism.* This type of spiritualism takes place when management is just as concerned about nurturing employee well-being as it is about profits. A practice such as a work/family program contributes to this style of corporate spiritualism.[7] The purpose of a work/family program is to make it easier for workers to effectively manage both work and personal life responsibilities. Flexible working hours and dependent-care assistance are prime examples, but even the presence of a dry cleaner on company premises can help workers balance the demands of work and personal life.

Company values are passed along to organization members as part of the process of **socialization**, the process of coming to understand the values, norms, and customs essential for adapting to the organization. As the individual observes others, he or she picks up hints as to what is acceptable behavior by watching other company employees in action. For example, a newcomer to the organization might observe the manager authorizing emergency funds for a worker whose house burned down. This would be an instance of the value of kindness and compassion in action.

Socialization
the process of coming to understand the values, norms, and customs essential for adapting to the organization

▶ Learning Objective 5.2 ▶

THE CLASSIFICATION AND CLARIFICATION OF VALUES

Because values can be related to anything we believe in, a large number of values exist. Several attempts have been made to classify values, and each one is closely tied to psychological needs. If you value something strongly, such as accomplishing worthwhile activities, it leads to a need such as achievement. If you value independence, it will most likely lead to a need for autonomy. The following classification of values involves needs and is linked to both career and personal life. The basis of the value classification is to categorize people into four types emphasizing different values and needs.[8]

Humanists are driven primarily by a need for self-awareness, personal growth, and a sense of being individual and unique. Humanism is their most important value. A humanist is likely to devote considerable time to self-help activities, including personal reflection and attending a workshop designed for personal growth, such as one given by Anthony Robbins.

Strategists highly value a sense of mastery and personal achievement. They are likely to say, "I am what I do." Strategists might believe that insight and understanding are important, but they place the highest value on tangible accomplishments. A typical strategist activity would be to undertake and complete a project such as fund-raising for a community center.

Pragmatists strive for a corner in the world anchored by power, influence, stability, and control. They search for roles and settings that provide them with formal power, respect, and prestige. A pragmatist, therefore, highly values career success in the traditional meaning of the term: high compensation and rank. A pragmatist would enjoy being a high-ranking manager in a business, government, or non-profit organization.

Adventurers place low value on status and conformity. Instead, they have a powerful drive for excitement and adventure. The adventurer might say, "I don't want to play it safe. I want to play often and big. Play is good. Just do it." The adventurer has high standing on the traits of risk taking and thrill seeking. An adventurer might enjoy working in the Arctic Circle as part of a team searching for underground petroleum reserves.

Another key value that influences both work and personal life is *conscientiousness*. As a personality trait, conscientiousness is regarded as one of the basic components of personality. But the same trait also functions as a value, with the conscientious person striving to be industrious, well organized, self-controlling, responsible, traditional, and virtuous.[9] Dozens of studies have demonstrated that workers with a high standing on conscientiousness tend to perform well in a wide variety of positions. As a result, employers look for conscientious workers when choosing among job candidates for both initial hiring and later promotion.[10]

Loyalty to the organization, as manifested in wanting to stay with or make supportive statements about an employer, is another key individual value with an impact on the job. Some people think that loyalty as a value is diminishing, partly because employers are quick to lay off employees when sales decrease or expenses mount. Loyalty to the employer often increases when fewer jobs are available and decreases when more jobs are available, such as during a time of economic prosperity.

Generational Differences in Values

Differences in values among people often stem from age, or generational differences. Workers older than fifty, in general, may have different values than people who are much younger. A subtle point, however, is that quite often generational values and attitudes we pick up at a certain age may persist for many years.[11] Assume that as a teenager and young adult, Jennifer develops a passion for using communication technology devices, as well as for living a balanced lifestyle (a fair balance between work and personal life). Although Jennifer has acquired these values early in life, the same values are likely to persist for many years. However, as Jennifer gets older, she may become more risk averse, such as not changing jobs unless forced to and obeying speed limits—with the increased conservatism being linked to age rather than her generation.

Generational differences in values have often been seen as a clash between baby boomers and members of Generation X and Generation Y. (Millennials make up approximately one-third of the U.S. workforce.) According to the stereotype, boomers see Generation X and Generation Y as disrespectful of rules, not willing to pay their dues, and being disloyal to employers. Generation X and Generation Y see boomers as worshipping hierarchy (layers of authority), being overcautious, and wanting to preserve the status quo.

The new generation following the Millennials (1981–2002) is referred to as the iGeneration, or Pluralist Generation, because of its acceptance of diversity. These are the individuals so preoccupied with smartphones that they prefer to text than talk with other individuals and want to stay connected to friends electronically.[12] A few athletic coaches have complained that players miss out on some key plays because they will not talk to each other on the field. Also, some customers complain that the youngest store associates hesitate to speak to a customer because talking to people is less preferred than sending them text messages.

Figure 5-1 summarizes these stereotypes with the understanding that massive group stereotypes like this are only partially accurate because there are literally millions of exceptions. For example, many baby boomers are fascinated with communication technology, and many members of Generation Y like hierarchy. Also, you may have observed

FIGURE 5-1

VALUE STEREOTYPES FOR SEVERAL GENERATIONS OF WORKERS

Baby Boomers (1946–1964)	Generation X (1961–1980)	Generation Y (1981–2002) Millennials
Uses technology as a necessary tool, but not obsessed with technology for its own sake	Tech-savvy; enjoys making some use of personal mobile devices for work purposes	Tech-savvy, and stays alert to new electronic devices that can be incorporated into work; often prefers to use personal rather than company electronic communication devices
Appreciates hierarchy	Teamwork very important	Teamwork very important, highly team focused
Tolerates teams but values independent work	Dislikes hierarchy	Dislikes hierarchy, prefers participation
Strong career orientation	Strives for work–personal life balance but will work long hours for now; prefers flexible work schedule	Strives for work–personal life balance, and may object to work interfering with personal life; expects flexible work schedule
More loyalty to organization	Loyalty to own career and profession	Loyalty to own career and profession and feels entitled to career goals
Favors diplomacy and tact	Candid in conversation	Quite direct in conversation
Seeks long-term employment	Will accept long-term employment if situation is right	Looks toward each company as a stepping-stone to better job in another company
Believes that issues should be formally discussed	Believes that feedback can be administered informally, and welcomes feedback	Believes that feedback can be given informally, even on the fly, and craves feedback
Somewhat willing to accept orders and suggestions	Often questions why things should be done in certain way	Frequently asks why things should be done in a certain way, and asks loads of questions
Willing to take initiative to establish starting and completion dates for projects	Slight preference for a manager's providing structure about project dates	Prefers structure on dates and other activities based on childhood of structured activities
Regards rewards as a positive consequence of good performance and seniority	Expects frequent rewards	Feels strong sense of entitlement to rewards, including promotions
Will multitask in front of work associates when it seems necessary	Feels comfortable in multitasking while interacting with work associates	Assumes that multitasking, including listening to music on earphones while dealing with work associates, is acceptable behavior
Prefers working at desk in company office	Eager to have the option of working from anywhere at any time	Prefers working from anywhere at any time; feels constrained when having to work in company office full time
Accepts and respects cultural diversity in organizations	Has favorable attitudes toward cultural diversity	Regards cultural diversity as a natural way of life
Believes that fully developed spoken communication is important	Perceives spoken communication to be a supplement to written electronic communication	Much prefers sending text messages and short e-mails to coworkers rather than talking

Note: Disagreement exists about which age brackets fit baby boomers, Generation X, and Generation Y, with both professional publications and dictionaries showing slight differences.
Source: "VALUE STEREOTYPES FOR SEVERAL GENERATIONS OF WORKERS" by Andrew J. DuBrin.

that many people in their fifties and sixties are so wedded to communication technology that they incessantly use their smartphone on and off the job. Now the vast majority of workers are tethered to communication technology, not just members of Generation X and Generation Y.

Heather Huhman, who has mentored people seeking entry-level positions, offers a useful perspective for understanding value-based generational difference. She contends that earlier generations have developed negative stereotypes about Gen Y people and offers the following advice for members of Gen Y to overcome such stereotypes, including dealing with these four stereotypes.[13]

1. **They are entitled.**   Remember to say frequently, "What can I do to help?" Offering help to others helps overcome the stereotype of being self-centered. Another approach is to suggest something of benefit to the organization, and to volunteer to develop it.

2. **They have a weak work ethic.**   Ask your supervisor to be specific about what he or she expects. The supervisor is likely to perceive the questioning as a sign of interest and commitment. At the same time, you are likely to get the information you need to perform your job well.

3. **They are self-centered.**   Show that you are a team player by being a good organizational citizen. (A team player is the opposite of being self-centered.) At the same time, displaying initiative and leadership will show that you want to help the company as well as coworkers.

4. **They are too casual in their speech (such as vocalized pauses and overuse of "like" and "you know").**   Using a camcorder and/or a speech coach, most people can learn to speak in a more refined and polished manner.

Although stereotypes do give us some general ideas, they can be insulting and patronizing. For example, many Gen Y people have highly polished speaking skills. At the same time, being a baby boomer does not automatically grant a person refined speaking skills.

Value Clarification

The values that you develop early in life are directly related to the kind of person you are and to the quality of the relationships you form.[14] Recognition of this fact has led to exercises designed to help people clarify and understand some of their own values. At times, the values you clarify will match with the value categories previously listed, including company values and generational differences in values. At other times, your personal value list will be different. The Applying Human Relations Exercise 5-1 at the end of the chapter gives you an opportunity to clarify your values.

THE MESH BETWEEN INDIVIDUAL AND JOB VALUES

Under the best of circumstances, the values of employees mesh with those required by the job. When this state of congruence exists, job performance is likely to be high. Suppose that Jacquelyn strongly values giving people with limited formal education an opportunity to work and avoid being placed on welfare. So she takes a job as a manager of a dollar store that employs many people who would ordinarily have limited opportunity for employment. Jacquelyn is satisfied because she and her employer share a similar value.

When the demands made by the organization or a superior clash with the basic values of the individual, he or she suffers from **person–role conflict**. The individual wants to obey orders but does not want to perform an act that seems inconsistent with his or her values. A situation such as this might occur when an employee is asked to produce a product that he or she feels is unsafe or is of no value to society. Another example of person–role conflict is illustrated in Figure 5-2.

Above all, Gen Y is tech savvy. Their lifestyle is all about technology. They are consumed by entertainment and accomplished at multitasking.
—*Elizabeth Gillespie*
President of marketing for Jones Lang LaSalle Americas Inc., a real estate firm

Person–role conflict
the demands made by the organization or a superior clash with the basic values of the individual

FIGURE 5-2

AN EXAMPLE OF PERSON–ROLE CONFLICT

Source: "AN EXAMPLE OF PERSON–ROLE CONFLICT" by Andrew J. DuBrin.

Sales Manager, High-Risk Bonds

Sales Rep with Strong Ethical Code

A manager of a commercial weight-reduction center resigned after two years of service. The owners pleaded with her to stay based on her excellent performance. The manager replied, "Sorry, I think my job is immoral. We sign up all these people with great expectations of losing weight permanently. Most of them do achieve short-term weight reduction. My conflict is that more than 90 percent of our clientele regain the weight they lost once they go back to eating standard food. I think we are deceiving them by not telling them up front that they will most likely gain back the weight they lose."

What constitutes a good fit between personal values and organizational values may change at different stages of a person's career because of a change in values. At one point in a person's career, he or she may think that founding a business is important because the new firm might create employment. At another stage of the same person's career, he or she might believe that working for the nonprofit sector is more meritorious.

A starting point in finding a good fit between individual and organizational values is to identify what type of work would be the most meaningful to you. After identifying your passion in terms of work, you would then seek an employment opportunity that provides such work. For example, a manager might discover that helping young people learn useful job skills brings her the most professional excitement. She might then seek an opportunity to manage a manufacturing apprenticeship program in her company.

A study with managers enrolled in an MBA program illustrates the importance of value congruence between the individual and the organization. When leaders were able to help group members perceive how the organization matched their values, work group effectiveness tended to increase.[15]

▶ **Learning Objective 5.3** ▶

The Importance of Being Concerned About Business Ethics

When asked why ethics (the moral choices a person makes) is important, most people would respond something to the effect that "Ethics is important because it's the right thing to do. You behave decently in the workplace because your family and religious values have taught you what is right and wrong." All this is true, but the justification for behaving ethically is more complex, as described next.[16]

A major justification for behaving ethically on the job is to recognize that people are motivated by both self-interest and moral commitments. Most people want to maximize gain for themselves. At the same time, most people are motivated to do something morally right. As one of many examples, vast numbers of people donate money to charity, although keeping that amount of money for themselves would provide more personal gain.

Corporate ethics are a major component of ethical behavior for workers. Many business executives want employees to behave ethically because a good reputation can enhance business. A favorable corporate reputation may enable firms to charge premium prices and attract better job applicants. A favorable reputation also helps attract investors, including mutual fund managers whose primary responsibility is to purchase stock in companies. Certain mutual funds, for example, invest only in companies that are environmentally friendly. Managers want employees to behave ethically because unethical behavior—for example, employee theft, lost production time, and lawsuits—is costly.

Behaving ethically is also important because many unethical acts are also illegal and can lead to financial loss and imprisonment. A company that knowingly allows workers to engage in unsafe practices might be fined, and the executives may be held personally liable. Furthermore, unsafe practices can kill people. Low ethics have also resulted in financial hardship for employees as company executives raid pension funds of other companies they purchase, sharply reducing or eliminating the retirement funds of many workers.

Extreme acts of unethical behavior can lead a company into bankruptcy, such as the famous scandals at Enron Corporation. Among the worst ethical violations were hiding financial losses by passing the losses on to phony subsidiaries, encouraging employees to invest their life savings in company stock that was doomed to failure, and creating power shortages in California to artificially inflate energy prices. Furthermore, company executives sometimes held business meetings at strip clubs—at company expense.[17]

A subtle reason for behaving ethically is that high ethics increases the quality of work life. Ethics provides a set of guidelines that specify what makes for acceptable behavior. Being ethical will point you toward actions that make life more satisfying for work associates. A company code of ethics specifies what constitutes ethical versus unethical behavior. When employees follow this code, the quality of work life improves. Several sample clauses from corporate (or company) ethical codes are as follows:

- Demonstrate courtesy, respect, honesty, and fairness.

- Do not use abusive language.

- Do not bring firearms, knives, or illegal drugs to work.

- Do not offer bribes.

- Maintain confidentiality of records.

- Do not harass (sexually, racially, ethnically, or physically) subordinates, superiors, coworkers, customers, or suppliers.

An example of a representative corporate, or company, code of ethics is presented in Figure 5-3. To the extent that all members of the organization abide by an ethical code, the quality of work life will improve. At the same time, interpersonal relations in

FIGURE 5-3

**A REPRESENTATIVE
CORPORATE CODE
OF ETHICS**

OUR COMPANY CODE OF ETHICS

- We demonstrate integrity, or sticking to our word, in our relationship with employees, customers, vendors, stockholders, and all other stakeholders.
- We show our commitment to our fellow employees by treating each other with respect and dignity.
- We practice equal opportunity for all our employees, customers, and suppliers, regardless of sex, race, ethnicity, age, or sexual orientation.
- We report our financial condition accurately by relying on generally accepted accounting principles.
- We strive for excellent performance in every position by each employee working up to his or her capacity.
- We maintain high standards of accountability by taking responsibility for our actions as individuals, team members, and as an entire company.
- We demonstrate our respect to consumers by providing the best products we can and adhering to the highest standards of ethical marketing practices.
- We are committed to following applicable local, state, and government regulations, and to protecting natural resources.
- Employees who violate our Code of Ethics are subject to discipline, including suspension, demotion, and even termination. Any employee accused of such violations will be given a fair hearing and receive due process.

organizations will be strengthened. To help raise your awareness of your own ethical thoughts and behaviors, take Human Relations Self-Assessment Quiz 5-1.

WHY BEING ETHICAL ISN'T EASY

As analyzed by Linda Klebe Treviño, an organizational behavior professor at Pennsylvania State University, and Michael Brown, a management professor at Penn State Erie, behaving ethically in business is more complex than it seems on the surface, for a variety of reasons.[18] To begin with, ethical decisions are complex. For example, someone might argue that hiring children for factory jobs in overseas countries is unethical. Yet, if these children lose their jobs, many would starve or turn to crime to survive. Second, people do not always recognize the moral issues involved in a decision. A handyman on a work assignment who finds a butcher knife under the bed might not think that he has a role to play in perhaps preventing murder. Sometimes language hides the moral issue involved, such as when the term *file sharing* replaces *stealing* in terms of online music.

Another complexity in making ethical decisions is that people have different levels of moral development. At one end of the scale, some people behave morally simply to escape punishment. At the other end of the scale, some people are morally developed to the point that they are guided daily by principles of justice and right, such as wanting to help as many people as possible. The environment in which we work also influences our behaving ethically. Suppose a restaurant owner encourages such practices as serving customers food that was accidentally dropped on the kitchen floor. An individual server is more likely to engage in such behavior to obey the demand of the owner.

Closely related to moral development is that some people have a tendency to *morally disengage,* or think in such a way as to avoid being moral without feeling distress. A product development specialist might morally disengage from selling a trade secret to a competitor by rationalizing that he or she is underpaid and therefore deserves supplementary income from working so hard. Workers with a strong tendency to morally disengage have

Human Relations Self-Assessment Quiz 5-1

The Ethical Reasoning Inventory

Describe how well you agree with each of the following statements. Use the following scale: disagree strongly (DS), disagree (D), neutral (N), agree (A), agree strongly (AS). Circle the number in the appropriate column.

		DS	D	N	A	AS
1.	When applying for a job, I would cover up the fact that I had been fired from my most recent job.	5	4	3	2	1
2.	Cheating only a few dollars in one's favor on an expense account is okay if a person needs the money.	5	4	3	2	1
3.	Employees should report on each other for wrongdoing.	1	2	3	4	5
4.	It is acceptable to give approximate figures for expense account items when one does not have all the receipts.	5	4	3	2	1
5.	I see no problem with conducting a little personal business on company time.	5	4	3	2	1
6.	Simply to make a sale, I would stretch the truth about a delivery date.	5	4	3	2	1
7.	I think it is okay for most workers to spend about one hour per day during work using Facebook, Twitter, or another social media site.	5	4	3	2	1
8.	I would flirt with my boss simply to get a bigger salary increase.	5	4	3	2	1
9.	If I received $500 for doing some odd jobs, I would report it on my income tax return.	1	2	3	4	5
10.	I see no harm in taking home a few office supplies.	5	4	3	2	1
11.	It is acceptable to read the e-mail and text messages of coworkers, even when not invited to do so.	5	4	3	2	1
12.	It is unacceptable to call in sick to take a day off, even if only done once or twice a year.	1	2	3	4	5
13.	I would accept a permanent, full-time job even if I knew I wanted the job for only six months.	5	4	3	2	1
14.	I would first check company policy before accepting an expensive gift from a supplier.	1	2	3	4	5
15.	To be successful in business, a person usually has to ignore ethics.	5	4	3	2	1
16.	If I felt physically attracted toward a job candidate, I would hire that person over a more qualified candidate.	5	4	3	2	1
17.	On the job, I tell the truth all the time.	1	2	3	4	5
18.	If a student were very pressed for time writing a paper, it would be acceptable to either have a friend write the paper or purchase one.	5	4	3	2	1
19.	I would authorize accepting an office machine for a thirty-day trial period, even if I knew we had no intention of buying it.	5	4	3	2	1
20.	I would never accept credit for a coworker's ideas.	1	2	3	4	5

Scoring and Interpretation:

Add the numbers you have circled to obtain your total score.

90–100 You are a strongly ethical person who may take a little ribbing from coworkers for being too straitlaced.

60–89 You show an average degree of ethical awareness and therefore should become more sensitive to ethical issues.

41–59 Your ethics are underdeveloped, but you at least have some awareness of ethical issues. You need to raise your level of awareness of ethical issues.

20–40 Your ethical values are far below contemporary standards in business. Begin a serious study of business ethics.

Source: "The Ethical Reasoning Inventory" by Andrew J. DuBrin.

been shown to engage in such behaviors as committing fraud and self-reported lying, cheating, and stealing.[19]

A major contributor to unethical behavior is an individual's greed and gluttony, or the desire to maximize self-gain at the expense of others. For example, a business owner might have a luxurious office, including rare art, built for personal use rather than having those funds available for salary increases, bonuses, or the construction of a much-needed additional restroom in the office.

Another major reason for unethical behavior in business is that goals sometimes reward unethical behavior, such as sales representatives being rewarded for sales with less attention to how the sale is accomplished. To enhance sales, a representative might then offer a bribe (or kickback) to the customer in order to attain the sale.

Ethics professors Max H. Bazerman of Harvard and Ann E. Tenbrunsel at the Notre Dame University explain that another reason for poor corporate ethics is *motivated blindness.* People tend to see what they want to see and easily block out contradictory information when it is in their interest to remain uninformed.[20] A mortgage broker intent on placing a lot of mortgages may be almost unconsciously motivated to overlook certain credit red flags on a mortgage application, such as the applicant having no savings account. To find red flags in the application represents a conflict of interest between selling the mortgage to a bank and making an honest appraisal of the mortgage application.

THE EXTENT OF ETHICAL PROBLEMS

The ethical misdeeds of executives have received substantial publicity in recent years. But ethical violations by rank-and-file employees also take place. A survey conducted by the Ethics Resource Center shows that 41 percent of the 6,400 workers surveyed said that they have observed misconduct on the job, such as lying, stealing, and sexual harassment. Also, about 9 percent of employees felt pressed to compromise their standards.[21]

Going beyond surveys of what individuals believe, some company practices of today might be considered unethical in terms of people getting harmed. Today, there is much less disgrace in a company declaring bankruptcy, thereby leaving many debts unpaid and abandoning employees' pensions. (The federal government is then forced to take over the pension plan and pays the workers a small percentage of the pension for which they were hoping.)

Two examples follow of the type of unethical conduct in business that many people find discouraging and unacceptable:

■ Avon Products Inc. was investigated for five years as to whether the company violated the Foreign Corrupt Practices Act by providing gifts or making payments to government officials in China and other countries in order to obtain licenses to sell its products. Prosecutors and regulators were seeking approximately $50 million to settle the claim.[22]

■ Vibram USA, the manufacturer of FiveFingers shoes, settled a multimillion-dollar class action lawsuit. The charge was that the company deliberately misled customers about the health benefits of "barefoot" running shoes. A specific charge was that Vibram's claims that the shoes reduced the risk of foot injury and strengthened foot and leg muscles constituted false advertising.[23]

An understanding of ethics must also recognize that consumers are frequently fraudulent, including making false insurance claims such as purposely damaging or burning their own property. Another major fraud is returning merchandise to a store that the customer intended to use only once, such as an expensive dress or a video camera. The latter activity is referred to in the trade as *de-shopping.* Two studies taken together found that regularly interacting with unethical customers poses a challenge for customer-contact workers. Dealing with unethical customers can lead to emotional exhaustion, which can negatively affect both work and personal life.[24]

FREQUENT ETHICAL MISTAKES AND VIOLATIONS

◀ **Learning Objective 5.4** ◀

Certain ethical mistakes, including illegal actions, recur in the workplace. Familiarizing yourself with these mistakes and violations can be helpful in monitoring your own behavior. Here we describe a number of common ethical problems faced by business executives as well as workers at lower job levels.[25]

Illegally Copying Software

A rampant ethical problem is whether to illegally copy computer software including software downloaded from the cloud. According to Apple Inc., the annual loss to piracy is more than $11 billion.[26] The illegal copying of software deprives software developers of profits they deserve for having produced the software. Such pirating also leads to the loss of potential jobs for many software developers because the companies that produce the software have less revenue.

Treating People Unfairly

Being fair to people means equity, reciprocity, and impartiality. Fairness involves the issue of giving people equal rewards for accomplishing equal amounts of work. The goal of human resource legislation is to make decisions about people based on their qualifications and performance—not on the basis of demographic factors such as sex, race, or age. A fair working environment is where performance is the only factor that counts (equity). Employer–employee expectations must be understood and met (reciprocity). Prejudice and bias must be eliminated (impartiality).

Treating people fairly—and therefore ethically—requires an underemphasis on political factors. Yet this ethical doctrine is not always easy to implement. It is human nature to want to give bigger rewards (such as fatter raises or bigger orders) to people we like.

> Follow the Platinum Rule: Treat people the way *they* wish to be treated.
> —*Eric Harvey and Scott Airitam*
> Authors of *Ethics 4 Everyone*

Sexual Harassment

Sexual harassment is a source of conflict and an illegal act. Sexual harassment is also an ethical issue because it is morally wrong and unfair. All acts of sexual harassment flunk an ethics test. Before sexually harassing another person, the potential harasser should ask, "Would I want a loved one to be treated this way?"

Conflict of Interest

Part of being ethical is making business judgments only on the basis of the merits or facts in a situation. Imagine that you are a supervisor who is romantically involved with a worker within the group. When it comes time to assign raises, it will be difficult for you to be objective. A **conflict of interest** occurs when your judgment or objectivity is compromised. Conflicts of interest often take place in the sales end of business. If a company representative accepts a large gift from a sales representative, it may be difficult to make objective judgments about buying from the representative. Yet being taken to dinner by a vendor would not ordinarily cloud one's judgment. Another common example of a conflict of interest is making a hiring decision about a friend who badly needs a job but is not well qualified for the position.

> **Conflict of interest**
> judgment or objectivity is compromised because of two competing ends that must be satisfied

Divulging Confidential Information

An ethical person can be trusted not to divulge confidential information unless the welfare of others is at stake. Suppose a coworker tells you in confidence that she is upset with the company and therefore is looking for another job. Behaving ethically, you do not pass this information along to your supervisor, even though it would help your supervisor plan for a replacement. Now suppose the scenario changes slightly. Your coworker tells you she is looking for another job because she is upset. She tells you she is so upset that she plans to destroy company computer files on her last day. If your friend does find another job, you might warn the company about her contemplated activities.

The challenge of dealing with confidential information arises in many areas of business that affect interpersonal relations. If you learned that a coworker was indicted for a crime, charged with sexual harassment, or facing bankruptcy, there would be a temptation to gossip about the person. A highly ethical person would not pass along information about the personal difficulties of another person.

Misrepresentation of Employment History

Many people distort in a positive direction information about their employment history on their job résumé, on their job application form, and during the interview. Distortion, or lying, of this type is considered unethical and can lead to immediate dismissal if discovered.

Ethical Violations with Computers and Information Technology

As computers have dominated the workplace, many ethical issues have arisen in addition to pirating software. One ethical dilemma that surfaces frequently is the fairness of tracking the websites a person visits and those from which he or she buys. Should this information be sold, like a mailing list? (Sometimes this tracking is harmless and humorous. A human relations professor was searching the Internet for articles about the *proactive personality*. Soon he would regularly see advertisements for the acne medication Proactiv® when he visited websites.) Another issue is the fairness of having an employee work at a keyboard for sixty hours in one week when such behavior frequently leads to repetitive-motion disorder. And is it ethical for workers to spend doing online shopping and placing bets online during the working day?

Causing Problems in Order to Take Credit for Fixing Them

A longstanding workplace issue involves employees who quietly cause problems so they can later take the credit for the problem's resolution.[27] The advantage derived from fixing problems is that such behavior is considered quite valuable by most employers. The problem repaired might be fictitious, or simply exaggerated. For example, a service manager at an automobile dealership pretended that many customers were complaining about the dimly lit waiting room. So he proceeded to improve the lighting and then told the owners of the dealership about how he had enhanced customer satisfaction.

Lying in Order to Look Good

Outright lying is a frequent form of unethical behavior. The most general purposes of lying are to look good and to protect oneself from punishment. Lies vary in intensity and seriousness, and this variation influences the extent of their ethical violation. Lying about how much profit a company made, for example, is much more serious than being untruthful about why one is late for work on a given day. Several studies have suggested that the average person tells one to two lies a day, and frequently at work.[28] The fact that lying is frequent does not make it ethical.

Engaging in Unethical Behavior to Benefit the Company

A final ethical mistake or violation concerns whether to engage in unethical behavior in order to help the company. This type of dilemma also contributes to unethical behavior in the workplace. Employees will be tempted to engage in unethical acts in order to benefit the company, in such ways as the following: (a) "cooking" numbers to boost the prediction of financial analysts' projections and stock values; (b) withholding information about the hazards of a pharmaceutical product; (c) neglecting to give customers correct change when the amount is small, such as a quarter.

Two studies found that workers were more likely to engage in unethical behavior when they identify with their employer and at the same time expect they will be rewarded for such behavior.[29] An example would be receiving a favorable performance evaluation for benefiting the company with unethical behavior.

Guidelines for Making Ethical Decisions and Behaving Ethically

◀ Learning Objective 5.5 ◀

Following guidelines for ethical behavior is the heart of being ethical. Although many people behave ethically without studying ethical guidelines, they are usually following guidelines programmed into their minds early in life. The Golden Rule exemplifies a guideline taught by parents, grandparents, and kindergarten teachers. In this section, we approach ethical guidelines from six perspectives: (a) developing the right character traits, (b) using a guide to ethical decision making, (c) developing strong relationships with work associates, (d) using corporate ethics programs, (e) following an ethical role model in the company, (f) following an applicable code of professional conduct, and (g) blowing the whistle on highly unethical and illegal conduct.

DEVELOPING THE RIGHT CHARACTER TRAITS

Character traits develop early in life, yet with determination and self-discipline, many people can modify old traits or develop new ones. A **character trait** is an enduring characteristic of a person that is related to consistent moral and ethical behavior. For example, if a person has the character trait of untruthfulness, he or she will lie in many situations. Conversely, the character trait of honesty leads to behaving honestly in most situations. A focus on character is considered important also because many social commentators and academic people are concerned that there is a decline in the development of character. The decline has contributed to such problems as a lowered sense of duty and personal integrity.[30]

Character trait
an enduring characteristic of a person that is related to consistent moral and ethical behavior

The Character Counts Coalition is an organization formed to encourage young people to develop fairness, respect, trustworthiness, responsibility, caring, and good citizenship. The coalition has developed a list of six key guidelines as a foundation for character development.[31] If you develop, or already have, these traits, it will be easy for you to behave ethically in business. As you read the following list, evaluate your own standing on each character trait. Remember, however, that extra effort is required to evaluate one's own character traits, because most people have an inflated view of their honesty and integrity.

1. **Trustworthiness.** Do what you say that you will do, and do things right.

2. **Respect.** Treat others with respect and follow the Golden Rule.

3. **Responsibility.** Do what you are supposed to do, be self-disciplined, and be accountable for your words and actions.

4. **Fairness.** Play by the rules, take turns and share.

5. **Caring.** Be kind and considerate, and express gratitude.

6. **Good citizenship.** Make your school and community better, be a good neighbor, and protect the environment.

If you score high on all of the preceding character traits and behaviors, you are an outstanding member of your company, community, and school. Your ethical behavior is superior.

USING A GUIDE TO ETHICAL DECISION MAKING

Ethical screening

running a contemplated decision or action through an ethics test, particularly when a contemplated action or decision is not clearly ethical or unethical

A powerful strategy for behaving ethically is to follow a guide for ethical decision making. Such a guide for making contemplated decisions includes testing their ethics. **Ethical screening** refers to running a contemplated decision or action through an ethics test. Such screening makes the most sense when the contemplated action or decision is not clearly ethical or unethical. If a sales representative were to take a favorite customer to KFC for lunch, an ethical screen would not be necessary. Nobody would interpret a bucket of chicken to be a serious bribe. Assume, instead, that the sales rep offered to give the customer an under-the-table gift of $1,000 for placing a large order with the rep's firm. The sales representative's behavior would be so blatantly unethical that conducting an ethical screen would be unnecessary.

Several guidelines, or ethical screens, have been developed to help the leader or other influence agent decide whether a given act is ethical or unethical, with all of them asking similar questions.[32] We present a typical guide here.

How morally correct was my decision?   This question is based on the idea that there are certain universally accepted guiding principles of rightness and wrongness, such as "Thou shall not steal." A person dining at a restaurant who is trying to cut back in expenses might contemplate giving a tip of 5 percent. Before doing so, he or she wonders, "Is this right?"

Was justice served by my decision?   According to the concept of justice, certain actions are inherently just or unjust. For example, it is unjust to fire a high-performing employee to make room for a less competent person who is a relative by marriage. Justice includes the idea that it is not just for people to get hurt by a decision, such as selling food supplements with dangerous side effects.

How comfortable would I be if the details of my decision or actions were made public in the media?   For example, would you be willing to post on Facebook or Twitter the outcome of a decision you made with respect to an ethical temptation, such as potential job discrimination?

What would you tell a young family member to do?   Would you say to a younger family member, "The way to write a good term paper is to pluck one from the Internet"?

Ethical issues that require a run through the guide are usually subtle rather than blatant, a decision that falls into the gray zone. You can use an ethical decision-making guide to help solve important human relations problems. Visualize yourself in the same or a similar predicament faced by Danielle.

Danielle and an acquaintance of hers, Ashley, were rivals for a promotion to supervisor of the pension department at a financial services firm. Ashley was often rude toward Danielle, making the rivalry more intense. Both were attending the same barbecue. It soon became apparent that Ashley was drinking way too much beer. Finally, Ashley jumped into the pool dressed in a tank top and cutoff jeans, while holding a bottle of beer in her left hand. Danielle was taking videos anyway, so she filmed Ashley's leap into the pool and obvious drunken behavior.

That night, Danielle thought she could place her rival Ashley in an unfavorable light by posting the video on YouTube and then having a friend alert an executive at the financial services firm to the availability of the video. Danielle hesitated long enough to think through the ethics of what she was doing, including how she would feel if her decision were made public. As a result, Danielle did not post the video to YouTube, and she also deleted the pool scene from her camcorder.

DEVELOPING STRONG RELATIONSHIPS WITH WORK ASSOCIATES

A provocative explanation of the causes of unethical behavior emphasizes the strength of relationships among people.[33] Assume that two people have close professional ties to each other, such as having worked together for a long time or knowing each other both on and off the job. As a consequence, they are likely to behave ethically toward one another on the job. In contrast, if a weak professional relationship exists between two individuals, either party is more likely to engage in unethical behavior. The owner of an auto service center is more likely to behave unethically toward a stranger passing through town than toward a long-time customer. The opportunity for unethical behavior between strangers is often minimized because individuals typically do not trust strangers with sensitive information or valuables.

The ethical-skill-building consequence of information about personal relationships is that building stronger relationships with people is likely to enhance ethical behavior. If you build strong relationships with work associates, you are likely to behave more ethically toward them. Similarly, your work associates are likely to behave more ethically toward you. The work associates we refer to are all your contacts.

USING CORPORATE ETHICS PROGRAMS

Many organizations have various programs and procedures for promoting ethical behavior. Among them are committees that monitor ethical behavior, training programs in ethics, and vehicles for reporting ethical violations. The presence of these programs is designed to create an atmosphere in which unethical behavior is discouraged and reporting on unethical behavior is encouraged.

Ethics Hotlines

Ethics hotlines are one of the best-established programs to help individuals avoid unethical behavior. Should a person be faced with an ethical dilemma, the person calls a toll-free line to speak to a counselor about the dilemma. Sometimes employees ask questions to help interpret a policy, such as, "Is it okay to ask my boss for a date?" or "Are we supposed to give senior citizen discounts to customers who qualify but do not ask for one?" At other times, a more pressing ethical issue might be addressed, such as, "Is it ethical to lay off a worker only five months short of his qualifying for a full pension?"

At times an ethical problem of such high moral intensity is presented that employee confidentiality cannot be maintained. But the ethics office handles the inquiries in as confidential a manner as practical and assigns them case identification numbers for follow-up.[34]

Ethics Training Program

Wells Fargo & Co., a mammoth bank, emphasizes both a code of conduct and ethics training. The company Code of Ethics and Business Conduct specifies policies and standards for employees, covering a variety of topics from maintaining accurate records to participating in civic activities. Each year, employees also participate in ethics training. Any Wells Fargo employee may ask questions or report ethical breaches anonymously using an ethics hotline or dedicated e-mail address. The company fires violators, dismissing about 100 people a year for misconduct ranging from conflicts of interest to cheating on incentive plans.

A group of human resource professionals said that no amount of training will ensure that employees will choose the ethical path in every situation. Also, which behavior is the most ethical is not always clear-cut. Nevertheless, the human resource specialists noted that training can start a useful dialogue about right and wrong behavior that employees could recall when faced with an ethical temptation.[35]

The Right Corporate Culture

A corporate ethics program works best when placed in a corporate culture that promotes ethical behavior. When top management holds meetings at luxury resorts and spends excessive amounts of money on entertainment, it is difficult to seriously preach the importance of ethics to their subordinates. Executives have to communicate regularly about the importance of high ethics and corporate values. For example, when sales representatives are asked about their total sales, they should also be asked how ethically they behaved in attaining the sales.

FOLLOWING AN ETHICAL ROLE MODEL IN THE COMPANY

An important influence on your ethical behavior can be the behavior of other people whom you regard as ethical role models. The role model is not necessarily a top-level manager. He or she could be the purchasing agent who refuses to accept tickets to sporting events from vendors, the coworker who goes on a business trip and returns the part of the travel advance not spent, or the supervisor who tells workers the truth about company problems that might affect them. According to a series of interviews, general categories of attitudes and behaviors that characterize ethical role models in organizations are as follows:

- Everyday interpersonal behaviors, such as taking responsibility for others

- High ethical expectations for oneself, such as working extra hours simply to make sure performance evaluations of group members were completed on time

- High ethical expectations for others, such as expecting others to avoid favoritism, including not recommending unqualified friends and relatives for jobs at the company

- Fairness in dealing with others, such as getting their input on a problem situation involving them

Quite often these role models were managers the participants in the study knew well rather than distant executives. As one of the interviewees in the study responded, "I had an opportunity to interact with him on a daily basis in close confines. I had the chance to see that the actions matched the verbal message."[36]

FOLLOWING AN APPLICABLE CODE OF PROFESSIONAL CONDUCT

Professional codes of conduct are prescribed for many occupational groups, including physicians, nurses, lawyers, paralegals, purchasing managers and agents, and real estate salespeople.

A useful ethical guide for members of these groups is to follow the code of conduct for their profession. If the profession or trade is licensed by the state or province, a worker can be punished for deviating from the code of conduct specified by the state. The code of conduct developed by the profession or trade is separate from the legal code but usually supports the same principles and practices. Some of these codes of conduct developed by the professional associations are fifty and sixty pages long, yet all are guided by the kind of ethical principles implied in the ethical decision-making guide described earlier. A representative principle would be to avoid conflicts of interest, such as a purchasing agent making a major purchase from a company he or she operates on the side.

BLOWING THE WHISTLE ON HIGHLY UNETHICAL AND ILLEGAL CONDUCT

The ethics hotline mentioned above and used by many companies is one way of reporting on unethical and illegal behavior. At times, a person may feel obliged to report extreme acts of unethical and illegal conduct directly to higher management or to a government agency. A **whistle-blower** is an employee who reports wrongdoing in the organization to parties who can take action. Although whistle-blowing might be ethical, it represents a challenge for the whistle-blower. The majority of workers who observe unethical or illegal behavior remain silent. More than one-half the time, the pleas of whistle-blowers are ignored. The Sarbanes-Oxley Act is supposed to prevent retaliation against whistle-blowers from top management. Yet negative consequences, such as being blocked from further promotions, often take place.

To avoid being perceived as simply a disgruntled employee who is seeking revenge, it is crucial that the whistle-blower has carefully documented facts to support his or her charges. When whistle-blowers do have strong documentation of their charges, the U.S. government will at times reward them handsomely. In an extreme example, in 2014 four whistle-blowers received approximately $170 million for aiding investigators obtain a record judgment of $16.65 billion from the Bank of America Corp. The fraud involved selling investments based on inflated evaluations of mortgages by Countrywide Financial Corp., a company the Bank of America acquired in 2008.[37]

Whistle-blower
an employee who reports wrongdoing in the organization to parties who can take action

Concept Review and Reinforcement

Summary and Review

Values, morals, and beliefs influence how a person behaves on the job, and values are closely tied in with ethics, the moral choices a person makes. Values are learned in several ways, as follows:

- Observing others or modeling
- Communication of attitudes by others
- Unstated but implied attitudes of others
- Later life influences, such as stories reported by the media
- Demands of employers that may help employees acquire new values, including corporate spiritualism

Values are closely tied to psychological needs. One way of categorizing values is as follows:

- Humanists (includes personal growth)
- Strategists (mastery and personal achievement)
- Pragmatists (power and control)
- Adventurers (excitement and adventure)

Conscientiousness, as well as kindness and compassion, are other values that influence both work and personal life.

Differences in values often stem from generational differences, such as members of Generation X and Generation Y being less concerned about hierarchy than are baby boomers. Earlier generations have developed negative stereotypes about Gen Y people, yet Gen Y people can often overcome these stereotypes.

Value clarification can lead to a better understanding of your values. When individual and job values mesh, performance may be higher. A person may suffer from person–role conflict when personal and job values clash. To find a good value fit, it helps to identify the type of work that would be most meaningful to you.

Business ethics are important to study for many reasons, including the following:

- People are motivated by both self-interest and moral commitments.

- A good ethical reputation can enhance business.
- Many unethical acts are illegal.
- High ethics increases the quality of work life because it provides guidelines for acceptable behavior.

Being ethical isn't easy, because ethical decisions are complex, people have different levels of moral development, our work environment influences our ethical behavior, workers are sometimes rewarded for being unethical, people often morally disengage, and people may engage in motivated blindness. Surveys reveal that unethical behavior is widespread. Also, much ethically questionable behavior exists, including companies declaring bankruptcy. Consumers also engage in unethical behavior, such as making false insurance claims.

Common ethical mistakes and violations include the following:

- Illegally copying software
- Treating people unfairly
- Sexual harassment
- Conflict of interest
- Divulging confidential information
- Misrepresentation of employment history
- Ethical violations with computers and information technology
- Causing problems in order to take credit for fixing them
- Lying in order to look good

Guidelines for making ethical decisions and behaving ethically include the following:

- Develop the right character traits (such as trustworthiness, respect, and citizenship).
- Use a guide to ethical decision making (the process of ethical screening).

- Develop strong relationships with work associates.
- Use corporate ethics programs.
- Follow an ethical role model in the company.
- Follow an applicable code of professional conduct.
- Blow the whistle on highly unethical and illegal conduct.

Questions for Discussion and Review

5.1 Identify several of your values that you think will help you succeed. Why do you think these values will help you?

5.2 A friend of yours is a vegan, and she receives an offer for what appears to be an ideal job at the headquarters of a group of restaurants that includes steak houses. She is worried about having a values clash if she accepts the position. What advice can you offer your vegan friend?

5.3 Get together in a brainstorming group to identify what you think might be a few values important to (a) Apple Inc. and (b) Nike. Support your reasoning.

5.4 To what extent have you found it true that some of the youngest members of the workforce are hesitant to talk to people because they prefer to send text messages?

5.5 Give an example of an action in business that might be unethical but not illegal.

5.6 A work associate or an acquaintance says to you "Don't worry about me. I am totally honest." How does such a statement influence your evaluation of the person's ethical behavior?

5.7 A 25-year-old is applying for a position as an assistant loan officer at a bank, and the bank is ready to make an offer. The hiring manager then decides against the offer when she discovers by Internet that the candidate spent one night in jail seven years ago after being arrested as an Occupy Wall Street demonstrator. How ethical is the hiring manager's decision?

5.8 Give an example of an action by top management or an immediate supervisor that would cause you to "blow the whistle."

5.9 The number of deaths and serious injuries caused by automobile and small-truck drivers sending and receiving text messages while driving continues to increase. What ethical responsibility should smartphone manufacturers and phone service providers have for preventing or reducing these accidents?

5.10 Some hospitals prohibit doctors from accepting any gift but a free lunch from pharmaceutical companies. Are these hospitals going overboard on ethics? Explain your reasoning.

Web Corner

Choosing a career based on values
www.careerplanning.about.com (Enter into the search box, "Consider Your Values When Choosing a Career.")

Learning more about business ethics
www.crimeradius.com (Focuses on the ethical responsibilities of business owners.)

Making ethical business decisions
http://www.decision-making-solutions.com (Enter into the search box, "Ethical decision making.")

INTERNET SKILL BUILDER
Demonstrating Company Values

Assume that you have accepted a position in your field with Rite Aid, the pharmacy giant. You want to fit in well with the company. One of your strategies is to demonstrate regularly that you conform to the company values of passion for our customers, caring neighbors, associate development, commitment to diversity, and so forth. Details about these values are found by visiting http://www.riteaid.com/about-us/mission-statement, or simply visit the company website and look for the values statement.

The skill aspect of this exercise is for you to explain in about twenty-five words how you will demonstrate that you have incorporated several of these values into your thinking and actions. For example, to demonstrate "Integrity In All We Do," you might say something to the effect of "Whenever I tell a supervisor or coworker that I will do something, I will follow through promptly. If the activity will take a long time, I will furnish a couple of progress reports."

Developing Your
Human Relations Skills

Applying Human Relations Exercise 5-1

Value Clarification

Learning how to clarify your values can be uplifting and, at the same time, can help you make career choices based on these values. Ideally, you might pursue career opportunities that give you an opportunity to satisfy your most important career values, such as "making an above-average income" pursuing a career in industrial sales. A person who values "helping people less fortunate than me" might pursue a career in youth work.

Rank from 1 to 20 the importance of the following values to you as a person. The most important value on the list receives a rank of 1; the least important a rank of 20. Use the space next to "Other" if the list has left out an important value in your life.

_____ Having my own place to live

_____ Having one or more children

_____ Having an interesting job and career

_____ Owning a vehicle

_____ Having a good relationship with coworkers

_____ Having good health

_____ Sending and receiving e-mail messages and text messages, and using the Internet

_____ Being able to stay in frequent contact with friends digitally

_____ Watching my favorite television shows

_____ Participating in sports or other pastimes

_____ Following a sports team, athlete, music group, or other entertainer

_____ Being a religious person

_____ Helping people less fortunate than me

_____ Loving and being loved by another person

_____ Having physical intimacy with another person

_____ Making an above-average income

_____ Being in good physical condition

_____ Being a knowledgeable, informed person

_____ Completing my formal education

_____ Other

1. Discuss and compare your ranking of these values with the person next to you.
2. Perhaps your class, assisted by your instructor, can arrive at a class average on each of these values. How does your ranking compare to the class ranking?
3. Look back at your own ranking. Does it surprise you?
4. Are there any surprises in the class ranking? Which values did you think would be highest and lowest?

Applying Human Relations Exercise 5-2

The Ethics of Whistle-Blowing

Read the two scenarios below about questionable ethical behavior, and decide whether they would warrant your blowing the whistle with a report to a government agency or upper management. Keep in mind the ethical decision-making guide as you think about being a whistle-blower in the situation.

■ In your work as a packaging specialist, you visit the ketchup section at one of the food-processing plants in your company. You notice one large vat of ketchup being used to fill bottles with two different labels. One label is for an upscale brand, and the other for a brand sold by a chain of discount general stores. You ask the department head how the company can sell the same ketchup for an upscale brand and a discount brand. She says with a wink, "Who would know the difference? We make great ketchup and sell it under different labels. If consumers want to pay almost double the price for a bottle of ketchup because it has a snob label, that's their problem not ours."

■ You are having your garage door replaced by a contractor who works for a national home-supply store. He has done a competent job and you congratulate him for the fine job. Before he leaves, the contractor asks you, "Do you have any other work you need done? I can do it for you on my own on a Sunday at about two-thirds the price _____ would charge. No need going through them when you need a home repair job."

Human Relations Class Activity

My Biggest Ethical Challenge and Its Resolution

The first step in this class activity is for each student to think of an ethical challenge, or temptation, he or she has faced in recent years and how he or she resolved the challenge. You may need about five minutes to think through your ethical challenge and its resolution. Students should keep in mind that they will be asked to share the scenario with classmates, so a scenario should be chosen that they would be comfortable sharing with others. Each student in the class, or perhaps volunteers, then makes about a two-minute presentation of his or her challenge and resolution. Here is an example contributed by a student named Danielle:

> About five years ago, I was facing financial pressures because of bills and things like that. I was due a $357 tax refund form the IRS, and I really needed the money. Then something bizarre happened. I received a refund for $357 one Monday, which pleased me no end. Then

it blew my mind when I received refund checks for $357 on Tuesday and Wednesday also. The money would have been so helpful. But then I thought of the ethical problems. The federal government is in worse shape than me and needs every penny. Also, what if I got audited?

> My resolution of the ethical dilemma was to contact the IRS on its website and explain my dilemma. Five weeks later I received a letter from the IRS instructing me to return the money. I hated sending those two extra refunds back, but I can sleep better knowing that I did the right thing.

The class will vote by secret ballot as to which three students presented ethical challenges and resolutions that were the most instructive for the rest of the class. The votes can be made on small slips of paper, or by computer if the classroom is so equipped. After the votes are tallied, the class might discuss why the scenarios receiving the most votes were so instructive.

PS: What would you have done if you had been in Danielle's position?

Human Relations Case Study 5–1

Am I Paid to Be My Manager's TV Repair Technician?

Karen worked for a division of a pharmaceutical company as a member of the technical support team. Among her many responsibilities was keeping the division's desktop computers, laptop computers, printers, and smartphones in working order. Gus, her manager, who had been with the company for about ten years, had a general understanding of what the tech support staff was doing, but he was more of an administrator than a specialist in communication technology.

Several times in recent weeks, Gus complained to Karen and a few other team members about a problem he was having with a digital television set connected to an internal (rabbit ears) antenna. During a lunch break, he explained to Karen,

> I'm going a little crazy. I have four television sets at home. The two big ones are satellite connected and they work just fine. I have a small set in the family room in the basement connected to rabbit ears, and the reception is reasonably good. I am picking up the digital signals with

a few halts here and there, but I am getting the reception I need.

> The problem I have is with a relatively new set connected in our upstairs bedroom. I did the channel scan about one year ago, and I was getting the network channels I needed. A few weeks ago I stopped receiving the channels I needed. All that was left was HSN (Home Shopping Network). I must have done a channel scan twenty times to try to fix the problem. Plus, I rotated the antenna a few times. I called tech support at the manufacturer of my set, and the rep couldn't help. He told me to telephone the FCC (Federal Communication Commission). I did that, followed the rep's instructions, and still no signal.

Karen agreed that Gus was facing a frustrating problem, but that many people using antennas on their TV sets have lost reception since the conversion from analog to digital in 2009.

A week later, Gus spoke to Karen again about his TV reception woes. He then asked Karen, "How about you coming over after work some night to help straighten out my TV problem? My wife and I would really appreciate your help. You're a great tech fixer."

Karen pondered for a moment, thinking that Gus was making an unreasonable demand. She replied, "Gus, let me think about your request. I really don't know a lot about TV reception. Also, I am pretty much tied up after work for a couple of weeks."

With a frown on his face, Gus said, "Karen, I know you can help. Please don't let me down."

Questions:

5.11 What do you see as any potential ethical issues in Gus's request that Karen attempt to fix his TV set reception problem?

5.12 What advice might you offer Karen for dealing with this problem?

5.13 How do Gus's demands fit into the category of expecting Karen to exhibit strong organizational citizenship behavior?

Human Relations Role-Playing Exercise 5–1

Dealing with an Unusual Request from the Boss

The case about the manager's request for tech support for his television set provides the background information for this role-play. The scenario is another meeting between Gus and Karen. One student plays the role of Gus, who is now increasingly frustrated that he cannot get the reception he wants. Just last week, he telephoned a television repair service and was told politely that he should simply hook up the set to cable or satellite TV. But Gus and his wife do not want any more wires running through their house. So this time, Gus is more insistent that Karen come over to his house to fix the problem.

Another person plays the role of Karen, who has thought through Gus's request some more, and she feels that his demand is both inappropriate and unethical. However, Karen still wants to maintain a good professional relationship with Gus.

Run the role-play for about five minutes. For both scenarios, observers rate the role-players on two dimensions, using a scale of 1 to 5 from very poor to very good. One dimension is "effective use of human relations techniques." The second dimension is "acting ability." A few observers might voluntarily provide feedback to the role-players in terms of sharing their ratings and observations. The course instructor might also provide feedback.

Human Relations Case Study 5–2

The Subprime Auto Loan Unit

Calvin is the director of the subprime auto loan unit of a large regional bank. He is aware the public, including politicians, do not take kindly to automobile loans issued to people with below-average credit ratings. He is also aware that Wells Fargo, one of the biggest banks in the country, has decided to reduce its exposure to subprime auto loans to 10 percent of all its auto loans. Yet Calvin also recognizes that subprime auto loans are important for many consumers. Today, he meets with a few members of his management team (Suzanne, Derek, and Gloria) to discuss his concerns.

Calvin: I am getting worried about our image. Let me tell you about some of my concerns. Our average interest rate for loans to our subprime and deep subprime loans is over 10 percent. Contrast this to rates of about 3.5 percent for our superprime and prime loans. We also know that the average interest paid for the life of the loan is about $9,000. Also, the repossession rate is climbing in recent months.

Suzanne: Calvin, you are the boss, but you are neglecting the reality of our loans. The majority of our customers would not be able to hold a job without personal transportation. If we don't lend them the money to purchase a car, they could not earn a paycheck. Our interest rates have to be high to cover our risks, but we enable many people to hold onto a job.

Derek: I, too, am concerned about our subprime and deep subprime loans. A few months after many of our customers purchase a vehicle, the loan is underwater. They owe more to us than their car is worth.

Gloria: Let's put this all in perspective. If the people who finance their vehicles through us could get low interest rates from a conventional bank or other lender, they would. We are the last resort for modest-income people with bad credit who need transportation.

Calvin: I agree that subprime and deep subprime loans do some good. But I have this uneasy feeling that we could be a little more ethical. Another problem is that the automobile dealers mark up the loans to give themselves an additional cut, so the auto buyers pay even higher interest rates and fees. Let's explore this issue a little more, later.

Questions

5.14 What ethical issues do you see in the unit of the bank in question making subprime and deep subprime loans at a much higher rate than loans granted to consumers with better credit ratings?

5.15 What recommendations can you make to Calvin so he would have less concern about issuing subprime and deep subprime loans?

Human Relations Role-Playing Exercise 5–2

Thinking through the Ethics of High-Cost Auto Loans

In this group role-play for four students, we have role-players for Calvin, Suzanne, Derek, and Gloria. The role-players examine the ethical issues of subprime and deep subprime loans. If any of the role-players are troubled by these auto loans to people with poor credit, they might offer a solution to the ethical problems.

Run the role-play for about five minutes. Observers rate the role-players on two dimensions, using a scale of 1 to 5 from very poor to very good. One dimension is "effective use of human relations techniques." The second dimension is "acting ability." A few observers might voluntarily provide feedback to the role-players in terms of sharing their ratings and observations. The course instructor might also provide feedback.

REFERENCES

1. Original story created from facts and observations in Bill Roberts, "Value-Driven HR," *HR Magazine*, March 2012, pp. 44–48; "About Juniper: The Juniper Way," www.juniper.net/us/en/company/profile/value/, p. 1, accessed March 6, 2015; "Corporate Culture Award of Distinction to Juniper Networks," *World's Most Ethical Companies Ranking*, www.peoplelink.com/blog/corporate-culture-award/, March 21, 2011, pp. 1–3; Dina Bass and Denni Hu, "Juniper CEO Resigns after Review over Customer Negotiation," www.bloomberg.com/news/articles, November 10, 2014, pp. 1–7.

2. Stephen Covey, *The 7 Habits of Highly Successful People* (New York: Free Press, 1989).

3. Ben Rand, "'On Track' at Kodak," *Democrat and Chronicle* (Rochester, NY), May 21, 2006, p. 4E.

4. Quoted in Judith Sills, "Kindness and Corporation," *Psychology Today*, March–April 2009, pp. 62–63.

5. David A. Lubin and Daniel C. Esty, "The Sustainability Imperative," *Harvard Business Review*, May 2010, pp. 42–50

6. Brian Stolle, "Core Values: How to Create a Sustainable Valuable High-Growth Company," *Forbes*, www.forbes.com, August 5, 2014, pp. 1–3; Jennifer Schramm, "Promoting Sustainability," *HR Magazine*, March 2001, p. 88.

7. Joanne Cole, "Building Heart and Soul," *HRfocus*, October 1998, pp. 9–10.

8. Douglas B. Richardson, "Know Thyself: An Easy Approach," Vault.com, 2012.

9. Brent W. Roberts, Oleksandr S. Chernyshenko, Stephen Stark, and Lewis R. Goldberg, "The Structure of Conscientiousness: An Empirical Investigation Based on Seven Major Personality Questionnaires," *Personnel Psychology*, Spring 2005, pp. 103–139.

10. A review of the evidence is Nicole N. Dudley et al., "A Meta-Analytic Investigation of Conscientiousness in the Prediction of Job Performance: Examining the Intercorrelations and the Incremental Validity of Narrow Traits," *Journal of Applied Psychology*, January 2006, pp. 40–57.

11. Opinion of Peter Cappelli cited in Erin White, "Age Is as Age Does: Making the Generation Gap Work for You," *The Wall Street Journal*, June 30, 2008, p. B6.

12. Sharon Jayson, "Tech Savvy 'iGeneration' Kids Multi-Task, Connect," *USA Today*, www.usatoday.com, February 10, 2010, p. 1; Max Mihelich, "Another Generation Rises," *Workforce Management*, May 2013, pp. 34–38.

13. Heather Huhman, "Avoiding Gen Y Stereotypes on the Job," *San Francisco Examiner* (www.examiner.com), December 3, 2008.

14. David C. McClelland, "How Motives, Skills, and Values Determine What People Do," *American Psychologist*, July 1985, p. 815.

15. Brian J. Hoffman, Bethany H. Bynum, Ronald F. Piccolo, and Ashley W. Sutton, "Person-Organization Value Congruence: How Transformational Leaders Influence Work Group Effectiveness," *Academy of Management Journal*, August 2011, pp. 779–796.

16. Linda K. Treviño and Katherine A. Nelson, *Managing Business Ethics: Straight Talk about How to Do It Right* (New York: Wiley, 1995), pp. 24–35; O. C. Ferrell, John Fraedrich, and Linda Ferrell, *Business Ethics: Ethical Decision Making and Cases*, 4th ed. (Boston: Houghton Mifflin, 2000), pp. 13–16; Anita Bruzzese, "Tools Take Ethics to the Real World," Gannett News Service, May 16, 2005.

17. Erin Kelly, "Unethical Behavior Is on Rise, Experts Fear," Gannett News Service, March 5, 2006.

18. Linda Klebe Treviño and Michael Brown, "Managing to Be Ethical: Debunking Five Business Ethics Myths," *Academy of Management Executive*, May 2004, pp. 69–82.

19. Celia Moore et al., "Why Employees Do Bad Things: Moral Disengagement and Unethical Organizational Behavior," *Personnel Psychology*, No. 1, 2012, pp. 1–48; Dean A. Shepherd, Holger Patzelt, and Robert A. Baron "'I Care about Nature but . . .': Disengaging Values in Assessing Opportunities That Cause Harm," *Academy of Management Journal*, October 2013, pp. 1251–1273.

20. Max H. Bazerman and Ann E. Tenbrunsel, "Ethical Breakdowns," *Harvard Business Review*, April 2011, p. 58.

21. "Survey: Workplace Misconduct at Historic Low," www.ethics.org, February 4, 2014, p. 1.

22. Joann S. Lublin, Joe Palazzolo, and Serena Ng, "Avon Near Settling U.S. Probe of Bribery," *The Wall Street Journal*, February 13, 2014, p. B1.

23. Jessica Hulett, "FiveFinger Shoes Owner? Come Get Your Refund" *Christian Science Monitor*, www.csmonitor.com, May 15, 2014, p. 1

24. Rebecca L. Greenbaum et al., "When the Customer Is Unethical: The Explanatory Role of Employee Emotional Exhaustion onto Work-Family Conflict, Relationship Conflict with Coworkers, and Job Neglect," *Journal of Applied Psychology*, November 2014, pp. 1188–1203.

25. Treviño and Nelson, *Managing Business Ethics*, pp. 47–64.

26. "Piracy Prevention," *Apple Legal Piracy Policy*, www.apple.com/legal, 2015, p. 1.

27. Phred Dvorak, "'Munchausen at Work': Employees Advance by Fixing Problems They Had Created," *The Wall Street Journal*, August 25, 2008, p. B4.

28. "Etc. Social Studies," *Bloomberg BusinessWeek*, February 4–February 10, 2013, p. 72.

29. Elizabeth E. Umphress, John B. Bingham, and Marie S. Mitchell, "Unethical Behavior in the Name of the Company: The Moderating Effect of Organizational Identification and Positive Reciprocity Beliefs on Unethical Pro-Organizational Behavior," *Journal of Applied Psychology*, July 2010, pp. 769–780.

30. Phillip London, *Character: The Ultimate Success Factor* (Jacksonville, FL: Fortis, 2013).

31. "The Six Pillars of Character®," https://charactercounts.org, © 2015, pp. 1–2.

32. Two such guides are James L. Bowditch and Anthony E. Buono, *A Primer of Organizational Behavior* (New York: Wiley, 2001), p. 4, and Curtis C. Verschoor, "What's Ethical? Here's a Simple Test," *Strategic Finance*, March 2000, p. 24.

33. Daniel J. Brass, Kenneth D. Butterfield, and Bruce C. Skaggs, "Relationships and Unethical Behavior: A Social Network

Perspective," *Academy of Management Review*, January 1998, pp. 14–31.

34. Daryl Koehn, "An Interview with William Griffin," www.stthom.edu/cbes/griffin.html. Accessed March 8, 2006.

35. Jean Thilmany, "Supporting Ethical Employees," *HR Magazine*, September 2007, p. 106.

36. Gary R. Weaver, Linda Klebe Treviño, and Bradley Agle, "'Somebody I Look Up To': Ethical Role Models in Organizations," *Organizational Dynamics*, Issue 4, 2005, pp. 313–330.

37. Dori Meinert, "Are You Listening?" *HR Magazine*, June 2014, pp. 58–66; Rick Bell, "Blowing the Whistle, Blowing Your Career," *Workforce*, December 2013, p. 12; Christina Rexrode and Timothy W. Martin, "Whistleblowers Score Big: Three Individuals, One Firm to Receive $170 Million in Bank of America Probe," *The Wall Street Journal*, December 20–21, 2014, p. B1.

CHAPTER 6

Problem Solving and Creativity

Fotolia

Outline

A few years ago in Australia, local Coca-Cola managers and ad agency representatives were brainstorming ideas for boosting the sales of Coke, which had gone sort of flat. The goal of the campaign would be to engage consumers in stores and online. An idea surfaced to distribute bottles and cans of Coke and Diet Coke with the 150 most popular names of teenagers and Millennials in Australia. The campaign, intended to be temporary, was labeled "Share a Coke." A small percentage of the Coca-Cola products were released with generic names, such as "Mom," "Dad," and "Mate." The first summer, Coke sold more than 250 million named bottles and cans in a country of under 23 million people. Driven by the success of the "Share a Coke" campaign, it soon spread to seventy countries. When the campaign hit the United States in 2014, sales of carbonated beverages for the Coca-Cola Co. rose 2 percent during the summer. The campaign used 250 first names, and the beverage containers also included warm terms such as "Friends," "BFF" (best friends forever), and "Family." Consumers were given the opportunity to type in any name they wanted on a Coca-Cola container posted on the company Facebook page and forward the photo to others.

Lucie Austin, one of the ad executives instrumental in launching the campaign, noted that having your name on a bottle or can of Coke is highly personal. She also said that the "Share a Coke" campaign capitalized on the global trends of self-expression and sharing in an emotional way. The success of "Share a Coke" suggests that it might be reintroduced in the future.[1]

The story about the successful Coca-Cola marketing campaign illustrates how creativity can be applied to business decisions. At the same time, the company's success with the campaign shows the importance of the human touch in attaining success in business. The general purpose of this chapter is to help you become a more effective and creative problem solver when working individually or within groups.

A **problem** is a gap between what exists and what you want to exist. If you are a website developer, and far fewer people are visiting your site than your company is hoping for, you have a problem. **Decision making** refers to choosing one alternative from the various alternative solutions that can be pursued. After exploring a number of possibilities for your website, you must choose one.

Learning Objectives ▶

After studying the information and doing the exercises in this chapter, you should be able to:

6.1 Understand how personal characteristics influence your ability to solve problems and make decisions.

6.2 Apply the problem-solving and decision-making steps to complex problems.

6.3 Summarize the characteristics of creative people.

6.4 Describe various ways of improving your creativity.

6.5 Know the basic steps in critical thinking.

6.6 Explain how multiple intelligences might help in problem solving and creativity.

Problem
gap between what exists and what you want to exist

Decision making
choosing one alternative from the various alternative solutions that can be pursued

◀ **Learning Objective 6.1** ▶

Personal Characteristics That Influence Your Problem-Solving Ability

Many personal characteristics influence the type of problem solver and decision maker you are or are capable of becoming. Fortunately, some personal characteristics that influence your decision-making ability can be improved through conscious effort. For instance, if you make bad decisions because you do not concentrate on the details of the problem, you can gradually learn to concentrate better. Most of the personal characteristics described next can be strengthened through the appropriate education, training, and self-discipline. Figure 6-1 outlines these characteristics.

COGNITIVE INTELLIGENCE, EDUCATION, AND EXPERIENCE

In general, if you are intelligent, well educated, and well experienced, you will make better decisions than people without these attributes. (The term *cognitive intelligence* refers to the intellectual, or traditional, type of intelligence that is necessary for such tasks as solving math problems and conjugating verbs.) Cognitive intelligence helps because, by definition, intelligence denotes the ability to solve problems. Education improves the problem-solving and decision-making process because it gives you a background of principles and facts on which to rely.

Experience facilitates decision making because good decisions tend to be made by people who have already faced similar situations in the past. All things being equal, would you prefer to take your computer problem to an experienced or an inexperienced specialist? Or what about flying with an experienced airline pilot?

EMOTIONAL INTELLIGENCE

Being able to deal effectively with your feelings and emotions and those of others can help you make better decisions. A worker with high emotional intelligence

FIGURE 6-1

INFLUENCES ON PROBLEM-SOLVING SKILL

Source: "INFLUENCES ON PROBLEM-SOLVING SKILL" by Andrew J. DuBrin.

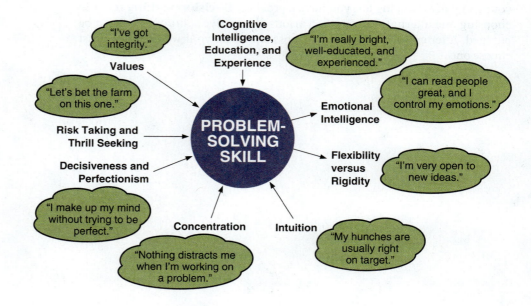

would be able to engage in such behaviors as sizing up people, pleasing others, and influencing them.

Emotional intelligence is important for decision making because how effective you are in managing your feelings and reading those of other people can affect the quality of your decisions. For example, if you cannot control your anger, you are likely to make decisions that are motivated by retaliation, hostility, and revenge. An example would be shouting and swearing at your team leader because of a work assignment you received. Your emotional intelligence could also influence your career decision making. If you understand your own feelings, you are more likely to enter an occupation or accept a position that matches your true attitude.

Another part of emotional intelligence related to problem solving is that contrary to common belief, experiencing intense emotions can facilitate decision making. Instead of attempting to block your emotions, you allow them to surface to facilitate making sharper decisions. A study with 101 members of stock investment clubs found that the investors who experienced more intense feelings achieved higher decision-making performance. Among the dozens of emotions and feelings recorded were "happy," "enthusiastic," "nervous," and "depressed." An equally important finding was that investors who were better able to identify and distinguish among their current feelings made better investment decisions. Understanding their feelings apparently enhanced their ability to control possible biases induced by these feelings.[2] For example, you might have exceptionally positive feelings about any company that directly assists animals, such as a pet food manufacturer. If you are aware of these feelings, it could prevent you from making the mistake of investing in a poorly managed dog and cat food company based on your love of animals.

FLEXIBILITY VERSUS RIGIDITY

Some people are successful problem solvers and decision makers because they approach every problem with a fresh outlook. They are able to avoid developing rigid viewpoints. Flexible thinking enables the problem solver to think of original—and therefore creative—alternative solutions to solving a problem. Another perspective on the same issue is that being open-minded helps a person solve problems well. In recent years, several major retailers have become more flexible in their thinking about inner cities as profitable locations for their stores.

INTUITION

Effective decision makers do not rely on careful analysis alone. Instead, they also use their **intuition**, an experience-based way of knowing or reasoning in which weighing and balancing of evidence are done automatically. Judgments and decisions reached through intuition are rapid, and they are largely unconscious; we are not completely aware of how we reached the decision.[3] Intuition appears to be composed of the interplay between knowing (intuition-as-expertise) and sensing (intuition-as-feeling). The best use of intuition, therefore, involves both bringing past facts in mind to deal with the situation and a sudden emotional hunch at the same time.[4] An experienced real estate developer might look at an old building and within ten minutes decide it would be a good investment to rehabilitate the structure. Based on hundreds of property evaluations, the developer knows that rehabilitating an old building can be profitable. At the same time, the developer visualizes what the old building would look like when rehabilitated.

Tim Cook, the CEO of Apple Inc., provides a useful insight into intuition. He explains that intuition is extremely critical in his job. According to Cook, the most important things in life, whether they are professional or personal, are decided on intuition. Although quantitative analysis is helpful, the decisions in life that are the most important are "gut calls."[5]

Intuition
an experience-based way of knowing or reasoning in which weighing and balancing of evidence are done automatically

Despite its merits, intuition has its drawbacks. Our hunches based on the combination of experience and emotion can sometimes lead us astray when a more analytical approach would have led to a better decision. For example, a charming and articulate job candidate might be chosen mostly on the basis of intuition. A background check based on rational analysis might have revealed that the candidate is a procrastinator and a criminal. One way to improve intuition is to get feedback on the decisions we make, so we can sharpen future decisions.[6] For example, a credit analyst in a bank profits from feedback about the future payment records of the loans he or she approved.

CONCENTRATION

Flow experience
total absorption in work; when flow occurs, things seem to go just right

Mental concentration is an important contributor to making good decisions. Many people who solve problems poorly do so because they are too distracted to immerse themselves in the problem at hand. In contrast, effective problem solvers often achieve the **flow experience**, total absorption in their work. When flow occurs, things seem to go just right. The person feels alive and fully attentive to what he or she is doing. As a byproduct of the flow experience, a good solution to a problem may surface. If you fail to concentrate hard enough, you may overlook an important detail that could affect the outcome of the decision. For example, a person about to purchase an automobile might be excited about the high gas mileage but forget to check the vehicle's ability to withstand a crash. A major factor affecting your ability to concentrate is how well rested you are. Being well rested helps you concentrate more, and being sleep deprived lowers concentration.[7] Negative stress can also adversely affect concentration, resulting in poorer decisions.

The accompanying self-assessment quiz gives you an opportunity to think about your ability to concentrate and focus.

DECISIVENESS AND PERFECTIONISM

Some people are ill suited to solving problems and making decisions because they are fearful of committing themselves to any given course of action. "Gee, I'm not sure, what do you think?" is their typical response to a decision forced on them. If you are indecisive, this characteristic will have to be modified if you are to become successful in your field. A manager has to decide which person to hire. And a photographer has to decide which setting is best for the subject. The combination of being indecisive and a perfectionist can lead to procrastination. Also, being a procrastinator can make one indecisive. Perfectionism contributes to delayed decision making because the person keeps working on a project before deciding to submit it to somebody else.

RISK TAKING AND THRILL SEEKING

The need for taking risks and seeking thrills is yet another personality characteristic that influences problem-solving skill. For some types of problems, the high-risk taker and thrill seeker is at an advantage. For example, an information technology specialist might have to engage in a risky maneuver to salvage data from a crashed hard drive. Risk taking and thrill seeking can also lead to poor problem solving and decision making, such as a merchandiser buying a huge inventory of a highly original fashion. The experienced decision maker needs to know when to take high risks and seek thrills and when to be more conservative.

Another influence on decision making related to risk is the common tendency to focus on avoiding loss—or being averse to taking a risk. According to the Nobel Prize–winning research of Daniel Kahneman and Amos Tverseky, an individual's response to loss is much more intense than his or her response to gains. This is one reason why so many people are tempted to hold onto a losing stock or refuse to leave a casino despite a long losing streak.[8]

Human Relations Self-Assessment Quiz   6-1

A Checklist of Behaviors and Attitudes Reflecting Good Concentration and Focus

Attitude or Behavior	Yes	No
1. I rarely miss a deadline on a work project.	❏	❏
2. When I begin a work activity, I am able to get started almost immediately.	❏	❏
3. When I am introduced to a person for the first time, I usually catch his or her name clearly.	❏	❏
4. I rarely read an entire news article from a print or electronic newspaper.	❏	❏
5. I find messages longer than a tweet difficult to follow.	❏	❏
6. I haven't read an entire book, except when reading a book was required for a course.	❏	❏
7. I have been able to perform well in a mental activity such as playing poker, chess, or checkers or doing a crossword puzzle.	❏	❏
8. I am good at spotting typographical and spelling errors while I am reading.	❏	❏
9. It is difficult for me to watch a movie, television, program, or sporting event without sending a tweet or a social media post about every five minutes.	❏	❏
10. I enjoy activities that force me to concentrate, such as meditation or yoga.	❏	❏
11. A few minutes after meeting a person for the first time, I can recall the color of his or her eyes.	❏	❏
12. I rarely ever lose or misplace items such as keys, handbag or wallet, gloves, or smartphone.	❏	❏
13. I have considerable difficulty in sticking with one activity for more than ten minutes.	❏	❏
14. While at the grocery store or supermarket, I usually neglect to purchase one or two items even if they are on my shopping list.	❏	❏
15. It is easy for me to listen carefully to the words when my national anthem is being played, such as at a sporting event.	❏	❏
16. I can fall asleep readily by thinking intently about something.	❏	❏
17. It is uncomfortable for me to have a meal without background noise, such as a television show, the radio, or other people talking around me.	❏	❏
18. At work or at play, I am so focused on what I am doing it seems that I am wearing blinders, as do horses.	❏	❏
19. I enjoy studying the details of whatever I am doing.	❏	❏
20. I spend far too much time trying to find electronic or paper documents.	❏	❏

Scoring and Interpretation:

The answers suggesting good concentration and focus are as follows:

1. Yes	6. No	11. Yes	16. Yes
2. Yes	7. Yes	12. Yes	17. No
3. Yes	8. Yes	13. No	18. Yes
4. No	9. No	14. No	19. Yes
5. No	10. Yes	15. Yes	20. No

The higher you scored out of the twenty questions, the more likely it is that you have good concentration and focus. Also, if it was a struggle for you to complete the checklist, you may have a problem with concentration and focus.

Source: "A Checklist of Behaviors and Attitudes Reflecting Good Concentration and Focus" by Andrew J. DuBrin.

VALUES OF THE DECISION MAKER

Values influence decision making at every step. The right values for the situation will improve problem solving and decision making, whereas the wrong values will lead to poor decisions. Ultimately, all decisions are based on values. A manager who places a high value on the well-being of employees tries to avoid alternatives that create hardships for workers. Another value that significantly influences problem solving and decision making is the pursuit of excellence. A worker who embraces the pursuit of excellence (and is therefore conscientious) will search for the high-quality alternative solution.

▶ **Learning Objective 6.2** ▶

The Problem-Solving and Decision-Making Steps

Whatever complex problem you face, it is best to use the standard problem-solving and decision-making steps as a guide. These steps are similar to the systematic approach used in the scientific method and also contribute to critical thinking as explained later in the chapter. Figure 6-2 summarizes the steps involved in problem solving and decision making. It assumes that problem solving should take place in an orderly flow of steps. Paying attention to this model is important because deviating too far will often result in decision failure, such as not exploring enough options before choosing to pursue a course of action.

Although the problem-solving and decision-making steps appear logical, we emphasize again that people are frequently not entirely rational when making decisions. Emotions and personality traits can cloud decision making.

FIGURE 6-2

PROBLEM-SOLVING AND DECISION-MAKING STEPS

Source: "PROBLEM-SOLVING AND DECISION-MAKING STEPS" by Andrew J. DuBrin.

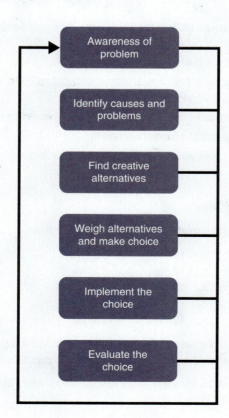

BE AWARE OF THE PROBLEM OR OPPORTUNITY

Problem solving and decision making begin when somebody is aware that a problem exists. In most decision-making situations, problems are assigned to a person. At other times, people create their own problems to solve, or they find problems. Scotch tape had its origins in 1930, when somebody noticed a problem. The story goes like this:

> Richard Drew, a banjo-playing engineer, was working for the Minnesota Mining and Manufacturing Co. (3M today), whose only product at the time was sandpaper. Drew was product testing one brand of sandpaper at a local body shop when he noticed that car painters were having trouble making clean dividing lines on two-color paint jobs. In 1925, as a solution to the problem, Drew invented a masking tape using crepe paper with lines of pressure-sensitive glue running along the edges. A problem encountered was that the tape kept falling off.
>
> An automotive painter told a 3M representative to "Take this tape back to those Scotch [negative stereotype that Scotch people are cheap] bosses of yours and tell them to put more adhesive on it." The bosses did, the tape worked, and the name was soon applied to the entire line of 3M tapes. Five years later, Drew overcame numerous production hurdles and developed the Scotch Brand Cellulose Tape that has become a worldwide staple. The first trial shipment of the new tape was sent to a Chicago firm specializing in package printing for bakery products. The response to the new cellulose tape was so positive that it was introduced to the market.[9]

After you are aware that a problem exists or have identified it, recognize that it may represent an important opportunity. If you are bothered enough by a problem facing your company, you might volunteer to be the person in charge of overcoming the problem. A related possibility is that sometimes you can begin solving a problem by recognizing an opportunity for its resolution. After three decades of working as an information technology professional, Bill Skees wanted to open a bookstore. He found that finding a suitable location was a big hurdle. Then one day, while walking around a town in northern New Jersey, he spotted an old karate studio for rent. Skees said the place was a mess but was on a busy street with adequate parking. After investing considerable time and energy in remodeling, Well Read New & Used Books was born.[10]

IDENTIFY CAUSES OF THE PROBLEM

The causes of problems should be diagnosed and clarified before any action is taken because they are not always what they seem to be on the surface. Some may be more complicated than suspected or may even be the wrong problem you need to solve in a particular situation.

Even when you have identified the general source of a problem, you may still need to dig further as to what, when, and where a problem *did not* occur. Suppose a friend talks about a fear of public speaking. By asking a few "but not" questions, you might be able to identify a major cause of the problem. Let's try out the method:

Your friend: I'm horribly afraid of public speaking. I hate going up in front of class.

You: But have you ever not been afraid of speaking to a group of people?

Your friend: Yes, I can remember once feeling okay speaking at a victory dinner for my high school soccer team. We came in first place in the region.

You: What did you talk about?

Your friend: I told a cute story about how my mother and father put a soccer ball in my crib. I hugged it every day like it was a teddy bear.

You: So why weren't you afraid of giving that talk?

Your friend: I knew what I was talking about. I didn't have to rehearse.

You: What else was different about the talk?

Your friend:	It wasn't like talking to strangers. I was just there with my buddies and our coaches.
You:	What you are really telling me is that public speaking is okay when you are well prepared and you are in comfortable surroundings?
Your friend:	Thanks for helping me understand my problem.

The accompanying Human Relations in Practice insert presents a classic example of recognizing the true problem.

FIND CREATIVE ALTERNATIVES

Creativity and imagination enter into problem solving and decision making. Successful decision makers have the ability to think of different alternatives. The person who pushes to find

Human Relations in Practice

The True Subarctic Oil Problem Gets Defined

Twenty years had elapsed since the 1989 *Exxon Valdez* oil spill, and cleanup crews were still struggling. Twenty-six thousand gallons of oil remained at the bottom of Prince William Sound. Multiple attempts to remove the oil from the sea had failed, including high-pressure hot water and mechanical cleanup with booms and skimmers. The problem was that because the petroleum was lying on the cold Arctic seabed, it was too viscous (sticky) to pump from barges to offshore collection stations. The Oil Spill Recovery Institute, a nonprofit organization established by the U.S. Congress, was called in to work on the problem. The institute framed it as one of "materials viscosity" rather than "oil cleanup." To attract a wider range of novel, potential solutions to the problem, the institute used language not specific to the petroleum industry.

The problem was posted in 2007, with the challenge of figuring out a way of separating frozen oil from water on the oil spill recovery barges. Within three months, more than two dozen potentially useful solutions from the entire world were submitted. The winning solution came from John Davis, a chemist in the cement industry. He had experience in pouring concrete, using a tool that vibrates the construction material to keep it in liquid form so it flows easily into cracks and crevices. He received $20,000 for his suggestion to modify commercially available construction equipment that would vibrate the frozen oil in order to keep it liquid and therefore possible to pump from the barges.

Davis, a habitual problem solver, said he thrives on the satisfaction of creating solutions to seemingly unsolvable problems. He donated part of his prize to research about environmental cleanup, and he used another part to fly to Alaska to observe his innovation in action.

Questions:

What was the true problem that needed to be defined? How can you use this classic story to help you refine your problem-solving skills?

Source: Original story created from facts and observations in the following sources: Dwayne Spradlin, "Are You Solving the Right Problem?" *Harvard Business Review,* September 2012, p. 90; Spradlin, "Are You Solving the Right Problem?" *Créativité Québec,* www.creativitequebec.ca, 2012, pp. 7–8; "Open Innovation: Exxon Valdez Cleanup," *IdeaConnection, Ltd.,* www.ideaconnection.com © 2007–2015, pp. 1–2.

one more alternative to a problem is often the person who finds a breakthrough solution. The more alternatives you generate, the more likely you are to find a useful solution to your problem. In the words of business strategy expert and consultant Gary Hamel, "Innovation is a numbers game. It takes 1,000 wacky ideas to find 100 things worth putting any money at all on, to find 10 ideas worth really investing in, to wind up with one really great idea."[11]

The personality trait of persistence is helpful in chasing down alternatives to your problem. Imagine that you are starting a small business on your own, and you need outside funding. Because so many people want to fund a business startup, you will have to chase down many possibilities. Conducting a thorough Internet search will be part of your persistence. A thorough Internet search includes using several different search terms, and using only the most popular search engine, Google. You also need to be flexible enough in your thinking when an unusual alternative presents itself, such as the man described above who located a site for his proposed bookstore in an old karate studio.

WEIGH ALTERNATIVES AND MAKE THE CHOICE

This stage refers simply to examining the pros and cons of the various alternatives in the previous stages and then making a choice. In a major decision, each alternative would have to be given serious consideration. The essence of decision making is selecting the right course of action to follow. You have to choose an alternative, even if it is not to go ahead with a new plan of action. For instance, after conducting a job campaign, you could decide *not* to change jobs. Instead of coming to a decision, some people overanalyze a problem. Do you suffer from "analysis paralysis," or do you make up your mind after a reasonable amount of thought?

In choosing an alternative, it is helpful to remember that most problems really have multiple solutions. You therefore do not have to be overly concerned with finding the only correct answer to your problem. For instance, there might be several effective ways of reducing the costs of running a department.

Another useful consideration about choices is that it is best to reduce the number of possible choices you have to make. With too many choices, you might freeze in terms of decision making, such as trying to choose one among fifteen different television sets. Psychology professor Barry Schwartz of Swarthmore College notes that as we face more and more options we become overloaded: "Choice no longer liberates, but debilitates. It might even be said to tyrannize."[12]

IMPLEMENT THE CHOICE

After you decide which course of action to take, you have to put the choice into effect. Some decisions are more difficult to implement than others. Decisions made by top management, for example, are sometimes so difficult to implement that they have to be reversed. An executive at a major online retailer announced a new policy that all customer problems would have to be resolved by e-mail and that the toll-free number for customer assistance would be disbanded. Hundreds of customers complained about the new policy by e-mail, and many customer accounts became inactive. The executive reconsidered the decision in terms of its effect on customer service and goodwill and reinstated the toll-free line. The general point is that in implementing many decisions, you must take the human element into consideration.

EVALUATE THE CHOICE

Decision making is not complete until the decision has been evaluated. Evaluation may take a considerable period of time because the results of your decision are not always immediately apparent. Suppose you receive two job offers. It might take several months to a year to determine whether you are satisfied with the job you accepted. It would be necessary to look at the factors you think are most important in a job. Among them might be "Is there opportunity for advancement?" "Are the people here friendly?" "Is the work interesting?"

Evaluating your choice would be further complicated by the difficulty of determining how you might have fared in the job you didn't accept. Now and then, you might obtain some information to suggest what that alternative held in store for you, as did a woman who turned down a job offer with a new and promising company. She questioned that decision until she read one morning a year later that the company had gone into bankruptcy.

What happens when your evaluation of a decision is negative? You go back to the drawing board, as the line and arrow on the left-hand side of Figure 6-2 indicate. Because your first decision was not a good one, you are faced with another problem situation. A helpful decision-making aid is to visualize what you would do if the alternative you chose proved to be dreadful, the **worst-case scenario**. Suppose, for example, you choose a job that proves to be unsuited to your talents. Would you resign as soon as your mistake became apparent, or would you sweat it out for a year to show some employment stability? Or would you retain the job while starting to look for a more suitable job? Developing a worst-case-scenario plan helps prevent you from becoming overwhelmed by a bad decision. Closely related to the worst-case scenario is establishing an **exit strategy** that determines in advance how you will get out of a bad decision, such as having joined a failing family business.

Worst-case scenario
helpful decision-making aid that involves visualizing what you would do if the alternative chosen proved to be dreadful

Exit strategy
determining in advance how to get out of a bad decision, such as having joined a failing family business

Creativity in Decision Making

Creativity is helpful at any stage of problem solving but is essential for being aware of problems, analyzing their causes, and searching for alternative solutions. Simply put, **creativity** is the ability to develop good ideas that can be put into action. Finding a creative idea usually involves a flash of insight as to how to solve a problem, such as that experienced by the person who thought of Scotch tape. The flash of insight might take place at your workplace or while you are engaged in other activity, such as jogging, walking, showering, or watching a movie. If you are aware that you have a problem to solve, the sudden insight is more likely to flash into your mind. For example, you might want to solve the problem of adding a couple more influential people to your network. So while you are taking out the garbage, the names of a couple of potential contacts might surface in your brain. Your mind has been working on your problem below your level of awareness.

When many people see or hear the word *creativity*, they think of a rarefied talent. A more helpful perspective is to recognize that not all creativity requires wild imagination. The emphasis here is on creativity applied to business and personal life rather than on creativity in science, technology, and the arts.

A major theme of this chapter is that the vast majority of people can improve their creativity. Creativity can be taught, learned, enhanced, and mastered. Current thinking is that creativity is a skill rather than a trait we inherit. In the words of two executives from a creativity firm who are also college professors, "Creativity is an activity you practice, not exclusively an inborn talent."[13] Creativity is highly valued in the workplace because it precedes **innovation**, the commercialization or implementation of creative ideas. A global positioning system (GPS) for consumer vehicles was a creative idea, but it was not truly innovative until it became a product on the market. Recognize, however, that *creativity* and *innovation* are sometimes used almost as synonyms.

Creativity
the ability to develop good ideas that can be put into action

Imagination is a very special thing, and we always try to find students with that ability.

—David Greenberg

Senior Vice President, human resources, for L'Oréal USA. Quoted in *The Wall Street Journal*, September 12, 2006, p. B8.

Innovation
the commercialization or implementation of creative ideas

MEASURING YOUR CREATIVE POTENTIAL

One way to understand creativity is to think through your tendencies toward having creative potential, such as in Human Relations Self-Assessment Quiz 6-2.

Human Relations Self-Assessment Quiz 6-2

Creative Personality Test

Answer each of the following statements as mostly true or mostly false. We are looking for general trends, so do not be concerned that under certain circumstances, your answer might be different in response to a particular statement.

	Mostly True	Mostly False
1. I think movies based on fictional stories are a waste of time, so I am more likely to watch a documentary.	____	____
2. You have to admit that some crooks are ingenious.	____	____
3. I pretty much wear the same style and colors of clothing regularly.	____	____
4. To me, most issues have a clear-cut right side or wrong side.	____	____
5. I enjoy it when my boss hands me vague instructions.	____	____
6. When I'm surfing the Internet, I sometimes investigate topics about which I know very little.	____	____
7. Leisure activities without a known purpose have very little appeal to me.	____	____
8. Taking a different route to work is fun, even if it takes longer.	____	____
9. From time to time, I have made friends with people of a different sex, race, religion, or ethnic background from myself.	____	____
10. Rules and regulations should be respected, but deviating from them once in a while is acceptable.	____	____
11. People who know me say that I have an excellent sense of humor.	____	____
12. I have been known to play practical jokes or pranks on people.	____	____
13. Writers should avoid using unusual words and word combinations.	____	____
14. Detective work would have some appeal to me.	____	____
15. I am much more likely to tell a rehearsed joke than make a witty comment.	____	____
16. Almost all advertising on television bores me.	____	____
17. Why write letters or send e-mail and text greetings to friends when there are so many clever greeting cards already available in the stores or online?	____	____
18. For most important problems in life, there is one best solution available.	____	____
19. Pleasing myself means more to me than pleasing others.	____	____
20. I'm enjoying taking this test.	____	____

Scoring and Interpretation:

Give yourself a plus 1 for each answer scored in the creative direction as follows:

1. Mostly False
2. Mostly True
3. Mostly False
4. Mostly False
5. Mostly True
6. Mostly True
7. Mostly False
8. Mostly True
9. Mostly True
10. Mostly True
11. Mostly True
12. Mostly True
13. Mostly False
14. Mostly True
15. Mostly False
16. Mostly False
17. Mostly False
18. Mostly False
19. Mostly True
20. Mostly True

A score of 15 or more suggests that your personality and attitudes are similar to those of a creative person. A score of between 9 and 14 suggests an average similarity with the personality and attitudes of a creative person. A score of 8 or less suggests that your personality is dissimilar to that of a creative person. You are probably more of a conformist and not highly open-minded in your thinking at this point in your life. To become more creative, you may need to develop more flexibility in your thinking and a higher degree of open-mindedness.

Source: "Creative Personality Test" by Andrew J. DuBrin.

▶ **Learning Objective 6.3** ▶

CHARACTERISTICS OF CREATIVE WORKERS

Creative workers tend to have different intellectual and personality characteristics from their less creative counterparts. Creative people are more mentally flexible than others, which allows them to overcome the traditional ways of looking at problems. The characteristics of creative workers can be grouped into three broad areas: knowledge, intellectual abilities, and personality.[14]

Knowledge

Creative thinking requires a broad background of information, including facts and observations. Knowledge supplies the building blocks for generating and combining ideas. This is particularly true because, according to some experts, creativity always comes down to combining things in a new and different way. A team of innovation researchers found that the most important discovery skill of a cognitive nature is the associating, defined as making connections, across seemingly unrelated fields. You can therefore become more creative by searching for associations.[15] For example, a smart watch combines such elements as a wristwatch, a smartphone, and a camera.

Intellectual Abilities

Insight
an ability to know what information is relevant, to find connections between the old and the new, to combine facts that are unrelated, and to see the "big picture"

Exceptionally high intelligence is not required to be creative, but creative people are good at generating alternative solutions to problems in a short period of time. According to Robert Sternberg, a professor of human development at Cornell University, the key to creative intelligence is **insight**, an ability to know what information is relevant, to find connections between the old and the new, to combine facts that are unrelated, and to see the "big picture."[16] (Again, the importance of combining ideas is emphasized.)

Creative people are able to think divergently. They can expand the number of alternatives to a problem, thus moving away from a single solution. Yet the creative thinker also knows when it is time to think convergently, narrowing the number of useful solutions. For example, the divergent thinker might think of twenty-seven different names for a website to sell high-fashion buttons. Yet, at some point, he or she will have to converge toward choosing the best name, such as www.chicbutton.com.

Personality

Creative self-efficacy
the belief that one has the knowledge and skills to produce creative outcomes

Creative people tend to have a positive self-image without being blindly self-confident. The self-confidence associated with worker creativity has been labeled **creative self-efficacy**, the belief that one has the knowledge and skills to produce creative outcomes. Creative self-efficacy is therefore a key psychological mechanism that supports solving problems creatively.[17] The marketing manager at MasterCard might say to her staff, "We have the same old problem. Only about 15 percent of the world's purchases are made with a credit card. How can we capture more of the 85 percent?" A staff member with high creative self-efficacy might respond, "Please let me form a small task force to work on this problem for a week. We will find you the answer you need."

The contribution of self-confidence to creativity was demonstrated in a study of a variety of employees and their supervisors in an agricultural processing firm. The study found that individuals who expected their ideas to be accepted increased their odds of having their ideas implemented. The odds of getting ideas accepted was also found to be higher for individuals who had the self-confidence and interpersonal skills of developing a network of people who would support their ideas.[18]

Creative people have the ability to tolerate the isolation necessary for developing ideas. Talking to others is a good source of ideas. Yet, at some point, the creative problem solver has to work alone and concentrate.

THE CONDITIONS NECESSARY FOR CREATIVITY

Creativity is not simply a random occurrence. Well-known creativity researcher and professor of business administration at Harvard Business School, Teresa M. Amabile, summarized twenty-two years of her research about creativity in the workplace. Her findings are also supported by others.[19] Creativity takes place when three components come together: expertise, creative thinking skills, and the right type of motivation. *Expertise* refers to the necessary knowledge to put facts together. The more ideas floating around in your head, the more likely you are to combine them in some useful way, as already described.

Creative thinking skills refers to how flexibly and imaginatively individuals approach problems. If you know how to keep digging for alternatives and to avoid getting stuck in the status quo, your chances of being creative multiply. Along these same lines, you are much more likely to be creative if you are intentionally seeking ideas, such as always being on the lookout for ways to save money. Persevering, or sticking with a problem to a conclusion, is essential for finding creative solutions. A few rest breaks to gain a fresh perspective may be helpful, but the creative person keeps coming back until a solution emerges. Or the creative idea might surface outside of the work setting, as described earlier.

The right type of *motivation* is the third essential ingredient for creative thought. A fascination with or passion for the task is much more important than searching for external rewards. Passion for the task and high intrinsic motivation contribute to a total absorption in the work and intense concentration, resulting in the flow experience. A creative businessperson, such as an entrepreneur developing a plan for worldwide distribution of a product, will often achieve the experience of flow. One analysis of creativity suggests that hard work and the love of the task can be at least as important as raw talent in ensuring creative success.[20] In addition to the internal conditions that foster creativity, five factors outside the person are key:

1. **An environmental need must stimulate the setting of a goal.** This is another way of saying, "Necessity is the mother of invention." For example, over a decade ago, independent hardware stores were faced with the challenge of large chains, such as Home Depot and Lowe's, driving them out of business. Many of these independent stores survived by forming buying alliances with each other so that they could purchase inventory in larger quantities—and therefore at lower prices. The independents also emphasize doing home repairs, such as fixing ripped screens and broken windows.

2. **Another condition that fosters creativity is enough conflict and tension to put people on edge.** The conflicts should be about ideas, not personality conflicts and name-calling. For example, a group member should be given time to defend his or her work, and then the ideas should be sharply criticized by the other group members.[21]

3. **Another external factor for creativity is encouragement, including a permissive atmosphere that welcomes new ideas.** A manager or team leader who encourages imagination and original thinking and does not punish people for making honest mistakes is likely to receive creative ideas from people. W. L. Gore is often cited among the world's most innovative companies. You may be familiar with their waterproof fabrics and guitar strings. The cornerstone of Gore's innovative culture has been a permissive atmosphere.[22]

4. **Humor is a key environmental condition for enhancing creativity.** Humor has always been linked to creativity. Humor gets the creative juices flowing, and effective humor requires creativity. Thomas Edison started every workday with a joke-telling session. Mike Vance, chair of the Creative Thinking Association of America, says, "Humor is unmasking the hypocritical. What makes us laugh often is seeing

how things are screwed up—then sometimes seeing how we can fix them. Whenever I go into a company and don't hear much laughter, I know it's not a creative place."[23]

5. **A positive mood often contributes to creativity.** Many people are at their creative problem-solving best, when in a good mood, but the relationship between mood and creativity is not so clear-cut. A study of over 200 employees in three high-tech industries found that a positive mood contributed to creativity.[24] A more recent study of the relationship between creativity and mood was conducted with Australian students working on their doctoral theses. It was found that a positive mood had the strongest link with creativity when students have the goal of competing favorably with others, and supervisory support is strong.[25]

Despite the theme of permissiveness in several of the conditions for enhancing creativity, constraints also have their place. Individuals or teams with budget constraints and time constraints sometimes find that these constraints help them rise to the occasion. Marissa Ann Mayer, CEO of Yahoo!, contends that constraints can actually speed product development. The people at Google often get a sense of just how good a new concept is if they simply prototype it (try it out) for a single day or week. Another constraint would be limiting team size to two or three people.[26]

▶ Learning Objective 6.4 ▶

Improving Your Creativity

Because of the importance of creative problem solving, many techniques have been developed to improve creativity. The goal of these experiences is to think like a creative problem solver. Such a person lets his or her imagination wander. He or she ventures beyond the constraints that limit most people. The result of thinking more creatively is to bring something new into existence. *Something new* can be a totally new creation or a combination of existing things and ideas. The new design of containers for prescription medicine is a representative example. Old prescription bottles were difficult to open and read, whereas the new prescription bottles are color-coded to specific medicines and easy to read and open. Nevertheless, many of the older-style prescription bottles are still in use.

BELIEVE THAT YOU CAN BE CREATIVE

As implied by creative self-efficacy, a starting point in increasing your creativity is to believe that you can. Acknowledge that you can solve problems with more imagination if you approach them with a different mindset. You can work up the confidence to solve a major problem creatively if you start small. For example, you might participate in an online forum to help develop a new idea for improving a product or service.[27]

CONCENTRATE INTENSELY ON THE TASK AT HAND

The ability to concentrate was mentioned earlier as a characteristic that contributes to effective problem solving in general. The ability to eliminate distractions also contributes mightily to generating new ideas. At times, we think we are thinking intently about our problem, yet in reality, we may be thinking about something that interferes with creativity. Among the office distractions that interfere with concentration are phone calls, a computer beep informing you of an incoming message, a person in the next cubicle talking loudly on the phone, and a friendly hello from a work associate walking past your cubicle. All the methods that follow for creativity enhancement require concentration.

OVERCOME TRADITIONAL MENTAL SETS

An important consequence of becoming more intellectually flexible is that you can overcome a **traditional mental set**, a fixed way of thinking about objects and activities. Overcoming traditional mental sets is important because the major block to creativity is to perceive things in a traditional way. All creative examples presented so far in this chapter have involved this process, and here is another one. An effective way of overcoming a traditional mental set (or thinking outside the box) is to challenge the status quo. If you want to develop an idea that will impress your boss or turn around an industry, you must use your imagination. Question the old standby that things have always been done in a particular way.

Traditional mental set
fixed way of thinking about objects
and activities

CONDUCT BRAINSTORMING AND BRAINWRITING SESSIONS

The best-known method of improving creativity is **brainstorming**, a technique by which group members think of multiple solutions to a problem. Using brainstorming, a group of six people might sit around a table generating new ideas for a product. During the idea-generating part of brainstorming, potential solutions are not criticized or evaluated in any way. In this way, spontaneity is encouraged. Brainstorming continues as a standard procedure for producing creative ideas in all types of organizations. If you engage in brainstorming on the job or in your personal life, you will be both solving a real problem and enhancing your creative thinking skills at the same time. Rules for brainstorming are presented in Figure 6-3. Brainstorming has many variations, including individuals submitting ideas via e-mail or a shared web page, and brainwriting.

Brainstorming
technique by which group members
think of multiple solutions to a problem

An important strategy for enhancing the outcome of brainstorming is to have intellectually and culturally diverse group members. Some group leaders purposely choose people of different problem-solving styles to encourage more diverse thinking. The logical type might have more "brainstorms" based on facts, whereas the intuitive type might have more brainstorms based on hunches. Cultural diversity is likely to improve brainstorming because people with different cultural experiences often bring different viewpoints to bear on the problem. A basic example is that when developing new food products, members with different ethnic backgrounds are chosen for a brainstorming group.

1. Use groups of about five to seven people.
2. Encourage the spontaneous expression of ideas. All suggestions are welcome, even if they are outlandish or outrageous. The least workable ideas can be edited out when the idea generation phase is completed.
3. Quantity and variety are very important. The greater the number of ideas, the greater the likelihood of a breakthrough idea.
4. Encourage combination and improvement of ideas. This process is referred to as *piggybacking* or *hitchhiking*.
5. One person serves as the secretary and records the ideas, perhaps posting them on a whiteboard or a computer with a projection device.
6. Do not overstructure by following any of the preceding rules too rigidly. Brainstorming is a spontaneous process.

FIGURE 6-3

RULES AND GUIDELINES FOR BRAINSTORMING

Source: "RULES AND GUIDELINES FOR BRAINSTORMING" by Andrew J. DuBrin.

Collecting wild ideas is only the start of the brainstorming process. After ideas are collected, the group or each member carefully evaluates and analyzes the various alternatives. (You also need to refine your ideas from brainwriting.) It is usually important to also specify the implementation details. For example, how do you actually convert an industrial robot into an amusement park ride?

In many situations, brainstorming alone produces as many or more useful ideas than does brainstorming in groups. **Brainwriting** is arriving at creative ideas by jotting them down yourself. Self-discipline is very important for brainwriting because some people have a tendency to postpone something as challenging as thinking alone. A variation of brainwriting is for group members to pass along their ideas from working alone to another member, who reads them and adds his or her own ideas.

Brainwriting
arriving at creative ideas by jotting them down

Brainwriting supports group brainstorming in two important ways. One approach is for team leaders to alert participants of the upcoming brainstorming session and encourage them to bring creative ideas into the meeting. A second approach is to permit participants to submit additional ideas up to twelve hours after the meeting. In this way, participants who were shy about submitting a particular idea in a group will have a voice.[28] Also, we often think of the right thing to say after an event—the phenomenon of "I wish I would have thought of that then instead of now."

ESTABLISH IDEA QUOTAS FOR YOURSELF

To enhance creativity, many companies assign idea quotas to workers. For example, workers might be instructed to bring one good idea for earning or saving money to every meeting. Establishing idea quotas is similar to brainwriting with a goal in mind. An easy way of getting started is to establish a monthly minimum quota of one creative idea to improve your personal life and one to improve your job or school performance. Although this exercise might take only about five minutes of thinking each month, it could have a tremendous impact on your life. After you have gained the skill of developing one good idea per month, you might up your quota to two or three ideas. As with any creative idea, you will need an action plan to make the idea a reality. For example, one creative idea might be "I will sell buried treasure on eBay." Next, you have to find the buried treasure or find a supplier, photograph the treasure, and so forth.

ENGAGE IN MULTICULTURAL EXPERIENCES

An analysis of many studies supports the assumption that multicultural experience fosters creativity.[29] *Multicultural experience* in this context refers to all direct and indirect experiences of encountering or interacting with people from foreign cultures. This definition is helpful because it suggests that travel to other countries is not the only way to obtain multicultural experience. For example, eating in a foreign-themed restaurant or interacting with people from another culture via the Internet would give you at least some multicultural experience.

Multicultural experience fosters creativity in several ways. First, you might obtain direct access to novel ideas and concepts from other cultures. For example, an American visitor to Japan might observe that many Japanese people read novels on their smart phones and then convince his or her company to start a similar service in the United States.

Second, multicultural living experience may allow people to recognize that the same surface behavior has different functions and implications. For example, in some cultures, leaving food on your plate is a compliment to the host, implying that you had enough food. In another culture, leaving food on the plate would suggest the food wasn't good. A stretch application of this concept is that the act of using a fountain pen might be perceived as (a) a means of signing an important document or as (b) a gesture of status. The latter is why expensive fountain pens still sell even if their practical use is limited.

Third, exposure to foreign cultures might shake up your thinking enough to access unconventional knowledge when back in your own culture. For example, you might observe that people in parts of Canada and Iceland actually pay to stay in a hotel made of ice and sleep in sleeping bags in their ice beds. As a hotel manager, you might say to yourself, "Maybe we can charge people to stay overnight in a swamp here in Florida."

Fourth, exposure to other cultures may lead to a psychological readiness to recruit ideas from unfamiliar sources and places. The well-traveled manager might now be more willing to ask entry-level workers for their suggestions on improving products, services, and work procedures. Or during "Bring Your Child to Work Day," the manager might ask the visiting children for useful suggestions.

Fifth, cultural exploration might foster a willingness to synthesize seemingly incompatible ideas from diverse cultures. For example, the rickshaws used in Asia sparked the idea for a similar service to provide transportation to businesspeople and tourists in crowded cities such as New York City and London. The modern rickshaw is usually bicycle-driven and referred to as a pedicab.

OBTAIN ADEQUATE PHYSICAL EXERCISE

Physical exercise plays an important role in preparing you for creative thinking. Physical movement stimulates the brain by bringing it more blood and oxygen. At the same time, the exercise may reduce stress that makes it difficult to concentrate enough to think creatively. Exercise also enhances activity in the frontal lobe, the region of the brain involved in abstract reasoning and attention. Participating in physical activity may also foster creativity because many flashes of insight occur while engaged in leisure pursuits.

Experiments conducted at Stanford University lend support to the importance of physical exercise for creativity. In one of the experiments, participants were tested indoors, both sitting and walking on a treadmill. The studies found that a person's creative output increased by an average of 60 percent while walking. The researchers concluded that walking opens up the free flow of ideas and could therefore be a robust way of enhancing creativity.[30]

The fact that physical activity can boost creative thinking should not be interpreted in isolation. Without other factors going for you, such as a storehouse of knowledge and passion for the task, physical exercise will not lead to mental breakthroughs.

SOLICIT FEEDBACK ON YOUR PERFORMANCE

An effective way of enhancing creativity on the job is to seek feedback on your performance from both your manager and your coworkers. Even if you are not asking for feedback on creative suggestions exclusively, the feedback process is likely to sharpen your imagination. An example of a feedback-seeking question would be "What did you think of my suggestion for reducing energy costs by encouraging employees to bring sweaters to the office?" The feedback refines your thinking, helping you develop ideas that others perceive to be imaginative.

A study demonstrating the link between feedback seeking and job creativity was conducted with 456 supervisor–employee pairs in four management consulting firms. Employees who asked for feedback directly, as well as looking around for indirect feedback, tended to be rated more highly on displaying creativity.[31] Examples of indirect feedback would be seeing positive mention of your performance in an e-mail or hearing a spontaneous comment about your work during a meeting.

TRY CREATIVE PROBLEM SOLVING WHEN YOU ARE NOT AT YOUR BEST

Many people believe that your best time for creative thinking is when you are well rested, and many people believe the opposite to true. When you are very fatigued, your mind loses its filtering mechanisms, enabling you to think more loosely and let in unusual thoughts. A study reported in *Scientific American* suggests that creative problem solving is most likely to occur when we are not at our best with respect to our circadian rhythms, those that determine whether you are a *morning-type* person or an *evening-type* person. The off-rhythm time is best when you are searching for an insight (aha!) moment. Here is a low-technology example of an insightful solution to a problem that occurred when the problem solver was not functioning at his or her best:

> A bus company in China kicked off a safe-driving campaign by hanging bowls of water over the heads of the bus drivers. To avoid getting doused with water, the drivers were forced to drive gently.[32] (We assume that the streets and roads were relatively smooth, so careful driving would avoid the douse.)

To make best use of the suggestion about circadian rhythms, we recommend you attempt creative problem solving at your worst, and then at your best, and observe the results. Begin experimenting with a task that is not of major consequence to your career or personal life.

PLAY THE ROLES OF EXPLORER, ARTIST, JUDGE, AND LAWYER

A method for improving creativity has been proposed that incorporates many of the suggestions already made. The method calls for you to adopt four roles in your thinking.[33]

1. **Be an explorer.** Speak to people in different fields and get ideas that you can use. For example, if you are a telecommunications specialist, speak to salespeople and manufacturing specialists.

2. **Be an artist by stretching your imagination.** Strive to spend about 5 percent of your day asking "what if" questions. For example, a sales manager at a fresh-fish distributor might ask, "What if some new research suggests that eating fish causes intestinal cancer in humans?" Also remember to challenge the commonly perceived rules in your field. Years ago, a supermarket executive at a discount grocer questioned why the supermarket should have to go to the expense of providing customers with bags. Today, several discount supermarkets require that customers have the choice of bringing their own bags or purchasing a bag at the store.

3. **Know when to be a judge.** After developing some wild ideas, at some point you have to evaluate them. Do not be so critical that you discourage your own imaginative thinking, but be critical enough to prevent attempting to implement weak ideas.

4. **Achieve results by playing the role of a lawyer.** Negotiate and find ways to implement your ideas within your field or place of work. The explorer, artist, and judge stages of creative thought might last only a short time toward developing a creative idea. Yet you may spend months or even years getting your brainstorm implemented. For example, it took a long time for the developer of the robotic bricklayer to finally get the product manufactured and distributed on a large scale.

How Critical Thinking Relates to Problem Solving and Creativity

◀ **Learning Objective 6.5** ◀

Another way of understanding and improving problem solving and creativity is to regard both processes as being part of critical thinking. Probably any course you have ever taken, including mathematics, chemistry, history, political science, and English literature, was aimed partially at improving your critical thinking. This is true because critical thinking is a broad concept that includes many different cognitive, or intellectual, behaviors that focus on problem solving. Whether or not there is widespread agreement on the meaning of critical thinking, the skill is in demand. Mentions of critical thinking on job postings have more than doubled in recent years.[34]

Critical thinking refers to solving problems and making decisions through a systematic evaluation of evidence.[35] A critical thinker can form his or her own opinion based on a variety of information. A person who thinks clearly and rationally is engaged in critical thinking, and the problem-solving steps described in this chapter help you think critically. Also, the suggestions for improving creativity will help you attain high-quality solutions to problems. Critical thinking proceeds in steps, as shown in Figure 6-4.

Critical thinking
solving problems and making decisions through a systematic evaluation of evidence

Step 1   is to have a healthy degree of skepticism about the argument or proposition being presented. Probe for logical flaws in the argument the other person might have made. The other person's emotional state might have made him or her a little irrational. Visualize yourself as a store manager in a chain of furniture stores. The CEO introduces a plan for saving money by firing two-thirds of the experienced full-time store associates and replacing them with part-time workers at modest wages. You are quite skeptical that this plan will help the company in the long run.

Step 2   is to evaluate the stated or unstated assumptions underlying the argument. You say to yourself, "The CEO is assuming that inexperienced part-time associates will sell as much furniture and accessories as our experienced associates did. He is also assuming that knowledge of the business does not count for much. Another assumption is that the part-timers who replace the full-timers will be as loyal, even if not given benefits. I doubt these assumptions are correct." Evaluating assumptions is important because a persuasive speaker will often influence us not to carefully evaluate the logic of his or her position.

FIGURE 6-4

STEPS IN CRITICAL THINKING

Source: "STEPS IN CRITICAL THINKING" by Andrew J. DuBrin.

Step 3 is to imagine and attempt to evaluate alternative arguments. Here are a couple of other assumptions you might make: "Experienced and knowledgeable store associates are the lifeblood of our business. They are worth the compensation they receive because they generate more business and create a greater base of satisfied customers. Many part-time workers might sell furniture as a supplement to their regular job. Instead of feeling committed to our company, they might have high turnover."

Step 4 is to make a decision. You have given careful thought to top management's plan, including having conducted some research. Your decision is to write an e-mail to the CEO that includes these thoughts: "I know we want to trim costs and increase profits. Our best profit generators are experienced, dedicated store associates. They give great decorating ideas to customers. Home Depot once tried to save money by dumping full-time associates. Customer service became so bad that the plan was reversed. Circuit City tried the same stunt of saving money by firing experienced store associates, and they went bankrupt."

Critical thinking is often difficult to accomplish for a variety of personal and situational factors that might prevent or limit us from critically evaluating a problem. The factors that influence problem-solving skills listed in Figure 6-1 might be considered potential constraints on critical problem solving. Here we highlight a few possible constraints.

One personal factor is a person's emotional state. When we are too emotional in a negative or positive direction, our ability to critically evaluate a situation is diminished. Another personal factor is cognitive skills, including knowledge and wisdom. A person who is mentally sharp and has more knowledge is better able to think critically than a person with fewer cognitive skills and less knowledge. (In the above example, being familiar with the Home Depot and Circuit City experiences in reducing the number of full-time associates was quite useful.)

Situational factors, including the atmosphere of the company, also influence critical thinking. For example, in some companies, critical thinking by employees about major issues is welcomed. In some other company atmospheres, critical thinking on issues outside your immediate area is discouraged. Another situational factor would be a crisis situation, such as a worker not taking time to reflect carefully on alternatives when he or she is charged with using company resources to establish an online retail business for his or her own profit. (The worker also did not engage in critical thinking when establishing the website.)

▶ **Learning Objective 6.6** ▶

How Multiple Intelligences Contribute to Problem Solving and Creativity

Multiple intelligences
the idea that people know and understand the world in distinctly different ways and learn in different ways and that they possess eight intelligences, or faculties, in varying degrees

Another approach to understanding the diverse nature of mental ability is the theory of **multiple intelligences**. According to Howard Gardner, people know and understand the world in distinctly different ways and learn in different ways. The concept of multiple intelligences also provides insights into problem solving and creativity because it suggests that people have different types of intelligences, or mental abilities, that can be called upon as needed to solve a particular problem. Individuals possess the following eight intelligences, or faculties, in varying degrees:

1. **Linguistic.** Enables people to communicate through language, including reading, writing, and speaking.

2. **Logical-mathematical.** Enables individuals to see relationships between objects and solve problems, as in calculus and statistics.

3. **Musical.**   Gives people the capacity to create and understand meanings made out of sounds and to enjoy different types of music.

4. **Spatial.**   Enables people to perceive and manipulate images in the brain and to re-create them from memory, as is required in making graphic designs.

5. **Bodily kinesthetic.**   Enables people to use their bodies and perceptual and motor systems in skilled ways, such as dancing, playing sports, and expressing emotion through facial expressions.

6. **Intrapersonal.**   Enables people to distinguish among their own feelings and acquire accurate self-knowledge.

7. **Interpersonal.**   Enables individuals to recognize and make distinctions among the feelings, motives, and intentions of others, as in managing or parenting.

8. **Naturalist.**   Enables individuals to differentiate among, classify, and utilize various features of the physical external environment.

Your profile of intelligences influences how you best learn and to which types of jobs you are best suited. Gardner believes that it is possible to develop these separate intelligences through concentrated effort. However, any of these intelligences might fade if not put to use.[36] The components of multiple intelligences might also be perceived as different talents or abilities. Having high cognitive intelligence would contribute to high standing on each of the eight intelligences.

The application of multiple intelligences applied to an everyday problem implies that the problem solver reaches into his or her bag of intelligences to use the right mix to solve the problem at hand. For example, if the problem facing you was how to raise some quick cash for a small business, you might decide to sell surplus equipment and furniture on an auction website such as eBay. To make the sale successful you might use your logical-mathematical intelligence to figure out reasonable pricing; your linguistic intelligence to accurately describe your offerings; and your spatial intelligence to post aesthetically pleasing photos of the furniture and equipment.

Concept Review and Reinforcement

Key Terms

Summary and Review

Problem solving occurs when you try to remove an obstacle that is blocking a path you want to take or when you try to close the gap between what exists and what you want to exist. Decision making takes place after you encounter a problem and you select one alternative from the various courses of action that can be pursued. Many traits and characteristics influence the type of problem solver you are now or are capable of becoming. Among them are the following:

- Cognitive intelligence, education, and experience
- Emotional intelligence
- Flexibility versus rigidity
- Intuition
- Concentration
- Decisiveness and perfectionism
- Risk taking and thrill seeking
- Values of the decision maker

The decision-making process outlined in this chapter uses both the scientific method and intuition for making decisions in response to problems. Decision making follows an orderly flow of events:

1. You are aware of a problem or create one of your own.
2. You identify causes of the problem.
3. You find creative alternatives.
4. You weigh the alternatives and make a choice.
5. You implement the choice.
6. You evaluate whether you have made a sound choice. If your choice was unsound, you are faced with a new problem, and the cycle repeats itself.

Creativity is the ability to look for good ideas that can be put into action. Innovation occurs when a creative idea is commercialized. Creative workers tend to have different intellectual and personality characteristics than their less creative counterparts. In general, creative people are more mentally flexible than others, which allows them to overcome the traditional way of looking at problems. Their characteristics are as follows:

- **Knowledge.** Creative thinking requires a broad background of information, including facts and observations. The most important discovery skill of a cognitive nature is making connections across seemingly unrelated fields.
- **Intellectual abilities.** Exceptional intelligence is not required for creativity, but creative people are good at generating alternative solutions to problems. The key to creative intelligence is insight, including the combination of ideas (associating). Creativity can stem from both fluid (raw) intelligence and crystallized (accumulated) intelligence.
- **Personality.** Instead of blind self-confidence, creative people have creative self-efficacy. Self-confidence helps in believing that one's creative ideas will be accepted. The ability to work in isolation and to concentrate is important.

Creativity takes place when three components come together:

1. Expertise
2. Creative thinking skills (being flexible and imaginative)
3. The right type of motivation (passion for the task and intrinsic motivation)

Four factors outside the person play a key role in fostering creativity: an environmental need, enough conflict and tension to put people on edge, encouragement from management, and the presence of humor. A positive mood often contributes to creativity. Constraints, such as time and budgets, can often enhance creativity.

Methods of improving your creativity include the following:

- Concentrate intensely on the task at hand.
- Overcome traditional mental sets.
- Conduct brainstorming and brainwriting sessions.
- Establish idea quotas for yourself.
- Engage in multicultural experiences.
- Obtain adequate physical exercise.
- Solicit feedback on your performance.
- Try creative problem solving when you are not at your best.
- Play the roles of explorer, artist, judge, and lawyer.

Another way of understanding and improving problem solving and creativity is to regard both processes as part of critical thinking. The process has four steps:

1. Be skeptical of the argument or proposition offered.
2. Evaluate the stated or unstated assumptions underlying the argument.
3. Imagine and attempt to evaluate alternative arguments.
4. Make a decision.

The idea of multiple intelligences can contribute to both problem solving and creativity because it recognizes that at least eight different types of intelligence, or faculties, can be applied to the problem at hand.

Questions for Discussion and Review

6.1 In what way might your present job, or any job you have held in the past, benefit from creative problem solving?

6.2 From time to time, McDonald's Corporation has experienced the problem of flat or declining sales at its restaurants (stores). What might be one or two of the company's underlying problems?

6.3 What would be some of the symptoms or signs of a "flexible thinker"?

6.4 How might being a low risk taker limit a person's chances for attaining a high level of career success?

6.5 Provide an example of how you have used intuition to your advantage in work or personal life.

6.6 Why does knowledge lead to creativity?

6.7 Provide an example of how a supervisor or teacher of yours encouraged you to be creative. How effective was this encouragement?

6.8 Why is being passionate about the task at hand almost essential for being creative?

6.9 How might having just a couple of creative ideas during your work life have a major impact on the success of your career?

6.10 Ask an experienced manager or professional how important creative thinking has been in his or her career. Be prepared to report back to class with your findings.

Web Corner

Problem-solving tools:

www.mindtools.com (Enter "problem solving" in the search box to be shown a variety of choices.)

Development of creative thinking:

www.cre8ng.com (Click on "MyLifePassion.Creativity".)

INTERNET SKILL BUILDER

Creativity Training

Millions of websites deal with creativity training, especially those that offer a course. CreativityGames.net is relatively unique because it offers you the opportunity to participate in creativity brain-training games that are stimulating and brief. Click on "Creativity Games" on the top bar.

Developing Your
Human Relations Skills

Applying Human Relations Exercise 6-1

Using the Problem-Solving Process

Imagine that you have received $2 million in cash with the income taxes already paid. The only stipulation is that you will have to use the money to establish some sort of enterprise, either a business or a charitable foundation. Solve this problem using the following worksheet. Describe what thoughts you have or what actions you will take for each step of problem solving and decision making.

I. *Be aware of the problem.* You have already been assigned the problem.
II. *Identify causes of the problem.* How did this problem come about?
III. *Find creative alternatives.* Think of the many alternatives facing you. Let your imagination flow and be creative.

	Alternatives	Advantages	Disadvantages
1.			
2.			
3.			
4.			
5.			

IV. *Weigh alternatives and make the choice.* Weigh the pros and cons of each of your sensible alternatives, and choose one course of action.
V. Implement the choice. Outline your action plan for converting your chosen alternative into action.
VI. Evaluate the choice. Do the best you can here by speculating how you will know if the decision you reached was a good one.

Applying Human Relations Exercise 6-2

Helping the Alliance Rubber Company Prosper

The Alliance Rubber Company, based in Hot Springs, Arkansas, is a leading manufacturer of rubber bands and related products, such as wristbands, and the Eraselet, a bracelet with an erasing capability. Today, you are gathered in a team to help Alliance Rubber think of a few new, commercially feasible uses of a rubber brand. You and your team members can regard your session as brainstorming for the purpose of product development. Top-level management instructs you to not be concerned about coming up with a foolish idea because silly ideas can become the germ of an idea for a breakthrough product.

Creative Problem Solving and Potholes

In most cities and towns that experience cold winters, the problems of potholes arises every year. By early spring, most municipalities have repaired almost all the potholes, taking up a big chunk of their maintenance budget. At the same time, city and town officials have to listen to hundreds, if not thousands, of complaints and jokes about the potholes. People post photos and videos of the biggest potholes they have found. Furthermore, potholes can lead to automobile accidents and many unwanted vehicle repairs by their owners. The next winter, the cycle repeats itself as water continues to seep into crevices, freeze, unfreeze, and create cracks.

The basic approach to this exercise is for problem-solving (or brainstorming) groups to suggest several solutions to resolving the pothole problem. Because this problem is so complex, with easy solutions not available, the groups may want to consult outside sources, such as websites, while engaging in problem solving.

After the various groups have completed their problem solving, it will be useful to compare solutions. Class discussion can then be held to answer the following questions:

1. Which solution to the problem of potholes seems the most feasible, and why?
2. Why has the problem of potholes been so resistant to solving for so many years?

Human Relations Case Study 6–1

Budget Vision Care Needs Ideas

Seth is the CEO of Budget Vision Care, a chain of twenty-five stores whose business is to provide low-price eyeglasses to consumers who cannot afford, or who do not choose to pay, standard prices for eyeware. The stores are located in neighborhoods with below-average income levels. Each store has a state-certified optician on premises. Most of the staff except for the store manager are part-time workers, which helps reduce payroll costs. The bottom line of eyeglasses begins with a price of about $25. The frames and lenses are purchased from the lowest-priced possible supplier from third-world countries.

Customer satisfaction has not been a major problem for Budget Vision Care because most of its customers understand that the eyeglasses they purchase at Budget are a good buy. The most consistent complaint, however, is that the eyeglasses are of low quality and break and bend easily. The frames often become misshapen after a few months of wear, and the lenses usually become detached if the eyeglasses fall on a hard surface.

With most of his customers having access to the Internet, Seth worries that dissatisfied customers might make negative social media posts about Budget Vision Care. Several media posts, for example, have stated that the company exploits the poor by selling them very low-quality frames. Seth is also concerned that the optician stores in major discount retailers such as Wal-Mart and Target will erode Budget Vision's market share.

Seth is so worried about the forces against his business that he decides to work on the problem with his top-management team. Seth said that he has been casually talking about the problem with his team, but he hasn't really put the problem on his agenda. Seth sends his team an e-mail about the necessity of finding new sources of revenue for the firm, and he alerts them to a meeting to work on the problem.

At the meeting, Seth says to the group, "Budget Vision Care is in trouble. Our revenues declined only 12 percent last year, but the handwriting is on the wall. The criticism of our business model is getting more vocal, with even the Better Business Bureau inquiring about the quality of our product. The big-box stores are breathing down our neck.

"I want you as the executive team to come up with a way of finding new sources of revenue for Budget Vision."

"No disrespect," said Kathy, the director of marketing. "But you are our leader. You are supposed to provide the breakthrough idea that will create a solid future for Budget Vision Care. We've often talked about broadening our services, but we usually hit the same brick wall. The most notable idea was the one about installing tattoo parlors in our stores because so many of our customers wear tattoos.

"I think the best idea we had was the one about selling lottery tickets in all the stores. But I think we ran into some potential legal problems."

Seth then said, "I don't disagree that as CEO maybe I should have the next great idea for Budget Vision. But I don't right now, so that's why I'm asking you for your creative suggestions."

José, the CFO said, "I think that we need to ask an even deeper question than where we can find new sources of revenue. We need to ask where to look and whom to ask about new lines of business."

Questions

6.11 To what extent do you think it is Seth's individual responsibility to furnish creative ideas for generating new business for Budget Vision Care?

6.12 In response to José's comment, where should the management team look for creative ideas for enlarging the revenue of Budget Vision Care?

6.13 From the standpoint of ethics, do you think Budget Vision Care should stay in business? Explain your reasoning.

Human Relations Role-Playing Exercise 6–1

Group Decision Making and Creativity

One student plays the role of Seth, who, during his meeting with the executive team, presses them to suggest at least one useful idea for expanding Budget Vision Care's top line (revenue) by either selling more of existing services or creating a new service. Several other students play the roles of members of the executive team. They enjoy this opportunity of group decision making as well as the chance to engage in creative thinking. Yet they also believe that it is Seth's role to exercise strong leadership by pointing Budget Vision Care in the right direction. Observers will look to see if this problem-solving session is likely to result in any innovations for Budget Vision Care.

Human Relations Case Study 6–2

Event Planner Kaitlin Could Use a Big Idea

Kaitlin has an exciting job at age thirty-two. She works for a public relations company as an event planner. The focus of her job is to coordinate all aspects of a large meeting, trade show, or convention for clients. She chooses the location for a meeting, makes hotel reservations, arranges for transportation, and takes care of hundreds of details. In addition, she is often asked to come up with a theme and décor for a meeting that will help entice people to attend the meeting, and to have fun while they are present.

Her company has just received a contract to arrange a regional meeting for a homebuilders' association. The president of the association, Sam, told Kaitlin, "We want this to be a meeting our members won't forget. You need to stay within budget, but I want everything to run smoothly, and for the meeting to be sensational at the same time. Come up with a theme for the meeting that is outrageously good."

As Kaitlin starts staring into her tablet computer, she thinks, "What great meeting theme can I dream up? Or if I can't do it myself, where should I go for ideas?"

Questions

6.14 What theme for a meeting do you suggest Kaitlin pursue?

6.15 How might Kaitlin go about solving the problem of needing a creative theme for the homebuilders' meeting?

Human Relations Role-Playing Exercise 6–2

Kaitlin Submits Her Big Idea

One student plays the role of Kaitlin, who later that day telephones Sam. She speaks in an excited tone and says, "I've got a powerful theme I want to run by you. I've done some brainstorming by myself, and I think that a superhero theme would be great. Everybody who attends the meeting will wear a necklace-style card indicating his or her favorite superhero. We will have superhero videos running on monitors for the entire meeting. For dinner the first night, each participant can dress as a superhero. What do you think?"

Another student plays the role of Sam, who thinks that Kaitlin's idea is on the foolish side. He responds, "Kaitlin, not a bad first try, but what else do you have?"

For both role-playing exercises, observers rate the role-players on two dimensions, using a scale of 1 to 5 from very poor to very good. One dimension is "effective use of human relations techniques." The second dimension is "acting ability." A few observers might voluntarily provide feedback to the role-players in terms of sharing their ratings and observations. The course instructor might also provide feedback.

REFERENCES

1. Original story created from facts and observations in the following sources: Mike Esterel, "'Share a Coke' Creates Pop in Sales," *The Wall Street Journal*, September 26, 2014, p. B5; Jay Moye, "Share a Coke: How the Groundbreaking Campaign Got Its Start 'Down Under,'" www.coca-colacompany.com September 25, 2014, pp. 1–6; "'Share a Coke' Campaign Grows Sales for First Time in 10 Years, WSJ Reports Coca-Cola's Big Idea Started in Australia by Toni McQuilken," *Ad Week*, www.adweek.com, September 26, 2014, pp. 1–4.

2. Myeong-Gu Seo and Lisa Feldman Barrett, "Being Emotional during Decision Making—Good or Bad? An Empirical Investigation," *Academy of Management Journal*, August 2007, pp. 923–940.

3. Erik Dane and Michael G. Pratt, "Exploring Intuition and Its Role in Managerial Decision Making," *Academy of Management Review*, January 2007, pp. 33–54.

4. Eugene Sadler-Smith and Erella Shefy, "The Intuitive Executive: Understanding and Applying 'Gut Feel' in Decision-Making," *Academy of Management Executive*, November 2004, p. 76.

5. Quoted in Josh Tyrangiel, "Tim Cook's Freshman Year," *Bloomberg Businessweek*, December 16, 2012, p. 78.

6. Lea Winerman, "What We Know without Knowing," *Monitor on Psychology*, March 2005, p. 52.

7. Christopher M. Barnes and John R. Hollenbeck, "Sleep Deprivation and Decision-Making Teams: Burning the Midnight Oil or Playing with Fire?" *Academy of Management Review*, January 2009, p. 64.

8. Research reported in Amy Cynkar, "A Towering Figure," *Monitor on Psychology*, April 2007, pp. 38–39.

9. Carol Polsky, "This Invention Is So Useful, It Has Stuck Around for 75 Years," *Newsday* syndicated story, May 13, 2000; Mary Bellis, "The History of Scotch Tape: Richard Drew (1886–1982)," About.com/Inventors, p. 1. Accessed January 25, 2012.

10. Kristi Essick, "Bookstore Opens a New Chapter," *The Wall Street Journal*, January 13, 2014, p. R8.

11. Quoted in Ann Pomeroy, "Cooking Up Innovation," *HR Magazine*, November 2004, pp. 49–50.

12. Cited in Dan Heath and Chip Heath, "Analysis of Paralysis," *Fast Company*, November 2007, p. 68.

13. Tom Kelley and David Kelley, "Reclaim Your Creative Confidence," *Harvard Business Review*, December 2012, p. 116.

14. Richard W. Woodman, John E. Sayer, and Ricky W. Griffin, "Toward a Theory of Organizational Creativity," *Academy of Management Review*, April 1993, pp. 293–321; Robert J. Sternberg, "Creativity as a Decision," *American Psychologist*, May 2002, p. 376; Kelley and Kelley, "Reclaim Your Creative Confidence," *Harvard Business Review*, pp. 115–118.

15. Research reported in Carolyn T. Geer, "Innovation 101," *The Wall Street Journal*, October 17, 2011, p. R5.

16. Robert J. Sternberg, ed., *Handbook of Creativity* (New York: Cambridge University Press, 1999).

17. Yaping Gong, Jia-Chi Huang, and Jiing-Lih Farth, "Employee Learning Orientation, Transformational Leadership, and Employees Creativity: The Mediating Role of Employee Creative Self-Efficacy," *Academy of Management Journal*, August 2009, p. 766.

18. Markus Baer, "Putting Creativity to Work: The Implementation of Creative Ideas in Organizations," *Academy of Management Journal*, October 2012, pp. 1102–1119.

19. Teresa M. Amabile, "How to Kill Creativity," *Harvard Business Review*, September–October 1998, pp. 78–79.

20. Teresa M. Amabile, "Beyond Talent: John Irving and the Passionate Craft of Creativity," *American Psychologist*, April 2001, p. 335.

21. Robert I. Sutton, "The Weird Rules of Creativity," *Harvard Business Review*, September 2001, p. 101.

22. Patrick J. Kiger, "Small Groups: Big Ideas," *Workforce Management*, February 27, 2006, p. 2.

23. Cited in Robert McGarvey, "Turn It On," *Entrepreneur*, November 1996, pp. 156–157.

24. Teresa M. Amabile, Sigal G. Barsade, Jennifer S. Mueller, and Barry M. Staw, "Affect and Creativity at Work: A Daily Longitudinal Text," *Harvard Business School Working Papers*, 2002–2003.

25. March L. To et al., "Within-Personal Relationships between Mood and Creativity," *Journal of Applied Psychology*, May 2012, pp. 599–612.

26. Marissa Ann Mayer, "Creativity Loves Constraints," *Businessweek*, February 13, 2006, p. 102; Alexia Tsotsis, "Marissa Mayer, Google's 'De Niro,' Reveals What She Asks Job Candidates," www.techcrunch.com, December 8, 2011, p. 1.

27. Kelley and Kelley, "Reclaim Your Creative Confidence," p. 116.

28. "Expand Brainstorming," *Manager's Edge*, November 2008, p. 6.

29. Angela Ka-yee Leung, William W. Maddux, Adam D. Galinksy, and Chi-yue Chiu, "Multicultural Experience Enhances Creativity: The When and How," *American Psychologist*, April 2008, pp. 169–181.

30. May Wong, "Stanford Study Finds Walking Improves Creativity," *Stanford Report*, http://news.standord.edu/news, April 24, 2014, pp. 1–3; Julia Savacool, "Waking Boosts Creativity, So Think on Your Feet," *USA Today*, June 1, 2014, p. 3U.

31. Katleen E. De Stobbeleir, Susan J. Ashford, and Dirk Buyens, "Self-Regulation of Creativity at Work: The Role of Feedback-Seeking Behavior in Creative Performance," *Academy of Management Journal*, August 2011, pp. 811–831.

32. Study reported in Cindi May, "The Inspiration Paradox: Your Best Creative Time Is Not When You Think," *Scientific American*, www.scientificamerican.com, March 6, 2012, pp. 1–3.

33. "Be a Creative Problem Solver," *Executive Strategies*, June 6, 1989, pp. 1–2.

34. Melissa Korn, "Bosses Seek Critical Thinking, but What Is It?" *The Wall Street Journal*, October 22, 2014.

35. Saul Kassin, *Psychology*, 2nd ed. (Upper Saddle River, NJ: Prentice Hall, 2001), p. 278. The critical thinking steps described in this section are from Kassin.

36. Howard Gardner, *Intelligence Reframed: Multiple Intelligence in the 21st Century* (New York: Basic Books, 1999); Mark K. Smith, "Howard Gardner and Multiple Intelligences," *The Encyclopedia of Informal Education*, www.infed.or/thinkers/gardner.htm, 2002, 2008, pp. 1–12.

CHAPTER 7

Personal Communication Effectiveness

Fotolia

Outline

Conrad is the CEO of Magnum Recyclers, a company whose primary business is refurbishing obsolete or unwanted computers from businesses and individuals. Magnum purchases its computers sometimes in bulk, and sometimes one at a time. Conrad explains that there is a big market for his revamped computers because many small businesses are looking to save money on computer purchases. Also, most of his customers have no particular need for computer hardware with the latest refinements because earlier models work quite well for them.

Business continues to expand, so Conrad has decided to hire another recycling representative whose responsibility it is to interface with customers who are selling old equipment or are purchasing refurbished computers. Based on personal observations and reports he has read, Conrad believes that empathy is one of the most important qualities of a recycling rep. He says, "Most of our customers are emotional about the old equipment they are parting with because it has enabled them to run their business. And business owners who purchase from us are very emotional about their companies. They expect us to understand that their enterprises are a big part of their life."

Today, Conrad is interviewing Julia for the recycling representative position. Her education, job experience, and communication skills all seem to be a good fit for the position. Thirty minutes into the interview, Conrad hits Julia with his question to measure empathy: "Julia, let's suppose that a customer comes to the office, looking a little confused. He says that he has run his plumbing business for years without computer support, other than a mobile device. But now he's getting too big to run the place with paper and pencil and a mobile phone. But he doesn't know what he should do about purchasing a computer. How would you respond to this guy?"

Julia thinks for about thirty seconds and then says she would respond about this way: "You must be proud of having built up such a successful business over the years. I understand that you are the third-generation owner. With all you have to do, it must be nerve-wracking to choose a computer. But I think we can make life easier for you. We have helped successful business owners like you in the past."

Conrad thought to himself, "This woman is good. She's got just the empathy we need for this position. If her references and background investigation check out, we'll make her a generous offer."

Learning Objectives ▶

After studying the information and doing the exercises in this chapter, you should be able to:

7.1 Explain the basic communication process.

7.2 Describe the nature and importance of nonverbal communication in the workplace.

7.3 Know how to use social media to enhance communication effectiveness.

7.4 Identify barriers to communication.

7.5 Know how to build bridges to communication.

7.6 Overcome many gender communication barriers.

7.7 Enhance your listening skills.

The story just presented illustrates one key aspect of interpersonal communication touched on in this chapter: the ability to listen to and empathize with another person. Furthermore, the story supports the relevance of studying communication skills. Communication is so vital that it has been described as the glue that holds organizations and families together. Most job foul-ups and personal relationship disputes are considered to be a result of communication problems. Furthermore, to be successful in work or personal life, you usually have to be an effective communicator. You can't make friends or stand up against enemies unless you can communicate with them. And you can't accomplish work through others unless you can send and receive messages effectively.

In this chapter, we explain several important aspects of interpersonal communication, such as the communication process, communicating with others via the social media, and overcoming various communication barriers. Many factors contribute to enhanced communication, leading in turn to more effective human relations. Explanation should also lead to skill improvement. For example, if you understand the steps involved in getting a message across to another person, you may be able to prevent many communication problems.

To personalize the subject of interpersonal communication effectiveness, you are invited to take Human Relations Self-Assessment Quiz 7-1.

Human Relations Self-Assessment Quiz   7-1

My Communication Effectiveness

Indicate the extent of your agreement with the following statements, using the following scale: Agree strongly (AS); Agree (A); about equal between agree and disagree (N); Disagree (D); Disagree strongly (DS). Because it is so easy to overrate our own communication effectiveness, it would be useful to also have somebody who has frequently observed you communicate to respond to the questions. Circle the best response to each of the ten statements.

Statement about Communication Effectiveness	AS	A	N	D	DS
	5	4	3	2	1
1. When I talk, people listen.	5	4	3	2	1
2. I almost never telephone or speak in person to another individual if it is possible to send him or her a text message.	1	2	3	4	5
3. I have received several compliments about the quality of presentations I have made in front of a group.	5	4	3	2	1
4. I have been told by at least a few people that I am a good listener.	5	4	3	2	1
5. I look away rather than maintain eye contact during a conversation with others.	1	2	3	4	5
6. My vocabulary continues to grow because I look up the meaning of words unfamiliar to me.	5	4	3	2	1
7. I often keep my hand over my mouth when I have an important message to deliver to another person.	1	2	3	4	5
8. During a conversation, I vary the loudness of my voice.	5	4	3	2	1
9. I often use text style spelling when sending messages about work or school. (For example, r u ok? LOL)	1	2	3	4	5
10. My social media postings are polite as well as being professional in appearance.	5	4	3	2	1

Scoring and Interpretation:

Add your scores, as indicated by the numbers you have circled. Assuming that your evaluations are reasonably accurate, use the following guide:

40 or higher   high communication effectiveness and a positive communication style.

21–39   average communication effectiveness and an average communication style.

20 or less   you need to improve your communication effectiveness and develop a more effective communication style.

Source: "My Communication Effectiveness" by Andrew J. DuBrin.

How Communication Takes Place

◀ Learning Objective 7.1 ◀

A convenient starting point in understanding how people communicate is to look at the steps involved in communicating a message. **Communication** is the sending and receiving of messages. A diagram of how the process takes place is shown in Figure 7-1. The theme of the model is that two-way communication involves three major steps and that each step is subject to interference or noise. Assume that Crystal, a customer, wishes to inform Tony, a used-car sales representative, that she is willing to make an offer of $9,000 on a used car. The price tag on the car is $9,750.

Step 1   **Sender encodes the message. Encoding** is the process of organizing ideas into a series of symbols, such as words and gestures, designed to communicate with the receiver. Word choice has a strong influence on communication effectiveness. The better a person's grasp of language, the easier it is for him or her to encode. Crystal says, "Tony, this car obviously is not in excellent condition, but I am willing to give you $9,000 for it."

Step 2   **Sender chooses one or more channels.** The message is sent via a communication channel or medium, such as voice, telephone, paper, e-mail, or text messaging. It is important to select a medium that fits the message. It would be appropriate to use the spoken word to inform a coworker that he swore under his breath at a customer. It would be less appropriate to send the same message through e-mail. Many messages on and off the job are sent nonverbally through the use of gestures and facial expressions. For example, a smile from a superior during a meeting is an effective way of communicating the message "I agree with you." Crystal has chosen the oral medium to send her message.

Step 3   **Receiver decodes the message.** In **decoding**, the receiver interprets the message and translates it into meaningful information. Decoding is the process of understanding a message. Barriers to communication are most likely to surface at the decoding step. People often interpret messages according to their psychological needs and motives. Tony wants to interpret Crystal's message as being that she

Communication
the sending and receiving of messages

Encoding
the process of organizing ideas into a series of symbols, such as words and gestures, designed to communicate with a receiver

Decoding
the process of understanding a message; the receiver interprets the message and translates it into meaningful information

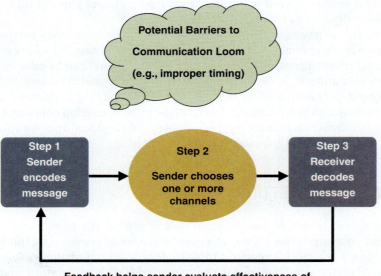

FIGURE 7-1

THE COMMUNICATION PROCESS

When sending a message to another person, one has to take into account potential barriers to communication. Feedback from the receiver helps clarify if the message has been interpreted as intended.

Source: "THE COMMUNICATION PROCESS" by Andrew J. DuBrin.

is very eager to purchase this car. Therefore he may listen attentively for more information demonstrating that she is interested in purchasing the car. Effective decoding is also dependent on the receiver understanding the words chosen by the sender. Breadth of vocabulary as well as cultural factors can influence the interpretation of a word or phrase. For example, if Crystal says the car is "bad," she could mean that the car is in poor condition *or* that it is wonderful, depending on her vernacular.

Decoding the message leads naturally to action: The receiver does something about the message. If the receiver acts in the manner the sender wants, the communication has been successful. If Tony says, "It's a deal," Crystal had a successful communication event. Many missteps can occur between encoding and decoding a message. **Barriers to communication** or unwanted interference or noise can distort or block a message. If Crystal has an indecisive tone and raises her voice at the end of her statement, it could indicate that she is not really serious about offering a maximum of $9,000 for the car.

Barriers to communication (or noise)
missteps that can occur between encoding and decoding a message; unwanted interference that can distort or block a message

▶ Learning Objective 7.2 ▶

Nonverbal Communication (Sending and Receiving Silent Messages)

Much of the communication among people includes nonspoken and nonwritten messages. These nonverbal signals are a critical part of everyday communication. As a case in point, *how* you say "thank you" makes a big difference in the extent to which your sense of appreciation registers. In **nonverbal communication**, we use our body, voice, or environment in numerous ways to help put a message across. Sometimes we are not aware how much our true feelings color our spoken message.

Nonverbal communication
using the body, voice, or environment in numerous ways to help get a message across

An important use of nonverbal communication in the workplace is to detect **mixed messages**, or a discrepancy between what a person says and how he or she acts.[1] An extreme example would be when a coworker says that she would like to join you on a special project. While she is expressing her agreement, her nostrils dilate, she looks down at the floor, her face twitches, and she twists her hair with her thumb and two fingers. Duh! This coworker really does not want to join your project, and you should question her about her sincerity.

Mixed messages
a discrepancy between what a person says and how he or she acts

One problem of paying attention to nonverbal signals is that they can be taken too seriously. Just because some nonverbal signals (such as yawning or looking away from a person) might reflect a person's real feelings, not every signal can be reliably connected with a particular attitude. Jason may put his hand over his mouth because he is shocked. Lucille may put her hand over her mouth because she is trying to control her laughter about the message. Here we look at seven categories of nonverbal communication that are generally reliable indicators of a person's attitude and feelings. We then describe briefly the use of nonverbal communication to detect lying.

ENVIRONMENT OR SETTING

Where you choose to deliver your message indicates what you think of its importance. Assume that your supervisor invites you over for dinner to discuss something with you. You will think it is a more important topic under these circumstances than if it were brought up when the two of you met in the supermarket. Other important environmental cues include room color, temperature, lighting, and furniture arrangement. A person who sits behind an large, uncluttered desk, for example, appears more powerful than a person who sits behind a small, cluttered desk.

Few people in an organization have the authority to control the physical factors of room color, temperature, and lighting, but there are exceptions. An office or building painted gray in the interior might suggest an impersonal, strictly business atmosphere. A business owner who keeps the temperature at 62°F during cold months or 75°F during warm months communicates a message of frugality.

DISTANCE FROM THE OTHER PERSON

How close you place your body relative to another person's also conveys meaning when you send a message. If, for instance, you want to convey a positive attitude toward another person, get physically close to him or her. Cultural differences must be kept in mind in interpreting nonverbal cues. A French male is likely to stand closer to you than a British male, even if they have equally positive attitudes toward you. A set of useful guidelines has been developed for estimating how close to stand to another person (at least in many cultures).[2] They are described here and diagrammed in Figure 7-2.

Intimate distance covers actual physical contact to about eighteen inches. Usually, it is reserved for close friends and loved ones or other people you feel affectionate toward. Physical intimacy is usually not called for on the job, but there are exceptions. For one, confidential information might be whispered within the intimate distance zone.

Personal distance covers from about one-and-a-half to four feet. In this zone it is natural to carry on friendly conversations and discussions. When people engage in a heated argument, they sometimes enter the personal distance zone. One example is a baseball coach getting up close to an umpire and shouting in his face.

FIGURE 7-2

FOUR CIRCLES OF INTIMACY

Source: "FOUR CIRCLES OF INTIMACY" by Andrew J. DuBrin.

Social distance covers from four to twelve feet and in general is reserved for interaction that is businesslike and impersonal. We usually maintain this amount of distance between ourselves and strangers, such as retail sales associates.

Public distance covers from twelve feet to the outer limit of being heard. This zone is typically used in speaking to an audience at a large meeting or in a classroom, but a few insensitive individuals might send ordinary messages by shouting across a room. The unstated message suggested by such an action is that the receiver of the message does not merit the effort of walking across the room.

People sometimes manipulate personal space in order to dominate a situation. A sales representative might move into the personal or intimate circle of a customer simply to intimidate him or her. Many people become upset when you move into a closer circle than that called for by the a situation. They consider it an invasion of their personal space, or their "territorial rights."

POSTURE

Certain aspects of your posture communicate a message. Leaning toward another individual suggests that you are favorably disposed toward his or her message. Leaning backward communicates the opposite. For example, leaning back in your chair with your arms crossed is often interpreted as negatively toned and "standoffish."[3] Openness of the arms or legs serves as an indicator of liking or caring. In general, people establish closed postures (arms folded and legs crossed) when speaking to people they dislike. Standing up straight generally indicates high self-confidence. Stooping and slouching could mean a poor self-image. In any event, there is almost no disadvantage to standing up straight.

A component of nonverbal communication related to posture is defensive positions that make people feel more protected, such as crossing their arms over their chests. During a group meeting, an indicator that the presenter's ideas are being rejected is when several participants cross their arms simultaneously. An exception might be that the meeting room is cold, a problem that can be clarified by the presenter asking if the room temperature is comfortable.[4]

Related to posture are the nonverbal signals sent by standing versus sitting. Sitting down during a conversation is generally considered to be more intimate and informal than standing. Standing up sends a message to the other person that it is time to leave. It also gives you the chance to be more attentive and polite in saying good-bye.

HAND GESTURES

Hand gestures are universally recognized as conveying specific information to others within the same culture. If you make frequent hand movements, you will generally communicate a positive attitude. If you use few gestures, you will convey dislike or lack of interest. An important exception here is that some people wave their hands vigorously while arguing. Some of their hand movements reflect anger. Another example is that open-palm gestures toward the other person typically convey positive attitudes. As will be described in Chapter 13, many hand gestures have culture-specific meanings.

It is often said that gestures speak louder than words, because if there is a discrepancy between words and gestures, the receiver will usually take your gestures more seriously. In general, more weight is given to nonverbal cues than to verbal cues when a discrepancy exists between the two.[5] Hand gestures are not unique in this regard. Nonverbal behaviors must match the spoken language, or people will tend to believe what is expressed nonverbally rather than verbally.[6]

Imagine that you have been interviewed for a job you really want. At the close of the interview, the interviewer looks at you with a solemn face, and his arms are crossed with his hands tucked under his armpits. He says in a monotone, "We will get back to you soon." Most likely, you will continue your job search.

FACIAL EXPRESSIONS AND EYE CONTACT

When used in combination, the head, face, and eyes provide the clearest indications of attitudes toward other people. Lowering your head and peering over your glasses, for instance, is the nonverbal equivalent of the expression "You're putting me on." As is well known, maintaining eye contact with another person improves communication with that person. To maintain eye contact, it is usually necessary to correspondingly move your head and face. Moving your head, face, and eyes away from another person is often interpreted as a defensive gesture or one suggesting a lack of self-confidence. Yet again, cultural differences can influence the meaning of eye contact. In some Asian cultures, looking down rather than maintaining eye contact is a sign of respect.

The face is often used as a primary source of information about how we feel. We look for facial clues when we want to determine another person's attitude. You can often judge someone's current state of happiness by looking at his or her face. The expression *sourpuss* attests to this observation. Happiness, apprehension, anger, resentment, sadness, contempt, enthusiasm, and embarrassment are but a few of the emotions that can be expressed through the face.

VOICE QUALITY

More significance is often attached to the *way* something is said than to *what* is said. A forceful voice, which includes a consistent tone without vocalized pauses, connotes power and control. Closely related to voice tone are volume, pitch, and rate of speaking. Anger, boredom, and joy can often be interpreted from voice quality. Anger is noted when the person speaks loudly with a high pitch and at a fast rate, with irregular inflection. Boredom is indicated by a monotone. Joy is often indicated by loud volume, high pitch, fast rate, upward inflection, and regular rhythm.

Avoiding an annoying voice quality can make a positive impact on others. The research of Jeffrey Jacobi, voice coach and founder of Jacobi Voice, provides some useful suggestions. A while back, he surveyed a nationwide sample of 1,000 men and women and asked, "Which irritating or unpleasant voice annoys you the most?" His results are still valid today. The most irritating quality was a whining, complaining, or nagging tone.

Jacobi notes that we are judged by the way we sound. He also contends that careers can be damaged by voice problems, such as those indicated in the survey: "We think about how we look and dress. And that gets most of the attention. But people judge our intelligence much more by how we sound than how we dress."[7]

PERSONAL APPEARANCE

Your external image plays an important role in communicating messages to others. Job seekers show recognition of this aspect of nonverbal communication when they carefully groom for a job interview. People pay more respect and grant more privileges to people they perceive as being well dressed and attractive. The meaning of being well dressed depends heavily on the situation and the culture of the organization. In an information technology firm, neatly pressed jeans, a stylish T-shirt, and clean sport shoes might qualify as being well dressed. The same attire worn in a financial services firm would qualify as being poorly dressed. In recent years, more formal business attire has made a comeback, as reflected in more space in department stores being devoted to suits for men and women.

Tattoos and body piercing represent another aspect of personal appearance that sends a strong nonverbal message. The message that tattoos and body piercing send, however, depends to a large extent on the values and preferences of the receiver. A positive message sent by visible tattoos and piercing is that the individual is cool, modern, fashionable, and youthful in outlook. A negative message is the person with visible tattoos and piercing is immature, daring, and nonconscientious. As the percentage of people wearing visible tattoos and body piercing continues to increase, less significance will probably be attached to them. For example, about thirty years ago when a man appeared in the office wearing a pierced earring, it was considered shocking. Today, the same behavior is unremarkable— at least to many people.

TOUCHING ANOTHER PERSON

Touch is a powerful vehicle for conveying such emotions as warmth, comfort, agreement, approval, reassurance, and physical attraction. Yet behavior involving touching in the workplace is governed by cultural attitudes and status.[8] Touching among people who are at approximately the same organizational rank is frequently used to convey agreement and reassurance. Touching between people of different ranks often indicates power and status differences, with the higher-ranking person more likely to initiate the touching. Concerns about sexual harassment and sexism have greatly limited the use of touching in the office. If professional sporting events are considered part of the workplace, then same-sex touching and hugging to express enthusiasm and approval are rampantly practiced.

Touching others on the on the job can be perceived positively or negatively, with hugging the most controversial. A generally accepted alternative to a full hug is to shake the other person's hand whileholding the other person's upper arm with the other hand.[9] (The same type of hug connotes power.)

LIE DETECTION THROUGH NONVERBAL COMMUNICATION

One workplace application of knowledge about nonverbal communication is to detect lies. A conservative approach is to regard certain indicators to suggest that a person might by lying, and then to investigate further the truthfulness of certain statements. For example, an employee suspected of selling employee Social Security numbers to an outside party might respond to any questioning about this theft with a quick, seemingly rehearsed answer. Further investigation, perhaps using a private detective, might be warranted.

It is important to recognize that surefire behavioral indicators of deception do not exist, that the behavior of liars is not consistently revealing. A team of three researchers who reviewed the evidence about human behavior and deception detection concluded that no researcher has documented a "Pinocchio response." (The nose of the fairy-tale character Pinocchio grew when he told a lie.) The finding means that there is no behavior or pattern of behavior that indicates deception in all people, in all situations.

What is known with reasonable certainty is that lying requires extra mental effort. The liar must think quite hard to cover up and create events that have not happened. The extra effort will show up in the nonverbal form: longer pauses between thoughts, and less use of hand and head movements that accompany speech. With respect to emotions, liars do appear to be more nervous than truth tellers. The facial expressions of liars tend to be less pleasant, their voices are pitched higher and more tense, their pupils are more dilated, and they fidget more.[10]

Using Social Media to Enhance Communication Effectiveness

◀ Learning Objective 7.3 ◀

Social media have become integrated into personal communication in personal life, and to some extent on the job. Many large companies have established their own social media sites for employee use. At one extreme, at the online retailer Zappos Inc., employees are encouraged to send tweets and Facebook postings all during the workday so they can be connected and be happy. At the other extreme, using social media on the job, except for a specific business purpose, can result in being disciplined. In Chapter 8, we explore the misuse of electronic communication, including overdependence.

The most frequent job use of social media is much like e-mail. Workers send brief messages to each other by making posts on the website, and top-level management might distribute a message to hundreds of workers simultaneously. Almost infinite knowledge exists about social networking, including its technology, application for building a personal network, and marketing. Included in this abundance of information are claims that Twitter and Facebook have completely transformed the way we live and have made e-mail obsolete. Our aim here is to simply list a few of the positive and negative communication skills associated with the use of social networking sites, including company social media sites.

POSITIVE COMMUNICATION SKILLS AND SOCIAL NETWORKING

The use of Twitter, Facebook, Instagram, and the like provides the serious worker with several opportunities for displaying positive communication and interpersonal skills:

1. **Demonstrate your loyalty by posting gracious comments about your employer.** Social networking sites present an open forum for your ideas about the company. You can demonstrate empathy and compassion for the mission of your company by commenting on an action taken by the company that you perceive as positive. An example: "I'm proud to work for the Jeep division of Fiat/Chrysler. My wife and our three children were caught in a snowstorm. I put my Cherokee into four-wheel drive and made it through the storm until we could find a motel. There were dozens of overturned vehicles, but we made it to safety. The vehicle stabilization feature is really functional."

2. **Demonstrate professional-level communication skills.** When making entries on Twitter in particular, many people feel compelled to write carelessly, foolishly, and viciously, along with using vulgarities. Demonstrate your professionalism by writing in a style suited for a printed newspaper, news website, or term paper. Remember that many influential people regard written communication skills as a subset of interpersonal skills.

3. **Pay deserved compliments to company personnel.** The ability to compliment others in a sensible way is an advanced interpersonal skill. Complimenting a person in private may be useful, but public compliments are welcome also. An example of a Facebook post of this nature: "I want everybody to know that Tom Barnes, our facilities manager, spearheaded the planting of a garden on the office building roof. We are saving the planet, one petunia at a time."

4. **Establish meaningful contact with workers far and wide.** The major purpose of social networking is to develop valuable contacts with many people with whom it would be difficult to maintain person-to-person or phone contact. Selective use of the social networking sites enables you to relate, at least on a written level, to a variety of people in your field. You might be able to enhance your cross-cultural skills by interacting

with professionals in different countries. (LinkedIn is particularly good for this purpose because so many of its members have a professional intent.)

5. **Display a desire to help others grow and develop.** Social networking sites afford an easy opportunity to point others toward helpful information, such as referring friends to useful websites and books. You can also alert people to dangers, such as a new scam related to earning large amounts of money working from home. Although the same type of alerts can be accomplished by e-mail, social networking sites do not require long distribution lists. By pointing people in the direction of useful information, you will be demonstrating part of a useful interpersonal and communication skill of helping others grow and develop. Instead of just writing about yourself on your post, include information that will help others.

6. **For professionally oriented websites, ask first before inviting another person to become a connection.** LinkedIn is the prime example of a social networking website where inviting unknown people to be a link or connection is unwelcome. Career specialist Liz Ryan recommends that when you meet a new acquaintance with whom you would like to make a connection on the site, first ask, "May I send you a LinkedIn invitation?" The reason is that LinkedIn urges users to connect only to people they know well and trust.[11]

NEGATIVE COMMUNICATION SKILLS AND SOCIAL NETWORKING

Social networking provides a setting for displaying negative as well as positive communication and interpersonal skills. In general, all of the positive opportunities mentioned above could be reversed to become negative. For example, instead of helping others grow and develop with postings on your site or their site, you slam and demean these people. Several adolescent suicides have been reported that appear to have been triggered by being insulted on a teen-oriented social networking site. The following list presents a few ways in which negative communication and interpersonal skills are sometimes displayed on social networking sites.

1. **Using social networking sites to eliminate face-to-face interactions with work associates.** As with e-mail, social networking sites provide an opportunity to avoid face-to-face interaction with coworkers, managers, and customers. However, the temptation is even greater with social networking sites because they tout the concept of being "friends" with people on your list of electronic contacts. A person might think consciously or subconsciously, "If my customer is already my friend, why should I have to talk to or personally visit him? Our relationship is already good." If all relationships could be built and maintained electronically, you would not need to be studying human relations.

2. **Posting confidential or derogatory information about your employer.** In the words of technology writer Bridget Carey, "Employees need to realize some conversations are privileged. Just because you're in a meeting about a new product, or worse, layoffs, doesn't mean you should be broadcasting to the world."[12] Posting negative information and insults about your employer demonstrates even lower emotional intelligence. Nasty comments about the employer, even if deserved, are often made out of uncontrolled anger. Hundreds of employees have been fired because of making inflammatory comments on social networking sites about their employers. Poor interpersonal skill is also displayed by joining a social networking group dedicated to destroying the reputation of your employer.

3. **Posting derogatory information and photos about a coworker.** Social networking site administrators generally do not edit posts, so anybody registered on the site can post dreadful comments about another person as a mean prank or a deliberate effort to ruin the target's reputation. YouTube can serve a similar evil purpose. Some of these negative posts reflect backstabbing because another person encourages you to engage in embarrassing behavior. He or she then quotes you or posts a photo or video of you engaged in outrageous behavior.

4. **Engaging in social networking at inappropriate times.** Many social networkers, "tweeters" in particular, are so habituated to visiting their favorite social networking site that they do so at inappropriate times, such as during work. Many office workers access their social networking sites during meetings. The interpersonal skill deficiency of accessing a social network site for nonbusiness purposes during working hours is that it reflects insensitivity and immaturity. (Print-related distractions would also be unwelcome, such as doing crossword puzzles in a meeting.) While dining in a restaurant for business or social purposes, it is considered highly inappropriate to access social media via a smartphone or tablet computer.

Despite all the emphasis on social media and other electronic forms of communication, many companies still see the value of face-to-face, in-person communication. The debate over the value of business travel, as described in the accompanying Human Relations in Practice box, focuses on the importance of building relationships in person.

Human Relations in Practice

Companies See the Relationship-Building Value of Business Travel

Cynthia is the CEO of a company that manufactures and sells industrial uniforms for a wide variety of companies, including security firms, banks, hospitals, and chain restaurants. During a meeting with her top-level managers, she pointed out that sales had declined about 20 percent during the recent year. She has been so concerned about this trend that she had asked Jeremy, the director of marketing, to investigate possible reasons for the decline, and how the problem might be resolved.

Jeremy told the group, as he had told Cynthia, that the company may have gone too far in cutting some expenses that had actually helped boost profits. He focused on the cutback in business travel as a factor that may have hurt sales. "We cannot forget," said Jeremy, "that ours is a business built on relationships. Other companies, including overseas competitors, can provide our customers with uniforms that work just fine. People do business with people they like.

"And the best way to get someone to like you is to have an in-person meeting, over a meal with wine included. Let me show you a few facts. Look at this slide." (Jeremy then flashed a PowerPoint slide on a screen, showing the following facts and observations.)

■ Business travel is related to corporate profit because in-person meetings help promote business.

■ The most profitable types of business travel are client meetings and participation in conventions and exhibitions.

■ Approximately 40 percent of prospective customers are converted to new customers with an in-person meeting, compared to 16 percent without such a meeting.

■ Despite the contribution of business travel to profits, a point of diminishing returns arrives when too much money is spent on travel.

Jeremy then presented a couple of observations made by marketing and communications consultant Rene Shimada Siegel in a business magazine article: "She wrote that there are few private offices any longer. People work in cubicles or open spaces so they can't have

(*continued*)

private conversations. That means when we talk to a client or potential client over the phone, we might not get to hear the most important information they can share.

"Another reason for visiting our customers is that relationships are built when people take the time to share information and learn more about each other. That happens more naturally in person than by phone or in an e-mail or text message. Siegel also reinforced what we already know: that you can read body language much better in person. And we all know that reading body language can help clinch a sale."

Cynthia then made a comment that was well received by the group. "Okay, let's take an experimental approach. Let's up our travel budget by 25 percent for the upcoming fiscal year. Jeremy can work with the sales representatives to prudently invest in business travel. But no sending customers to the Super Bowl or Mardi Gras just to sell a handful of uniforms."

Question:

What really is it about an in-person meeting that is more effective for sales than electronic messages and even videoconferencing (technologies such as Skype included)?

Source: Original story with a few supporting facts contained in the following: Alice Lesch Kelly, "Finding Value in Business Travel," *About.com. Business Travel,* http://businesstravel.about.com, accessed January 29, 2012, p. 1; Rene Shimada Siegel, "5 Reasons You Need to Meet in Person," www.Inc.com, February 29, 2012, pp. 1–3; Rieva Lesonsky, "Why Face to Face Meetings Still Matter," www.smallbiztrends.com, April 7, 2011, pp. 1–5.

▶ **Learning Objective 7.4** ▶

Frequent Barriers to Communication

Communication rarely proceeds as effectively as we would like. Many different factors filter out a message on its way to the intended receiver, shown as potential barriers in Figure 7-1. In this section, we look at some of the human barriers to communication. If you are aware of their presence, you will be better able to overcome them.

Routine or neutral messages are the easiest to communicate. Communication roadblocks are most likely to occur when a message is complex, is emotionally arousing, or clashes with the receiver's mental set. An emotionally arousing message would deal with such topics as job security or money. A message that clashes with a receiver's mental set requires that person to change his or her familiar pattern of receiving messages. The next time you order a meal in a restaurant, order dessert first and an entrée second. The server will probably not "hear" your dessert order because it deviates from the normal ordering sequence. The barriers described here are as follows:

1. Sending a self-centered message

2. One-way communication

3. Different interpretation of words (semantics)

4. Credibility of the sender and mixed signals

5. Distortion and filtering of information

6. Different perspectives and experiences

7. Emotions and attitudes

8. Communication overload

   9. Improper timing

  10. Poor communication skills

  11. Cultural and language barriers

SENDING A SELF-CENTERED MESSAGE

If you send a self-centered message, your communication effectiveness will be limited. It's much more effective to frame your message in terms of what you can do for the other person. Suppose a person in need of money wants to sell food supplements to a friend. Mentioning financial need is a very self-centered message. It could be made less self-centered:

> *Very self-centered.* "You've got to buy a few food supplements from me. I can't meet my credit card payments."

> *Less self-centered.* "Would you be interested in purchasing a few food supplements that would bring you more energy and help you live longer? If your answer is yes, I can help you."

Similarly, when you are applying for a new position or promotion, a weak message is to explain that you need the money associated with the job. It is much better to ask for the position in terms of your potential contribution to the organization, such as resolving a complex problem.

ONE-WAY COMMUNICATION

Effective communication proceeds back and forth. An exchange of information or a transaction takes place between two or more people. Person A may send messages to person B to initiate communication, but B must react to A to complete the communication loop. One reason written messages sometimes fail to achieve their purpose is that the person who writes the message cannot be sure how it will be interpreted. One written message that is subject to many interpretations is "Your idea is of some interest to me." (How much is *some*?) Face-to-face communication helps clarify meanings.

A quick way to bring about the exchange of information necessary for two-way communication is to ask a question. An example here would be "Are you clear on what I mean by a *good customer*?"

DIFFERENT INTERPRETATION OF WORDS (SEMANTICS)

Semantics is the study of the meaning and changes in the meaning of words or symbols. These different meanings can create communication barriers. Often the problem is trivial and humorous; at other times, semantic problems can create substantial communication barriers. Consider first an example of trivial consequence.

Semantics
the study of the meaning and changes in the meaning of words or symbols

An older supervisor told a new hire to the unit that her work so far was "good as gold." The young worker looked perplexed and frowned. The supervisor then asked, "Don't you like your work to be good as gold?" The new employee said, "I thought you were giving me negative feedback. Gold goes up and down in price so often that I've been told it's not so good."

Of greater consequence is the use of a word or term without thorough explanation that could cause people to act in an unintended direction. An example is for a manager to use the term *restructure* when speaking to employees or outsiders. Four common interpretations of the word are the following: (1) refinance the company debt, (2) declare bankruptcy, (3) change the organization structure, or (4) lay off many workers. A negative consequence of not knowing the true meaning of the term would be for a competent employee to seek employment elsewhere because he or she feared being laid off.

A contributing factor to most problems of semantics is that a word or expression with multiple possible meanings is used without clarification and explanation. Language scholar Kees van Deemter observes that most words have fuzzy boundaries, so it is helpful to clarify key words for the target.[13] For example, when referring to our "wealthy customers," it is good to clarify what is meant by a *wealthy* customer. Perhaps the reference is to those customers in the top 2 percent income bracket. Or the reference might be to the top 1 percent, or even 50 percent.

CREDIBILITY OF THE SENDER AND MIXED SIGNALS

Mixed signals

type of message in which the sender might recommend one thing to others yet behave in another way

The more trustworthy the sender of the message, the greater the probability that the message will get through clearly. In contrast, when the sender has low credibility, many times it will be ignored. Communications can also break down for a subtle variation of low credibility. The disconnect occurs from **mixed signals**, a type of message in which the sender might recommend one thing to others yet behave in another way himself or herself. (Observe that *mixed message* as described earlier has a different meaning.) A team leader might tell others that a tidy worker is a productive worker. However, his or her own cubicle contains a four-month supply of empty soft-drink cans, and old papers consume virtually every square inch of his or her desk.

Mixed signals also refers to sending different messages about the same topic to different audiences. For example, company representatives might brag about the high quality of the company's products in public statements. Yet, on the shop floor and in the office, the company tells its employees to cut costs whenever possible to lower costs.

DISTORTION AND FILTERING OF INFORMATION

A great problem in sending messages is that people receiving them often hear what they want to hear. Without malicious intent, people modify your message to bolster their self-esteem or improve their situation. An incident that occurred between Danielle and her supervisor is fairly typical of this type of communication barrier. Danielle asked her supervisor when she would be receiving a salary increase. Regarding the request as far-fetched and beyond the budget at the time, Danielle's supervisor replied, "Why should the company give you a raise when you are often late for work?"

Danielle *heard* her supervisor say, "If you come to work on time regularly, you will receive a salary increase." One month later, Danielle said to her supervisor that she had not been late for work in a month and should now be eligible for a raise. Her supervisor replied, "I never said that. Where did you get that idea?"

Filtering of information refers to the barrier to effective communication that takes place when a person softens bad news to avoid a negative reaction from the receiver. For example, a plant manager might tell the CEO that the accident rate in the plant "slipped upward a little." When the CEO later finds out that accidents went up 25 percent, the plant manager might then be perceived as a dishonest communicator.

DIFFERENT PERSPECTIVES AND EXPERIENCES

People perceive words and concepts differently because their experiences and vantage points differ. On the basis of their perception of what they have heard, most people believe that all homeless people live in the street, parks, or public buildings such as libraries. In reality, many homeless people live in temporary housing such as shelters provided by the community.

Cultural differences create different perspectives and experiences, such as workers from Eastern cultures tending to have high respect for authority. A worker from India might more readily accept a message from the boss than would his or her counterpart from California or Sweden. In the last two places, workers have a more casual attitude toward authority.

EMOTIONS AND ATTITUDES

Have you ever tried to communicate a message to another person while that person is emotionally aroused? Your message was probably distorted considerably. Another problem is that people tend to say things when emotionally aroused that they would not say when calm. Similarly, a person who has strong attitudes about a particular topic may become emotional when that topic is introduced. The underlying message here is try to avoid letting strong emotions and attitudes interfere with the sending or receiving of messages. If you are angry with someone, for example, you might miss the merit in what that person has to say. Calm down before proceeding with your discussion or attempting to resolve the conflict. Emotional intelligence makes a key contribution in this situation.

COMMUNICATION OVERLOAD

A major communication barrier facing literate people is being bombarded with information. **Communication overload** occurs when people are so overloaded with information that they cannot respond effectively to messages. As a result, they experience work stress. Workers at many levels are exposed to so much electronic, printed, and spoken information that their capacity to absorb it is taxed. The problem is worsened when low-quality information is competing for your attention. An example is a flashing pop-up ad informing you that you have just won a free laptop computer, and all you have to do is follow a link to claim your prize. The human mind is capable of processing only a limited quantity of information at a time. Workers who intentionally multitask, such as reading instant messages and filling in a spreadsheet at the same time, aggravate the problem of communication overload. More information about this problem is in Chapter 8, about communication in the workplace, and Chapter 16 about developing good work habits.

Communication overload
phenomenon that occurs when people are so overloaded with information that they cannot respond effectively to messages

IMPROPER TIMING

Many messages do not get through to people because they are poorly timed. You have to know how to deliver a message, but you must also know *when* to deliver it. Sending a message when the receiver is distracted with other concerns or is rushing to get somewhere is a waste of time. A specific example is that your message might be wasted when you contact someone who is getting set to leave for a lunch break at the moment. Furthermore, the sender may become discouraged and therefore will not repeat the message later.

The art of timing messages suggests not to ask for a raise when your boss is in a bad mood or to ask a new acquaintance for a date when he or she is preoccupied. However, do ask your boss for a raise when business has been good, and do ask someone for a date when you have just done something nice for that person and have been thanked.

POOR COMMUNICATION SKILLS

A message may fail to register because the sender lacks effective communication skills. The sender might garble a written or spoken message so severely that the receiver finds it impossible to understand. Also, the sender may deliver the message so poorly that the receiver does not take it seriously. A common deficiency in sending messages is to communicate with low conviction by using *wimpy* words, backpedaling, and qualifying. Part of the same idea is to use affirmative language, such as saying "when" instead of "if." Also, do not use phrases that call your integrity into question, such as "to be perfectly honest" (implying that you usually do not tell the truth).[14] To illustrate, here are three statements that send a message of low conviction to the receiver: "I think I might be able to finish this project by the end of the week"; "It's possible that I could handle the assignment you have in mind"; "I'll do what I can."

Communication barriers can result from deficiencies within the receiver. A common barrier is a receiver who is a poor listener. Improving listening skills is such a major strategy for improving communication skills that it receives separate mention later in this chapter.

CULTURAL AND LANGUAGE BARRIERS

Communication barriers in work and personal life can be created when the sender and receiver come from different cultures and are not fluent in each other's language. Quite often, cultural differences and language differences exist at the same time. A cultural difference creating a barrier to communication often takes this form: A supervisor from a culture that emphasizes empowering (giving power to) employees is giving instructions to an employee from a culture that believes the boss should make all the decisions. In response to a question from the subordinate, the supervisor says, "Do what you think is best." The subordinate has a difficult time understanding the message because he or she is waiting for a firm directive from the boss.

Limited understanding of another person can sometimes be attributed to cultural differences. For example, a supervisor might send a message to Lana, a South Korean American in her group, that she can win an Employee of the Month award if she increases her productivity by 5 percent. Lana does not receive the message well because according to her cultural beliefs, it is negative behavior to stand out from the group. (After Lana assimilates more into the American culture, she will most likely receive the message more clearly.)

At times, language barriers cause accidents. Many foreign-language-speaking construction workers in the United States encounter accidents because they do not clearly understand the instructions about danger.

A notable problem with language barriers has stemmed from the practice of *offshoring* (sending overseas) customer service and call center positions to India, as well as Mexico and the Philippines. For Mexicans and Filipinos, English is usually their second language so they have an accent unfamiliar to many Americans. Although English might be the primary or strong second language of Indian workers, it is not a type of English familiar to many Americans. As a result, many Americans who are not familiar with the accents of English-speaking Indians will say, "I can't understand the person who is trying to help me." Many of these people hang up in frustration. Several U.S.-based telecommunication companies have therefore reestablished customer service centers in the United States.

To help overcome cultural and language barriers, many companies invest considerable time and money in cross-cultural training, as will be explained in Chapter 14.

▶ **Learning Objective 7.5** ▶

Building Bridges to Communication

With determination and awareness that communication roadblocks and barriers do exist, you can become a more effective communicator. It would be impossible to remove all barriers, but they can be minimized. The following ten techniques are helpful in building better bridges to communication.

1. Appeal to human needs, and time your messages.

2. Repeat your message assertively, using more than one channel.

3. Have a positive attitude, and be persuasive.

4. Discuss differences in frames of reference.

5. Check for comprehension and feelings through feedback.

6. Minimize defensive communication.

7. Combat communication overload.

8. Use mirroring to establish rapport.

9. Engage in small talk and positive gossip.

10. Solicit feedback on your communication effectiveness.

APPEAL TO HUMAN NEEDS, AND TIME YOUR MESSAGES

People are more receptive to messages that promise to do something for them. In other words, if a message promises to satisfy a need that is less than fully satisfied, you are likely to listen. The person in search of additional money who ordinarily does not hear low tones readily hears the whispered message, "How would you like to earn $600 in one weekend?"

Timing a message properly is related to appealing to human needs. If you deliver a message at the right time, you are taking into account the person's mental condition at the moment. A general principle is to deliver your message when the person might be in the right frame of mind to listen. The right frame of mind includes such factors as not being preoccupied with other thoughts, not being frustrated, being in a good mood, and not being stressed out. (Of course, all this severely limits your opportunity to send a message!)

REPEAT YOUR MESSAGE ASSERTIVELY, USING MORE THAN ONE CHANNEL

You can overcome many communication barriers by repeating your message several times. An assertive message is clear and direct, without being too aggressive or passive (such as using wimpy expressions.) It is usually advisable not to say exactly the same thing so as to avoid annoying the listener with straight repetition. Repeating the message in a different form is effective in another way: The receiver may not have understood the message in the way in which it was first delivered. Repetition, like any other means of overcoming communication roadblocks, does not work for all people. Many people who repeatedly hear the message "Text messaging while driving is dangerous" are not moved by it. It is helpful to use several methods of overcoming roadblocks or barriers to communication.

A generally effective way of repeating a message is to use more than one communication channel. For example, follow up a face-to-face discussion with an e-mail message or phone call or both. Your body can be another channel or medium to help impart your message. If you agree with someone about a spoken message, state your agreement and also shake hands over the agreement. Can you think of another channel by which to transmit a message?

A study conducted with project managers found that these people typically send the same message to the same recipient using more than one medium, and they send the messages in sequence. The redundant messages were most likely to be employed when the project was facing a threat to achieving a goal on time.[15]

HAVE A POSITIVE ATTITUDE, AND BE PERSUASIVE

A positive attitude helps a person communicate better in speaking, writing, and nonverbally. Being positive is a major factor in being persuasive, as mentioned previously in avoiding wimpy words. Developing a positive attitude is not always easy. A starting point is to see things from a positive perspective, including looking for the good in people and their work. If your work is intrinsically motivating, you are likely to have a positive attitude. You would then be able to communicate about your work with the enthusiasm necessary.

Figure 7-3 summarizes key ideas about persuasive communication, a topic most readers have very likely studied in the past.[16] If you can learn to implement most of the ten suggestions, you are on your way toward becoming a persuasive communicator. In addition, you will need solid facts behind you, and you will need to make skillful use of nonverbal communication.

DISCUSS DIFFERENCES IN FRAMES OF REFERENCE

Frame of reference
mental model, viewpoint, or perspective

Another way of understanding differences in perspectives and experiences is to recognize that people often have different frames of reference that influence how they interpret events. A **frame of reference** is a mental model, viewpoint, or perspective. When two people with different frameworks look at a situation, a communication problem may occur. For instance, one person may say, "I have just found the *ideal* potential mate." To this person, an *ideal* mate would be a person who was kind, caring, considerate, in good health, gainfully employed, and highly ethical. The listener may have a perception of an *ideal* potential mate as someone who has a superior physical appearance and is wealthy (a traditional stereotype). Until the two people understand each other's frame of reference, meaningful communication about the prospective mate is unlikely. The solution to this communication clash is to discuss the frame of reference: Each party in this exchange defines his or her perception of an ideal mate.

CHECK FOR COMPREHENSION AND FEELINGS THROUGH FEEDBACK

Don't be a hit-and-run communicator. Such a person drops a message and leaves the scene before he or she is sure the message has been received as intended. It is preferable to ask for feedback. Ask receivers for their understanding or interpretation of what you said. For example, you might say after delivering a message, "What is your understanding of our agreement?" Also use nonverbal indicators to gauge how well you delivered your message. A blank expression on the receiver's face might indicate no comprehension. A disturbed, agitated expression might mean that the receiver's emotions are blocking the message.

A comprehension check increases in importance when possible cultural and language barriers exist. A simple direct inquiry about comprehension is often effective, such as, "Is what I said okay with you?" or "Tell me what I said." A friendly facial expression should accompany such feedback checks; otherwise your inquiry will come across like a challenge.

In addition to looking for verbal comprehension and emotions when you have delivered a message, check for feelings after you have received a message. When a person speaks, we too often listen to the facts and ignore the feelings. If feelings are ignored, the true meaning and intent of the message are likely to be missed, thus creating a communication barrier. Your boss might say to you, "You never seem to take work home." To clarify what your boss means by this statement, you might ask, "Is that good or bad?" Your boss's response will give you feedback on his or her feelings about getting all your work done during regular working hours.

FIGURE 7-3

KEY PRINCIPLES OF PERSUASIVE COMMUNICATION

Source: "KEY PRINCIPLES OF PERSUASIVE COMMUNICATION" by Andrew J. DuBrin.

1. *Know exactly what you want.* First, clarify ideas in your mind.
2. *Never suggest an action without describing its end benefit.* Explain how your message will benefit the receiver. *Reciprocity* is a key principle of persuasion. If you want another person to do something, be clear about how you will reciprocate, which could mean the benefit the other person will receive.
3. *Have a reputation as a trustworthy source of information.* Most persuasion techniques have a trust component included. If people have found you to be trustworthy in the past, you are more likely to be persuasive in the present.
4. *Use powerful words.* Sprinkle your speech with phrases like "bonding with customers" and "vaporizing the competition."
5. *When you speak, begin with your headline—the most important point.* After the headline, provide more information as needed. To come up with the right headline, imagine what you would say if you had only ten minutes to deliver your message. An environmental specialist might begin a message to management with "My new program will help us save the planet."
6. *Minimize raising your pitch at the end of sentences.* Part of being persuasive is not to sound unsure and apologetic.
7. *Back up conclusions with data.* You will be more persuasive if you support your spoken and written presentations with solid data, but do not become an annoyance by overdoing it.
8. *Minimize "wimp" phrases.* See discussion under "Poor Communication Skills" in this chapter.
9. *Avoid or minimize common language errors.* Do not say "could care less," when you mean "couldn't care less," or "orientated" when you mean "oriented." Because language standards have loosened so much in everyday talk, a person who speaks with precision is likely to stand out.
10. *Avoid overuse of jargon and clichés.* To feel "in" and cool, many workers rely heavily on jargon and clichés, such as referring to their "fave" (for *favorite*) product or saying that "at the end of the day," something counts. It is also helpful to minimize the use of catchphrases like "bottom line," "quantum leap," and "cutting edge." It is best to avoid or minimize unprofessional expressions such as "you guys," "like," and "awesome." The problem is that if you make frequent use of overused expressions, you may give the impression of not thinking critically.
11. *Frame your position in the direction you want.* Describe in a positive way the option you want the receiver to choose, or describe in a negative way the option you don't want the receiver to choose. For example, if you want to convince others of the advantages of global outsourcing, you might refer to it as "seeking wage rates that will make us competitive." If you want to convince others of the disadvantages of global outsourcing, you might refer to it as "shipping jobs from our country overseas."
12. *Explain that there is limited opportunity to capitalize on your offer.* According to persuasion principle of *scarcity*, people desire what is rare. If you make statements such as "There is only one left in stock," or "We have only one position left on our team," you will often be persuasive.
13. *Speak with a big-picture perspective instead of presenting small details.* People who present ideas in a broad, abstract manner, looking at the big picture rather than presenting small details tend to be perceived as powerful. A big picture usually points to an overall direction. The higher the level of the position the person speaking holds, the more a big picture is expected. Yet a person at any organizational level can appear more powerful by using a big picture, such as a team leader saying to the group, "We are moving at a pace that will be the envy of many other teams in the company."

When you send a message, it is also helpful to express your feelings in addition to conveying the facts. For example, "Our customer returns are up by 12 percent [fact], and I'm quite disappointed about those results [feelings]." Because feelings contribute strongly to comprehension, you will help overcome a potential communication barrier.

MINIMIZE DEFENSIVE COMMUNICATION

Defensive communication
tendency to receive messages in such a way that one's self-esteem is protected

Distortion of information was described previously as a communication barrier. Such distortion can also be regarded as **defensive communication**, the tendency to receive messages in such a way that our self-esteem is protected. Defensive communication is also responsible for people sending messages to look good. For example, when criticized for achieving below-average sales, a store manager might shift the blame to the sales associates in her store. Overcoming the barrier of defensive communication requires two steps. First, people have to acknowledge the existence of defensive communication. Second, they have to try not to be defensive when questioned or criticized. Such behavior is not easy because of **denial**, the suppression of information we find uncomfortable. For example, the store manager previously cited would find it uncomfortable to think of herself as being responsible for below-average sales.

Denial
the suppression of information one finds uncomfortable

COMBAT COMMUNICATION OVERLOAD

You can decrease the chances of suffering from communication overload by such measures as carefully organizing and sorting information before plunging ahead with reading. Speed-reading may help, provided that you stop to read carefully the most relevant information. Or you can scan through downloaded reports, hard-copy reports, magazines, and websites looking for key titles and words that are important to you. Recognize, however, that many subjects have to be studied carefully if you are to derive benefit. It is often better to read thoroughly a few topics than to skim through lots of information. Dealing with the challenges of e-mail is discussed in Chapter 8.

USE MIRRORING TO ESTABLISH RAPPORT

Mirroring
form of nonverbal communication to overcome communication barriers by subtly imitating another; used to improve rapport with another person

Another approach to overcoming communication barriers is to improve rapport with another person. A form of nonverbal communication, called **mirroring**, can be used to establish such rapport. To mirror someone is to subtly imitate that individual. The most successful mirroring technique for establishing rapport is to imitate the breathing pattern of another person. If you adjust your own breathing rate to someone else's, you will soon establish rapport with that person. Mirroring sometimes takes the form of imitating the boss in order to communicate better and win favor. Many job seekers now use mirroring to get in sync with the interviewer. Is this a technique you would be willing to try?

Mirroring takes practice to contribute to overcoming communication barriers. It is a subtle technique that requires a moderate skill level. If you mirror (or match) another person in a rigid, mechanical way, you will appear to be mocking that person. And mocking, of course, erects rather than tears down a communication barrier.

ENGAGE IN SMALL TALK AND POSITIVE GOSSIP

The terms *small talk* and *gossip* have negative connotations for the career-minded person with a professional attitude. Negative gossip can badly damage a person's reputation, such as spreading the story that the company's chief security officer was recently arrested for shoplifting. Nevertheless, the effective use of small talk and gossip can help a person melt communication barriers. Small talk is important because it contributes to conversational skills, and having good conversational skills enhances interpersonal communication. A helpful technique is to collect tidbits of information to use as small talk to facilitate work-related or heavy-topic conversation in personal life. Keeping informed about current events, including sports, television, and films, provides useful content for small talk.

Being a source of *positive gossip* brings a person power and credibility. (*Positive gossip* is the passing along of information of a constructive nature that does not harm or demean another individual.) Workmates are eager to communicate with a person who is a source of not-yet-verified developments. Having such inside knowledge enhances your status and makes you a more interesting communicator. Positive gossip would include such tidbits as mentioning that the company will be looking for workers who would want a one-year assignment in Europe or that more employees will soon be eligible for profit-sharing bonuses. Employment law specialist Lynne Elsaguirre says that the key to making good use of gossip is to avoid petty gossip, such as "Did you hear that the IT guy dumped his girlfriend?"[17] Spreading negative gossip will often erode your attractiveness to other people.[18]

SOLICIT FEEDBACK ON YOUR COMMUNICATION EFFECTIVENESS

It may require courage and a strong desire to improve, but soliciting feedback on your communication effectiveness can help overcome barriers. Asking a question electronically rather than in person is often effective because the other person has more time to reflect on the answer and perhaps give you a couple examples of your communication effectiveness or ineffectiveness. Here are a couple of candid answers in response to the question, "How well am I communicating with you?"

I'd say quite well both in the way you speak, and in your written messages.

When you're nervous, you're not so good at communicating. You put your hand over your mouth, and you look down at the floor.

As with most forms of feedback about the self, the same comment made by more than one person is more reliable than one random comment. If three or four people make a similar comment about a communication error you are making, you know you have an area for improvement.

Overcoming Gender Barriers to Communication

◀ Learning Objective 7.6 ◀

Another strategy for overcoming communication barriers is to deal effectively with potential gender differences. Despite the movement toward equality of the sexes in the workplace, substantial interest exists in identifying differences in communication style between men and women. People who are aware of these differences face fewer communication problems between themselves and members of the opposite sex.

As we describe these differences, recognize that they are group stereotypes. Individual differences in communication style are usually more important than group styles (men versus women). Here we will describe the major findings of gender differences in communication patterns.[19]

1. **Women prefer to use conversation for rapport building and social connections.** For most women, the intent of conversation is to build rapport and connections with people.

Women are therefore more likely to emphasize similarities, to listen intently, and to be supportive.

2. **Men prefer to use talk primarily as a means to preserve independence and status by displaying knowledge and skill.** When most men talk, they want to receive positive evaluations from others and maintain their hierarchical status within the group. Men are therefore more oriented to giving a *report*, whereas women are more interested in establishing *rapport*.

3. **Women want empathy, not solutions.** When women share feelings of being stressed out, they seek empathy and understanding. If they feel they have been listened to carefully, they begin to relax. When listening to the woman, the man may feel blamed for her problems or that he has failed the woman in some way. To feel useful, the man might offer solutions to the woman's problem.

4. **Men prefer to work out their problems by themselves, whereas women prefer to talk out solutions with another person.** Women look on having and sharing problems as an opportunity to build and deepen relationships. Men are more likely to look on problems as challenges they must meet on their own. Similarly men are more hesitant to ask questions when faced with a problem, and women gather information by asking questions. The communication consequence of these differences is that men may become uncommunicative when they have a problem.

5. **Men tend to be more directive and less apologetic in their conversation, whereas women are more polite and apologetic.** Women are therefore more likely to frequently use the phrases "I'm sorry" and "thank you," even when there is no need to express apology or gratitude. Men less frequently say they are sorry, because they perceive communications as competition, and they do not want to appear vulnerable.

6. **Women tend to be more conciliatory when facing differences, whereas men become more intimidating.** Again, women are more interested in building relationships, whereas men are more concerned about coming out ahead.

7. **Men are more interested than women in calling attention to their accomplishments or hogging recognition.** One consequence of this difference is that men are more likely to dominate discussions during meetings. Another consequence is that women are more likely to help a coworker perform well. In one instance, a sales representative who had already made her sales quota for the month turned over an excellent prospect to a coworker. She reasoned, "It's somebody else's turn. I've received more than my fair share of bonuses for the month."

8. **Women are more likely to use a gentle expletive, whereas men tend to be harsher.** For example, if a woman locks herself out of the car, she is likely to say, "Oh dear." In the same situation, a man is likely to say, "Oh _____." (Here we could be dealing with both a sex and a generational difference, with recent generations of women being more likely to swear than previous generations.)

9. **Women use the words "I," "me," and "mine" more frequently.** It is generally thought that men use "I" more, because men are more narcissistic and self-congratulatory. Yet recent research from several studies, and across cultures, indicates that women make more frequent use of "I," "me," and "mine." The reason appears to be that women are more aware of their internal state. In contrast, men use more articles such as "a," "an," and "the." The implication is that men talk more frequently about objects and things. Women also make more frequent use of the third-person pronouns, "he," "she," and "they," because women talk more about people and relationships.[20]

How can the information just presented help overcome communication problems on the job? As a starting point, remember that gender differences often exist. Understanding these differences will help you interpret the communication behavior of people. For example, if a male coworker is not as polite as you would like, remember that he is simply engaging in gender-typical behavior. Do not take it personally.

A woman can remind herself to speak up more in meetings because her natural tendency might be toward holding back. She might say to herself, "I must watch out to avoid gender-typical behavior in this situation." A man might remind himself to be more polite and supportive toward coworkers. The problem is that although such behavior is important, his natural tendency might be to skip saying "thank you."

Men and women should recognize that when women talk over problems, they might not be seeking hard-hitting advice. Instead, they may simply be searching for a sympathetic ear so they can deal with the emotional aspects of the problem.

A general suggestion for overcoming gender-related communication barriers is for men to improve communication by listening with more empathy. Women can improve communication by becoming more direct.

Enhancing Your Listening Skills

◀ Learning Objective 7.7 ◀

Improving your receiving of messages is another part of developing better face-to-face and telephone communication skills. Unless you receive messages as they are intended, you cannot perform your job properly or be a good companion. Listening is a particularly important skill for anybody whose job involves solving problems for others because you need to gather information to understand the nature of the problem. Improving employee listening skills is important because insufficient listening is extraordinarily costly. Listening mistakes lead to reprocessing letters and e-mail messages, rescheduling appointments, reshipping orders, and recalling defective products. Effective listening also improves interpersonal relationships because people like to feel understood and respected.

A fundamental reason so many people do not listen well is because of the difference between the average speed of talking and the average speed of processing information. Humans speak at an average pace of 110 to 200 words per minute. In contrast, they can understand or process information in the range of 400 to 3,000 words per minute.[21] As a result, the mind tends to wander while listening to the slow pace of the sender talking. Human Relations Self-Assessment Quiz 7-2 is designed to help you think about your listening effectiveness.

ACTIVE LISTENING

A major component of effective listening is to be an **active listener**. The active listener listens intensely, with the goal of empathizing with the speaker. **Empathy** means understanding another person's point of view. If you understand the other person's paradigm, you will be a better receiver and sender of messages. Empathy does not necessarily mean that you sympathize with the other person. For example, you may understand why some people are forced to beg in the streets, but you may have very little sympathy for their plight. As described in the chapter opener, empathy is a valuable job behavior.

Active listener
person who listens intensely, with the goal of empathizing with the speaker

Empathy
understanding another person's point of view

Accepting the Sender's Figure of Speech

A useful way of showing empathy is to accept the sender's figure of speech. If you do so, the sender feels understood and accepted. Also, if you reject the person's figure of speech by rewording it, the sender may become defensive. Many people use the figure of speech "I'm stuck" when they cannot accomplish a task. You can facilitate smooth communication by a response such as "What can I do to help you get unstuck?" If you respond with something like "What can I do to help you think more clearly?" the person is forced to change mental channels and may become defensive.[22]

Human Relations Self-Assessment Quiz   7-2

Common Listening Mistakes

Number	Statement about Listening	Not a Problem	Need Improvement
1.	I often finish people's sentences for them, to save time.	❑	❑
2.	When another person talks to me, I usually attempt to do something else, such as glancing at my smartphone or looking at what's on my television screen.	❑	❑
3.	I change the subject quickly and frequently when someone is talking to me.	❑	❑
4.	I tune out right away when someone is telling me something I strongly disagree with.	❑	❑
5.	I ask, "What did you say?" a few times in every conversation even though my hearing is okay.	❑	❑
6.	As soon as I disagree with something somebody tells me, I laugh at him or her.	❑	❑
7.	I become bored quickly when I am not the person doing the talking in a conversation.	❑	❑
8.	I often answer my own questions with a statement such as "How are you today? You seem fine."	❑	❑
9.	I rarely remember a person's name after hearing it once.	❑	❑
10.	I never recall somebody saying to me, "Thanks for listening."	❑	❑

Scoring and Interpretation:

Assuming that you have enough self-insight to respond accurately to the ten statements, if you answered "Not a Problem" to at least eight of the statements you are a good listener. If you responded "Need Improvement" to eight or more of the statements, you are advised to work on your listening skills.

Source: "Common Listening Mistakes" by Andrew J. DuBrin.

Feedback and Paraphrasing

Paraphrase
repeating in one's own words what a sender says, feels, and means

As a result of listening actively, the listener can feed back to the speaker what he or she thinks the speaker meant. Feedback of this type relies on both verbal and nonverbal communication. Feedback is also important because it facilitates two-way communication. To be an active listener, it is also important to **paraphrase**, or repeat in your own words, what the sender says, feels, and means. In your paraphrasing, avoid rewording a person's figure of speech so long as that phrase is acceptable to you. You might feel awkward the first several times you paraphrase. Therefore, try it with a person with whom you feel comfortable. With some practice, it will become a natural part of your communication skill kit. Here is an example of how you might use paraphrasing:

Other Person: I'm getting ticked off at working so hard around here. I wish somebody else would pitch in and do a fair day's work.

You: You're saying that you do more than your fair share of the tough work in our department, and it's ticking you off.

Other Person: You bet. Here's what I think we should be doing about it. . . .

After you have paraphrased, it is sometimes helpful to ask the person you listened to whether your impression of what he or she said is correct. Your goal is not to make others repeat themselves but to extend the conversation so you can obtain more useful details.[23]

Minimize Distractions

If feasible, keep your phone and your computer screen out of sight when listening to somebody else. Having distractions in sight creates the temptation to glance away from the message sender. At the start of your conversation, notice the other person's eye color to help you establish eye contact. (But don't keep staring at his or her eyes!) A major technique of active listening is to ask questions rather than making conclusive statements. Asking questions provides you with more useful information. Suppose a teammate is late with data you need to complete your analysis. Instead of saying, "I must have your input by Thursday afternoon," try, "When will I get your input?"

Allow the Sender to Finish His or Her Sentence

Be sure to let others speak until they have finished. Do not interrupt by talking about you, jumping in with advice, or offering solutions unless requested. It is equally bad for careful listening to finish the sentence of a sender. Almost all people prefer to complete their own thoughts, even when dealing with a close work associate or family member. You have probably noticed that when you start to enter a phrase into an Internet search engine, suddenly you are given about ten choices that are not necessarily what you are planning to write. (Of course, this is responding to writing and not really listening, but the overtaking of your thinking is the same.)

Ask Open-Ended Questions

A key part of listening is to keep the conversation flowing. One of the most effective ways to keep the conversation flowing is to ask open-ended questions that invite the other person to provide information rather than responding yes or no. An open-ended question about providing help to a coworker would be "How else can I help you get this task accomplished?" A closed-end question would be "Are you getting enough help from me?"

Minimize Words That Shut Down Discussion

According to executive coach Marshall Goldsmith, an especially useful approach to keep conversation going in most work situations is for the listener to minimize certain negatively toned words that frequently shut down conversation. When you say, "no," "but," or "however," you effectively shut down or limit the conversation. No matter what words follow, the sender receives a message to the effect, "You are wrong and I am right." Even if you say, "I agree, but . . ." the shutdown message still comes through. The other person is likely to get into the defensive mode.

After the person has finished talking, there are times it will be appropriate to say, "no," "but," or "however."[24] Assume, for example, that a worker says to the business owner that the company should donate one-third of its profits to charity each year. The owner might then reply, "I hear you, but if we give away all that money, our profits will be too slim to grow the business."

Another way to block the free flow of communication is to make a shutdown response when someone asks, "Do you have the time to discuss something important?" The shutdown response is "I'm busy right now, but go ahead anyway." The person who approached you is likely to feel slighted and might even leave the message unsaid.

Control Your Biases

A subtle barrier to active listening is that a personal bias might prevent you from paying careful attention to the message sender. If you have preconceived ideas that the message sender has little to offer, you might not listen to that person carefully.[25] A hospital administrator might not think that a custodial worker has much to offer about patient satisfaction. The administrator would therefore not listen to the worker's suggestions for improving the patient experience.

Personal Communication Style

Personal communication style
verbal and nonverbal communication style for a unique approach to sending and receiving information

In this chapter we have described many aspects of how people communicate, including gender-specific tendencies. How you combine verbal and nonverbal communication becomes part of your **personal communication style**, or your unique approach to sending and receiving information. Your personal communication style is a major component of your personality because it differentiates you from others. Hundreds of styles are possible, including the following:

- Katherine speaks loudly, smiles frequently, and moves close to people when speaking. Her communication style might be described as aggressive.

- Oscar speaks softly, partially covers his mouth with his hand while talking, and looks away from others. His communication style might be defined as passive or wimpy.

- Tim speaks rapidly, uses a colorful vocabulary, smiles frequently, and makes sweeping gestures. His communication style might be defined as flamboyant.

Concept Review and Reinforcement

Key Terms

Communication, 175
Encoding, 175
Decoding, 175
Barriers to communication
(or noise), 176
Nonverbal communication, 176

Mixed messages, 176
Semantics, 185
Mixed signals, 186
Communication overload, 187
Frame of reference, 190
Defensive communication, 192

Denial, 192
Mirroring, 192
Active listener, 195
Empathy, 195
Paraphrase, 196
Personal communication style, 198

Summary and Review

Communication is the sending and receiving of messages. Therefore, almost anything that takes place in work and personal life involves communication. The steps involved in communication are sending, transmission over a channel, and decoding.

Nonverbal communication, or silent messages, is an important part of everyday communication. Nonverbal communication includes the following:

- Environment or setting in which the message is sent
- Distance from the other person
- Posture
- Hand gestures
- Facial expressions and eye contact
- Voice quality
- Personal appearance
- Touching another person

Nonverbal communication can be used to detect lying, such as a higher pitched voice and fidgeting.

Positive interpersonal and communication skills associated with social networking include (a) demonstrating your loyalty by making gracious comments about your employer, (b) demonstrating professional-level communication skills, (c) paying deserved compliments to company personnel, (d) establishing meaningful contact with workers far and wide, (e) displaying a desire to help others grow and develop, and (f) asking before inviting another person to be a connection.

Negative communication and interpersonal skills associated with networking include (a) using social networking sites to eliminate face-to-face interactions with work associates, (b) posting confidential or derogatory information about your employer, (c) posting derogatory information and photos about a coworker, and (d) engaging in social networking at inappropriate times.

Barriers to communication are most likely to occur when messages are complex or emotional or clash with the receiver's mental set. Communication roadblocks include the following:

- Sending self-centered messages
- One-way communication
- Semantics
- Credibility of the sender and mixed signals
- Distortion and filtering of information
- Different perspectives and experiences
- Emotions and attitudes
- Communication overload
- Improper timing
- Poor communication skills
- Cultural and language barriers

Strategies to overcome communication roadblocks include these:

- Appealing to human need and timing your messages
- Repeating your message assertively, using more than one channel
- Having a positive attitude and being persuasive
- Discussing differences in frames of reference
- Checking for comprehension and feelings through feedback
- Minimizing defensive communication
- Combating communication overload
- Using mirroring to establish rapport
- Engaging in small talk and positive gossip
- Soliciting feedback on your communication effectiveness

Some opinion and evidence exist about gender differences in communication style. For example, women prefer to use conversation for rapport building, and men prefer to use talk primarily as a means to preserve independence and status by displaying knowledge and skill. Understanding gender differences will help you interpret the communication behavior of people.

Improving your receiving of messages is another part of developing better communication skills. Unless you receive messages as intended, you cannot perform your job properly or be a good companion. A major component of effective listening is to be an active listener. The active listener uses empathy and can feed back to the speaker what he or she thinks the speaker meant.

Active listening also involves:

- Accepting the sender's figure of speech
- Feedback and paraphrasing
- Minimizing distractions
- Allowing the sender to finish his or her sentences
- Asking open-ended questions
- Minimizing words that shut down discussion

How you combine verbal and nonverbal communication becomes your personal communication style.

Questions for Discussion and Review

7.1 What could you do to demonstrate to your immediate manager that you are empathetic (have empathy skills)?

7.2 Many people contend they communicate much more formally when on the job and much more informally (including using a more limited vocabulary) when among family members and friends. What do you see as the potential advantages and disadvantages of using two communication styles?

7.3 Why is nonverbal communication so important for the effectiveness of a manager or sales representative?

7.4 Hugging in the workplace is still frequent, but why is it that you are unlikely to be hugged by (a) a sales associate in a retail store, (b) your medical care provider, or (c) the mechanic who repairs your vehicle?

7.5 Assume that a person who is intent on a career in business chooses to have several tattoos. Which type of tattoo is likely to send the most positive message about his or her maturity and seriousness?

7.6 "Hey" has become a widely used salutation for e-mail messages and, often, social media posts. Give an example of a situation for which you think "Hey" is an inappropriate salutation, and explain why.

7.7 Watch an episode of *Shark Tank* on television, or reflect back on a few episodes if you do watch the show. What advantage do the in-person appeals for funding on the show offer over sending e-mails or text messages?

7.8 Based on your own observations, identify a term or phrase in the workplace that creates semantic problems.

7.9 So what if differences in communication patterns between men and women have been identified? What impact will this information have on your communication with men and women?

7.10 How would you rate the persuasive communication skills of the current president of the United States? Have you any suggestions as to how the president could improve?

Web Corner

Effective listening:
www.forbes.com (Enter into search box "10 Steps to Effective Listening")

Exploring nonverbal communication:
http://nonverbal.ucsc.edu/

INTERNET SKILL BUILDER

The Importance of Communication Skills

How important are communication skills in your present or intended field? Conduct an Internet search for several different positions in your field, using both job search sites and the career section of companies that have openings in your field. Investigate the job qualifications. What conclusions do you reach about the importance of communication skills for obtaining or holding a job in your present or future specialty? An example would be to enter Caterpillar/Careers into your search engine. Caterpillar is a stable, worldwide company that has thousands of job openings. Track down a position of interest to you, such as "team leader" or "administrative assistant." See if communication skills are mentioned as a qualification.

Developing Your Human Relations Skills

Applying Human Relations Exercise 7-1

I Want This Position

The purpose of this exercise is to practice your persuasive skills using a topic of interest to many people: being hired for an attractive position. One by one, students make a presentation in front of the class, presenting a persuasive argument as to why they merit the attractive position they have applied for. The instructor will decide whether to use a handful of volunteers or the entire class. The audience represents the hiring manager. The student will first explain the nature of the position. (Use your imagination here.) Next, make a three-minute convincing argument as to why you merit a job offer. You will probably have about fifteen minutes to prepare, inside or outside of class.

After the presentations, volunteers will offer feedback on the effectiveness of selected presentations. During the presentations of the other students, make a few notes about the presenter's effectiveness. You may need a couple of minutes between presenters to make your notes. Consider these factors:

- Overall, how convincing was the presenter? If you were the hiring manager, would you give him or her a favorable recommendation for being hired?
- Which techniques of persuasion did he or she use?
- What aspect of the presentation was unconvincing or negative?
- What lessons did you take away from this exercise about persuasive communication?

Applying Human Relations Exercise 7-2

Active Listening

Before conducting the following role-plays, review the suggestions for active listening in this chapter. The suggestion about paraphrasing the message is particularly relevant because the role-plays involve emotional topics.

The Cost-Cutting Coworker

One student plays the role of a coworker who has just been appointed as the cost-cutting coordinator for the department. The cost cutter has decided to explain his or her new responsibilities to coworkers one at a time before calling a group meeting. He or she wants to emphasize how everybody has an important role in saving the company money, even in such minor initiatives as copying on two sides of a sheet of paper and not throwing out pencils until they are less than three inches long. The second worker decides to listen intently to the first worker. Other class members will rate the second student on his or her listening ability.

The Jubilant Innovation Award Winner

One student plays the role of a coworker who has just been notified that she has won a $2,000 innovation award from the company for her suggestion about a tooth whitener for dogs. She is eager to talk about the award and how she developed such a great idea.

Another student plays the role of a coworker she corners to discuss her triumph. The second worker decides to listen intently to her description of her accomplishment but is pressed for time. Other class members will rate the second student on his or her listening ability.

When evaluating the active listening skills of the role-players, consider using the following evaluating factors, on a scale of 1 (low) to 5 (high):

Evaluation Factor	Rating 1 2 3 4 5
1. Maintained eye contact	
2. Showed empathy	
3. Paraphrased what the other person said	
4. Focused on the other person instead of being distracted	
5. Asked questions	
6. Let the other person speak until he or she was finished	

Total Points: _____

Human Relations Class Activity

How Good Should Our Communication Skills Be?

"How good do my communication skills have to be to succeed in the workplace?" is a question on the minds of many career-oriented people. The purpose of this exercise is to observe the verbal and nonverbal communication skills of people who appear to have succeeded in their careers. The class in its entirety will observe a business leader or sports leader, such as a coach or an athletic director, being interviewed on television. Business channels and sports channels might be a good source of material, as might YouTube. CNBC is another potential source of useful interviews. The transmission can be real-time or previously recorded, and it should last approximately five to ten minutes.

As you observe the leader (or perhaps two leaders) on television or on the Internet, grade the person or persons on two dimensions: verbal communication skills and nonverbal communication skills. Use a standard A though F system. Back up your grading with a few written comments, such as

"Great eye contact with the interviewer," or "Dull, unanimated person. Put me to sleep." Also, attempt to answer the following questions:

1. What kind of impact is the presenter having on your classmates? To answer this question, take a few quick peeks around the room during the presentation, and observe the nonverbal communication of your classmates.
2. To what extent would this person be a good communications role model for me?
3. What, if any, communication tips did I learn from the person or persons in the interview(s)?

A couple of minutes after the grading and written observations are completed, the class will discuss some of the student observations. Be alert to whether consensus exists about the quality of the communication skills observed.

Human Relations Case Study 7–1

Totally Connected Alan

Alan is an operations supervisor at a regional distribution center for a large online consumer-goods shopping website. He enjoys his position and sees it as an important job on the path to attaining his long-range goal of becoming the vice president of logistics (the movement of goods) at his present company or another one. Alan perceives himself to be a high-tech professional who relies on constant communication to get his job done. "You won't find me using dinosaur technologies around the office," says Alan. "I'm totally connected."

A few of Alan's coworkers and his boss wonder sometimes if Alan isn't pushing his fascination with communication technology too far. When Alan attends a physical meeting with his group, he keeps his smartphone at hand and his laptop open. He usually begins the meeting with a statement to the effect, "As I tweeted you folks early this morning, here is what we need to accomplish today."

Kim, one of the logistics specialists in Alan's group, commented to a friend, "Yesterday, Alan was walking down the hall and was about twenty feet from my cubicle. He had something important to tell me about a misplaced shipment.

So he sends me a text message instead of just entering my cubicle. I received his text message about two hours later because of a delay on the server. Alan was upset that I didn't respond more quickly to his message."

Alan believes the workers should receive frequent feedback on performance rather than wait for the year-end review. To provide feedback to the members of his department, Alan relies mostly on posting messages on Facebook and sending tweets. A recent Facebook post to one worker was "Good job on verifying the identity of the mysterious customer, but why did it take you so long?" A recent tweet to another worker was "U updated address database gr8. U r totally Superwoman."

Questions

7.11 To what extent are the people criticizing Alan simply out of touch with modern technology?

7.12 What suggestions might you have for Alan to improve his use of communication technology in the office?

7.13 How might Alan improve his written communication skills in order to qualify for the position of vice president of logistics?

Human Relations Role-Playing Exercise 7–1

Feedback about Feedback

One student plays the role of Juan, the worker who received the Facebook posting from Alan about taking so long on the assignment. Juan sends Alan a text message requesting a five-minute, face-to-face meeting about the Facebook posting. Juan is a private person who objects to receiving feedback in a public space such as a social media site. Another student plays the role of Alan, who thinks that giving feedback about job performance on Facebook is entirely appropriate.

Human Relations Case Study 7–2

Charlotte, the Aspiring Restaurant Manager

Charlotte spent the first three years in her restaurant-management career in two different North Dakota locations of a national restaurant chain. She began as a server, then hostess to help her thoroughly learn the business. As planned, Charlotte was then assigned as an assistant manager in one of the restaurants. Her responsibilities included planning menus, assisting with the hiring of wait staff, and organizing banquets. Six months later, Charlotte met with Kevin, the restaurant manager, to discuss her progress as assistant manager.

Kevin opened the conversation by asking Charlotte how she was enjoying her work as the assistant manager at the restaurant. Charlotte answered, "It's really nice that you asked me how I like my job. I mean, an assistant manager is really not an important person. I kind of like my job even if it's not so very cool and impressive."

"How could this assistant manager position be better for you?" asked Kevin.

"I don't know for sure," said Charlotte. "Well, maybe if I didn't have so many different tasks to perform at once, my job would probably be better."

"Could you please be more specific?" asked Kevin.

"I'm not exactly sure because I don't like to accuse anybody of anything," responded Charlotte. "But maybe some people around here could understand that that an assistant manager can't work on five problems at the same time."

"Are you certain about that?" asked Kevin.

"Okay, maybe I'm exaggerating the problem a little," said Charlotte. "I'm so sorry."

With an exasperated expression, Kevin said, "If you want to achieve success in restaurant management, you've got to come across with more conviction."

Questions

7.14 What evidence do you see that Charlotte needs to come across with more conviction?

7.15 What do you recommend that Charlotte do to become a more persuasive communicator?

Human Relations Role-Playing Exercise 7–2

Charlotte Communicates Persuasively

One student plays the role of Charlotte, who has requested another meeting with Kevin to further discuss her progress as an assistant manager. Charlotte has taken quite seriously Kevin's recommendations that she communicate more persuasively. The student who plays the role of Kevin will listen attentively to judge her ability to communicate more persuasively. Conduct the role-play for about seven minutes, and provide feedback to both role players about their communication effectiveness.

For both role-plays, observers rate the role-players on two dimensions, using a scale of 1 to 5 from very poor to very good. One dimension is "effective use of human relations techniques." The second dimension is "acting ability." A few observers might voluntarily provide feedback to the role-players in terms of sharing their ratings and observations. The course instructor might also provide feedback.

REFERENCES

1. Linda Talley, "Body Language: Read It or Weep," *HR Magazine*, July 2010, p. 64.
2. Edward T. Hall, "Proxemics—A Study of Man's Spatial Relationships," in *Man's Image in Medicine and Anthropology* (New York: International Universities Press, 1963); Pauline E. Henderson, "Communication without Words," *Personnel Journal*, January 1989, pp. 28–29.
3. William A. Gentry, book review in *Personnel Psychology*, Summer 2010, p. 500.
4. Talley, "Body Language," pp. 64–65.
5. Carol Kinsey Gorman, *The Nonverbal Advantage: Secrets and Science of Body Language at Work* (San Francisco: Berrett-Koehler, 2008).
6. Nick Morgan, "How to Become an Authentic Speaker," *Harvard Business Review*, November 2008, p. 116.
7. Jeffrey Jacobi, *The Vocal Advantage* (Upper Saddle River, NJ: Prentice Hall, 1996).
8. John V. Thrill and Courtland L. Bovée, *Excellence in Business Communication*, 5th ed. (Upper Saddle River, NJ: Prentice Hall, 2002), p. 38.
9. Peggy Drexler, "The Delicate Protocol of Hugging," *The Wall Street Journal*, September 14–15, 2013, p. C3.
10. Mark G. Frank, Melissa A. Menasco, and Maureen O'Sullivan, "Human Behavior and Deception Detection," in John G. Voeller, ed., *Handbook of Science and Technology Security*, Vol. 5 (New York: John Wiley, 2008), pp. 2–3; Eric Benac, "Nonverbal Ways to Tell Someone Is Lying," www.ehow.com, accessed February 2, 2012.
11. Liz Ryan, "How's Your LinkedIn Etiquette?" *Denver Post* www.denverpost.com/business, May 18, 2004, pp. 3–4.
12. Bridget Carey, "Bosses Should Set Social Networking Rules," *Miami Herald* www.miamiherald.com, August 11, 2009, p. 1.
13. Kees van Deemter, *Not Exactly: In Praise of Vagueness* (New York: Oxford University Press, 2010).
14. "Avoid Words That Mar Your Image," *Administrative Professional*, January 2009, pp. 30–32.
15. Paul Leonardi, Neeley Tseda, and Elizabeth M. Gerber, "How Managers Use Multiple Media: Discrepant Events, Power and Timing in Redundant Communication," *Organization Science*, January–February, 2012, pp. 98–117.
16. Several of the ideas are from Charles Harrington Elster, "Cubicle Conversation," *The Wall Street Journal*, July 23, 2008, p. A15; Kevin Elkenberry, "5 Thoughts on Persuasion," *Executive Leadership*, July 2014, p. 7; "Talk in Headlines," *Manager's* Edge, April 2008, p. 8. For more details about point 9 in 7-4, see Brian Fugere, Chelsea Hardaway, and Jon Warshawsky, *Why Business People Speak like Idiots* (New York: Free Press, 2005); statements 2 and 12 are based on the principles of persuasion developed by Robert Cialdini, as summarized in Michael Price, "Tapping Our Powers of Persuasion," *Monitor on Psychology*, February 2011, p. 28; Joel Stein, "Could You Explain It Less Clearly," *Bloomberg Businessweek*, July 21–July 27, 2014, p. 63.
17. Cited in Mandi Woodruff, "Why You Should Start 'Gossiping' at the Office," www.finance.yahoo.com, December 12, 2014, p. 2.
18. Nancy B. Kurland and Lisa Hope Pelled, "Passing the Word: Toward a Model of Gossip and Power in the Workplace," *Academy of Management Review*, April 2000, pp. 428–438.
19. John Gray, *Men Are from Mars, Women Are from Venus* (New York: HarperCollins, 1992); Deborah Tannen, "The Power of Talk: Who Gets Heard and Why," *Harvard Business Review*, September–October 1995, pp. 138–148; Laurie Arliss, *Gender Communication* (Englewood Cliffs, NJ: Prentice Hall, 2005).
20. James W. Pennebaker, "Your Use of Pronouns Reveals Your Personality," *Harvard Business Review*, December 2011, p. 33.
21. One source of this widely quoted statistic is Jared Sandberg, "Bad at Complying? You Might Just Be a Very Bad Listener," *The Wall Street Journal*, September 25, 2007, p. D1.
22. Daniel Araoz, "Right-Brain Management (RBM): Part 2," *Human Resources Forum*, September 1989, p. 4.
23. Cited in "Five Keys to Effective Listening," *Black Enterprise*, March 2005, p. 113.
24. Ideas from Marshall Goldsmith cited in "Eliminate Bad Words," *Manager's Edge*, special issue, 2008, p. 5.
25. "Overcome Barriers to Listen Better," *Executive Leadership*, December 2014, p. 2; Sue Shellenbarger, "Tuning Out: Listening Becomes a Rare Skill," *The Wall Street Journal*, July 22, 2014, p. D1.

Fotolia

CHAPTER **8**

Communication in the Workplace

Outline

Carlton is the director of operations for a chain of five health and fitness clubs in his region. Part of his responsibilities is to promote memberships, including both finding new members and getting existing members to renew their memberships. The club had received many nasty complaints in the past when it billed customers automatically for re-signing their membership annually. As a result, the club sends electronic messages and postal mailings to re-sign members each year. Carlton delegates almost all the direct work for obtaining renewals to a few young staff members.

During the three most recent years, the percent of re-signings has decreased even though two new people were added to the marketing staff. Carlton dug into why re-signings were decreasing at the same time that the marketing activity had increased. As Carlton reviewed a log of how marketing for re-signings was conducted, he noted that e-mailings, text messaging, and social media posts had increased substantially. In contrast, the number of direct phone calls to members encouraging them to renew their membership had decreased. When Carlton was asked about the mix of communication techniques to encourage renewals, he was basically told that talking on the telephone is too old-fashioned. One staff member responsible for communicating with members said, "A lot of our members are young like us, and they don't like to talk. They text and write e-mails, but talking is so yesterday."

Carlton told the marketing staff that they might be missing out on the importance of phone calls as a supplement to texting and e-mails to encourage renewals. He explained, "Most of our guests love the club. A call from one of us is friendly. It's not like we're an energy company trying to get people to switch suppliers. Let's boost the number of phone calls we make to existing members to see the impact on club renewals."

The staff members agreed to conduct a more intensive telephone campaign to supplement the text messaging, e-mailing, and social media posts. Six months later, Carlton noted to his satisfaction that renewals had increased 18 percent, which was enough to substantially improve profits at the club. Carlton presented the data to the staff members and thanked them for their cooperation in going along with the modified marketing technique.

Learning Objectives ▶

After studying the information and doing the exercises in this chapter, you should be able to:

8.1 Describe the formal channels of communication within organizations.

8.2 Describe the informal channels of communication within organizations.

8.3 Identify the challenges to interpersonal communication created by communication technology.

8.4 Be ready to do an effective job of conducting or participating in a business meeting.

The story about the health club illustrates the importance of companies giving careful consideration to the mode of communication they use to attain business results, and that different modes of communication might be required for different purposes. Effective communication contributes to organization success in many ways, such as keeping employees informed as to what needs to be accomplished and identifying problems before they cripple a company. For example, a lab technician might quickly warn his or her manager that a new food supplement being sold by the company has an unacceptably high level of mercury, thereby avoiding a recall and lawsuits. In this chapter, we study communication in organizations from several perspectives: formal and informal communication channels, the communication challenges created by information technology, and having productive group meetings.

▶ **Learning Objective 8.1** ▶

Formal communication channels
the official pathways for sending information inside and outside an organization

Formal Channels of Communication Within Organizations

Messages in organizations are sent over both formal (official) and informal (unofficial) channels. **Formal communication channels** are the official pathways for sending information inside and outside an organization. The primary source of information about formal channels is the organization chart. It indicates the channels the messages are supposed to follow. By carefully following an organization chart, an entry-level worker would know how to transmit a message to someone in the executive suite. Formal communication channels are often bypassed through information technology. Using e-mail, instant messaging, and intranets, anybody can send a message to anybody else in the organization. During an emergency, workers are also likely to bypass formal channels, such as a technician telephoning the plant manager directly about a chemical spill.

COMPANY BLOGS AND SOCIAL MEDIA SITES AS FORMAL CHANNELS

The company blog is a widely used formal mode of communication, paralleling the use of blogs in private life. Many companies have abandoned their own blogs in favor of using the public blogs of Facebook and Twitter to communicate with the public. Quite often a posting on Facebook or Twitter leads directly to a company website, so the posting is simply a link to the website itself or a blog. However, the website might contain a blog.

Blogs originated by consumers are often used to complain about products or services and less often to compliment a company. At the same time, the company can use an external blog to defend its reputation when under attack. For example, the company might have received a large number of negative Facebook and Twitter posts because it reduced the healthcare benefits of retirees. The blog might explain that although company management wants to provide the best it can for retirees, it still needs enough cash to stay in business.

Blogs were first used by business to communicate with customers in a personal, direct manner and perhaps form a bond with them. The blog can provide customers with a behind-the-scenes look at the company. Blogs can be useful in bringing a company and its customers together through the open sharing of ideas, issues, events, and feedback.[1] Today, the vast majority of business corporations have entered the *blogosphere,* if you include Facebook, Twitter, and LinkedIn as blogs.

The blog communicates business information but with a soft, human touch. For example, the McDonald's blog explains some of the ways in which it gives back to the community, such as sponsoring athletic teams for children and engaging in neighborhood cleanup campaigns. The company blog can also be used to communicate with employees in a relaxed, casual tone. Employees, as well as customers, can interact through a blog by providing comments that are a source of valuable feedback to management and also communicated directly to other visitors to the site.

An individual who establishes a blog on his or her own to chat about the employer creates an *informal* rather than a formal channel—when the blog is not authorized by the company. Bloggers who publish negative information about their employer, or publish unprofessional photos of themselves run the risk of being fired. The rationale behind these firings is that the employee is making unwarranted use of his or her association with the company. To prevent problems of negativity appearing on personal blogs by employees, many companies now establish guidelines, such as "no disclosure of negative information about the company," "no nude photos," or "no profanity."

A general guideline for the use of offensive blogs is that a person's First Amendment right to free speech is not protected if it defames a company or divulges trade secrets on a web posting. As explained by Nancy Flynn, executive director of the ePolicy Institute, "You could find yourself on the wrong side of a civil lawsuit."[2]

SOCIAL NETWORKING WEBSITES, INTRANETS, AND WEBINARS

Formal communication channels in the workplace have kept pace with Internet-based communication technology. An important implication of this development is that workers at all levels are expected to use these channels to send and receive messages and to work collaboratively with each other. Here we describe three key Internet-based workplace communication channels: social networking websites, intranets, and webinars.

Social Networking Websites

As a majority of workers have become members of social networking websites such as Facebook, LinkedIn, Twitter, and Instagram, these sites have become natural channels for members of the same company to communicate. Research by the consultancy McKinsey and Company shows that more than one half of all firms use some type of social media to facilitate employees collaborating and exchanging information.[3] Because of their more widespread membership, Facebook and Twitter are more likely to be used as official workplace communication channels. Also, these social media sites have networks dedicated to companies or coworkers.

A major purpose of company social networking sites is to satisfy employee preferences for being connected to each other electronically. Many employers recognize that social networks are a platform for connecting to others preferred by many young employees and many older ones as well. Many employees would prefer to communicate with coworkers by posting a message on a social networking site than speaking to the coworker or even sending him or her an e-mail.

The use of social networking technologies on the job is quite similar to their use in personal life. Members are allowed to create profiles of themselves and link up with others in a virtual community.[4] The focus on the workplace site, however, is to communicate work-related messages. The sites are also useful for workers offering support to each other, such as encouraging another Facebook member when he or she is facing a challenging problem. Another official use of social networking by corporations is for recruiting workers, with many companies posting positions on these sites. Also, site members can pass along recruiting information to their network friends.

Yet another business application of social networks is to connect workers looking for mentors among more experienced workers who are available for mentoring. Members create profiles, ask questions of potential mentors, and arrange for in-person meetings. The same software has a "praise" tab, enabling site members to write quick notes of appreciation to each other.

Social networking sites also have an application that rests at the border between a formal and an informal communication channel. For example, all employees might be encouraged to join Facebook so they can network with each other and build their working relationships. Facebook becomes a virtual watercooler. In the words of Jeremy Burton, CEO of Serena Software Inc., "Social networking tools like Facebook can bring us back together, help us to get to know each other as people, help us understand our business and our products, and help us better serve our customers."[5]

A concern about social networking sites in the workplace is that they facilitate spending time on nonwork matters, such as pausing to watch a coworker's surfing video instead of reviewing his or her input. Nestlé USA has created a social network with its own firewall. Employees can post content related to nutrition and health but are prohibited from using the site for dating or selling products or services.[6] Another problem is that the same social networking site that displays a professional presence might present unprofessional images and content.

Assume that your vice president of finance sends you a finance message from her Facebook page. Will you take her seriously when her page also includes photos of her mud wrestling in a bikini? (This is the reason that many companies implement a company-specific social networking site rather than a public site.)

Intranets

Intranet
a company version of the Internet with the basic purpose of giving employees a central place to find what they need amidst a sea of digital information

An **intranet** is essentially a company version of the Internet with the basic purpose of giving employees a central place to find what they need amidst a sea of digital information. The intranet serves as a useful communication channel because updated information is readily available to workers, and the information is centralized, current, and correct. For example, an employee might want to know the company's per diem allowance for meals while traveling. Instead of having to send an e-mail to the boss or human resources department, the employee can search the intranet.

The intranet is also used for much more than a file for routine information. More advanced uses include posting a video displaying a new product or service, describing the company's stand on a particular environmental issue, or posting a motivational message from the CEO. The company might also post a vision statement focusing on its exciting plans for the future. Another useful purpose is to use the intranet as a storage place for the minutes of meetings.

An intranet can also have a wiki feature in which workers are encouraged to add information of their own to certain content. Employee interaction of this type is helpful when those adding input are well informed and serious. The wiki approach facilitates worker collaboration, including the modification of documents as needed. The on-the-spot modification replaces sending hundreds of e-mails with attachments back and forth. To guard against misinformation being circulated, the company restricts which content allows for employee interaction. For example, the company cannot allow employees to modify per diem meal allowances.

Some company intranets have added a human touch with such features as a phone book, menus from the company cafeteria, a classified ad section, and a dating site. Again, we see how a formal communication channel can also serve an informal, social purpose.

Webinars

Webinar
a web-based method of holding a seminar

Another formal communication channel is a web-based method of holding a seminar, referred to as a **webinar**. The speaker sends information to participants, who can interact with the conference presenter by computer. Collaboration is possible through such means as asking and answering questions. A telephone hookup is also typically used, including a speakerphone so many people at the same time can tune in on the information flow. Slides are displayed throughout the presentation.

The participants in the webinar often are working alone, yet they can be gathered in groups at one or more locations. The meetings can include PowerPoint presentations and streaming videos. Chat is another possible feature, so participants can react to the points raised by other participants.

Webinars as a formal communication channel are efficient and save travel costs and time, but, like some other forms of communication technology, they have a limited human touch. For example, it is more difficult to inspire a worker with a message to his or her computer screen than an in-person message complete with many nonverbal cues.

COMMUNICATION CHANNELS FOR MANAGING CRISES

Many companies have developed formal communication channels for managing crises, such as fires and explosions, massive product recalls, financial scandals, and terrorist attacks. One of the most crucial parts of a disaster plan is how to communicate with the company's workforce during a crisis. A key part of the challenge is to locate and reestablish contact with employees who may be scattered in the streets or stranded in airports around the world. Aon Corporation, an international insurance, risk-management, and consulting company, improvised to use its website as an official communication channel during the crisis of September 11, 2001. A company official said, "With everything else down, we decided to use the company website. That seemed like the only option we had."[7]

A more subtle type of crisis is widespread employee fear that the company might lay off large numbers of workers or go out of business. An effective communication strategy is for top management to quickly allay fear if the company is not truly in danger, particularly when suggestions of an impending bankruptcy have been reported in the media.

During more recent crises, such as the earthquake in Japan in 2011, multinational companies made extensive use of intranets and social media to disseminate messages about whether or not company employees were accounted for. Calming messages about the search for the missing were also sent via social media.

COMMUNICATION DIRECTIONS

Another aspect of formal communications is the directions messages follow in the organization. Messages in organizations travel in four primary directions: downward, upward, horizontally, and diagonally, as illustrated in Figure 8-1.

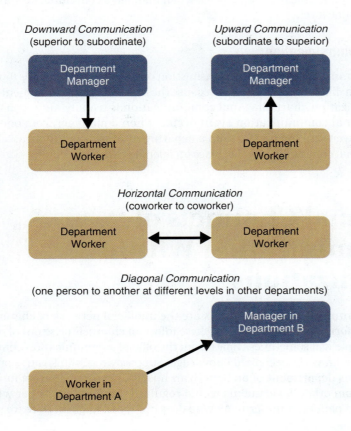

Downward Communication
(superior to subordinate)

Upward Communication
(subordinate to superior)

Horizontal Communication
(coworker to coworker)

Diagonal Communication
(one person to another at different levels in other departments)

FIGURE 8-1

COMMUNICATION DIRECTIONS IN ORGANIZATIONS
Communication in organizations can take place in four directions: downward, upward, horizontally, and diagonally.

Source: "COMMUNICATION DIRECTIONS IN ORGANIZATIONS" by Andrew J. DuBrin.

Downward Communication

Downward communication
the transmission of messages
from higher to lower levels in an
organization

Downward communication is the flow of messages from one level to a lower level. It is typified by a middle manager giving orders to a lower-level supervisor or by top management sending announcements to employees. Information is sometimes transmitted from a higher level to a lower one without the sender inviting a response. When this occurs, the feedback built into two-way communication is lost.

Upward Communication

Upward communication
the transmission of messages
from lower to higher levels in an
organization

Open-door policy
communication channel that is
structured upward that allows
employees to bring a gripe to top
management's attention without first
checking with the employee's manager

Upward communication is the transmission of messages from lower to higher levels in an organization. It is the most important channel for keeping management informed about problems within the organization. Simply talking regularly to employees improves upward communication. An **open-door policy** is a more structured upward communication channel that allows employees to bring a complaint to top management's attention without first checking with their manager. Managers who are willing to listen to bad news without becoming upset at the messenger are more likely to receive upward communication. Upward communication is more widely used in less bureaucratic firms than in highly bureaucratic firms. Almost all executives contend that they value upward communication, although the majority of employees may not think so.

Horizontal Communication

Horizontal communication
sending messages among people at
the same organization level

Horizontal communication is sending messages among people at the same organization level. It often takes the form of coworkers from the same department talking to one another. Horizontal communication is the basis for cooperation and collaboration. When coworkers are not sharing information with and responding to one another, they are likely to fall behind schedule. Also, efforts are duplicated and quality suffers. Another type of horizontal communication takes place when managers communicate with other managers at the same level.

Diagonal Communication

Diagonal communication
the transmission of messages to
higher or lower organizational levels in
different departments

Diagonal communication is the transmission of messages to higher or lower organizational levels in different departments. Because these pathways are infrequently spelled out on the organization chart, diagonal communication is usually an *informal* channel. A typical diagonal communication event occurs when a manager from one department contacts a lower-ranking person from a department outside of his or her chain of command. Diagonal communication becomes an *informal* pathway.

▶ **Learning Objective 8.2** ▶

Informal Channels of Communication Within Organizations

**Informal communication
channels**
unofficial networks of channels that
supplement the formal channels

Informal communication channels are the unofficial network of channels that supplements the formal channels. Most of these informal channels arise out of necessity. For example, people will sometimes depart from the official communication channels to consult with a person with specialized knowledge. Suppose an administrative professional in the admissions department of an American hospital spoke and wrote fluent German. Employees from other departments would regularly consult him or her when they are dealing with a patient from Germany who does not speak English. Here we study several aspects of informal communication channels: communities of practice, networks of contacts, the grapevine, rumors, chance encounters, and management by walking around.

NETWORKS OF CONTACTS

Perhaps the most useful aspect of informal communication channels is that they enable workers to accomplish many tasks they would not be able to if they relied exclusively on formal channels. The network of contacts often means in practice that an individual worker might be in touch with people in his or her formal and informal channels to get work accomplished. However, the emphasis is on the informal communication channels. Here we describe several variations of networks of contacts that are primarily informal.

Communities of Practice

Two professors at the Warwick Business School, Richard McDermott and Douglas Archibald, have studied how work gets accomplished at many technical companies. A key conclusion they reached is that informal employee networks, or **communities of practice**, are an inexpensive and efficient vehicle for specialists to share knowledge and ideas. Effective communities of practice often assume responsibility for key problems. The communities of practice deliberately seek to expand the network of contacts so difficult technical problems can be conquered. A pharmaceutical specialist might ask, "Who can I consult to help me figure out how to stop the spread of fungus infections in people who continue to come in contact with others?" At Pfizer, these informal employee networks are responsible for helping drug developers make difficult decisions on drug safety issues.

A key feature of these communities of practice is that experts from different parts of the company share tidbits of knowledge, such as scattered information about drug safety. As a result, they work under an informal structure. Yet these networks are so effective, that some companies now consider them to be part of the formal structure.[8]

Communities of practice
informal employee networks

The Shadow Organization and Social Network Analysis

Some observers believe that the network of contacts explains how work really gets accomplished. According to this viewpoint, all companies have hidden **shadow organizations** where much of the real work gets done.[9] For example, in most firms, there are "tech fixers" who supplement—but do not replace—the technical support center. Suppose a worker is stuck with an information technology problem, such as being unable to access the e-mail system with his or her desktop computer. The worker might get in immediate contact with a tech fixer (whose formal job responsibilities do not include solving technical problems outside his or her department) for help with the problem.

The shadow organization is revealed by **social network analysis**, the mapping and measuring of relationships and links between and among people, groups, and organizations.[10]

The nodes in the network are the people, and the links show relationships or flow between and among the nodes as shown in Figure 8-2. Social network analysis helps explain how work gets accomplished in a given unit, as is shown in the interactions among Susan, Tim, and Tara on the right side of Figure 8-2. Perhaps the three of them mutually discuss credit risks. The interrelations can become quite complicated because of the number of people and the interactions among them.

Social network analysis helps management survey maps of the informal interactions among employees that can lead to innovative ideas. At the same time, the maps can point to areas where workers should be collaborating but are not. In this way, the maps help facilitate knowledge sharing. The maps can also be used to pinpoint the interactions one manager has so he or she can give the information to a successor.

Shadow organizations
where much of the real work gets accomplished, the shadow organization is revealed by network analysis, which traces who talks to whom

Social network analysis
the mapping and measuring of relationships and links between and among people, groups, and organizations that reveals the shadow organization

FIGURE 8-2

A BASIC UNIT OF A SOCIAL NETWORK ANALYSIS

Source: "A BASIC UNIT OF A SOCIAL NETWORK ANALYSIS" by Andrew J. DuBrin.

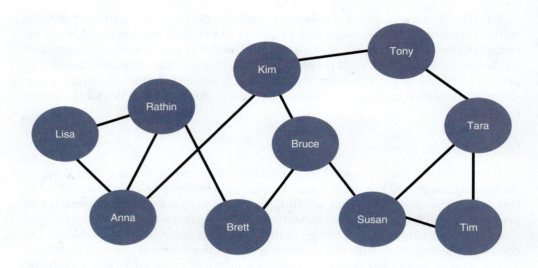

Another insight gleaned for social network analysis is that the line indicates who trusts whom because they exchange ideas and go to each other for advice. According to corporate anthropologist Karen Stephenson, knowing who trusts whom is as important as knowing who reports to whom. Finding out who trusts whom is part of the social network analysis and is revealed by asking employees questions such as the following:[11]

- Whom do you go to for a quick decision?
- Whom do you hang out with socially?
- Whom do you turn to for advice?
- Whom do you go to with a good idea?
- Whom do you go to for career advice?

An important implication of having a reasonable number of positive contacts in a network is that the individual is more likely to feel attached to the organization, and therefore less likely to quit.[12] This finding makes sense because having a positive network contributes to job satisfaction, which is positively related to staying with an employer.

Your network of contacts can also extend outside the organization. A real estate developer, for example, might have contacts inside a bank who inform him of upcoming foreclosures. In this way, the developer can make an early appraisal of the property to be ready with an effective bid on the foreclosed property. The mortgage specialist in the bank is part of the real estate developer's network of contacts.

A subtle perspective about social network analysis maps is that more connections aren't necessarily the best for the organization. If one person is too connected, he or she could be a bottleneck. Also, it is okay for some workers who spend a lot of time with customers or have expertise in highly specialized areas to show up on the outside of the web of interactions.

Human Relations Self-Assessment Quiz 8-1 gives you an opportunity to think about the quality of the contacts in your network.

Human Relations Self-Assessment Quiz   8-1

The Strength of My Network of Contacts

To help you think through the effectiveness of your network of contacts, respond "Mostly Yes" or "Mostly No" to the following statements.

Statement about Contacts	Mostly Yes	Mostly No
1. I know at least ten people I could contact to give me advice about solving a work problem.	❏	❏
2. At least 95 percent of the people I am in touch with in the social media are people I have never met in person or talked to on the phone.	❏	❏
3. I am in touch with the majority of people in my network at least once a month.	❏	❏
4. The majority of my network members are doing well in their careers or are good students.	❏	❏
5. Most of the people I follow on Facebook, Twitter, or other social media sites are celebrities I have never met or will never meet.	❏	❏
6. I almost never bother telephoning or seeing someone in person whom I can contact through a social media website.	❏	❏
7. I would take advantage of the opportunity to attend a professional networking event, such as a face-to-face meeting of "tweeters."	❏	❏
8. I have a few people in my network who hold positions that I aspire to.	❏	❏
9. I am much more concerned about the quality of the people in my network than the quantity.	❏	❏
10. When I encounter a person who holds a good position, or who appears to have the potential to be influential, I invite him or her to become a member of my social media network.	❏	❏

Scoring and Interpretation:

Give yourself 1 point for the following answers: Mostly Yes to questions 1, 3, 4, 7, 8, 9, and 10; Mostly No to questions 2, 5, and 6. If you scored 7 or more points, it appears that you have established or are establishing a strong professional network. If you scored between 0 and 6, you may not be establishing a strong professional network. Furthermore, you might be wasting time on social media sites that you could be investing in career advancement.

THE GRAPEVINE

The **grapevine** is the major informal communication channel in organizations. The *grapevine* refers to the tangled pathways that can distort information. The term referred originally to the snarled telegraph lines on the battlefield during the U.S. Civil War. The grapevine is often thought to be used primarily for passing along negative rumors and negative gossip. Gossips sometimes use the Internet and e-mail as channels for transmitting negative gossip. Facebook and Twitter are increasingly used to pass along gossip, often in the form of a question, such as "Is it true that one of our vice presidents was caught speeding in a company car?" When left to fester, gossip can cause individuals chagrin and also lead to turnover, conflict, and lawsuits. Gossip often increases when workers are bored or lack ample information about company events.

Managers can often stop negative gossip by confronting the source of the gossip, demanding that he or she stop. Positive gossip, however, makes a contribution to the

> **Grapevine**
> major informal communication channel in organizations; the grapevine refers to the tangled pathways that can distort information

organization because trading information strengthens ties among workers and humanizes the workplace. Gossip can be viewed as the glue that binds social groups together.[13] An example of positive gossip would be "I heard management is considering adding a paid holiday next year. Everyone with five or more service years gets his or her birthday off from work." (You may recall the discussion in Chapter 7 in relation to building bridges to communication.)

The grapevine is sometimes used purposely to disseminate information along informal lines. For example, top management might want to hint to employees that certain work will be outsourced (sent to another company or outside the country) unless the employees become more productive. Although the plans are still tentative, feeding them into the grapevine may result in improved motivation and productivity.

Rumors

Rumors are an important informal communication force within organizations, and they tend to thrive in organizations with poor formal communication, such as a penitentiary. Rumors are an important early source of information and are readily spread through personal texting and social media posts. A problem with inaccurate rumors is that they can distract workers, create anxiety, and decrease productivity. A frequent byproduct of false rumors about company relocation or a pending merger is that some of the more talented workers leave in the hopes of more stable employment.

CHANCE ENCOUNTERS AND MANAGEMENT BY WALKING AROUND

Chance encounter
unscheduled informal contact between managers and employees

Another informal channel of significance is the **chance encounter**. Unscheduled informal contact between managers and employees can be an efficient and effective communication channel. Many years ago, John P. Kotter, professor of leadership at Harvard Business School, found that effective managers do not confine their communication to formal meetings.[14] Instead, they collect valuable information during chance encounters. Spontaneous communication events may occur in the cafeteria, near the water fountain, in the halls, and on the elevator. In only two minutes, the manager might obtain the information that would typically be solicited in a thirty-minute meeting or through a series of e-mail or text-messaging exchanges. A representative question might be "What seems to be the buzz on our newest product?"

Management by walking around
managers intermingle freely with workers on the shop floor or in the office, as well as with customers; enhances open communication

One important communication channel can be classified as either formal or informal. **Management by walking around** involves managers intermingling freely with workers on the shop floor or in the office, as well as with customers. By spending time in personal contact with employees, the manager enhances open communication. During contacts with employees the manager will often ask questions such as, "How are you enjoying your work?" or "What bottlenecks have you encountered today?" Because management by walking around is systematic, it could be considered formal. However, a manager who circulates throughout the company is not following the formal paths prescribed by the organization chart. Management by walking around differs from chance encounters in that the latter are unplanned events; the former occur intentionally.

Another perspective on management by walking around is that it is similar to a physician making rounds to visit his or her hospital patients. Instead of visiting patients, the manager drops by to see employees and engages in brief, informal conversations. Sample questions to ask on rounds include "What is working well today?" "Do you have the tools and equipment you need to do your job?" "Is there anything I could do better?"[15] Recognizing the nature of the rounds, the employees are likely to respond with brief, spontaneous, and useful feedback—assuming the manager making the rounds is trusted!

OPEN WORK SPACES AND INFORMAL COMMUNICATION

An architectural approach to enhancing informal communication in organizations is to make extensive use of open office spaces. (Work space in manufacturing, construction, mills, and refineries has always been open.) Based on the ease of face-to-face communication without the presence of many offices, cubicles, or partitions, collaboration and creativity are often enhanced. The open work space is also designed to increase informality and decrease formality. Several conference rooms are usually available for private conversations. Open office spaces are often accompanied by shared workspaces in which a desk is not permanently assigned to one worker.[16]

The open office space does facilitate more informal communication, but it also violates the human need for privacy and the opportunity to work without the continuous distraction of being surrounded by other people. Employees who want to hold a private conversation sometimes resort to holding a conversation in a stairwell or a vehicle in the company parking lot.[17] The noise and confusion found in many open-office spaces have increased the desire of working from home for many individuals.

The accompanying Human Relations in Practice insert illustrates the use of open work spaces to enhance informal communication among employees.

Human Relations in Practice

Pharmaceutical Giant GSK Uses Collaborative Work Spaces

Things you will find upon arriving for work each morning at GlaxcoSmithKline (GSK) in Philadelphia's Navy Yard: A tranquility room for prayer, a rooftop perch with city views for impromptu meetings, work stations that allow for typing at a keyboard while simultaneously walking two miles per hour on the treadmill, and a fairly good chance that at some point during the day you will bump into the CEO.

What you won't find anywhere in the 208,000-square-foot space: a desk of your own. GSK's office design embraces an open-space philosophy and uses "hoteling." All workers, even top management, are assigned to "neighborhoods"—areas of workers engaged in related tasks—but no one has a permanent desk.

Many employees work at computer terminals standing. Everyone is encouraged to float—in the cafeteria on top of the deck beside a green roof filled with indigenous plants, on a sofa in a quiet room, or in the lobby. The idea is that chance encounters will spark conversations and collaboration that would not happen when creative minds are moored to a single assigned desk. GSK calls it "smart working." The arrangement also saves a lot of money because 1,300 employees at this facility are crammed into office space that is one-quarter the size of the space they previously occupied.

Spokeswoman Jennifer Armstrong says about the open-space office design, "On a global basis, GSK is transitioning to collaborative workspaces whenever possible to foster better communication and idea sharing. GSK is taking down office and cubicle walls so employees can see and talk to one another." The goals, according to Armstrong, are to enhance collaboration and trust, break down hierarchical barriers, reduce e-mailing and formal meetings, and help decisions get made more quickly. Furthermore, the open spaces promote more physical movement during the day and ultimately enable the company to better serve patients.

GSK management recognizes that the open office space is not always ideal, especially when privacy is needed. Quiet rooms of various sizes exist for solitary acts such as writing and private conversations involving sensitive or proprietary subjects. Larger rooms are available for group meetings that are not meant to be interrupted. Each floor comes with a concierge who helps with the use of spaces both discrete and shared. As for heading off unwelcome conversational advances, three clip-on signs send a clear message: green for "Come on over," yellow for "I'll be right back," and red for "Please do not disturb."

Questions:

How would personality traits influence how much workers would enjoy working in an open office space? Should a pharmaceutical firm require workers to be in close physical contact with other workers who are carrying germs or do not practice good personal hygiene?

Source: Adapted from "Cost Efficient Open-Space Office Designs: Ditching Desks—and Privacy," *Knowledge@Wharton*, http://knowledge.wharton.upenn.edu, June 19, 2013, pp. 1–4.

▶ **Learning Objective 8.3** ▶

Challenges to Interpersonal Communication Created by Communication Technology

Rapid advances in information (or communication) technology may enable workers to communicate more easily and quickly than they could even a few years ago. Although social media, including social networking, blogs, and photo sharing websites receive the most attention, other forms of communication technology are influential. Quite often, the influence has been positive, but at other times, the effectiveness of interpersonal communication has decreased. Six developments that illustrate the impact of information technology on interpersonal communication are e-mail, presentation technology, telephones and voice mail, telecommuting, multitasking, and overconfidence in computer-generated data. (The author realizes that traditional telephones are not usually considered part of communication or information technology, but they, too, are electronic devices that create communication challenges.)

E-MAIL AND COMMUNICATION AMONG PEOPLE

E-mail, including text messaging, is the information technology system with the most dramatic impact on interpersonal communication in the current era. The major impact of e-mail on interpersonal communication is that written messages replace many telephone and in-person exchanges. Furthermore, workers exchange e-mails much more frequently than they telephoned each other in the past. Team members often keep in regular contact with each other without having lengthy meetings or phone conversations.

E-mail, including attachments of graphics and videos, has become the dominant form of communication on the job. Several potential communication problems that e-mail and instant messaging create should be kept in mind to minimize these problems.

Indiscriminate Message Sending

A major problem with e-mail is that it encourages indiscriminate sending of messages. Some professional workers receive an average of three hundred e-mail messages per day, and some workers check their e-mail over thirty times an hour. Some of these workers make cynical comments such as, "My job is answering e-mail" or "I answer e-mail during the day and do my work at night and on weekends."

Donna Rawady, an executive coach, hints at a factor generating so much e-mail. The system has created unreasonable expectations on worker's time.[18] Many employees have become programmed to check their e-mail around the clock. The mental set becomes "So long as I am checking e-mail, why not send a few messages?" Some workers conduct virtual joke-telling contests over e-mail, with some of the jokes being perceived as offensive by many other workers. The proliferation of electronic junk mail (spam) has prompted most company officials to take corrective action, such as the installation of spam filters.

A guiding principle for sending e-mails is to respect other people's time by not over-loading them with messages.[19] For example, you might question why you have the right to send a work associate five e-mails in one day unless your job absolutely requires the delivering of so much information or asking so many questions.

To minimize feeling overwhelmed by e-mail, it is best to schedule blocks of time for sending and answering e-mail, assuming you have the type of work that allows you to limit e-mail. Checking about once per hour would leave more time for other work activities. It is also useful to disable all the buzzes, beeps, and other alerts built into the e-mail system.[20] Consider also that sometimes a brief telephone conversation will help clarify an issue that might otherwise require a dozen e-mail or text-message exchanges. A representative example would be explaining how to fix a mechanical problem by phone rather than through sending e-mail messages back and forth.

Many successful people control e-mail, rather than letting it control them. Excessive use of e-mail drains company productivity because workers who receive an e-mail typically spend about four minutes reading it and recovering from the interruption before they can return to other work. But for workers like an online customer service representative, dealing with e-mail is their entire job.

Too Much Informality

The informal style of many e-mail exchanges can lead a person to believe that incorrect spelling, poor grammar, and disconnected thoughts are acceptable in all forms of business communication. The opposite is true. To appear professional and intelligent, writers of business e-mail messages should use correct spelling, grammar, capitalization, and punctuation. A conflict here, however, is that some professional people have begun to incorporate the informal writing style into their e-mails, including the lowercase *i* instead of *I*. A few of the popular search engines show a spelling error when capitals are used properly, such as in capitalizing the first letter of a person's name.

E-mail has become a tool for office politicians who search for ways to look good themselves and make others look bad. Many office politicians use e-mail to give credit to themselves for their contributions to a project, perhaps using a companywide distribution list. When something goes wrong, such as a failed project, the office politician will inform hundreds of people that it was not his or her fault.

Avoidance of In-Person Reprimands

Many supervisors and other workers use e-mail to reprimand others because, by sending a message over the computer, they can avoid face-to-face confrontation. E-mail is well suited for managers who would prefer to avoid face-to-face contact with group members. Harsh messages sent over e-mail create several problems. First, it is shocking to be reprimanded or insulted in writing. Second, the person cannot offer a defense except by writing back an e-mail message explaining his or her position. Third, the recipient, not knowing what to do about the harsh message, may brood and become anxious.

Alternatives to E-mail

Some business firms have counterattacked the problems associated with e-mail by shifting to related technologies, as mentioned in relation to social networking sites and intranets. The major problem counterattacked is the time drain of sending and responding to e-mail messages. Alternatives to e-mail also focus on enhancing collaboration by reducing the need for exchanging so many e-mails, such as seeing all the relevant information on a subject on one screen.

Among the e-mail replacements are private workplace wikis, blogs, instant messaging, RSS, and more elaborate forms of groupware that allow workers to create websites for the team's use on a specific project. (*RSS* is the abbreviation for really simple syndication, which enables people to subscribe to the information they need.) A wiki is a site that allows a group of people to comment on and edit each other's work. As a result, a wiki can be a useful tool for sharing knowledge as well as publicly displaying which workers are willing to publicly display their bright ideas. E-mail will probably remain strong for one-to-one communication, but the tools just mentioned will be relied on more heavily for collaboration.[21]

Figure 8-3 presents suggestions for good etiquette when using e-mail, including messaging. The good etiquette leads to more productive use of e-mail.

FIGURE 8-3

E-MAIL AND MESSAGING ETIQUETTE

Many of the problems associated with e-mail and messaging can be avoided or minimized by practicing good etiquette in relation to e-mails and text messages. A few suggestions are as follows:

- Insert an informative subject line. The effective use of e-mails begins with an informative subject line that tells the receiver why he or she would want to open your e-mail. For example, "Budget Meeting 8:30 a.m., Friday April 17" is a more effective subject than "Budget."
- Focus your e-mail on one major topic, and when possible start a fresh e-mail rather than to keep on adding to a chain of messages (or "threads"). If you include an attachment explain in a few words why the reason for the attachment.
- Use a professional writing style. First, organize your thoughts to avoid sending e-mails with confusing, incomplete, or missing information. Check carefully for grammatical and typographical errors, including the fact that some word processing programs automatically change a word you intended, such as converting "be able" to "bobble."
- Do not use e-mail to criticize a coworker or boss, and send copies to other people. Similarly do not pressure a coworker by requesting help from him or her and sending a copy to the person's boss.
- Go light on emoticons and emojis, such as, ☺ ✌ 📱. Although they are entertaining, they are better suited for social than work purposes. Also, avoid "LOL" in a professional e-mail.

USE PRESENTATION TECHNOLOGY TO YOUR ADVANTAGE

PowerPoint presentations have been frequently criticized for their bullet points and clip art, but they remain part of the modern world. Speakers in all types of organizations supplement their talk with computer slides, such as those created with Power-Point, and often organize their presentation around them. Many people want presentations reduced to bulleted items and eye-catching graphics. (Have you noticed this tendency among students?) The communication challenge here is that during an oral presentation, the predominant means of connection between sender and receiver is eye contact. When an audience is constantly distracted from the presenter by movement on the screen, sounds from the computer, or lavish colors, eye contact suffers, as does the message.

One of the biggest challenges is to learn how to handle equipment and maintain frequent eye and voice contact at all times. Several professionals in the field of business communication offer these sensible suggestions for overcoming the potential communication barrier of using presentation technology inappropriately:[22]

■ **Reveal points only as needed.** Project the computer slides only when needed, and use a cursor, laser pointer, or metal pointer for emphasis.

■ **Talk to the audience, not the screen.** A major problem with computer slides is that the presenter as well as the audience is likely to focus continually on the slide. If the presenter minimizes looking at the slide and spends considerable time looking at the audience, it will be easier to maintain contact with the audience. A related problem is when the speaker simply reads the slides to the audience without adding other content.

■ **Keep the slide in view until the audience gets the point.** A presenter will often flash a slide without giving the audience enough time to comprehend the meaning of the slide. It is also important for presenters to synchronize the slides with their comments.

■ **Reduce the text on each page of your PowerPoint presentation to a bare minimum.** Few people can really listen to you and read your slides at the same time, even if they think they are effective at multitasking. For many audiences, using the text as an outline of your talk, or talking points, is the most effective use of the slides.

■ **Make sure to triple-check your presentation for spelling errors.** A spelling error projected on a screen can quickly become a joke passed around the room.

The point, again, is not to avoid the new technologies for communication but to use them to your advantage skillfully.

IMPROVE YOUR TELEPHONE, VOICE MAIL, AND SPEAKERPHONE COMMUNICATION SKILLS

A direct way of overcoming communication barriers is to use effective telephone and voice mail communication skills, because these two communication media often create communication problems. Also, many businesses attract and hold onto customers because their representatives interact positively with people through the telephone and voice mail (as suggested in the opening case). Many other firms lose money, and nonprofit organizations irritate the public, because their employees have poor telephone and voice mail skills. Furthermore, despite the widespread use of computer networks, a substantial amount of work among employees is still conducted via telephone and voice mail. For example, investment firms, such as Merrill Lynch, do not send sensitive financial information by e-mail but instead rely on telephone conversations.

Although telephones are still important for business, the traditional office phone is on the edge of being transformed technologically, combining the advantages of telephones and computers. One such device is labeled Switch. It enables the user to dial voice calls by computer and then switch devices in the middle of the call and observe documents exchanged with the receiver of the message. Conference-call participants automatically receive a ring.[23] (This system resembles the widespread practice of making a telephone call and accessing relevant information on the computer during the call.)

Speakerphones present some of their own communication challenges. Small noises, such as crumpling paper, eating crunchy food, and placing a handset on a hard desk, magnify when broadcast over a speakerphone. If other people are present in the office, advise the person you are telephoning at the beginning of the conversation.[24] Doing so may save a lot of embarrassment, such as the caller making negative comments about your boss or coworker. Most of the previous comments about overcoming communication barriers apply to telephone communications, including speakerphones. Keep in mind these four representative suggestions for improving telephone effectiveness:

- Vary your voice tone and inflection to avoid sounding bored or uninterested in your job and the company.

- Smile while speaking on the phone—somehow a smile gets transmitted over the telephone wires or optic fibers!

- Although multitasking has become the mode, when speaking on a telephone do not conduct a conversation with another person simultaneously, do not read e-mails, and do not have a television or radio playing in the background. (The last point is a challenge for people who work from home.) Business callers expect your undivided attention.

- Do not eat while talking on the phone, even though it is widely practiced. Many people are repelled by the sound of a person eating while talking—much like talking with food in your mouth in a restaurant. Loudly slurping a beverage is also objectionable to most people.

- Avoid offending customers by inappropriate use of smartphones. As a face-to-face sales representative, if you are going to use the phone to access information or take notes, explain your intention to customers in advance. Then return full attention to the meeting without stopping to check for messages.[25]

TELECOMMUTING AND THE REMOTE WORKFORCE

Telecommuter
employee who works at home or another offsite location full-time or part-time and sends output electronically to a central office

A **telecommuter** is an employee who works at home or other offsite location full-time or part-time and sends output electronically to a central office. An estimated 20 to 30 million people in the United States work at home, out of their cars, or as corporate employees working on the premises of the corporation's customer. Collectively, they are referred to as the remote workforce.[26] Information technology companies rely the most heavily on the distributed workforce. Yet there are exceptions with both Yahoo! and Google strongly limiting remote working. The majority of people who work at home do so only a day or two per week at their residence. Also, millions of people work from their homes in self-employment.

Concerns about lengthy commutes, contagious diseases, and the high cost of gasoline have made working at home even more attractive for many workers in recent years.

Say your phone number slowly. I can't tell you how many people have zipped through it.

—*Michael Shepley*
owner of a public relations firm in New York City

Some people believe that the pollutants from driving a gasoline-powered vehicle contribute to global warming. Furthermore, some people find workplaces to have too many interruptions and distractions, such as meetings and conversations with coworkers and superiors.

Advantages of Telecommuting

An analysis of forty-six studies involving close to 13,000 employees found many important advantages of telecommuting. Remote workers tend to be more productive, are less likely to quit, and have higher job satisfaction than those who spend the entire workweek in the office. Employees gained the most benefits from telecommuting when managers granted them flexibility on when and how they worked from home or another remote location, such as an Internet café. An example of flexibility would be letting teleworkers be on the job outside the confines of a rigid schedule, such as from 9 a.m. until 5 p.m.[27]

A study conducted at Ctrip, a travel agency in Shanghai, China, found that employees working from home showed a 13 percent increase in performance. About 9 percent of the improvement was from working five more minutes per shift because of fewer breaks and sick days. Of the productivity increases, 4 percent stemmed from more telephone calls per minute, attributed to a quieter working environment.[28]

For the advantages of remote work to materialize, workers have to be judged on measured output rather than the time invested. An example of measured output for a teleworker would be the number of medical claims applications produced in a week.

Interpersonal Communication Problems

Telecommuters can communicate abundantly via electronic devices, but they miss out on the face-to-face interactions so vital for dealing with complex problems. Another communication problem telecommuters face is feeling isolated from activities at the main office and missing out on the encouragement and recognition that take place in face-to-face encounters. (Of course, many telecommuters prefer to avoid such contact.) Many telecommuters have another communications problem: Because they have very little face-to-face communication with key people in the organization, they believe they are passed over for promotion. Most telecommuters spend some time in the traditional office, yet they miss the day-by-day contact.

To combat the problem of isolation, most companies schedule some face-to-face time with remote workers, perhaps every few months. At a minimum, a supervisor might phone the teleworkers at least once a week or hold a monthly videoconference.

Characteristics of Successful Telecommuters

A worker needs the right personality characteristics and work habits to be successful as a remote worker. Successful telecommuters should be able to work well without supervision and be highly self-disciplined to avoid falling prey to the many distractions at home or another remote location. You also need to be able to work well in isolation and not be dependent on frequent interaction with coworkers or a supervisor. High-maintenance employees who need frequent praise and attention are much better suited for working in a traditional office than for telework.[29]

THE MULTITASKING MOVEMENT

A major consequence of electronic communication devices is that they encourage multitasking, for good or for bad. It has become standard communication practice for many workers to read e-mail and text messages while speaking on the phone, to surf the Internet while in a business meeting, and to check text messages while listening to a presentation. Some customer-contact workers even conduct cell phone conversations with friends while serving customers. Many workers are now using two or three computer monitors so they can write reports while attending to e-mail. Multitasking has become a way of life for many members of Generation Y, who grew up studying while watching television and chatting with their friends on a cell phone.

The Benefits of Multitasking

Advocates of multitasking contend that it increases productivity, such as accomplishing two or more tasks at once. A prime example is Sergio Marchionne, the chairman of Fiat Chrysler. He works intensely, often through the nights on flights from Turin, Italy, to the United States; usually carries several smartphones at once; and accesses his phone while talking to another person. He is also dependent on cigarettes.[30] Many workers contend that it makes them more productive to access e-mail messages while seated at a meeting.

Cognitive Problems Associated with Multitasking

Only a small proportion of workers can multitask successfully. Cognitive psychologist David Strayer of the University of Utah defines a *supertasker*, as a person who can juggle two demanding tasks without pausing or making mistakes. About 2.5 percent of the population is successful at multitasking. Strayer's experiments indicate that while most people think they can handle several tasks simultaneously, most people cannot accomplish the feat. The human brain does not really do two things at once but toggles between the task that places heavy burdens on attention, memory, and focus.[31]

Performing more than one demanding cognitive activity at once lowers accuracy and productivity, because you can devote 100 percent of your attention to only one task at a time. Would you want a brain surgeon to operate on a loved one while he or she chatted on the phone with an investment consultant? Would you want your tax accountant to e-file your return while making calculations on someone else's return?

The multitasking problem is more acute for complex and demanding tasks that require action planning, such as deciding how to respond to a customer complaint or solving an accounting problem. Highly practiced and routine tasks, such as sealing an envelope, suffer less from multitasking.

According to Basex, an IT research and consulting firm, the average worker dealing with information loses 2.1 hours of productivity every day to electronic interruptions and distractions. Multitasking costs the U.S. economy an estimated annual productivity loss of $997 billion and a minimum of 28 billion hours of lost work time. The primary productivity drainers are e-mail alerts, instant messages, buzzing smartphones, and cell phones. (Yet, used properly, these productivity drainers can be productivity enhancers, as explained in Chapter 16.) A contributing problem is that the more you multitask by checking your messages, the more you feel the need to check them.[32]

Interpersonal Consequences of Multitasking

Another byproduct of the multitasking movement with implications for interpersonal relationships is that electronic devices have facilitated breaking down the distinction between work and personal life. While out of the office, including vacations, it is easy to be in frequent contact with the office digitally. On the positive side, the wired worker can be more productive, such as providing input on an important work issue at any time. Also, if you take care of a few work problems while away from the office, you will be less

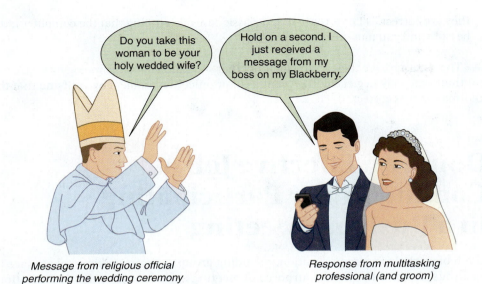

Message from religious official performing the wedding ceremony

Response from multitasking professional (and groom)

FIGURE 8-4

MULTITASKING CAN BLUR THE DISTINCTION BETWEEN WORK AND PERSONAL LIFE

Source: "MULTITASKING CAN BLUR THE DISTINCTION BETWEEN WORK AND PERSONAL LIFE" by Andrew J. DuBrin.

overwhelmed with work when you return. On the negative side, interpersonal relationships may become impoverished because the wired worker concentrates less on friends and family even during leisure time, as illustrated in Figure 8-4.

Digital connectivity in the form of multitasking can weaken human connections in another way. When talking to people face-to-face it is more polite to focus on them rather than paying attention to your smartphone or computer screen. We caution, however, that some people in the workplace regard multitasking while you are talking to them as acceptable and typical behavior.

Whether communication in the workplace is formal or informal, electronic or printed, the human touch should be included for the highest level of effectiveness. Many of the points already made about informal communication illustrate this statement.

OVERCONFIDENCE IN COMPUTER-GENERATED DATA

A subtle communication problem from heavy reliance on computers is that many people regard computerized data as infallible. Neglected in this assumption is the reality that humans, with all their possible shortcomings, entered the data into the computer. Communication problems occur because somebody acts on the computer-generated data and neglects to challenge or double-check the data. The same person might be unwilling to listen to a plea that the information is incorrect. As a result, the computer-generated data creates a barrier to listening. Two examples follow of the phenomenon in question, and you can probably provide a personal example.

■ A woman named Beatrice applied for a position as a front-desk clerk at a hotel. It appeared to the woman that she would be hired, but she was turned down at the last moment. She was told that a Google check revealed that she had been involved in an armed robbery of a convenience store several years ago. Beatrice explained that the Beatrice from the robbery had the same name, but they were not the same person. The hiring manager said, "Sorry, we rely heavily on Google results." (The error here was not validating the Google entry about the criminal Beatrice.)

■ Your bank statement indicates that you are overdrawn by $251. You review your statement three times and are convinced that you have a positive balance of $85. The bank officer shuts you off by saying, "All our calculations are done by computer, so they are correct." (The error here is a classic case of assuming that the computer must be right and you must be wrong.)

The message from these examples is not that communication technology was in error but that somebody neglected to prevent a communication problem by verifying that the information was correct.

▶ **Learning Objective 8.4** ▶

Doing an Effective Job of Conducting or Participating in a Business Meeting

Much of workplace communication, including group decision making, takes place in meetings. Among the many purposes of meetings are disseminating information, training, building team spirit, and problem solving, including brainstorming. Meetings consume considerable work time. At Seagate Technology, for example, an analysis found that work teams were spending more than twenty hours per week at meetings.[33] When conducted properly, meetings accomplish the purpose. Yet, when conducted poorly, meetings represent a substantial productivity drain. The following suggestions apply to those who conduct physical and electronic meetings, and some are also relevant for participants. Videoconferencing is sometimes used to conduct meetings with people in dispersed locations, as is teleconferencing. The globalization of business, as well as interest in reducing travel costs, has increased the demand for videoconferencing. By following these nine suggestions, you increase the meeting's effectiveness as a communication vehicle.

1. **Start with a key meeting outcome.**   Before the meeting is called, the meeting leader defines the one thing that must be accomplished to consider the meeting a success. The outcome in mind is best framed even before establishing the agenda, because knowing what should be accomplished will help establish the agenda.[34] To illustrate, a hospital administrator establishes the key meeting outcome of "find new ways to shorten waiting time in the emergency room." The agenda might then include discussing what other hospitals have done to shorten waiting times in the emergency room.

2. **Meet only for valid reasons.**   Many meetings lead to no decisions because they lacked a valid purpose in the first place. Having an agenda for the meeting is a valid reason because the agenda is an important purpose for getting together. Meetings are necessary only in situations that require coordinated effort and group decision making. E-mails and intranet exchanges can be substituted for meetings when factual information needs to be disseminated and discussion is unimportant. When looking to meet for valid reasons, be aware of possible cultural differences in the motives for having a meeting. In many cultures, meetings are conducted to build relationships. For example, a key to doing business in Asia is to get to know work associates on a personal level before getting down to problem solving, buying, or selling. So for an Asian manager, conducting a meeting to build personal relationships *is* a valid reason. For many Americans, also, an important purpose of face-to-face meetings is to build relationships.

3. **Start and stop on time, and offer refreshments.**   Meetings appear more professional and action oriented when the leader starts and stops on time. If the leader waits for the last member to show up, much time is lost and late behavior is rewarded. Stopping the meeting on time shows respect for the members' time. Offering refreshments is another tactic for emphasizing the importance of the meeting and also enhances

satisfaction with the meeting. Agree in advance on when and if there will be a break, to reduce anxiety about when the break will occur.

4. **Keep comments brief and to the point.** A major challenge facing the meeting leader is to keep conversation on track. Verbal rambling by participants creates communication barriers because other people lose interest. An effective way for the leader to keep comments on target is to ask the contributor of a non sequitur, "In what way does your comment relate to the agenda?"

5. **Encourage critical feedback and commentary.** Meetings are more likely to be fully productive when participants are encouraged to be candid with criticism and negative feedback. Openness helps prevent groupthink and also brings important problems to the attention of management.

6. **Strive for wide participation.** One justification for conducting a meeting is to obtain a variety of input. Although not everybody is equally qualified to voice a sound opinion, everyone should be heard. A skillful leader may have to limit the contribution of domineering members and coax reticent members to voice their ideas. Asking participants to bring several questions to the meeting will often spur participation. The meeting leader should not play favorites by encouraging the participation of some members and ignoring others. If the meeting leader spends the entire time making a PowerPoint presentation, participation will be discouraged. The slides should supplement the meeting and be starting points for discussion.

7. **Solve small issues ahead of time with e-mail or other forms of electronic communication.** Meetings can be briefer and less mundane when small issues are resolved ahead of time. E-mail is particularly effective for resolving minor administrative issues and also for collecting agenda items in advance. Intranets and blogs can serve the same purpose.

8. **Consider "huddling" when quick action is needed.** A huddle is a fast-paced, action-oriented way to bring workers together into brief meetings to discuss critical performance issues. A department store manager might bring together five floor managers ten minutes before opening to say, "We have a lineup of about 500 customers waiting to get in because of our specials today. Is everybody ready for the rush of excitement? What problems do you anticipate?" The huddle is particularly important when it would be difficult for the workers to attend a long meeting. Huddles are often accomplished standing up, which helps keep the meetings brief. In these situations, you have to literally "think on your feet," meaning that you have to make your point quickly. Standup meetings are usually quite brief, so you do not have much time to reflect on what you are saying.

9. **Ensure that all follow-up action is assigned and recorded.** All too often, even after a decision has been reached, a meeting lacks tangible output. Distribute a memo summarizing who is responsible for taking what action and by what date.

10. **Minimize distractions during the meeting.** The group should agree on whether meeting participants will be allowed to use laptop computers for purposes other than recording information in the meeting. Agree also on whether using phones and text messaging is acceptable during the meeting. Tim Brown, CEO of design firm IDEO, believes that it is unacceptable to use a smartphone during a meeting because engaging with the people present is important.[35] If handouts are used, allow participants enough time to read them so one person is not presenting while the others are reading. Ensure beforehand that computer-related equipment, such as the projector, is working and that it is compatible with the presenter's software.

A project manager reports that a major distraction in videoconferences is the clickety-clack of people on a keyboard and not focusing on the meeting, sniffing, and talking out of turn on top of others.[36]

Concept Review and Reinforcement

Summary and Review

Messages in organizations are sent over both formal (official) and informal (unofficial) channels. Three key aspects of the formal channels are as follows:

- The company blog is a type of formal communication that might also be placed on social networking websites. It communicates business information with a soft, human touch.
- Formal communication channels in the workplace have kept up with Internet-based communication technology. Four such channels are social networking sites (such as Facebook), intranets, wikis, and webinars.
- Many companies have developed formal communication channels for managing crises, such as fires and terrorist attacks.
- Messages in organizations travel in four primary directions: downward, upward, horizontally, and diagonally. An open-door policy facilitates upward communication.
- An informal communication channel supplements the formal channel.
- A major informal communication channel is the network of contacts that employees use to accomplish work, sometimes referred to as the *shadow organization*. Communities of practice are an informal channel that has often slipped into being a formal channel. Social networking analysis is used to map the shadow organization.
- The grapevine is the major informal communication channel, and it carries rumors and gossip.
- Chance encounters between managers and employees foster informal communication, as does management by walking around.

- An architectural approach to enhancing informal communication is to make extensive use of open office space. Two risks, however, are frustrating the need for privacy and creating a distracting work environment.

Communication technology creates challenges for interpersonal communication, despite all its advantages, as follows:

- E-mail, including instant messaging and text messaging, has the most dramatic impact on interpersonal communication in organizations. Some workers are overwhelmed by e-mail, whereas others have the system under control.
- E-mail encourages informal, unprofessional communication, and the system is too often used to play office politics.
- E-mail should be used to supplement, not to substitute for, face-to-face negotiations.
- Some business firms have counterattacked the problems associated with e-mail by shifting to related technologies.
- Presentation technology creates challenges of its own, including the need to learn how to handle equipment and maintain eye contact at the same time. It is important to talk to the audience and not the screen and to reduce the text on each page to a bare minimum.
- Effective telephone and voice mail communication skills are helpful in overcoming communication problems. Remember to vary your voice tone and avoid multitasking while speaking.
- Telecommuters are now referred to as the remote or distributed workforce.

■ Telecommuters may miss out on the face-to-face interactions necessary for dealing with complex problems.

■ Telecommuting is also a challenge because it lacks a solid human connection.

■ Electronic communication facilitates the multitasking that is so popular with Generation Y.

■ Advocates of multitasking claim it enhances productivity.

■ The bulk of scientific evidence suggests that performing more than one demanding cognitive activity at once lowers accuracy and productivity. Mental output and depth of thought deteriorate while multitasking.

■ Multitasking has facilitated breaking down the distinction between work and personal life.

■ A subtle communication problem from heavy reliance on computers is that many people regard computerized data as infallible. As a result, the user of the data might not listen to pleas that the information is incorrect.

Much of workplace communication takes place in meetings. Among the many suggestions for productive meetings are the following:

■ Start with a key meeting outcome.
■ Meet only for valid reasons.
■ Start and stop on time, and offer refreshments.
■ Solve small issues ahead of time with e-mail.
■ Minimize distractions during the meeting.

Questions for Discussion and Review

8.1 Suppose you thought that the CEO of your company was moving the company in the wrong direction, and you wanted to tell him or her. Explain which communication channel you would choose to deliver your message.

8.2 How might understanding the informal communication pathways in your organization help you become a more effective worker?

8.3 Why do so many businesspeople object to receiving an e-mail or text message in all caps?

8.4 A growing number of workers in entry-level positions are told they have been fired by text messages. What concerns do you have about this approach to dismissing workers?

8.5 What do you think would be the advantages and disadvantages of having a "no e-mail on Friday" policy at a busy office?

8.6 Give three examples of business situations in which telephone conversations still play a key role.

8.7 Many large banks provide customers an opportunity to interact with a bank representative through a video-conferencing device that is as clear as HDTV (high-definition television), the bank representative is situated at headquarters while the customer is at a branch. What is your evaluation of the communication effectiveness of this approach in providing customer service?

8.8 Provide an example from your own life in which multitasking has enhanced your performance.

8.9 Give an example from your own life in which multitasking has lowered your performance.

8.10 Why are face-to-face meetings still so popular even in high-technology companies?

Web Corner

Suggestions for writing better e-mails
http://www.mindtools.com/ (Enter into the search box, "Writing effective e-mails.")

How to run an effective business meeting
http://www.meetingwizard.org (Information appears directly on the front page.)

INTERNET SKILL BUILDER

Social Media and Productivity

Use your preferred search engine or engines to identify two business settings in which the use of social media resulted in higher worker productivity or increased sales. Identify what the company did correctly with social media that led to the good result.

Developing Your
Human Relations Skills

Applying Human Relations Exercise 8-1

Designing an Office for a Virtual-Customer Agent

Work in a team to design a home office for a virtual-customer agent, a worker whose responsibilities are to fill orders for merchandise for three different companies. The agent receives calls through a toll-free number and then uses the computer to enter the order. He or she also processes orders online. The office in question will be placed somewhere in a three-bedroom house that also has a family room, a kitchen, a basement, and an enclosed porch.

While designing the office, include such factors as the layout of the furniture and equipment, the equipment needed, and any decorations. Keep in mind ergonomic factors that focus on making the equipment easy to use and with low risk for physical problems such as carpal tunnel syndrome and backaches. Because the virtual-customer agent will have to pay for the office setup, derive a tentative budget.

Draw your design on any convenient format, such as a flip chart, whiteboard, blackboard, or computer screen. Your team leader might be asked to present the design to the rest of the class so class members can compare the effectiveness of each design. Class members evaluating the home office design might use the following evaluation factors in addition to whatever their intuition suggests:

- To what extent does the office design help reduce possible conflict with other people living in the same household?
- How might this design offer productivity advantages over a conventional office?
- When and if customers or company representatives call into this office, how professional will the setup sound?
- How will this office design contribute to job satisfaction?

Applying Human Relations Exercise 8-2

Evaluating a Business Meeting

The class organizes into teams of about six students to conduct a meeting to formulate plans for building temporary housing for homeless people downtown in your city or a nearby city. Three other students, or the entire class, will observe the meeting. This exercise should take about thirty-five minutes, and it can be done inside or outside of class. Each team takes on the assignment of formulating plans for building temporary shelters for the homeless. The dwellings you plan to build, for example, might be two-room cottages with electricity and indoor plumbing. During the time allotted to the task, formulate plans for going ahead with shelters for the homeless. Consider dividing up work by assigning certain tasks to each team member. Sketch out tentative answers to the following questions: (a) How will you obtain funding for your venture? (b) Which homeless people will you help? (c) Where will your shelters be? (d) Who will do the actual construction?

After the meeting is completed, the three observers will provide feedback to the team members about the effectiveness of the meeting, using the following criteria:

1. How effective was the teamwork? Support your conclusion with an example of specific behavior.
2. How well did group members stay on track in terms of focusing on their goal?
3. Did the team members make any introductory warm-up comments to help build rapport?
4. To what extent was the participation among team members balanced?
5. Did the team move toward any conclusions or action plans?
6. Choose another criterion you think might be relevant.

Company Messages on Company Websites or YouTube

Each class member is asked to search company websites, YouTube, or Hulu for a serious message to employees or other stakeholders, such as customers and stockholders. If you choose YouTube or Hulu, the video you choose should appear to have been authentically prepared by a company representative, not the work of a prankster. Finding a serious message might take some digging because so many corporate messages posted on YouTube or Hulu are strictly for entertainment purposes. But it is also possible to find video messages on an occasional company website.

At some point the class meets in a setting where it is possible to project videos on a large screen. Even if the screen is a large monitor for a PC, the activity will work. Depending on how much class time is available for the project, about six volunteers project their chosen video on the screen. As class

members watch the selection of videos, form an impression of the communication effectiveness of each video. Answer such questions as:

- What message is the business organization really getting across to its intended audience?
- How convincing is the video in sending its message?
- How sincere does the message appear to be?

After students have reflected on the videos, have a brief class discussion of the answers to the above questions.

Human Relations Case Study 8–1

I Want to Get into the Loop

Lisa, an order fulfillment specialist, was informed by her supervisor that many managers in the company were now using social network analysis, in an attempt to figure out which associates other workers were turning to for help and friendship. The results of the social network analysis were not yet being used directly for salary increases or performance reviews. However, a list was being compiled of the most influential employees based on the social network analysis.

Very concerned about the social network analysis, Lisa expressed her uneasiness to her best friend in the company, Dion, a technical support specialist. She said, "Dion, I feel that I am going to be shut out of promotional possibilities here. The way I understand this new social network analysis, if other workers don't contact you much, you score pretty low on the network analysis. My problem is not that I have enemies here. It's just that hardly anybody ever asks me anything. For example, the only question I received this week was whether or not it was still raining."

Dion asked Lisa, "What have you done lately to get more people to rely on you for advice and friendship?"

Lisa replied, "I want to get into the loop, but I don't know how. Maybe I could wear clothing that was a little more stylish. Maybe I could send out tweets telling everybody what a star I am. I really just don't know what to do to upgrade my number of contacts."

"Maybe we can set aside some time next week to figure out how to make you a network star," said Dion with a smile.

Questions

8.11 To what extent should Lisa be concerned about showing up frequently on the company social network analysis?

8.12 What advice might you offer Lisa and Dion to help make her a "network star"? (In addition to your own analysis, you might find some ideas in Chapter 9 about getting along with people.)

Human Relations Role-Playing Exercise 8–1

Lisa Builds Her Network

One student plays the role of Lisa, who wants to be part of the network of more people. She spots Clyde, a marketing associate, sitting alone in the company cafeteria. She decides to see if she can become part of Clyde's network because she

has heard that Clyde is influential in the company. Another student plays the role of Clyde, who likes to develop network members only if they have something to offer. Run the scenario for about five minutes.

An Office Design Built for Outgoing People

Ashley is the CEO of Luxury Luggage, a designer and manufacturer of upscale luggage as well as cases for smartphones, laptop computers, and tablet computers. Luxury Luggage has a large central office in a ninety-year-old downtown building. The supplier network of companies that manufacture and ship luggage and covers is located throughout the world. Despite the intense competitiveness of the business for luggage and electronic-device covers, the company has survived.

Up until recently, the office space for Luxury was divided into closed offices for higher-ranking individuals, cubicles, open space, and conference rooms. Ashley, however, read a few articles about how open work areas help companies become more democratic and encourage communication, collaboration, and creativity. She also read about the advantages of the top executives working out in the open on worktables, among all the other workers.

With the help of a design consultant, Ashley redesigned the office space to be totally open, with just a few conference rooms for holding discussions with major customers, such as retail store executives. Ashley and her executive team moved their offices out into the open.

Within two months, praise and complaints about the new office design trickled in to Ashley. Those people who liked the new design talked about the ease of interacting with their coworkers, including being able to talk to them without using e-mail, texting, or the telephone. In contrast, Alberto,

the head of product design, presented a very negative view of the new office design to Ashley. He insisted that the two discuss his concerns in a restaurant booth, so they could have some privacy.

Over a glass of wine, and before placing the dinner order, Alberto jumped right into his concerns: "Ashley, the new office design is a playground for chatty, outgoing people. They love jabbering away during the day, waving to people, and getting someone else's input before reaching even a simple decision. But you are destroying the spirit of our more introverted employees, who are really the heart of a product design business. These people need to think in solitude, unbothered by the buzz and cell phones of coworkers. A good example is Magnolia, our top luggage and cover designer. She told me she has to create her designs at night and on weekends so she can think straight without interruptions."

Ashley responded, "I hear you, Alberto. I am just trying to be modern in laying out our office. I will give your concerns some more thought. We love both our outgoing and more reserved staff members."

Questions

8.13 What action, if any, should Ashley take in response to Alberto's concerns about the new office layout at Luxury Luggage?

8.14 If Luxury Luggage decides to retain its open office design, how might the company accommodate the needs of more reserved people?

The Open Office-Space Discussion

One student plays the role of Ashley, who has decided to investigate the effectiveness of the open-office-space design for enhancing communication, collaboration, and creativity. She therefore conducts an interview with Magnolia about the new office arrangement in a conference room designed for customer contact. Another student plays the role of Magnolia, who is frustrated, angry, and about ready to quit. Ashley attempts to both

calm down Magnolia and convince her of the value of the open-space-office design.

For both role-plays, observers rate the role-players on two dimensions, using a scale of 1 to 5 from very poor to very good. One dimension is "effective use of human relations techniques." The second dimension is "acting ability." A few observers might voluntarily provide feedback to the role-players in terms of sharing their ratings and observations. The course instructor might also provide feedback.

REFERENCES

1. Steven Snell, "Corporate Blog Design: Trends and Examples," *Smashing Magazine*, www.smashingmagazine.com, August 20, 2009, pp. 1–70.
2. Cited in Erika D. Smith, "Web Opens Another Defensive Front for Companies," *Indianapolis Star*, syndicated story, July 1, 2007.
3. "The Value of Schmoozing in the Age of Social Media," *Knowledge@Wharton*, http://knowledge.wharton.upenn.edu, October 22, 2014, p. 1.
4. Ed Frauenheim, "Social Revolution," *Workforce*, October 22, 2007, pp. 1, 28–37.
5. Cited in Bill Roberts, "Social Networking at the Office," *HR Magazine*, March 2008, pp. 81–83.
6. p. 82.
7. Patrick Kiger, "Lessons from a Crisis: How Communication Kept a Company Together," *Workforce*, November 2001, p. 28.
8. Richard McDermott and Douglas Archibald, "Harnessing Your Staff's Informal Networks," *Harvard Business Review*, March 2010, pp. 82–89.
9. Mark Hendricks, "The Shadow Knows," *Entrepreneur*, January 2000, p. 110; Jennifer Reingold and Jia Lynn Yang, "What's Your OQ?" *Fortune*, July 23, 2007, pp. 98–106.
10. Valdis Krebs, "Social Network Analysis: A Brief Introduction," www.orgnet.com, Copyright © 2000–2011, 2014, Valdis Krebs.
11. Cited in Ethan Watters, "The Organization Woman," *Businessweek*, April 10, 2006, pp. 106–110.
12. Vijaya Venkataramani, Guiseppe (Joe) Labianca, and Travis Grosser, "Positive and Negative Workplace Relationships, Social Satisfaction, and Organizational Attachment," *Journal of Applied Psychology*, November 2013, pp. 1028–1039.
13. Samuel Greengard, "Gossip Poisons Business: HR Can Stop It," *Workforce*, July 2001, pp. 26–27; Lea Winerman, "Have You Heard the Latest?" *Monitor on Psychology*, April 2006, pp. 56–57.
14. John P. Kotter, *The General Managers* (New York: Free Press, 1991).
15. "Making Rounds like a Physician," *Manager's Edge*, February 8, 2006, as adapted from Quint Studer, *Hardwiring Excellence* (Gulf Breeze, FL: Fire Starter Publishing, 2005).
16. Lana Burtolot, "What Is the Office of the Future?" *Entrepreneur*, August 2013, pp. 44–50.
17. Sue Shellenbarger, "Indecent Exposure: The Downsides of Working in a Glass Office," *The Wall Street Journal*, January 4, 2012, pp. D1, D2.
18. Cited in Enid Abelo, "Don't Underrate Old-Fashioned Communication," *Democrat and Chronicle*, September 26, 2010, p. 3E.
19. "10 Rules to Reverse the Email Spiral," *Office Manager Today*, December 2012, p. 6.
20. Marsha Egan, "E-Mail Overload? Three Ways to Tame Your In Box," *Christian Science Monitor*, March 17, 2011, pp. 1–2.
21. Michelle Conlin, "E-Mail Is So Five Minutes Ago: It's Being Replaced by Software That Promotes Real-Time Collaboration," *Businessweek*, November 28, 2005, pp. 111–112; Luis Suarez, "I Freed Myself from E-mail's Grip," *New York Times*, nytimes.com June 29, 2008.
22. Jean Mausehund and R. Neil Dortch, "Presentation Skills in the Digital Age," *Business Education Forum*, April 1999, pp. 30–32; Michael Patterson, "The Pitch Coach," *BusinessWeek SmallBiz*, Fall 2005, p. 61.
23. Shira Ovide, "Office Phone Calls Make a Comeback," *The Wall Street Journal*, March 13, 2015, p. B6.
24. John T. Adams III, "When You're on a Speakerphone, Don't Make Noise," *HR Magazine*, March 2001, p. 12.
25. Alex Williams, "Mind Your BlackBerry or Mind Your Manners," *New York Times*, www.nytimes.com, June 21, 2009, p. 2.
26. Based on 2014 U.S. Bureau of Labor Statistics.
27. Ravi S. Gajendran and David A. Harrison, "The Good, the Bad and the Unknown about Telecommuting: Meta-Analysis of Psychological Mediators and Individual Consequences," *Journal of Applied Psychology*, November 2007, p. 1524.
28. "Telecommuters vs. Office Workers: Who's More Productive?" *SiliconANGLE*, http://siliconangle.com, October 14, 2013, pp. 2–3.
29. "Telecommuting Tips," *Manager's Edge*, December 2007, p. 1.
30. Larry P. Vellequette, "Marchionne Is Fiat Chrysler's Miracle Worker," *Automotive News*, www.autonews.com, December 1, 2014, p. 1.
31. Kat McGowan, "Meet the Super-Taskers," *Psychology Today*, January–February 2014, p. 64.
32. Susan G. Hauser, "'Mindfulness' over Matter of Multitasking," *Workforce Management*, December 2012, p. 10; Joe Robinson, "E-Mail Is Making You Stupid," *Entrepreneur*, March 2010, pp. 61, 62; Stephanie Pappas, "Digital Overload: Is Your Computer Frying Your Brain?" *Live Science*, www.livescience.com, November 9, 2010, pp. 1–3.
33. Sue Shellenbarger, "Stop Wasting Everyone's Time," *The Wall Street Journal*, December 3, 2014, p. D1.
34. "Never Hold Another Bad Meeting," *Manager's Edge*, October 2008, p. 6.
35. "Bringing Design to Blue Chips: Tim Brown, CEO, IDEO," *Fortune*, November 12, 2007, p. 32.
36. Comment made in "Feedback," *Entrepreneur*, January 12, 2014, p. 14.

Fotolia

CHAPTER **9**

Specialized Tactics for Getting Along with Others in the Workplace

Outline

Chloe is the manager of the service department of a large, successful automobile dealership. She has a staff of twenty-five people, including the shop manager, the credit manager, an accountant, and several bookkeepers and receptionists. Today, Chloe has her annual performance review with Larry, the president of the dealership. She enjoys working at the dealership and reporting to Larry, whose leadership she admires and respects. A couple of minutes into the performance review, Larry asks Chloe how she thinks she has performed during the previous year. Chloe has rehearsed for the moment, and she says to Larry, "Thank you for giving me a chance to give you a rundown. Here's what I think, I've accomplished this year:

"You wanted us to keep an eye on costs. Our service department went 9 percent under budget this year. You wanted us to enhance customer satisfaction. Our Internet surveys, as revealed by the outside firm conducting them, showed an overall customer satisfaction rate of 85 percent—way above the industry average.

"You have made it clear that most of our profit comes from service rather than sales. It's the after-sale business that keeps us afloat. Our service revenue climbed 15 percent this year. Our body shop was booming, and we even sold a lot of tires although we charge much more than tire stores.

"You would be pleased to know that our employee turnover is about 10 percent. That's much lower than our competitors'."

Larry responded, "Chloe, you have given me great data to work with in evaluating your performance. I have an even clearer picture of what the service department is doing to make our dealership succeed."

The story about the proactive behavior of the service manager illustrates the importance of creating a good impression with the boss, based on legitimate accomplishments. This chapter presents information about developing productive relationships with three major groups of work associates: managers, coworkers, and customers. Along the way, we include information about coping with difficult bosses. The ability to deal effectively with others in the work environment and to influence them for constructive purposes can be framed as **political skill**. The term refers to a combination of social astuteness with the capacity to adjust and adapt behavior to the demands of different situations. As a result, the person with political skill inspires trust and support and controls and influences the responses of others. At the same time, he or she appears genuine and sincere.[1]

Learning Objectives ▶

After reading the information and doing the exercises in this chapter, you should be able to:

9.1 Select several tactics for developing a good relationship with your manager or team leader.

9.2 Deal effectively with a problem manager.

9.3 Describe methods of getting along with coworkers.

9.4 Identify tactics that help a person become a good team player.

9.5 Specify approaches to building good relationships with customers.

Political skill
a combination of social astuteness with the capacity to adjust and adapt behavior to the demands of different situations

Developing a Good Relationship with Your Manager or Team Leader

Getting along well with your manager is the most basic strategy of getting ahead in your career. If you cannot gain favor with the boss, it will be difficult to advance to higher positions or earn much more money. Obtaining good performance reviews and receiving favorable work assignments also depends on a good relationship with the person to whom you report. Workers who have good relationships with their manager have more job security than those with poor relationships. Your manager or team leader is always the person who is contacted first when someone wants to determine what kind of employee you are. Usually this information is sought when you are being considered for transfer, promotion, or a position with another firm.

In this section, we present a variety of approaches that lead to constructive relationships with an immediate superior. The goal is to be legitimately perceived as a strong contributor to your work unit.

CREATE A POSITIVE FIRST IMPRESSION

A logical starting point in developing a good relationship with the person to whom you report is to create a positive first impression. Peter Stephens, a managing director of internships at the Washington Center for Internships and Academic Seminars, offers this advice: "Before setting foot in the office, become a sponge. Exhaust your online resources and briefing materials to absorb anything you can about the organization. On the first day, show you are ready to work by walking in on time and exuding a can-do attitude." Equally important is to show that you are acclimating to the organizational culture by learning people's names and treating everyone with respect and civility.[2]

ACHIEVE GOOD JOB PERFORMANCE

Maintaining good job performance remains the most effective strategy for impressing your manager. When any rational manager evaluates a group member's performance, the first question asked is "Is this employee getting the job done?" And you cannot get the job done if you are not competent. Many factors contribute to whether you can become a competent performer. Among them are your education, training, personality characteristics, job experience, and special skills, such as being able to organize your work. Factors external to you, such as having a supportive boss and cooperative coworkers, also contribute to good performance.

An advanced way of displaying good job performance is to assist your manager with a difficult problem he or she faces. Your manager, for example, might need to operate equipment outside his or her area of expertise. If you show the manager how to operate the equipment, he or she will think highly of your job performance.

An effective way of enhancing your job performance is to offer alternative solutions to complex problems. In this way, you are more likely to follow a path favored by your boss, leading to good performance reviews. The director of a senior living residence asked an administrator to find a way to reduce the number of falls by residents—a problem that plagues people of advanced age. Instead of suggesting one idea, the administrator offered several suggestions, as follows:

- Let's check to see if all our residents use footwear with appropriate treads.

- Instruct our healthcare aides to coach all our residents about the proper use of canes.

- The entire staff should check periodically to see if our residents are making good use of handrails at the facility.

A subtle issue about performing well to please your manager is that your manager has to be aware of your good performance and give you proper credit. One useful approach is to assist your boss by keeping him or her informed about exactly what work you are doing, the problems you are solving, and the successes you have attained.[3]

DISPLAY A STRONG WORK ETHIC

A strong **work ethic** is a firm belief in the dignity and value of work and therefore is important for favorably impressing a manager. An employee with a strong work ethic will sometimes be excused if his or her performance is not yet exceptional. This is true because the manager assumes that a strong work ethic will elevate performance eventually. Six suggestions follow for demonstrating a strong work ethic:

1. Work hard and enjoy the task.   By definition, a person with a strong work ethic works diligently and has strong internal motivation. The person may appreciate external rewards yet appreciates the importance of any work that adds value to society.

2. Demonstrate competence even on minor tasks.   Attack each assignment with the recognition that each task performed well, however minor, is one more career credit. A minor task performed well paves the way for your being given more consequential tasks.

3. Take the initiative by assuming personal responsibility for problems.   An employee with a problem will often approach the manager and say, "We have a tough problem to deal with." The connotation is that the manager should be helping the employee with the problem. A better impression is created when the employee takes the initiative by saying, "I have a tough problem to deal with, and I would like your advice." This statement implies that you are willing to assume responsibility for the problem and for any mistake you may have made that led to the problem.

4. Assume responsibility for free-floating problems.   A natural way to display a strong work ethic is to assume responsibility for free-floating (nonassigned) problems. Taking the initiative, or being proactive, on even a minor task, such as ordering lunch for a meeting that is running late, can enhance the impression one makes on a manager.

5. Get your projects completed promptly.   A byproduct of a strong work ethic is an eagerness to get projects completed promptly. People with a strong work ethic respect deadlines imposed by others. Furthermore, they typically set deadlines of their own more tightly than those imposed by their bosses.

6. Accept undesirable assignments willingly.   Look for ways to express the attitude "Whether this assignment is glamorous and fun is a secondary issue. What counts is that it is something that needs doing for the good of the company."

BE DEPENDABLE AND HONEST

Dependability is a critical employee virtue. If an employee can be counted on to deliver as promised and to be at work regularly, that employee has gone a long way toward impressing the boss. A boss is uncomfortable not knowing whether an important assignment will be accomplished on time. If you are not dependable, you will probably not get your share of important assignments. Honesty is tied to dependability because a dependable employee is honest about when he or she will have an assignment completed. Dependability and honesty are important at all job levels. One of the highest compliments a manager can pay an employee is to describe the employee as dependable. Conversely, it is considered derogatory to call any employee undependable.

Work ethic
a firm belief in the dignity and value of work and therefore important for favorably impressing a manager

Don't' wait to be told what to do. . . . Pitch in when you have the time to do so.

—*Joni Daniels*
Principal and founder of Daniels & Associates

BE A GOOD ORGANIZATIONAL CITIZEN

An especially meritorious approach to impressing key people is to demonstrate organizational citizenship behavior. If people engage only in work included in their job description, an "it's not my job" mentality pervades. An effective way to impress your manager, therefore, is to demonstrate that you are not constrained by a job description. If something needs doing, you will get it done regardless of whether it is your formal responsibility.

An impressive way of stepping outside your job description is to be proactive. Anticipate problems, even when the manager had not planned to work on them. Instead of working exclusively on problems that have been assigned, the worker is perceptive enough to look for future problems. Anticipating problems impresses most managers because it reflects an entrepreneurial, take-charge attitude. An example of anticipating a future problem took place at a large supermarket chain. A marketing specialist noted that dollar stores were growing at such a rapid pace that sales would soon be hurt at the supermarket. In response, the chain soon developed a bottom-price section that helped stem the loss of sales to dollar stores.

CREATE A STRONG PRESENCE

A comprehensive approach to impressing your manager or team leader and other key people in the workplace is to create a strong presence, keeping yourself in the forefront. Such actions impress key people and simultaneously help advance your career. Stephanie Sherman, a career consultant, offers this advice for creating a strong presence:

- Get involved in high-visibility projects, such as launching a new product or redesigning work methods. Even an entry-level position on such a project can help a worker get noticed.

- Get involved in teams because they give you an opportunity to broaden your skills and knowledge.

- Get involved in social and community activities of interest to top management, such as those sponsored by the company. Behave professionally, and use your best manners.

- Create opportunities for yourself by making constructive suggestions about earning or saving money. Even if an idea is rejected, you will still be remembered for your initiative.

- Show a willingness to take on some of the tasks that your manager doesn't like to do but would be forced to do if you did not step in.[4]

A powerful way of creating a strong presence with a newly appointed manager is to take the initiative to state that you want to be part of his or her team. Instead of acting envious toward the new manager, approach the person with a statement to this effect: "I am experienced in my job, and I want to help. I may not be perfect, but I accept your goals for our unit."[5]

FIND OUT WHAT YOUR MANAGER EXPECTS OF YOU

You have little chance of doing a good job and impressing your manager unless you know what you are trying to accomplish. Review your work goals and ask clarifying questions. An example would be "You told me to visit our major customers who are sixty days or more delinquent on their accounts. Should I also visit the three of these customers who have declared bankruptcy?" In addition to having a clear statement of your goals, it is helpful to know the priorities attached to them. In this way you will know which task to execute first.

A subtle aspect of understanding the expectations of your boss is adapting to his or her preferred style of work. Managers vary in terms of wanting written versus oral briefings. Some managers prefer to receive e-mail messages from you regularly, others once a week. Many managers want to be treated informally, much like being a coworker. A minority of managers want to be treated as if they were royalty. Matching your work style to the work style of your boss can help build a strong relationship between the two of you.

MINIMIZE COMPLAINTS

Being open and honest in expressing your feelings and opinions is part of having good human relations skills. Nevertheless, this type of behavior, when carried to excess, could earn you a reputation as a whiner. Few managers want to have a group member around who constantly complains about working conditions, coworkers, working hours, pay, and so forth.

Another important reason a boss usually dislikes having a direct report (subordinate) who complains too much is that listening to these complaints takes up considerable time. Most managers spend a disproportionate amount of time listening to the problems of a small number of ineffective or complaining employees.

To make valid complaints to the manager, complain only when justified. And when you do offer a complaint, back it up with a recommended solution. Anyone can take potshots at something. The valuable employee is the person who supports these complaints with a constructive action plan. An example follows of a complaint, supported by action plans for its remedy.

> When a potential customer wants a discount of more than 3 percent, we have to receive authorization from you. The problem is that you may be out of contact with us temporarily, even by your phone. The 3 percent rule was probably established before there were so many overseas suppliers. If authorization were required only for discounts of 5 percent or more, we could close more sales quickly.

One possibility for minimizing the need for complaints is to attempt to look at decisions from the boss's point of view. The company might decide to prohibit workers from using text messaging for personal reasons during working hours. Instead of complaining that the prohibition on text messages is unjust, the worker might attempt to understand why company management thinks instant messages lower productivity.

AVOID BYPASSING YOUR MANAGER

A way to embarrass and sometimes infuriate your manager is to repeatedly go to his or her superior with your problems, conflicts, and complaints. Such bypasses have at least three strongly negative connotations. One is that you don't believe your boss has the power to take care of your problem. Another is that you distrust his or her judgment in the matter at hand. A third is that you are secretly launching a complaint against your manager.

The boss bypass is looked on so negatively that most experienced managers will not listen to your problem unless you have already discussed it with your immediate superior. There *are* times, however, when running around your manager is necessary, such as when you have been unable to resolve a conflict directly with him or her (see the following section). Should your manager be involved in highly immoral or illegal actions, such as sexual harassment or taking kickbacks from vendors, a boss bypass might be warranted. But even under these circumstances, you should politely inform your manager that you are going to take up your problem with the next level of management.

If your boss is unable or unwilling to take care of the problem, you might consider contacting your boss's superior. Nonetheless, considerable tact and diplomacy are needed. Do not imply that your manager is incompetent but merely that you would like another opinion about the issues at stake. If an organization has a formal system for filing complaints, such as an open-door policy, it can be used to substitute for a boss bypass but should be used only when you are unable to resolve a problem with your boss.

ENGAGE IN FAVORABLE INTERACTIONS WITH YOUR MANAGER

The many techniques described previously support the goal of engaging in favorable interactions with your manager. Human Relations Self-Assessment Quiz 9-1 contains a list of behaviors used by employees to create positive interactions with their supervisors. Use these behaviors as a guide for skill building.

According to a synthesis of findings by organizational behavior professor Cecily D. Cooper at the University of Miami, an effective way of ingratiating yourself with your boss, as well as with others in the workplace, is to make effective use of humor. **Ingratiating** is an attempt to increase one's attractiveness to others, so as to influence their behavior. The most effective type of humor for building a relationship with the boss should be work related and hint at a strength of the boss, department, or company. If the humor is well received, it helps build a relationship with the manager (or other targets of the humor as well).[6] Here's an attempt at ego-building humor that worked well with one vice president. The department administrative

Ingratiating
describing an attempt to increase one's attractiveness to others to influence their behavior

---

Human Relations Self-Assessment Quiz   9-1

Manager Interaction Checklist

Use the following behaviors as a checklist for achieving favorable interactions with your present manager or a future one. The more of these actions you engage in, the higher the probability that you are building a favorable relationship with your manager.

1. Express agreement with manager's opinion whenever I truly agree.
2. Ask for assistance in areas in which I know that my manager enjoys giving assistance or providing an opinion.
3. Am polite toward my manager, including smiling frequently and expressing appreciation.
4. Avoid profanity in front of my boss, even if he or she uses profanity on the job.
5. Bring forth solutions to important problems facing the group or organization.
6. Contribute willingly to payroll deductions for charity such as United Way.
7. Put considerable effort into working on problems that I know are important to my manager.
8. Almost never miss or be late for a meeting called by my manager.
9. Almost always get a work assignment done on time.
10. Often volunteer to help my manager accomplish a significant task.
11. Compliment my manager when he or she has accomplished something substantial.
12. Occasionally take on work that is outside my job description and then explain to my manager what I did and why I did it.
13. Almost never complain about work or personal life to my manager.
14. In a meeting, explain to the group why I think the manager's new idea will work.
15. Inform my boss should I hear that a customer or client enjoys our product or service.
16. Make only positive social networking posts about my manager or the company.

Source: "Manager Interaction Checklist" by Andrew J. DuBrin.

assistant said, "Herb, we all know what a reputation you've developed in the company. When you are promoted to CEO, will you invite us all to the big bash you will schedule in Las Vegas?"

Delivering Bad News

Although favorable interactions with a manager are valuable for relationship building, there are times when a group member has to deliver bad news. For example, you might have to inform the manager about a roof that caved in at a company location, or of customer complaints about a new product. You want to avoid being the messenger who is punished because he or she delivered bad news. Attempt to be calm and businesslike. Do not needlessly blame yourself for the problem. Mention that *we are* or *the company is* facing a serious challenge. If possible, suggest a possible solution, such as, "I have already investigated a temporary location we can use until the damage is repaired."

Cross-Cultural Factors

When working to establish a good relationship with your manager, keep in mind that cultural factors could influence how a given tactic should be modified for best effectiveness. An example would be that displaying a strong work ethic to a supervisor from Japan would be different from displaying the same work ethic to a manager from France. The Japanese manager might think that working fifty-five hours a week indicates a strong work ethic, whereas the French manager might think that forty hours a week of hard work is exceptional. Another cultural factor in establishing a good relationship could be the amount of respect shown to the manager. A typical American manager might expect an informal, friendly relationship, with the two of you acting like equals. However, a manager from China might expect much more respect. In one situation, a manager from China in charge of a chemistry lab in the United States became angry when workers addressed him by his first name. He expected to be addressed as "Dr." plus his last name.

Coping with a Problem Manager

◀ Learning Objective 9.2 ◀

At some point in their careers, many people face the situation of dealing with a problem manager—one who makes it difficult for the subordinate to get the job done. The problem is sometimes attributed to the boss's personality or incompetence. A frequent personality problem is being a **bully**, a cruel and aggressive boss who intimidates and verbally abuses subordinates. Bullying bosses frequently use the techniques of berating the skills of a subordinate in front of coworkers, spreading rumors, disrupting the person's work, and screaming at him or her.[7] People who report to a bully often feel belittled and sapped of energy.

Here we describe several constructive approaches to dealing with the delicate situation of working for a problem manager.

Bully
a cruel and aggressive boss who intimidates and verbally abuses subordinates

REEVALUATE YOUR MANAGER

Some employees think they have problem managers when those bosses simply have major role, goal, or value differences. (A role in this context is the expectations of the job.) The problem might also lie in conflicting personalities, such as being outgoing or shy. Another problem is conflicting perspectives, such as being detail oriented as opposed to taking an overall perspective. The differences just noted can be good or bad, depending on how they are viewed and used. For example, a combination of a detail-oriented group member with an "overall perspective" boss can be a winning combination.[8]

If your immediate manager has recently begun to react too harshly toward you and other members of the unit, consider that the boss might now be under pressure from upper management. The boss could also be experiencing personal problems, such as a broken relationship or heavy debt.[9] After the boss resolves these issues, he or she might stop being a problem manager. A related way of understanding why the boss is abusive is that the boss may be the recipient of abusive management. A study conducted with over 1,000 employees from a variety of industries found that abusive behavior on the part of higher management is related to supervisors behaving abusively. A supervisor who is abused abuses his or her own work unit.[10]

Another approach to being more cautious in evaluating your manager is to judge slowly and fairly. Many decisions your manager makes may prove to be worthwhile if you give the decisions time. Top management at your company might issue an order that employees cannot surf the Internet for personal reasons on the job. You might think this rule is unfair and treats workers like adolescents. If you wait for the result of the decisions, you might find that productivity improves. Another benefit might be that many workers no longer have to work late because they save time by not surfing.

CONFRONT YOUR MANAGER ABOUT THE PROBLEM

A general-purpose way of dealing with a problem manager is to confront the problem and then look for a solution. A beginning point in confronting a manager is to gently ask for an explanation of the problem. Suppose, for example, you believed strongly that your team leader snubs you because he or she dislikes you. You might inquire gently, "What might I be doing wrong that is creating a problem between us?" A related approach is to point out to the manager that you are concerned about not meeting his or her expectations, and that you want to perform well on the job. Next, ask what you can do to better meet his or her expectations.[11]

Micromanagement
the close monitoring of most aspects of group member activities by the manager

Confrontation can also be helpful in dealing with the problem of **micromanagement**, the close monitoring of most aspects of group member activities by the manager. "Looking over your shoulder constantly" is an everyday phrase for micromanagement. If you feel that you are being supervised so closely that it is difficult to perform well, confront the situation. Say something of this nature: "I notice that you check almost all my work. Do you doubt my ability to perform my job correctly?" As a consequence, the manager might explain why he or she is micromanaging or begin to check on your work less frequently.

Despite the usefulness of confrontation about a problem with your manager, diplomacy is still important, particularly because the boss has more formal authority than you. Your confrontation should reflect a concern about performing well, not a need to strike back at your manager. Career coach Deb Koen writes that if your aim is to stay with your company, direct your energy at coming to an understanding so that the two of you can get along well enough to have a productive working relationship.[12]

OVERRESPOND TO THE MANAGER'S PET PEEVES

If your boss has a pet peeve, cater to that demand. (A pet peeve is something that annoys us, even though it is not of major significance.) A worker might know that his or her boss likes orders to get processed immediately. (The boss's pet peeve is a delay in the processing of an order.) So the worker attempts to process an order upon arrival. The best approach is to do an honest job of staying on top of any task that your boss deems to be extra important.

LEARN FROM YOUR MANAGER'S MISTAKES

Just as you can learn from watching your manager do things right, you can also learn from watching him or her do things wrong. In the first instance, we are talking about using your manager as a positive model. Modeling of this type is an important source of learning on

If you're not looking at your work relationships as a resource, you should be. Relationships need to be nurtured and developed, like any other skill or asset. Assess the quality of your relationships, and make a concerted effort to improve the ones lower on the scale.

—*Steve Arneson*

Statement from this leadership coach appeared in his column, "Evaluate Your Work Relationships," San Francisco Examiner, www.examiner.com, January 8, 2009, p. 1.

the job. Using a superior as a negative model can also be of some benefit. As an elementary example, if your manager criticized you in public and you felt humiliated, you would have learned a good lesson in effective supervision: Never criticize a subordinate publicly. By serving as a negative example, your manager has taught you a valuable lesson.

A general point about coping with a problem manager is that conscientious workers are better able to cope with abusive supervision. This conclusion stems from a study of insurance claims processors in India, suggesting that abusive supervision tended to have little impact on employees who scored high on the personality trait of conscientiousness.[13]

Building Good Coworker Relationships

◀ Learning Objective 9.3 ◀

Developing productive relationships with coworkers is a challenge for many workers. If you are unable to work cooperatively with others you are unlikely to be recommended for promotion to a supervisory position. It will also be difficult to hold onto your job. Poor relationships with coworkers can lead to frustration, stress, and decreased productivity, whereas getting along with them makes the workplace more satisfying. You need their cooperation and support, and they need yours. When workers need help in getting a job done, they will choose a coworker who is congenial over one who might have the edge in expertise.[14] Furthermore, the leading reason employees are terminated is not poor technical skills but inability or unwillingness to form satisfactory relationships with others on the job. In this section, we describe basic tactics for developing and maintaining good coworker relationships, as outlined in Figure 9-1.

If your goal is to become part of the *in-crowd* in your work group, building coworker relationships is all the more important. According to clinical psychologist and author Judith Sills, the in-crowd is the group of cool kids at your office, those with access to the boss, power, and information.[15] A relevant point here is that to become part of the select informal group, you must work extra hard at cultivating members of that group.

FIGURE 9-1

APPROACHES TO BUILDING COWORKER RELATIONSHIPS

Source: "APPROACHES TO BUILDING COWORKER RELATIONSHIPS" by Andrew J. DuBrin.

HAVE HIGH SELF-ESTEEM AND BE AT THE CENTER OF A COMMUNICATION NETWORK

A starting point in building effective coworker relationships is to have the right personality structure and to be at the center of a communications network. Brent A. Scott, a professor of management at Michigan State University, and Timothy A. Judge, a professor of industrial/organizational psychology at Notre Dame University, conducted two studies to investigate what made workers popular, or generally accepted by their peers.

The study with the most informative results involved 139 healthcare employees from twenty-two groups of a large hospital, with most of the work being conducted in teams. Popularity was measured in terms of how well the employee was liked by coworkers on a 1-to-5 scale. Self-esteem was measured by significant others of the study participants completing a core self-evaluation quiz about the participant. (You will recall having completed the core self-evaluation quiz in Chapter 2, which focuses on self-esteem.) Work communication centrality was measured by asking each coworker to "check the names of people with whom you communicate as part of the job during a typical workweek."

The results showed that having a high core self-evaluation (including self-esteem) and being at the center of communications was related to popularity. The more popular employees also received more citizenship behavior from coworkers and less incidences of counterproductive, or disruptive, behavior—both of which reflect better coworker relationships.[16]

DEVELOP ALLIES THROUGH BEING CIVIL

People who are courteous, kind, cooperative, and cheerful develop allies and friends in the workplace. Practicing basic good manners, such as being pleasant and friendly, is also part of being civil. Being civil helps make you stand out, because many people believe that crude, rude, and obnoxious behavior has become both the norm and a national problem. Uncivil behaviors characteristically involve rudeness and discourteousness. A study of three midwestern business organizations across different industries found that 86 percent of the employees surveyed said they had experienced some form of incivility within the last year.[17] Examples of incivility include the following:

- A salesperson makes sarcastic comments about another employee in front of a customer.

- A coworker initiates cell phone calls while listening to a presentation at a meeting.

- One worker continues responding to e-mail messages while another is talking to him in person.

- One worker gives a dirty look to another during a meeting.

- A person whistles or sings constantly in the office (an intensely annoying behavior for many people).

Being civil also involves not snooping, not spreading malicious gossip, and not weaseling out of group presents, such as shower or retirement gifts. In addition, it is important to be available to coworkers who want your advice as well as your help in times of crisis.

Closely related to being civil is maintaining a positive outlook. Everyone knows that you gain more allies by being optimistic and positive than by being pessimistic and negative. Nevertheless, many people ignore this simple strategy for getting along well with others. Coworkers are more likely to solicit your opinion or offer you help when you are perceived as a cheerful person.

Human Relations Self-Assessment Quiz   9-2

The Civil Behavior Checklist

To help you think through the civility of your behavior in relation to coworkers, respond "Mostly Yes" or "Mostly No" to the following statements.

Number	Statement about Behavior	Mostly Yes	Mostly No
1.	If a coworker says something that contains a factual error, I let the coworker finish the sentence before I explain the error.	_____	_____
2.	When a coworker and I are walking together and approaching a door, I will typically open the door and let him or her go through the door first.	_____	_____
3.	When a coworker makes a small mistake, I will often say something to the effect of "What's wrong with you?"	_____	_____
4.	I frequently shout out vulgarities when in the presence of coworkers.	_____	_____
5.	When I learn about something outstanding a coworker has accomplished, I quickly compliment him or her in writing or in speaking.	_____	_____
6.	I ignore most e-mails and text messages coworkers send me unless the subject is urgent.	_____	_____
7.	I routinely check messages on my smartphone when a coworker is talking to me in person.	_____	_____
8.	I sometimes poke fun at coworkers who have a foreign accent.	_____	_____
9.	When I see a coworker for the first time at the beginning of a workday, I will smile even if I am in a bad mood.	_____	_____
10.	If a coworker asked me for help with a problem close to quitting time, I would gladly spend about fifteen minutes trying to help with the problem.	_____	_____

Scoring and Interpretation:

Give yourself 1 point for the following answers: Mostly Yes to questions 1, 2, 5, 9, and 10; Mostly No to questions 3, 4, 6, 7, and 8. If you scored 8 or more points, it appears that you behave civilly toward coworkers. If you scored between 0 and 7, you may be perceived as uncivil even in today's world. Furthermore, you might be developing the reputation of a person without good enough human relations skills to be promoted.

Source: "The Civil Behavior Checklist" by Andrew J. DuBrin.

Human Relations Self-Assessment Quiz 9-2 provides an opportunity to think about the civility of your own behavior.

MAKE OTHER PEOPLE FEEL IMPORTANT

A fundamental principle of fostering good relationships with coworkers and others is to make them feel important. Making others feel important is honest because everybody in an organization has a contribution to make, including the CEO, payroll coordinator, and parking lot attendant. Although the leader has primary responsibility for satisfying this recognition need, coworkers also play a key role. One approach to making a coworker feel important would be to bring a notable accomplishment of his or hers to the attention of the group. Human Relations Self-Assessment Quiz 9-3 gives you an opportunity to think through your tendencies to make others feel important.

MAINTAIN HONEST AND OPEN RELATIONSHIPS

Self-disclosure

the process of revealing one's inner self to others

In human relations, considerable importance is attached to maintaining honest and open relationships with other people. The mechanism underlying openness is **self-disclosure**, the process of revealing your inner self to others. A person with a high degree of self-disclosure is open, whereas a person with a low degree of self-disclosure is closed. Nevertheless, you must be careful of excessive self-disclosure. Many people feel uneasy if another person is too self-revealing. The overly candid person risks being rejected. For instance, if you communicate all your negative feelings and doubts to another person, that person may become annoyed and pull away from you. It would be too open to tell an office mate, "I am ticked off that the manager has us sharing the same cubicle, but I'll put up with it until you quit or are fired."

Sharing too much with coworkers can also be annoying, as suggested by the acronym BYB (blabbing your business). Many people have become desensitized to the reality that some aspects of personal life are best left private.[18] For example, a coworker might feel uncomfortable if told about a pending relationship breakup, a family member who was just convicted of a crime, or an annoying rash.

Human Relations Self-Assessment Quiz   9-3

How Important Do I Make People Feel?

Indicate on a scale of 1 to 5 how frequently you act (or would act if the situation presented itself) in the ways indicated: very infrequently (VI), infrequently (I), sometimes (S), frequently (F), very frequently (VF). Circle the number in the column that best fits your answer.

		VI	I	S	F	VF
1.	I do my best to correctly pronounce a coworker's name.	1	2	3	4	5
2.	I avoid letting other people's egos get too big.	5	4	3	2	1
3.	I brag to others about the accomplishments of my coworkers.	1	2	3	4	5
4.	I recognize the birthdays of friends in a tangible way.	1	2	3	4	5
5.	It makes me anxious to listen to others brag about their accomplishments.	5	4	3	2	1
6.	After hearing that a friend has done something outstanding, I shake his or her hand.	1	2	3	4	5
7.	If a friend or coworker recently received a degree or certificate, I would offer my congratulations.	1	2	3	4	5
8.	If a friend or coworker finished second in a contest, I would inquire why he or she did not finish first.	5	4	3	2	1
9.	If a coworker showed me how to do something, I would compliment that person's skill.	1	2	3	4	5
10.	When a coworker starts bragging about a family member's accomplishments, I do not respond.	5	4	3	2	1

Total Score _____

Scoring and Interpretation:

Total the numbers corresponding to your answers.

40 to 50 points—Suggests that you typically make people feel important.

16 to 39 points—Suggests that you have a moderate tendency toward making others feel important.

10 to 15 points—Suggests that you need to develop skill in making others feel important. Study this chapter carefully.

Source: "How Important Do I Make People Feel?" by Andrew J. DuBrin.

Giving coworkers frank but tactful answers to their requests for your opinion is one useful way of developing open relationships. Assume that a coworker asks your opinion about a document he intends to send to his boss. As you read it, you find it somewhat incoherent and filled with spelling and grammatical errors. An honest response to this document might be "I think your idea is a good one, but I think your memo needs more work before that idea comes across clearly."

Accurately expressing your feelings also leads to constructive relationships. If you arrive at work upset over a personal problem and appearing obviously fatigued, you can expect some reaction. A peer might say, "What seems to be the problem? Is everything all right?" A dishonest reply would be "Everything is fine. What makes you think something is wrong?" In addition to making an obviously untrue statement, you would also be perceived as rejecting the person who asked the question.

If you prefer not to discuss your problem, an honest response on your part would be "Thanks for your interest. I am facing some problems today. But I think things will work out." Such an answer would not involve you in a discussion of your personal problems. Also, you would not be perceived as rejecting your coworker. The same principle applies equally well to personal relationships.

BE A TEAM PLAYER

◀ Learning Objective 9.4 ◀

An essential strategy for developing good relationships with coworkers is to be a team player. A **team player** is one who emphasizes group accomplishment and cooperation rather than individual achievement and not helping others. Team play is important because of the emphasis on having teams of workers decide how to improve productivity and reduce costs. You will also have to be a team player if you reach the pinnacle of power in your organization. Executives are expected to be good team players as well as individual decision makers. But team play is even more important on the way to becoming an executive, because impatience and making unilateral decisions are more tolerated in the executive suite. Being an effective team player is important because without such capability, collaborative effort is not possible.

Team player
one who emphasizes group accomplishment and cooperation rather than individual achievement and not helping others

Here we describe a representative group of behaviors that contribute to team play. In addition, engaging in such behavior helps you be perceived as a team player.

1. Share credit with coworkers. A direct method of promoting team play is to share credit for good deeds with other team members. Instead of focusing on yourself as the person responsible for a work achievement, point out that the achievement was a team effort. You will make a poor team player if you try to grab all the glory for ideas that work and distance yourself from ideas that do not work. An effective team member wants all other members to succeed. You will stand out by praising the people you work with rather than hogging any praise for the team.

2. Display a helpful, cooperative attitude. Working cooperatively with others is virtually synonymous with team play. Cooperation translates into such activities as helping another worker with a computer problem, covering for a teammate when he or she is absent, and making sure a coworker has the input required from you on time. A helpful cooperative attitude is the main component of organizational citizenship behavior.

3. To establish trust, keep confidential information private and give honest opinions. Trust is important for teamwork because trust is a major contributor to cooperation.[19] Confidential information a teammate shares with you should not be shared with others. Trust is exceedingly difficult to regain after a person has been betrayed. Giving honest opinions helps develop trust because the recipient of your honesty will regard you as a person of integrity. However, tact and diplomacy are still important. A dishonest opinion can often be detected through your nonverbal cues, such as discomfort in your voice tone.

Assume that a friend of yours is starting a business selling antique toys over the Internet. She asks you if you like her proposed domain name, www.OldjunkRus.com. You think the name is both ridiculous and an infringement on the Toys "R" Us name; yet you say, "Hey, terrific" with a sickened look on your face. You might lose some of your friend's trust.

4. Share information and opinions with coworkers. Teamwork is facilitated when group members share information and opinions. This is true because one of the benefits of group effort is that members can share ideas. The result is often a better solution to problems than would have been possible if people worked alone. The group thus achieves **synergy**, a product of group effort whereby the output of the group exceeds the output possible if the members worked alone.

Another important aspect of sharing information and opinions with teammates is to provide technical expertise, or knowledge of the task. Most people are selected for a work team primarily because of their specialized knowledge. To use your expertise to advantage, you must be willing to share it with teammates. Some experts perceive their specialized knowledge as a source of power. As a consequence, they are hesitant to let others share their knowledge for fear of losing power.

5. Provide emotional support to coworkers. Good team players offer each other emotional support. Such support can take the form of verbal encouragement for ideas expressed, listening to a group member's concerns, or complimenting achievement. An emotionally supportive comment to a coworker who appears to be experiencing stress might be "This doesn't look like one of your better days. What can I do to help?" Figure 9-2 illustrates providing emotional support to a coworker.

6. Follow the Golden Rule. The ancient adage "Treat others the way you would like them to treat you" provides a firm foundation for effective teamwork. Although some may dismiss the Golden Rule as a syrupy platitude, it still works. For example, you would probably want someone to help you with a perplexing problem, so you take the initiative to help others when you have the expertise needed.

7. Avoid actions that could sabotage or undermine the group in any way. Frequently criticizing group members directly or complaining about them to outsiders works against the best interest of the group. Members within the group, as well as the team leader, will most likely hear that you criticized them to an outsider, thus doing severe damage to your ability to work cooperatively with them.

Synergy
a product of group effort whereby the output of the group exceeds the output possible if the members worked alone

FIGURE 9-2

AN EXAMPLE OF PROVIDING EMOTIONAL SUPPORT TO A COWORKER

Source: "AN EXAMPLE OF PROVIDING EMOTIONAL SUPPORT TO A COWORKER" by Andrew J. DuBrin.

Coworker facing an emotionally draining problem

Emotionally supportive coworker

8. Attend company-sponsored social events. A worker's reputation as a team player is often judged both on the job and in company-sponsored social events, such as parties, picnics, and athletic events. If you attend these and participate fully, your reputation as a team player will be enhanced. Company-sponsored social events are also important because they provide an opportunity to build rapport with coworkers. Rapport, in turn, facilitates teamwork.

9. Avoid backstabbing. A special category of disliked behavior is **backstabbing**, an attempt to discredit by underhanded means, such as innuendo, accusation, and the like. A backstabber might drop hints to the boss, for example, that a coworker performs poorly under pressure or is looking for a new job. Sometimes the backstabber assertively gathers information to backstab a coworker. He or she might engage another worker in a derogatory discussion about the boss and then report the coworker's negative comments back to the boss. A person who develops a reputation as a backstabber will receive poor cooperation from coworkers. The person might also be considered untrustworthy by management, thus retarding his or her own career.

These nine points contribute specifically to effective team play. Recognize also that all other actions directed toward good coworker relationships will enhance team play.

> **Backstabbing**
> an attempt to discredit others by underhanded means such as innuendo, accusation, or the like

FOLLOW GROUP STANDARDS OF CONDUCT

The basic principle to follow in getting along with coworkers is to follow **group norms**. These refer to the unwritten set of expectations for group members—what people ought to do. Norms become a standard of what each person should do or not do within the group. Norms also provide general guidelines for reacting constructively to the behavior of coworkers. Norms are a major component of the **organizational culture**, or values and beliefs of the firm that guide people's actions. In one firm, the norms and culture may favor hard work and high quality. In another firm, the norms and culture may favor a weaker work ethic.

Group norms also influence the social aspects of behavior on the job. These aspects of behavior relate to such things as the people with whom to have lunch, getting together after work, joining a company team, and the type of clothing to wear to work. Sharing laughter, such as poking positive fun at coworkers, is another example of an important social behavior linked to a group norm.

Workers learn about norms through both observation and direct instruction from other group members. If you do not deviate too far from these norms, the group will accept much of your behavior. If you deviate too far, you will be subject to much rejection and feelings of isolation. In some instances, you might even be subjected to verbal abuse if you make the other employees look bad.

Getting along too well with coworkers has its price as well. The risk of conforming too closely to group norms is that you lose your individuality. You become viewed by your superiors as "one of the office gang" rather than a person who aspires to move up in the organization. It is important to be a good team player, but to advance in your career, you must also find a way to distinguish yourself, such as through creative thinking and outstanding performance.

> **Group norms**
> unwritten set of expectations for group members—what people ought to do; basic principle to follow in getting along with coworkers
>
> **Organizational culture**
> values and beliefs of the firm that guide people's actions

EXPRESS AN INTEREST IN THE WORK AND PERSONAL LIVES OF COWORKERS

Almost everyone is self-centered to some extent. Thus, people favor topics closely related to themselves, such as their children, friends, hobbies, work, or possessions. Sales representatives rely heavily on this fact in cultivating relationships with established customers. They routinely ask the customer about his or her hobbies, family members, and work activities. You can capitalize on this simple strategy by asking coworkers and friends questions such as these:

How is your work going? (*highly recommended*)

How did you gain the knowledge necessary for your job?

How does the company use the output from your department?

How did your son enjoy computer camp?

Closely related to expressing interest in others is to investigate what you have in common with your peers, both professionally and personally. You might identify common interests, such as a focus on the company's market share, or a personal interest, such as hiking.

A danger in asking questions about other people's work and personal life is that some questions may not be perceived as well intentioned. There is a fine line between honest curiosity and snooping. You must stay alert to this subtle distinction.

USE APPROPRIATE COMPLIMENTS

An effective way of developing good relationships with coworkers and friends is to compliment something with which they closely identify, such as their children, spouses, hobbies, or pets. Compliments are also effective because they are a form of flattery. Paying a compliment is a form of positive reinforcement, rewarding somebody for doing something right. The right response is therefore strengthened or reinforced. A compliment is a useful multipurpose reward.

Another way of complimenting people is through recognition. The suggestions made earlier about making people feel important are ways of recognizing people and therefore are compliments. Investing a small amount of time in recognizing a coworker can pay large dividends in terms of cultivating an ally. Recognition and compliments are more likely to create a favorable relationship when they are appropriate. *Appropriate* in this context means that the compliment fits the accomplishment. Praise that is too lavish may be interpreted as belittling and patronizing. Let's look at the difference between an appropriate and an exaggerated compliment over the same issue.

An executive secretary gets a printer operating that was temporarily not printing documents.

Appropriate compliment. Nice job, Stephanie. Fixing the printer took considerable skill. We can now resume making hard copies of documents.

Exaggerated compliment. Stephanie, I'm overwhelmed. You're a world-class printer specialist. Are there no limits to your talents?

Observe that the appropriate compliment is thoughtful and is proportionate to what Stephanie accomplished. The exaggerated compliment is probably wasted because it is way out of proportion to the magnitude of the accomplishment.

An important factor in making effective use of compliments is not to use them in a manipulative way to attain personal gain. An example would be to compliment a coworker and then follow up the compliment with a request to cover for you for a couple of hours while you take care of personal business.

FACE MATURELY THE CHALLENGE OF THE OFFICE ROMANCE

A final aspect of getting along with coworkers to be considered here is dealing with the challenge of an office romance. The office has become a frequent meeting place, with more romances beginning at work than over the Internet. A survey conducted by *Workforce* indicated that 56 percent of respondents said they had a workplace relationship; 17 percent of women and 11 percent of the men said the romance led to a long-term relationship. Also of note, 20 percent of women and 9 percent of men said they dated the boss.[20]

People often work closely in teams and other joint projects, thus creating the conditions for romance to take place. Another basic reason why office romances are so frequent is that familiarity builds emotional and physical attraction.

Company Policies about Office Romances

Office romances can be disruptive to morale and productivity. Coworker romances are a more widespread potential problem because more romances take place between coworkers on the same level than between superiors and subordinates. The emphasis on *potential* is important because most coworker romances do not create problems. According to a study conducted by Ryerson University professor Nina Cole, most coworkers are not disturbed by office romances if they do not have a negative impact on the workplace. The potential negative impacts include lowering productivity and demotivating coworkers.[21]

To help deal with the potential negative aspects of office romance, some companies have established policies covering such relationships, including written agreements. Either written, or implied, most companies are opposed to office romances between two people who are married to other people. Many companies have policies about breaking up the reporting relationship between a superior and a subordinate who become romantically involved with each other. In small companies, the potential problems of an office romance are more difficult to manage. Everyone is aware of the romance, and transfers to different departments for the pair involved are more difficult to arrange.[22]

The purpose of the consensual relationship contract (also referred to as a *love contract*) is to avoid sexual harassment and retaliation lawsuits when the office romance terminates, especially when the two people are not at the same organizational level.[23] The contract is likely to emphasize that both parties must mutually and voluntarily consent to the social relationship. Furthermore, the policy states that the social relationship must not affect job performance or negatively impact the company's business. The contract will often specify what type of behavior is appropriate, such as eating lunch together in the company cafeteria. Inappropriate behavior, such as spending time together in a supply closet for purposes of romantic activity, is also specified.

Companies worry about negative consequences stemming from office romances, such as sexual harassment claims, low morale of coworkers, lowered productivity from the couple involved in the romance, and an unprofessional atmosphere. Yet an important positive consequence to employers of an office romance is that while the relationship is working well, the couple may have a heightened interest in coming to work. Also, romance can trigger energy that leads to enhanced productivity.

Be Discreet with the Office Romance

Sensitivity is required to conduct an office romance that does not detract from your professionalism. It is important not to abuse company tolerance of the coworker romance. Do not invite the person you are dating to meals at company expense, take him or her on nonessential business trips, or create projects to work on jointly. Strive to keep the relationship confidential and restricted to after hours. Minimize talking to coworkers about the relationship. Engaging in personal conversations during work time or holding hands in the company cafeteria is unprofessional and taboo. Such behavior as holding hands or kissing in public view is regarded as poor office etiquette.

Should your coworker romance terminate, you face a special challenge. You must now work together cooperatively with a person toward whom you may have angry feelings. Few people have the emotional detachment necessary to work smoothly with a former romantic involvement. Extra effort, therefore, will be required by both of you.

What should you do if you and your boss seem suited for a long-term commitment? Why walk away from Mr. or Ms. Right? My suggestion is that if you do become romantically involved, one of you should request a transfer to another department. Many office romances do lead to happy marriages and other long-term relationships. At the start of the relationship, however, use considerable discretion.

Cultural factors can mediate (influence) the most effective approach for getting along with coworkers. Although there is a strong tendency for people from another country to quickly adapt to the culture of your country, you still have to be sensitive to cultural differences for rapport building. An example would be for an American not to be disappointed when a British coworker offers modest, instead of effusive, compliments for a job well done. The American might have just won a sales contest and informs her British coworker of the feat. He responds, "Certainly, in the right direction." (Your disappointment might come across as a frown or some other subtle rejection.)

▶ **Learning Objective 9.5** ▶

Building Good Relationships with Customers

Business success is built on good relationships, as emphasized repeatedly by business advisers. An employee whose thoughts and actions are geared toward helping customers has a **customer service orientation**. Good service is the primary factor that keeps customers coming back, leading to more profits. Customer loyalty is therefore a major goal for almost all business firms. Occasionally, a place of business does not want the same person back, such as a bankruptcy counseling service. Nevertheless, the financial counselor still wants loyalty in the form of referrals for other services.

Customer service orientation
approach of employee whose thoughts and actions are geared toward helping customers

An overall approach to dealing effectively with customers is to be a good organizational citizen with respect to customer relationships. You gear a lot of out-of-your-way effort to customer relationships. Specific behaviors of this type are presented in Figure 9-3. Time-tested suggestions for high-level customer service are presented next.[24] Taken together, these suggestions will help you bond with a retail or industrial customer,

FIGURE 9-3

SERVICE-ORIENTED ORGANIZATIONAL CITIZENSHIP BEHAVIORS
Source: "SERVICE-ORIENTED ORGANIZATIONAL CITIZENSHIP BEHAVIORS" by Andrew J. DuBrin.

A few specific service-oriented organizational citizenship behaviors are as follows:

- I encourage people in my network, including family members and friends, to use my company's products and services.
- I am courteous and respectful toward all customers even if I am having a bad day or I dislike something about the customer.
- I solicit ideas from other employees on how we can serve customers better and get more repeat business.
- I study our products and services regularly in order to be well informed, and helpful to customers.

forming a close and valued ongoing relationship. You will be able to implement principles of good service more readily if you are treated well by your employer. Satisfied employees create satisfied customers.

1. Establish customer satisfaction goals.   Decide jointly with your manager how much you intend to help customers. Find answers to questions such as the following: "Is your company attempting to satisfy every customer within ten minutes of his or her request?" "Are you striving to provide the finest customer service in your field?" Your goals will dictate how much and the type of effort you put into pleasing customers.

2. Engage in proactive customer service performance.   A key principle of providing good customer service is to be proactive about customer demands. The job description provides a general guide to servicing customers. Proactive customer service is characterized by a self-starting and forward-thinking approach to customer service. Proactive customer service workers take the initiative, rather than waiting to be prompted by their supervisors, coworkers, or customers.[25] An estimator for a roofing company might engage in such proactive behavior by telling a prospective customer, "We would love to replace your roof. But you will first have to hire another contractor to replace your fireplace chimney. It is about to crumble and would severely damage any roof we might install." A useful research finding is that proactive service providers typically have high general self-efficacy: They are confident of their ability to help customers.

3. Strive for the "wow" experience.   One of the most effective ways to be proactive about pleasing a customer is to provide an unusually sensitive and warm surprise, often referred to as a "wow" experience. As a daily activity at every Ritz-Carlton hotel around the world, the staff meets to share "wow" stories. The stories accomplish two important ends. First, they offer workers local recognition in front of peers. Second, the wow stories reinforce the values each employee is expected to demonstrate as a Ritz-Carlton "ambassador" (being part of the hotel brand experience).[26] An example of a wow experience might be helping a wheelchair user get into her minivan without being asked.

4. Understand your customer's needs and place them first.   The most basic principle of selling is to identify and satisfy customer needs. Many customers may not be able to express their needs clearly. Also, they may not be certain of their needs. To help identify customer needs, you may have to probe for more information. For example, an associate in a consumer electronics store may have to ask, "What uses do you have in mind for your television receiver aside from watching regular programs? Will you be using it to display digital photographs, videos, phone alerts, and the Internet?" Knowing such information will help the store associate identify which television receiver will satisfy the customer's needs.

After you have identified customer needs, focus on satisfying them rather than doing what is convenient for you or the firm. Assume, for example, that the customer says, "I would like to purchase twelve Samsung tablet computers for our field staff." The sales representative should not respond, "How about Acer tablets, we have an overload of them in our warehouse?" The sales rep might, however, offer a discount for Acer tablets if such action fits company policy.

Customer needs also have to be understood when the customer has a problem. A large-scale study of contact-center and self-service interactions revealed a simple truth about satisfying customers. What customers really want, and do not always receive, is just a satisfactory solution to their service issue.[27] For example, a customer who purchased a new SUV might want a windshield leak repaired. Sealing this leak means much more in terms of customer loyalty than giving the customer a free oil change.

5. Show care and concern.   A major customer complaint is that service providers do not care enough about their problems. For example, Delta Air Lines conducted customer feedback surveys indicating that customers write to the airline saying, "No one cared or apologized" when something went wrong, such as a canceled flight or lost baggage.[28]

During contacts with your customer, show concern for his or her welfare. Ask questions such as the following: "How have you enjoyed the office lounge chairs you bought here a while back?" "How are you feeling today?" After asking the question, project a genuine interest in the answer. A strictly business approach to showing care and concern is to follow up on requests, such as by phone or e-mail. A follow-up is effective because it completes the communication loop between two people.

6. Communicate a positive attitude. A positive attitude is conveyed by factors such as appearance, friendly gestures, a warm voice tone, and good telephone communication skills. If a customer seems apologetic about making a heavy demand, respond, "No need to apologize. My job is to please you. I'm here to serve." One reason a positive attitude is important is that hostility by the customer contact person leads to customer dissatisfaction. Lorna Doucet, a professor of organizational behavior at the University of Illinois, conducted a study in the telephone service center for a large retail bank. She found that hostility by the service provider had the strongest negative effect on customers when it was combined with low technical performance (poor answers) by the call center representative. (Perceived hostility was measured by questionnaires.) Hostility was more tolerated if the customers received the answers they needed.[29]

7. Make the buyer feel good. A fundamental way of building a customer relationship is to make the buyer feel good. Also, make the buyer feel good because he or she has bought from you. Offer compliments about the customer's healthy glow or a report that specified vendor requirements (for an industrial customer). Explain how much you value the customer's business. An effective feel-good line is "I enjoy doing business with you." Smiling is a useful technique for making the customer feel good. Also, smiling is a natural relationship builder and can help you bond with your customer. Yet guard against smiling constantly or inappropriately because your smile then becomes meaningless. False smiling if carried out regularly is stressful, so look for opportunities to smile genuinely.

Another basic way of making the buyer feel good is to thank a major customer in writing, such as a handwritten note or a social media post. Mention how much you appreciate the customer's continuing business.

8. Be helpful rather than defensive when a customer complains. Take a complaint professionally rather than personally. Listen carefully and concentrate on being helpful. The upset customer cares primarily about having the problem resolved and does not care whether you are at fault. Use a statement such as "I understand this mistake is a major inconvenience. I'll do what I can right now to solve the problem." Complaints that are taken care of quickly and satisfactorily will often create a more positive impression than mistake-free service. Another way of being helpful is to ask for enough details about what went wrong so that you can begin resolving the problem. Explain as soon as possible how you are going to fix the problem.

9. Invite the customer back. The southern U.S. expression "Y'all come back, now!" is well suited for good customer service. Specific invitations to return may help increase repeat business. The more focused and individualized the invitation, the more likely it is to have an impact on customer behavior. ("Y'all come back, now!" is sometimes used too indiscriminately to be effective.) Pointing out why you enjoyed doing business with the customer and what future problems you could help with is an effective technique. Another way of encouraging the customer to return is to explain how much you value him or her.

10. Avoid rudeness. Although rudeness to customers is obviously a poor business practice, the problem is widespread. Rudeness by customer contact personnel is a major problem from the employer's standpoint. Be aware of subtle forms of rudeness, such as

Human Relations Self-Assessment Quiz   9-4

Am I Being Rude?

Following is a list of behaviors of customer contact workers that would be interpreted as rude by many customers. Indicate whether you have engaged in such behavior in your dealings with customers or whether you are likely to do so if your job does involve customer contact.

	Yes	No
1. I talk to a coworker while serving a customer.	_____	_____
2. I conduct a phone conversation with someone else while serving a customer.	_____	_____
3. I address customers by their first names without having their permission or knowing if such informality is company policy.	_____	_____
4. I address customers as "you guys."	_____	_____
5. I chew gum or eat candy while dealing with a customer.	_____	_____
6. I laugh when customers describe an agonizing problem they are having with one of our company's products or services.	_____	_____
7. I minimize eye contact with customers.	_____	_____
8. I say the same thing to every customer, such as "Have a nice day," in a monotone.	_____	_____
9. I accuse customers of attempting to cheat the company before carefully investigating the situation.	_____	_____
10. I hurry customers when my break time approaches.	_____	_____
11. I comment on a customer's appearance in a flirtatious, sexually oriented way.	_____	_____
12. I sometimes complain about or make fun of other customers when I am serving a customer.	_____	_____

Scoring and Interpretation:

The more of these behaviors you have engaged in, the ruder you are and the more apt you are to lose potential business for your company. If you have not engaged in any of these behaviors, even when faced with a rude customer, you are an asset to your employer. You are also tolerant.

Source: "Am I Being Rude?" by Andrew J. DuBrin.

complaining about your job or working hours in front of customers. To elevate your awareness level about rudeness among customer contact personnel, take the Human Relations Self-Assessment Quiz 9-4.

11. Exert emotional effort and engage in deep acting with respect to emotions. A study of 5,000 consumers worldwide indicated that customers are passionate about and impacted by the emotional connection with employees. One way of making this connection is through **emotional effort**, the work employees invest to express the emotional response customers expect. A happy customer might expect a cheerful response, whereas an angry customer might expect patience and empathy.[30]

Deep acting with respect to emotions plays a role in customer service. In many customer service situations, it is helpful for the customer service provider to modify his or her inner emotions in order to please the customer. For example, the manager of a pet cemetery might learn to feel truly sad when dealing with customers, and the manager of a sporting goods store might learn to experience true joy when selling children's trophies to

Emotional effort
the work employees invest to express the emotion customers expect

parents. Service providers who engage in deep acting are likely to benefit financially. A study with Dutch waiters and taxi drivers found that deep acting was associated with higher tips.[31] An example is that the taxi driver might imagine how he or she would feel if a trip to a funeral home were necessary, as needed by the passenger.

12. Keep electronic communications professional and polite. Many customer interactions take place by phone, e-mail, and website interactions. These electronic interactions are as important as those conducted face-to-face. The suggestions for proper e-mail etiquette and phone interactions described in Chapter 7 apply here. Above all, avoid the same informal breeziness that you might use in electronic interaction with friends. Be sure to check with company policy if it is acceptable to address customers by their first name only, as is widely practiced today.

13. Speak to the customer in his or her preferred language, even if you can speak his or her native language. In our multicultural world, a situation arises occasionally that gets at a subtle point in being sensitive and responsive to the needs of the client. The general point is to accept the customer's desire to speak in your language, even if you know his or her native language.

Assume that you are a tax preparer who is bilingual in English and German. A client, Gunther, enters your office. He speaks to you in English with a German accent, most likely because he has chosen to work on his English and is proud of his command of his second language. Because you can speak German fluently, you insist on communicating with him in German. You might think you are pleasing Gunther by speaking German, but if Gunther continues to speak in English that means he wants to speak English while having his taxes prepared. If you continue to speak in German with Gunther, you are likely to frustrate him and lose a repeat client.

The preceding thirteen points emphasize the importance of practicing good human relations with customers and having a customer service orientation. Good customer service stems naturally from practicing good human relations.

As you deal with customers in our culturally diverse and enriched workplace, remember also to be aware of possible cross-cultural differences. Be alert to customs that could make a difference in terms of the customer feeling good about his or her experience with you. An illustrative cultural difference is that in the typical Asian family, older family members accompany younger members when a major purchase, such as a home, is being contemplated. Although the older family members may stay in the background, they might be a major financial and emotional influence on the purchase. So the eager real estate agent should not act as if the older family members are simply along for the ride. Instead, the agent should show respect by presenting vital details to all the family members, not only the couple making the purchase.

Concept Review and Reinforcement

Key Terms

Political skill, 235
Work ethic, 237
Ingratiating, 240
Bully, 241
Micromanagement, 242

Self-disclosure, 246
Team player, 247
Synergy, 248
Backstabbing, 249
Group norms, 249

Organizational culture, 249
Customer service orientation, 252
Emotional effort, 255

Summary and Review

Adequate interpersonal skills are necessary for success in business. Developing a favorable relationship with your manager is the most basic strategy of getting ahead in your career. Specific tactics for developing a good relationship with your manager include the following:

- Create a positive first impression.
- Achieve good job performance.
- Display a strong work ethic. (Use such means as demonstrating competence on even minor tasks, assuming personal responsibility for problems, and completing projects promptly.)
- Demonstrate good emotional intelligence. (Deal effectively with the emotional responses of coworkers and customers.)
- Be dependable and honest.
- Be a good organizational citizen. (Be willing to work for the good of the organization even without the promise of a specific reward.)
- Create a strong presence. (Keep yourself in the forefront.)
- Find out what your manager expects of you.
- Minimize complaints.
- Avoid bypassing your manager.
- Engage in favorable interactions with your manager. (At times, you may have to deliver bad news.)

Coping with a manager you perceive to be a problem is part of getting along with him or her. The bully is a frequent type of problem manager. Consider the following approaches:

- Reevaluate your manager to make sure you have not misperceived him or her.
- Confront your manager about your problem. Often this problem is a case of being micromanaged.

- Overrespond to the manager's pet peeves.
- Learn from your problem manager's mistakes.

Methods and tactics for building coworker relationships include the following:

- Have high self-esteem and be at the center of a communication network.
- Develop allies through being civil.
- Make other people feel important.
- Maintain honest and open relationships (including self-disclosure).
- Be a team player. (Observe the nine approaches reported here.)
- Follow group standards of conduct.
- Express an interest in the work and personal life of coworkers.
- Use appropriate (nonexaggerated) compliments.
- Face maturely the challenge of the office romance.

Team player approaches include sharing credit, maintaining a cooperative attitude, establishing trust, sharing information and opinions, providing emotional support, practicing the Golden Rule, avoiding sabotaging or undermining actions, sharing the glory, and avoiding backstabbing.

Job success also requires building good relationships with customers. Techniques for providing high-level customer service include:

- Establishing customer satisfaction goals
- Engaging in positive customer service performance
- Striving for the "wow" experience
- Understanding your customer's needs and placing them first

- Showing care and concern
- Communicating a positive attitude
- Making the buyer feel good
- Being helpful rather than defensive when a customer complains
- Inviting the customer back
- Avoiding rudeness

- Exerting emotional effort and engaging in deep acting with respect to customers' emotions
- Keeping electronic communications professional and polite
- Speaking to the customer in his or her preferred language, even if you can speak his or her native language.

Questions for Discussion and Review

9.1 If team leaders don't have as much power as a regular manager, why is it still important to build a good relationship with your team leader?

9.2 How can a worker implement the tactic "engage in favorable interactions with your manager" without appearing to be "kissing up" to the boss?

9.3 Give an example of a Facebook post or tweet a person could write to make a coworker feel important.

9.4 Suppose a coworker apparently dislikes you. Explain which two techniques described in this chapter you think would be the most effective in building a positive relationship with that person.

9.5 Provide an example of a *group standard of conduct* in any place you have worked. What led you to conclude that the particular behavior was a group standard of conduct?

9.6 What would be an example of an *appropriate compliment* you might deliver to a coworker who made a suggestion that saved the company $1 million annually in shipping costs?

9.7 If rudeness is so widespread today, why bother being polite and considerate on the job?

9.8 Considering that consumers post a lot of crazy comments on social networking sites, why should company management be concerned about these negative posts?

9.9 Visualize yourself as the manager of a hotel, and two of the guests checking in are celebrating their sixtieth wedding anniversary. How might you and your staff deliver the wow experience to these guests?

9.10 Ask a person who has achieved job success what he or she thinks are two important ways of getting along with coworkers and customers. Compare notes with classmates.

Web Corner

Getting along with your boss and coworkers

http://careerplanning.about.com (Enter into search box "Getting along with your boss and coworkers.")

Improving relationships with the boss

www.forbes.com (Enter into search box "14 tips for improving your relationship with your boss")

Creating the wow experience for customers

www.deliveringhappiness.com (Enter "wow experience.")

INTERNET SKILL BUILDER

Workplace Relationships

Visit http://careers.homedepot.com, and proceed to "Our Culture." Identify which skills mentioned relate to workplace relationships, including communication skills and self-understanding. Reflect back on any time you have visited a Home Depot or a competitor's store. How realistic is Home Depot about the interpersonal and personal skills required for a sales associate? If you happen to know a Home Depot employee, obtain his or her input in formulating your answer to the preceding question.

Developing Your Human Relations Skills

Applying Human Relations Exercise 9-1

Giving Good Customer Service

Role-players in this exercise will demonstrate two related techniques for giving good customer service: Showing care and concern and making the buyer feel good. The role-players will carry out the scenarios in front of the class. For both role-plays, the provider of customer service should think through before starting the role-play what specifically he or she is attempting to accomplish. For example, the role-player might ask himself or herself, "How am I going to show care and concern?" or "What am I going to do to make the buyer feel good?"

Scenario 1: Providing the Wow Experience One student plays the role of a sales associate at a mattress store meeting with a couple who are seriously considering purchasing one of the most expensive mattresses in the store: a model that has electronic controls governing the temperature and firmness of the mattress on both sides. The sales associate eagerly wants to close the sale and decides to deliver a wow experience to ensure that the deal goes through. Two other students play the couple, who have never even heard of a wow experience, as they contemplate this major purchase.

Scenario 2: Make the buyer feel good A couple, played by two role-players, enter a new-car showroom to examine a model they have seen advertised on television. Although they are not in urgent need of a new car, they are strongly interested.

Customer Service Evaluation Factors	1 VP	2 P	3 A	4 G	5 VG
1. Maintained eye contact					
2. Was warm and supportive					
3. Smiled appropriately					
4. Displayed positive attitude					
5. Showed genuine concern					
6. Made buyer feel good					
Customer Evaluation Dimensions	**1 VP**	**2 P**	**3 A**	**4 G**	**5 VG**
1. Behaved realistically					
2. Showed respect for service provider					
3. Treated provider like a professional					
4. Showed appreciation for service provider's effort					

The sales representative is behind quota for the month and would like to close a sale today. The rep decides to use the tactic "make the buyer feel good" to help form a bond.

The rest of the class will provide some constructive feedback, and perhaps compliments, to the role-players. Use the evaluation dimensions in the table to help you evaluate the effectiveness of the customer service providers and customers. Use a scale of 1 to 5 in making your ratings: 1 = very poor, 2 = poor, 3 = average, 4 = good, and 5 = very good.

Other comments about the role-players:

Applying Human Relations Exercise 9-2

The Thirty-Second Elevator Speech

A longstanding tip in career development and impressing higher-ups is to make a thirty-second impromptu presentation when you have a chance encounter with a key person in your organization. If you work in an office tower, the chance encounter is likely to take place on an elevator—and it is generally frowned on to have long conversations in an elevator. So the term *elevator speech* developed, describing a brief opportunity to impress a key person. Imagine that you have a chance encounter with a high-ranking executive in your area on the elevator or escalator, in the parking lot, during a company picnic, or at some other location. You then give that person a thirty-second pitch geared to make a positive impression. Because you must boil your pitch down to thirty seconds, you will need to prepare for a long time. (Give credit to President Abraham Lincoln for that insight.)

About six different pairs (impresser and person to be impressed) will carry out this role-play in front of the class. The evaluators will put themselves in the role of the target key person of the thirty-second evaluation. Consider using the following scale and answering the two questions:

_____ Wow, I was impressed. (5 points)

_____ I was kind of impressed with the person I ran into. (4 points)

_____ He or she left me with at least an average impression. (3 points)

_____ I found the person to be somewhat annoying. (2 points)

_____ That person I met left me with a terrible impression. (1 point)

1. What I liked about person's thirty-second pitch:
2. What I saw as possible areas for improvement:

Find a mechanism to feed back some of your observations to the role-players. Volunteer to present the findings in class, give the person your comments on notepaper, or send him or her an e-mail.

Human Relations Class Activity

How We Got in Good with the Boss

The purpose of this class activity is to further understand what workers have actually done to develop a positive relationship with a present or former boss. This activity would require about forty-five minutes of class time for a class of approximately thirty students. The first step is for each person to think through, and write down, an effective tactic he or she has used in developing a good relationship with a manager, past or present. Any type of work experience counts. If you have no formal work experience, perhaps the experience can be related to sports or a club. Include in your analysis how the boss reacted to the tactic.

After about four minutes of class time have been invested in thinking through the tactic-and-result scenarios, students will come up in front of the class one by one to present their findings. Presentations should be about sixty seconds. After all students have presented, have a brief class discussion centering on these points:

1. Which two tactics appeared to be the most frequently mentioned?
2. Which two tactics appeared to be the most creative?
3. Which one or two tactics gave you a useful idea for the future?
4. How closely do some of the tactics conform to the suggestions for developing a relationship with the manager or team leader presented in the text?

Human Relations Case Study 9–1

Leah Cultivates Her Coworkers

Leah was happy to find a position as a scanning technician at a business-process-outsourcing company, Expert Resource, Inc. A major part of the Expert's business was converting paperwork related to human resource management into digital form. Clients would mail their forms, such as medical claims, to Expert. Scanning technicians would then insert the claim forms into large scanning machines to make the conversion to digital. Clients would then have digital instead of paper documents for health claims and other human resource records.

The scanning technicians had to interact with other employees in several ways. Many of the claims received contained illegible identifying information, so they had to be sent to a security department that attempted to obtain the proper identification for the forms. The scanning technicians were expected to help level the workload among the technicians. For example, if one of the technicians was

overwhelmed, and another was caught up, the latter was supposed to help out the former. Also, the company frequently held small celebrations in the office. A typical celebration would be to hold a brunch in honor of a new employee joining the company.

Leah believed that if she performed well in her position as scanning technician, she would be eligible for promotion to the information technology department. Eventually being promoted to a supervisor position was also within the realm of possibility. Leah also recognized that having good skills and speed in scanning documents were not sufficient to be promoted to a supervisory position. Her size-up of the situation was that being a good team player would be required to be considered for promotion. Leah then set out to develop the reputation of being a good team player.

The next Monday morning, Leah arrived at the office with a box of donuts that she placed in the break room, with a note attached that said, "Enjoy your coffee or tea this morning with a treat from your coworker Leah." Several of the other scanning technicians thanked Leah; however, one technician said to her, "Why did you bring us donuts? You're not our supervisor."

A week later, Leah implemented another tactic designed to boost her reputation as a team player. She sent an e-mail to the other technicians informing them that they were free to send her an e-mail or text message anytime they were overloaded with documents to scan. Leah said that she would help the overloaded coworker so long as she was caught up on her own work.

A week later Leah reflected, "I think I am developing a reputation as a good team player, but I can't give up yet. I think I know a way to really cement being regarded as a strong team player." Leah then wrote an e-mail to the other scanning technicians, as well as her supervisor. The e-mail read in part:

We all know that it takes a village to raise a child. But did you also know that it takes a group of friendly and cooperative coworkers to get a scanning technician up to speed? I want to thank you all for your cooperation and friendliness. You have been very helpful to me.

Questions

9.11 How effective do you think Leah's initiatives are in helping her develop a reputation as a strong team player?

9.12 If you were Leah's supervisor, how would you react to the e-mails she sent to the group?

9.13 What advice might you offer Leah to help her advance her reputation as a team player?

Human Relations Role-Playing Exercise

Cecilia Objects to Leah's Teamwork Tactics

One student plays the role of Leah who receives a text message at 11 p.m. from Cecilia, another scanning technician in the department. The message reads, "Cut it out. You are trying too hard to make us happy." Concerned about the message, Leah returns the message and says she will talk to Cecilia in the office. During break time, she visits Cecilia at her cubicle and attempts to explain how she is trying to be a good team player. Another student plays the role of Cecilia, who is willing to listen to Leah but does not like her attempts at building teamwork.

Human Relations Class Study 9–2

How Far Should Tom Go to Keep His Client Happy?

Tom is a sales consultant in the wealth management group at a well-established financial services firm. He manages the financial portfolios of many high-income professionals and also has several institutions as clients. The institutions include a few colleges, hospitals, and nonprofit agencies. These institutions purchase some of their investments through Tom's firm.

Tom is an average performer as a sales consultant, which translates into an income in the top 2 percent of wage earners. He is satisfied with the nature of his work as well as his income. At the moment, one of Tom's biggest challenges is to decide how much time to invest in managing one client, a large hospital. Deborah, the hospital's pension fund manager, never seems to be quite satisfied. She sends Tom an e-mail almost every day and telephones him almost every week with a question about how well or how poorly the investments placed through his firm are doing. (Tom's firm, like other financial services firms, places very limited information in e-mail messages.)

Tom explained to his manager the challenges he was facing with Deborah in these words: "We both agree that keeping this hospital account is important. But how high-maintenance can a client get before we set a limit to how much service we can provide? When the few mutual funds we have invested in for the hospital head down in value at the same time, she wants a fifteen-minute phone call to reassure her that the funds will rebound."

"When Deborah decides that the hospital should invest more money in one of our funds, she almost insists that I take her to lunch. The problem is that these lunches wind up taking about two-and-one-half hours out of my day, travel and time in the restaurant included. Another problem is that Deborah insists on so much documentation about her investments through us. She could really find some of this documentation on financial websites on her own."

"What have you told Deborah so far about the amount of time she is consuming in managing her account?" asked Tom's manager.

Tom said, "I have only given her the smallest hint so far. I said that our firm valued her account, and we will do what

we can to satisfy her and the hospital, but that sometimes I need a little more time to get back to her."

Questions

9.14 To what extent is Tom neglecting the idea that client's needs come first and that his goal is to please the client?

9.15 Should Tom be direct with Deborah and tell her that she is consuming too much time for the amount of business the hospital is giving his firm?

9.16 What advice might you offer Tom to maintain a good relationship with Deborah without the relationship being too disruptive to his own work schedule?

Human Relations Role-Playing Exercise

Tom Confronts High-Maintenance Deborah over the Phone

One student plays the role of Tom, who feels that Deborah is consuming too much of his time but still wants to retain her as a client. He receives another call from Deborah, who wants to discuss the mix of investments in her portfolio. Tom thinks the time might be right to set limits on Deborah's demands. Another student plays the role of Deborah, who thinks that she is worth of the highest level of client service.

For the scenarios in the role-plays accompanying both cases, observers rate the role-players on two dimensions, using a scale of 1 to 5 from very poor to very good. One dimension is "effective use of human relations techniques." The second dimension is "acting ability." A few observers might voluntarily provide feedback to the role-players in terms of sharing their ratings and observations. The course instructor might also provide feedback.

REFERENCES

1. Timothy P. Munyon, James K. Summers, Katin A. Thomson, and Gerald R. Ferris, "Political Skill and Work Outcomes: A Theoretical Extension, Meta-Analytic Investigation, and Agenda for the Future," *Personnel Psychology*, No. 1, 2015, p. 145.

2. Quoted in Heather Huhman, "Ten Ways to Impress Your Boss during the First Week," *Entry Level Careers Examiner*, www.examiner.com, December 4, 2008, p. 1.

3. Judith Sills, "How to Improve Your Credit Rating," *Psychology Today*, March–April 2008, p. 67.

4. Quoted in Anita Bruzzese, "Get the Boss to Take Notice of You," Gannett News Service, April 21, 1997.

5. Kevin P. Coyne and Edward J. Coyne, Sr., "Surviving Your New CEO," *Harvard Business Review*, May 2007, p. 66.

6. Cecily D. Cooper, "Just Joking Around? Employee Humor Expression as Ingratiatory Behavior," *Academy of Management Review*, October 2005, pp. 765–776.

7. Robert I. Sutton, cited in Ellen Simon, "Purge Jerks at Work, Says Author," Associated Press, March 18, 2007; Spencer Morgan, "Office Bullying," *Bloomberg Businessweek*, November 1–November 7, 2010, p. 76.

8. J. Kenneth Matejka and Richard Dunsing, "Managing the Baffling Boss," *Personnel*, February 1989, p. 50.

9. Debra Auerbach, "Conquer Your Bad Boss Conflicts," *CareerBuilder* (published in *Democrat and Chronicle*), April 7, 2013. p. 2F.

10. Mary Bardes Mawritz et al., "A Trickle-Down Model of Abusive Supervision," *Personnel Psychology*, Number 2, 2012, pp. 325–357.

11. Debra Auerbach, "Repairing Relationships with Your Boss," *CareerBuilder* (published in *Democrat and Chronicle*), August 11, 2013, p. 2E.

12. Deb Koen, "Ways to Deal with Difficult Bosses," *Democrat and Chronicle*, October 11, 2009, p. 2E.

13. Amit K. Nandkeolyar et al., "Surviving an Abusive Supervisor: The Joint Role of Conscientiousness and Coping Strategies," *Journal of Applied Psychology*, January 2014, pp. 138–150.

14. Janet Banks and Diane Coutu, "How to Protect Your Job in a Recession," *Harvard Business Review*, September 2008, p. 113.

15. Judith Sills, "Hanging with the In-Crowd," *Psychology Today*, November–December 2007, pp. 65–66.

16. Brent A. Scott and Timothy A. Judge, "The Popularity Contest at Work: Who Wins, Why, and What Do They Receive?" *Journal of Applied Psychology*, January 2009, pp. 20–33.

17. Cited in Donna M. Owens, "Incivility Rising: Researchers Say Workers Might Not Have the Time to Be Civil," *Human Resource Management*, February 2012, p. 33; Christine M. Pearson and Christine L. Porath, "On the Nature, Consequences and Remedies of Workplace Incivility: No Time for 'Nice'? Think Again," *Academy of Management Executive*, February 2005, pp. 7–18.

18. Elizabeth Bernstein, "Thank You for Not Sharing," *The Wall Street Journal*, May 7, 2013, pp. D1, D4; Bernstein, "You Did What? Spare the Office the Details," *The Wall Street Journal*, April 6, 2010, p. D1.

19. Andrew C. Wicks, Shawn L. Berman, and Thomas M. Jones, "The Structure of Optimal Trust: Moral and Strategic Implications," *Academy of Management Review*, January 1999, p. 99.

20. "Crazy Little Thing Called Love," *Workforce*, February 2015, p. 13.

21. Nina Cole, "A Workplace Romance: A Justice Analysis, *Journal of Business and Psychology*, December 2009, pp. 363–372.

22. Barbara Haislip, "A Little Romance, a Lot of Problems?" *The Wall Street Journal*, February 3, 2014, p. R4.

23. Laura Tiffany, "How Useful Are Love Contracts?" *Entrepreneur*, October 2008, p. 84.

24. Some of the ideas in the list are from Linda Thornburg, "Companies Benefit from Emphasis on Superior Customer Service," *HR Magazine*, October 1993, pp. 3–22, 46–49; Jena McGregor, "When Service Means Survival," *Businessweek*, March 2, 2009, pp. 026–033.

25. Steffen Raub and Hui Liao, "Doing the Right Thing without Being Told: Joint Effects of Initiative Climate and General Self-Efficacy on Employee Proactive Customer Service Performance," *Journal of Applied Psychology*, May 2012, pp. 651–667.

26. Carmine Gallo, "Wow Your Customers the Ritz-Carlton Way," *Executive Leadership*, April 2011, p. 4.

27. Matthew Dixon, Karen Freeman, and Nicholas Toman, "Stop Trying to Delight Your Customers," *Harvard Business Review*, July–August 2010, pp. 116–122.

28. Scott McCartney, "Delta Sends Its 11,000 Agents to Charm School," *The Wall Street Journal*, February 3, 2011, p. D3.

29. Lorna Doucet, "Service Provider Hostility and Service Quality," *Academy of Management Journal*, October 2004, pp. 761–771.

30. Sharon Daniels, "Developing Customer-Centric Employees to Enrich Your Customers' Experience," *Workforce*, March 2013, p. S3.

31. Ute R. Hüsheger et al., "When Regulating Emotions at Work Pays Off: A Diary and an Intervention Study on Emotion Regulation and Customer Tips in Service Jobs," *Journal of Applied Psychology*, March 2015, pp. 263–277.

Fotolia

Outline

onnectria, based in St. Louis, Missouri, is a world leader in cloud hosting. The company provides cloud computing to more than 1,000 customers in thirty countries. In addition to its reputation as a technologically advanced company, Connectria is known for its No Jerks Allowed® company philosophy. A "jerk" refers in general to an obnoxious, difficult person you would recognize immediately even if you cannot define the term *jerk*. Rich Waidmann, president and CEO of Connectria, says that the company has established a unique culture where every employee goes the extra mile to take care of customers. Being a jerk is also not allowed within the company. The no-jerks-allowed policy is designed to foster a respectful work relationships among employees, customers, partners, and vendors.

Avoiding jerky behavior has many implications for customers. Hosting that is not jerk-free has rigid contracts, policies, and procedures and is also bureaucratic, slow, and challenging to work with. In contrast, being jerk-free allows for flexible contracts, policies, and procedures to meet a customer's business need and is also fast and easy to deal with.

Waidmann has launched the No Jerks Allowed movement to encourage other employers to do the same. He says that the trigger for starting the movement was some pretty horrible, jerky work experiences when he started his tech career, including running into a lot of big egos: "It felt like any time you asked a question it couldn't be stupider." Waidmann also says that being kind and considerate can go a long way toward making the workplace, and the world in general, a better place.[1]

Learning Objectives ▶

After studying the information and doing the exercises in this chapter, you should be able to:

10.1 Identify reasons why conflict between people takes place so often.

10.2 Pinpoint several helpful and harmful consequences of conflict.

10.3 Choose an effective method of resolving conflict.

10.4 Improve your negotiating skill.

10.5 Pinpoint tactics for dealing effectively with difficult people.

10.6 Develop anger management skills.

The company just described, intent on creating a civil workplace for employees and customers, points to the reality that conflict arises frequently, often based on the actions of difficult people. Being able to manage conflict successfully enables the workers involved to function more peacefully, and the company to get more work done. **Conflict** is a condition that exists when two sets of demands, goals, or motives are incompatible. For example, if a person wants a career in retailing yet also wants to work a predictable eight-hour day with weekends off, that person faces a conflict. He or she cannot achieve both goals. A conflict can also be considered a dispute, feud, or controversy.

Our approach to studying conflict includes explaining why so much conflict exists, constructive approaches to resolving conflict, dealing with difficult people, and the management of anger.

Conflict
condition that exists when two sets of demands, goals, or motives are incompatible

▶ **Learning Objective 10.1** ▶

Why So Much Conflict Exists

Many reasons exist for the widespread presence of conflict in all aspects of life. All these reasons are related to the basic nature of conflict: the fact that not every person can have what he or she wants at the same time. As with other topics in this text, understanding conflict helps you develop a better understanding of why people act as they do. Here we describe nine key sources of conflict.

COMPETITION FOR LIMITED RESOURCES

A fundamental reason you might experience conflict with another person is that not everybody can get all the money, material, supplies, or human help they want. Conflict also ensues when employees are asked to compete for prizes, such as bonuses based on individual effort or company-paid vacation trips. Because the number of awards is so limited, the competition becomes intense enough to be regarded as conflict. Conflict stemming from limited resources has become prevalent as so many companies attempt to reduce expenses. Many units of the organization have to compete for the limited money available to hire new people or purchase new technology.

DIFFERENCES OF OPINION ON WORK-RELATED ISSUES AND RIGHTS

A natural source of conflict in the workplace centers on differences of opinion about work-related issues, including whose idea will work the best. One member of the design team for a luxury sports car might insist the paneling should be composed mostly of wood. Another might say that the car could get by with plastic paneling, saving the company considerable money. The two members might therefore be in conflict.

Conflict over rights will often take the form of one group or individual feeling that it has the right to engage in certain behavior despite a rule or custom denying that right. Smoking is forbidden in almost all workplaces, with some employers forbidding workers to smoke anywhere on the property—especially at a medical facility. The smokers who have to walk or drive about a half mile become quite upset with the nonsmokers who have blocked what they consider their right to smoke immediately outside of a building. A frequent conflict over custom is when some office workers believe they have the right to wear low-cut jeans and shirts that display their midriff to work, but the company officials say that such clothing is unacceptable.

INCIVILITY

In Chapter 9, incivility was described as a frequent problem in getting along with coworkers. Incivility toward work associates can also be regarded as a major contributor to workplace conflict. In a survey of nearly 3,000 participants, 96 percent of workers said they had experienced uncivil behavior.[2] According to the research of Christine Porath of Georgetown University, after being a victim of workplace rudeness and hostility, two-thirds of employees said their performance declined. Four-fifths of employees indicated that they lost time worrying about the unpleasant incident, while two-thirds wasted time avoiding the offender. About one-eighth quit because of being treated uncivilly by a coworker.[3]

The relationship between incivility and conflict is twofold. First, being treated in an uncivil manner, such as being sworn at by a boss or coworker, usually leads to a dispute with that person. Second, conflict emerges because one cannot satisfy the goal of having a relatively calm workplace while at the same time being treated uncivilly. A frequently reported form of incivility leading to conflict is when one employee steals a coworker's lunch from the office refrigerator for himself or herself. The person whose lunch was stolen often goes into a rage.

Snubbing, or ignoring, others is another type of uncivil behavior leading to conflict. A **micro-inequity** is a small, semiconscious message we send with a powerful impact on

Micro-inequity

small, semiconscious message sent with a powerful impact on the receiver the receiver. A micro-inequity might also be considered a subtle slight. Conflict occurs because a person's feelings are hurt, and he or she feels trivialized. Two examples of workplace micro-inequities follow:

- You check your messages on a phone or computer screen while a coworker is talking to you. (You are devaluing the other person's time and trivializing his or her importance.)

- A manager dismisses the first idea offered in a meeting by responding, "Okay, so who would like to get the ball rolling?" (The person who offered the idea feels as if his or her suggestion is not even worth consideration and therefore has hurt feelings.)[4]

A recent laboratory study of incivility in the form of insulting the ideas of others, provides insight into the consequences of instigating incivility. The research suggested that observers of incivility have an immediate negative reaction toward the uncivil person and might attempt to punish the instigator, for example, by not being willing to work with him or her.[5]

PERSONALITY CLASHES AND DRAMA

Many disagreements on the job stem from the fact that some people simply dislike each other. A **personality clash** is thus an antagonistic relationship between two people based on differences in personal attributes, preferences, interests, values, and styles. People involved in a personality clash often have difficulty specifying why they dislike each other. The end result, however, is that they cannot maintain an amiable work relationship. A strange fact about personality clashes is that people who get along well may begin to clash after working together for a number of years. Many business partnerships fold because the two partners eventually clash.

You are probably familiar with "drama" in personal life, such as the person who demands a "drama-free" relationship or says, "I'm drama-free." Drama takes the form of an obstacle to what you want to attain and often functions like a personality clash because the dramatic person does not get along with you.[6] Instead, he or she might blame you for a problem or be so preoccupied with personal problems that working smoothly with you is extremely difficult. A coworker who introduces drama might say, "I know that we are supposed to investigate these missing funds together, but I am facing a personal emergency today."

> **Personality clash**
> antagonistic relationship between two people based on differences in personal attributes, preferences, interests, values, and styles

AGGRESSIVE PERSONALITIES AND WORKPLACE BULLIES

Coworkers naturally disagree about topics, issues, and ideas. Yet some people convert disagreement into an attack that puts down other people and damages their self-esteem. As a result, conflict surfaces. **Aggressive personalities** are people who verbally and sometimes physically attack others frequently. Verbal aggression takes the form of insults, teasing, ridicule, and profanity. The aggression may also be expressed as attacks on the victim's character, competence, background, and physical appearance. When people are verbally abused, they are put on the defensive, making them feel uncomfortable.[7] Aggressiveness can also take the extreme form of the shooting or knifing of a former boss or colleague by a mentally unstable worker recently dismissed from the company.

Aggressive personalities are also referred to as *bullies*. **Workplace bullying** refers to hurtful treatment of others in the workplace that is malicious and typically repeated. Bullying includes tirades by managers as well as more subtle approaches to undermining employees, such as overloading them with responsibilities to facilitate their failing. Among their typical behaviors are interrupting others, ranting in a loud voice, and making threats. A typical attitude of a bullying boss is "My way or the highway," sending the message that the employee's suggestions are unwelcome.

The best way to stand up to a bully, whether he or she is a boss or a coworker, is to document every incident and every detail, including who witnessed the bullying act. The documentation should then be shown to an objective authority, such as the human

> **Aggressive personalities**
> people who verbally and sometimes physically attack others frequently

> **Workplace bullying**
> hurtful treatment of others in the workplace that is malicious and is typically repeated

resources manager. It is helpful for the documentation to include data about damaging effects, such as lost productivity and time lost from work.[8]

Although bullying is troublesome and creates discomfort for many people, it is only considered illegal when it involves job discrimination, such as verbally harassing older but not younger workers. So it may not be nice, but it is legal to be a jerk at work.[9]

PASSIVE-AGGRESSIVE PERSONALITIES

Passive-aggressive personality

a person who appears to enthusiastically and readily respond to another person's request or demand while acting in ways that negatively and passively resist the request

Another form of aggressive behavior that contributes to job conflict is when someone creates problems by not doing something that needs to get accomplished. (Passive aggression is a deliberate and disguised way of expressing hidden anger.) A **passive-aggressive personality** is a person who appears to enthusiastically and readily respond to another person's request or demand while acting in ways that negatively and passively resist the request.[10] The passive-aggressive coworker might say that he will bring some key information to a meeting, yet when the meeting arrives he contends that he became too busy to gather the information. Another form of passive-aggressive behavior is for a person to say that he or she wanted to phone you about an urgent problem but that his or her phone battery was dead (or "ran out of minutes"). Human Relations Assessment Quiz 10-1 presents a checklist of common symptoms and behaviors of a passive-aggressive personality.

Human Relations Self-Assessment Quiz | 10-1

Am I Dealing with a Passive-Aggressive Personality?

At times, you may be wondering why you are in so much conflict with a person who on the surface does not appear to be an angry, conflict-prone person. Your problem could be that you are dealing with a passive-aggressive personality. Carefully observe that person's behavior to look for certain telltale indictors of passive aggression. Check the signs and symptoms that he or she has displayed at least several times.

1. Keeps forgetting to take care of problems ☐
2. Procrastinates on so many work-related matters ☐
3. Won't make a decision ☐
4. Says nothing when asked why a task was not completed ☐
5. Performs many tasks inefficiently ☐
6. Sulks rather than expressing anger directly ☐
7. Tends to blame other people and equipment for not getting an assignment accomplished ☐
8. Often has an excuse for not doing something important ☐
9. Makes frequent derogatory comments about coworkers and superiors when those people are not present ☐
10. Often expresses enthusiasm for an activity but then fails to follow through ☐

Scoring and Interpretation:

If the person you are evaluating receives a score of 8, 9, or 10, he or she will be a difficult person to work with, especially from the standpoint of dependability. He or she will probably be demoted or fired. In the meantime, attempt to implement some of the suggestions for dealing with difficult people presented later in this chapter.

Source: "Am I Dealing with a Passive-Aggressive Personality?" by Andrew J. DuBrin.

A key component of passive aggression that creates problems is that the person who is angry often has a pleasant exterior. His or her acts of forgetfulness and lack of follow-through on assignments are driven by anger.

CULTURALLY DIVERSE TEAMS AND FACTIONAL GROUPS

Conflict often surfaces as people work in teams whose members vary in many ways. Ethnicity, religion, and gender are three of the major factors that lead to clashes in viewpoints. Differing educational backgrounds and work specialties can also lead to conflict. Workers often shut out information that doesn't fit comfortably with their own beliefs, particularly if they do not like the person providing the information. When these conflicts are properly resolved, diversity lends strength to the organization because the various viewpoints make an important contribution to solving a problem. Groups that are reminded of the importance of effective communication and taught methods of conflict resolution usually can overcome the conflict stemming from mixed groups.[11]

Another form of diversity occurs when groups contain different factions, such as those representing two different companies that merged. Often the factional group consists of two subgroups, each with several representatives, such as a cost-cutting task force consisting of three representatives each from marketing, operations, and finance. The potential for conflict within factional groups increases when the subgroups differ substantially in demographic characteristics such as age, gender, and educational levels.[12]

COMPETING WORK AND FAMILY DEMANDS

Balancing the demands of work and family life is a major challenge facing workers at all levels. Yet achieving this balance and resolving these conflicts is essential for being successful in career and personal life. The challenge of achieving balance is particularly intense for employees who are part of a two-wage-earner family. A heavy workload also intensifies the conflict because the person feels compelled to work long hours at the office, in addition to taking work home. Frequent business travel is another major contributor to work–family conflict.

Work–family conflict occurs when the individual has to perform multiple roles: worker, spouse or partner, and often parent. From the standpoint of the individual, this type of conflict can be regarded as work interfering with family life. From the standpoint of the employer, the same conflict might be regarded as family life interfering with work. Being a single parent can lead to even stronger work–family conflict when the other parent does not help manage unanticipated problems. An example would be managing the situation of a sick child not being able to attend school and refused from day care also because of the illness. The opportunity to minimize work–family conflict is important to many workers. An American Psychological Association survey found that 67 percent of workers said they choose to stay with their employer because their job fits well other components of their life.[13]

Work–family conflict
conflict that occurs when an individual has to perform multiple roles: worker, spouse or partner, and often parent

The patterns of work–family conflict undergo subtle changes over time. The younger generation today expects fathers to contribute more to child care and women to contribute more to family income.

Incompatible Demands

Attempting to meet work and family demands is a frequent source of conflict because the demands are often incompatible. Imagine having to attend your child's championship soccer game and then being ordered at the last minute to attend a late-afternoon meeting. As revealed in a study with working adults, another complication of work–family conflict is that when family life interferes with work, the person will often feel guilty. Guilt will be experienced also by some people who feel that work interferes with family life.[14] Feelings of guilt arise because the person might feel that when one is being paid for doing a job, the job should have higher priority than taking care of personal issues. Or the person might feel guilty because he or she believes that family remains a higher priority than work.

Work can conflict with family demands, but family demands can also interfere with work, such as family responsibilities making business travel difficult. Many people who want to advance their career find it difficult because they have to limit the hours they invest in work. A recent synthesis of thirty-three studies found that emotional strain can result from both work interfering with family and family interfering with work. The strain often includes a lowered feeling of well-being.[15]

Multitasking to Deal with the Conflict

Some people attempt to resolve their work–family conflict by doing some work at family and personal events. Watch any Little League baseball game, high school tennis match, or youth soccer match, and you will see parents at the sidelines busily engaged with their smartphones conducting work. Equally extreme is a recent trend for young people to do office work while on a date.

Flexible Work Arrangements to Reduce the Conflict

The general solution to work–family conflict is to have workplaces where employees have a choice of when, where, and how they do their work.[16] Employer initiatives to help reduce work–family conflict include flexible working hours, the opportunity to work at home, child care centers, and parental-leave programs. Flexible working hours enable parents to meet such challenges as taking a child for a medical appointment during the day and then making up the work time during the evening.

A prime example of implementing flexible work arrangements (or flex work) to help reduce work–family conflict is the medical device manufacturer Medtronic Inc. A major component of flex work at Medtronic is the opportunity to work at home three or four days per week. A senior compliance officer in the Singapore office notes that the flexible work schedule allows her to work from home occasionally, which helps her to attain a better work–family balance. (She also says that working from home provides her an opportunity to exert creative thinking without distraction from the office.)[17]

Flexible work arrangements now pay more attention to the needs of fathers to balance work and family demands. For example, furniture manufacturer Herman Miller Inc. offers fathers two weeks of paid paternity leave after the birth or adoption of a child.[18] Many fathers in other organizations do not take paternity leave because parental leave is not legally required in the United States.

The Role of Work Group Support

The intensity of work–family conflict can sometimes be softened by a supportive work group. Other members of the work group might share experiences, offer suggestions, and perhaps even lend a hand, such as taking care of a few errands for the coworker attempting to juggle work and family demands. A survey of over 2,400 faculty members was conducted at a midwestern university, exploring how the work group might influence work–family conflict. A major finding of the study was that individuals who received high levels of social support from their work group reported lower levels of work–family conflict than those who received less social support.[19]

Cultural Differences

Cross-national differences based on culture can influence the extent to which workers experience work–family conflict. A study of 5,270 managers from twenty countries investigated how much work interfered with family life. Four clusters of countries were studied: the individualistic (Anglo) cluster versus three collectivistic cultures (Asia, Eastern Europe, and Latin America). A collectivistic culture highly values the group. A finding was that work interfering with family life led to more dissatisfaction and intention to quit for people in individualistic than in collectivistic societies. The researchers suggested that people in the collectivistic society might be more likely to remain loyal to the employer. Also, managers who value collectivism are more apt to respond to adverse conditions with greater affiliation toward coworkers.[20] A study with immigrant Latinos in the poultry-processing industry also suggested that workers with collectivistic beliefs experience less work–family conflict. For this group of Latinos, work is necessary and a vital method of ensuring family well-being.[21]

SEXUAL HARASSMENT: A SPECIAL TYPE OF CONFLICT

Many employees face conflict because they are sexually harassed by a supervisor, coworker, or customers. **Sexual harassment** is an unwanted sexually oriented behavior in the workplace that results in discomfort or interference with the job. It can include an action as violent as rape or as subdued as telling a sexually toned joke. The word *unwanted* is important for understanding sexual harassment. When workers enjoy or welcome sexual behavior, such as joking and flirting, that behavior is not considered harassment.[22] Sexual harassment creates conflict because the harassed person has to make a choice between two incompatible motives. One motive is to get ahead, keep the job, or have an unthreatening work environment. But to satisfy this motive, the person is forced to sacrifice the motive of holding onto his or her moral values or preferences. For example, a person might say, "I want a raise, but to do this, must I submit to being fondled by my boss?"

Here we focus on the types and frequency of sexual harassment and guidelines for dealing with the problem.

Types, Frequency, and Effects of Harassment

Two types of sexual harassment are legally recognized. Both are violations of the Civil Rights Acts of 1964 and 1991 and are therefore a violation of your rights. Union contracts also prohibit sexual harassment. In quid pro quo sexual harassment, the individual suffers loss (or threatened loss) of a job benefit as a result of his or her negative response to a request for sexual favors. The demands of a harasser can be blatant or implied. An implied form of quid pro quo harassment might take this form: A manager casually comments to one of his or her employees, "I've noticed that workers who become very close to me outside of the office get recommended for bigger raises."

The other form of sexual harassment is hostile-environment harassment. Another person in the workplace creates an intimidating, hostile, or offensive working environment. No tangible loss or psychological injury has to be suffered under this form of sexual harassment. Two frequent types of environmental harassment are displaying pornography and making sexually oriented comments about a coworker.

A major problem in controlling sexual harassment in the workplace is that most workers understand the meaning and nature of quid pro quo harassment but are confused about what constitutes the hostile-environment type. For example, some people might interpret the following behaviors to be harassing, whereas others would regard them as friendly initiatives: (a) calling a coworker "sweetie" and (b) saying to a subordinate, "I love your suit. You look fabulous." Judges, lawyers, and human resource specialists might also disagree on what constitutes hostile-environment harassment. Another confusing factor is that a plaintiff is likely to win a claim only if the employer failed to respond appropriately, such as counseling the perpetrator.[23]

Managers and human resource professionals respond to many sexual harassment claims related to sexually explicit photos sent via text messaging, a practice referred to as

Sexual harassment
unwanted sexually oriented behavior in the workplace that results in discomfort or interference with the job

"sexting" or "textual harassment." Closely related is the transmission of sexually oriented and pornographic content over social media during working hours.

Surveys, as well as the opinions of human resource professionals, suggest that somewhere between 50 and 60 percent of women are sexually harassed at least once in their careers. One study found that women in male-dominated organizations, such as a construction company, tend to be harassed more frequently than women in female-dominated organizations, such as a community service center. The same study found that women in male-dominated organizations who had relatively masculine personalities were sexually harassed the most. A "masculine" personality would include being highly aggressive and cold rather than warm.[24]

Aside from being an illegal and immoral act, sexual harassment has negative effects on the well-being of its victims. The negative effects of sexual harassment toward women were documented by University of Calgary psychology professors Chelsea R. Willness and Kibeom Lee and business professor Piers Steel. The researchers analyzed data from forty-one studies involving nearly 70,000 respondents. Sexual harassment experiences were associated with the negative outcomes of:

■ Decreased job satisfaction

■ Lower commitment to the employer

■ Withdrawing from work, such as being absent more frequently, escapist drinking, and a desire to quit

■ Decreased productivity for both the individual and the work group

■ Physical and mental health problems

■ Symptoms of posttraumatic stress disorder

The negative effects in the list were more likely to occur when the climate (or culture) was more tolerant of sexual harassment.[25] For example, "flashing" women is considered to be part of the hazing ritual for recently hired women workers in certain male-dominated manufacturing settings.

Racial harassment can result in the same type of conflict as sexual harassment, and much of the information presented here about sexual harassment applies to racial harassment. Racially offensive comments and jokes can be considered in violation of the same civil rights legislation as sexual harassment.[26]

Guidelines for Preventing and Dealing with Sexual Harassment

Decreasing or eliminating sexual harassment is a major goal among many employers. The U.S. Equal Employment Opportunity Commission (EEOC) identified eradicating sexual harassment as a key priority in an enforcement plan for 2013–2016.[27] A starting point in dealing with sexual harassment is to develop an awareness of the types of behavior that are considered sexual harassment. Often the difference is subtle. Suppose, for example, you placed copies of two nudes painted by Renoir, the French painter, on a coworker's desk. Your coworker might call that harassment. Yet, if you took that same coworker to a museum to see the originals of the same nude paintings, your behavior would usually not be classified as harassment. This example illustrates that the setting of the words or behavior influences whether they are harassing. College courses in understanding and dealing with pornography often show adult (sexually explicit) films as part of the curriculum. If an accounting professor in a college of business showed the same films to accounting students, he or she would most likely be charged with sexual harassment.

Education about the meaning of sexual harassment is therefore a basic part of any company program to prevent sexual harassment. The situation and your tone of voice, as well as other nonverbal behavior, contribute to perceptions of harassment. For example, the statement "You look wonderful" might be perceived as good-natured versus harassing, depending on the sender's voice tone and facial expression. Many human resource directors have formulated policies to help guard against the use of social media for harassment. Such a policy dictates that sending explicit sexual messages or photos to employees is inappropriate workplace behavior according to the company code of conduct.[28]

The easiest way to deal with sexual harassment is to speak up before it becomes serious. The first time it happens, respond with statements such as "I won't tolerate that kind of talk," "I dislike sexually oriented jokes," or "Keep your hands off me." Write the harasser a stern letter shortly after the first incident. Confronting the harasser in writing dramatizes your seriousness of purpose in not wanting to be sexually harassed. If the problem persists, say something to the effect of "You're practicing sexual harassment. If you don't stop, I'm going to exercise my right to report you to management."

Don't leave any room for doubt that the behavior or words you heard were unwelcome. Recurring incidents should be reported to the immediate manager, a higher-level manager, or a human resources official. When the harasser is the manager, of course, reporting the incident to him or her is ineffective. In the typical situation, the employer will keep the information it gathers as confidential as possible, consistent with state, provincial, and federal laws. Both the accused and the complainant will have a chance to present the case.

Whether you are the accused employee, the complaining one, or a potential witness, confidentiality is crucial in dealing with accusations of harassment. Two people have their reputations on the line, and you may not have all the facts.

A recommended approach to dealing with continuing harassment from the same person or persons is to maintain a dated log of the incidents. If the incidents are severe, such as unwanted groping or hugs, a copy of the log might be sent to a high-level manager in the company and a human resources professional. The principle here is that any type of documentation is better than none when dealing with a workplace issue of legal consequences.

Guidelines for Dealing with False Accusations of Sexual Harassment

Many workers will be falsely charged with sexual harassment for such reasons as revenge related to another issue, a desire to get attention, or a misunderstanding of what constitutes sexual harassment. A strategy for defending against false accusations of sexual harassment is to establish the reputation of never engaging in sexual harassment. Among the possibilities here are (a) open no pornographic websites at work, (b) never touch women or men in the workplace except for a handshake, fist-bump, or an occasional sideways hug in a group setting, (c) do not confer with another person face-to-face unless the door is open to an office or cubicle, and (d) don't make sexually toned comments or tell sexually oriented jokes.

When falsely charged with sexual harassment, the person should present a detailed account of his or her side of the story and point out that false accusations can be considered libel. The testimony of any witness to the alleged incident would also be helpful.

The Good and Bad Sides of Conflict   ◀ Learning Objective 10.2 ◀

Conflict over significant issues is a source of stress. We usually do not suffer stress over minor conflicts, such as having to choose between wearing one sweater or another. Handled properly, moderate doses of conflict can be beneficial. Some of the benefits that might arise from conflict can be summarized around the following key points. Figure 10-1 outlines the positive as well as the negative consequences of conflict.

FIGURE 10-1

THE GOOD AND BAD SIDES OF CONFLICT

Conflict between people and groups can have both positive and negative consequences.

Source: "THE GOOD AND BAD SIDES OF CONFLICT" by Andrew J. DuBrin.

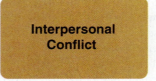

Interpersonal Conflict

Positive Consequences

- Talents and abilities emerge
- Need satisfaction leads to good feelings
- Unity after conflict
- Prevents premature agreement and poor decisions

Negative Consequences

- Poor well-being
- Wasted time and energy
- Financial and emotional costs
- Fatigue
- Self-interest dominates
- Workplace violence

1. Talents and abilities may emerge in response to conflict. When faced with a conflict, people often become more creative than they are in a tranquil situation. Assume that your employer told you that it would no longer pay for your advanced education unless you used the courses to improve your job performance. You would probably find ways to accomplish such an end. The late Steve Jobs of Apple Inc. was well-known for his tirades against engineers and designers when he disliked a product feature or product they suggested. As a result, the recipients of the tirade often came back with an improved product or product feature. A study conducted with employees in a long-term healthcare organization found that as a result of mild conflict about job tasks, the workers often acquired more job-related information.[29] As a result, they often performed their job better.

2. Conflict can help you feel better because it satisfies a number of psychological needs. By nature, many people like a good fight. As a socially acceptable substitute for attacking others, you might be content to argue over a dispute on the job or at home.

3. As an aftermath of conflict, the parties in conflict may become united. Two battling supervisors may become more cooperative toward each other in the aftermath of confrontation. A possible explanation is that the shared experience of being in conflict with each other *sometimes* brings the parties closer.

4. Conflict helps prevent people in the organization from agreeing too readily with each other, thus making some very poor decisions. Groupthink is the situation that occurs when group members strive so hard to get along that they fail to critically evaluate each other's ideas.

Despite the positive picture of conflict just painted, it can also have detrimental consequences to the individual, the organization, and society. These harmful consequences of conflict make it important for people to learn how to resolve conflict:

1. Prolonged conflict can be detrimental to some people's emotional and physical well-being. As a type of stress, prolonged conflict can lead to such problems as heart disease and chronic intestinal disorders. In one consultant firm, a woman aged fifty-two suffered a stroke after prolonged work–family conflict. She struggled to balance long, intense working hours and the demands of two adolescent children.

2. Relationships damaged by conflict can have consequences that impede individual, group, and organizational performance.   When coworkers have a falling out, the repercussions for the people in conflict as well as their coworkers can include emotional strain, poor listening, reduced information processing, distraction from work tasks, and a lowering of commitment and satisfaction. As a result, performance suffers for the individual, the group, and the organization.[30]

3. People in conflict with each other often waste time and energy that could be put to useful purposes.   Instead of fighting all evening with your roommate, the two of you might fix up your place. Instead of writing angry e-mail messages back and forth, two department heads might better invest that time in thinking up ideas to save the company money.

4. The aftermath of extreme conflict may have high financial and emotional costs.   Sabotage—such as ruining machinery or destroying a company database—might be the financial consequence. At the same time, management may develop a permanent distrust of many people in the workforce, although only a few of them are saboteurs.

5. Too much conflict is fatiguing, even if it does not cause symptoms of emotional illness.   People who work in high-conflict jobs often feel spent when they return home from work. When the battle-worn individual has limited energy left over for family responsibilities, the result is more conflict. (For instance, "What do you mean you are too tired to visit friends?" or "If your job is killing your interest in having friends, find another job.")

6. People in conflict will often be much more concerned with their own interests than with the good of the family, organization, or society.   An employee in the shipping department who is in conflict with his supervisor might neglect to ship an order. And a gang in conflict with another might leave a park or beach strewn with broken glass.

7. Workplace violence erupts, including the killing of managers, previous managers, coworkers, and customers, as well as spouses and partners.   Intense conflict can release anger, leading to aggressive behavior and violence. People involved in an unresolved domestic dispute sometimes storm into the partner's workplace to physically attack him or her. Unresolved conflict and frustration from financial, marital, or other domestic problems increase the odds of a person "going ballistic" at work. Violence has become so widespread that homicide is currently the fourth leading cause of fatal occupational injuries in the United States, with approximately 500 workplace homicides annually.[31] Most of these deaths result from a robbery or commercial crime. Many of these killings, however, are perpetrated by a disgruntled worker or former employee harboring an unresolved conflict.

Techniques for Resolving Conflicts

◀ Learning Objective 10.3 ◀

Because of the inevitability of conflict, a successful and happy person must learn effective ways of resolving conflict. An important general consideration is to face conflict rather than letting conflict slide or smoothing over it. Ignoring or smoothing over conflict does little to resolve the real causes of conflict and seldom leads to an effective long-term solution. Here we concentrate on methods of conflict resolution that you can use on your own. Most of them emphasize a collaborative or win–win philosophy. Several of the negotiating and bargaining tactics described may be close to the competitive orientation. Human Relations Self-Assessment Quiz 10-2 gives you the opportunity to think through your style of managing conflict.

Human Relations Self-Assessment Quiz 10-2

Collaborative versus Competitive Styles of Conflict Management

Answer on a scale of 1 to 5 how well you agree with each of the following statements: disagree strongly, disagree, neutral, agree, and agree strongly.

	Disagree Strongly	Disagree	Neutral	Agree	Agree Strongly
1. I like to see the other side squirm when I resolve a dispute.	5	4	3	2	1
2. Winning is everything when it comes to settling conflict.	5	4	3	2	1
3. After I have successfully negotiated a price, I like to see the seller smile.	1	2	3	4	5
4. I have a "smash-mouth" attitude toward resolving conflict.	5	4	3	2	1
5. In most conflict situations, one side is clearly right, and the other side is clearly wrong.	5	4	3	2	1
6. I think there are effective alternatives to strikes for settling union versus management disputes.	1	2	3	4	5
7. The winner should take all.	5	4	3	2	1
8. Conflict on the job is like a prize fight: The idea is to knock out the opponent.	5	4	3	2	1
9. I like the idea of tournaments in which first-round losers receive another opportunity to play.	1	2	3	4	5
10. Nice guys and gals usually finish first.	1	2	3	4	5

Scoring and Interpretation:

Add the point value of your scores to obtain your total. Scores of 40 and higher suggest that you prefer a *collaborative*, or *win–win*, approach to resolving conflict. You tend to be concerned about finding long-term solutions to conflict that will provide benefits to both sides. Scores of 39 and lower suggest that you prefer a *competitive* approach to resolving conflict. You want to maximize gain for yourself, with little concern about the welfare of the other side. In an organization that emphasizes collaboration, this approach to conflict resolution may not be welcome.

Source: "Collaborative versus Competitive Styles of Conflict Management" by Andrew J. DuBrin.

Before attempting to resolve a conflict, it is prudent to first consider if the issue is important enough to risk the potential negative consequences of resolving the conflict. Might you be labeled as a troublemaker? Might you damage an otherwise good relationship with your boss? For example, if you find out that a coworker received a slightly higher bonus than you, it might not be worth confronting your boss. In general, it is best not to enter into conflict with people with much more formal power than you, such as confronting the CEO about spending so much money on advertising.[32]

BEING ASSERTIVE

Several of the techniques for resolving conflict described here require assertiveness. Learning to express your feelings to make your demands known is also an important aspect of becoming an effective individual in general. Expressing your feelings helps you establish good relationships with people. If you aren't sharing your feelings and attitudes with other people, you will never get close to them.

As implied previously, **assertive people** state clearly what they want or how they feel in a given situation without being abusive, abrasive, or obnoxious. People who are assertive are open, honest, and up-front because they believe that all people have an equal right to express themselves honestly. Another representative assertive behavior is to ask for clarification rather than contradicting a person with whom you disagree. The assertive person asks for clarification when another person says something irritating, rather than hurling insults or telling the other person he or she is wrong. For example, assume someone says to you, "Your proposal is useless." Aggressively telling the person, "You have no right to make that judgment," shuts out any possible useful dialogue. You will probably learn more if you ask for clarification, such as, "What is wrong with my proposal?"

Assertive
characteristic of people who state clearly what they want or how they feel in a given situation without being abusive, abrasive, or obnoxious; open, honest, and up-front people who believe that all people have an equal right to express themselves honestly

CONFRONTATION AND PROBLEM SOLVING LEADING TO WIN–WIN

A highly recommended way of resolving conflict is **confrontation and problem solving**. It is a method of identifying the true source of conflict and resolving it systematically. The confrontation in this approach is gentle and tactful rather than combative and abusive. It is best to wait until your anger cools down before confronting the other person to avoid being unreasonable. Reasonableness is important because the person who takes the initiative in resolving the conflict wants to maintain a harmonious working relationship with the other party. Also, both parties should benefit from the resolution of the conflict.

Confrontation and problem solving
the most highly recommended way of resolving conflict; method of identifying the true source of conflict and resolving it systematically

Win–Win Conflict Resolution

Assume that Jason, the person working at the desk next to you, whistles loudly while he works. You find the whistling to be distracting and annoying; you think Jason is a noise polluter. If you don't bring the problem to Jason's attention, it will probably grow in proportion with time. Yet you are hesitant to enter into an argument about something a person might regard as a civil liberty (the right to whistle in a public place). An effective alternative is for you to approach Jason directly in this manner:

You: Jason, may I talk to you about a little problem that is bugging me?

Jason: Go ahead. I don't mind listening to a problem.

You: My problem is that when you whistle, it distracts me and grates on my nerves. It may be my problem, but the whistling does bother me.

Jason: I guess I could stop whistling when you're working next to me. It's probably simply a nervous habit.

An important advantage of confrontation and problem solving is that you deal directly with a sensitive problem without jeopardizing the chances of forming a constructive working relationship in the future. One reason that the method works so effectively is that the focus is on the problem at hand and not on the individual's personality.

The intent of confrontation and problem solving is to arrive at a collaborative solution to the conflict. The collaborative style reflects a desire to fully satisfy the desires of both parties. It is based on the philosophy of **win–win**, the belief that after conflict has been resolved, both sides should gain something of value. The user of win–win approaches is genuinely concerned about arriving at a settlement that meets the needs of both parties or at least that does not badly damage the welfare of the other side. When collaborative approaches to resolving conflict are used, the relationships among the parties are built on and improved.

Win–win
belief that after conflict has been resolved both sides should gain something of value

Here is an example of a win–win approach to resolving conflict. A manager granted an employee a few hours off on an occasional Friday afternoon because she was willing to be on call for emergency work on an occasional weekend. Both parties were satisfied with the outcome, and both accomplished their goals.

Another way of achieving win–win solutions to conflict is to address conflict in relation to productivity. Be prepared to discuss your differences with another person by completing statements such as the following:[33]

"What I would like to change about the current situation is . . ."

"What I am willing to do to bring about that change is . . ."

"The one issue I cannot give in on is . . ."

Following the win–win mindset, these three phrases reflect a willingness to work on the problem together. Even the nonnegotiable point about not giving in is expressed positively.

Win–Lose Conflict Resolution

The opposite approach to win–win conflict resolution is *win–lose,* in which one side attempts to maximize gain at the expense of the other side. Win–lose is also referred to as a *zero-sum game,* in which one side wins nothing and the other side wins everything. Many people believe that win–lose is the best approach to resolving conflict—and that is one reason so much conflict goes unresolved in the form of physical attacks on people and bankruptcies. A person with a competitive orientation is likely to engage in power struggles in which one side wins and the other loses. "My way or the highway" is a win–lose strategy.

If faced with an adversary who has a win–lose orientation, a plausible defense is to keep on pointing out the benefits of finding a solution that fits both sides. A sales representative for a company that makes steel buildings (often used for warehousing) was about to be laid off because of poor business. He proposed to his boss, "Please give me one more chance. Give me just enough salary to pay my rent and feed our newborn child. All the rest of my income will come from commissions on the sales I make." The owner conceded, and the sales rep did earn his way, so a win–lose situation emerged into a win–win.

DISARM THE OPPOSITION

Disarming the opposition
method of conflict resolution in which you disarm the criticizer by agreeing with his or her criticism

When in conflict, your criticizer may be armed with valid negative criticism of you. The criticizer is figuratively clobbering you with knowledge of what you did wrong. If you deny that you have made a mistake, the criticism intensifies. A simple technique has been developed to help you deal with this type of manipulative criticism. **Disarming the opposition** is a method of conflict resolution in which you disarm the criticizer by agreeing with his or her criticism of you. The technique assumes that you have done something wrong. Disarming the opposition generally works more effectively than counterattacking a person with whom you are in conflict.

Another reason disarming the opposition is effective is that it implies you are apologizing for a mistake or an error you have made. An apology often gets the other person on your side or at least softens the animosity. By offering an apology and regretting your mistake, you are likely to gain sympathy from the person who disapproves of what you have done or whom you have wronged.

Agreeing with criticism made of you by a manager or team leader is effective because it puts you in a position to ask that manager's help in improving your performance. Most managers and team leaders recognize that it is their responsibility to help employees overcome problems, not merely to criticize them. Imagine that you have been chronically late in submitting reports during the past six months. It is time for a performance review, and you know you will be reprimanded for your tardiness. You also hope that your boss will not downgrade all other aspects of your performance because of your tardy reports. Here is how disarming the situation would work in this situation:

Your boss:	Have a seat. It's time for your performance review, and we have a lot to talk about. I'm concerned about some things.
You:	So am I. It appears that I'm having a difficult time getting my reports in on time. I wonder if I'm being a perfectionist. Do you have any suggestions?
Your boss:	I like your attitude. I think you can improve on getting your reports in on time. Maybe you are trying to make your reports perfect before you turn them in. Try not to figure out everything to four decimal places. We need thoroughness around here, but we don't want to overdo it.

REFRAMING (INCLUDING COGNITIVE RESTRUCTURING AND ASKING QUESTIONS)

Another useful approach to resolving conflict is to reexamine or *reframe* the conflict situation by looking at it in a different light. What follows are two practical approaches to reframing, one by searching for the positives in the situation and the other by asking questions.

Reframing through Cognitive Restructuring

An indirect way of resolving interpersonal conflict is to lessen the conflicting elements in a situation by viewing them more positively. According to the technique of **cognitive restructuring**, you mentally convert negative aspects into positive ones by looking for the positive elements in a situation. How you frame or choose your thoughts can determine the outcome of a conflict situation. Your thoughts influence your actions. If you search for the beneficial elements in the situation, there will be less area for dispute. Although this technique might sound like a mind game to you, it can work effectively.

> **Cognitive restructuring**
> technique of mentally converting negative aspects into positive ones by looking for the positive elements in a situation

Imagine that a coworker of yours, Ted, has been asking you repeated questions about how to carry out a work procedure. You are about ready to tell Ted, "Go bother somebody else; I'm not paid to be a trainer." Instead, you look for the positive elements in the situation. You say to yourself, "Ted has been asking me a lot of questions. This does take time, but answering these questions is valuable experience. If I want to become a manager, I'll have to help group members with problems."

After having completed this cognitive restructuring, you can then deal with the conflict situation more positively. You might say to Ted, "I welcome the opportunity to help you, but we need to find a mutually convenient time. In that way, I can better concentrate on my own work." To get started with cognitive restructuring, do Applying Human Relations Exercise 10-1 at the end of the chapter.

Reframing by Asking Questions

Another way to use reframing is to step back, take a deep breath, and then ask all or some of the following questions about the conflict situation arising within the work group:

- Do I fully understand the situation?

- Is the person really angry at me or just worried and anxious?

■ Do I have all the facts?

■ What is the real issue here?

■ How would I want to be treated if the situation were reversed?

By taking such an approach, you are more likely to communicate effectively and constructively with coworkers when conflict situations arise. You carefully talk through the issues rather than becoming explosive, defensive, and argumentative. A useful scenario for reframing through questioning would be when a coworker accuses you of not carrying your fair share of the workload.[34]

APPEAL TO A THIRD PARTY AND THE GRIEVANCE PROCEDURE

Now and then, you may be placed in a conflict situation in which the other party either holds most of the power or simply won't budge. Perhaps you have tried techniques such as confrontation and problem solving or disarming the opposition, yet you cannot resolve your conflict. In these situations, you may have to enlist the help of a third party with power—more power than you or your adversary has. Among such third parties is your common boss, a union steward, or the human resource manager. Filing a lawsuit against your adversary is another application of the third-party technique, such as filing an age-discrimination charge.

In some situations, simply implying that you will bring in a third party to help resolve the conflict situation is sufficient for you to gain advantage. Many conflicts about sexual harassment, as well as ethnic and racial harassment, are resolved through third-party appeal.

Grievance procedure

formal process of filing a complaint and resolving a dispute within an organization

Another way of appealing to a third party is the **grievance procedure**—the formal process of filing a complaint and resolving a dispute within an organization. It can also be regarded as a formal (officially sanctioned) method of resolving conflict, in which a series of third parties are brought into the picture. In a unionized firm, the steps in the grievance procedure are specified in the written contract between management and labor. The grievance procedure is a key part of a labor agreement because one of the union's goals is to obtain fair treatment for union members. An example of a grievance about favoritism would be "I get the worst assignments because I'm not one of the boss's fishing buddies." An example of a grievance about discrimination would be "I didn't get the transfer to the receptionist job because I'm fifty-five years old."

The steps in the grievance procedure may vary from one to six, depending on the labor agreement or company procedures. A summary of four typical steps in a grievance procedure is presented next and outlined in Figure 10-2. If the company does not have a labor union, a specialist from the human resources department might serve as a third party.

Step 1 **Initiation of the formal grievance.** Suppose that an employee feels that he or she has been treated unfairly or that his or her rights have been violated in some way. The employee then files a grievance with the supervisor (or team leader). Most grievances end at step 1 by conversation among the employee, the union steward (if the workers are represented by a labor union), and the supervisor. At this stage, it makes sense to use some of the techniques for resolving conflict already described. (If the workforce is not represented by a union, another type of grievance procedure might be used.)

Step 2 **Second level of management.** If the steward, supervisor or team leader, and employee cannot reach a satisfactory solution to the conflict, it goes to the next-highest level in the organization. At this point, the grievance must be documented in writing by both sides. Which people are involved at this level

FIGURE 10-2

THE GRIEVANCE PROCEDURE

Step 1:   Initiation of formal grievance

Employee files grievance, and discussion is held with employee, supervisor or team leader, and union steward.

If not settled

Step 2:   Second-level manager

Grievance now goes to next-highest level of management and must be documented in writing by both sides.

If not settled

Step 3:   Higher-level manager and local union president

Higher-level officials from both union and employer step in to settle dispute.

If not settled

Step 4:   Arbitration

Independent arbitrator is called in to settle the issue.

Source: "THE GRIEVANCE PROCEDURE" by Andrew J. DuBrin.

depends on the size of the firm. In a small firm, a high-ranking manager might be involved in step 2.

Step 3   A higher-level manager and the local union president. If the grievance is not resolved at step 2, higher-level officials from both the union and the employer become involved in settling the dispute. A general principle is that at each higher step in the grievance process, comparable levels of management from both company and union face each other, or a higher-level representative from the human resources department might be involved.

Step 4   Arbitration. If the grievance cannot be settled at the lower steps, an independent arbitrator may be called in to settle the issue. Only about 1 percent of grievances go all the way to arbitration. Arbitration is often used as an alternative to a strike. The arbitrator has the authority to settle the dispute and must be a person acceptable to both sides.

In a small organization, step 2 is sometimes omitted. After the grievance is discussed with the union steward, and it is not resolved, the grievance is taken to the chief executive or business owner, and then to arbitration if necessary.[35]

Mediation is often confused with arbitration. A mediator is a third party who enters a controversy but holds no power of decision. The mediator helps the two sides find a resolution to their conflict. Relatively few labor agreements allow for mediation, yet mediation might be used to settle a strike. A mediator works like a marriage counselor by helping both sides come to agreement by themselves.

The grievance processes described are formal and legalistic. Nevertheless, to represent your interests well, it is helpful to use the informal conflict-resolution techniques described earlier, such as confrontation and problem solving.

► **Learning Objective 10.4** ►

Negotiating and bargaining
situation of conferring with another
person to resolve a problem

NEGOTIATION AND BARGAINING TACTICS

Conflicts can be considered situations calling for **negotiating and bargaining**, conferring with another person to resolve a problem. When you are trying to negotiate a fair price for an automobile, you are also trying to resolve a conflict. At first, the demands of both parties seem incompatible. After haggling for a while, you will probably reach a price that is satisfactory to both sides. Negotiation has many applications in the workplace, including buying, selling, arriving at a starting salary or raise, and deciding on a fair compensation for a contract worker. Negotiation may also take place with coworkers when you need their assistance. For example, you might need to strike a bargain with a coworker to handle some of your responsibilities if you are faced with a temporary overload.

A sampling of negotiating tactics to help you resolve conflict is presented next. As with other techniques of resolving conflict already presented, choose those that best fit your style and the situation. Many people feel awkward at the prospect of negotiating with a stranger, yet by learning and practicing new skills most people can become better negotiators.

Deal with Your Anxiety about the Upcoming Negotiation

A big challenge with negotiation is that it is anxiety-provoking for many people. Harvard Business School professor Alison Wood Brooks offers a suggestion for dealing with this challenge that supports all the negotiating tactics described below. She recommends that you deal with the anxiety that often precedes entering negotiations by reframing anxiety as excitement. Think of yourself as being excited rather than nervous about the upcoming negotiation.

Also, build your confidence by practicing negotiation when the opportunity presents itself, such as negotiating for more time to complete an important project.[36] It is also important to recognize that you will probably experience heavy emotion during negotiation, so be prepared to use your emotional intelligence to advantage.[37] As a basic example, you might be so excited about negotiating a car price that you forget that color choice or a sun roof is important for you.

Create a Positive Negotiating Climate

Negotiation proceeds much more swiftly if a positive tone surrounds the session, so it is helpful to initiate a positive outlook about the negotiation meeting. A good opening line in a negotiating session is "Thanks for fitting this meeting into your hectic schedule." Nonverbal communication such as smiling and making friendly gestures helps create a positive climate. A calm voice helps build the trust necessary for creating a positive climate.

In negotiating with coworkers for assistance, a positive climate can often be achieved by phrasing demands as a request for help. Most people will be more accommodating if you say to them, "I have a problem, and I wonder if you could help me with it." The problem might be that you need the person's time and mental energy. By giving that person a choice of offering you help, you have established a much more positive climate than by demanding assistance.

Another way of creating a positive negotiating climate is to validate the other side's position by describing his or her position in your own words (a form of paraphrasing). Make a positive comment to the other person that emphasizes the value in the relationship.[38]

Assume that you are renting a condominium, and the owner wants to raise the rent 10 percent for next year. You might state, "I recognize that your costs are rising. You are also a great landlord. But 10 percent more rent is a little beyond my budget."

Listen First to Investigate What the Other Side Wants

Listening skills are also part of effectiveness in negotiation. Negotiation professional Bobby Covie says, "There's a saying among negotiators that whoever talks the most during a negotiation loses." Being the first to listen helps establish trust. Listening also involves paying attention to what the other side is saying.[39] A person might begin a negotiating session claiming to want a bigger share of the division budget. Yet careful listening might indicate that he really is looking for his department to receive more respect and attention. So the issue is not financial.

As shown in the example just presented, listening helps you dig for information as to why the other side wants what it does.[40] If the other side wants a bigger budget just to have more respect, there are less expensive ways to grant respect than granting a bigger share of the budget. Perhaps the manager can give the person a classier job title, rename the department, or appoint the person to head a task force. For example, the head of marketing is renamed "chief of brands," and her department "brand development."

Allow Room for Compromise, but Be Reasonable

The basic strategy of negotiation is to begin with a demand that allows room for compromise and concession. Anyone who has ever negotiated the price of an automobile, house, or used furniture recognizes this vital strategy. If you are a buyer, begin with a low bid. (You say, "I'll give you $160 for that painting" when you are prepared to pay $190.) If you are the seller, begin with a high demand. (You say, "You can have this painting for $230" when you are ready to sell it for as low as $150.) As negotiations proceed, the two of you will probably arrive at a mutually satisfactory price. This negotiating strategy can also be used for such purposes as obtaining a higher starting salary or purchasing excess inventory.

Common sense, and perhaps greed, propels many negotiators to allow *too much* room for compromise. They begin negotiations by asking way beyond what they expect to receive or offering far less than they expect to give. As a result of these implausible demands, the other side may become hostile or antagonistic or walk away from the negotiations. Beginning with a plausible demand or offer is also important because it contributes to a positive negotiating climate.

Focus on Interests, Not Positions

Rather than clinging to specific negotiating points, keep your overall interests in mind and try to satisfy them. A negotiating point might be a certain amount of money or a concession that you must have. Remember that the true object of negotiation is to satisfy the underlying interests of both sides. Among the interests you and the other side might be trying to protect are money, lifestyle, power, and the status quo. For example, instead of negotiating for a particular starting salary, your true interests might be to afford a certain lifestyle. If the company pays all your medical and dental coverage, you can get by with a lower salary. Or your cost of living might be much lower in one city than in another. Therefore you can accept a lower starting salary in the city with a lower cost of living.

Make a Last and Final Offer

In many circumstances, presenting a final offer will break a deadlock. You might frame your message something like this: "All I can possibly pay for your guitar is $250. You have my number. Call me when it is available at that price." Sometimes the strategy will be countered by a last and final offer from the other side: "Thanks for your interest. My absolute minimum price for this guitar is $300. Call us if that should seem okay to you." One of you will probably give in and accept the other person's last and final offer.

Allow for Saving Face

We have saved one of the most important negotiating and conflict resolution strategies for last. Negotiating does not mean that you should try to squash the other side. You should try to create circumstances that will enable you to continue working with that person if it is necessary. People prefer to avoid looking weak, foolish, or incompetent during negotiation or when the process is completed. If you do not give your opponent an opportunity to save face, you will probably create a long-term enemy.

Saving face could work in this way. A small-business owner winds up purchasing an intranet system for about twice what he originally budgeted. After the sale is completed, the sales rep says, "I know you bought a more professional intranet rig than you originally intended. Yet I know you made the right decision. You will be able to boost productivity enough with the intranet to pay back the cost of the system in two years."

▶ **Learning Objective 10.5** ▶

Difficult people
a coworker is classified as difficult if he or she is uncooperative, disrespectful, touchy, defensive, hostile, or even very unfriendly

Dealing with Difficult People

A major challenge in resolving conflict is dealing constructively with **difficult people**. A worker is classified as difficult if he or she is uncooperative, disrespectful, touchy, defensive, hostile, or even very unfriendly. Difficult people are responsible for much of the conflict in the workplace. The difficult person often meets or exceeds performance standards, yet annoys coworkers and superiors.[41] Other symptoms of being a difficult person include bullying and incivility.

A few nasty, lazy, or incompetent workers can ruin the performance of a team or organization. It takes time to deal with the problems difficult people create, and their distracting behavior is often contagious.[42] Managers have the primary responsibility for keeping the office running smoothly, yet much of the day-by-day dealings with difficult people are coworker interactions. Many companies take the problem of difficult people quite seriously, including the Connectria ban on office jerks described in the chapter opener. Five examples of difficult people follow:

- **The lone wolf.** Can't stand being part of anything: a team, a project, or group functions. Independent to a fault—makes no attempt to hide solitary preferences.

- **Chicken Little.** No matter how sunny things seem to be, will always find a cloud to cast a shadow. ("What a great website we have. Twenty thousand unique visitors in the first week." "Yeah, but are more than 1 percent buying anything?")[43]

- **The high-maintenance person.** Requires so much assistance, special attention, and extra help that it wears you down. No matter what type of help you offer, he or she wants a little more. If you bring a high-maintenance worker a soft drink, he or she is likely to say, "Didn't they have any decaffeinated soft drinks?"

- **The office magpie.** Always eager to chat and assumes that other workers want to do likewise. Whenever he or she is not faced with a pressing deadline, barges into your workspace to shoot the breeze. Also known to send dozens of e-mails, along with chatty personal comments, over the same issue.[44]

- **The destructive hero.** A high-performing person whose contributions to the organization make it difficult to fire the person, despite his or her being an egotist, a prima donna, and a poor team player. He or she can also be characterized as a brilliant jerk. The destructive hero intimidates coworkers and lowers morale.[45]

In dealing with difficult coworkers, as well as difficult bosses, it is important to recognize that their problems could go much deeper than those of the types of individuals mentioned. Such individuals could be suffering from a **personality disorder**. Such a disorder is a pervasive, persistent, inflexible, maladaptive pattern of behavior that deviates from expected cultural norms. The disorder is learned early in life and causes distress to the person and/or conflicts with others. The bullies and passive-aggressive personalities described earlier usually have a personality disorder. If your difficult coworker has a severe personality disorder, the techniques described in the following paragraphs will not work as well as they would with a difficult person who has a mild disorder. About 5 to 10 percent of the population suffer from a personality disorder, and the negative behavior is the most likely to be triggered by heavy stress.

Here we present eight widely applicable approaches for dealing with difficult people. Keep in mind that dealing with a difficult coworker requires grace and a firm grip on your own patience and temperament.

Personality disorder
a pervasive, persistent, inflexible, maladaptive pattern of behavior that deviates from expected cultural norms

Take Problems Professionally, Not Personally

A key principle in dealing with difficult people is to take what they do professionally, not personally. Difficult people are not necessarily out to get you. You may simply represent a stepping-stone for them to get what they want.[46] For example, if a coworker insults you because you need his help Friday afternoon, he probably has nothing against you personally. He just prefers to become mentally disengaged from work that Friday afternoon. Your request distracts him from mentally phasing out of work as early as he would like.

Give Ample Feedback

The primary technique for dealing with counterproductive behavior is to feed back to the difficult person how his or her behavior affects you. Focus on the person's behavior rather than on characteristics or values. If a Chicken Little type is annoying you by constantly pointing out potential disasters, say something to this effect: "I have difficulty maintaining my enthusiasm when you so often point out the possible negatives." Such a statement will engender less resentment than saying, "I find you to be a total pessimist, and it annoys me."

Feedback can also be useful in dealing with a bully by pointing out how you recognize the bullying and how you find it to be unacceptable. For example, "You have insulted me three times this morning. Maybe you want to lower my self-confidence, but it is not working. I find most of your criticism to be pointless and mean-spirited."

Listen and Respond

Closely related to giving feedback is listening and responding. Give the difficult person ample opportunity to express his or her concerns, doubts, anger, or other feelings. Face the person directly and maintain eye contact. Then acknowledge your awareness of the person's position.[47] An example: "Okay, you tell me that management is really against us and therefore we shouldn't work so hard." After listening, present your perspective in a way such as this: "Your viewpoint may be valid based on your experiences. Yet, so far, I've found management here to be on my side." This exchange of viewpoints is less likely to lead to failed communication than if you are judgmental with a statement such as "You really shouldn't think that way."

Use Tact and Diplomacy in Dealing with Annoying Behavior

Coworkers who irritate you rarely do annoying things on purpose. Tactful actions on your part can sometimes take care of these annoyances without your having to confront the problem. You might try one woman's method of getting rid of office pests: She keeps a file open on her computer screen and gestures to it apologetically when someone overstays a visit.

Sometimes subtlety doesn't work, and it may be necessary to diplomatically confront the coworker who is annoying you. A useful approach is to precede a criticism with a compliment. Here is an example of this approach: "You're one of the best people I've ever worked with, but one habit of yours drives me bananas. Do you think you could let me know when you're going to be late getting back to the office after lunch?"[48]

Use Nonhostile Humor

Nonhostile humor can often be used to help a difficult person understand how his or her behavior is blocking others. Also, the humor will help defuse conflict between you and that person. The humor should point to the person's unacceptable behavior yet not belittle him or her. Assume that you and a coworker are working jointly on a report. For each idea that you submit, your coworker gets into know-it-all mode and informs you of important facts that you neglected. An example of nonhostile humor that might jolt the coworker into realizing that his or her approach is annoying is as follows:

> If there is ever a contest to choose the human with a brain that can compete against cloud storage, I will nominate you. But even though my brain is limited to human capacity, I still think I can supply a few facts for our report.

Your humor may help the other person recognize that he or she is attempting to overwhelm you with facts at his or her disposal. You are being self-effacing and thereby drawing criticism away from your coworker. Self-effacement (self-criticism) is a proven humor tactic.

Avoid Creating a Dependency on You

A trap to avoid with many difficult people, and especially the high-maintenance person, is to let him or her become too dependent on you for solutions to problems. In your desire to be helpful and supportive to coworkers, you run the risk of creating a dependency. A difficult person might be pestering you to regularly help solve some of his or her most challenging work problems. The high-maintenance worker might ask you to look up a fact with a search engine, reboot a stalled computer, or help scrape ice from the windshield and windows of his or her car. You may want to be a good organizational citizen, yet you also need more time for your own work, and you do not want to make the person too dependent on you.[49] As an antidote to the problem, make frequent statements such as, "You know how to use Google," or "Perhaps you can scrape the ice yourself, because I have to do the same thing with my SUV."

Reinforce Civil Behavior and Good Moods

In the spirit of positive reinforcement, when a generally difficult person is behaving acceptably, recognize the behavior in some way. Reinforcing statements would include "It's fun working with you today" and "I appreciate your professional attitude." Two office bully specialists, Kathi Elster and Patricia Barnes, observe that an effective tactic for dealing with a mean bully is to befriend that person.[50]

The tactics for dealing with difficult people described require practice to be effective. Also, you may have to use a combination of the eight tactics described in this section to deal effectively with a difficult person. The point of these tactics is not to outmanipulate or subdue a difficult person but to establish a cordial and productive working relationship.

▶ **Learning Objective 10.6** ▶

Suggestions for Managing Anger

Limited ability to manage anger damages the careers and personal lives of many people. The ability to manage your anger, and the anger of others, is an important human relations skill now considered to be part of emotional intelligence. Managing anger is also part of dealing with bullies because they are usually angry people. A person who cannot manage anger well cannot take good advantage of his or her cognitive intelligence. As an extreme example, a genius who swears at the manager regularly will probably lose his or her job despite being so talented.

Although the emotion of anger is relatively easy to observe, it is more complicated than it appears on the surface. Psychologist Raymond Novaco, who developed the term *anger management*, points out that anger does not occur by itself. Rather, it is embedded with many other emotions, including sadness, grief, and shame. One implication of this finding is that you would have to manage a feeling such as sadness before you prevent your anger from surfacing frequently.[51]

Concerns about employees becoming violent have prompted many companies to offer employees training in anger management. Also, employees who become verbally abusive on the job are often sent to such training. Anger-management training is likely to encompass most of the suggestions presented next. Our concern here is with several tactics for managing your own anger and that of others effectively.

MANAGING YOUR OWN ANGER

A starting point in dealing with your anger is to recognize that at its best, anger can be an energizing force that can fuel ambition and creativity.[52] In contrast, explosive outbursts of anger can be self-destructive. Recent evidence suggests that an intensely angry episode increases eightfold the risk of a heart attack among adults. Anger can also spike blood pressure and trigger strokes and irregular heartbeats.[53]

Instead of letting it be destructive, channel your anger into exceptional performance. If you are angry because you did not get the raise you thought you deserved, get even by performing so well that there will be no question you deserve a raise next time. Develop the habit of expressing your anger before it reaches a high intensity. Tell your coworker that you do not appreciate his or her listening to an iPod while you are having dinner together the first time the act of rudeness occurs. If you wait too long, you may wind up grabbing the iPod and slamming it to the floor.

As you are about to express anger, *slow down.* (The old technique of counting to ten is still effective.) Slowing down gives you the opportunity to express anger in a way that does not damage your relationship with the other person. Following your first impulse, you might say to the other person, "You're a stupid fool." If you slow down, this might translate into "You need training on this task."

Closely related to slowing down is a technique taught in anger-management programs: Think about the consequences of what you do when you are worked up. Say to yourself as soon as you feel angry, "Oops, I'm in anger mode now. I had better calm down before I say something or do something that I will regret later." To gauge how effectively you are expressing your anger, ask for feedback. Ask a friend, coworker, or manager, "Am I coming on too strong when I express my negative opinion?"

Most anger-management programs focus on emotional intelligence, especially understanding why you are frustrated, annoyed, or upset. You then learn to find a calm, constructive means to get what you need, rather than lose your temper. Assume that you join a high-tech company, and that you are given no tech support to help you hook up your desktop computer to the company network. If you have an anger problem, you would start swearing and perhaps throw a tantrum about the lack of support. A more emotionally intelligent approach to your problem would be to calmly ask one of your new coworkers for some technical assistance.

Here are a few additional suggestions from a variety of anger-management specialists for managing your own anger:[54]

■ Reframe the situation as in the cognitive restructuring ideas presented earlier in this chapter. For example, "I won't go ballistic because the airline lost my baggage. Instead, I will look upon this as an opportunity in problem solving."

■ Find a constructive solution to the problem at hand. For example, "So, I didn't get the big raise I anticipated. Instead, I will look for ways to cut my expenses 4 percent this year."

■ Get a medical checkup and stay physically healthy if possible. Medical conditions such as diabetes, chronic pain, and low testosterone and low estrogen can make people irritable.

■ Calculate the cost of your anger. For example, your reputation may suffer enormously, blocking you from good career opportunities, or you might even get fired.

■ Pay more attention to the important things in life rather than exploding over small incidents. Be aware that most frustrations, inconveniences, and insults are trivial and temporary.

MANAGING ANGER IN OTHER PEOPLE

A variation of confrontation and problem solving has developed specifically to resolve conflict with angry people: confront, contain, and connect. *Confront* in this context means that you jump right in and get agitated workers talking to prevent future blowups. The confrontation, however, is not aimed at arguing with the angry person. If the other person yells, you talk more softly. *Contain* refers to moving an angry worker out of sight and out of earshot. At the same time, you remain impartial. The supervisor is advised not to choose sides or appear to be a friend.

You *connect* by asking open-ended questions such as "What would you like us to do about your concern?" to get at the real reasons behind an outburst. Using this approach, one worker revealed he was upset because a female coworker got to leave early to pick up her daughter at day care. The man also needed to leave early one day a week for personal reasons but felt awkward making the request. So instead of being assertive (explicit and direct) about his demands, he flared up.

An important feature of the confront–contain–connect technique is that it provides angry workers a place where they can vent their frustrations and report the outbursts of others: Workers need a safe outlet to talk through anger and not feel they will put their job in jeopardy."[55]

Another useful suggestion in dealing with an angry person is to be aware of your own nonverbal communication. Guard against confrontational body language such as finger pointing or rolling the eyes. Stay out of the employee's personal space, and avoid touching, even if meant to be reassuring.[56]

CHOOSING A TACTIC FOR RESOLVING A CONFLICT OR MANAGING ANGER

How does a person know which of the tactics or strategies presented in this chapter will work best for a given problem? The best answer is to consider both your personality and the situation. With respect to your personality, or personal style, pick a tactic for resolving conflict that you would feel comfortable using. One person might say, "I would like the tactic of making a last and final offer because I like to control situations." Another person might say, "I'll avoid disarming the opposition for now. I don't yet have enough finesse to carry out this technique."

In fitting the strategy to the situation, it is important to assess the gravity of the topic for negotiation or the conflict between people. A woman might think, "My boss has committed such a blatant act of sexual harassment that I had best take this up with a higher authority immediately." Sizing up your opponent can also help you choose the best strategy. If she or he appears reasonably flexible, you might try to compromise. Or if your adversary is especially upset, give that person a chance to simmer down before trying to solve the problem.

Concept Review and Reinforcement

Summary and Review

Conflict occurs when two sets of demands, goals, or motives are incompatible. Such differences often lead to a hostile or antagonistic relationship between people. A conflict can also be considered a dispute, feud, or controversy. Among the reasons for widespread conflict are the following:

- Competition for limited resources
- Differences of opinion on work-related issues and rights

Incivility

- Personality clashes and drama
- Aggressive personalities, including bullies

Passive-aggressive personalities

- Culturally diverse teams and factional groups
- Competing work and family demands
- Sexual harassment

Sexual harassment is one of two types: quid pro quo (a demand for sexual favors in exchange for job benefits) and creating a hostile environment. It is important for workers to understand what actions and words constitute sexual harassment and how to deal with the problem.

The benefits of conflict include the emergence of talents and abilities, constructive innovation and change, and increased unity after the conflict is settled. Among the detrimental consequences of conflict are physical and mental health problems, wasted resources, the promotion of self-interest, and workplace violence.

Techniques for resolving conflicts with others include the following:

- Being assertive. Be explicit in expressing your demands without being too aggressive.

- Confrontation and problem solving leading to win–win. Get to the root of the problem and resolve it systematically. The intention of confrontation and problem solving is to arrive at a collaborative solution to the conflict. The opposite of win–win is win–lose, where each side attempts to maximize gain at the expense of the other.
- Disarm the opposition. Agree with the criticizer and enlist his or her help.
- Reframing. One approach is to use cognitive restructuring by mentally converting negative aspects into positive ones by looking for the positive elements in a situation. Also use reframing by asking questions such as "Have I missed something important?"
- Appeal to a third party (such as a government agency), including using a grievance procedure (a formal organizational procedure for dispute resolution), used extensively in unionized companies.
- Use negotiation and bargaining tactics, including creating a positive negotiating climate; listening first to investigate what the other side wants; allowing room for compromise but being reasonable; focusing on interests, not positions; making a last and final offer; and allowing for face-saving.

Deal effectively with difficult people, including the following:

- Take problems professionally, not personally.
- Give ample feedback.
- Listen and respond.
- Use tact and diplomacy in dealing with annoying behavior.
- Use nonhostile humor.

- Avoid creating a dependency on you.
- Reinforce civil behavior and good moods.

Limited ability to manage anger damages the careers and personal lives of many people. The ability to manage anger is part of emotional intelligence. In managing your own anger, remember that anger can be an energizing force, but if outbursts are not controlled your cardiac system can be damaged.

- Express your anger before it reaches a high intensity.
- As you are about to express your anger, slow down.

- Ask for feedback on how you deal with anger.
- In dealing with the anger of others, use the method of confront, contain (move the angry worker out of sight), and connect (ask open-ended questions to get at the real reason behind the outburst).

In choosing a tactic for resolving conflict, consider both your personality or style and the nature of the situation facing you. The situation includes such factors as the gravity of the conflict and the type of person you are facing. Also, think through whether you are so conflict-prone and angry that you are being ostracized from the group.

Questions for Discussion and Review

10.1 Why are person-to-person meetings often better for resolving conflict than sending written messages back and forth?

10.2 Imagine that after two weeks on a new job that you want, your boss begins to treat you in a bullying, intimidating manner. What would you say to that boss?

10.3 Many male managers who confer with a female worker in their offices leave the door open to avoid any charges of sexual harassment. Are these managers using good judgment, or are they being overly cautious?

10.4 Suppose one member of your work team of five people is passive-aggressive. How might that affect the productivity of the team?

10.5 Identify several occupations in which conflict resolution skills are particularly important.

10.6 Visualize a person taking the road test part of obtaining a driver's license. The candidate has done a poor job of parallel parking, and the examiner looks at him or her with a frown and says, "Not very impressive." How can this candidate make the best use of the tactic "disarming the opposition"?

10.7 How might a person use cognitive restructuring to help deal with the conflict of having received a below-average raise while expecting an above-average raise?

10.8 Which negotiating tactic are you the most likely to use the next time you face a situation in which negotiation is possible? Explain the reason for your choice.

10.9 Suppose a company has a "no jerks allowed" policy. Who should have the right to decide which people are "jerks"?

10.10 Suppose you thought the reason that a coworker was a difficult person was because he or she had a true personality disorder. Would you recommend to that person directly that he or she seek mental health treatment? Explain your reasoning.

Web Corner

Combating sexual harassment

www.nolo.com (Enter "combating sexual harassment" in the search slot, which provides several useful articles prepared by a legal staff.)

Controlling your anger

www.mayoclinic.org (Enter "controlling your anger" in the search slot.)

Dealing with difficult people

www.howdini.com (Enter "dealing with difficult people" in the search slot to see a video about the subject.)

INTERNET SKILL BUILDER

Conflict Resolution

Despite all the information available about resolving conflict in the workplace and in personal life, resolving conflict successfully remains difficult. Search the Internet to find a brief case history of successful conflict resolution in the workplace, in community life, or in personal life. Analyze the case to identify which approach or approaches to conflict resolution covered in this chapter were employed. Be prepared to share your findings with other class members.

Human Relations Application Exercises

Applying Human Relations Skill-Building Exercise 10-1

Win–Win Conflict Resolution

The owner of a large restaurant with a combined wait and kitchen staff of twenty people receives official word from the state that minimum wages for these workers will have to be increased by four dollars per hour. He and his accountant conclude that if he pays the new minimum wage, the restaurant will have to close because almost all profits will be wiped away, and he might have to operate at a loss. Assume that you, along with a few other teammates, do not want to lose your jobs, and you know that the restaurant owner does not want to close the business. Come up with a win–win solution to resolve this conflict of the restaurant owner wanting to stay in business, yet being forced into a situation of making no money or perhaps losing money.

Applying Human Relations Exercise 10-1

Reframing through Cognitive Restructuring

The following are examples of negative statements about others in the workplace. In the space provided, cognitively restructure (reframe) each comment in a positive way.

Negative: Nancy is getting on my nerves. It takes her two weeks longer than anyone else on the team to complete her input.

Positive:

Negative: Rob is so obsessed with sports he is hurting my productivity. Where does it say in the employee handbook that I have to spend thirty minutes on Monday listening to Rob's comments on his team's weekend performance? Doesn't he know that I have a job to do and that I just don't care about his team?

Positive:

Negative: My boss is driving me crazy. He's forever telling me what I did wrong and making suggestions for improvement. He makes me feel like I'm in elementary school.

Positive:

Human Relations Class Activity

Negotiating for a Bigger Raise

During good times and bad times, most people would like to receive a bigger raise than the one the company or immediate manager has decided to grant. But it is not widely known which negotiating tactic or tactics are likely to be the most effective. The purpose of this class activity is to conduct a survey of written comments about the best way to negotiate for a bigger raise than management probably had in store for you (assuming that you are not self-employed). In addition, the class will attempt to categorize the three most frequently occurring tactics. Following the text, the categories include "be the first to listen," "allow room for compromise, but be reasonable," "make a last and final offer," and so forth.

Method of data collection: Each class member sends an e-mail or text message to two experienced working adults in his or her network, perhaps including himself or herself. Ask the person to complete the following sentence:

The best way to negotiate for a bigger raise for yourself is to _____.

After collecting the responses, send them to a master e-mail or web page for your class.

Method of analysis: After every class member has taken the opportunity to review the master file, each student compiles (a) what he or she considers the three most frequently used approaches to asking for a bigger raise and (b) which negotiating and bargaining tactics these approaches best fit. Here is an example for clarification: Suppose one of the most frequently used approaches is for the person wanting a bigger raise to state something to this effect: "Give me a bigger raise or I'll look elsewhere." This approach might be classified as "Make a last and final offer."

The analysis by individuals is then sent back to the master e-mail or website to prepare a final summary of the results. The class might then hold a discussion as to any takeaway lessons from this exercise.

Human Relations Case Study 10–1

Diego Feels Sexually Harassed

Twenty-eight-year-old Diego is the director of warehousing and order fulfillment at a machine tool company that employs 400 people. He is proud to hold such an important position this early in his career, and he is also proud to be part of a company that builds machines that enable other companies to manufacture products. Diego reports to Sylvia, a fifty-four-year-old woman who is the director of manufacturing.

Diego respects Sylvia's knowledge of manufacturing, as well as most of her management and leadership skills. Yet Diego has come to find his relationship with Sylvia to be awkward. He thinks that Sylvia is getting too personal and a little unprofessional in her relationship with him. Diego started to document these incidents to help clarify his thinking, and to present his side of the story should it ever be needed:

- Sylvia often pinches my arm or shoulder during or after a conversation.
- I accepted a luncheon invitation of hers on January 15. We dined at a fine restaurant. She almost made no mention of work but kept asking me questions about my personal life, such as whether I had a girlfriend.

- On February 16, she told me for about the fifth time that she is a young widow, and that she is very lonely.
- When I arrived home on March 26, there was a FedEx box at my door. Inside the box was a luxurious sweater, with a note saying, "For you, nice guy. Hugs and kisses, Sylvia."
- On April 12, Sylvia sent me a text saying, "Have you ever wondered what your boss would look like in a Victoria's Secret outfit?"

Diego is worried about these episodes. He wants to maintain a good working relationship with Sylvia but has zero interest in getting romantically involved with her. Diego is even wondering if he should file a sexual harassment complaint against his boss.

Questions

10.11 What advice can you offer Diego about dealing with his relationship with Sylvia?

10.12 What advice can you offer Sylvia about dealing with her relationship with Diego?

10.13 To what extent do you think Diego is being sexually harassed? If you think Diego is a sexual harassment victim, what actions should he take?

Human Relations Role-Playing Exercise

Diego Deals with an Advance by Sylvia

One student plays the role of Diego, who is concerned that the attempts by Sylvia to develop a personal relationship with him have gone too far. He receives a text from Sylvia asking him to drop by her office ASAP. Another student plays

the role of Sylvia, who has a surprise for Diego when he meets her at his office. She says she has two front-row seats for an upcoming professional basketball game and then says casually, "If you could make it to the game with me, we could talk loads about the manufacturing challenges we are facing."

Human Relations Case Study 10–2

Ashley Uses Passion as an Excuse

Ashley works as a price estimator in the division of a large electronics company that manufactures and sells security systems to business firms. She holds a degree in electronics technology and has extensive knowledge about security systems. In recent years, her company has prospered because of heightened concerns about security. However, the market for security systems in her area has become saturated because virtually every firm has a security system. New business for the division comes mostly from getting companies to switch to her company, or from security system upgrades with existing customers.

As a result of the security business having stabilized in the geographic area, the atmosphere in the office has become tense. Workers have become less calm and pleasant than previously. Ashley, who has had a volatile personality since early childhood, has become tenser than her coworkers. During a recent proposal to upgrade the security system at a pharmaceutical warehouse, her company's sales representative accused Ashley of providing a cost estimate too high to clinch the deal. Ashley replied, "You are a sad (expletive) salesperson. You will tell a prospective client anything just to bag a sale. So long as you get your commission, you don't

care if the company loses money on the project." Ashley offered no apology for her outburst.

A week later at a department meeting to discuss goals for the year, Ashley said to the group, including the manager, "Goal setting for me is a dumb (expletive) idea. I will have no work to do unless this time-wasting, expense-account-hogging sales group gets off its butt and makes some sales."

Horrified, the manager said to Ashley, "You are being totally unprofessional. Please apologize to the sales group."

Ashley said, "Okay, maybe I shouldn't be so truthful in what I say. I can't help it. I'm a passionate person who wants results for the company."

Questions

10.14 To what extent does Ashley being "passionate" justify her expression of anger toward coworkers?

10.15 What do you recommend that Ashley's manager and coworkers do to make her a less difficult person in the office?

10.16 What career advice might you offer Ashley? (Or does she need any advice?)

Human Relations Role-Playing Exercise

Ashley Lashes Out

One student plays the role of the sales representative who accuses Ashley of providing a cost estimate too high to clinch the deal with the pharmaceutical warehouse. Another student plays the role of Ashley, who lashes back at the sales rep. The goal of the sales representative is to be treated in a more civil manner by Ashley. The rep also wants Ashley to get more into a problem-solving mode. Ashley, in turn, thinks that the rep is more interested in bagging a sale than making money for the company.

Observers rate the role-players for both exercises on two dimensions, using a scale of 1 to 5 from very poor to very good. One dimension is "effective use of human relations techniques." Focus on the rep's ability to effectively deal with Ashley's anger and hostility. The second dimension is "acting ability." A few observers might voluntarily provide feedback to the role players in terms of sharing their ratings and observations. The course instructor might also provide feedback.

REFERENCES

1. Original story created from facts and observations in the following sources: Minda Zetlin, "6 Powerful Reasons to Create a 'No Jerks Allowed' Rule in Your Workplace," *Inc.com*, www.inc.com, March 18, 2015, pp. 1–3; Scott Azzolina, "Connectria Launches No Jerks Allowed Store," www.connectria.com March 23, 2015, pp. 1–3; "Connectria Named to CRN's Top 100 Hosting and MSP 500," http:finance.yahoo.com, February 26, 2015, pp. 1–5; Justin Lee, "Connectria Hosting Rebrands Corporate Policy and Website," www.thewhir.com, June 28, 2013, pp. 1–2; "Connectria: The Jerk Free Company®," www.nonjerksasllowed.com, March 2015, pp. 1–3.

2. Research reported in Rachel Feintzeig, "When Co-Workers Don't Play Nice," *The Wall Street Journal*, August 28, 2013, p. B6.

3. Research reported in Susan G. Hauser, "The Degeneration of Decorum," *Workforce Management*, January 2011, pp. 16–21.

4. The examples, but not the interpretations, are from Julie Fawe, "Why Your Boss May Start Sweating the Small Stuff," *Time*, March 20, 2006, p. 80.

5. Tara C. Reich and M. Sandy Hershcovis, "Observing Workplace Incivility," *Journal of Applied Psychology*, January 2015, pp. 203–215.

6. Marlene Chism, "Drop the Curtain on Workplace Drama," *Communication Briefings*, June 2011, p. 5.

7. Siobhan Leftwich, "Hey, You Can't Say That! How to Cope with Verbally Abusive People," *Black Enterprise*, January 2006, p. 95.

8. Cindy Krischer Goodman, "Workplace Bullies Bearing Down," *McClatchy Newspapers*, www.detnews.com, July 11, 2011, pp. 1–2.

9. Frank Kalman, "Bullying, Bigotry and a Bill to Prevent Picking on All Personnel," *Workforce*, January 2014, pp. 22–23.

10. Diane A. Safer, "Passive-Aggressive Behavior," *NYU Langone Medical Center*, www.med.nyu, pp. 1–2. Copyright © 2012 EBSCO Publishing.

11. Angela Pirisi, "Teamwork: The Downside of Diversity," *Psychology Today*, November–December 1999, p. 18.

12. Jiatao Li and Donald C. Hambrick, "Factional Groups: A New Vantage on Demographic Faultlines, Conflict, and Disintegration in Work Teams," *Academy of Management Journal*, October 2005, pp. 794–813.

13. Norman B. Anderson, "Psychologists' Role in Work-Life Fit Is More Important than Ever," *Monitor on Psychology*, November 2012, p. 9.

14. Beth A. Livingston and Timothy A. Judge, "Emotional Responses to Work–Family Conflict: An Examination of Gender Role Orientation among Working Men and Women," *Journal of Applied Psychology*, January 2008, pp. 207–216.

15. Christoph Nohe et al., "The Chicken or the Egg? A Meta-Analysis of Panel Studies of the Relationship between Work-Family Conflict and Strain," *Journal of Applied Psychology*, March 2015, pp. 522–536.

16. Henry G. Jackson, "Flexible Workplaces: A Business Imperative," *HR Magazine*, October 2011, p. 10.

17. Ed Frauenheim, "Special Report: Flex Wok," *Workforce Management*, June 2013, p. 29; Medtronic, www.medtronic.com, p. 2. © 2015 Medtronic.

18. Mike Ramsey, "Not Your Father's Workplace," *HR Magazine*, November 2014, pp. 21–22.

19. Devasheesh P. Bhave, Amit Kramer, and Theresa M. Glomb, "Work-Family Conflict in Work Groups: Social Information Processing, Support, and Demographic Dissimilarity," *Journal of Applied Psychology*, January 2010, pp. 145–158.

20. Paul E. Spector et al., "Cross-National Differences in Relationships of Work Demands, Job Satisfaction, and Turnover Intentions with Work–Family Conflict," *Personnel Psychology*, Winter 2007, pp. 805–835.

21. Joseph G. Gryzwacz et al., "Work–Family Conflict: Experiences and Health Implications among Immigrant Latinos," *Journal of Applied Psychology*, July 2007, pp. 1119–1130.

22. Jennifer L. Berdhal and Karl Aquino, "Sexual Behavior at Work: Fun or Folly?" *Journal of Applied Psychology*, January 2009, p. 34.

23. Curt Levey, "Sexual Harassment's Legal Morass," *The Wall Street Journal*, November 7, 2011, p. A19.

24. Jennifer Berdahl, "The Sexual Harassment of Uppity Women," *Journal of Applied Psychology*, March 2007, pp. 425–437.

25. Chelsea R. Willness, Piers Steel, and Kibeom Lee, "A Meta-Analysis of the Antecedents and Consequences of Workplace Sexual Harassment," *Personnel Psychology*, Spring 2007, pp. 127–162; Christopher D. Nye, Bradley Brummel, and Fritz Drasgow, "Understanding Sexual Harassment Using Aggregate Construct Models," *Journal of Applied Psychology*, November 2014, pp. 1204–1221.

26. Domenick Carmagnola and R. Shane Kagan, "Racially Offensive Comments and Jokes Supported Harassment Claim," *HR Magazine*, September 2012, p. 99.

27. Jonathan A. Segal, "Stamping Out Harassment: Prevent Systemic Workplace Hostility," *HR Magazine*, June 2014, p. 111.

28. Lisa Mainiero and Kevin J. Jones, "Sexual Harassment versus Workplace Romance: Social Media Spillover and Textual Harassment in the Workplace," *Academy of Management Perspectives*, August 2013, p. 198.

29. Gergana Todorova, Julia B. Bear, and Laurie R. Weingart, "Can Conflict Be Energizing? A Study of Task Conflict, Positive Emotions, and Job Satisfaction," *Journal of Applied Psychology*, May 2014, pp. 451–467.

30. Hong Ren and Barbara Gray, "Repairing Relationship Conflict: How Violation Types and Culture Influence the Effectiveness of Restoration Rituals, *Academy of Management Review*, January 2009, p. 105.

31. "Workplace Violence," *Occupational Safety and Health Administration*, www.osha.gov, pp. 1–2, accessed March 31, 2015.

32. Sue Shellenbarger, "To Fight or Not to Fight? When to Pick Workplace Battles," *The Wall Street Journal*, December 17, 2014, pp. D1, D2.

33. "Complete These to Control Conflict," *Communication Briefings*, May 2010, p. 2.

34. "Conquer Conflict with This Technique," *Manager's Edge*, September 7, 2005, as adapted fom Maria Broomhower, "Dissolving Conflict through Reframing," http://www.conflict911.com.

35. Stephen P. Robbins and David A. DeCenzo, *Supervision Today!* 4th ed. (Upper Saddle River, NJ: Pearson Prentice Hall, 2004), p. 438.

36. Alison Wood Brooks, "Defusing Anxiety," *Executive Leadership*, September 2014, p. 7.

37. Kimberlyn Leary, Julianna Pillemer, and Michael Wheeler, "Negotiating with Emotion," *Harvard Business Review*, January–February 2013, pp. 96–103.

38. "To Agree or Disagree?" *Chicago Tribune Career Builder*, November 4, 2007, Section 6, p. 1.

39. Quoted in Brenda Goodman, "The Art of Negotiation," *Psychology Today*, January–February 2007, p. 65.

40. Deepak Malhotra and Max H. Bazerman, "Investigative Negotiation," *Harvard Business Review*, September 2007, pp. 72–78.

41. Peggy Drexler, "The Value of Office 'Disrupters,'" *The Wall Street Journal*, February 15–16, 2014, p. C3.

42. Robert Sutton, "How a Few Bad Apples Ruin Everything," *The Wall Street Journal*, October 24, 2011, p. R5.

43. The first two types are from a brochure for ETC w/Career Track, Boulder, CO.

44. Matt Vilano, "How to Shush the Office Magpie," *New York Times*, www.nytimes.com, accessed December 25, 2005.

45. John Grossman, "The Long Odds of Reforming an Employee Who Is a 'Destructive Hero,'" *New York Times*, www.nytimes.com, October 29, 2014, pp. 1–4.

46. Dru Scott, *Customer Satisfaction: The Other Half of Your Job* (Los Altos, CA: Crisp Publications, 1991), p. 16.

47. "Master Dealing with Difficult People," *Manager's Edge*, March 2009, p. 8.

48. Jane Michaels, "You Gotta Get Along to Get Ahead," *Woman's Day*, April 3, 1984, p. 58.

49. Lin Grensing-Pophal, "High-Maintenance Employees," *HR Magazine*, February 2001, p. 89.

50. Kathi Elster and Patricia Barnes, "Field Guide to Office Bullies," *Bloomberg Businessweek*, November 26–December 2, 2012, p. 95.

51. Cited in Melinda Beck, "When Anger Is an Illness," *The Wall Street Journal*, March 9, 2010, p. D6.

52. Joann Ellison Rodgers, "Go Forth in Anger," *Psychology Today*, March–April, 2014, p. 75.

53. Jeanne Whalen, "Angry Outbursts Really Do Hurt Your Health, Doctors Find," *The Wall Street Journal*, March 24, 2015, pp. D1, D4.

54. Beck, "When Anger Is an Illness," p. D6.

55. Kathleen Doheny, "It's a Mad, Mad Corporate World," *Working Woman*, April 2000, pp. 71–72.

56. "How to Handle an Angry Employee: 6 Tips," *Manager's Legal Bulletin*, January 1, 2015, p. 1.

CHAPTER **11**

Becoming an Effective Leader

Fotolia

Outline

Veteran fashion executive Paula Schneider took on one of the biggest leadership challenges of her career when in January 2015, she was appointed as the CEO of American Apparel. Based in Los Angeles, the company had become North America's largest apparel manufacturer. The company is also a distributor and retailer of casual clothing, operates 265 retail stores in twenty countries, and employs 10,000 employees. The company is a champion of equal rights for everyone, antibullying, and immigration reform

The leadership challenge for Schneider was that despite the brand being so well known, the company had lost $310 million in five years and was heavily in debt, and the former CEO faced multiple sexual harassment lawsuits. Another problem was that the company was perceived by many as being pornographic, particularly because of the semidressed young men and women featured in their advertising and in in-store poster photos.

Schneider needed to create order out of the chaos that existed in the company, without sacrificing the soul of the company, which includes a heavy reliance on normcore. (The term refers to unisex fashion trends, characterized by average-looking clothing.) Schneider saw her roles as "getting everybody in their lane and understanding that we have a common goal." Restoring order to the company also meant better forecasting of which fashions would be in demand, and getting the clothing produced on time and shipped to the stores.

Prior to joining American Apparel, Schneider was an experienced executive with a strong track record in design, merchandising, sales, manufacturing, finance, and human resources. As president of Warnaco, a company that makes swimsuits for Speedo and Calvin Klein, she upped profits 25 percent in two years.

Schneider is warm and likable. She is also a nuts-and-bolts leader, meaning that she believes in hiring people systematically, giving direction to people, and drawing up organization charts. She reaches out to employees to get their input on major decisions. One of Schneider's main goals at American Apparel is to tone down its oversexed image, yet keep the company edgy and committed to social causes.[1]

Learning Objectives ▶

After studying the information and doing the exercises in this chapter, you should be able to:

11.1 Identify personal traits and characteristics of effective leaders.

11.2 Identify behaviors and skills of effective leaders.

11.3 Understand the nature of leadership style and the importance of the leader adapting to the situation.

11.4 Know what needs to be done to get along well with group members.

11.5 Map out a tentative program for developing your leadership potential and skills.

11.6 Describe several challenges involved in being a first-time leader.

To become CEO of American Apparel, Schneider no doubt had many good leadership qualities, including the ability to provide structure and direction to others. **Leadership** is the process of bringing about positive changes and influencing others to achieve group goals, along with coordinating the pursuit of these goals.[2] The key words in understanding leadership are *change* and *influence*. A leader often challenges the status quo and brings about improvements. A leader also influences people to do things that they would not do otherwise, such as achieve higher performance. We therefore measure the effectiveness of leaders in terms of the results they attain, such as running a profitable medical clinic or a winning athletic team. In short, the leader makes a difference, particularly with respect to driving performance.[3]

The study of leadership warrants your attention because today people at all levels in the organization are expected to exert some leadership. Organizations seek people to exert leadership at all levels by giving many of them an opportunity to engage in such tasks as motivating others and setting goals. Even if your job title or job description does not include the mention of management responsibility, you will often be called on to be a temporary leader, such as being appointed the head of a committee or project. Our approach to the vast topic of

Leadership
the process of bringing about positive changes and influencing others to achieve worthwhile goals

leadership encompasses the attributes and behaviors of leaders, leadership style, getting along with subordinates, and developing your leadership potential.

► **Learning Objective 11.1** ►

Traits and Characteristics of Effective Leaders

A major thrust to understanding leaders and leadership is to recognize that effective leaders have the "right stuff." In other words, certain inner qualities contribute to leadership effectiveness in a wide variety of situations. **Leadership effectiveness** in this context means that the leader helps the group accomplish its objectives without neglecting satisfaction and morale. The characteristics that contribute to effectiveness depend somewhat on the situation. A supervisor in a meatpacking plant and one in an information technology department will need different combinations of personal characteristics. The situation includes such factors as the people being supervised, the job being performed, the company, and the cultural background of employees.

In the next several pages, we describe some of the more important traits and characteristics of leaders. Many of these traits and characteristics can be developed and refined. Figure 11-1 outlines the seven key traits.

PROACTIVITY

Leadership is often regarded as taking the initiative to accomplish something, and a key aspect of proactivity is initiative taking. A person with a **proactive personality** has a relatively stable tendency to bring about environmental change.[4] He or she makes things happen as part of the work role. As a result, the leader with a proactive personality is more likely to influence people and bring about constructive change. Proactivity is important for leaders at all levels and has a big impact in top-level positions. A study conducted in a

Leadership effectiveness
inner quality of a leader who helps the group accomplish its objectives without neglecting satisfaction and morale

Proactive personality
a person with a relatively stable tendency to bring about environmental change

FIGURE 11-1

SEVEN KEY LEADERSHIP TRAITS

Source: "SEVEN KEY LEADERSHIP TRAITS" by Andrew J. DuBrin.

large packaged-goods company found that proactive senior managers set higher goals for their units, which facilitated attaining more revenue. It was also found that when employees trusted their manager, high goals were more likely to lead to high sales.[5]

SELF-CONFIDENCE AND COURAGE

Self-confidence is necessary for leadership because it helps assure group members that activities are under control. The confidence centers on a belief that a person has the knowledge, skills, and abilities associated with leading others. Assume you are a manager in a company that is facing bankruptcy. You would probably hope that the CEO behaves in a confident, assured manner. The leader who functions best is self-confident enough to reassure others and to appear in control. But if the leader is so self-confident that he so she will not admit errors, listen to criticism, or ask for advice, that too creates problems.

Self-confidence often takes the form of the courage to face the challenges of taking prudent risks and taking initiative in general. Courage comes from the heart, as suggested by the French word for heart, *coeur*. Leaders must be able to face up to responsibility and be willing to put their reputations on the line, even if this means taking a course of action others would not advise.

Being confident and courageous does not exclude a leader from also displaying humility. People who are too confident and courageous will often neglect to welcome input from others or listen to criticism. Being too self-confident can also lead to the person to ignore potential problems, thinking, "I can handle whatever comes my way." A leader with an appropriate degree of humility will also admit to having made a mistake and is therefore willing to change course. For example, a leader who decided against hiring experienced store associates because they cost too much found that customer service suffered, resulting in lower sales. The leader then added a few more experienced store associates, and customer service again improved.

> As a leader, display a healthy level of humility. Humility is a different source of inner strength, meaning that you're open to input from others; admitting mistakes and most importantly, understanding your own limitations.
> —*Derica W. Rice*
> VP and CFO of Eli Lilly and Company. Quoted in Sonia Alleyne and Annya M. Lott, "The 100 Most Powerful Executives in Corporate America," *Black Enterprise*, February 2009, p. 116.

EMOTIONAL INTELLIGENCE

Emotional intelligence is considered a major contributor to leadership effectiveness because leadership involves so much working with the emotions and feelings of other people. A useful component of emotional intelligence for leaders is the ability to display warmth before attempting to influence others with knowledge and facts. A body language approach to projecting warmth is to lean forward in a friendly manner to signal interest and engagement.[6]

Here is an example of a leader applying emotional intelligence: Meg Whitman, the former eBay CEO, was appointed to the chief position at Hewlett-Packard Co., after the company had just fired its second top executive within a year and had faced several scandals. On her first day on the job, Whitman sought to reassure employees and calm the storm. She told employees at a town hall meeting that HP needed to earn back their trust and respect following her predecessor's turbulent eleven months.[7] A key point of this example is that Whitman could sense that company employees needed calming down at the moment more than they needed to hear about new business strategies or projected financial results.

TRUSTWORTHINESS AND CHARACTER

Being trustworthy or honest contributes to being an effective leader. An effective leader is supposed to *walk the talk*, thereby showing a consistency between deeds (walking) and words (talking). In this context, **trust** is defined as a person's confidence in another individual's intentions and motives and in the sincerity of that individual's words. Leaders must be trustworthy, and they must also trust the group members. Behaving in an ethical manner contributes to being perceived as trustworthy. For example, a store manager who

Trust
a person's confidence in another individual's intentions and motives and in the sincerity of that individual's words

Integrity
a consistency in the values a person professes and in the person's behavior

makes sure that store associates are fully compensated for their overtime work is likely to be trusted about other matters as well. **Integrity** is also related to trust because it refers to a consistency to the values a person professes and the person's behavior. For example, a team leader who says that feedback to employees is essential will show integrity when he or she provides feedback to employees regularly.

It takes a leader a long time to build trust, yet one brief incident of untrustworthy behavior can destroy it. An example of untrustworthy behavior would be using company money for private purposes or sexually harassing a team member. Leaders are usually allowed a fair share of honest mistakes. In contrast, dishonest mistakes quickly erode leadership effectiveness. Trust in company leadership also contributes to business success. According to surveys conducted by Linda Stewart, lower performing companies have lower levels of trust.[8]

Character
doing the right things despite outside pressures to do the opposite; includes leaving enduring marks that set one person apart from another; being moral

Having certain character traits contributes to being trustworthy and being perceived as a trustworthy person. **Character** in this context refers to doing the right things despite outside pressures to do the opposite. Being of good character also includes leaving enduring marks that set one apart from another.[9] To be of good character is to be moral. Three traits that contribute to good character are honesty, loyalty, and compassion.

Human Relations Self-Assessment Quiz 11-1 gives you the opportunity to think about your level of trustworthiness and honesty.

STRONG WORK MOTIVATION AND HIGH ENERGY

Leadership positions tend to be both physically and mentally demanding. A successful leader must be willing to work hard and long to achieve success. Many business leaders often work sixty-hour weeks, as do a large number of business owners. Many leaders appear to be driven by a need for self-fulfillment. Another fundamental reason strong work motivation is required for effectiveness is that a person has to be willing to accept the heavy responsibility that being a supervisor entails. As one department manager said, "Whoever thought being a manager would mean that I would have to fire a single parent who has three children to feed and clothe?"

Working long and hard contributes to a leader being able to lead by personal example, or being a good role model for subordinates. More specifically, if the leader shows good organizational citizenship behavior through extra-hard work, group members are likely to model this behavior.[10]

COGNITIVE SKILLS

Cognitive skills
problem-solving and intellectual skills

Cognitive skills, as well as personality, are important for leadership success. Problem-solving and intellectual skills are referred to collectively as **cognitive skills**. The term *cognition* refers to the mental process or faculty by which knowledge is gathered. To inspire people, bring about constructive changes, and solve problems creatively, leaders need to be mentally sharp. A synthesis of 151 different studies examining the relationship between intelligence and leadership performance found a slight positive relationship between the two variables. But when the leader's job emphasized playing an active role in making decisions about the work of the group (such as helping solve technical problems), intelligence showed a higher relationship with performance.[11]

A distinguishing cognitive skill of many successful leaders is to think strategically, or understand the big picture instead of focusing on the major purpose of the organizational unit.[12] A small-thinking team leader might invest considerable time in focusing on how the team can save a few dollars in such matters as turning off lights when away from the desk or cubicle. A more strategic thinking team leader would spend considerable time in thinking about how the team can contribute to the success of the business.

Human Relations Self-Assessment Quiz 11-1

The Trustworthiness and Honesty Checklist

Check whether each of the actions and attitudes in the list below are generally true or generally false. Responding to this checklist is difficult because you are required to be objective and honest about your trustworthiness.

Number	Statement about Trustworthiness	Generally True	Generally False
1.	I do my best to tell the truth even it makes me look bad or appear to be guilty.	_____	_____
2.	More than one person has referred to me as a pathological liar.	_____	_____
3.	When I agree to a date for completing a project, I am usually late anyway.	_____	_____
4.	I minimize telling people what they want to hear.	_____	_____
5.	My promises almost always match what I actually carry out.	_____	_____
6.	Many people have referred to me as being reliable.	_____	_____
7.	When (or if) I receive too much change from a restaurant server or a store cashier, I give the extra money back.	_____	_____
8.	I give out lots of false compliments just to make friends.	_____	_____
9.	I am undependable.	_____	_____
10.	I admit to my faults and attempt to make the necessary improvements.	_____	_____

Scoring and Interpretation:

Give yourself one point for the following answers: Generally True to questions 1, 4, 5, 6, 7, and 10; generally false to questions 2, 3, 8, and 9. If you scored 8 or more points, you are most likely a trustworthy person, and these types of attitudes and behaviors will be an asset to you as a leader. If you scored between 0 and 7, you are likely to be perceived as untrustworthy by many people. Being perceived as untrustworthy could make it difficult for you to be promoted to a leadership position or to be effective as a leader. A caution again is that it is quite difficult to be honest with oneself about one's honesty, so perhaps take this quiz again in one week.

Source: "The Trustworthiness and Honesty Checklist" by Andrew J. DuBrin.

A cognitive skill of major importance is *knowledge of the business,* or technical competence. An effective leader has to be technically or professionally competent in some discipline, particularly when leading a group of specialists. It is difficult for the leader to establish rapport with group members when he or she does not know what they are doing. A related damper on leadership effectiveness is when the group does not respect the leader's technical skill. Good practical intelligence (*street smarts*) is also part of an effective leader's intellectual makeup. A leader with high practical intelligence could size up a good opportunity without spending an extensive amount of time analyzing what could possibly go wrong. Knowledge of the business sometimes takes the form of a leader getting involved in small details about products, such as the CEO of an automotive company providing input about the design of door handles or buttons.

CHARISMA

An important quality for leaders at all levels is **charisma**, a type of charm and magnetism that inspires others and makes them loyal to the leader. Charismatic leaders are typically

Charisma
type of charm and magnetism that inspires others; important quality for leaders at all levels

assertive because they are eager to reach out to others and express their feelings and thoughts. Research indicates that many charismatic leaders have a moderate degree of narcissism, which enhances their distinctiveness.[13] Not every leader has to be charismatic, yet to be an effective leader you often need some degree of this personality quality. Being charismatic helps leaders form better relationships with workers, who might then work harder for them. A charismatic leader who inspires people therefore contributes to attaining results or being effective.

A leader's charisma is determined by the subjective perception of him or her by other people. Therefore, it is impossible for even the most effective leaders to inspire and motivate everyone. Even popular business leaders are disliked by some of their employees. For example, the late Steve Jobs, cofounder of Apple Inc., was regarded as charismatic and inspirational by many employees and company outsiders. Yet, he was also perceived to be arrogant, obnoxious, and tyrannical by many others who worked with him because of his explosive temper and second-guessing their decisions. Jobs admitted to being obnoxious on occasion, but he was so convinced that he was almost always right that such behavior was warranted. Charisma encompasses many traits and characteristics. Here we focus on vision, passion, enthusiasm, excitement, and humor.

Vision

Top-level leaders need a visual image of where the organization is headed and how it can get there. The person with vision can help the organization or group establish a vision. The progress of the organization depends on the executive having a vision, or an optimistic version of the future. Another essential part of having a vision is for leaders to make sure that others around them also understand the direction. Selling the vision is often attained by having vigorous discussions with many people about the proposed future.

Effective leaders project ideas and images that excite people and therefore inspire employees to do their best. Leadership positions of lesser responsibility also call for some vision. Each work group in a progressive company might be expected to form its own vision, such as "We will become the best accounts receivable group in the entire auto replacement parts industry."

Vision, like other leadership characteristics, usually has the biggest impact when combined with one or more other characteristics. Leaders need a vision of what needs to be accomplished, combined with the courage and execution skills to make it happen.

Passion, Enthusiasm, and Excitement

Charismatic leaders are passionate about their work and their group members. Part of the reason charismatic leaders can readily be passionate, enthusiastic, and excited is that they tend to be extraverted. The extraversion is most strongly associated with the type of charismatic leader who brings about major changes in the organization or an organizational unit.[14] Upon joining American Apparel, CEO Paula Schneider explained how much she loved the brand, and that her daughters had shopped at the stores for many years. Entrepreneurial leaders, who are often charismatic, are characteristically passionate about their enterprises and their product and services. Tim Talley, the founder of U-Lace (elasticized shoelaces), notes that the difference between entrepreneurs and most other imaginative people is not their ideas for new products. Rather, it is the desire to bring those ideas to life, regardless of any missteps along the way.[15]

Because of their contagious excitement, charismatic leaders stimulate group members. Workers respond positively to enthusiasm, especially because enthusiasm may be perceived as a reward for good performance. Enthusiasm is also effective because it helps build good relationships with group members. Spoken expressions of enthusiasm include such statements as "great job" and "I love it." The leader can express enthusiasm nonverbally through gestures, nonsexual touching, and so forth.

An important positive consequence of the passion and enthusiasm of the leader is that they contribute to the emotional well-being of group members. A study with forty-eight groups of firefighters found that firefighters under the command of a charismatic officer were happier than those groups reporting to supervisors low in charisma.[16]

The emotional state of followers (group members) is also significant for understanding how charisma works. When people are in a state of emotional arousal, such as facing a crisis or an unusual success, they are more ready to perceive a leader as being charismatic.[17] A historically important example is when Chrysler Corporation was facing bankruptcy in the late 1970s. Chairman Lee Iacocca spearheaded a federal government loan to save the company. In the process, the name Iacocca became almost synonymous with charisma. Chrysler employees, as well as suppliers and many others, were in dire need of a charismatic leader.

Sense of Humor

Humor is a component of charisma and a contributor to leadership effectiveness. Humor helps leaders influence people by reducing tension, relieving boredom, and defusing anger. The most effective form of humor by a leader is tied to the leadership situation. It is much less effective for the leader to tell rehearsed jokes. A key advantage of a witty, work-related comment is that it indicates mental alertness. A canned joke is much more likely to fall flat. An example of a witty comment by a leader that took place in relation to high involuntary employee turnover is "I know we are a great training ground for competitors, but we've got to stop our generosity."

A caution about charisma is that it is not entirely dependent on personal characteristics but also on what a person accomplishes. Achieving outstanding results may lead to being perceived as charismatic. An example would be if an almost-forgotten coach suddenly has an outstanding season and is then described as charismatic.

Although inherited characteristics, such as energy, contribute to charisma, most people can develop some charismatic qualities. Figure 11-2 presents suggestions for becoming more charismatic.

FIGURE 11-2 SUGGESTIONS FOR BECOMING MORE CHARISMATIC

Following are a number of suggestions for behaving charismatically, all based on characteristics and behaviors often found among charismatic leaders and other charismatic persons.

1. **Communicate a vision.** A charismatic leader offers an exciting image of where the organization is headed and how to get there. A vision is more than a forecast because it describes an ideal version of the future of an entire organization or an organizational unit, such as a department.
2. **Make frequent use of metaphors and analogies.** To inspire people, the charismatic leader uses colorful language and exciting metaphors and analogies. Develop metaphors to inspire people around you. To pick up the spirits of her maintenance group, a maintenance supervisor told the group, "We're a lot like the heating and cooling system in a house. A lot of people don't give us much thought, but without us, their lives would be very uncomfortable."
3. **Inspire trust and confidence.** Make your deeds consistent with your promises. Get people to believe in your competence by making your accomplishments known in a polite, tactful way.
4. **Be highly energetic and goal oriented.** Impress others with your energy and resourcefulness. To increase your energy supply, exercise frequently, eat well, and get ample rest. You can also add to an image of energy by raising and lowering your voice frequently and avoiding a slow pace.
5. **Be emotionally expressive and warm.** In dealing with team members, refer to your feelings at the time, such as "I'm excited because I know we are going to hit our year-end target by mid-October." Nonverbal emotional expressiveness, such as warm gestures and frequent (nonsexual) touching of group members, also exhibits charisma.
6. **Increase and decrease vocal pitch abruptly.** When addressing a group of people, stretch your voice to the lower and higher limits, thereby varying your pitch in a commanding way.
7. **Make ample use of true stories.** An excellent way of building rapport is to tell stories that deliver a message. Storytelling adds a touch of warmth to the teller and helps build connections among people who become familiar with the same story.

(Continued)

FIGURE 11-2 (*Continued*)

8. **Smile frequently, even if you are not in a happy mood.** A warm smile seems to indicate a confident, caring person, which contributes to a perception of charisma.

9. **Be candid.** Practice saying directly what you want rather than being indirect and evasive. If you want someone to help you, don't ask, "Are you busy?" Instead, ask, "Can you help me with a problem I'm having right now?"

10. **Make everybody you meet feel that he or she is quite important.** For example, at a company social gathering, shake the hand of or fist-bump every person you meet. Also, thank people frequently both orally and by written notes.

11. **Use nonverbal signals of self-confidence.** Practice having good posture. Minimize fidgeting, scratching, foot tapping, and speaking in a monotone. Walk at a rapid pace without appearing to be panicked. Dress fashionably without going to such an extreme that people notice your clothes more than they notice you. Shake hands firmly without creating pain, and make enough eye contact to notice the color of the other person's eyes. When you take that much trouble, you project care and concern.

12. **Take personal risks.** Charismatic leaders are typically risk takers, and risk taking adds to their charisma. Risks you might take include suggesting a bright but costly idea and recommending that a former felon be given a chance in your firm.

13. **Demonstrate to others that you are passionate about what you want others to accomplish.** Speak in an animated voice, use bold positive and negative facial expressions, and make ample use of gestures including making a fist.

Source: "SUGGESTIONS FOR BECOMING MORE CHARISMATIC" by Andrew J. DuBrin.

▶ **Learning Objective 11.2** ▶

Behaviors and Skills of Effective Leaders

The personal traits, skills, and characteristics just discussed help create the potential for effective leadership. A leader also has to *do* things that influence group members to achieve good performance. The behaviors or skills of leaders described next contribute to productivity and morale in most situations. Before studying the behaviors and skills of effective leaders, do Human Relations Self-Assessment Quiz 11-2. The exercise will help you understand how ready you are to assume a leadership role. Taking the quiz will also give you insight into the type of thinking that is characteristic of leaders.

PRACTICE STRONG ETHICS

Being trustworthy facilitates a leader practicing strong (or good) ethics, which is the study of moral obligation, or separating right from wrong. Ethics deals with doing the right thing by employees, customers, the environment, and the law. Practicing good ethics contributes to effective leadership for several reasons. Workers are more likely to trust an ethical leader than an unethical leader, which helps the leader gain the support of the group. Good ethics serves as a positive model for group members, thus strengthening the organization. Also, ethical leaders help group members avoid common ethical pitfalls in the workplace. Many of these unethical practices, as listed next, can lead to lawsuits against the company. Three examples are (a) lying or misrepresenting facts, (b) suppressing grievances and complaints, and (c) covering up accidents and failing to report health and safety standards.

To simplify a complex issue, an effective leader practices the Golden Rule: *Do unto others as you would have others do unto you.*

DIRECTION SETTING

Given that leaders are supposed to bring about change, they must point people in the right direction. Setting a direction includes the idea of establishing a vision for the organization or a smaller group. An example of direction setting by a top-level manager would be for the chief executive officer of a toy company to decide that the company should now

Human Relations Self-Assessment Quiz   11-2

Readiness for the Leadership Role

Indicate the extent to which you agree with each of the following statements. Use a scale of 1 to 5: (1) disagree strongly, (2) disagree, (3) neutral, (4) agree, (5) agree strongly. If you do not have leadership experience, imagine how you might react to the questions if you were a leader.

1.	It is enjoyable having people count on me for ideas and suggestions.	1	2	3	4	5
2.	It would be accurate to say that I have inspired other people.	1	2	3	4	5
3.	It's a good practice to ask people provocative questions about their work.	1	2	3	4	5
4.	It's easy for me to compliment others.	1	2	3	4	5
5.	I like to cheer up people even when my own spirits are down.	1	2	3	4	5
6.	What my team accomplishes is more important than my personal glory.	1	2	3	4	5
7.	Many people imitate my ideas.	1	2	3	4	5
8.	Building team spirit is important to me.	1	2	3	4	5
9.	I would enjoy coaching other members of the team.	1	2	3	4	5
10.	It is important to me to recognize others for their accomplishments.	1	2	3	4	5
11.	I would enjoy entertaining visitors to my firm even if it interfered with my completing a report.	1	2	3	4	5
12.	It would be fun for me to represent my team at gatherings outside our department.	1	2	3	4	5
13.	The problems of my teammates are my problems, too.	1	2	3	4	5
14.	Resolving conflict is an activity I enjoy.	1	2	3	4	5
15.	I would cooperate with another unit in the organization even if I disagreed with the position taken by its members.	1	2	3	4	5
16.	I am an idea generator on the job.	1	2	3	4	5
17.	It's fun for me to bargain whenever I have the opportunity.	1	2	3	4	5
18.	Team members listen to me when I speak.	1	2	3	4	5
19.	People have asked to me to assume the leadership of an activity several times in my life.	1	2	3	4	5
20.	I've always been a convincing person.	1	2	3	4	5

Total Score _____

Scoring and Interpretation:

Calculate your total score by adding the numbers circled. An interpretation of the scoring is as follows:

90–100	High readiness for the leadership role
60–89	Moderate readiness for the leadership role
40–59	Some uneasiness with the leadership role
39 or less	Low readiness for carrying out the leadership role

   If you are already a successful leader and you scored low on this questionnaire, ignore your score. If you scored surprisingly low and you are not yet a leader, or you are currently performing poorly as a leader, study the statements carefully. Consider changing your attitude or your behavior so that you can legitimately answer more of the questions with a 4 or 5. Studying the rest of this chapter will give you additional insight into the leader's role that may be helpful in your development as a leader.

Source: "Readiness for the Leadership Role" by Andrew J. DuBrin.

diversify into the bicycle business. A current example is that Jeff Immelt, the CEO of GE, has moved the company more into industrial products and away from consumer products and services, such as appliances and loans for vehicles. Direction setting by a team leader would include encouraging the group to strive toward error-free work from this point forward or to collaborate more with each other to form a true team.

HELP GROUP MEMBERS REACH GOALS AND ACHIEVE SATISFACTION

Effective leaders help group members in their efforts to achieve goals according to the path–goal theory of leadership.[18] In a sense, they smooth out the path to reaching goals. One important way to do this is to provide the necessary resources to group members. An important aspect of a leader's job is to ensure that subordinates have the proper tools, equipment, and human resources to accomplish their objectives.

Another way of helping group members achieve goals is to reduce frustrating barriers to getting work accomplished. A leader who helps group members cut through minor rules and regulations would be engaging in such behavior. In a factory, a supervisory leader has a responsibility to replace faulty equipment, make sure unsafe conditions are corrected, and see that troublesome employees are either rehabilitated or replaced.

Another important general set of actions characteristic of an effective leader is looking out for the satisfaction of the group. Small things sometimes mean a lot in terms of personal satisfaction. One office manager fought for better beverage facilities for her subordinates. Her thoughtfulness contributed immensely to job satisfaction among them. Giving group members emotional support is another effective way of improving worker satisfaction. An emotionally supportive leader would engage in activities such as listening to group members' problems and offering them encouragement and praise. Encouragement can also take the form of asking group members to identify and fix whatever is holding them back.[19] For example, with encouragement from her head nurse, a new nurse admitted that her knowledge of calculating fractions and percentages was not good enough for dispensing certain medications. The newcomer nurse then set about to study the arithmetic she needed. (Again, basic human relations skills contribute to leadership effectiveness.)

Current findings suggest that a powerful approach to enhancing job satisfaction is for leaders to help group members make progress in meaningful work. Even small steps forward boost the feeling that workers are on their way toward achieving something worthwhile.[20] Visualize a leader in a shipyard directing hundreds of workers toward building a cruise ship—a meaningful task for many people. To enhance satisfaction, the leader might ask frequently what he or she could do to help overcome any barriers to getting work done and might also keep workers informed about how well they were progressing against schedule.

SET HIGH EXPECTATIONS

Pygmalion effect
leader's ability to elevate worker performance by the simple method of expecting them to perform well; the manager's high expectations become a self-fulfilling prophecy

In addition to making expectations clear, it is important for leaders to set high expectations for group members. Effective leaders consistently hold group members to high standards of performance. The owner of a Kia dealership might say, "I see that our customer satisfaction ratings have been about 80 percent. From now on, I want to hear back from regional headquarters that our ratings average 95 percent. We'll figure out together how to do it." If you as a leader expect others to succeed, they are likely to live up to your expectations. This mysterious phenomenon has been labeled the **Pygmalion effect**. (In Chapter 3, we discussed the origins of this idea based on Greek mythology in relation to the Galatea effect, or setting high expectations for oneself.)

The point of the Pygmalion effect is that the leader can elevate performance by the simple method of expecting others to perform well. The manager's high expectations become a self-fulfilling prophecy. Why high expectations lead to high performance could be linked to self-confidence. As the leader expresses faith in the group members' abilities to perform well, they become more confident of their skills. Also, when a managerial leader believes that a group member will succeed, the manager communicates this belief without realizing it.

ENGAGE IN FACE TIME AND GIVE FREQUENT FEEDBACK ON PERFORMANCE

Discussions with several business executives reinforce a vital human relations aspect of leadership: No good substitute exists for being in the same room with a subordinate.[21] How much face time is necessary is difficult to estimate, but enough time must be established to feel that a personal relationship exists between the leader and the subordinate. One of the most meaningful and productive activities during face time is to provide the subordinate feedback on performance, with even a casual comment such as, "I notice that you just surpassed quota this morning."

Another reason that face time with group members is useful for leaders is that it encourages conversation. A conversation in this context is a frank exchange of ideas and information that can be helpful in solving work problems, similar to management by walking around. By talking with employees instead of simply issuing orders, the leader facilitates employee engagement because conversations with leaders help build a connection with the company.[22]

Effective leaders provide such feedback regularly, even if outside of face time. Often, a simple e-mail message can be effective feedback, such as, "Sue, the financial analysis you prepared for our client today was exactly the information he needed to purchase a $300,000 variable annuity. Thanks so much." Less effective leaders, in contrast, often avoid confrontation and give limited positive feedback. An exception is that some ineffective leaders become involved in many confrontations; they are masters at reprimanding people!

ASK THE RIGHT QUESTIONS

Leaders do not need to know all the answers. Instead, a major contribution can be to ask the right questions. Although being knowledgeable about the group task is important, there are many times when asking group members penetrating questions is more important. In today's complex and rapidly changing business environment, the collective intelligence of group members is needed to solve problems. Quite often, a leader does not have the answer to a problem, so asking questions is important. Also, asking questions rather than giving answers is the natural method of helping group members become better problem solvers. Here are sample questions a leader might ask group members to help them meet their challenges:

- What are you going to do differently to reduce by 50 percent the time it takes to fill a customer order?

- Can you figure out why the competition is outperforming us?

BE A SERVANT LEADER

A humanitarian approach to leadership is to be a **servant leader**, one who serves group members by working on their behalf to help them achieve their goals, not the leader's goals. The idea behind servant leadership, as developed by Robert K. Greenleaf, is that

Servant leader
one who serves group members by working on their behalf to help them achieve their goals, not the leader's goals

leadership stems naturally from a commitment to service. Serving others, including employees, customers, and the community, is the primary motivation for the servant leader. The servant leader is passionate about the people he or she works with and for.[23] Leaders who score high on the traits of agreeableness and extraversion are the more likely to be perceived as servant leaders.[24] Servant leadership encompasses many different acts, all designed to make life easier or better for group members. Several acts or aspects of servant leadership are mentioned next.

- **Humble servant.** A good starting point is for the leader to see himself or herself as a humble servant ("I'm here to serve you"). The leader downplays his or her ego to support the talents of others. Servant leaders also look for the opportunity to lend assistance directly to employees, such as a supermarket manager bagging groceries during an unanticipated rush of business. A servant leader would also provide the tools people needed to accomplish their work, such as fighting for enough money for the budget to purchase expensive new equipment.

- **Good listener.** A servant leader emphasizes listening to subordinates, because you cannot help people if you do not understand their concerns. Sam Palmisano, the former chairman and CEO of IBM, believes strongly in the listening aspect of servant leadership. He believes that effective leaders listen instead of making themselves the center of attention.[25]

- **Realistic about what can be done.** Although a servant leader is idealistic, he or she recognizes that one individual cannot accomplish everything. So the leader listens carefully to the array of problems facing group members and then concentrates on a few. As the head of a nurses' union told the group, "I know you are hurting in many ways. Yet I think that the work overload issue is the biggest one, so we will head into negotiations working on obtaining sensible workloads. After that, we will work on job security."

- **Development of subordinates.** Another important behavior of servant leaders is that they want subordinates to grow and succeed. They demonstrate genuine concern for the career growth of group members by providing emotional support and mentoring.[26] As a result, a servant leader is likely to be perceived as a good coach.

The evidence for the contribution of servant leadership is encouraging. A study of ninety-six employees working in seventy-one restaurants of the same chain found that servant leaders tended to set up a culture of prioritizing the needs of others above their own. The culture is formed as the workers model the servant leader approach. As a result, the restaurant workers performed better and the restaurants became more profitable.[27] A study with seventy-one teams in five banks indicated that servant leadership at the team level is associated with team effectiveness. Servant leadership was measured by team members rating their leader on a scale with items such as "My manager seems to care more about my success than his or her own." Team performance was measured by members of upper-level management rating the team's performance on a 1-to-7 scale.[28]

► **Learning Objective 11.3** ►

Leadership Style and Style Flexibility

Leadership style
a leader's characteristic way of behaving in a variety of situations

Understanding the traits, behaviors, skills, and attitudes of leaders points to another major approach to explaining leadership. A **leadership style** is a leader's characteristic way of behaving in a variety of situations. Here we look at the classic dimensions of leadership style, participative leadership, and style flexibility or adaptability.

THE CLASSIC DIMENSIONS OF CONSIDERATION AND INITIATING STRUCTURE

Leadership styles have been characterized in many ways, beginning in the 1950s with studies at the Ohio State University conducted with factory supervisors and military personnel.[29] Most approaches to leadership style are variations, refinements, and expansions of this pioneering work. The researchers asked group members to describe their supervisors by responding to questionnaires. Leaders were also asked to rate themselves on leadership dimensions (activities they performed). Two main dimensions were identified that accounted for the vast majority of a leader's activity: "consideration" and "initiating structure."

Consideration is the degree to which the leader creates an environment of emotional support, warmth, friendliness, and trust. Recent research conducted in eighty-one organizations around the world has also identified that supportive frontline leaders tend to be effective.[30] The leader creates this environment by being friendly and approachable and looking out for the welfare of the group. He or she also keeps the group informed about new developments and does small favors for the group, such as getting the break area repainted. In other words, the leader focuses on the human relations aspect of work.

Initiating structure means organizing and defining relationships in the group by engaging in such activities as assigning specific tasks, specifying procedures to be followed, scheduling work, and making expectations clear. In other words, the leader provides structure for the group and focuses on the work.

More recent research on consideration and initiating structure suggests that when employees receive the amount of consideration and structure they think the need, they tend to be more satisfied.[31] For example, Fred will be happier when he receives what he perceives to be the right amount of consideration from supervisor Seth. And when Paula receives the amount of structure and instructions from Seth, she will be satisfied.

Leaders have been categorized with respect to how much emphasis they place on the two dimensions of consideration and initiating structure. As implied by Figure 11-3, the two dimensions are not mutually exclusive. A leader can achieve high or low status on both dimensions. For example, an effective leader might contribute to high productivity yet still place considerable emphasis on warm human relationships. A leader's style could be characterized in terms of which one of the four boxes he or she fits into in Figure 11-3.

> **Consideration**
> the degree to which the leader creates an environment of emotional support, warmth, friendliness, and trust

> **Initiating structure**
> organizing and defining relationships in the group by engaging in such activities as assigning specific tasks, specifying procedures to be followed, scheduling work, and making expectations clear

THE PARTICIPATIVE (TEAM) LEADERSHIP STYLE

For the past forty years, the participative leadership style has received the most attention because this style enables the leader to share decisions with the group and capitalize on

FIGURE 11-3

FOUR COMBINATIONS OF INITIATING STRUCTURE AND CONSIDERATION

A leader's behavior can be described in terms of four different combinations of consideration and initiating structure. For example, a leader who emphasizes both giving group members a high degree of structure and paying close attention to their needs would be characterized as "high structure and high consideration," the upper right box.

Source: "FOUR COMBINATIONS OF INITIATING STRUCTURE AND CONSIDERATION" by Andrew J. DuBrin.

Participative leader

leader who shares decision-making authority with the group; motivates group members to work as a team toward high-level goals

the talents of the group. By definition, a **participative leader** shares decision-making authority with the group. At his or her best, the participative leader motivates group members to work as a team toward high-level goals. Encouraging employees to participate in making decisions is the major approach to empowerment. Participative leadership is often favored because workers are more willing to implement decisions when they are involved in formulating the decisions. Involving employees in decision making is also important because it facilitates collaboration. When group members participate in making decisions, they usually share knowledge with each other in order to make good decisions.[32] Participative leadership encompasses so many different behaviors that it is useful to divide it into three subtypes: consultative, consensus, and democratic.

Consultative Leaders

Consultative leader

leader who solicits opinions from the group before making a decision, yet does not feel obliged to accept the group's thinking; this type of leader makes it clear that he or she alone has the authority to make the final decisions

A **consultative leader** solicits opinions from the group before making a decision yet does not feel obliged to accept the group's thinking. Leaders of this type make it clear that they alone have authority to make the final decisions. A standard way to practice consultative leadership would be to call a group meeting and discuss an issue before making a decision. An example of a consultative leader is Tim Cook, the CEO of Apple Inc. He communicates freely with employees throughout the company and solicits their opinion. Cook sends many e-mails to Apple employees, whom he addresses as "Team."[33]

Consensus Leaders

Consensus leader

leader who encourages group discussion about an issue and then makes a decision that reflects the consensus of the group members

A **consensus leader** encourages group discussion about an issue and then makes a decision that reflects the consensus of the group members. Consensus-style leaders thus turn over more authority to the group than do consultative leaders. The consensus style sometimes results in long delays in decision making because every party involved has to agree. The problem of delays can be minimized if group members are given a deadline to reach an agreement.

Democratic Leaders

Democratic leader

leader who confers final authority on the group; functions as a collector of opinion and takes a vote before making a decision (in extreme cases, sometimes referred to as a free-rein leader)

A **democratic leader** confers final authority on the group. He or she functions as a collector of opinion and takes a vote before making a decision. The group usually achieves its goals when working under a democratic leader. Democratic leadership has more relevance for community activities than for most work settings.

When democratic leaders turn over too much authority to the group, they are referred to as laissez-faire (or free-rein) leaders. Laissez-faire leadership works only with highly motivated and self-sufficient individuals. Otherwise, group members left completely on their own may become dissatisfied and unproductive. A study with over 2,000 Norwegian workers found that workers managed with a laissez-faire style were likely to suffer from role ambiguity, or not knowing what is expected. As a result, these workers were stressed and anxious, often guessing if they were focusing on the correct tasks and establishing the right priorities.[34]

Autocratic leader

leader who attempts to retain most of the authority granted to the group; autocratic leaders make all the major decisions and assume subordinates will comply without question

In contrast to the participative leader is the leader/manager who makes decisions more independently. An **autocratic leader** attempts to retain most of the authority granted to the group. Autocratic leaders make all the major decisions and assume subordinates will comply without question. Leaders who use this style give minimum consideration to what group members are likely to think about an order or decision. Group members sometimes see an autocrat as rigid and demanding.

Although the autocratic leadership style is not in vogue, many successful leaders are autocratic. Among them are *turnaround managers,* those who specialize in turning around failing organizations or rescuing them from crises. The autocratic style generally works best in situations where decisions have to be made rapidly or when group opinion is not needed. Yet in most crises, such as earthquakes, product recalls, and workplace violence, the leader might consult with subordinates quickly, then make a rapid decision.

Human Relations Self-Assessment Quiz 11-3 gives you the opportunity to measure your present or potential leadership style.

Human Relations Self-Assessment Quiz 11-3

What Style of Leader Are You or Would You Be?

Answer the following questions, keeping in mind what you have done, or think you would do, regarding the scenarios and attitudes described.

Number		Mostly True	Mostly False
1.	I am more likely to take care of a high-impact assignment myself than turn it over to a group member.	_____	_____
2.	I would prefer the analytical aspects of a manager's job rather than working directly with group members.	_____	_____
3.	An important part of my approach to managing a group is to keep the members informed almost daily of any information that could affect their work.	_____	_____
4.	It's a good idea to give two people in the group the same problem and then choose what appears to be the best solution.	_____	_____
5.	It makes good sense for the leader or manager to stay somewhat aloof from the group, so he or she can make a tough decision when necessary.	_____	_____
6.	I look for opportunities to obtain group input before making a decision, even on straightforward issues.	_____	_____
7.	I would reverse a decision if several of the group members presented evidence that I was wrong.	_____	_____
8.	Differences of opinion in the work group are healthy.	_____	_____
9.	I think that an activity to build team spirit, such as the team fixing up a poor family's house on a Saturday, is an excellent investment of time.	_____	_____
10.	If my group were hiring a new member, I would like the person to be interviewed by the entire group.	_____	_____
11.	An effective team leader today uses e-mail, text messaging, or collaboration sites for about 98 percent of communication with team members.	_____	_____
12.	Some of the best ideas are likely to come from the group members rather than the manager.	_____	_____
13.	If our group were going to have a banquet, I would get input from each member on what type of food should be served.	_____	_____
14.	I have never seen a statue of a committee in a museum or park, so why bother making decisions by a committee if you want to be recognized?	_____	_____
15.	I dislike it intensely when a group member challenges my position on an issue.	_____	_____
16.	I typically explain to group members what method they should use to accomplish an assigned task.	_____	_____
17.	If I were out of the office for a week, most of the important work in the department would get accomplished anyway.	_____	_____
18.	Delegation of important tasks is something that is very difficult for me.	_____	_____
19.	When a group member comes to me with a problem, I tend to jump right in with a proposed solution.	_____	_____
20.	When a group member comes to me with a problem, I typically ask that person something such as "What alternative solutions have you thought of so far?"	_____	_____

(*continued*)

Scoring and Interpretation:

The answers in the participative/team-style leader direction are listed below. Give yourself one point for each answer that matches the scoring key.

1. Mostly false	8. Mostly true	15. Mostly false
2. Mostly false	9. Mostly true	16. Mostly false
3. Mostly true	10. Mostly true	17. Mostly true
4. Mostly false	11. Mostly false	18. Mostly false
5. Mostly false	12. Mostly true	19. Mostly false
6. Mostly true	13. Mostly true	20. Mostly true
7. Mostly true	14. Mostly false	

If your score is 15 or higher, you are most likely (or would be) a participative/team-style leader. If your score is 5 or lower, you are most likely (or would be) an authoritarian style leader.

Skill Development:

The quiz you just completed is also an opportunity for skill development. Review the twenty items and look for implied suggestions for engaging in participative leadership. For example, item 20 suggests that you encourage group members to work through their own solutions to problems. If your goal is to become an authoritarian leader (one who makes decisions primarily on his or her own), the items can also serve as useful guidelines. For example, item 19 suggests that an authoritarian leader looks first to solve problems for group members

Source: "What Style of Leader Are You or Would You Be?" by Andrew J. DuBrin.

STYLE FLEXIBILITY AND ADAPTABILITY

Although *leadership style* refers to a person's characteristic approach to dealing with leadership tasks, effective leaders adapt their style to fit the situation. For example, a leader might typically use a consensus style, yet when managing a crisis, he or she might become more authoritarian, giving subordinates directions in a hurry without waiting to achieve agreement among group members. Furthermore, an analysis of hundreds of studies suggests that leadership should be defined as "doing the right thing at the right time."[35] The leader makes the decision or chooses the action that fits the circumstances. An example might be transferring a valuable worker to a temporary assignment rather than firing him or her because of too little work for that individual at the moment.

Rule of Thumb for Style Flexibility

A rule of thumb for attaining style flexibility is to give considerable guidance, direction, and coaching to a worker who has low motivation or capability in terms of accomplishing the task. In contrast, give less guidance, direction, and coaching to a worker with high motivation and capability. The preceding is perhaps the best established finding about providing leadership to others.

Adapting Leadership Style to Cultural Values

Another way in which leadership style flexibility can be important is when it has to be adapted to fit cultural values. (Chapter 13 provides more information about these values.) Visualize an autocratic manager from France being sent to a Swedish subsidiary, where

Swedes strongly value democracy and status equality. The Swedish workers might not take too kindly to the French manager's autocratic behavior. And the French manager might dislike not being treated with great respect.

Techniques for a Leader Getting Along Well with Subordinates

◀ Learning Objective 11.4 ◀

The concepts already mentioned in this chapter, as well as other information you have studied about getting along with people, apply to a leader getting along well with subordinates. We spotlight this topic by presenting a well-documented theory about leader–member relationships, as well as a few illustrative principles.

THE LEADER–MEMBER EXCHANGE MODEL

One of the most popular leadership models focuses on the quality of leader–member relations. The **leader–member exchange (LMX) model** recognizes that leaders develop unique working relationships with each group member.[36] A leader might be considerate and compassionate toward one team member, yet rigid and unfeeling toward another. Leaders usually face constraints on their time, so the number of high-quality relationships they can form with subordinates is limited. As a result, leaders might be selective about which group members they develop close relationships with.[37] Figure 11-4 illustrates the fact that a leader might have different quality exchanges with different group members.

Leader–member exchange (LMX) model

leadership model that focuses on the quality of leader–member relations; recognizes that leaders develop unique working relationships with each group member

Samantha

Darlene

Boris

Jack

Samantha, I love the way you learn so quickly.

Darlene, do you think you are in the right career?

Boris, you have great potential to move up in the company.

Jack, can't you ever get things right the first time?

FIGURE 11-4

AN EXAMPLE OF THE LEADER–MEMBER EXCHANGE MODEL IN ACTION

The leader has a different quality of relationship with each member in the group.

Source: "AN EXAMPLE OF THE LEADER-EXCHANGE MODEL IN ACTION" by Andrew J. DuBrin.

Each relationship between the leader/manager and employees differs in quality. One subset of employees, the in-group, is given additional rewards, responsibility, and trust in exchange for their loyalty and performance. In contrast, another subset of employees (the out-group) is treated in accordance with a more formal understanding of the supervisor–subordinate relationship. The leader's first impression of a group member's competency heavily influences whether he or she becomes a member of the in-group or the out-group.

In-group members have attitudes and values similar to the leader and interact frequently with the leader. Out-group members have less in common with the leader and operate somewhat detached from the leader. The one-to-one relationships have a major influence on the subordinate's behavior in the group. Members of the in-group become part of a smoothly functioning team headed by the formal leader. Out-group members are less likely to experience good teamwork. Being a member of the in-group facilitates achieving high productivity and satisfaction. Out-group members receive less challenging assignments and are more likely to quit because of job dissatisfaction.[38]

The specific relevance of the LMX model for getting along with group members is that if the leader establishes good relationships with group members, higher productivity and satisfaction is likely to occur. Here is an example of how a good exchange between a leader and an employee can enhance productivity and satisfaction:

> Malcolm is a project manager at a company that makes modular (manufactured) housing. The project he heads is for the construction of patio homes for retirement communities. Beverly, one of the engineering technicians assigned to Malcolm's project, is just beginning her career. Malcolm recognizes that Beverly is talented and ambitious but that she needs guidance to get on the right track. He therefore sends her friendly text messages and e-mails from time to time commenting on her progress and the quality of her work. Malcolm also has positive face-to-face interactions with Beverly, offering her encouragement and suggestions. For example, one time Malcolm said to Beverly, "I know that you like perfection but we can't incorporate features into our patio homes that will jack up the price too high."

Because of the encouragement and mentoring Beverly received from Malcolm, she worked extra hard and felt as if she was growing professionally. As she told the company HR rep, "I'm so glad I joined this company. With Malcolm as my project manager, I'm growing professionally every day."

As with most topics in human relations, when you dig into the research about LMX, there are subtle points to be discovered. A study of LMX with 375 commercial bank employees in eighty-two teams found that when workers had positive exchanges with their boss, they performed better as rated by customers. However, when there was considerable variation in the quality of leader–member relations, team coordination was disrupted and performance suffered a little.[39] (When the boss has "pets" teamwork can suffer.)

SUGGESTIONS FOR ATTAINING GOOD RELATIONSHIPS WITH SUBORDINATES

A key part of leadership is forming good relationships with people, so getting along with subordinates is essential. If you are a leader and your subordinates do not like you, it will be difficult for the group to achieve high productivity and satisfaction. A sampling follows of time-tested principles for attaining good relationships with subordinates.

1. Solicit opinions before taking action. In the spirit of participative leadership, find out what group members think of your potential action, even on relatively small matters such as selecting a restaurant for a department banquet. Subordinates will be pleased that their input matters, and they will be more cooperative in implementing your decision. Listening to opinions is an essential tool of the participative leader or manager, and it is also an excellent way of cultivating subordinates. To be listened to is to be respected and considered important.

2. **Ask how you can make their jobs better.**   An excellent relationship builder with subordinates is playing an active role in facilitating the jobs of subordinates running more smoothly. Toward this end, ask such questions as "What drives you the craziest about the processes around here?" and "If you could have a fantasy tool that made your job easier, what would it be?"[40]

3. **Give out recognition.**   Most people are recognition-deprived, so being a boss who recognizes the contributions of subordinates goes a long way toward building positive relationships with them. Effective forms of recognition include thank-you notes and face-to-face comments, such as "You really helped us out in a jam, and I appreciate it." You will learn more about recognition in Chapter 12, on motivation.

4. **Be courteous.**   Many managers are rude to subordinates, so showing courtesy will help you build relationships with your direct reports. Being courteous to subordinates would include such acts as responding quickly to e-mail messages, returning phone calls, not multitasking when subordinates are talking to you, not keeping people waiting for you, and not belittling them.

5. **Look for opportunities to say yes to requests.**   Repeated refusals on requests can be demoralizing and demotivating for employees, especially when the request is feasible. Some requests, such as asking for a cash bar in the lunchroom, must be refused. But look for opportunities to say yes. A useful guideline is when a group member makes a request, avoid automatically replying, "We cannot do that." Instead, ask yourself, "Can we do that?"[41]

6. **Provide leader political support.**   A comprehensive way of establishing good relationships with subordinates is to use your influence to help the group accomplish its tasks, including getting the resources its needs. **Leader political support** refers to political acts and influence techniques by the leader to provide followers with the resources they need to accomplish individual, group, or organizational objectives.[42] (This idea is included in the path–goal theory mentioned above.) Assume that Cheryl is the manager of a distribution facility that badly needs a new mechanical system for moving goods through the warehouse, and that budgets are tight. Cheryl uses her contacts with the vice president of manufacturing to free up funds for the system, thereby exercising leader political support.

Another aspect of political support is to bring forth the demands of group members to higher management and then fight for these demands, such as needing new equipment. Carrying out this principle enhances your stature among group members and helps you win their support.

Leader political support
political acts and influence techniques used by the leader to provide followers with the resources they need to accomplish individual, group, or organizational objectives

Developing Your Leadership Potential

◀ Learning Objective 11.5 ◀

Developing your leadership potential is possible because both nature and nurture contribute to leadership effectiveness. Just as in playing music or sports, you need certain talents to begin with, such as good eye–hand coordination, but with practice, you can improve. Almost anything you do to improve your individual effectiveness will have some impact on your ability to lead others. If you strengthen your self-confidence, improve your memory for names, study this text carefully, read studies about leadership, or improve your physical fitness (giving you more energy), you stand a good chance of improving your leadership potential. Seven modes of advancement might be kept in mind if you are seeking to improve your leadership potential:

1. **General education and specific training.**   Almost any program of career training or education can be considered a program of leadership development. Courses in human relations, management, or applied psychology have obvious relevance for someone currently occupying or aspiring to a leadership position. Many of today's leaders in profit

and nonprofit organizations hold formal degrees in business. Specific training programs will also help you improve your leadership potential. Among them might be skill development programs in interviewing, employee selection, listening, cross-cultural training, budgeting, planning, improving work habits, resolving conflict, and communication skills. After acquiring knowledge through study, you then put the knowledge into practice as a leader.

The late leadership scholar Warren G. Bennis emphasized that becoming a leader involves continual learning, development, and the reinvention of the self.[43] "Reinvention" in this sense could mean rethinking your assumptions about people or even changing careers into one you found that was a better fit with your values.

2. Leadership development programs. A focused way of improving your leadership potential is to attend development programs designed specifically to improve your ability to lead others and develop self-confidence. A popular type of leadership development program, called *offsite training*, includes such far-reaching activities as rope climbing, preparing gourmet meals, and performing standup comedy. We return to this topic in Chapter 12 about motivation and team building.

3. Acquire broad experience. Because leadership varies somewhat with the situation, a sound approach to improving leadership effectiveness is to attempt to gain supervisory experience in different settings. On-the-job experience remains a helpful way of improving leadership effectiveness, yet it can reach the point of diminishing returns.[44] Obtaining fresh ideas and insights from the study of leadership therefore remains important.

A person who wants to become an executive is well advised to gain supervisory experience in at least two different organizational functions, such as customer service and finance. Support for this viewpoint can be found from the work of Personnel Decisions International, a firm that specializes in leadership development. A long-term study found that first-level supervisors are more likely to succeed if they have cross-functional experience (having worked in different departments).[45]

First-level supervisory jobs are an invaluable starting point for developing your leadership potential. It takes considerable skill to manage a fast-food restaurant effectively or to direct a public playground during the summer. First-level supervisors frequently face situations in which subordinates are poorly trained, poorly paid, and not well motivated to achieve company objectives. Taking a turn as a team leader is also valuable experience for developing leadership skills.

4. Modeling effective leaders. Carefully observe a capable leader in action and incorporate some of his or her approaches into your own behavior. You may not be able to or want to become that person's clone, but you can model (imitate) what the person does. For instance, most inexperienced leaders have a difficult time confronting others with bad news. Observe a good confronter handle the situation and try his or her approach the next time you have some unfavorable news to deliver. The biography or autobiography of a leader whom you admire is another source of ideas for modeling an effective leader.

5. Obtain feedback on your leadership performance and behavior. The several approaches described in Chapter 1 for learning about the self are also applicable for leadership development. However, it is also important to receive feedback directly related to leadership performance and behavior, such as asking an observer how well you motivated others during a meeting. Many organizations help leaders develop by providing them systematic feedback from several raters, such as subordinates, superiors, and customers. The ratings are anonymous, which enhances objectivity but also invites cruel and thoughtless comments. A widely used feedback instrument of this type is the **360-degree survey**, designed to gather information about how a leader can be more effective. Such feedback can be helpful in suggesting which traits and behaviors you particularly need to develop.

360-degree survey
a feedback instrument designed to gather information about how a leader can be more effective

6. Self-development of leadership characteristics and behavior. Study the leadership characteristics and behaviors described in this chapter. As a starting point, identify several attributes you think you could strengthen within yourself, given some self-determination. For example, you might decide that with effort, you could improve your passion and enthusiasm. You might also believe that you could be more emotionally supportive of others.

7. Practice self-leadership. One of the most effective ways of becoming a leader is to begin by leading yourself, or practicing **self-leadership**. According to this concept, workers are capable of leading themselves to some extent. You influence yourself without waiting for an external leader to lead you, much like taking the initiative to accomplish something worthwhile or being a good organizational citizen. Charles C. Manz, a professor of business leadership at the University of Massachusetts, says that self-leadership extends as far as setting your own standards and objectives. Recognize, however, that you still have to accomplish what your leader wants you to accomplish, but you can go beyond the minimum required in your job.[46]

> **Self-leadership**
> leading oneself; influencing oneself without waiting for an external leader to lead; all organizational members are capable of leading themselves to some extent

Key Challenges of Being a First-Time Leader

◀ Learning Objective 11.6 ◀

Another way of preparing for becoming a leader for the first time is to think through some of the inevitable challenges that the first-time leader faces, as described next.

1. Uncertainty about how much time to spend leading versus doing individual tasks. Leaders at all levels spend some time as individual contributors, including preparing budgets, thinking of ideas for new products, and making financial deals. As a new leader, you have to work with your manager and perhaps your direct reports to find the right balance between doing and leading.

2. Overcoming the resentment of the people in the group who wanted your leadership position. If you are selected from among the group to be the new leader, you will have to deal with the resentment and envy of several direct reports who wanted your position. It can be helpful to deal openly with the issue with such statements as "I know that other people would be equally qualified to be the leader of the group. Yet management has chosen me for this position, at least for now. I respect your expertise and I need your contribution. I also want your respect for me in my job as the chosen leader."

3. Building relationships and fostering teamwork quickly enough. As a new leader, a high priority is to build constructive relationships with subordinates as quickly as possible, using many of the techniques described earlier in this chapter. Several direct reports who were your former coworkers may attempt to manipulate you and take advantage of prior friendships to receive special treatment. It is essential to build a professional, merit-based team climate as soon as possible. In the words of career coach Aya Fubara Eneli, "Friendships work best between equals. If you were already friends with some of the staff, expect those relationships to change. It's difficult to be a friend while giving orders and judging performance."[47]

4. Overcoming the need to be liked by everybody. The most admired leaders at every level are rarely liked by everybody. By the nature of their roles, leaders make decisions that not everybody agrees with. The changes you bring about may hurt the feelings of some people and jeopardize their positions. Your role is to establish and implement goals that will result in the greatest good.

Concept Review and Reinforcement

Summary and Review

Leadership is the process of bringing about positive changes, influencing others to achieve worthwhile goals, and coordinating the pursuit of these goals. Effective leadership is needed at the top of organizations, but supervisors and team leaders also need to provide effective leadership. Effective leaders have the "right stuff." Certain traits and characteristics contribute to leadership effectiveness in many situations. Among them are the following:

- Proactivity
- Self-confidence and courage
- Emotional intelligence
- Trustworthiness and character
- Strong work motivation and high energy
- Cognitive skills and openness to experience
- Charisma (vision, passion, enthusiasm, excitement, and humor)

Behaviors and skills of an effective leader (one who maintains high productivity and morale) include these:

- Practicing strong ethics
- Direction setting
- Helping group members reach goals and achieve satisfaction
- Setting high expectations (the Pygmalion effect)
- Engaging in face time and giving frequent feedback on performance
- Asking the right questions
- Being a servant leader

Leadership style is a leader's characteristic way of behaving in a variety of situations. Most approaches to understanding leadership style stem from the two dimensions of consideration and initiating structure. Leaders can be characterized with respect to how much emphasis they place on these two dimensions.

Participative leaders share decisions with the group and capitalize on the talents of the group. The subtypes of participative leadership are consultative, consensus, and democratic. In contrast to the participative leader is the autocratic leader/manager who makes decisions more independently.

Effective leaders tend to adapt their style to the situation, such as a consensus leader becoming authoritarian during a crisis. The effective leader does the right thing at the right time. In general, workers with low motivation and capability need more guidance, direction, and coaching. Cultural values, such as a belief in collectivism, can influence which style is best.

According to the leader–member exchange (LMX) model, leaders develop unique working relationships with each group member. If the leader establishes good relationships with group members, higher productivity and satisfaction are likely to occur.

Time-tested principles for attaining good relationships with subordinates include:

- Soliciting opinions before taking action
- Asking how you can make their jobs better
- Giving out recognition
- Being courteous

- Looking for opportunities to say yes to requests
- Providing leader political support

Many activities in life can in some way contribute to the development of a person's leadership potential. Seven recommended avenues for improving your leadership potential or leadership skills are as follows:

- General education and specific training
- Leadership development programs
- Acquiring broad experience
- Modeling effective leaders
- Obtaining feedback on your leadership performance and behavior

- Self-developing leadership characteristics and behavior
- Practicing self-leadership

First-time leaders face key challenges, such as:

- Uncertainty about how much time to spend on leading versus doing individual tasks
- Overcoming the resentment of the people in the group who wanted your leadership position
- Building relationships and fostering teamwork quickly enough
- Overcoming the need to be liked by everybody

Questions for Discussion and Review

11.1 Provide an example of something a leader motivated or inspired you to do that you would not have done without his or her presence.

11.2 If cognitive skills are really important for being an effective leader, what can a future leader do to enhance his or her cognitive skills?

11.3 Why does being charismatic often make a leader more effective?

11.4 Create a vision for a large company you admire.

11.5 Provide an example of how you might use the Pygmalion effect in working with subordinates or with a child you have or might have.

11.6 In what way is the professor in this course a *servant leader* in his or her relationship with the students in the class?

11.7 How might being close friends with several members of the group you are leading interfere with your ability to lead that group?

11.8 Give an example of a specific action taken by a present or former boss that helped cultivate good relationships with subordinates. Also, identify an action that hurt relationships with subordinates.

11.9 In what way might being a playground supervisor or a shift supervisor in a fast-food restaurant help a person prepare for a high-level leadership position in the future?

11.10 In what way does your program of study contribute to your development as a leader?

Web Corner

Overview of leadership
www.ccl.org

Leadership development programs
www.academyleadership.com

Servant leadership
http://greenleaf.org

INTERNET SKILL BUILDER

Charisma Development

Visit www.core-edge.com to search for additional ideas for charisma development. Go to the section on charisma, and read a couple of case histories to uncover ideas you might try to enhance your charisma. Watch the video "A Conversation on Charisma." After digging through core-edge.com, list two concrete ideas you might implement to enhance your charisma.

Also answer these questions: (a) What is charismatology? and (b) What is your rating of the charisma of the presenter in the video?

Developing Your
Human Relations Skills

Human Relations Application Exercises

Applying Human Relations Exercise 11-1

Developing Your Charisma

An effective way of developing your leadership potential is to project a more charismatic image, even if you do not truly make over your personality. If you appear more charismatic to others, they are more likely to respond to your leadership. Also, if you project a more charismatic image, you are more likely to be nominated for leadership positions and assignments. Following is a checklist of the suggestions for becoming more charismatic as presented in Figure 11-2. As you go through the list, select two or three ideas that you would be willing to try in the next two weeks. Note that some of the suggestions are much easier than others to implement in the short range.

Charisma Suggestions (see Figure 11-2 for explanations)	Yes, I Will Try It
1. Communicate a vision.	❏
2. Make frequent use of metaphors and analogies.	❏
3. Inspire trust and confidence.	❏
4. Be highly energetic and goal oriented.	❏
5. Be emotionally expressive and warm.	❏
6. Make ample use of true stories.	❏
7. Smile frequently, even if not in a happy mood.	❏
8. Be candid.	❏
9. Make everybody you meet feel that he or she is important.	❏
10. Multiply the effectiveness of your handshake.	❏
11. Use nonverbal signals of self-confidence.	❏
12. Take personal risks.	❏
13. Demonstrate that you are passionate about what you want to accomplish.	❏

Now that you have made your choice of suggestions, try them out with other people, including students, athletic team members, coworkers, or members of a community group. After your experience, answer the following questions:

1. How did people react to me when I attempted to be more charismatic?
2. How can I use this approach more effectively next time? (How should I fine-tune my approach?)
3. Are these approaches to charisma enhancement making any contribution to my development as a leader?

Applying Human Relations Exercise 11-2

My Personal Leadership Journal

A potentially important tool in your development as a leader is to maintain a journal or diary of your leadership experiences. Make a journal entry within twenty-four hours after you carried out a leadership action of any kind, or failed to do so when the opportunity arose. You will therefore have entries dealing with leadership opportunities both capitalized on and missed. An example: "A few of my neighbors were complaining about trash flying around the neighborhood on trash pick-up days, particularly when the wind was strong. I took the initiative to send e-mails and flyers to neighborhood residents discussing what could be done about the problem. I suggested that people pack their recycling boxes more tightly. I also suggested ever so politely that people should pick up their own flying trash. Soon the problem nearly disappeared."

Also include in your journal such entries as comments you receive on your leadership ability, leadership traits that you appear to be developing, and leadership ideas about which you learn. Also, keep a list of leadership articles and books you intend to read. You might also want to record observations about significant acts of leadership or leadership blunders that you have observed in others, either firsthand or through the media.

Review your journal monthly, and make note of any progress you think you have made in developing your leadership skills. Also consider preparing a graph of your progress in developing leadership skills. The vertical axis can represent skill level on a 1-to-100 scale, and the horizontal axis might be divided into time intervals, such as calendar quarters.

Applying Human Relations Exercise 11-3

Analyzing the Leadership Effectiveness of a Past or Present Supervisor

Visualize a current supervisor or one to whom you reported in the past. Analyze his or her approach to leadership based on your own observations and perhaps comments you heard from coworkers. Consider also the results the leader achieved. Your evaluation should be based on the supervisor's traits and characteristics, including charisma, leadership style, and ability to get along with group members. Conclude your brief report with several suggestions for how the supervisor in question might become a more effective leader. Share your evaluation with your supervisor if you think it is positive and constructive.

Human Relations Class Activity

"Some Good Leadership Advice I Received"

Here is an opportunity for you to obtain some potentially useful information for your present or future career as a leader. Each class member contacts an experienced person in his or her network to get one brief piece of advice about his or her leadership development. Among the potential experienced people are business executives, business owners, human resource professionals, public officials, former instructors, athletic coaches, parents, or other family members. You might contact the person through an e-mail, text message, phone call, or social networking site. Try an approach of this nature: "I'm doing a class activity for a unit on leadership in a human relations course. Would you be willing to give me about two sentences of advice for helping me become a leader or develop my present leadership skills?" (You will most likely encounter a strong willingness to help by almost anybody you contact.)

Record the advice you receive in written form. During class, each student, or a number of volunteers, will make about a one-minute presentation sharing the leadership advice received. After all the presentations, hold a class discussion centering on these points:

- What was the most frequent advice offered?
- What was the most useful advice offered?
- What advice would most likely backfire?
- How helpful for my leadership development was this activity?

Human Relations Case Study 11–1

Firing up the Bus Drivers at Interstate Transport

Kristen is the southeast regional manager for Interstate Transport, an interstate bus service. The company has been thriving as more and more travelers seek to avoid the high cost of air travel or traveling by a personal vehicle. Rational or not, the fear of potential airplane crashes has also boosted the number of bus passengers. Kristen is the leader for the bus drivers, terminal employees, and bus maintenance workers.

Kristen is satisfied with the profitability of her region, yet she, as well as top-level management in the company, thinks she could do better. Dressed in disguise, Kristen takes the occasional trip on a bus, and she also pays a few "mystery passengers" to take a bus trip and make observations about the service. A conclusion Kristen comes to about these trip observations is that the bus drivers are not excited about their work.

She observes that some of the drivers engage the passengers and act interested in the welfare of passengers. For example, driver Billy Joe announces at the beginning of a trip, "I am here to drive you safely and on time. I want all

you passengers to respect each other on this coach, and to be as polite as possible." Driver Ruby often tells her passengers, "I thank you all for being on this bus. We will get you where you want to be on time, and safely. I also want to thank you all for helping fight highway congestion and saving fuel by taking the bus." In contrast, many of the bus drivers make only the minimum number of comments necessary and do so with an emotional flatness.

Kristen then reflects, "If some of the drivers are not inspired, it could be my fault. I should exercise inspirational leadership, but it won't be easy. We are already paying drivers all we can afford. Maybe every driver should have a plastic vision statement that could be placed on a key chain. I will come up with a plan of inspiration by next week."

Questions

11.11 What leadership technique do you recommend that Kristen use to fire up the bus drivers?

11.12 What do you think of a key-chain vision statement?

Kristen Attempts to Inspire a Group of Bus Drivers

One student plays the role of Kristen, who conducts a meeting with a sample of five bus drivers, all of whom are paid their regular hourly rate during the meeting. Kristen tries her best to be an inspirational leader. Five other students play the roles of the drivers, not all of whom feel they need to be inspired. For example, one of the drivers whispers to another, "What's wrong with this 'girl'? Does she think we're not doing our job?"

What Kind of Leader Is Danny Wong?

Danny Wong, a claims supervisor at an insurance company, recently took a leadership development course sponsored by his company. The major thrust of the course was to teach supervisors how to implement participative leadership and management. The course leader said, "Today, almost all employees want to get involved. They want a say in important decisions affecting them. The era of the know-it-all manager has long passed."

Wong was mildly skeptical about the course leader's universal endorsement of participative leadership. Yet he decided that if this is what the company wanted, he would adopt a more participative style. Six months after the leadership development program was completed, the human resources department attempted to evaluate its impact. One part of the program evaluation was to speak to employees about how the course influenced their boss's approach to supervision.

Rick Alluto, the company training director, conducted several of the interviews with employees. He spoke first with Amy Green, a claims analyst who reported to Danny. Rick told Amy that her answers would be confidential. He said that the purpose of these interviews was to evaluate the effectiveness of the leadership training program, not to evaluate the supervisor.

Amy responded, "It would be okay with me if Danny did hear my comments. I have nothing very critical to say. I think the leadership training program was useful. Danny is a much better manager now than in the past. He's much more aware that the people in his group have something useful to contribute. Danny asks our opinion on many issues.

"I'll give you an example. Danny was going to order a new office copier and printer. In the past, he might have just ordered a new copier and printer and told us when it was going to be delivered. Instead, Danny held three meetings to decide on which brand of copier and printer would best meet our needs. Three of us chose a copier that everybody in the office, including the new office assistant, agreed would be best."

Rick then spoke to Kent Nelson, another claims analyst reporting to Danny. Kent said he appreciated the fact that the interviews would be confidential. However, he hoped that the drift of his comments would get back to Danny so long as he was not identified. Kent offered this evaluation:

"Danny has gone downhill as a manager ever since he took your leadership development program. He has been lazier than ever. Danny always did have a tendency to pass off too much work to employees. Now, he's gone overboard. The recent purchase of the photocopier and printer is a good example. Too many people spent too much time deciding on which machine to purchase. To make matters worse, a committee of three people was formed to research the possibilities. It seems to me that we can make better use of working time.

"If Danny keeps up this approach to supervision much longer, he won't have a job. We will be doing all his work. How can you justify a supervisor's salary if other people are doing his work?"

Rick thought to himself, "I wonder if Amy and Kent are talking about the same supervisor. Their comments make it difficult for me to know whether the development program is getting the job done."

Questions

11.13 How do you explain the different perceptions of Amy and Kent?

11.14 What suggestions can you offer Danny for making better use of the consensus leadership style?

11.15 What is the counterargument to Kent's point about Wong not justifying his pay?

Danny Wong Attempts to Practice Participative Leadership

One student plays the role of Danny Wong, who has gathered his group to make recommendations for speeding up the processing of claims within the office. He has some ideas of his own but wants to practice participative leadership and decision making. Several other students play the roles of claims analysts within the group who are asked for their suggestions. At least one of the analysts within the group believes that Danny himself should be making the suggestions for improving the efficiency of processing claims.

Run the role-play for about ten minutes. Observers will provide feedback on how well Danny implements participative decision making, yet still not exerting leadership.

REFERENCES

1. Original story created from facts and observations in the following sources: Liza Darwin, "Exclusive: Can This Woman Save American Apparel?" *Refinery29*, www.refinery29.com, March 5, 2015, pp. 1–4; Clare O'Connor, "New CEO Paula Schneider: How I'll Fix American Apparel," www.forbes.com, January 22, 2015, pp. 1–6: Shan Li, "American Apparel's Culture Shift: New CEO Aims to Eliminate Risqué Ads, Restore Order," *Tribune Newspapers*, March 27, 2015, p. 5; "American Apparel Names Paula Schneider as CEO, Terminates Dov Charney," http://investors.americanapparel.net, December 16, 2014, p. 1.

2. Claudio Feser, Fernanda Mayoi, and Ramesh Srinivasan, "Decoding Leadership: What Really Matters," *McKinsey & Company*, www.mckinsey.com, January 2015, pp. 1–3.

3. Mark Van Vugt, Robert Hogan, and Robert B. Kaiser, "Leadership, Followership, and Evolution, *American Psychologist*, April 2008, pp. 182–183.

4. Thomas S. Bateman and J. Michael Grant, "The Proactive Component of Organizational Behavior: A Measure and Correlates," *Journal of Organizational Behavior*, March 1993, p. 103.

5. Craig D. Crossley, Cecily D. Cooper, and Tara S. Wernsing, "Making Things Happen through Challenging Goals: Leader Proactivity, Trust, and Business-Unit Performance," *Journal of Applied Psychology*, May 2013, pp. 540–549.

6. Amy J. C. Cuddy, Matthew Kohut, and John Feffinger, "Connect, Then Lead," *Harvard Business Review*, July–August 2013, p. 61

7. Ben Worthen, "Whitman Takes Charge," *The Wall Street Journal*, September 24–25, 2011, p. B1.

8. Cited in John Patrick Pullen, "The Bottom Line," *Entrepreneur*, June 2013, p. 65.

9. Cassie R. Barlow, Mark Jordan, and William H. Hendrix, "Character Assessment: An Examination of Leadership Levels," *Journal of Business and Psychology*, Summer 2003, p. 563.

10. Tal Yaffe and Ronit Kark, "Leading by Example: The Case of Leader OCB," *Journal of Applied Psychology*, July 2011, pp. 806–826.

11. Timothy A. Judge, Amy E. Colbert, and Remus Ilies, "Intelligence and Leadership: A Quantitative Review and Test of Theoretical Positions," *Journal of Applied Psychology*, June 2004, pp. 542–552.

12. David Goldsmith, "Change Your View of Leadership," *HR Magazine*, June 2013, p. 111.

13. Emily Grijalva et al., "Narcissism and Leadership: A Meta-Analytic Review of Linear and Nonlinear Relationships," *Personnel Psychology*, No. 1, 2015, pp. 1–47.

14. Joyce E. Bono and Timothy A. Judge, "Personality and Transformational and Transactional Leadership: A Meta-Analysis," *Journal of Applied Psychology*, October 2004, pp. 901–910.

15. Cited in Todd Clausen, "U-Lace Ties Up New Deals," *USA Today Money*, October 15, 2014, p. 8A.

16. Amir Erez et al., "Stirring the Hearts of Followers: Charismatic Leadership as the Transferal of Affect," *Journal of Applied Psychology*, May 2008, pp. 602–613.

17. Juan Carlos Pastor, Margarita Mayo, and Boas Shamir, "Adding Fuel to the Fire: The Impact of Followers' Arousal on Ratings of Charisma," *Journal of Applied Psychology*, November 2007, pp. 1584–1596.

18. Robert T. Keller, "A Test of the Path–Goal Theory of Leadership with Need for Clarity as a Moderator in Research and Development Organizations," *Journal of Applied Psychology*, April 1989, pp. 208–212.

19. "Carrot & Stick Failing? Try Encouragement," *Executive Leadership*, July 2007, p. 4.

20. Teresa Amabile and Steven Kramer, *The Progress Principle: Using Small Wins to Ignite Joy, Engagement, and Creativity at Work* (Boston: Harvard Business Review Press, 2011).

21. Joann S. Lublin, "Managers Need to Make Time for Face Time," *The Wall Street Journal*, March 18, 2015, p. B6.

22. Boris Groysberg and Michael Slind, "Leadership Is a Conversation," *Harvard Business Review*, June 2012, pp. 78–79.

23. Robert K. Greenleaf, *The Power of Servant Leadership: A Journey into the Nature of Legitimate Power and Greatness* (San Francisco: Berrett-Koehler, 1998); James C. Hunter, *The World's Most Powerful Leadership Principle: How to Become a Servant Leader* (New York: Crown Business, 2004).

24. Emily M. Hunter et al., "Servant Leaders Inspire Servant Followers: Antecedents and Outcomes for Employees and the Organization," *The Leadership Quarterly*, April 2013, pp. 316–331.

25. "The Best Advice I Ever Got," *Fortune*, May 12, 2008, p. 74.

26. Robert C. Liden et al., "Servant Leadership and Serving Culture: Influence on Individual and Unit Performance," *Academy of Management Journal*, October 2014, pp. 1434–1452.

27. Ibid., p. 162.

28. Jia Hu and Robert C. Liden, "Antecedents of Team Potency and Team Effectiveness: An Examination of Goal and Process Clarity and Servant Leadership," *Journal of Applied Psychology*, July 2011, pp. 851–862.

29. Ralph M. Stogdill and Alvin E. Coons, eds., *Leader Behavior: Its Description and Measurement* (Columbus: The Ohio State University Bureau of Business Research, 1957).

30. Feser, Mayoi, and Srinivasan, "Decoding Leadership," pp. 1–2.

31. Lisa Schurer Lambert et al., "Forgotten but Not Gone: An Examination of Fit between Leader Consideration and Initiating Structure Need and Received," *Journal of Applied Psychology*, September 2012, pp. 913–930.

32. Donna M. Owens, "Is Management Obsolete?" *HR Magazine*, May 2012, p. 28.

33. Jessica E. Vascellaro, "Apple in His Own Image," *The Wall Street Journal*, November 2, 2011, p. B1.

34. Anders Skogstad et al., "The Destructiveness of Laissez-Faire Leadership Behavior," *Journal of Occupational Health Psychology*, N. 1, 2007, pp. 80–92.

35. Gary Yukl and Richard Lepsinger, *Flexible Leadership: Creating Value by Balancing Multiple Challenges and Choices* (San Francisco: Jossey-Bass, 2004).

36. George Graen and J. F. Cashman, "A Role-Making Model of Leadership in Formal Organizations: A Developmental Approach," in J. G. Hunt and L. I. Larson, eds., *Leadership Frontiers* (Kent, OH: Kent State University Press, 1975), pp. 143–165.

37. Robert Eisenberger et al., "Leader–Member Exchange and Affective Organizational Commitment: The Contribution of Supervisor's Organizational Embodiment," *Journal of Applied Psychology*, November 2010, p. 1085.

38. Robert P. Vecchio, "Are You In or Out with Your Boss?" *Business Horizons*, Vol. 29, 1987, pp. 76–78.

39. Alex Ning Li and Hui Liao, "How Do Leader–Member Exchange Quality and Differentiation Affect Performance in Teams? An Integrated Multilevel Dual Process Model," *Journal of Applied Psychology*, September 2014, pp. 847–866.

40. "Personalize Your Management Style," *Manager's Edge*, June 2007, p. 3.

41. "Motivate by Telling Staffers 'Yes,'" *Manager's Edge*, May 2007, p. 4.

42. B. Parker Ellen III, Gerald R. Ferris, and M. Ronald Buckley, "Leader Political Support: Reconsidering Leader Political Behavior," *The Leadership Quarterly*, December 2013, pp. 842–857.

43. "Warren G. Bennis, Leadership Guru," in *Business: The Ultimate Resource* (Cambridge, MA: Perseus Publishing, 2002), p. 969.

44. D. Scott DeRue and Ned Wellman, "Developing Leaders via Experience: The Role of Developmental Challenge, Learning Orientation, and Feedback Availability," *Journal of Applied Psychology*, July 2009, pp. 859–875.

45. Donna M. Owens, "Success Factors: The Right Experience Can Increase Your Leadership Potential," *HR Magazine*, August 2008, pp. 87–88.

46. Craig L. Pearce and Charles C. Manz, "The New Silver Bullet of Leadership: The Importance of Self- and Shared Leadership in Knowledge Work," *Organizational Dynamics*, No. 2, 2005, p. 133.

47. Quoted in Sonja D. Brown, "Congratulations, You're a Manager, Now What?" *Black Enterprise*, April 2006, p. 104.

CHAPTER **12**

Motivating Others and Developing Teamwork

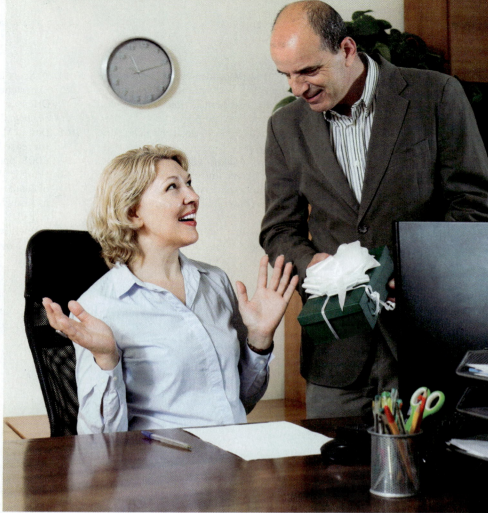

Fotolia

Outline

When Matt Ehrlichman was twenty-one years old, he raised enough money from Seattle, Washington, investors to found Thriva LLC, a company that developed software to assist sporting camps and summer camps run the registration system online. The company grew to sixty-five employees and more than 1,000 customers before it was sold to ACTIVE Network. Ehrlichman stayed on with ACTIVE as the chief strategy officer.

At age thirty-four, Ehrlichman launched Porch, a website that matches home improvement specialists with people seeking home improvements. Contractors are able to display home improvement projects they have successfully completed. Porch has compiled data on 90 million projects, usually including photos and project costs. The company's database includes 1.5 million home-improvement professionals. Porch generates revenue by charging contractors for market insights and promotional exposure in specific geographic regions.

A major breakthrough for Porch took place when home improvement giant Lowe's incorporated the company's software in all 1,700 of its locations. Porch also functions as a platform for homeowners to "tell the story of their houses," similar to the way you can describe your career on LinkedIn.

Ehrlichman attributes his substantial business success to his ability to select and build high-performing teams. Upon winning the 2014 USA Today Entrepreneur of the Year award, Ehrlichman said that he was surprised and humbled, but that all the credit goes to his team.

Ehrlichman speaks frequently with aspiring entrepreneurs and sticks with the same mantra: The business owner must be selective about who is hired and make sure that the people hired match the culture. He says that the Porch motto is "No jerks, no ego, no bureaucracy." He also advises business start-ups to have a fun team that jokes around while at work.

Ehrlichman's formal education has provided the foundation for his business and technology career. He holds a bachelor of science degree in entrepreneurial engineering, as well as a master of science degree in management science and engineering, both from Stanford University.[1]

The accomplishments of the home improvement website illustrate the importance of building successful teams and having a motivated workforce. In this chapter, we describe a variety of theories and practices for motivating others, including recognition. We also describe the closely related topic of developing teamwork, because approaches to getting a team or group working well are essentially techniques of motivation. One of the biggest motivational challenges facing managers and team leaders is to get the team working together smoothly.

▶ **Learning Objective 12.1** ▶

Diagnosing Work Motivation

Motivation

concept with two widely used meanings: (1) an internal state that leads to effort expended toward objectives and (2) an activity performed by one person to get another to accomplish work

An eternal challenge for people responsible for the work of others is to get them to perform at a high level. **Motivation** has two widely used meanings: (1) an internal state that leads to effort expended toward objectives and (2) an activity performed by one person to get another to accomplish work. Usually the manager is doing the motivating, yet many people in the workplace have a need to motivate others. To accomplish their work, people must motivate individuals who report to them, coworkers, supervisors, and customers. Understanding how to motivate others, therefore, is essential to your success. It is often important to motivate groups of people, such as a team, in addition to motivating people one at a time.

Knowledge of motivation is particularly important in the current era because so many workers do not feel identified with their work or their employers, as described in the discussion of worker engagement in Chapter 3. A starting point in being able to motivate people and groups is to understand what outcomes or payoffs they want from their work. If you know what a person wants—and the person knows what he or she wants—you are in a better position to motivate that person. Questions can be asked in person or through a survey.[2] Basic questions might include:

■ What could this job offer you that would make you work at your best?

■ What might the company do to make you excited about your job?

■ How can I (or we) make your job a wonderful experience for you?

■ What would make you feel really good about your job?

A person's behavior is often more revealing than what he or she says. You might therefore also gain some diagnostic insights by observing what elements of the job or work situation strongly interest the subordinate. For example, one team member might display enthusiasm primarily when there is an opportunity to do exciting work. Another team member might be excited primarily when a weekend or holiday approaches. You could tentatively conclude that the first person is motivated by exciting work and the second by time off from work.

▶ **Learning Objective 12.2** ▶

Motivation Through Empowerment, Job Design, and Various Forms of Positive Reinforcement

Among the standard practices for employee motivation are empowerment, job design, and various forms of positive reinforcement, including financial incentives, recognition, and praise.

EMPOWERMENT

A comprehensive strategy for employee motivation is to grant workers more power by enabling them to participate in decisions affecting themselves and their work.

Empowerment basically involves passing decision-making authority and responsibility from managers to employees. A key point is that the leader shares power with group members. Because group members have some power, they can influence the manager, such as giving him or her guidance.

Workers experience a greater sense of self-efficacy and ownership of their jobs when they share power. According to this logic, **empowerment** is the process by which a manager shares power with team members, thereby enhancing their feelings of self-efficacy. Because the worker feels more effective, empowerment contributes to intrinsic motivation. The individual has a choice in initiating and regulating actions, such as in deciding how to perform a particular task.[3] Sharing power with team members enables them to feel better about themselves and perform at a higher level. Teams as well as individuals can be empowered. An example of empowering a team would be to give it responsibility for developing a new product.

Empowerment
process by which a manager shares power with team members, thereby enhancing their feelings of self-efficacy

Empowerment as Shared Leadership

Another way of understanding empowerment is that it involves **shared leadership**, or the leader granting group members authority to carry out some of the leadership activities. Instead of relying exclusively on the designated head of the group for leadership, the group members guide and influence themselves. The shared leadership is particularly useful when group members have certain technical knowledge they need to accomplish the work and the leader lacks this knowledge. At any given period of time, the group member with the key knowledge, skills, and abilities for the task at hand becomes the person in charge. As an extreme example, if a hurricane attacked the building the person who would take charge would be someone with experience in dealing with a hurricane. But the leader of the group plays an important role in coaching the team members in how to assume leadership responsibility.[4]

Shared leadership
the leader granting group members authority to carry out some of the leadership activities

> Visualize a group of environmental specialists seeking ways to make an existing office building environmentally friendly. All group members have specialized knowledge of their own that they want to share with coworkers and influence them with. The leader steps back to allow this shared leadership take place, such as one group member influencing others to plant a garden on the roof to help moderate temperature and absorb carbon dioxide.

An analysis of forty-two studies about shared leadership indicates that it shows a positive relationship with team effectiveness. In support of the example just presented, it appears that shared leadership contributes more to team effectiveness when the task is complex.[5]

Two Forms of Empowerment

Employee empowerment often takes the form of giving customer-contact employees more freedom in making decisions. At the same time, the employees are encouraged to exercise initiative and imagination (such as figuring how to satisfy an unusual customer demand), and they are rewarded for doing so.

Although customer-contact employees are empowered, they are still given overall direction and limits to the extent of their authority. One limit is that a customer service worker cannot overturn a company rule, thereby creating a health or safety hazard. For example, a hotel receptionist would not be authorized to allow a guest to park in a fire safety zone just because a space close to the hotel was not available at the time.

Self-managed work groups are another frequent form of empowerment because they make many decisions on their own rather than relying on a supervisor. Representative of this approach are the self-managed groups within the customer-financing division of Hewlett-Packard. The teams are empowered to make decisions on their own on how to allocate resources, and to establish priorities for reaching major goals.[6]

MOTIVATION THROUGH JOB DESIGN AND INTERESTING WORK

To understand how the work itself contributes to motivation, we look at the foundation theory of this approach followed by later applications of the theory.

The Two-Factor Theory of Work Motivation

Two-factor theory of work motivation
two different sets of job factors; one set, the motivators, or satisfiers, can motivate and satisfy workers; the other set, dissatisfiers, or hygiene factors, can only prevent dissatisfaction

The late Frederick Herzberg developed the pioneering **two-factor theory of work motivation**. According to this theory, there are two different sets of job factors.[7] One set, the motivators (or satisfiers), can motivate and satisfy workers. The other set, dissatisfiers (or hygiene factors), can only prevent dissatisfaction. Motivators relate to higher-order needs, whereas hygiene factors relate to lower-order needs.

The two-factor theory explains how to design jobs to make them motivational. The motivational elements are the intrinsic, or job content, factors that make a job exciting. Motivator factors include achievement, recognition, advancement, responsibility, the work itself, and personal growth possibilities. The extrinsic, or job context, factors are hygienic. Although they are health maintaining and desirable, they are not motivational. Examples of hygiene factors are pay, status, job security, working conditions, and quality of leadership. Herzberg believed that motivation increases when one combines pay with a motivator such as challenging work.

According to the theory, only the presence of motivator factors leads to more positively energized behavior. For example, challenging work will motivate many people to exert increased effort. If intrinsic factors, such as challenging work, are not present, the result is neutral rather than negative, and the worker will feel bland rather than angry or unhappy.

Although the presence of hygiene (or extrinsic) factors is not motivational, their absence can cause dissatisfaction, as in the following illustration. A police captain reported that when officers were assigned old patrol cars, they complained frequently, but when assigned brand-new patrol cars, they did not express much appreciation. Nor did they increase their productivity as measured by the number of citations issued.

The two-factor theory has made two lasting contributions to work motivation. First, it has helped managers realize that money is not always the primary motivator. Second, it has spurred much of the interest in designing jobs to make them more intrinsically satisfying, as described next. A major problem with the two-factor theory is that it deemphasizes individual differences and glosses over the importance of hygiene factors in attracting and retaining workers. Hygiene factors such as good benefits and good company management satisfy and motivate many people and keep them committed to the firm.

Intrinsic Motivation and Job Enrichment

Intrinsic motivation
a person's beliefs about the extent to which an activity can satisfy his or her needs for competence and self-determination

Many human relations and management experts contend that if you make jobs more interesting, there may be less need for motivating people with external rewards. Also, attempting to motivate people by external rewards may not be sufficient. Motivating people through interesting work is based on the principle of **intrinsic motivation**, which refers to a person's beliefs about the extent to which an activity can satisfy his or her needs for competence and self-determination. Instead of looking to somebody else for rewards, a person is motivated by the intrinsic, or internal, aspects of the task.

Prosocial motivation
the desire to expend effort to help other people

Intrinsic motivation contributes even more to productivity when combined with **prosocial motivation**, the desire to expend effort to help other people. People who are agreeable by nature are more likely to have strong prosocial motivation. A study was conducted with fund-raising callers whose task was to telephone alumni to raise money for the university. A major finding was that those callers who experienced both intrinsic and prosocial motivation tended to have high productivity in terms of calls made and funds raised.[8]

Job enrichment refers to making a job more motivating and satisfying by adding variety and responsibility. A job is considered enriched to the extent that it demands more of an individual's talents and capabilities. As the job becomes more meaningful to you, you become better motivated and, it is hoped, more productive. Unless you want an enriched job, these positive results may not be forthcoming. Substantial research and practical experience have gone into enriching jobs. Three noteworthy characteristics of an enriched job are direct feedback, client relationships, and new learning.[9]

Direct feedback occurs when a worker receives immediate knowledge of the results he or she is achieving. This evaluation of performance can be built into the job (such as a highway patrol officer catching a speeder) or provided by a supervisor. *Client relationship* refers to an employee having a client or customer to serve, whether that client is inside or outside the organization. In this regard, both a customer service representative and a hairstylist have enriched jobs.

New learning takes place when a job incumbent feels that he or she is growing psychologically, including acquiring new skills. In contrast, an impoverished job allows for no new learning. The information technology component built into most jobs provides ample opportunity for new learning, as would learning a second language to relate better to customers in another country. Another perspective on new learning is that it has positive effects beyond immediate motivation.

A basic example of job enrichment is as follows: Instead of simply putting an accounts payable specialist in charge of more accounts, put the same person in charge of following up on the calls, talking with collection agencies, and redesigning the workflow.[10]

Going beyond the formal theory of job enrichment, interesting work also includes having a sense of purpose as you may have studied in relation to self-motivation and goal setting. An example of a bold mission leading to interesting work for most people would be working on a community redevelopment project or finding a cure for childhood leukemia.

MOTIVATION THROUGH POSITIVE REINFORCEMENT

Rewarding a worker for achieving a certain result or behaving in a particular way is a widely used motivational tactic and has become ingrained in our culture in work and personal life. **Positive reinforcement** means increasing the probability that behavior will be repeated by rewarding people for making the desired response. The phrase *increasing the probability* means that positive reinforcement improves learning and motivation but is not 100 percent effective. The phrase *making the desired response* is also noteworthy. To use positive reinforcement properly, a reward must be contingent on doing something right. Simply paying somebody a compliment or giving the person something of value is not positive reinforcement. Because financial incentives, recognition, and praise are given for attaining a given goal, they function as positive reinforcement.

Positive reinforcement is easy to visualize with well-structured jobs, such as data entry or producing parts. Yet positive reinforcement is also used to encourage desired behavior for those in highly paid, complex jobs. An accountant who developed a new method for the company getting paid faster might be rewarded with two extra days of vacation.

Rules for the Effective Use of Positive Reinforcement

Although using rewards to motivate people seems straightforward, positive reinforcement requires the systematic applicant of rules. The rules are specified from the standpoint of the person trying to motivate another individual, such as a group member, coworker, supervisor, or customer. The same rules also apply to motivating a work group.

Job enrichment
making a job more motivating and satisfying by adding variety and responsibility

◀ **Learning Objective 12.3** ◀

Positive reinforcement
increasing the probability that behavior will be repeated by rewarding people for making the desired response; improves learning and motivation

Rule 1: State Clearly What Behavior Will Lead to a Reward. The nature of good performance, or the goals, must be agreed on by the manager and group member. Clarification might take this form: "We need to decrease by 40 percent the number of new credit card customers who have delinquent accounts of sixty days or more."

Rule 2: Choose an Appropriate Reward. An appropriate reward is effective in motivating a given person and is feasible from the standpoint of the individual or the company. If one reward does not motivate the person, try another. One person might be motivated by time off from work, another by an interesting assignment, and a third by an e-mail note of praise with a copy to a high-ranking executive. Many employees are strongly motivated by the possibility of receiving a promotion, especially because promotions offer the prospect of more status and higher pay. The importance of choosing the right reward underscores the fact that not all rewards are reinforcers. A reward is something of perceived value by the person receiving the reward, but if the reward does not strengthen the desired response (such as wearing safety goggles), it is not a true reinforcer.[11]

Rule 3: Supply Ample Feedback. Positive reinforcement cannot work without frequent feedback to individuals. Feedback can take the form of simply telling people they have done something right or wrong. Brief e-mail or text messages or handwritten notes are other forms of feedback. Effective motivators make extensive use of handwritten thank-you notes.

Intermittent rewards
sustaining desired behaviors longer and slowing down the process of behaviors fading away when they are not rewarded

Rule 4: Schedule Rewards Intermittently. Rewards should not be given on every occasion of good performance. **Intermittent rewards** sustain desired behaviors longer and also slow down the process of behaviors fading away when they are not rewarded. If each correct performance results in a reward, the behavior will stop shortly after a performance in which the reward is not received. Another problem is that a reward given continuously may lose its impact. A practical value of intermittent reinforcement is that it saves time. Few managers or team leaders have enough time to dispense rewards for every correct action by group members.

Rule 5: Make the Rewards Follow the Observed Behavior Closely in Time. For maximum effectiveness, people should be rewarded soon after doing something right. A built-in, or intrinsic, feedback system, such as software working or not working, capitalizes on this principle. E-mail and text messages are again useful here because it would be difficult for the manager or team leader to congratulate in person team members who work in another location.

Rule 6: Make the Reward Fit the Behavior. People who are inexperienced in applying positive reinforcement often overdo the intensity of spoken rewards. When an employee does something of an ordinary nature correctly, a simple word of praise such as "Good job" is preferable to something like "Fantastic performance." A related idea is that the magnitude of the reward should vary with the magnitude of the accomplishment.

Rule 7: Make the Rewards Visible. Another important characteristic of an effective reward is the extent to which it is visible, or noticeable, to other employees. When other workers notice the reward, its impact multiplies because other people observe what kind of behavior is rewarded.[12] Rewards should also be visible, or noticeable, to the employee. A reward of $5 per week added to a person's paycheck might be hardly noticeable, after payroll deductions. However, a bonus check for $200 might be very noticeable.

Rule 8: Change the Reward Periodically. Rewards do not retain their effectiveness indefinitely. Employees and customers lose interest in striving for a reward they have received many times in the past. This is particularly true of a repetitive statement such as

"Nice job" or "Congratulations." It is helpful for the person giving out the rewards to compile a list of potential rewards and try different ones from time to time.

Positive reinforcement has a long history of improving productivity on the job, including the control of absenteeism. In recent years, positive reinforcement has been applied to encouraging employees to participate in company wellness and fitness programs, as well as to attain the goals of the program. For example, some wellness programs offer cash incentive payments and gift cards for stopping smoking or losing weight. Twenty-four percent of companies responding to a survey tied incentives to progress in measures such as an employee's blood pressure or body mass index (a measure that takes into account weight in relation to height).[13]

FINANCIAL INCENTIVES AS POSITIVE REINFORCEMENT

Money is a natural motivator, and no program of motivation can exclude the role of financial compensation. Even the most ardent critics of the motivational power of money recognize that nonfinancial motivators are effective only when compensation is considered to be fair and adequate. When workers are preoccupied with not being paid fairly, they are less likely to respond to other approaches to motivation. When money is used as a motivator, it becomes a positive reinforcer because a person receives more money for performing well.

A challenge in understanding the role of money and other forms of compensation is that they are not pure concepts. High pay is also closely associated with other outcomes, such as status and recognition. Thus, a person may work hard to earn more money as a way of achieving more status and recognition. Here we describe programs making pay partially contingent on performance, individual factors that influence the effectiveness of financial incentives, and problems with financial incentives.

Linking Compensation to Performance

Many employers make a systematic effort to link some portion of pay to performance to make pay more motivational. **Variable pay** (or *merit pay*) is an incentive plan that intentionally pays good performers more money than poor performers. Employees receive more money by excelling on performance measures such as number of sales or number of computer programs completed. Whatever the specific plan, employees receive a base level of pay along with a bonus related to performance. The better your performance as measured by your employer, the higher your pay. Linking salary increases to good performance helps employers spare the cost of giving too many workers a pay boost. At the same time, such plans are perceived to be useful in retaining valuable employees.

Another approach to relating pay to performance is to link bonuses to results obtained by the work group or the entire company. A companywide bonus plan ties individual merit pay to overall company or division performance, such as a year-end bonus based on company profits. The financial results on which the bonuses are determined can be measured at the division, group, business unit, or company level. Sometimes the bonus is based on a combination of the levels mentioned.

Personal Factors Influencing the Power of Financial Incentives

Individual differences profoundly influence the motivational power of financial incentives. Workers who attach a high value to financial incentives will be more motivated by money than those who attach a low value. A major influencing factor is that money is a good motivator when you need it badly enough. Money has a motivational pull for most people who think that they need more money. Once people have enough money to pay for all those things they think are important in life, money may lose its effectiveness. There

Variable pay
incentive plan that intentionally pays good performers more money than poor performers

are tremendous individual differences in what people classify as necessities, such as some people regarding membership in a golf club to be a necessity.

Tolerance for risk taking also influences the power of financial incentives. A relevant example is that industrial sales representatives vary in the ratio of salary to commissions they find motivational. A high risk taker would prefer most of compensation based on commissions because of the possibility of higher earnings. A lower risk taker would prefer a higher proportion of compensation based on salary because more income is guaranteed.[14]

Problems Created by Financial Incentives

Despite their effectiveness as motivators, financial incentives also create human problems. A major concern is that financial rewards can lead a person to focus on rewards rather than the joy built into exciting work. Another problem is that after people receive several increases based on performance, merit pay comes to be perceived as a right or entitlement. A person who does not receive a merit increase one quarter often feels that he or she has been punished. Another problem with cash awards is that they sometimes interfere with teamwork as employees concentrate on individual financial rewards.

Also, pay-for-performance plans can prompt executives, corporate professionals, and sales representatives to focus on achieving exceptional financial results, sometimes by unethical means. The problems sometimes associated with goals, such as not caring how you reach your goal, are closely linked to the pursuit of financial rewards. For example, a manufacturer might sell to the public a baby crib known to be dangerous in order to attain a quarterly financial goal.

MOTIVATION THROUGH RECOGNITION AND PRAISE

William James, the well-regarded nineteen-century philosopher and psychologist, wrote, "The deepest principle of human behavior is the craving to be appreciated."[15] The workplace provides a natural opportunity to satisfy the **recognition need**, the desire to be acknowledged for one's contributions and efforts and to feel important. A manager can thus motivate many employees by making them feel important, or at a minimum, saying "Thank you" for a job well done. Employee needs for recognition can be satisfied both through informal recognition and by establishing formal recognition programs. If the recognition prize is made contingent on achievement, the recognition program functions like positive reinforcement. Limited recognition and praise given to employees can have substantial negative consequences for an employer. Gallup Inc. research found that a lack of recognition and praise for good work is responsible for a 10 to 20 percent difference in revenue and productivity.[16]

Recognition need
the desire to be acknowledged for one's contributions and efforts and to feel important

Praise as Recognition

Praising workers for good performance is closely related to informal recognition. An effective form of praise describes the worker's performance rather than merely making an evaluation. Describing good performance might take this form: "You turned an angry customer into an ally who referred new business to us." A more general evaluation would be "You are great with angry customers."

Although praise costs no money and requires only a few minutes of time, many workers rarely receive praise. According to the American Psychological Association "Stress in America" survey, only 46 percent of respondents agree or strongly agreed with the statement, "Overall, I am satisfied with the employee recognition practices of my employer."[17] Managers and team leaders therefore have a good opportunity to increase motivation by the simple act of praising good deeds. Other informal approaches to recognizing good performance include taking an employee to lunch, a handshake from the manager or team leader, and putting flowers on an employee's desk.

Tailor Praise to Individual Preferences

An advanced use of praise is to tailor the praise to the needs of the person being praised, much like the diagnostic approach to motivation. A study with workers who perceived themselves to be technically oriented found that they have a more negative attitude toward being flattered (a strong form of praise). Instead, they prefer a laid-back, factual statement of how they made a contribution. (An example: "Your solution to the problem saved us 30 percent in raw material costs.") Conversely, people who perceived themselves as less technically oriented were more positively disposed toward being flattered. (An example: "I love it. What a fantastic solution to our problem.")[18]

Another example of differences in response to recognition and praise is that not every employee wants to receive the accolade of "employee of the month" or to receive public recognition. A cultural difference is that many Asian workers prefer that praise be given privately or shared with the team publicly.[19] Team recognition rather than individual recognition is often more effective in Japan.

Company Recognition Programs

Formal recognition programs are more popular than ever as companies attempt to retain the right employees and keep workers productive who worry about having no private work area. Recognition programs are also regarded as one of the best ways to drive employee engagement. An Aon Hewitt survey found that recognition ranked just after career opportunities and pay as a driver of engagement.[20] The reason could be that employees become more emotionally attached to an employer who appreciates them.

Company recognition programs include awarding watches and jewelry for good service, plaques for good performance, and on-the-spot cash awards (about $50 to $100) for good performance. On-the-spot small bonuses for doing something exceptional sometimes take the form of a gift certificate for out-of-the-ordinary performance such as having identified a major safety hazard before it became a problem.

Because so many workers are not in face-to-face contact with their managers, managers often deliver verbal recognition by e-mail or telephone. Furthermore, some recognition programs are administered through websites in which the employee can choose from among a list of possible awards.

Human Relations Self-Assessment Quiz 12-1 gives you an opportunity to think about how some of the motivators described in this chapter might apply to you.

Strategies and Tactics for Building Teamwork

So far in this chapter, we have studied how leaders and managers can influence subordinates by direct use of motivational techniques. Team leaders, as well as other managers, also need to use techniques that influence subordinates to work well together in a team. Influencing others is similar to motivating them. In this section, we describe methods for building **teamwork**, work done with an understanding and commitment to group goals on the part of all team members.[21]

◄ **Learning Objective 12.4** ◄

The team with the best players wins.
—*Jack Welch*

Former CEO of GE, now with Sprayer/Jack Welch Management Institute

Teamwork
work done with an understanding and commitment to group goals on the part of all team members

Human Relations Self-Assessment Quiz   12-1

My Own Motivators

Listed below are ten job factors that are motivators for many workers. Check the factors or motivators that apply to you.

Number	Job Factor or Motivator	Would Motivate Me	Would Not Motivate Me
1.	Promise of a 10 percent salary increase for good performance	_____	_____
2.	Opportunity to do work on an exciting assignment	_____	_____
3.	Threat of being fired if I do not meet performance standards	_____	_____
4.	A fancy new job title with no pay increase	_____	_____
5.	Promise of two extra weeks of vacation per year	_____	_____
6.	Promise of one-step promotion for good performance	_____	_____
7.	Time off from job to do volunteer work in community	_____	_____
8.	Recognition placed on company website	_____	_____
9.	Opportunity to mentor other workers if I perform well	_____	_____
10.	Opportunity to work on project of my choosing if I perform well	_____	_____

Scoring and Interpretation:

The more of the ten factors that you said would motivate you, the more readily you are or will be a motivated worker. Checking the following job factors suggests that you are more motivated by external factors: 1, 3, 4, 5. 6, and 8. Checking the following job factors suggests that that you are motivated by internal factors: 2, 7, 9, and 10.

Source: "My Own Motivators" by Andrew J. DuBrin.

Team

a small number of people who are committed to common goals and approaches to which they hold themselves mutually accountable

Group

a collection of people who interact with one another and are working toward some common purpose; a team approaches being a supergroup

The term *team* is used frequently in human relations, yet it merits a formal definition. A **team** is a small number of people who are committed to common goals and approaches to which they hold themselves mutually accountable. A **group** is slightly different because it has less emphasis on teamwork. It is a collection of people who interact with one another and are working toward some common purpose. All teams are groups, but not all groups are teams: A team approaches being a supergroup. For a collection of people to function well as a team or a group, they must collaborate, such as in solving problems together.

In the following sections, we describe more about how groups function because such knowledge can indirectly help the manager or leader do a better job of developing teamwork. An analogy is that if a professor understands how people learn, he or she can be more effective at teaching.

Good teamwork enhances, but does not guarantee, a successful team. For example, a group with excellent teamwork might be working on improving a product or service no longer valued by the company or customers. No matter what the output of this team, it will probably be ignored. A list of strategies and tactics for building teamwork follows.

1. Select qualified members. A starting point in developing good teamwork is to select members for the team who are interested in and qualified to be strong team members. The hiring manager or team leader should look for individuals who have enjoyed and performed well on teams in the past, both on and off the job. A study conducted in a manufacturing organization with highly interdependent teams found that being conscientious and extraverted and having knowledge about teamwork were positively related to good job performance as a team member.[22]

2. Be well motivated yourself.   A basic strategy for motivating the team toward teamwork or another worthwhile purpose is for the team leader to be well motivated, thereby being a good role model. The importance of the group leader being well motivated was demonstrated in a study with customer service representatives at a large travel agency franchise. The specific finding of the study was that when team leaders had strong motivation to adopt a new technology, the motivation to adopt increased for the representatives. Modeling took place because when the team leaders adopted the new technology, so did the customer service representatives. Charismatic team leaders were the most successful in motivating the workers to adopt the new technology.[23]

Part of the motivational effect of charisma stems from positive thinking. A study conducted in Taiwan with eighty-five retail sales teams involving 365 team members found that leaders' positive mood enhanced various aspects of team performance. Objective measures of team performance included commissions and premiums, whereas subjective measures consisted of evaluations of team members provided by the team leaders.[24]

3. Have urgent, constructive purpose.   Another early step is to help team members believe they have an urgent, constructive purpose. An example would be "If we don't patch this software problem, we will get 95 percent returns." A demanding performance challenge helps create and sustain the team. Rewards should stem from meeting the challenge. The urgent, constructive purpose often stems from the team's mission, such as "eliminating or reducing environmental hazards while manufacturing our HD television screens."

4. Compete against a common enemy.   Competing against a common enemy is one of the best-known methods of building team spirit. It is preferable that the adversary is external, such as an independent diner competing against franchised family restaurants.

5. Have a culture of teamwork.   A primary strategy for teamwork promotes the attitude that working together effectively is an expected norm. Developing such a culture of teamwork generally proves difficult when a strong culture of individualism exists within the firm. Pacific Investment Management Co. recently replaced an authoritarian and self-centered chief investment officer with Daniel Ivascyn. The new CIO announced that the firm was shifting from a founder-driven management structure to one that emphasizes teamwork.[25]

The team leader can communicate the norm of teamwork by making frequent use of words and phrases that support teamwork. Emphasizing the words *team members* or *teammates,* along with deemphasizing the words *subordinates* and *employees,* helps communicate the teamwork norm. The norm of teamwork is also fostered by having a code of conduct to which members agree. Provisions of the code might include "Never abandon a teammate" and "Never humiliate a teammate." Showing respect for all team members is a strong method of communicating the norm of teamwork. A useful method of showing respect is to never joke about the errors or shortcomings of a team member in the presence of others.

As a team leader, you can contribute to a culture of teamwork by remembering to share credit with teammates whenever you receive a compliment for what the group has accomplished. Tell the group directly about the praise. Or if the praise is given publicly, make a statement in front of the team, such as, "I appreciate the compliment, but I could not have done it without Gus, Jennifer, Fred, and Constance." Although, this sentiment is widely expressed, it still has a positive impact on teamwork.

6. Use the consensus decision-making style.   Using the consensus decision-making style provides another way to reinforce teamwork. A sophisticated approach to enhancing teamwork, it feeds team members valid facts and information that motivate them to work together. New information prompts the team to redefine and enrich its understanding of the challenge it is facing, thereby focusing on a common purpose. The consensus decision-making style helps develop teamwork also because the team members feel empowered because they feel involved in decision making. As the team members share in decision making, they are likely to develop a cooperative spirit.

7. Minimize micromanagement. To foster teamwork, the manager should minimize micromanagement, or supervising group members too closely and second-guessing their decisions. Micromanagement can hamper a spirit of teamwork because team members do not feel in control of their own work. A relatively frequent example of a team leader being a micromanager (or *control freak*) is dictating which type font should be used on team reports.

8. Reward the team as well as individuals. One high-impact strategy for encouraging teamwork rewards the team as well as individuals. The most convincing team incentive is to calculate compensation partially on the basis of team results. For a more general reward strategy, managers apply positive reinforcement whenever the group or individuals engage in behavior that supports teamwork. For example, team members who took the initiative to have an information-sharing session can be singled out and praised for this activity. The use of team-based incentives began in manufacturing, but it has spread to hospitals and health systems. Rewards are typically tied to specific goals, such as increased patient satisfaction or a reduction in accounts receivable.[26]

9. Send members to offsite training. Another option available to organizations for enhancing teamwork comes through experiential learning, such as sending members to offsite (or outdoor) training. Participants acquire teamwork skills by confronting physical challenges and exceeding their self-imposed limitations. (As mentioned in Chapter 11, offsite training is also used for leadership development.) In rope activities, which are typical of outdoor training, participants attached to a secure pulley with ropes climb ladders and jump off to another spot.

A day at an auto-racing track, another form of outdoor training for elite teams, provides team members with an opportunity to drive at racecar speeds in some kind of cooperative venture. Getting the team to work together in doing a social good, such as repairing a rundown house in a poor neighborhood, is another popular form of team building. Gourmet cooking as a team is now popular for teamwork development because so much cooperation is required to get the meal prepared correctly.

All of these challenges require teamwork rather than individual effort, hence their contribution to team development. Offsite training generally offers the most favorable outcomes when the trainer helps the team members comprehend the link between such training and on-the-job behavior.

10. Encourage communication among virtual team members. A special challenge in developing good teamwork is when the members are geographically dispersed, as in a virtual team. Because the members communicate with each other mostly by e-mail and group software, they lose out on the face to-face interaction useful for building teamwork. A technologically advanced approach is for the virtual team members to use online team rooms, where everyone can see the state of work in progress and interact with each other simultaneously.[27] (The setup is much like a blog for team member use.) Bringing the group together for an occasional face-to-face meeting is also helpful in building teamwork.

An indirect way of encouraging communication among virtual team members is to engage in shared leadership, which encourages the exchange of information and joint problem solving. Shared leadership is also associated with higher performance in virtual teams.[28]

11. Make appropriate use of a team slogan, logo, and clothing. Many teams and groups in the workplace will develop closer ties when they identify with a team logo and slogan that might be emblazoned on T-shirts, coffee mugs, pencils, and pens. The purpose of the symbols is to remind the group that they are part of a greater whole.[29] For some work situations, such as a group of financial planners or tax consultants, such gimmicks might be inappropriate. Yet, for many groups, such as manufacturing employees, call center workers, and distribution center specialists, the team slogan, logo, and clothing might work well. The team members should be encouraged to develop the slogan and logo. For example, a group of dog and cat groomers might label themselves the Proud Pet Champions and use a logo of a cartoon dog and cat next to "PPC" in large letters.

Understanding Group Dynamics to Improve Teamwork Development and Motivation

◀ **Learning Objective 12.5** ◀

An indirect way of a leader being effective at developing teamwork and motivating team members is to be knowledgeable about how groups operate. **Group dynamics** refers to the forces operating in groups that affect how members work together. To help zero in on this vast body of knowledge, we feature four practical topics: the stages of group development, team member roles, the problem of groupthink, and the characteristics of an effective work group.

Group dynamics
the forces operating in groups that affect how members work together

STAGES OF GROUP DEVELOPMENT

Key to understanding the nature of work groups is to know what the group does (the content) and how it proceeds (the process). A key group process is the group's development over time. To make this information more meaningful, relate it to any group to which you have belonged for at least one month. Understanding the stages of group development can lead to more effective group leadership or membership. The five group stages are shown in Figure 12-1 and described next.[30]

Stage 1. Forming. At the outset, members are eager to learn what tasks they will be performing, how they can benefit from group membership, and what constitutes acceptable behavior. Members often inquire about rules they must follow. Confusion, caution, and communality are typical during the initial phase of group development.

Stage 2. Storming. During this "shakedown" period, individual styles often come into conflict. Hostility, infighting, tension, and confrontation are typical. Members may argue to clarify expectations of their contributions. Coalitions and cliques may form within the group, and one or two members may be targeted for exclusion. Subgroups may form to push for an agenda of interest to them. (Despite the

FIGURE 12-1

THE STAGES OF GROUP DEVELOPMENT

Most Groups Follow a Predictable Sequence of Stages

Source: THE STAGES OF GROUP DEVELOPMENT by Andrew J. DuBrin.

frequency of storming, many workplace groups work willingly with one another from the outset, thus skipping stage 2.)

Stage 3. Norming. After storming comes the quieter stage of overcoming resistance and establishing group standards of conduct (norms). Cohesiveness and commitment begin to develop. The group starts to come together as a coordinated unit, and harmony prevails. Norms stem from three sources. First, the group itself quickly establishes limits for members, often by effective use of glares and nods. For example, the team member who swears at the leader might receive angry glances from other members. Second, norms may also be imposed that are derived from the larger organization and from professional codes of conduct. A third source of norms might be an influential team member who inspires the group to elevate its performance or behavior. The head of an audit team might say, "Let's develop the reputation of an audit team that is the most professional and objective in the industry."

Stage 4. Performing. When the group reaches the performing stage, it is ready to focus on accomplishing its key tasks. Issues concerning interpersonal relations and task assignment are put aside as the group becomes a well-functioning unit. Intrinsic motivation and creativity are likely to emerge as the group performs. At their best, members feel they are working "for the cause," much like a political campaign team or a team bringing a breakthrough product to market.

Stage 5. Adjourning. Temporary work groups are abandoned after their task has been accomplished, much like a project team created to erect an office tower. The same group members, however, have developed important relationships and understandings they can bring with them should they be teammates in the future. The link between adjourning and forming shown in Figure 12-1 is that many groups do reassemble after one project is completed. The link between stages 1 and 5 would not apply to a group that disbanded and never worked together again.

A key managerial challenge is to help the group move past the first three stages into performing. At times, group members may have to be notified that they are spending too much time on process issues and not enough on the task at hand.

TEAM MEMBER ROLES

A major challenge in learning to become an effective team member is to choose the right roles to occupy. A **role** is a tendency to behave, contribute, and relate to others in a particular way. It is helpful for the leader to understand these roles as he or she attempts to get the group working together smoothly. For example, the leader might want to make sure that all positive roles are filled. If you carry out positive roles, you will be perceived as a contributor to team effort. If you neglect carrying out these roles, you will be perceived as a poor contributor. Human Relations Self-Assessment Quiz 12-2 will help you evaluate your present inclinations toward occupying effective roles as a team member. In this section, we describe a number of the most frequently observed positive roles played by team members. We also mention a group of negative roles.

According to the role theory developed by Meredith Belbin and his group of researchers at Belbin Associates, there are nine frequent roles occupied by team members.[31] All of these roles are influenced to some extent by an individual's personality.

1. **Creative problem solver.** The creative problem solver is creative, imaginative, and unorthodox. Such a person solves difficult problems. A potential weakness of this role is that the person tends to ignore fine details and becomes too immersed in the problem to communicate effectively.

Human Relations Self-Assessment Quiz   12-2

Team Player Roles

For each of the following statements about team activity, check mostly agree or mostly disagree. If you have not experienced such a situation, imagine how you would act or think if placed in that situation. In responding to the statements, assume that you are taking the questionnaire with the intent of learning something about yourself.

		Mostly Agree	Mostly Disagree
1.	It is rarely that I ever miss a team meeting.	_____	_____
2.	I regularly compliment team members when they do something exceptional.	_____	_____
3.	Whenever I can, I avoid being the note taker at a team meeting.	_____	_____
4.	From time to time, other team members come to me for advice on technical matters.	_____	_____
5.	I like to hide some information from other team members so I can be in control.	_____	_____
6.	I welcome new team members coming to me for advice and learning the ropes.	_____	_____
7.	My priorities come first, which leaves me with very little time to help other team members.	_____	_____
8.	During a team meeting, it is not unusual for several other people at a time to look toward me for my opinion.	_____	_____
9.	If I think the team is moving in an unethical direction, I will say so explicitly.	_____	_____
10.	Rarely will I criticize the progress of the team even if I think such criticism is deserved.	_____	_____
11.	It is not unusual for me to summarize the progress in a team meeting, even if not asked.	_____	_____
12.	To conserve time, I attempt to minimize contact with my teammates outside of our meetings.	_____	_____
13.	I intensely dislike going along with a consensus decision if the decision runs contrary to my thoughts on the issue.	_____	_____
14.	I rarely remind teammates of our mission statement as we go about our work.	_____	_____
15.	Once I have made up my mind on an issue facing the team, I am unlikely to be persuaded in another direction.	_____	_____
16.	I am willing to accept negative feedback from team members.	_____	_____
17.	Simply to get a new member of the team involved, I will ask his or her opinion.	_____	_____
18.	Even if the team has decided on a course of action, I am not hesitant to bring in new information that supports another position.	_____	_____
19.	Quite often I talk negatively about one team member to another.	_____	_____
20.	My teammates are almost a family to me because I am truly concerned about their welfare.	_____	_____
21.	When it seems appropriate, I joke and kid with teammates.	_____	_____
22.	My contribution to team tasks is as important to me as my individual work.	_____	_____
23.	From time to time, I have pointed out to the team how we can all improve in reaching our goals.	_____	_____
24.	I will fight to the last when the team does not support my viewpoint and wants to move toward consensus.	_____	_____
25.	I will confront the team if I believe that the members are thinking too much alike.	_____	_____
	Total Score		_____

(continued)

Scoring and Interpretation:

Give yourself one point (+1) for each statement you gave in agreement with the keyed answer. The keyed answer indicates carrying out a positive, as opposed to a negative, role.

1. Mostly agree	10. Mostly disagree	19. Mostly disagree
2. Mostly agree	11. Mostly agree	20. Mostly agree
3. Mostly disagree	12. Mostly disagree	21. Mostly agree
4. Mostly agree	13. Mostly disagree	22. Mostly agree
5. Mostly disagree	14. Mostly disagree	23. Mostly agree
6. Mostly agree	15. Mostly disagree	24. Mostly disagree
7. Mostly disagree	16. Mostly agree	25. Mostly agree
8. Mostly agree	17. Mostly agree	
9. Mostly agree	18. Mostly agree	

20–25   You carry out a well above average number of positive team roles. Behavior of this type contributes substantially to being an effective team player. Study the roles in this chapter to further build your effectiveness as a team member.

10–19   You carry out an average number of positive team roles. Study carefully the roles described in this chapter to search for ways to carry out a greater number of positive roles.

0–9   You carry out a substantially above-average number of negative team roles. If becoming an effective team player is important to you, you will have to diligently search for ways to play positive team roles. Study the information about roles in this chapter carefully.

Source: "Team Player Roles" by Andrew J. DuBrin.

2. **Resource investigator.**   The resource investigator is extraverted and enthusiastic and communicates freely with other team members. He or she will explore opportunities and develop valuable contacts. A potential weakness of this role is that the person can be overly optimistic and may lose interest after the initial enthusiasm wanes.

3. **Coordinator.**   The coordinator is mature, confident, and a natural team leader. He or she clarifies goals, promotes decision making, and delegates effectively. A downside to occupying this role is that the person might be seen as manipulative and controlling. Some coordinators delegate too much by asking others to do some of the work they (the coordinators) should be doing.

4. **Shaper.**   The shaper is challenging and dynamic and thrives under pressure. He or she will use determination and courage to overcome obstacles. A potential weakness of the shaper is that he or she can be easily provoked and may ignore the feelings of others.

5. **Monitor–evaluator.**   The monitor–evaluator is even tempered, engages in strategic (big-picture and long-term) thinking, and makes accurate judgments. He or she sees all the options and judges accurately. A potential weakness of this role occupant is that he or she might lack drive and the ability to inspire others.

6. **Team worker.**   The team worker is cooperative, focuses on relationships, and is sensitive and diplomatic. He or she is a good listener who builds relationships, dislikes confrontation, and averts friction. A potential weakness is that the team worker can be indecisive in a crunch situation or crisis.

7. **Implementer.**   The implementer is disciplined, reliable, conservative, and efficient. He or she will act quickly on ideas and convert them into practical actions. A potential weakness is that the implementer can be inflexible and slow to see new opportunities.

8. **Completer–finisher.** The completer–finisher is conscientious and eager to get the job done. He or she has a good eye for detail and is effective at searching out errors. He or she can be counted on for finishing a project and delivering on time. A potential weakness is that he or she can be a worrier and reluctant to delegate.

9. **Specialist.** The specialist is a single-minded self-starter. He or she is dedicated and provides knowledge and skill in rare supply. A potential weakness of the specialist is that he or she can be stuck in a niche with little interest in other knowledge and may dwell on technicalities.

The weaknesses in the roles point to problems the team leader or manager can expect to emerge, and therefore allowances should be made. Belbin refers to these potential problems as *allowable weaknesses,* because allowances should be made for them. To illustrate, if a team worker has a tendency to be indecisive in a crisis, the team should not have high expectations of the team worker when faced with a crisis. Team workers will be the most satisfied if the crisis is predicted and decisions involving them are made before the pressure mounts.[32]

Another perspective on team roles is that team members will sometimes engage in *self-oriented roles.* Members will sometimes focus on their own needs rather than those of the group. The individual might be overly aggressive because of a personal need, such as wanting a bigger budget on his or her project. The individual might hunger for recognition or power. Similarly, the person might attempt to dominate the meeting, block others from contributing, or serve as a distraction. One of the ploys used by distracters recently is to engage in cell phone conversations during a meeting and blaming it on "those people who keep calling me."

The many roles just presented overlap somewhat. For example, the implementer might engage in specialist activities. Do not be concerned about the overlap. Instead, pick and choose from the many roles as the situation dictates—regardless of whether overlap exists.

The behavior associated with the roles just described is more important than remembering the labels. For example, remembering to be creative and imaginative is more important than remembering the specific label *creative problem solver*.

THE PROBLEM OF GROUPTHINK (TOO MUCH CONSENSUS)

For a team to be truly effective, somebody has to step forth and say, "The emperor has no clothes," when the group is making an outrageously bad decision. Often the shaper or monitor–evaluator plays this role. **Groupthink** is a deterioration of mental efficiency, reality testing, and moral judgment in the interest of group solidarity. Simply put, groupthink is an extreme form of consensus. The group atmosphere values getting along with each other more than getting things done.[33] The group thinks as a unit, believes it is impervious to outside criticism, and begins to have illusions about its own invincibility. As a consequence, the group loses its powers of critical analysis.

One historically important example of groupthink took place in relation to the explosion of the space shuttle *Challenger*. According to several analyses of the incident, NASA managers were so committed to reaching space program objectives that they ignored safety warnings from people both within and outside the agency. As reported in an internal NASA briefing paper dated July 20, 1986, both astronauts and engineers expressed concern that the agency's management had a groupthink mentality. Of related significance, the management style of NASA managers is characterized by a tendency not to reverse decisions and not to heed the advice of people outside the management group. The analysis of their styles was conducted by a series of management-style tests administered several years prior to the *Challenger* explosion.[34]

Groupthink appears to have contributed to several of the major financial scandals of several years ago involving major investment banks. Several such scandals have

Groupthink
a deterioration of mental efficiency, reality testing, and moral judgment in the interest of group solidarity; extreme form of consensus

resurfaced. The investment banks in question offered mortgage-backed securities to the public without informing their clients that the mortgages behind these securities were high risk. When homeowners defaulted on their mortgages, the securities lost considerable value or became worthless. Groupthink was probably involved because highly paid, intelligent individual financial executives most likely would not have attempted frauds of this magnitude. (Or the bankers involved simply had low ethics.)

The negative aspects of groupthink can often be prevented if the team leader, or a member, encourages all team members to express doubts and criticisms of proposed solutions to the problem or suggested courses of action. It is also helpful to periodically invite qualified outsiders to meet with the group and provide suggestions.

▶ **Learning Objective 12.6** ▶

Characteristics of an Effective Work Group

Groups, like individuals, have characteristics that contribute to their uniqueness and effectiveness. Effectiveness includes such factors as objective measures of production (for example, units produced), favorable evaluations by the manager, and worker satisfaction. In understanding how groups can be effective, keep in mind that a justification for forming groups and teams is that they can produce more than the sum of the individual

FIGURE 12-2

KEY CHARACTERISTICS OF EFFECTIVE TEAMS AND WORK GROUPS

1. The team has clear-cut goals linked to organizational goals so that group members feel connected to the entire organization. Group members are empowered so they learn to think for themselves rather than expecting a supervisor to solve all the difficult problems.

2. Group members are assigned work they perceive to be challenging, exciting, and rewarding. As a consequence, the work is self-rewarding.

3. Members depend on one another to accomplish tasks and work toward a common goal. The group believes in itself and that it can accomplish an interdependent task. Group members who engage in *social loafing* (not doing their fair share) are advised by other group members and the team leader that they must perform at an acceptable level. Complementary skills within the team facilitate the interdependence, such as one member being strong on details, and another member good at seeing the big picture.

4. Members receive extensive training in technical knowledge, problem-solving skills, and interpersonal skills. Also, the team develops *team cognition,* in which knowledge important to the group is organized and distributed within the group, allowing for appropriate action.

5. Group size is generally about six people, rather than ten or more.

6. Team members have good intelligence, creative problem-solving skills, and personality factors, such as conscientiousness and pride that contribute to good performance.

7. There is honest and open communication among group members and with other groups in the organization.

8. Members have the philosophy of working as a team—twenty-five brains, not only fifty hands.

9. Members are familiar with their jobs, coworkers, and the work environment. This experience adds to their expertise. The beneficial effects of experience may diminish after a while because the team needs fresh ideas and approaches.

10. The team has emotional intelligence in the sense that it builds relationships both inside and outside the team. Included in emotional intelligence are norms that establish mutual trust among members, a feeling of group identity, and group efficacy. (Emotional intelligence for individual group members is more important when the worker is involved in tasks involving interactions with people.)

11. Stronger-performing group members assist weaker-performing group members accomplish their task, particularly when the performance of the "weakest link" in the group is key for group performance.

Sources: Crystal I. C. Chien Farh et al., "Emotional Intelligence, Teamwork Effectiveness, and Job Performance: The Moderating Role of Job Context," *Journal of Applied Psychology*, July 2012, pp. 890–900; Claus W. Langred, "Too Much of a Good Thing? Negative Effects of High Trust and Individual Autonomy in Self-Managing Work Teams," *Academy of Management Journal,* June 2004, pp. 385–399; Leslie A. DeChurch and Jessica R. Mesmer-Magnus, "The Cognitive Underpinnings of Effective Teamwork: A Meta-Analysis," *Journal of Applied Psychology,* January 2010, pp. 32–53; Mimi Bacilek, "Build Team with Complementary Skills," *USA Today Money,* February 18, 2014, p. 6B.

members, that is, have synergy. As the late Stephen Covey explained, to synergize is to combine the efforts, power, and positive energy of people who come together in order to accomplish a goal. The process of synergizing also multiplies the value all participants bring to the interaction.[35]

For a group to be effective, the members must strive to act like a group or team. Also, the task given to the group or team should require collective effort instead of being a task that could be better performed by individuals. For example, many customers would prefer to be called on by an individual sales representative rather than by a sales team, so for some customers the rep should work individually rather than in a team effort. As shown in Figure 12-2, and based on dozens of different studies, effective work group and team characteristics can be grouped into eleven factors. The accompanying Human Relations in Practice describes two highly effective work groups.

Human Relations in Practice

The Fuel-Cell Automobile Team at Toyota

The success of the Mirai, the fuel-cell automobile designed and manufactured by Toyota, is in the hands of an elite group of workers. A fuel-cell engine is powered by a fuel-cell stack combining hydrogen with oxygen to produce water. A stream of electricity is generated in the process. The only waste or emission is a small amount of water. Some of the hydrogen is produced by rotting garbage. To fuel the vehicle, you fill up with compressed hydrogen gas that combines with oxygen from the atmosphere. The process takes a few minutes and powers the vehicle for about 300 miles.

To test a prototype of the vehicle, the original group of nine workers logged more than 1 million miles. On trips lasting weeks at a time, the group based in California took the vehicle from Yellowknife, Canada, to Death Valley, California. The test car started immediately after being left overnight in the -30°F is not very cold at Yellowknife, whereas a support vehicle failed to start.

At Toyota City, Japan, the Mirai is manufactured by a team of thirteen skilled workers, who were selected for their talent and potential. The team assembles three cars a day, after receiving a painted body from another section of the plant. The assembly activity is regarded as a *dojo,* or training studio, for craftsmanship. Team members spend two years learning how to assemble much of the car by hand. The production process for the Mirai resembles that used to produce a boutique sports car. In place of a belt moving the vehicle from one area to another, it is pushed by group members between areas. The hands-on approach is designed to guarantee an attention to quality.

Toyota President Akio Toyoda says that the factory where the Mirai is produced is not so advanced. Instead, the company relies on the work of its skilled employees.

Question:

Why might it be important for members of the fuel-cell team who tested the vehicle, as well as the team that assembles the vehicle, to be good team players?

Source: Original story created from facts and observations in the following sources: Alex Taylor III, "Tire Kicking Toyota Style," *Fortune,* April 28, 2014, p. 80; "See How Toyota Mirai Fuel Cell Car Is Made," www.autoblog.com, February 24, 2015. pp. 1–16; Yoko Kubota, "Toyota's Mirai Fuel-Cell Car: 13 Workers Make Three per Day," *Japan Realtime/The Wall Street Journal*, February 24, 2015, pp. 1–2; "Toyota's Futuristic, Freak Fuel-Cell Car," http://money.cnn.com, December 18, 2014, pp. 1–3.

Concept Review and Reinforcement

Summary and Review

Motivating others toward good performance begins with the diagnosis of motivation. Diagnostic questions might include "What could this job offer you that would make you work at your best?" Diagnosis should also include observing the subordinate's behavior in terms of what interests him or her.

Empowerment is a comprehensive motivational strategy that grants workers more power by enabling them to participate in decisions affecting them and their work:

- Empowerment contributes to intrinsic motivation.
- Empowerment is commonplace in the service industry.
- Empowered employees must still be given overall direction and limits to the extent of their authority.

Motivation can take place through job design and interesting work. The two-factor theory of work motivation explains how to design jobs to make them more motivational. According to the theory, one set of factors, the motivators or satisfiers, can motivate and satisfy workers. The other set, dissatisfiers, or hygiene factors, can only prevent dissatisfaction.

If you make jobs more interesting, there may be less need for motivating people with external rewards. Motivating people through interesting work is based on the principle of intrinsic motivation. Such motivation contributes even more to productivity when combined with prosocial (helping others) motivation.

Job enrichment makes a job more motivating and satisfying through means such as the following:

- Direct feedback to the job incumbent
- The opportunity for client relationships
- New learning

Rules for effectively using positive reinforcement to motivate employees include the following:

- State clearly what behavior will lead to a reward.
- Choose an appropriate reward.
- Supply ample feedback.
- Schedule rewards intermittently.
- Make the rewards follow the observed behavior closely in time.
- Make the reward fit the behavior.
- Make the rewards visible.
- Change the reward periodically.

Financial incentives are a natural motivator and are a form of positive reinforcement. Such incentives have multiplied in importance as companies struggle to stay afloat in worldwide competition. Money is also tied in with recognition. Key issues about financial incentives include the following:

- To make pay more motivational, many employers link pay to performance, such as in variable pay and financial bonuses.
- Personal factors influence the power of financial incentives, including the value the worker attaches to money and his or her need for money.
- Financial incentives can cause problems, including workers attaining good financial results by unethical means and focusing more on rewards than on the joy built into exciting work.

Motivation through recognition and praise is an important motivational strategy because the workplace provides a natural opportunity to satisfy the recognition need. Praising workers for good performance is closely related to informal recognition. Many workers rarely receive praise. An advanced use of praise is to tailor the praise to the needs of the person. Formal recognition programs are important for employee retention as well as motivation.

Team leaders as well as other managers need to use techniques that influence subordinates to work well together as a team. Among the many suggestions presented in the chapter for building teamwork are the following:

- Select members for the team who are interested in being and qualified to be strong team members.
- Help team members believe they have an urgent, constructive purpose.
- Use the consensus decision-making style.
- Reward the team as well as individuals.
- Have a culture of teamwork.
- Encourage communication among virtual team members.

Understanding how groups operate (group dynamics) helps a leader effectively build teamwork. One useful concept is the stages of group development: forming, storming, norming, performing, and adjourning. Team members occupy various roles, including the following:

- Resource investigator
- Coordinator
- Monitor–evaluator
- Completer–finisher
- Specialist

A key potential problem with group effort is groupthink, or extreme consensus. The problem can be lessened by team members occupying a critical role.

An effective work group has characteristics that contribute to its uniqueness and effectiveness, as outlined in Figure 12-2. For a group to be effective, the members must strive to be a team and work on a task that requires collective effort.

Questions for Discussion and Review

12.1 How could diagnosing the motivational wishes and needs of employees save a company a lot of money when launching motivational programs?

12.2 What objection might some employees have to being empowered?

12.3 In what way does job enrichment appeal to the pride some people have in their work?

12.4 How can a professional-level worker use smiling as a form of positive reinforcement?

12.5 Visualize a cafeteria worker who observes an employee seated at a table who is choking to death. The cafeteria worker runs over and squeezes the employee back to normal breathing (the Heimlich maneuver). What kind of reward would fit the cafeteria worker's behavior?

12.6 A small percentage of sales representatives work strictly on commission. What negative impact might this pay arrangement have on customers?

12.7 What type of recognition on the job would be motivational for you? How do you know?

12.8 Assume that Jennifer from the tech support center gets rid of a nasty virus in your tablet computer. What is likely to be an effective statement of praise for her?

12.9 Give an example of one or two group norms that a team of firefighters might have.

12.10 Identify several of the characteristics of an effective work group that one of your favorite restaurants possesses. Justify your reasoning the best you can.

Web Corner

Suggestions for motivating professional-level employees
www.forbes.com (Enter "motivating professional-level employees" into search box.)

Gourmet cooking as a team-building exercise
www.recipeforsuccess.com

Teamwork posters
www.art.com (Enter "teamwork posters" in search box.)

INTERNET SKILL BUILDER

Motivating Employees

Visit www.nelson-motivation.com, and enter "video clips" into the search box. Watch a video clip of one of Bob Nelson's talks. After watching the video, answer the following questions:

12.1 What have I learned that I could translate into a skill for motivating employees?

12.2 Which theory, or approach, to motivation does Nelson emphasize in his presentation?

Developing Your Human Relations Skills

Applying Human Relations Exercise 12-1

The Job Enrichment Squad

Work individually or in small groups to develop skill in enriching several standard jobs by making them more interesting, challenging, and responsibility oriented. As part of your analysis, see if you can find someone who has held such a job (either you or a group member), and interview the job incumbent for some ideas. You might e-mail or text as an alternative or supplement to telephone or face-to-face interviews. Choose three from among the following positions:

- Supermarket cashier
- Highway toll collector
- Custodial worker at an educational institution
- Home health aide
- Car wash attendant
- Call center operator for service with mobile phones

In your problem-solving activity and in your interviews, seek answers to these basic questions: (a) What is the most boring part of this job? (b) What is the most exciting part of this job? (c) What is the most demotivating part of the job? (d) What is the most motivating part of the job? (e) Find an answer to any other questions or issues you think are relevant.

After you have completed your analysis, prepare a report of about two brief paragraphs as to how the specific job can be more motivational through job design.

Applying Human Relations Exercise 12-2

Team Member Roles

A team of approximately six people is formed to conduct a twenty-minute meeting on a significant topic of their choosing. The possible scenarios follow:

Scenario A: Management Team A group of managers is pondering whether to lay off one-third of the workforce to increase profits. The company has had a tradition of caring for employees and regarding them as the company's most precious asset. But the CEO has said privately that times have changed in our competitive world, and the company must do whatever possible to enhance profits. The group wants to think through the advisability of laying off one-third the workforce and explore other alternatives.

Scenario B: Group of Sports Fans A group of fans has volunteered to find a new team name to replace Pit Bulls for the local basketball team. One person among the group of volunteers believes that the name Pit Bulls should be retained because it signifies strength and intensity. The other members of the group believe that a name change is in order, but they lack any good ideas for replacing a mascot team name that has endured for more than fifteen years..

Scenario C: Community Group A community group is attempting to launch an initiative to help battered adults and children. Opinions differ strongly as to what initiative would be truly helpful to these people. Among the alternatives are establishing a shelter for battered people, giving workshops on preventing violence, and self-defense training. Each group member with an idea strongly believes that he or she has come up with a workable possibility for helping with the problem of battered people.

While the team members are conducting their heated discussion, other class members make notes on which team members carry out which roles. Watching for the nine different roles, as well as the self-oriented roles, can be divided among class members. For example, the people in the first row might look for examples of the creative problem solver. Use the role worksheet that follows to help make your observations. Summarize the comment that is indicative of the role. An example would be noting in the shaper category: "Linda said naming the team the Environmentalists seems like too much of an attempt to be politically correct."

Creative problem solver _____

Team worker _____

Resource investigator _____

Implementer _____

Coordinator _____

Completer–finisher _____

Shaper _____

Specialist _____

Monitor–evaluator _____

Self-oriented roles _____

Human Relations Class Activity

A Survey of Positive Motivators

As explained in this chapter, positive reinforcement works well as a motivational technique only when the right (effective) motivators (or reinforcers) are used. Plenty of written information is available about what constitutes effective motivators, including recognition. For this class activity, you will collect fresh data about effective motivators. The steps are as follows:

1. Each student completes the following sentence: "The most effective form of positive reinforcement I ever received on the job (or in school, sports, or community activity) was _____."
2. Each student submits his or her answer to a class database. If the class has a website, intranet, or similar centralized method of collecting input, simply submit your answer using that medium. If you do not have such a system, simply send an e-mail or instant message to every class member with your answer.
3. Each student, or a few volunteers, will then compile a list of the five most effective motivators, based on how frequently the motivator was mentioned. For example, perhaps four class members completed the sentence with a response such as "I was given a gift certificate for having been an outstanding performer."
4. If the class size is large enough, look for possible sex differences in preference for motivators.
5. Hold a class discussion of (a) how well you think the class findings might fit many different work settings and (b) how useful this activity has been in giving you ideas for motivating workers.

Human Relations Case Study 12–1

Squeezing Out Higher Motivation from Dental Hygienists

Cindy is the office manager at Craig Dental Arts, a large dental practice headed by Ben Craig, DDS. One of Cindy's many responsibilities is to coordinate the online satisfaction surveys patients are asked to complete a couple of days following their visit with a dental hygienist. A large part of the revenue from the dental practice stems from visits with the hygienists. As a result, Cindy scans the patient replies looking for clues about patient satisfaction with the seven dental hygienists Craig employs full-time and part-time.

During a discussion about the status of the dental practice with Dr. Craig, Cindy comments, "It looks like our patients are generally satisfied with hygienist staff, but I don't see a wave of enthusiasm. A passion for the service they are receiving seems to be missing. I wonder if our dental hygienists are strongly motivated to provide exceptional dental care."

Ben responds, "I wonder the same thing. When I talk to our hygienists individually, they don't seem so excited about their work. A good example is Raoul. I asked him how his work was going, and he said, 'Okay, but after you have scraped the tartar from 5,000 different teeth, it gets a little repetitious and dull.' The other day, I asked Lauren how she liked her work with patients, and she told me, 'Not bad. I am very happy today because now I get four consecutive days off.'

Cindy says, "Maybe we have a motivation problem. Do you think we should give the hygienists bonuses when they receive great comments on the patient surveys? Or maybe we should have an award for the dental hygienist of the month. How about putting motivational posters on the wall?"

Ben concludes the conversation, "We are dealing with professionals, so we don't want to be too hokey. Yet we should think through a good approach to motivating our hygienist staff toward more outstanding patient care."

Questions

12.11 What suggestion might you offer Craig Dental Arts for enhancing the motivation of the hygienist staff?

12.12 How advisable would it be for Cindy and Ben to discuss the possible motivational problem with the hygienist staff?

12.13 How valid is Dr. Craig's concern about a motivational program being too hokey?

Human Relations Role-Playing Exercise

A Motivational Meeting with the Dental Hygienists

One student plays the role of Cindy and another the role of Ben. The two are conducting a group meeting to discuss with the hygienists (a) if they have a motivation problem, and (b) if a problem exists, what the dental practice might do to increase their motivation. Seven other students play the role of hygienists, a couple of whom do not understand the relevance of this meeting.

Observers rate the role-players on two dimensions, using a scale of 1 to 5 from very poor to very good. One dimension is "effective use of human relations techniques." Look carefully to see if Cindy and Ben do a reasonable job of diagnosing a motivational problem. The second dimension is "acting ability." A few observers might voluntarily provide feedback to the role-players in terms of sharing their ratings and observations. The course instructor might also provide feedback.

Human Relations Case Study 12–2

Ruth Waves a Red Flag

Carlos is the team leader of a cost reduction team within a baked-goods company that produces bakery products under its own label, as well as private labels for grocery store chains such as Giant and Winn-Dixie. Top-level management formed the team to arrive at suggestions for reducing costs throughout the organization. A transcript of one of the meetings is presented next.

Carlos: We've been gathering information for a month now. It's about time we heard some specific suggestions.

Jack: At the top of my list is cutting pension benefits. Our pension payments are higher than the minimum required by law. Our medical benefits are way above average. If we cut back on pension benefits, no current employees would be adversely affected.

Melissa: I like your analysis, Jack. No sense risking laying off employees just to keep retirees happy.

Jordan: We should make absolutely certain there are no legal complications here. Then we can sharpen our cost-cutting knives and dig right in.

Gunther: I'd support cutting pension benefits. It would probably reduce expenses more dramatically than the ways I have uncovered.

Carlos: There seems to be consensus so far that we should considered making recommendations about cutting pension benefits. Ruth, what do you think?

Ruth: I think it is much too early to reach consensus on such a sensitive issue. Cutting pension benefits would create panic among our retirees. Our older employees would be screaming as well. We'll have an avalanche of negative publicity in the media.

Jordan: Hold on, Ruth. I said the team should first check out this idea with the legal department.

Ruth: Just because cutting pension benefits could squeeze by legally doesn't mean that it's a good idea. We haven't examined the negative ramifications of cutting pension benefits. Let's study this issue further before word leaks out that we're taking away the golden egg.

Carlos: Maybe Ruth has a point. Let's investigate this issue further before making a recommendation.

Questions

12.14 What role, or roles, is Ruth occupying on the cost reduction team?

12.15 How effective does Ruth appear to be in her role?

12.16 What role, or roles, is Jack occupying on the cost reduction team?

12.17 How effective does Jack appear to be in his role?

12.18 How effective is Carlos in his role as a team leader?

REFERENCES

1. Original story created from facts and observations in the following sources: Marco della Cava, "Porch CEO Matt Ehrlichman Credits Great Team for Success," *USA Today Money*, December 11, 2014, pp. 5B, 6B; Todd Bishop, "Fast-Growing Porch Tops 100 Employees, Seeks New CTO, Consolidates Operations at New Seattle HQ," www.geekwire.com, February 14, 2014, pp. 1–6; "Best Advice I Ever Got: Matt Ehrlichman," *Inc.*, www.inc.com, September 23, 2013, p. 1; "Our Story: The House That Built Porch," http://aboutporch.com, pp. 2–4, accessed April 15, 2015.

2. John Sullivan, "Personalizing Motivation," *Workforce Management*, March 27, 2006, p. 50.

3. Gretchen M. Spreitzer, "Psychological Empowerment in the Workplace: Dimensions, Measurement, and Validation," *Academy of Management Journal*, October 1995, pp. 1443–1444.

4. Craig L. Pearce, Charles C. Manz, and Henry P. Sims Jr., "Is Shared Leadership the Key to Team Success?" *Organizational Dynamics*, July–September 2009, p. 238.

5. Danni Wang, David A. Waldman, and Zhen Zhang, "An Analysis of Shared Leadership and Team Effectiveness," *Journal of Applied Psychology*, March 2014, pp. 181–198.

6. Irv Rothman, "Teamwork at Its Best," *Executive Leadership*, December 2013, p. 3.

7. Frederick Herzberg, Bernard Mausner, and Barbara Synderman, *The Motivation to Work*, 2nd ed. (New York: Wiley, 1959); Herzberg, *Work and the Nature of Man* (Cleveland: World Publishing, 1966).

8. Adam M. Grant, "Does Intrinsic Motivation Fuel the Prosocial Fire? Motivational Synergy in Predicting Persistence, Performance, and Productivity," *Journal of Applied Psychology*, January 2008, pp. 48–58.

9. Frederick Herzberg, "The Wise Old Turk," *Harvard Business Review*, September–October 1974, pp. 70–80.

10. David Javitch, "Getting Your Employees Excited Again," *Entrepreneur*, August 7, 2006.

11. Fred Luthans and Alexander Stajkovic, "Reinforce for Performance: The Need to Go beyond Pay and Even Rewards," *Academy of Management Executive*, May 1999, p. 52.

12. Steven Kerr, *Ultimate Rewards: What Really Motivates People to Achieve* (Boston: Harvard Business School Publishing, 1997).

13. Matt Dunning, "More Companies Linking Rewards, Penalties to Wellness Program Results, *Workforce*, www.workforce.com, August 9, 2012, pp. 1–2.

14. Doug J. Chung, "How to *Really* Motivate Salespeople," *Harvard Business Review*, April 2015, p. 58.

15. Cited in Ken Blanchard, Vicki Stanford, and David Witt, "Singing the Praises of Praises," *Workforce*, April 2014, p. 39.

16. Cited in ibid., p. 37.

17. Reported in "Employees Want More Recognition, Growth Opportunity," *Monitor on Psychology*, May 2011, p. 12.

18. Andrew J. DuBrin, "Self-Perceived Technical Orientation and Attitudes toward Being Flattered," *Psychological Reports*, Vol. 96, 2005, pp. 852–854.

19. Charlotte Garvey, "Meaningful Tokens of Appreciation: Cash Awards Aren't the Only Way to Motivate Your Workforce," *HR Magazine*, August 2004, p. 103.

20. Susan Ladika, "Companies Recognize the Importance of Recognition," *Workforce*, December 2013, p. 52.

21. Jon R. Katzenbach and Douglas K. Smith, "The Discipline of Teams," *Harvard Business Review*, March–April 1993, p. 112.

22. Frederick P. Morgeson, Matthew H. Reider, and Michael A. Campion, "Selecting Individuals in Team Settings: The Importance of Social Skills, Personality Characteristics, and Teamwork Knowledge," *Personnel Psychology*, Autumn 2005, pp. 583–611.

23. Jan Wieseke et al., "How Leaders' Motivation Transfers to Customer Service Representatives," *Journal of Service Research*, No. 2, 2011, pp. 214–233.

24. Joseph C. Santora, "Do Happy Leaders Make for Better Team Performance?" *Academy of Management Perspectives*, November 2011, pp. 88–90; Nai-Wen Chi, Yen-Yi Chung, and Wei-Chi Tsai, "How Do Happy Leaders Enhance Team Success? The Mediating Role of Transformational Leadership, Group Affective Tone, and Team Processes," *Journal of Applied Social Psychology*, June 11, pp. 1421–1454.

25. Katy Burne, Kirsten Grind, and Tom Lauricella, "New Pimco Captain's Style: More Team Spirt, Less TV," *The Wall Street Journal*, October 1, 2014, p. C1.

26. Matt Bolch, "Rewarding the Team," *HR Magazine*, February 2007, p. 92.

27. Ann Majchrzak, Arvind Malhgotra, Jeffrey Stamps, and Jessica Lipnack, "Can Absence Make a Team Grow Stronger?" *Harvard Business Review*, May 2004, pp. 131–137.

28. Julia E. Hoch and W. J. Kozlowski, "Leading Virtual Teams: Hierarchical Leadership, Structural Supports, and Shared Team Leadership," *Journal of Applied Psychology*, May 2014, pp. 390–403.

29. "5 Ways to Create Team Motivation," *Manager's Edge*, November 2007, p. 4.

30. J. Steven Heinen and Eugene Jacobsen, "A Model of Task Group Development in Complex Organizations and a Strategy of Implementation," *Academy of Management Review*, October 1976, pp. 98–111.

31. R. Meredith Belbin, "Belbin Team-Roles," in *Business: The Ultimate Resource* (Cambridge, MA: Perseus Publishing, 2002), pp. 966–967.

32. From a review of Meredith Belbin, *Management Teams: Why They Succeed or Fail*, 2nd ed. (London: Butterworth Heinemann, 2004), by Colin Thomson appearing at http://www.accountingweb.co.uk. March 13, 2005.

33. Irving L. Janis, *Victims of Groupthink: A Psychological Study of Foreign Policy Decisions and Fiascos* (Boston: Houghton Mifflin, 1972), pp. 39–40; Glenn Whyte, "Groupthink Reconsidered," *Academy of Management Review*, January 1989, pp. 40–56.

34. Kenneth A. Kovach and Barry Bender, "NASA Managers and *Challenger*: A Profile of Possible Explanations," *Personnel*, April 1987, p. 40.

35. Stephen R. Covey, *The Seven Habits of Highly Effective People* (New York: Simon & Schuster, 1989).

CHAPTER **13**

Diversity and Cross-Cultural Competence

Fotolia

Outline

Loews Hotels (not Lowe's, the home-improvement giant) is a group of eighteen elegant luxury hotels and resorts located throughout the United States. The company grew from a small family-owned winter resort in New Jersey over sixty years ago. Loews is distinctive in many ways, including the breathtaking guest rooms and lobbies. Another aspect of the company's distinctiveness is its commitment to multiculturalism, in both words and actions.

A major multicultural initiative at the corporate level is the minority business enterprise program that provides qualified business firms the opportunity to become partners of Loews Hotels. After a small company submits a profile online to Loews, the profile is evaluated and entered into the company database. Among the products and services bought from minority companies are operating supplies and equipment, food and beverage, logistics services, and utilities. The criteria for becoming a partner of Loews include hospitality references, competitive prices, and a minimum three-year business history.

The Loews Coronado Bay, a high-end resort hotel in San Diego, California, provides an example of appreciating multiculturalism at the hotel level. Barbara Vale, the director of human resources, says that the employees are treated with the same level of respect given to guests. A specific focus is ensuring the comfort of the hotel's employees, who are predominantly Asian, Filipino, and Latino. Cafeteria meals are free and reflect the tastes of each cultural group. Furthermore, Vale keeps records of important holidays and celebrations for each culture. As a human touch, on the Mexican Mother's Day, every Latina mother working at the hotel receives a rose.[1]

Learning Objectives ▶

After studying the information and doing the exercises in this chapter, you should be able to:

13.1 Explain some of the major ways in which cultures differ from one another.

13.2 Describe techniques for improving cross-cultural relations.

13.3 Be sensitive to potential cultural bloopers.

13.4 Be prepared to overcome cross-cultural communication barriers.

13.5 Be aware of additional ways in which organizations use diversity to advantage.

13.6 Be aware of some of the legal aspects of working in a culturally diverse environment.

The story about Loews illustrates the point that welcoming diversity has become an established practice in large, successful organizations. As a result, being able to work well with people from diverse groups, including other cultures both outside and inside your own country, is important for career success. To work well with diverse groups, it is helpful to make a distinction between two types of diversity. *Surface-level diversity* is about differences in visible characteristics, such as gender, race, ethnicity, and physical status. *Deep-level diversity* is about differences in underlying psychological characteristics, such as personality, attitudes, values, and sexual orientation.[2] For example, as a team member, you might encounter surface-level diversity, but you will almost always encounter deep-level diversity.

Being able to relate to a culturally diverse customer base is also necessary for success. Not only is the workforce becoming more diverse, but business has also become increasingly international or globalized. Small- and medium-size firms, as well as corporate giants, are increasingly dependent on trade with other countries. Furthermore, with the large number of jobs sent overseas, more U.S. workers will have contact with personnel in foreign countries.

Customers often take a careful look at the diversity of their supplier. Retailers are also involved in globalization because so many store customers are immigrants. Many companies are using bilingual websites to convert online browsers into in-store customers. Similarly, some retailers are hiring store associates with foreign-language skills and updating store signs and displays to appeal to immigrants. The globalization of business therefore increases the relevance of cross-cultural skills.

The consultancy McKinsey & Company conducted a study that confirms the potential benefits of diversity to business. Companies in the top quartile for racial and ethnic diversity are 30 percent more likely to outperform their competitors. Companies in the top quartile for gender diversity are 15 percent more likely to have better financial returns than others in the industry.[3]

This chapter presents ideas and techniques you can use to sharpen your ability to work effectively with people from diverse backgrounds, or to be *inclusive* in your relationships with people. We also include a discussion of antidiscrimination legislation that protects the rights of workers, as well as specific company initiatives dealing with diversity.

▶ **Learning Objective 13.1** ▶

Major Dimensions of Differences in Cultural Values

Culture
a learned and shared system of knowledge, beliefs, values, attitudes, and norms

Everything we do in work and personal life is influenced by a combination of heredity and culture, or nature and nurture. You might be thirsty at this moment because a genetically produced mechanism in your brain tells you it is time to ingest fluid. But if you choose to drink bottled water, or papaya juice with a coworker, you are engaging in culturally learned behavior. **Culture** is a learned and shared system of knowledge, beliefs, values, attitudes, and norms. As such, culture includes an enormous amount of behavior. Here we describe eight dimensions of cultural values that help us understand how cultures differ from each other.[4] In other words, various cultures value different types of behavior.

Recognize that these dimensions are stereotypes, representing a typical value for a person in a given culture. You might find, for example, that most Chinese people are oriented more toward the group than seeking individual recognition, but you might meet some Chinese people who are egotistical and self-centered.

1. **Individualism versus collectivism.** At one end of the continuum is individualism, a mental set in which people see themselves first as individuals and believe that their own interests take priority. Members of a society who value individualism are more concerned with their careers than with the good of the firm. Members of a society who value collectivism, in contrast, are typically more concerned with the organization or the work group than with themselves. An example of individualistic behavior would be to want to win an "employee of the month" award; an example of collectivistic behavior would be to want to win an award for the team. Highly individualistic cultures include the United States, Canada, and the Netherlands. Japan and Mexico are among the countries that strongly value collectivism. But with the increasing emphasis on teamwork in American culture, more U.S. workers are becoming collectivistic.

2. **Acceptance of power and authority.** People from some cultures accept the idea that members of an organization have different levels of power and authority. In a culture that believes in concentration of power and authority, the boss makes many decisions simply because he or she is the boss. Group members readily comply because they have a positive orientation toward authority, including high respect for elders. In a culture that accepts power and authority less, employees do not recognize a power hierarchy. They accept directions only when they think the boss is right or when they feel threatened. Cultures that readily accept power and authority include France, China, Malaysia, and India. Countries that have much less acceptance of power and authority are the United States and, particularly, the Scandinavian countries (for example, Sweden).

3. **Materialism versus concern for others.** In this context, *materialism* refers to an emphasis on assertiveness and the acquisition of money and material objects. It also means deemphasizing caring for others. At the other end of the continuum is concern for others, an emphasis on personal relations, and a concern for the welfare of others. Materialistic countries include Japan and Italy. The United States is considered to be moderately materialistic. For example, the high participation rates in charities suggest that Americans are interested in the welfare of others, and therefore not totally materialistic. Scandinavian countries all emphasize caring as a national value.

4. Formality versus informality.   A country that values formality attaches considerable importance to tradition, ceremony, social rules, and rank. At the other extreme, informality refers to a casual attitude toward these same aspects of culture. Workers in Latin American countries highly value formality, such as lavish public receptions and processions. Americans, Canadians, and Scandinavians are much more informal. Most of the world is becoming more informal through such practices as an emphasis on using the first name only during business introductions and talking with customers over the phone.

5. Urgent time orientation versus casual time orientation.   Individuals and nations attach different importance to time. People with an urgent time orientation perceive time as a scarce resource and tend to be impatient. People with a casual time orientation view time as an unlimited and unending resource and tend to be patient. Americans are noted for their urgent time orientation. They frequently impose deadlines and are eager to get started doing business. Asians and Middle Easterners, in contrast, are patient negotiators. Many corporate workers and entrepreneurs engaged in international business recognize the importance of building relationships slowly overseas.

6. Work orientation versus leisure orientation.   A major cultural difference is the number of hours per week and weeks per year people expect to invest in work versus leisure or other nonwork activities. American corporate professionals typically work about fifty-five hours per week, take forty-five-minute lunch breaks, and take two weeks of vacation. Japanese workers share similar values with respect to time invested in work. In contrast, many European countries have a shorter workweek with longer vacations. As European governments have accumulated enormous debt, there has been a move by several governments to lengthen workweeks.

7. High-context versus low-context cultures.   Cultures differ in how much importance they attach to the surrounding circumstances, or context, of an event. People from a high-context culture place more emphasis on *how* something is said rather than *what* is said. (They emphasize nonverbal communication.) For example, a person from a high-context culture is not likely to take you seriously if you smile when you say that you do not like his or her service.

High-context cultures make more extensive use of body language as part of their emphasis on nonverbal communication. Some cultures, such as the Hispanic and African American cultures, are high context. In contrast, Northern European cultures are low context and make less use of body language. The Anglo-American culture is considered to be medium-low context. People in low-context cultures seldom take time in business dealings to build relationships and establish trust.

8. Social support seeking.   This dimension refers to the degree to which people seek out others to help them with difficult problems through such means as listening, offering sympathy, and giving advice. Asians and Asian Americans are more reluctant to explicitly request support from close others than are European Americans. The hesitancy comes about because the Asians and Asian Americans are more concerned about negative relationship consequences, such as disrupting group harmony or receiving criticism from the other person. Another possible reason for the hesitancy is that Asians and Asian Americans expect social support without having to ask.[5]

The eight cultural values mentioned contribute to understanding how cultural differences contribute to diversity, but many other factors also lead to cultural differences. Among these factors would be the region of the country in which a person was raised and whether the person lives in a large city, a small city, or a rural area. Socioeconomic class is a major contributor to cultural differences. For example, people from a higher socioeconomic class are likely to place more value on physical exercise and fitness, leading to better health.[6] One possible explanation is that people with higher disposable income can afford to invest in physical health.

One example of how cultural values can influence workplace behavior can be found in how McDonald's restaurants are operated around the world. In the United States, a manager is more likely to arrive at a solution to a workplace issue. In China, the manager might be quicker to seek approval from a supervisor based on the value of collectivism.[7] Another example is that studies conducted with participants recruited on the Internet found that workers with a high power-distance orientation were more likely to accept abusive supervision. (A high power-distance value prompts workers to think that the boss has the authority to be nasty.[8])

MULTICULTURAL IDENTITIES AND THE CULTURAL MOSAIC

Multicultural identities

individuals who incorporate the values of two or more cultures because they identify with both their primary culture and another culture or cultures

Another complexity about understanding cultural differences is that many people have **multicultural identities** because they identify with both their primary culture and another culture or cultures. As a consequence, these people may incorporate the values of two cultures. Being bilingual contributes to having two cultural identities because it is easier to identify with a foreign culture when one speaks the language of that culture.[9] Recent evidence suggests that multicultural workers are often good at solving complex problems, leading multicultural teams, and negotiating with workers from other cultures.[10]

Young people develop a global identity that gives them a feeling of belonging to a worldwide culture. The feeling of belongingness enables them to communicate with people from diverse places when they travel, when others travel to where they live, and when they communicate globally using e-mail, social media, and the telephone. Television and movies also help us develop a global identity.

Further, according to this theory, people retain a local identity along with their global identity. Young people in India provide an apt example. The country has a rapidly growing high-tech sector led mostly by young people. Yet most of these well-educated young people still cling to local traditions, such as a marriage arranged by the parents and the expectation that they will care for their parents in old age.[11]

Another complexity of culture is that a person's country is but one cultural influence. For example, people from the upper socioeconomic group within one country or ethnic group might value education and the use of grammatically correct speech more than people from a lower socioeconomic group.

The Cultural Mosaic

Cultural mosaic

an individual's unique mixture of multiple cultural identities that yields a complex picture of the cultural influences on that person

The fact of multicultural identities and different values among people from the same country and ethnic groups has been labeled the cultural mosaic by management professors Georgia T. Chao from Michigan State University and Henry Moon of Emory University. The **cultural mosaic** refers to an individual's unique mixture of multiple cultural identities, which yields a complex picture of the cultural influences on that person. Rather than choosing a particular "tile," such as race, gender, or country of origin, people develop an identity based on a mix of smaller tiles.[12] Every reader of this text is probably an example of a cultural mosaic. One of thousands of possible examples is that one person could derive a cultural identity from being (a) a U.S. citizen, (b) an African American, (c) a Baptist, (d) a male, (e) a musician, (f) a football player, (g) an accountant, and (h) a Southerner.

Religious Values

The religious value part of the cultural mosaic often affects when people are willing to work or not work. One potential cultural clash is that the rights of an individual to freely practice and observe religious beliefs sometimes collide with company goals. Differences in religious practices must be recognized because the number of religions in the workplace has increased substantially.

Religious diversity can create problems as more companies move to 24/7 (around-the-clock, seven-days-per-week) schedules. Employers therefore need more flexibility from employees, yet religious beliefs often limit times at which employees are willing to work.

The message for improved understanding is that employers must recognize workers' religious beliefs. At the same time, workers must understand the importance of a company meeting the demands of the marketplace, such as having twenty-four-hour customer service support. Workers, for example, can trade off working on each other's religious holidays.

APPLYING KNOWLEDGE OF CULTURAL DIFFERENCES IN VALUES

How might you use this information about cultural differences to improve your interpersonal relationships on the job? A starting point would be to recognize that a person's national values might influence his or her behavior. Assume that you wanted to establish a good working relationship with a person from a high-context culture. Make sure your facial expression fits the content of your words. For example, do not smile when, as a supervisor, you say, "No, you cannot take off tomorrow afternoon to have your French poodle groomed." You would also want to emphasize body language when communicating with that individual. A related point is that people from high-context cultures are more likely to touch and kiss strangers. As Fernando, who was raised in the Dominican Republic and is studying in the United States, said, "In my country, I hug people I meet for the first time. When I do it here, they think I'm very rude."

Approaches to Improving Cross-Cultural Relations

◀ Learning Objective 13.2 ◀

By now you are probably aware of how to improve cross-cultural relations by avoiding some of the mistakes already mentioned or implied, such as relying too heavily on group stereotypes. In this section, we take a systematic look at approaches you can use on your own along with training programs designed to improve cross-cultural relations. The methods and techniques for such improvement are outlined in Figure 13-1. Human Relations Self-Assessment Quiz 13-1 provides an opportunity to think about your cross-cultural skills and attitudes that could influence your ability to develop good cross-cultural relations.

Methods and techniques

1. Develop cultural sensitivity and cultural intelligence.
2. Focus on the individual rather than groups.
3. Respect all workers and cultures.
4. Value cultural differences.
5. Minimize cultural bloopers.
6. Participate in cultural training.
7. Participate in diversity training.

Improved cross-cultural relations

FIGURE 13-1

IMPROVING CROSS-CULTURAL RELATIONS

Source: "IMPROVING CROSS-CULTURAL RELATIONS" by Andrew J. DuBrin

Human Relations Self-Assessment Quiz 13-1

Cross-Cultural Skills and Attitudes

Following are skills and attitudes important for relating effectively to coworkers in a culturally diverse environment.

	Applies to Me Now	Not There Yet
1. I have spent some time in another country.	_____	_____
2. At least one of my friends is deaf or blind or uses a wheelchair.	_____	_____
3. Currency from other countries is as real as the currency from my own country.	_____	_____
4. I can read in a language other than my own.	_____	_____
5. I can speak in a language other than my own.	_____	_____
6. I can write in a language other than my own.	_____	_____
7. I can understand people speaking in a language other than my own.	_____	_____
8. I would feel comfortable reporting to a physically disabled boss.	_____	_____
9. My friends include people of races different from my own.	_____	_____
10. My friends include people of different generations.	_____	_____
11. I feel (or would feel) comfortable having a friend with a sexual orientation different from mine.	_____	_____
12. My attitude is that although another culture may be very different from mine, that culture is equally worthwhile.	_____	_____
13. I would be willing to (or already do) hang art from different countries in my home.	_____	_____
14. I would accept (or have already accepted) a work assignment of more than several months in another country.	_____	_____
15. I have a passport that has not expired.	_____	_____

Interpretation:

If you checked "Applies to Me Now" for ten or more of the preceding items, you most likely function well in a multicultural work environment. If you answered "Not There Yet" to ten or more of the preceding items, you need to develop more cross-cultural awareness and skills to work effectively in a multicultural work environment. You will notice that being bilingual gives you at least four points on this quiz.

Source: "Cross-Cultural Skills and Attitudes" by Andrew J. DuBrin.

DEVELOP CULTURAL SENSITIVITY AND CULTURAL INTELLIGENCE

Cultural sensitivity

an awareness of and a willingness to investigate the reasons why people of another culture act as they do

To relate well to someone from a foreign country, you must be alert to possible cultural differences. When working in another country, you must be willing to acquire knowledge about local customs. When working with people from different cultures, even from your own country, you must be patient, adaptable, flexible, and willing to listen and learn.

The characteristics mentioned are part of **cultural sensitivity**, an awareness of and a willingness to investigate the reasons why individuals of another culture act as they do.[13] If you have cultural sensitivity, you will recognize certain nuances in customs that will help you build better relationships with people from cultural backgrounds other than your own. A business executive said he found it frustrating that he was unable to receive a clear "yes" or "no" when talking by telephone with a colleague in Indonesia. The executive failed to take into account the importance of building a relationship and the effectiveness of in-person communication. Lacking in cultural sensitivity, he projected his home-country norms onto his Indonesian colleague.[14]

Cultural sensitivity is sometimes referred to as *multicultural savvy* because you are smart enough to work well in different cultures. An example would be sizing up quickly whether the people you are visiting in a work context are task focused or relationship focused.[15] To draw another cultural stereotype, suppose Jan, a Northerner is visiting a plant in the Deep South of the United States on a mission to help the plant install a new cloud-computing system. Using her multicultural savvy, Jan observes that the IT (information technology) staff at the plant want to get to know her a little before jumping into the complexities of cloud computing (the group has a relationship focus for the moment). So at lunch Jan does not talk about cloud computing until she senses that the group is ready to focus on the task.

One approach to enhancing cultural sensitivity is to keep in mind the types of cultural differences mentioned throughout this chapter, even down to such details as holding a fork in your left hand when dining in England and India. Another approach is to raise your antenna and observe carefully what others are doing. Suppose you are on a business trip to a different region of your country and are invited to have dinner at the plant general manager's house. You notice that she takes off her street shoes on entering the house. You do likewise to establish better rapport, even if your host says, "Oh, please don't bother." It is obvious from your host's behavior that she observes a "shoe code" in her house.

An advanced aspect of cultural sensitivity is to be able to fit in comfortably with people of another culture by observing the subtle cues they give about how a person should act in their presence. **Cultural intelligence (CQ)** is an outsider's ability to interpret someone's unfamiliar and ambiguous behavior the same way that person's compatriots would.[16] (*CQ* refers to a "cultural quotient.") With high cultural intelligence a person would be able to figure out what behavior would be true of all people and all groups in a culture, such as rapid shaking of a clenched fist to communicate anger. Also, the person with a high CQ could figure out what is peculiar to a particular group and those aspects of behavior that are neither universal nor peculiar to this group.

Similar to emotional intelligence, cultural intelligence encompasses several different aspects of behavior. The four sources of cultural intelligence relate to the metacognitive, the cognitive, the emotional/motivational, and the physical, explained as follows:[17]

1. **Metacognitive (higher-order intelligence).** The metacognitive aspect of cultural intelligence refers to high-level problem-solving ability used to organize and understand cultural knowledge. Even thinking that there is much to be learned in a new cultural interaction requires considerable intelligence.

2. **Cognitive (the head).** The cognitive part of CQ refers to what a person knows and how he or she can acquire new knowledge. Here you acquire facts about people from another culture, such as their passion for football (soccer in North America), their business practices, and their promptness in paying bills. Another aspect of this source of cultural intelligence is figuring out how you can learn more about the other culture.

3. **Emotional/motivational (the heart).** The emotional/motivational aspect of CQ refers to energizing one's actions and building personal confidence. You need both confidence and motivation to adapt to another culture. A man on a business trip to the Ivory Coast in Africa might say to himself, "When I greet a work associate in a restaurant, can I really pull off kissing him on both cheeks. What if he thinks I'm weird?" With strong motivation, the same person might say, "I'll give it a try. I kind of greet my grandfather the same way back in the United States."

4. **The body (physical).** The body aspect of CQ is the action component. The body is the element for translating intentions into actions and desires. Kissing the same-sex African work associate on both cheeks is the *physical* aspect previously mentioned. We often have an idea of what we should do, but implementation is not so easy. You might know, for example, that when entering an Asian person's home you should take off your shoes, yet you might not actually remove them—thereby offending your Asian work (or personal life) associate.

Cultural intelligence (CQ)
an outsider's ability to interpret someone's unfamiliar and ambiguous behavior in the same way that person's compatriots would

These ideas are abstract, so an example will help clarify.

An American sales representative is attempting to interpret a "Japanese smile." First, she needs to recognize that thinking about cultural differences is worthwhile. Second, she needs to observe the various cues provided in addition to the smile itself (such as head scratching) to assemble them into a meaningful whole. This helps her understand what that Japanese representative is really experiencing. Third, she must be motivated to persist despite the ambiguity of the situation. Fourth, she must take the right actions to respond appropriately, such as saying, "I am pleased that we are in agreement."

To practice high cultural intelligence, the high-order intelligence, mind, heart, and body have to work together. If any of these elements are deficient, she will be less effective in dealing with the Japanese company representative. All four aspects of CQ must work in unison. You have to figure out how you have to act with people from another culture, you need motivation and confidence to change, and you have to translate your knowledge and motivation into action. So when you are on a business trip to South Korea, go ahead and bow when you are introduced to the plant manager.

A study conducted with 305 real estate agents at twenty-six real estate firms in the United States indicated that cultural intelligence really does translate into business results. Agents with higher motivational cultural intelligence, as measured by a questionnaire, tended to have more sales with customers from cultures different than their own. The effects of good motivational cultural intelligence were even stronger (more sales) when the firm was perceived to be culturally intelligent and had a positive climate with respect to diversity.[18]

FOCUS ON INDIVIDUALS RATHER THAN GROUPS

Understanding broad cultural differences is a good starting point in building relationships with people from other cultures. Nevertheless, it is even more important to get to know the individual rather than relying exclusively on an understanding of his or her cultural group. A consultant in the area of cross-cultural relations suggests that the best way to know individuals is to build personal relationships with people and not to generalize.[19]

Focusing on individuals rather than groups is sometimes difficult because people tend to hold on strongly to cultural stereotypes. Evidence that these stereotypes are strong comes from an experiment with college students who were purposely presented with stereotype-busting strangers. One of these stereotype busters was a young Asian American woman with a thick southern drawl. (She was really a hired actress trained by a voice coach to learn an accent specific to Charleston, South Carolina.) Students worked in pairs with either a stereotype buster or a person whose behavior was consistent with the stereotype. Students paired with a stereotype buster performed less well on a word-finding game, showed more physical signs of stress, and they smiled less frequently. Watching a participant's initial meeting with one of the surprising partners was revealing according to the experimenter, Wendy Berry Mendes of Harvard University: "She'd begin the introduction with, 'Hi, I'm Jenny and I'm from Charleston, South Carolina,' and our participants just froze and stared at this truly surprising person. Their body posture stayed closed and more defensive during the interaction."[20]

One lesson for cross-cultural relations to be learned from this experiment is to focus on the individual's characteristics and try not to be upset because the person's behavior is not consistent with your stereotype of how he or she is supposed to behave. For example, many Americans find it strange when they meet a black businessperson with a British or French accent. As one American tourist said when visiting Paris, "I didn't know black people spoke French."

RESPECT ALL WORKERS AND CULTURES

An effective strategy for achieving cross-cultural understanding is to simply respect all others in the workplace, including their cultures, as suggested in the opening case about Loews. An important component of respect is to believe that although another person's culture is different from yours, it is equally worthwhile. Respect comes from valuing differences, such as one person speaking Standard English and the other favoring American Sign Language. Respecting other people's customs can translate into specific attitudes, such as respecting one coworker for wearing a yarmulke on Friday or another for wearing an African outfit to celebrate Kwanzaa. An aspect of respecting all workers is the importance of respecting the rights of majorities, including white males.

Another way of showing respect for all workers and cultures is to develop supportive peer relations in the workplace with people from different cultural groups. A supportive relationship includes a feeling of closeness and trust, the sharing of thoughts and feelings, and the feeling that one is able to seek assistance from another. Such respect in the form of support doubles in importance because the creativity advantage of a diverse group is more likely to surface when there is a supportive relationship among coworkers who differ demographically.

Another way of respecting all workers and cultures is to practice **sexual equity**, parity among heterosexual, gay, lesbian, bisexual, and transgender employees. The last four groups have come to be referred to collectively as LGBT. Sexual equity most frequently takes the form of an employer offering healthcare coverage for same-sex domestic partners.[21] When same-sex people are married, healthcare coverage for the spouse is legally required.

True respect of any group goes beyond company policies and extends to informal social behavior. A group of workers who invited a transgender coworker (one who had switched sexes) for an after-work drink would be showing him or her total respect. (For some people, however, religious beliefs would make showing such respect difficult.)

Sexual equity
parity among heterosexual, gay, lesbian, bisexual, and transgender employees

VALUE CULTURAL DIFFERENCES

Recognizing cultural differences is an excellent starting point in becoming a **multicultural worker**, one who can work effectively with people of different cultures. More important, however, is to *value* cultural differences. The distinction goes well beyond semantics. If you place a high value on cultural differences, you will perceive people from other cultures to be different but equally worthwhile. You cannot motivate anyone, especially someone of another culture, until that person first accepts you.[22]

A challenge in showing respect for other cultures is not to act revolted or shocked when a member of another culture eats something that lies outside your area of what is acceptable as food. Some Westerners are shocked and repelled to find that some Easterners eat insects, cats, dogs, sheep's eyeballs, chicken soup containing the feet, and rattlesnakes. Some Easterners are shocked and repelled to find that Westerners eat a sacred animal such as cow and are surprised about popcorn.[23]

A well-documented advantage stemming from valuing cultural differences is creative problem solving. A diversity of viewpoints within the group can enhance group creativity. Another perspective on the contribution of cultural differences to creativity is that multicultural experience helps us become more creative ourselves.[24] In practice, this finding could mean that working with different cultural groups within the same company, or outside the company, would facilitate workers becoming more creative problem solvers. Broadening your perspective helps develop your flexible thinking. A more specific advantage is that exposure to different cultures might trigger a profitable idea that you could transport to your own culture. For example, cottages of about 500 square feet found in many cultures outside the United States now have a small but growing market in the United States.

Multicultural worker
one who can work effectively with people of different cultures

RECOGNIZE YOUR OWN CULTURAL BIASES

A potential barrier to working smoothly with people from cultures other than our own is an almost unconscious tendency to react positively or negatively toward those people from a particular culture or demographic group. Let us begin with a seemingly harmless example. Your positive bias toward Indians is that they are careful and methodical in executing work tasks. Consequently, when you are in a busy department store, you go to the checkout line with an Indian cashier without even thinking why. A negative bias would be a person rejecting a job offer because his or her supervisor would be a person of about age seventy. The bias might be that the applicant perceives an older person as intellectually slow, living in the past, and technology challenged. Having bias is human nature. A challenge is therefore learning how to manage those biases appropriately, such as asking yourself whether you have prejudged anybody lately based on his or her culture.

Human Relations Self-Assessment Quiz 13-2 offers you an opportunity to think candidly about cultural biases you might have.

Human Relations Self-Assessment Quiz 13-2

The Personal Biases and Prejudices Checklist

Check whether each of the attitudes, beliefs, and actions in the list below are generally true or generally false. Responding to this checklist is difficult because you are required to be objective and honest about your biases and prejudices.

Number	Statement about Biases and Prejudices in Relation to People	Generally True	Generally False
1.	I can imagine a woman being an effective president of the United States.	_____	_____
2.	I would feel comfortable if my boss were a midget.	_____	_____
3.	I would be fearful of any woman wearing a covering over her face in an airport.	_____	_____
4.	It makes sense to charge higher interest rates for loans and mortgages to minority group members even if their credit rating is above average.	_____	_____
5.	If I or a loved one needed brain surgery, I would want the surgery performed only by a male Caucasian brain surgeon.	_____	_____
6.	During a major athletic contest, such as a basketball or soccer game, I would want a black person to take the game-deciding shot.	_____	_____
7.	I would prefer not to be a passenger on an airplane if the pilot were older than age fifty.	_____	_____
8.	My like or dislike for President Barack Obama had nothing to do with his being African American (or mixed race).	_____	_____
9.	When I am uncertain about a person's race or ethnic background, I often ask, "What are you?"	_____	_____
10.	If I needed a financial planner, I would never hire one who was under age thirty-five.	_____	_____

Scoring and Interpretation:

Give yourself one point for the following answers: Generally True to questions 3, 4, 5, 6, 7, 9, and 10; generally false to questions 1, 2, and 8. If you scored 5 or more points, you most likely have biases and prejudices that hold you back a little from having strong cross-cultural relations. If you scored between 0 and 4, you are likely to be perceived as an unbiased person, and one whose biases and prejudices create very few problems in interpersonal relationships. Being perceived as unbiased and unprejudiced could facilitate you getting along well with coworkers and being selected for a leadership position. A caution is that it is quite difficult to be honest with oneself about one's level of bias and prejudice, so perhaps take this quiz again in one week.

Source: "The Personal Biases and Prejudices Checklist" by Andrew J. DuBrin.

MINIMIZE CULTURAL BLOOPERS

◀ **Learning Objective 13.3** ◀

An effective way of being culturally sensitive is to minimize actions that are likely to offend people from another culture based on their values and customs. Cultural bloopers are most likely to take place when you are visiting another country. The same bloopers, however, can also be committed with people from a different culture within your own country. To avoid these bloopers, you must carefully observe persons from other cultures. Studying another culture through reading is also helpful. Even small behaviors, such as asking for ketchup to accompany an omelet while in France, can strain a business relationship.

E-commerce has created new opportunities for creating cultural bloopers. Website developers and the workers responsible for adding content must have good cross-cultural literacy, including an awareness of how the information might be misinterpreted. Here are two examples of potential problems:

- Numerical date formats can be readily misinterpreted. To an American, 4/9/15 would be interpreted as April 9, 2015 (or 1915!). But many Europeans would interpret the same numerical expression as September 4, 2015.

- Colors on websites must be chosen carefully. For example, in some cultures, purple is the color of royalty, whereas in Brazil purple is associated with death.

Keep two key facts in mind when attempting to avoid cultural mistakes. One is that members of any cultural group show individual differences. What one member of the group might regard as an insensitive act another might welcome. Recognize also that one or two cultural mistakes will not peg you permanently as a boor. Figure 13-2 will help you minimize certain cultural bloopers.

FIGURE 13-2

CULTURAL MISTAKES TO AVOID WITH SELECTED CULTURAL GROUPS

Western Europe	
Great Britain	• Asking personal questions. The British protect their privacy.
	• Thinking that a businessperson from England is unenthusiastic when he or she says, "Not bad at all." English people understate positive emotion.
France	• Expecting to complete work during the French two-hour lunch.
	• Attempting to conduct significant business during August—*les grandes vacances* (vacation time).
Italy	• Eating too much pasta, as it is not the main course.
	• Handing out business cards freely. Italians use them infrequently.
Spain	• Expecting punctuality. Your appointments will usually arrive twenty to thirty minutes late.
	• Make the American sign for "okay" with your thumb and forefinger. In Spain (and many other countries) this is vulgar.
Scandinavia (Denmark, Sweden, Norway)	• Being overly conscious of rank in these countries. Scandinavians pay relatively little attention to a person's place in the hierarchy.
	• Introducing conflict among Swedish work associates. Swedes go out of their way to avoid conflict.
Greece	• Saying good-bye by using the American handshake. Greeks regard this practice to be an insult.
Asia	
All Asian countries	• Pressuring an Asian job applicant or employee to brag about his or her accomplishments. Asians feel self-conscious when boasting about individual accomplishments and prefer to let the record speak for itself. In addition, they prefer to talk about group rather than individual accomplishments.
	• Giving gifts with four items such as four dollars or four boxes of candy because the number four connotes death in many Asian countries.

(Continued)

FIGURE 13-2 (*Continued*)

Japan	• Shaking hands or hugging Japanese (as well as other Asians) in public. Japanese consider the practices to be offensive. • Looking directly in the eye of a business acquaintance for more than a few seconds. • Not interpreting "We'll consider it" as "no" when spoken by a Japanese businessperson. Japanese negotiators mean "no" when they say, "We'll consider it." • Knocking the competition (Japanese are typically cordial toward competitors). • Not giving small gifts to Japanese when conducting business. Japanese are offended by not receiving these gifts. • Giving your business card to a Japanese businessperson more than once. Japanese prefer to give and receive business cards only once.
China	• Not taking a business card presented to you seriously, such as quickly stuffing it in your pocket. • Using a strong handshake instead of a limp one. Insisting on a handshake rather than a polite bow. • Giving a clock as a gift can backfire because the Mandarin word for "to give clocks" resembles "to attend to a dying relative." • Making cold calls on Chinese business executives. An appropriate introduction is required for a first-time meeting with a Chinese official.
Korea	• Saying no. Koreans feel it is important to have visitors leave with good feelings.
India	• Telling Indians you prefer not to eat with your hands. If the Indians are not using cutlery when eating, they expect you to do likewise.
Thailand	• Pointing the soles of your shoes toward another person. Be aware of this potential mistake when sitting.

Mexico and Latin America

Mexico	• Flying into a Mexican city in the morning and expecting to close a deal by lunch. Mexicans build business relationships slowly.
Most Latin American countries	• Attempting to impress Brazilians by speaking a few words of Spanish. Portuguese is the official language of Brazil. • Wearing elegant and expensive jewelry during a business meeting. Most Latin Americans think people should appear more conservative during a business meeting.

Note: A cultural mistake for Americans to avoid when conducting business in most countries outside the United States and Canada is to insist on getting down to business quickly. Other stereotyped American traits to avoid are aggressiveness, impatience, and frequent interruptions to get your point across. North Americans in small towns also like to build a relationship before getting down to business. Another general mistake for Americans is to use a familiar, laid-back style in locales where "business casual" is unacceptable and first names are reserved for family and friends.

Source: CULTURAL MISTAKES TO AVOID WITH SELECTED CULTURAL GROUPS by Andrew J. DuBrin. A couple of points about China are based on *How to Impress Your Chinese Boss* by Eric Spitznagel.

Avoiding cultural bloopers might also be framed as being *politically correct*. The point of political correctness is to avoid offending anybody. As an American when visiting India, you would therefore not say to your hosts, "Eating with your hands is disgusting." Nor would you say to an Inuit (aka Eskimo), "Killing seals is barbaric."

PARTICIPATE IN CULTURAL TRAINING

Cultural training
set of learning experiences designed to help employees understand the customs, traditions, and beliefs of another culture

For many years, companies and government agencies have prepared their workers for overseas assignments. The method most frequently chosen is **cultural training**, a set of learning experiences designed to help employees understand the customs, traditions, and beliefs of another culture. In today's diverse business environment and international marketplace, learning about individuals raised in different cultural backgrounds has become more important. Many industries therefore train employees in cross-cultural relations.

Cultural training is considered essential for international workers involved with people from other cultures because negotiating styles differ across cultures. For example, the Japanese prefer an exchange of information to confrontation. Russians, in contrast, enjoy combat in negotiations.[25] (Again, we are dealing with cultural stereotypes.)

Much of the information presented in this chapter, such as understanding cultural values and bloopers, is often incorporated into cultural training. Here we look at two perspectives on cultural training: (1) training for domestic employees and (2) foreign-language training.

Cultural Training for Domestic Employees

Many employees who never leave the country work with people from around the globe, so cultural training has been extended also to domestic employees. "Whether a multinational or a start-up business out of a garage, everybody is global these days," says Dean Foster, the head of an international consultancy in New York. A specific example is that managers at a mining and exploration company in Britain sought cross-cultural training because the company was unsuccessful in winning business from an American company. During the training, the company learned that the proposal turned off Americans because it started with ten pages listing all the risks inherent in the venture and how much money would be lost if it failed.

The cultural training consultant pointed out that Americans often perceive failure to be a learning experience, so the American company considered the proposal to be negative. The British, however, were following their cultural value of being risk averse. When the British company rewrote the proposal with a positive spin, they received a signed contract the next day. "Differences got overlooked because we both speak English," said the consultant.[26]

Foreign-Language Training

Learning a foreign language is often part of cultural training or can also be a separate activity. Knowledge of a second language is important because it builds better connections with people from other cultures than does relying on a translator. Speaking another language can help build rapport with customers and employees who speak that language. Companies invest heavily in helping employees learn a target language because it facilitates conducting business in other countries. Nissan Motor Co. offers language training to its employees because the company recognizes the value of cross-cultural skills.[27]

Many multinational companies have downplayed the importance of American workers being fluent in a second language because English has become the standard language of commerce. Despite the merits of this observation, speaking and writing well in the language of your target can help establish rapport. Another value of foreign-language training is to better communicate with subordinates, coworkers, and customers. For example, it is estimated that in the United States, nearly two-thirds of construction workers do not speak English as their primary language. Construction supervisors who speak Spanish can prevent many accidents.[28]

From a career perspective, being fluent in a second language is considered important, if not essential, for a variety of positions, including the following: human resource managers, registered nurses, police officers and detectives, and concierges. (A concierge ensures that hotel guests receive excellent service, including arranging or giving advice on transportation.)[29] Medical specialists and firefighters also find second-language skills to be quite helpful. Clients under stress, such as an injured person, are likely to revert to their native tongue. To the extent that the location of the job is in a bilingual culture, such as Phoenix, Los Angeles, or El Paso, being fluent in Spanish is all the more important.

As with any other skill training, these investments can only pay off if the trainee is willing to work hard developing the new skill outside the training session. It is unlikely that almost anyone can develop conversational skills or learn much grammar in another language by listening to foreign-language CDs or taking classes for thirty days. The quick training program, however, helps you develop a base for further learning.

PARTICIPATE IN DIVERSITY TRAINING

The general purpose of cultural training is to help workers understand people from other cultures. Understanding can lead to dealing more effectively with them as work associates or customers. **Diversity training** has a slightly different purpose. It attempts to bring about workplace harmony by teaching people how to get along with diverse work associates. Quite often, the program is aimed at minimizing open expressions of racism and sexism. Diversity training deals with both surface-level diversity (e.g., race) and deep-level diversity (e.g., autism).

Recognizing Differences

Diversity training emphasizes that everybody is different in some way and that all these differences should be appreciated. As the U.S. Office of Civil Rights explains, "Diversity is a term used broadly to refer to many demographic variables, including but not limited to race, religion, color, gender, national origin, disability, sexual orientation, age, education, geographic origin, and skill characteristics."[30]

Diversity training emphasizes *inclusion,* or including everybody when appreciating diversity. Figure 13-3 presents a broad sampling of the ways in which workplace associates can differ from one another. All these differences are tucked under the welcoming *diversity umbrella.* Studying this list can help you anticipate the type of differences to understand and appreciate in a diverse workplace. The differences include cultural as well

Diversity training

program that attempts to bring about workplace harmony by teaching people how to get along with diverse work associates; often aimed at minimizing open expressions of racism and sexism

FIGURE 13-3

THE DIVERSITY UMBRELLA

Source: "THE DIVERSITY UMBRELLA" by Andrew J. DuBrin.

- Race
- Sex or gender
- Religion
- Age (young, middle-aged, and old)
- Generation differences, including attitudes (e.g., baby boomers versus Generation Y)
- Ethnicity (country of origin)
- Education
- Abilities
- Mental disabilities (including attention deficit disorder)
- Physical status (including hearing status, visual status, being able-bodied, being a wheelchair user)
- Values and motivation
- Sexual orientation (heterosexual, homosexual, bisexual, transsexual)
- Marital status (married, single, cohabitating, widow, widower)
- Family status (children, no children; two-parent family, single-parent family, grandparent family; opposite-sex parents, same-sex parents)
- Personality traits
- Functional background (area of specialization, such as marketing, manufacturing)
- Technology interest (high tech, low tech, technophobe)
- Weight status (average, obese, underweight, anorexic)
- Hair status (full head of hair, bald, wild hair, tame hair, long hair, short hair)
- Style of clothing and appearance (dress up, dress down, professional appearance, casual appearance, tattoos, body piercing, including multiple earrings, nose rings, lip rings)
- Tobacco status (smoker versus nonsmoker, chewer versus nonchewer)
- Your creative suggestion

as individual factors. Individual factors are also important because people can be discriminated against for personal characteristics as well as group characteristics. Many people who are disfigured, for example, believe they are held back from obtaining a higher-level job because of their disfigurement, such as a facial birthmark.

Another important part of diversity training is to develop empathy for diverse viewpoints. To help training participants develop empathy, representatives of various groups explain their feelings related to workplace issues. The accompanying Human Relations in Practice illustrates developing empathy for differences.

Human Relations in Practice

The Empathy-for-Differences Diversity-Training Exercise

Human relations consultant Tamara had been invited into the refinery division of a large petroleum company to conduct diversity training. Company leadership thought that many refinery workers were too traditional in their thinking to recognize the importance of understanding differences among workers. Tamara begins with a basic exercise for developing empathy for differences. Each group member takes a turn explaining how he or she has been perceived as different by others at least once, and how that perception made him or her feel. A few excerpts from the session follow:

Herb: As you can see, I'm six foot seven, so I get a lot of dumb comments about my height. The most stupid question is "How's the weather up there?" I also get asked to change lightbulbs for people, and to move heavy furniture. All these comments about my height aggravate me.

Mindy: I'm from a very small, rural town. At least ten people have asked me if I dated my brother or cousins. I hate the negative perception that small-town people are so desperate they have to date family members.

Ken: I'm an African American petroleum engineer. So many people have congratulated me on working my way up from poverty. Little do they know that my father is a professor and my mother is a physician. It's deep-rooted prejudice to think that almost no black people come from successful upper-middle-class families. This type of prejudice discourages me.

Sue: I'm a Chinese American computer coder. I've been in the profession for ten years. The few supervisors I've had all think that I want to code for the rest of my life and don't want to work with people. I wish my supervisor would listen to me and understand that I want to be a leader of people, not only write computer code.

Nick: I'm a senior, past the typical retirement age. So a lot of people treat me like an old man. They ask me if I've found a place to retire yet. Even worse, coworkers rarely talk to me about technology. I never get invited to go out for a drink with the office gang. I feel frustrated because the fact that I'm still working means that I'm a regular employee, not a has-been.

After the rest of the group presented their stories about how they had been perceived as different, a group discussion was moderated by Tamara about the significance of the session. Consensus was reached (a) that we are all different in some way, and (b) that we shouldn't jump to conclusions about people until we first get the facts.

Questions:

What do you perceive as the value of this diversity-training exercise about empathy for differences?

Another approach used in diversity training to recognize differences is for workers to simulate having a specific disability. Two such approaches are to walk around the office or training room blindfolded and using a cane to simulate blindness, or to navigate around the property using a wheelchair.[31] By simulating a specific disability, the worker might develop a better appreciation of the hurdles the disabled worker faces.

Diversity training sometimes includes providing guidelines for dealing with different groups and individuals to help create a positive work environment. A segment of a diversity program geared toward creating a positive environment for people with physical disabilities is likely to suggest things you should not say to or ways you should not behave toward these individuals:

- Speaking slowly or loudly to a wheelchair user.

- "I don't even think of you as a person with a disability."

- "But you look so good."[32]

Concerns about Diversity Training

During diversity training programs too many angry feelings are expressed and negative stereotypes are reinforced, leading to strained relationships. At worst, majority groups sometimes feel that they are targeted for having held back minority groups. Diversity training might be considered patronizing because the majority of participants are already respectful of people different from themselves and know how to work harmoniously with a wide variety of people. Even when diversity training attains its goal of enhanced cross-cultural understanding, the training may not lead to enhanced promotional opportunities for women and minorities. Diversity training must therefore be integrated into other aspects of human resource management, such as career management.[33]

▶ **Learning Objective 13.4** ▶

Overcoming Cross-Cultural Communication Barriers

A key part of developing good cross-cultural relations is to overcome or prevent communication barriers stemming from cultural differences. Personal life, too, is often culturally diverse, leading to culturally based communication problems. The information about avoiding cultural bloopers presented in this chapter might also be interpreted as a way to prevent communication barriers. Here we describe eight additional strategies and tactics to help overcome cross-cultural communication barriers.

1. Be alert to cultural differences in customs and behavior. To minimize cross-cultural communication barriers, recognize that many subtle job-related differences in customs and behavior may exist. For example, people from many Asian cultures typically feel uncomfortable providing negative feedback to a supervisor because they value power distance.

2. Use straightforward language and speak slowly and clearly. When working with people who do not speak your language fluently, speak in an easy-to-understand manner. Be patient for many reasons, including the fact that your accent in your native tongue may not be the same as the person from whom your target learned your language. (For example, English as learned in Scotland is quite different from English as learned in Ohio.) Minimize the use of idioms and analogies specific to your language. For example, in North America the term *a slam dunk* means a sure thing. A person from another culture may not understand this phrase yet be hesitant to ask for clarification. Speaking slowly is also important because even people who read and write a second language at an expert level may have difficulty catching the nuances of conversation. Facing the person from another culture directly also improves communication because your facial expressions and lips contribute to comprehension.

Speaking slowly and clearly is more effective at overcoming communication barriers than shouting at a person who does not understand your language well. For example, some Americans visiting other countries will shout at a restaurant server, "DON'T YOU SPEAK ENGLISH?" Shouting makes people defensive, including shouting at blind people to enhance comprehension. (Because the blind person cannot see a person's lips to enhance understanding, speaking clearly and not murmuring is helpful.) Also, a deaf person who reads lips will usually not understand words better when the speaker shouts.

3. Observe cultural differences in etiquette. Violating rules of etiquette without explanation can erect immediate communication barriers. A major rule of etiquette is that in most countries, people in high-status positions expect to be treated with respect. Formality is important, unless you are invited to act otherwise. When visiting a company in Japan, for example, it is best to be deferent to (appeal to the authority of) company dignitaries. Visualize yourself as a company representative of a high-tech American firm that manufactures equipment for legally downloading music over the Internet. You visit Sony Corporation in Japan to speak about a joint venture. On meeting the marketing vice president, bow slightly and say something to the effect of "Mr. _____, it is my honor to discuss doing business with Sony." Do not commit the etiquette mistake of saying something to the effect of "Hi, Charlie. How's the wife and kids?" (An American actually said this at a Japanese company shortly before being escorted out the door.)

4. Be sensitive to differences in nonverbal communication. Stay alert to the possibility that a person from another culture may misinterpret your nonverbal signal. To use positive reinforcement, some managers will give a sideways hug to an employee or will touch an employee's arm. People from some cultures resent touching from workmates and will be offended. Koreans in particular dislike being touched or touching others in a work setting.

5. Do not be diverted by style, accent, grammar, or personal appearance. Although all these superficial factors are related to business success, they are difficult to interpret when judging a person from another culture. It is therefore better to judge the merits of the statement or behavior. A brilliant individual from another culture may still be learning your language and thus make basic mistakes in speaking your language. He or she might also not have developed a sensitivity to dress style in your culture.

A major cross-cultural communication problem arises when an American on the telephone cannot understand the version of English spoken by the customer service or technical support representative at a call center. Americans who can understand people well only from their own geographic region are likely to have the most difficulty in understanding the overseas technical support or customer service representative. The problem has been particularly acute with customers seeking technical assistance for prepaid cell phones. For example, the rep from the Philippines might ask the American caller to enter a long series of numerals—a challenging task even if you are familiar with the other person's accent. In recognition of the potential cross-cultural communication barriers that occur with overseas call centers, the trend toward such outsourcing is slowing down.

6. Listen for understanding, not agreement. When working with diverse teammates, the differences in viewpoints can lead to conflict. To help overcome such conflict, follow the LUNA rule: Listen for Understanding, Not Agreement. In this way you gear yourself to consider the viewpoints of others as a first resort. For example, some older workers may express some intense loyalty to the organization, whereas their younger teammates may speak in more critical terms. By everyone listening to understand, they can begin to appreciate each other's perspectives and accept differences of opinion.[34] Listening is a powerful tool for overcoming cross-cultural communication barriers.

7. **Be attentive to individual differences in appearance.**   A major cross-cultural insult is to confuse the identity of people because they are members of the same race or ethnic group. Research suggests that people have difficulty seeing individual differences among people of another race because they code race first, such as thinking, "He has the nose of an African American." However, people can learn to search for more distinguishing features, such as a dimple or eye color.[35]

8. **Ask questions to clarify potential misunderstandings.**   Many cross-cultural communication barriers can be avoided by asking questions to clarify potential misunderstandings. Even when speaking the same language, cultural traditions might lead to misunderstanding. For example, a representative from a foreign company might say that he or she "would be honored to try your product." However, "being honored" might imply that the person wants to try the product for free. Because many people think in terms of the metric system, it is often important for an American to ask for a translation into the American system. A woman from Italy might say that a machine weighs 2000 kilograms. To avoid misunderstanding, the American might ask, "How many pounds is that?"

▶ **Learning Objective 13.5** ▶

Additional Ways in Which Organizations Use Diversity to Advantage

To both make possible and capitalize upon diversity, organizations take many initiatives, as already implied or mentioned in this chapter. Here we describe briefly four specific programs and processes aimed at capitalizing upon workplace diversity: creating diverse teams; matching organization diversity with community diversity; physical accommodations for workers with physical disabilities; and employee network groups. The work versus personal life accommodations described in Chapter 10 in relation to conflict resolution can also be regarded as an initiative for benefiting from diversity.

DIVERSE TEAMS

A building block for diversity is to staff teams, as well as other work groups, with members who are different from each other in some important respect. As mentioned previously, diversity within the group can enhance creativity. Diversity within the group can be among many factors, including ethnic background, race, gender, income level, educational background, and field of specialty.

Educational background and specialty field are emphasized here because many people are not aware that there is more to diversity than race, ethnicity, and gender. Consultant Ann Evangelista explains that race and gender are only the tip of the diversity iceberg. Diversity also stems from an individual's personal and professional background, personal interests, geographic upbringing, personality traits, and approach to problem solving.[36]

An example of diversity based personality-trait and problem-solving style is that a work team can benefit from members who are detail-oriented as well as those who prefer to look at the big picture. One member might have a creative idea, such as "We would satisfy customers better if our waiting lines were shorter." Another member with good skill in detailed thinking might develop a revised process that would decrease the time customers spend waiting in line for service.

MATCHING ORGANIZATIONAL DIVERSITY WITH COMMUNITY DIVERSITY

A standard practice for many business, education, and government organizations is to approximately match diversity within the organization to that of diversity within the community. Home Depot is a good example because its mix of store associates approximately matches the cultural diversity within the community, such as one-third of the associates being Latino in a section of Chicago that is about one-third Latino. Cultural diversity also extends to the executive suites; consumer products companies in particular have a leadership team that is culturally diverse. Prime examples include Home Depot, PepsiCo, Coca-Cola, and McDonald's.

ACCOMMODATIONS FOR PEOPLE WITH PHYSICAL DISABILITIES

Many organizations practice diversity by making special accommodations for people with physical disabilities, thereby making the workplace more inclusive. These accommodations include making it easier for wheelchair users to navigate the workplace and providing software that makes it possible for the visually impaired and blind workers to perform their tasks. According to an ongoing study by the Job Accommodations Network, 57 percent of accommodations for disabled workers do not cost money, while they usually cost the employer about $500.[37]

The Canadian bank CIBC has been at the forefront of hiring people with physical disabilities, with about 4 percent of CIBC's 40,000 plus Canadian employees having a physical disability. Among the accommodations are automatic doors to facilitate people with limited physical ability getting around.[38]

EMPLOYEE NETWORK (AFFINITY) GROUPS

Another company initiative toward recognizing diversity is to permit and encourage employees to form **employee network (or affinity) groups**. The network group is composed of employees throughout the company who affiliate on the basis of a group characteristic such as race, ethnicity, sex, sexual orientation, or physical ability status. Group members typically have similar interests and look to the groups as a way of sharing information about succeeding in the organization.

Allstate has at least seven employee network groups running at any given time. Two examples are 3AN (Allstate Asian American Network) and ANGLES (Allstate Network of Gay and Lesbian Employees and Supporters). The mission statement of 3AN is "3AN develops leaders of tomorrow through professional development, networking, cultural awareness, and knowledge sharing." The group's vision statement is "Leverage the diverse experiences of Asian Americans at Allstate to create value that supports Allstate."[39]

Employee network groups sometimes play a functional role in the organization in addition to the social role. For example, a Latino group at a food company might make product suggestions that would be strongly appealing to Latinos.

A caution about employee network groups is that they can result in employees segregating rather than integrating themselves into the workforce, thereby defeating the purpose of diversity initiatives. A relevant example here is that if an organization has no concern about an employee's sexual orientation with respect to hiring or promotion, why should gay and lesbian workers single themselves out by joining a network group for gay, lesbian, and transgender employees?

A fitting conclusion to the discussion of initiatives for organizations to obtain the most value from diversity is that company leadership should set the example. Interviews were conducted with twenty-four CEOs in companies known for their success with

Employee network (or affinity) groups
network group of employees throughout the company who affiliate on the basis of a group characteristic such as race, ethnicity, sex, sexual orientation, or physical ability status

cultural diversity, such as MasterCard, Merck, and Nissan. Among the ways these executives led by example was to meet regularly with employee network groups and diversity councils.[40]

▶ **Learning Objective 13.6** ▶

Legal Aspects of Working in a Culturally Diverse Environment

In this chapter, we have emphasized the interpersonal aspects of building good relationships with work associates who are demographically and culturally diverse. The legal side of diversity focuses on such matters as protecting workers from being discriminated against, such as not being denied a job you are qualified for because of race, gender, age, or physical disability. A major purpose of these laws is to help all workers be treated fairly. According to one analysis, the groups disadvantaged in the U.S. workplace are women, people of color, sexual minorities, and people with disabilities.[41] Note that not all members of these groups are disadvantaged, including the reality that in 2015 the CEO of American Express was an African American man and the CEO of Xerox Corp. was an African American woman.

Legislation may help advance the rights of many workers, but it does not require workers to develop constructive relationships with each other or to develop cultural intelligence. Here we look briefly at relevant employment legislation, as well as affirmative action.

FEDERAL LAWS PROHIBITING JOB DISCRIMINATION

Workers are protected by a series of federal laws that prohibit job discrimination. In addition, states, provinces (Canada), and municipalities have their own laws governing fair treatment of employees. Furthermore, many employment lawyers bring forth lawsuits for discrimination not specifically mentioned in federal laws. For example, a job candidate might claim that he or she was denied a position for which he or she was qualified because he or she was obese. A state or local judge could then decide whether the claim was justified. The general purpose of job discrimination laws is to protect individuals who have been disadvantaged in the past because of demographic (not cultural) characteristics. Employment legislation began with prohibiting employment discrimination based on race, color, religion, sex, or national origin. Figure 13-4 summarizes federal Equal Employment Opportunity (EEO) laws. These laws apply to all private employers, state and local governments, and educational institutions that employ fifteen or more individuals.

An effective way of understanding how these laws might affect the individual is to specify the discriminatory practices prohibited by these laws. Under Title VII of the Americans with Disabilities Act (ADA) and the Age Discrimination in Employment Act (ADEA), it is illegal to discriminate in any aspect of employment, including hiring and firing; compensation, assignment, or classification of employees; transfer, promotion, layoff, or recall; job advertisements; recruitment; testing; use of company facilities; training and apprenticeship programs; fringe benefits; pay, retirement plans, and disability leave; or other terms and conditions of employment. Discriminatory practices under these laws also include the following:

1. Harassment on the basis of race, color, religion, sex, national origin, disability, or age

2. Retaliation against an individual for filing a charge of discrimination, participating in an investigation, or opposing discriminatory practices

- Title VII of the Civil Rights Act of 1964 (Title VII) prohibits employment discrimination based on race, color, religion, sex, or national origin.
- The Equal Pay Act of 1963 (EPA) protects men and women who perform substantially equal work in the same establishment from sex-based wage discrimination.
- The Age Discrimination in Employment Act of 1967 (ADEA) protects individuals who are forty years of age or older.
- Title I and Title V of the Americans with Disabilities Act of 1990 (ADA) prohibits employment discrimination against qualified individuals with disabilities in the private sector and in state and local governments.
- Sections 501 and 505 of the Rehabilitation Act of 1973 prohibit discrimination against qualified individuals with disabilities who work in the federal government.
- The Civil Rights Act of 1991 provides, among other things, monetary damages in cases of intentional employment discrimination.
- Title II of the Genetic Information Nondiscrimination Act of 2008 makes it illegal for companies to discriminate against employees for insurance purposes, based upon genetic testing. The employee cannot be discriminated against due to family medical history either. The employer is not allowed to ask for genetic testing to be done nor ask for genetic testing results of a fetus being carried either by the employee or a family member of the employee.

The U.S. Equal Employment Opportunity Commission (EEOC) enforces all of these laws. EEOC also provides oversight and coordination of all federal equal employment opportunity regulations, practices, and policies.

Source: FEDERAL LAWS PROHIBITING JOB DISCRIMINATION.

FIGURE 13-4

FEDERAL LAWS PROHIBITING JOB DISCRIMINATION

3. Employment decisions based on stereotypes or assumptions about the abilities, traits, or performance of individuals of a certain sex, race, age, religion, or ethnic group or individuals with disabilities

4. Denying employment opportunities to a person because of marriage to, or association with, an individual of a particular race, religion, national origin, or an individual with a disability. Title VII also prohibits discrimination because of participation in schools or places of worship associated with a particular racial, ethnic, or religious group.

Although all of these forms of discrimination may appear clear-cut, a good deal of interpretation is required to decide whether a given employee is the subject of discrimination. For example, assume that a woman files a charge of sexual harassment. Later, she is bypassed for promotion. She claims she is now the victim of discrimination, yet the company claims that she did not have the appropriate interpersonal skills to be promoted to a supervisory position.

Among the remedies awarded to individuals judged to be discriminated against are back pay, promotion, reinstatement, and the employer paying attorney's fees and court costs. Compensatory and punitive damages are also possible.

ADDITIONAL EXAMPLES OF LEGISLATION AND COURT RULINGS TO ENSURE EQUAL RIGHTS

The federal legislation described previously set the stage for a wide variety of laws and judicial rulings to prevent employment discrimination and thereby protect the rights of workers. Similar legislation is found in Canada, as well as European and some Asian countries.

Here we highlight a few representative examples of how the rights of workers against discrimination are protected beyond major federal legislation summarized in Figure 13-4.[42]

■ **Unconscious bias.** Several court rulings have recognized that unconscious prejudice and bias can prevent women and people of color from achievement and advancement after they have joined an employer. One example is a class-action suit against Wal-Mart involving more than 2 million women (*Dukes et al. v. Wal-Mart Stores Inc.*, 2004).

■ **Protection for people with disabilities.** The Ticket to Work and Work Incentives Improvement Act of 1999 and the Workforce Investment Act of 1998 both focus on increased workforce participation for people with disabilities. For example, the 1998 act mandates state attention to developing employment programs, including career centers to help the disabled. (A problem remains in implementing disability legislation in unambiguously defining the meaning of *disability*. For example, one worker was fired for downloading pornography on his desktop computer. He sued, claiming he had a *disability* of pornography addiction. The judge supported the company.)

■ **State laws protecting the employment rights of lesbian, gay, bisexual, or transgender (LGBT) workers.** By 2015, eighteen states and the District of Columbia had laws protecting LGBT workers from being fired because of their sexual orientation or gender identity. Three other states have legal protection of only sexual orientation. Connecticut is an example of a state that protects the rights of LGBT workers. Employers of more than three employees are forbidden from refusing to hire, discharge, or discriminate against any person in compensation, or in terms, conditions, or privileges of employment because of sexual orientation. The law covers most significant job actions such as hiring, firing, failure to promote, demotion, excessive discipline, harassment, and different treatment of the employee. In addition, employment agencies may not participate in discrimination by refusing to properly classify or refer people for employment, or to otherwise discriminate because of sexual orientation. Labor unions also are forbidden from denying membership based on sexual orientation.

In addition to state laws, President Barack Obama issued executive orders that provide employment protections to all federal workers, as well as federal contractors and subcontractors who conduct business of more than $10,000 with the federal government in one year.[43]

AFFIRMATIVE ACTION

Affirmative action
programs that comply with antidiscrimination laws and attempt to correct past discriminatory practices

A key aspect of implementing the spirit and letter of antidiscrimination law in the United States has been affirmative action programs. **Affirmative action** consists of complying with antidiscrimination laws and correcting past discriminatory practices. During 1965, President Lyndon Johnson signed an executive order prohibiting federal contractors from discriminating in employment decisions on the basis of race, color, religion, sex, or national origin. Government contractors are also required to take affirmative action to ensure that all individuals have an equal opportunity for employment.

Under an affirmative action program, employers actively recruit, employ, train, and promote minorities and women, groups that have been discriminated against by an employer in the past. As a result, women and minority group members have been underrepresented in certain positions. Part of an affirmative action plan might be to actively recruit Latino business graduates to place them in a company management-training program.

Affirmative action has been the subject of continuing debate. Proponents of affirmative action believe that it provides the opportunity many people need to prove their capability and earn just rewards. Opponents of affirmative action believe that it provides preferential treatment for certain groups and winds up discriminating against workers who are qualified but do not fit an affirmative action category.

Concept Review and Reinforcement

Culture, 354
Multicultural identities, 356
Cultural mosaic, 356
Cultural sensitivity, 358

Cultural intelligence (CQ), 359
Sexual equity, 361
Multicultural worker, 361
Cultural training, 364

Diversity training, 366
Employee network (or affinity) groups, 371
Affirmative action, 374

Summary and Review

Being able to work well with people from other cultures, both outside and inside your own country is important for career success. Eight dimensions of cultural values that help us understand how cultures differ from one another are as follows:

- Individualism versus collectivism
- Acceptance of power and authority
- Materialism versus concern for others
- Formality versus informality
- Urgent time orientation versus casual time orientation
- Work orientation versus leisure orientation
- High-context versus low-context cultures (with an emphasis on body language)
- Social support seeking

Many people have multicultural identities because they identify with their own culture as well as other cultures. Similarly, according to the cultural mosaic, people have a rich mixture of cultural identities. The religious value part of the cultural mosaic often affects when people are willing to work or not work. It is important to be alert to possible cultural differences.

Seven specific methods and techniques for improving cross-cultural relations are as follows:

- Develop cultural sensitivity (be aware of differences) and cultural intelligence (metacognitive, cognitive, emotional, and body components).
- Focus on individuals rather than groups.
- Respect all workers and cultures (including practicing sexual equity).
- Value cultural differences (this also involves showing respect).

- Recognize your own cultural biases.
- Minimize cultural bloopers (embarrassing mistakes).
- Participate in cultural training, including foreign-language training.
- Participate in diversity training, or learning to get along with diverse work associates.

Cross-cultural communication barriers can often be overcome by the following:

- Being alert to cultural differences in customs and behavior.
- Using straightforward language and speaking slowly and clearly.
- Observing cultural differences in etiquette.
- Being sensitive to differences in nonverbal communication.
- Not being diverted by style, accent, grammar, or personal appearance.
- Listening for understanding, not agreement.
- Being attentive to individual differences in appearance.
- Asking questions to clarify potential misunderstandings.

Additional ways in which organizations use diversity to their advantage are as follows:

- Diverse teams
- Matching organizational diversity with community diversity
- Accommodations for people with physical disabilities
- Employee network (affinity) groups

The legal side of diversity focuses on such matters as protecting workers from discrimination, but it is not part of developing cross-cultural competence. Workers are protected by a series of federal, state, and municipal laws that govern fair treatment of employees. It is illegal to discriminate in any aspect of employment including hiring and firing, compensation, and recruitment. Legislation and court rulings continue to emerge to ensure the equal rights of workers. Affirmative action programs consist of complying with antidiscrimination laws and correcting past discriminatory practices.

Questions for Discussion and Review

13.1 In what way might having a high acceptance for power and authority make it difficult for a person to work well on a team that has very little supervision?

13.2 Identify three positive stereotypes about cultural groups that are related to job behavior. (An example would be the observation that Mexican laborers are known for their hard work and dependability.)

13.3 When you meet someone from another culture, what can you do to demonstrate that you respect that person's culture?

13.4 Provide an example of cultural insensitivity of any kind that you have seen, read about, or could imagine.

13.5 In an era of welcoming cultural diversity, does a company have the right to exclude employees with visible body piercings from any type of positions?

13.6 Suppose a company wants to promote cross-cultural understanding. Should the executives then discourage employees from one racial or ethnic group from forming a club or sitting together in the company cafeteria? Explain your position.

13.7 Several large consumer firms in recent years have hired African Americans into the CEO position, with the companies not mentioning race in announcements about the appointment. To what extent do you think these firms missed an opportunity to publicize their welcoming of cultural diversity?

13.8 It has been often observed that many automobile sales representatives are biased against women customers. How might this bias (if true) be evident on the sales floor of the dealer?

13.9 As mentioned in the chapter, a current approach to cultural diversity is to point to and celebrate differences among employees. Who should decide on which differences to celebrate, such as some employees thinking that women should not be allowed to drive a vehicle?

13.10 How might you be able to convert cross-cultural skills into higher income and job status for yourself?

Web Corner

Cultural training

www.slrobbins.com (Contains videos of S. L. Robbins conducting cultural-awareness training sessions.)

Cultural diversity

www.diversityinc.com

INTERNET SKILL BUILDER

Developing Your Multicultural Skills

A useful way of developing skills in a second language and learning more about another culture is to use as a home page (the page that appears when you open the Internet) a page written in your target language. In this way, each time you go the Internet on your own computer, your home page will contain fresh information in the language you want to develop your knowledge of.

Assume that your target language is French. Enter a phrase such as "French language newspaper" or "French current events" in the search box. Once you find a suitable choice, insert that newspaper as your cover page. The search engine might have brought you to www.france2.fr or www.cyberpresse.ca. These websites keep you abreast of French and French Canadian international news, sports, and cultural events—written in French. Now, every time you access the Internet, you can spend a few minutes becoming multicultural. The foreign-language site is also likely to have a few brief videos featuring native speakers, not only news commentators. You can save a lot of travel costs and time using the Internet to help you become multicultural.

Developing Your Human Relations Skills

Applying Human Relations Exercise 13-1

Avoiding Cultural Mistakes

Refer to Figure 13-2, "Cultural Mistakes to Avoid with Selected Cultural Groups." Review the list of cultural groups listed. After you have chosen one or two cultural groups, imagine how and where you might have an opportunity to relate to someone from one of these culture groups. During the next thirty days, look for an opportunity to relate to a person from another culture in the way described in these suggestions. You may have to be creative to find a target with whom you can practice your cross-cultural skills. Before approaching your target, answer these questions:

1. What would be my usual approach to dealing with a person from that culture? (An example here would be as follows: "Usually when I visit the neighborhood convenience store operated by a Korean family, I attempt to place the money for purchases directly in the hands of the cashier.")

2. What will I do differently after studying the suggestions in Figure 13-2? ("Because touching a Korean's hand might be uncomfortable for him or her, I will lay the money on the counter and let the cashier pick it up.")

Observe the reaction of the other person for feedback on your cross-cultural effectiveness. Then assess whether your approach to improving cross-cultural relations had any effect on your target.

Applying Human Relations Exercise 13-2

Developing Empathy for Differences

Class members go up to the front of the room one by one and give a brief presentation (perhaps two or three minutes) of any way in which they have been perceived as different and how they felt about this perception. The difference can be of any kind, relating to characteristics such as ethnicity, race, field of study, physical appearance, height, weight, hair color, or body piercing. An example heard frequently from information technology students is as follows: "When I'm out socially, people are forever asking me about some software problem they are facing. They think I know all about every software package ever written. Even worse, they think I have no life outside of computers. Why should I want to talk about computer problems when I'm partying?"

After each member of the class has presented (perhaps even the instructor), class members discuss what they learned from the exercise. Points to look for include the following:

- What pattern do you see in the ways people perceive themselves to be different?
- What is the most frequent difference reported by class members?
- What kind of perceptions by others seem to hurt the most?

It is also important to discuss how this exercise can improve relationships on the job. What would be at least one takeaway from the exercise?

Cultural Gaffes in Both Directions

Many analyses of cross-cultural relations emphasize the mistakes Americans make in dealing with people from other cultures, as described in Figure 13-2. But people from non-American cultures also make mistakes in dealing with Americans. An example would be an Iranian businessperson who did not take an American company manager seriously because she was a woman.

The class assignment here is for students to collect two cross-cultural gaffes (or mistakes): one made by an American in relation to a person from another culture and one made by a foreigner in relation to an American. Use any method of gaffe collection you want, including conversations with people you know, your own observations, e-mails, blogs, or Internet search engines.

At a time designated by the instructor, each student or a number of volunteers present their gaffes in front of class. The gaffes can be presented in about two minutes. As class members present the gaffes, look for (a) frequently occurring gaffes and (b) lessons to be learned from these gaffes. An example of a lesson would be how to use this information about gaffes to improve cross-cultural relations.

Chantal Struggles with a Big Sale in Mexico City

Chantal is a key sales representative at her company, which sells and installs large-scale heating and air-conditioning systems in new buildings as well as those undergoing renovation. Chantal often makes an initial visit to a potential customer, and she is then backed up by a sales engineer as well as several technicians. Chantal was sent down to Mexico City to meet with the executive team that was converting a beautiful old church into condominium units.

Chantal knew that the sale and service on this potential contract were worth three million U.S. dollars (or about 40 million Mexican pesos). Chantal met with the executive team at the construction company on Friday morning for an all-day discussion of her company's services. All was going well, and Chantal could picture a big commission and loads of exciting work coming her way. The executive team then invited Chantal to stay over on Saturday and Sunday, attend a big soccer game, dine at a couple of restaurants, and tour the city.

Chantal thought the invitation was excessive in terms of her personal time, so she attempted to tactfully decline the invitation. The representative of the team seemed taken back, but he said that he understood that she had a busy schedule.

When Chantal returned to her office on Monday morning she found an e-mail message from the lead executive on the condominium development team. He said that he liked what her company had to offer but that they would need much more time to study her proposal. He also pointed out that in Mexico developing a good relationship comes first before signing a contract.

Chantal was horrified and wondered what she did wrong. She was wondering what to do next to nail down this giant contract.

Questions

13.11 What might the executive have been referring to in terms of "developing a good relationship before signing a contract"?

13.12 What significance might the weekend stay offered to Chantal have had for the condominium development team?

13.13 What advice can you offer to Chantal from a cross-cultural value standpoint to attempt to salvage this giant contract?

Chantal Tries to Win Back Those Potential Pesos

One student plays the role of Chantal, who pleads on the phone with the condominium representative to have another chance to win the contract for her firm. She decides that she wants to demonstrate how important relationship building is to her and to her firm. Another person plays the role of Hugo, the lead executive on the condominium development project. He dislikes the American attitude of getting down to business so quickly, but he has some sympathy for Chantal's sincerity.

Observers rate the role-players on two dimensions, using a scale of 1 to 5 from very poor to very good. One dimension is "effective use of human relations techniques." For Chantal, focus on how well she demonstrates a sincere interest in developing a good relationship with the Mexican team. The second dimension is "acting ability." A few observers might voluntarily provide feedback to the role-players in terms of sharing their ratings and observations. The course instructor might also provide feedback.

Human Relations Case Study 13–2

Akiak Wants to Fit In

Akiak Nori was raised in Noorvik, Alaska, and then attended a career school in Juneau, Alaska, majoring in electronic technology. Approaching graduation, Akiak sorted out dozens of job offers he had obtained, several of which did not even require an in-person interview.

Nori accepted a position with a construction company in International Falls, Minnesota, because of the job opportunities and the long brisk winters that would be natural and comfortable for him. Akiak was assigned to a construction team for new buildings. He was also assigned maintenance work for existing electronic systems in office buildings, factories, and mills.

Akiak's goal from the first day on the job was to perform well and fit in with his coworkers. He recognized that fitting in with a non-Eskimo group would require some patience on his part. Akiak had been counseled by several teachers that patience was not one of his strong points.

During employee orientation, two other new employees asked Akiak if his name meant kayak in Eskimo language. With a smile, Akiak replied, "No, it means brave. I guess my parents thought I would have to be brave to grow up in Noorvik, where you have to be tough to survive."

Later that morning, Akiak was asked if ice fishing and seal hunting were his two favorite sports. "Not at all," said Akiak. "We had a first-rate hockey rink in town, so I got to love hockey. And I'm a Minnesota Viking (professional football team) fan. That's why I took a job in Minnesota." (Said with a smile.)

During lunch, Mary, another new employee asked Akiak, "Tell me Akiak, are you an Eskimo? Or are you an Inuit? I don't want to make a mistake."

Akiak responded, "It's no mistake to call me an Eskimo. It's no mistake to call me an Inuit. Some people think that the term Eskimo is wrong, and that we should be called Inuit. It doesn't matter to me or to my friends and family. We like both terms.

"Yet, Mary, the mistake you are making is not thinking of me as just another American. Alaska is one of the fifty states. We vote. We pay and receive Social Security. And we learn English in school, and we eat at McDonald's."

"I'm sorry," said Mary. "I was just trying to be friendly."

Ned, the supervisor of the orientation program, said to the group, "I think we have asked Akiak enough about his cultural heritage for now. Yet I have just one favor to ask Akiak. I wish he would show us how he positions his arm, head, and body to spear a big fish."

Akiak said with a sarcastic tone, "Time out. I'm taking a break from this orientation right now. I have to go back to my igloo and chew on some frozen fish."

Question.s:

13.14 What does this case tell us about cultural sensitivity?

13.15 How might Akiak's coworkers have related better to him during the orientation?

13.16 How might Akiak have done a better job of relating to his new coworkers so far?

13.17 Does Akiak have an *attitude* (meaning negative attitude problem)?

Human Relations Role-Playing Exercise

Building a Relationship with an Eskimo Electronic Technician

Several class members play the role of new workers at the company in International Falls, Minnesota, as described in the case presented above. One of the other new workers is Akiak Nori. You want to welcome him and help him feel part of the group. At the same time, you believe that recognizing his Eskimo heritage would be part of showing respect for his culture. Yet you do not want to be patronizing or make Akiak feel that he is a curiosity. Another student plays the role of Akiak, who regards himself an American, yet is also proud of his Eskimo heritage.

Conduct this role-play for about seven minutes. Observers rate the role-players on two dimensions, using a scale of 1-to-5 from very poor to very good. One dimension is "effective use of human relations techniques." Focus on the cross-cultural sensitivity of the workers attempting to build a relationship with Akiak. Also provide feedback about Akiak's interpersonal skills. The second dimension is "acting ability." A few observers might voluntarily provide feedback to the role-players in terms of sharing their ratings and observations. The course instructor might also provide feedback.

REFERENCES

1. Original story created from facts and observations in the following sources: Susan G. Hauser, "The Clone Danger," *Workforce Management*, April 13, p. 40; "Loews Hotels," *Hospitalityonline*, www.hospitalityonline.com, accessed April 19, 2015, pp. 1–2; "Loews Hotel Employment Opportunity," www.hcareers.com, accessed April 19, 2015, pp. 1–3; "Love Hospitality? We'd Love to —Meet You," *Loews Hotels, Resorts*, www.loewshotels.com, accessed April 20, 2015, pp. 1–3.

2. Kristen M. Klein and Mo Wang, "Deep-Level Diversity and Leadership," *American Psychologist*, December 2010, pp. 932–933.

3. Vivian Hunt, Dennis Layton, and Sara Prince, "Why Diversity Matters," *McKinsey & Company*, www.mckinsey.com, January 2015, pp. 1–3.

4. Geert Hofstede, *Culture's Consequences: International Differences in Work-Related Values* (Beverly Hills, CA: Sage, 1980). Updated and expanded in "A Conversation with Geert Hofstede," *Organizational Dynamics*, Spring 1993, pp. 53–61; Manasour Javidan, Peter W. Dorfman, May Sully de Luque, and Robert J. House, "In the Eye of the Beholder: Cross-Cultural Lessons in Leadership from Project GLOBE," *Academy of Management Perspectives*, February 2006, pp. 69–70.

5. Heejung S. Kim, David K. Sherman, and Shelley E. Taylor, "Culture and Social Support," *American Psychologist*, September 2008, pp. 518–526.

6. Adam P. Cohen, "Many Forms of Culture," *American Psychologist*, April 2009, p. 197.

7. Janet Wiscombe, "McDonald's Corp.," *Workforce Management*, November 2010, p. 38.

8. Huiwen Lian, D. Lance Ferris, and Douglas J. Brown, "Does Power Distance Exacerbate or Mitigate the Effects of Abusive Supervision? It Depends on the Outcome," *Journal of Applied Psychology*, January 2012, pp. 107–123.

9. Carlin Flora, "Double Talk," *Psychology Today*, September–October 2010, p. 75.

10. Stacey R. Fitzsimmons, "Multicultural Employees: A Framework for Understanding How They Contribute to Organizations," *Academy of Management Review*, October 2013, p. 537.

11. Jeffrey Jensen Arnett, "The Psychology of Globalization," *American Psychologist*, October 2002, pp. 777–778.

12. Georgia T. Chao and Henry Moon, "The Cultural Mosaic: A Methodology for Understanding the Complexity of Culture," *Journal of Applied Psychology*, November 2005, pp. 1128–1140.

13. Arvind V. Phatak, *International Dimensions of Management* (Boston: Kent, 1983), p. 167.

14. Tsedal Neeley and Robert Steven Kaplan, "What's Your Language Strategy?" *Harvard Business Review*, September 2014, p. 76.

15. Kathryn Tyler, "Global Ease," *HR Magazine*, May 2011, pp. 41–42.

16. P. Christopher Earley and Elaine Mosakowski, "Cultural Intelligence," *Harvard Business Review*, October 2004, p. 140.

17. Jacob Eisenberg et al., "Can Business Schools Make Students Culturally Competent? Effects of Cross-Cultural Management Courses on Cultural Intelligence," *Academy of Management Learning & Education*, December 2013, pp. 603–621; Earley and Mosakowski, "Toward Cultural Intelligence: Turning Cultural Differences into Workplace Advantage," *Academy of Management Executive*, August 2004, pp. 154–155.

18. Xiao-Ping Chen, Dong Liu, and Rebecca Portnoy, "A Multi-Level Investigation of Motivational Cultural Intelligence, Organizational Diversity Climate, and Cultural Sales: Evidence from U.S. Real Estate Firms," *Journal of Applied Psychology*, January 2012, pp. 93–106.

19. Todd Raphael, "Savvy Companies Build Bonds with Hispanic Employees," *Workforce*, September 2001, p. 19.

20. Experiment reported in Christopher Munsey, "Stereotype-Busting Can Spur Stress, Reduce Cognitive Performance," *Monitor on Psychology*, June 2007, p. 11.

21. Diane Cadrain, "Sexual Equity in the Workplace," *HR Magazine*, September 2008, pp. 44–50.

22. Gunnar Beeth, "Multicultural Managers Wanted," *Management Review*, May 1997, p. 17.

23. A few of these tasty morsels are from Lillian H. Chaney and Jeannette S. Martin, *Interpersonal Business Communication*, 3rd ed. (Upper Saddle River, NJ: Pearson Prentice Hall, 2004), p. 190.

24. Angela Ka-yee Leung, William W. Maddux, Adam G. Galinsky, and Chi-yue Chiu, "Multicultural Experience Enhances Creativity: The When and How," *American Psychologist*, April 2008, pp. 169–181.

25. Marc Diener, "Culture Shock," *Entrepreneur*, July 2003, p. 77.

26. The quotes in this section as well as the general idea are from Tanya Mohn, "Learning to Work with a Culture, Even from a Distance," *New York Times*, www.nytimes.com, March 8, 2010, pp. 1–4.

27. Sarah Fister Gale, "Now, You're Speaking My Language," *Workforce Management*, July 2013, p. 10.

28. James L. Curtis and Craig B. Simonsen, "Fatal Falls and Accidents Involving Foreign-Born and English-as-a-Second-Language-Speaking Workers in the US," *Environmental & Safety Law Update*, www.environmentalsafetyupdate.com, March 8, 2013, p. 1.

29. Matt Tarpey, "7 Promising Jobs for Bilingual Workers," *CareerBuilder*, March 15, 2015, p. 2F.

30. Definition from the U.S. Department of the Interior, Office of Civil Rights, as quoted in Janet Perez, "Diversity Inside-Out," *Hispanic Business*, April 2006, p. 64.

31. Todd Henneman, "Making the Pieces Fit," *Workforce Management*, August 2011, pp. 12–18.

32. "7 Things Never to Say to People with Disabilities," www.diversityinc.com/things-not-to-say, May 27, 2008, pp. 1–2.

33. Katerina Bezrukova, Karen A. Jehn, and Chester S. Spell, "Reviewing Diversity Training: Where We Have Been and Where We Should Go," *Academy of Management Learning & Education*, June 2012, pp. 207–227.

34. "Use Team's Diversity to Best Advantage," *Executive Strategies*, April 2000, p. 2.

35. Siri Carpenter, "Why Do 'They All Look Alike'?" *Monitor on Psychology*, December 2000, p. 44.

36. Cited in "All Inclusive: Bringing Workplace Diversity to Higher Level," *Chicago Tribune Career Builder*, March 11, 2012, p. 16.

37. Sarah Fister Gale, "The Untapped Talent Pool of People with Disabilities," *Workforce*, September 14, 2014, p. 10.

38. Terrence Belford, "Opening Doors for Employees with Disabilities," *Toronto Star*, www.thestar.com June 13, 2008.

39. "Allstate Diversity," www.allstate.com/diversity, accessed April 22, 2015.

40. Boris Groysberg and Katherine Connolly, "Great Leaders Who Make the Mix Work," *Harvard Business Review*, September 2013, p. 76.

41. Ruth E. Fassinger, "Workplace Diversity and Public Policy," *American Psychologist*, May–June 2008, p. 252.

42. pp. 262–265; "Bush Signs Genetic Anti-Discrimination Bill," Associated Press, May 21, 2008.

43. Max Mihelich, "The Changing Landscape of LGBT Discrimination Laws," *Workforce*, October 14, 2014, p. 22.

Fotolia

CHAPTER **14**

Getting Ahead in Your Career

Outline

Jason, an experienced elevator installer and repair technician, was applying for a position as a supervisor of elevator technicians. Jason had the experience, technical skills, and people skills he believed qualified him for this high-paying and demanding position. He recognized that although not many people possessed this relatively rare skills set, a couple of other qualified candidates were applying for the position.

The interview appeared to be going quite well, as Jason answered routine questions about his education, experience, strengths, needs for improvement, and career goals. Gloria, the interviewing manager, then said to Jason, "Tell me about a time you were under heavy pressure in your work as an elevator-repair technician, and what you did about the problem."

After a ten-second pause to collect his thoughts, Jason responded, "It was 5 p.m. on a Tuesday. We received an emergency alert from the property manager of a downtown office building in which our company had installed the elevators. An elevator full of people was stuck between the sixteenth and seventeenth floors. My supervisor called this a red alert and asked me take the first steps in working on the problem. If we did not free these people within an hour, our company's reputation would be in shambles.

"My first step was to jump onto the computer and use our advanced diagnostic software to figure out what might be wrong. Within ten minutes, I discovered that a few commands on the elevator computer system had fallen out of position. I regulated the commands and phoned the property manager that the elevator should now be functioning normally. Everybody involved in this horrible glitch, including the people stuck on the elevator, was relieved and happy."

Gloria said to Jason, "Great response. We need a supervisor who can stay cool under heavy pressure." A few days later, Jason did receive and accept a job offer at even higher pay than he expected.

The excerpt from a job interview just presented illustrates what can be a vital part of moving ahead in today's world: responding effectively to a question relating to job behavior and skill. This chapter offers many useful approaches to career advancement, but our discussion of career advancement is preceded by the necessary first step of conducting a job campaign.

We have divided the vast information about career advancement into three sections. The first section deals with approaches to managing or taking control of your own behavior to advance or retain a good position. The second section deals with approaches to exerting control over your environment to improve your chances for success. The third section deals with networking, the most widely accepted career advancement strategy. To begin relating career development to yourself, do Human Relations Self-Assessment Quiz 14-1.

Human Relations Self-Assessment Quiz   14-1

The Career Development Inventory

Career development activities inevitably include answering some penetrating questions about yourself, such as the twelve questions that follow. You may need several hours to do a competent job answering these questions. After individuals have answered these questions by themselves, it may be profitable to hold a class discussion about the relevance of the specific questions. A strongly recommended procedure is for you to date your completed inventory and put it away for safekeeping. Examine your answers in several years to see (a) how well you are doing in advancing your career and (b) how much you have changed.

Keep the following information in mind in answering this inventory: People are generous in their self-evaluations when they answer career development inventories, so you might want to discuss some of your answers with somebody who knows you well.

1. How would you describe yourself as a person?
2. What are you best at doing? Worst?
3. What are your two biggest strengths or assets?
4. What skills and knowledge will you need to acquire to reach your goals?
5. What are your two biggest accomplishments?
6. Write a two-paragraph synopsis of your career, pretending that you have just retired.
7. What would be the ideal job for you?
8. What career advice can you give yourself?
9. Describe the two peak work-related experiences in your life.
10. What are your five most important values (the things in life most important to you)?
11. What goals in life are you trying to achieve?
12. What do you see as your niche (spot where you best fit) in the current world?

Source: "The Career Development Inventory" by Andrew J. DuBrin.

▶ **Learning Objective 14.1** ▶

The Basics of Conducting a Job Search

The purpose of this section is to provide a review of a few key ideas that you need to conduct a successful job search, including sources of job leads, preparation of a cover letter and job résumé, and performing well in a job interview. Recognizing that few people stay with one employer for an entire career, conducting a job search is an important part of career development. Although job search knowledge is readily available, this concise information can be used as a refresher and a reminder to be systematic in finding a new position. We also present a few fine points to help give you an edge over those who do the minimum necessary to find a new position.

TARGET YOUR JOB SEARCH

A job search begins with a reasonably flexible description of the type of job or jobs for which you are looking. Flexibility is called for because with so many different jobs available, it is difficult to be too specific. Also, flexibility with respect to the type of employer is important. For example, many job seekers overlook the possibilities of working for the U.S. government or their state government. The federal and state governments hire graduates in dozens of fields, and the starting pay is competitive with similar private-sector jobs.

Your chances of finding suitable employment are directly proportional to the number of positions that will satisfy your job objectives. One person with a degree in information technology might be interested exclusively in working in the information systems division of a major corporation. Another person with the same background is willing to work in the information technology field for a large company, a small company, a high-tech start-up, a government agency, a hospital, or an educational institution. The second person has a better chance than the first of finding a job in a geographic location he or she wants.

Closely tied in with the type of work you are seeking is the type of organization in which you would prefer to work. You are much more likely to be successful in your new job and your career when you find a good **person–organization fit**, the compatibility of the individual and the organization. In other words, what type of organizational culture (or atmosphere) would fit you best? Your job satisfaction will be higher, and you are likely to stay longer with an employer, when there is a good person–organization fit. In addition to fitting in well with the organization, it is also important to fit your job, group, and supervisor.[1]

Unless you have had exposure to different types of organizations, you may have only tentative ideas about a good person–organization fit for yourself. Questioning people who work at different places can provide you with some useful clues. A vital source of input about a prospective employer is present and past employees. Further, plant tours open to the public can provide valuable tips about what it is like to work in a particular firm.

Visits to stores, restaurants, and government agencies will provide informal information about the general nature of working conditions in those places. Using the Internet to find facts about a company has become standard practice. The Internet search includes the firm's website as well as news stories about the company. Also, the time spent talking to your prospective supervisor and coworkers is time well spent.

Person–organization fit
the compatibility of the individual and the organization

LAUNCH YOUR JOB SEARCH WITH A POSITIVE ATTITUDE

Most job seekers recognize the importance of being positive and optimistic during the job search, particularly when they do not find the right job almost immediately. You need to project a positive attitude in face-to-face conversations, e-mail responses, and text messages; during a video interview; and when asking people in your network for help. A study conducted with 245 students searching for a full-time position reinforces the idea that a positive attitude is beneficial. The students with positive affect (emotion) were able to stay better motivated, and to control procrastination, leading to better job search results. For example, positive affect was positively related to obtaining second interviews. It appeared that positive affect energized job seekers, leading to more energy, enthusiasm, and alertness.[2]

BE AWARE OF QUALIFICATIONS EMPLOYERS ARE SEEKING

A constructive early stage of conducting a job search is to be aware of what qualifications many employers are seeking. What you are looking for in an employer must be matched against what an employer is looking for in an employee. If you are aware of what employers are seeking, you can emphasize those aspects of yourself when applying for a position. For example, applicants for almost any type of position should emphasize their information technology skills and learning ability. Vicki Swisher, an employment placement specialist, says that learning agility is what employers are looking for in all new hires.[3]

Job interviewers and hiring managers do not all agree on the qualifications they seek in employees. Nevertheless, a number of traits, characteristics, skills, and accomplishments are important to many employers. Human Relations Self-Assessment Quiz 14-2 summarizes these qualifications in a way that you can apply to yourself as you think about your job hunt.

Human Relations Self-Assessment Quiz   14-2

Qualifications Sought by Employers

Directions:

Following is a list of qualifications widely sought by prospective employers. After reading each qualification, rate yourself on a 1-to-5 scale by circling the appropriate number: 1 = very low, 2 = low, 3 = average, 4 = high, 5 = very high.

1. Appropriate education for the position under consideration and satisfactory grades	1	2	3	4	5
2. Relevant work experience	1	2	3	4	5
3. Communication and other interpersonal skills	1	2	3	4	5
4. Motivation and energy	1	2	3	4	5
5. Problem-solving ability (intelligence) and creativity	1	2	3	4	5
6. Judgment and common sense	1	2	3	4	5
7. Adaptability to change, including ability to take on tasks not directly part of your field of expertise	1	2	3	4	5
8. Emotional maturity (acting professionally and responsibly)	1	2	3	4	5
9. Teamwork (ability and interest in working in a team effort)	1	2	3	4	5
10. Positive attitude (enthusiasm about work and initiative)	1	2	3	4	5
11. Emotional intelligence (ability to deal with your own feelings and those of others)	1	2	3	4	5
12. Customer service orientation (wanting to meet customer needs)	1	2	3	4	5
13. Up-to-date information technology skills	1	2	3	4	5
14. Ability and willingness to continue to study and learn about the job, company, and industry	1	2	3	4	5
15. Likableness and sense of humor	1	2	3	4	5
16. Dependability, responsibility, and conscientiousness (including good work habits and time management)	1	2	3	4	5
17. Willingness and ability to work well with coworkers and customers from different cultures	1	2	3	4	5
18. Ethical behavior toward customers and company employees and obedience to laws and regulations	1	2	3	4	5
19. Ability to relate well to customers (even if not in a formal customer contact position)	1	2	3	4	5
20. Ability to use social networking sites for business purposes	1	2	3	4	5

Interpretation:

Consider engaging in some serious self-development, training, and education for items on which you rated yourself low or very low. If you accurately rated yourself as 4 or 5 on all the dimensions, you are an exceptional job candidate.

Source: "Qualifications Sought by Employers" by Andrew J. DuBrin.

FINDING JOBS THROUGH NETWORKING AND THE INTERNET

Two cornerstone principles of conducting a job campaign are to use several different methods and to keep trying. These two principles should be applied because most approaches to job finding are inefficient yet effective. *Inefficient* refers to the fact that a person might have to make many contacts to find only one job. Yet the system is *effective* because it does lead to a desired outcome: finding a suitable position. Here we look at two of dozens of possible routes for conducting a job search: networking and the Internet.

Survey results vary as to which methods employers find the most useful in discovering suitable job candidates. A survey conducted by TheHRSpecialist.com found that the five most effective methods are as follows: career websites, 34 percent; employee referrals, 31 percent; newspaper classifieds, 12 percent; employment services, 12 percent; and social networking (such as Facebook, LinkedIn), 9 percent.[4] These results may be surprising to job hunters who think that newspaper ads are obsolete and that social media dominate in job searches.

Networking (Contacts and Referrals)

The most effective method of finding a job is through personal contacts who might then refer you to a potential employer. **Networking** is the process of establishing a group of contacts who can help you in your career. Networking is particularly helpful because it taps you into the *internal job market.* This market is the large array of jobs that haven't been advertised and are usually filled by word of mouth or through friends and acquaintances of employees. More jobs are found by a referral from a personal contact than through any other more formal sources, such as recruitment sites on the Internet or print advertising. Furthermore, the most consistent piece of advice about conducting a job search is to use networking extensively.

Networking has become a confusing term because it refers to in-person networking as well as to establishing contacts by use of social networking websites. Whether the source of your contact is in-person or online, the result is the same for job-hunting purposes as long as the contact is valuable. For example, an influential contact is worth much more than a social media "friend" or "follower" whom you have never spoken to, and who has a connection to employers.

The best way to reach the jobs in the internal market is by getting someone to recommend you for one. When looking for a job, it is therefore important to tell every potential contact of your job search. Be able to tell your story briefly, in terms of your experience, your strengths, and the type of work you are seeking.[5] The more influential the person, the better. Be specific about the type of job you are seeking. To use networking effectively, it may be necessary to create contacts aside from those you already have.

Potential sources of contacts for your network include the following: friends, family members, faculty and staff, athletic team members, professional associations, and career and job fairs. Attending job fairs also illustrates the point that every feasible method of job finding should be attempted. Recruiters who are looking to fill specific positions might be present at the job fair, along with those recruiters who are looking only to build relationships for the future.

Joining online networking sites, such as Facebook, Twitter, LinkedIn, and Pinterest, has become standard practice for conducting a job search. Pinterest is particularly useful if you have images and photos about your work that you might want to display. For example, you might have organized a warehouse for improved productivity, and you want to display photos of and drawings of what you accomplished. Although social media sites are less effective than other sources of job candidates, their influence continues to grow. A major purpose of these sites is for members to help each other find jobs. Some sites emphasize professional contacts, whereas others focus on developing friendships. The contacts you might develop through social media sites can lead to information about job openings.

Networking
the process of establishing a group of contacts who can help you in your career

If you use Twitter as part of your job search, it is important to create a professional profile, as well as updates. *CareerBuilder* recommends that you include a link to your online résumé, LinkedIn profile, a Pinterest board with professional accomplishments, and perhaps your blog.[6]

Many employers recruit directly through these sites, such as companies having a Facebook site or a link to their career website. The usefulness of online networking increases when you meet face-to-face a few of the most promising contacts. Another contribution of social networking websites to job finding is that hiring managers sometimes look through these websites to find potential candidates. The best candidates are invited to submit a résumé or be interviewed by telephone. However, this process works better for website members who are experienced and have unusual expertise.

An important caution about networking: Too many people are consuming too much of other people's time to help them with their job searches. Keep your request for assistance brief and pointed. Ask to reciprocate in any way you can. For example, you might prepare a chart or conduct research for a manager who gave you a job lead. Bothering influential network members too frequently can lead to your being ignored as a pest or high-maintenance person.

Websites for Job Finding

Using the Internet, for little or no cost, the job seeker can post a résumé or scroll through hundreds of job opportunities. Websites such as CareerBuilder, Monster, and Dice are job boards that give employers access to résumés submitted by job hunters. It is also helpful to look for job websites for a specific field, such as information technology, finance, or sales. Job search engines, such as Indeed and SimplyHired, scan the web and aggregate listings from job boards, specialty websites, and employer career websites. SimplyHired emphasizes that you can explore millions of jobs with one job search, and it gives you the opportunity to search within specific fields, such as sales, and office and administration.

The employment section of company websites can be as effective as general job boards in finding job leads. Google is an example of an employer that has dropped the use of job boards in favor of job candidates contacting the company directly.[7] Another Internet approach to finding jobs is to simply insert the position you are seeking, such as "accounts payable specialist," "banquet manager," or "surgical technician," into a search engine. You are likely to find recruiters and employers claiming to have such a position open.

Job hunting on the Internet can lead to a false sense of security. When you use a job search engine, your résumé is cast over a wide net, and hundreds of job postings can be explored. As a consequence, the job seeker may think that he or she can sit back and wait for a job offer to come through e-mail, from your niche on a social networking site, or into your website. In reality, the Internet is only one source of leads and should be used in conjunction with other job-finding methods. Thousands of other job seekers can access the same job openings, and many of the positions listed have already been filled.

A major challenge of job hunting through the Internet is finding a way to speak to a company representative about your application. Telephoning the human resources department of a large company usually leads to a voice mail system with a lengthy menu, and rarely a return call. A plausible approach to making a personal contact is to call the main number of your target company and get connected to the operator. Ask for the department where you hope to work, and you may be able to establish a personal contact—provided that you do not encounter another lengthy menu.

Although online networking is standard practice, building relationships face-to-face is a key component of the job search. Lauren Milligan, the founder of a career-coaching service says that technology tools have not changed the fact that people prefer to hire somebody they like. Meeting face-to-face will often enhance your likableness.[8]

THE JOB RÉSUMÉ AND COVER LETTER

◀ **Learning Objective 14.2** ◀

The job résumé and job interview remain an essential part of the job search. Almost all employers will expect to see your résumé. We mention this basic observation because some people think a résumé is obsolete and should be replaced with a biographical story, a job sample, or a statement of how you can bring about change in an organization. A review of the basics of the two job-finding methods is essential for most job seekers.

Preparing an Effective Job Résumé

The major purpose of a résumé is to market yourself to a prospective employer. The résumé therefore presents a targeted message that will help you obtain a job interview, not a job. You need a résumé both as an outside candidate and often when seeking a transfer within a large firm. Effective résumés are straightforward, factual presentations of a person's experiences, education, skills, and accomplishments. The word *factual* is important because employers frequently verify facts presented on résumés, and gross inaccuracies lead to immediate rejection of the candidate. Some job seekers hire an outside agency to provide a seal of verification to their résumé. The seal is based on a background-screening investigation that confirms relevant information, such as work history and formal education.[9] Many employers still prefer to pay for their own background investigations.

A challenge in preparing an effective résumé is to suit many different preferences; for example, some people spell *résumé* with the acute accents (*résumé* is a French word) and some without. Searching through job search books and websites, you will find hundreds of different opinions as to what constitutes an effective job résumé. Résumé preparation is a broad topic, yet many of the major points are described in the following list.

1. **Length.** Résumé length illustrates how employers hold different opinions about the best résumé format. For people of limited job experience, a one-page résumé is usually sufficient. For candidates with more experience, two pages may suffice.

2. **General construction.** Information about résumé construction is readily available. Using the search engine term *sample job résumé*, you will find dozens of potential models to consider. Done properly, a résumé can lead to an interview with a prospective employer. Done poorly, it will block you from further consideration. *Poorly* refers to such features as misspellings, misuse of words, disorganization, lack of accurate contact information, too many abbreviations and acronyms, and too many unaccounted-for blocks of time.

Job candidates who are found to have misrepresented facts on a résumé (such as pretending to have graduated from a particular school) are immediately disqualified. If references are included on a résumé, they should be valid. *CareerBuilder* surveyed 2,500 hiring managers and found out that 30 percent regularly find false or misleading references on the résumés of job candidates.[10]

Figure 14-1 presents a representative job résumé for a recent college graduate. The sample illustrates the reality that almost all potential employers expect to find on your résumé information about your skills, education, and experience and your contact information.

Note that the traditional sections of the "job objective" and "references upon request" have been intentionally omitted from this sample résumé. The reason is that these two sections are considered old-fashioned by many job search specialists. Your job objective will be implied by the position you are applying for or in the cover letter, and references will be asked for, most likely during the interview. Also note that the résumé has substituted "retail and customer experience" for the more general "work experience."

3. **Keyword importance.** Keywords are an essential part of résumé construction because prospective employers screen for these words both visually and electronically. **Keywords** are terms for skills, certifications, job activities, and other qualifications sought for a particular job. Although keywords vary according to the position in question, here is

Keywords
terms for skills, certifications, job activities, and other qualifications sought for a particular job

FIGURE 14-1 A SAMPLE JOB RÉSUMÉ FOR A RECENT COLLEGE GRADUATE

Maria Gravista

622 Reynolds Avenue, Lexington, KY 40502 mgravista@yahoo.com 502-617-8278 Facebook, Twitter, and LinkedIn pages under my name. Personal website: www.MariaGravista.com.

Profile

Sales and customer service specialist with solid basic business skills, eager to help her employer and customers and advance in responsibilities. Good work experience for my age, including teamwork. Speak and write fluently in English and Spanish.

Key Accomplishments and Skills

Spearheaded department store inventory liquidation of $50,000, and introduced new line of merchandise at the same time. Helped recruit and select ten part-time store associates in a one-month time frame.

Work well with Windows and Macintosh operating systems, Microsoft and Apple office suites. Set up and conduct marketing on social media sites including Facebook, Twitter, and LinkedIn. Work well with Adobe Photoshop, Picasa, and PowerPoint. Website development. Prepare thorough reports, and analyze quantitative and qualitative data well. Can converse with work associates and customers in English and Spanish.

Formal Education

2014–2017: Western Kentucky Valley College: Associate degree in business and marketing, with information technology minor. 3.25 GPA. Captain of soccer team. Vice president of marketing club.

2010–2014: Benjamin Franklin High School, Lexington, KY. Graduated with high honors and was class president. Captain of soccer team, played shooting guard on basketball team for three seasons.

Retail and Customer Experience

2011–2017: Majestic Department Store, Lexington, KY: Began as shelf-stocking clerk, then worked as store associate in women's clothing, jewelry, TV, and consumer electronics. Assigned to projects on inventory liquidation and merchandising. Received outstanding performance reviews.

2007–2010: Newspaper delivery girl for *Kentucky Gazette*. Well liked by customers, and complimented for making my deliveries on time even during inclement weather. Received four awards as Gazette Carrier of the Month.

2012–present: Work with family eBay store to purchase goods from dollar stores and Wal-Mart, and resell in European markets.

Source: "A SAMPLE JOB RÉSUMÉ FOR A RECENT COLLEGE GRADUATE" by Andrew J. DuBrin.

a sampling: *cost reduction, revenue enhancement, customer satisfaction, social media marketing, Google optimization, business process improvement, diversity skills, Mandarin Chinese.* Another use of keywords is to match them in the best possible way to the position applied for, such as using the word *maintenance* several times in the résumé when applying for a position as a maintenance supervisor at a factory. Keywords can also be those action verbs and terms that indicate positive results, such as *achieved, improved,* and *built.*

Keywords must be chosen carefully because so many job searchers use the same buzzwords to describe themselves, such as *think outside the box, best of breed, results-driven, outstanding, motivated,* and *dynamic.*[11] *Creative* is the most-used adjective in LinkedIn profiles, according to a review of millions of user pages on the site. As a result, describing yourself as "creative" may appear to be noncreative. When choosing a buzzword to describe yourself, it is best to provide evidence that you merit the descriptor. For example, if you say you are *results-driven,* describe some results you have attained for an employer.

4. Customization and relevance. Customize your résumé somewhat to fit the position under consideration, rather than sending a generic version to all prospective employers. The cover letter, as mentioned later, makes the major contribution to customization.

Customizing your résumé could mean emphasizing your sales accomplishments of any type if you are applying for a sales position or highlighting your community activities when applying for a position as an administrator at a nonprofit organization.

Customization helps you prepare a résumé that focuses more on relevance than chronology. You concentrate on presenting experiences and accomplishments that are pointedly relevant to the position under consideration, rather than emphasizing a chronological listing of your job experiences. For example, in applying for a position as an assistant hotel manager, you would highlight any activity that related to hotel work, even being on a member of the wait staff or a playground supervisor.[12]

5. Skills and accomplishments. Whichever style of résumé you choose, it should include a section about your job-related skills and accomplishments. A *skill* is an activity, such as preparing a PowerPoint presentation, compiling a research report on consumer preferences, or translating documents from Spanish to English. Most employers hire for skills, so being specific about your skills in a résumé is essential. (Skill description is also quite important during a job interview.) Skills can be based on academic pursuits, paid work, volunteer work, and sometimes sports, such as a team captain mentioning "activity scheduling" as a skill. Remember, though, that a skill is something you can do now and does not refer to a course you once took, unless you have practiced the skill learned in the course. The skills mentioned on your résumé might be incorporated into the profile section.

The importance of listing key skills has increased dramatically in recent years because, according to an expert on employment software at IBM, about 90 percent of large companies use applicant tracking systems to search résumés for the right skills and experience.[13]

Quantifying accomplishments and making objective statements is helpful in creating a positive self-presentation, yet it is not always feasible to do so. Two examples of making your accomplishments more tangible would be as follows:

Reduced home invasions by 28 percent during my three years in my precinct (police captain)

Revised medical billing process resulting in 37 percent fewer patient complaints about errors in medical bills (business administration analyst in hospital)

6. Additional information about you. To provide prospective employers with information about yourself beyond the résumé, you might provide a link to your personal website or page on LinkedIn or a similar social networking site. The site becomes a permanent online home for your credentials. In this way, the employer has a choice about obtaining additional information, but you are not forcing the representative to obtain the information to review your credentials. Take care to ensure that your social media profiles match your résumé. Job descriptions on your profile that do not match the ones on your résumé could arouse suspicion in the prospective employer.[14]

An important caution about a personal website is that it can backfire if it appears to be an overblown, narcissistic statement about who you are. Also, most hiring managers or human resource specialists will conduct an Internet search to learn more about you, including searching for your name on the most frequently used social media sites.[15]

The Cover Letter

A résumé should be accompanied by a cover letter explaining who you are and why you are applying for a particular position. Many companies now require a cover letter as part of the application process, as do many city and county governments. The cover letter customizes your approach to a particular employer, whereas the résumé is more general. (It is also often recommended to modify your résumé to suit a particular position or similar positions.) The cover letter can be more influential than a résumé in deciding who receives an interview offer.

Sometimes it is helpful to prepare an attention-getting cover letter in which you make an assertive statement about how you intend to help the employer deal with an important problem. A person applying for a credit manager position might state, "Let me help you improve your cash flow by using the latest methods for getting customers to pay on time, or even early."

The cover letter should contain a few short paragraphs and focus on the skills and background you will bring to the job. Follow this material with a brief bullet-point list of your accomplishments. If possible, mention a company insider in your network, and then close the cover letter with appreciation for any consideration your qualifications might be given. If you do not have the name of the contact person, use a salutation such as "Dear Purchasing Manager." The ubiquitous "Hi" or "Hey" are best confined to e-mails, text messages, and social networking sites.

Figure 14-2 presents a traditional, yet brief, cover letter. Use this approach if you are concerned about being too bold in your cover letter, or if you are applying to a highly traditional business firm. Modify any sample letter to fit the particular circumstance and your individuality to avoid making it appear that you are using a template, and therefore not thinking independently.

THE SUCCESSFUL JOB INTERVIEW

A successful job campaign results in one or more employment interviews. Screening interviews are often conducted by phone, particularly for customer contact positions requiring telephone skills. Prepare a thirty-second presentation of yourself including your name, your schooling, your job experience, and the type of job you want. Keep working at your presentation until you reduce it to thirty seconds of clear, useful information. During the interview, make sure to avoid background noises and multitasking in order to communicate a professional image.

More extensive interviews are usually conducted in person. Being interviewed by one person at a time is still standard practice. Many firms, however, also conduct panel (or group) interviews in which the job candidates speak to several prospective work associates at the same time. Often, the group interview is conducted in a casual environment, such as a restaurant or company cafeteria. The candidate may not be aware that meeting with the group is actually an interview and that he or she is being judged.

A list of key observations about the employment interview follows. A general guide for performing well in a job interview is to present a positive but accurate self-picture.

FIGURE 14-2

A TRADITIONAL COVER LETTER

Source: "A TRADITIONAL COVER LETTER " by Andrew J. DuBrin.

27 Running Brook Road Baton Rouge, Louisiana 70801 (507) 825-6742 swooden@aol.com
Ms. Melissa Flowers Director of Human Resources Medical Supplies Corporation 7385 South Clinton Avenue New Orleans, Louisiana 70130

Dear Ms. Flowers:

Please accept my application for the position of purchasing assistant, posted on your company website, and also in the *Times Picayune,* March 27.

My company, Wentworth Industries, is currently sending its manufacturing operations to Malaysia, and my position will be terminated on April 30. I am strongly interested in being considered a candidate for the position of purchasing assistant. As shown in my résumé, I have the following key qualifications:

- Two years of experience in a purchasing department, including one year as an office assistant and one as a purchasing assistant
- An appropriate academic background with a major in business administration
- Courses in purchasing and inventory management, and computer applications

Thank you for considering my application.

Cordially,

Sara Wooden

Sara Wooden

As with the job résumé, there is more written and filmed about the job interview than one person could process in a lifetime.

1. **Practice the job interview, as well as prepare.**   Becoming a skillful interviewee requires practice. You can acquire this practice as you go through the job-finding process. In addition, you can rehearse simulated job interviews with friends and other students. Practice answering the questions posed in Figure 14-3. You might also think of several questions you would not like to be asked and develop answers for them. Think through how you have handled difficult job situations, such as dealing with a tight deadline or resolving conflict with a customer, so you can describe these situations during an interview. Preparing for the interview also includes arriving well rested to project the image of a well-motivated person.

   Preparing a video of the practice interviews is especially helpful because it provides feedback on how you presented yourself. In watching the playback, pay particular attention to your spoken and nonverbal communication skills. Then make adjustments as needed. Many colleges of business and career schools require students to be videotaped before they go out on job interviews.

   As is well known, preparing for the interview means knowing relevant facts about the potential employer as gleaned from its website, articles about the company, and speaking with anybody you know affiliated with the company. The suggestions made about finding a good person–organization fit are also relevant for interview preparation. Explain why you are a good fit for the organization. For example, when applying for a position with United Airlines, describe your love for airplane travel, and how often you and your family have flown United.

   Prepare also by inquiring about the most appropriate attire for the interview. Professional-style dress, such as a suit is usually best, yet some companies prefer that job candidates wear business casual. Even if the CEO wears a hoodie to work, such as at Facebook, you still want to appear more professional at your interview.

   Mel Wolfgang, a head recruiter for the Boston Consulting Group, offers a caution about interview preparation. Do not be so well prepared with answers that you appear to be scripted, and therefore not giving truly honest answers to some questions.[16]

FIGURE 14-3

TWELVE QUESTIONS FREQUENTLY ASKED OF JOB CANDIDATES

Source: "TWELVE QUESTIONS ASKED OF JOB CANDIDATES" by Andrew J. DuBrin.

The following questions are of the same basic type and content encountered in most employment interviews. Practice answering them in front of a friend, camcorder, or mirror.

1. Why did you apply for this job?
2. What are your short-term and long-term goals?
3. What are your strengths?
4. What are your areas for improvement? (Or what are your weaknesses?)
5. Why should we hire you?
6. What do you know about our firm?
7. Describe how well you work under pressure.
8. Here's a sample job problem. How would you handle it?
9. Why did you leave your last job?
10. What negative information about you is likely to show up when we conduct a background check of you?
11. Why would hiring you make us more profitable (or stay within budget)?
12. What are your accomplishments?
13. Give me an example of a time in which you took the initiative on the job.
14. What is your opinion of your online presence?
15. Do you have any questions?

Note: Questions 7 and 8 are often asked as part of a behavioral interview.

2. **Explain how you can help the prospective employer.**   An effective job-getting tactic is to explain to a prospective employer what you think you can do to help the company. Look for opportunities to make brief explanations of how your skills can benefit the company. If you were applying for a billing specialist position in a company that you knew was having trouble billing customers correctly, you might make this statement: "Here is how I would apply my skill and experience in setting up billing systems to help develop a billing system with as few glitches as possible." Or you might state that your previous employer had a billing problem and then explain how you helped solve the problem.

   Telling a story about an accomplishment will help explain how you can help the company and will also humanize your presentation. For example, a person applying for a position as a supervisor of collection agents might tell a story about her experience as a collection agent when she one time rowed a boat out to a person's yacht to talk about a repayment schedule.

Behavioral interview
a candidate is asked how he or she handled a particular problem in the past

3. **Respond well to a behavioral interview (work sample).**   A key aspect of evaluating a candidate is the **behavioral interview**, in which the person is asked how he or she handled a particular problem in the past. Such an interview is essentially a job sample, as described in the chapter opener. An example of a behavioral interview question is as follows: "Tell me how you dealt with an angry customer. What was the problem, and what was the outcome?" Behavioral interviews are used frequently because they seem more related to job behavior than personal characteristics, general interview impressions, or test scores. Of course, this assertion neglects the important fact that a person with strong potential may never have handled the type of job situation presented yet could do so in the future. Google is but one example of a company that relies heavily on sample work tests to evaluate job candidates for professional-level positions.[17]

4. **Be prepared to discuss your strengths and weaknesses (developmental opportunities).**   Most interviewers will ask you to discuss your strengths and developmental opportunities. (These and other frequently asked questions are presented in Figure 14-3.) Knowledge of your strengths hints at how good your potential job performance will be. If you deny having areas for improvement, you will appear uninsightful or defensive. When describing your weaknesses, it is helpful to also describe how you overcame a problem or your action plan for dealing with the problem. For example, "Two people told me that my people skills were not nearly as good as my technical skills. I then invested time and money in strengthening my people skills. I took an interpersonal skills course that really helped me."

   Some candidates describe developmental opportunities that could be interpreted as strengths. A case in point: "I have been criticized for expecting too much from myself and others." Do you think this approach is unethical?

5. **Ask a few good questions.**   Many interviewers expect the job candidate to ask a few questions that relate to the heart of the job or the nature of the organization. Two such questions are (a) "What would I have to accomplish in this position that would make me an outstanding performer?" and (b) "What kind of organizational culture do you have?" Having a couple of questions to ask in advance is also helpful because many interviewers ask, "What questions do you have?"

6. **Smooth out rough spots in your background.**   Problems and concerns about your background will often be expressed during a job interview, although they will often prevent you from receiving an interview. About 95 percent of employers routinely conduct background investigations of prospective employees. A background investigation by a firm hired for the purpose could include speaking to neighbors and coworkers about your reputation. In addition, the investigator may delve into your driving record, check for criminal charges or convictions, survey your credit record, and find out whether you have had disputes with the government about taxes.

   Any job seeker who has severe negative factors in his or her background cannot readily change the past. Yet the job seeker can receive copies of a credit bureau report to make sure it is fair and accurate. If inaccuracies exist, or certain credit problems have been resolved, the credit report might be changed in the applicant's favor. Or bring up the negative credit rating during an interview to present your side of the story. Perhaps you had cosigned a loan for a friend who fell behind on his or her payments. It might also be possible to obtain a more favorable reference from an employer by making a polite request.

7. **Be ready for a video interview.**   To save time and travel money, some employers are using camcorders to conduct job interviews or to screen a candidate before inviting him or her to visit the company. Skype is often the technology of choice. If you are interviewed from home, take precautions to create a professional setting. Eliminate clutter from view. If your computer equipment does not project clear images and sound, perhaps you can be interviewed from another location with better equipment. Decrease or eliminate background noises such as a television set playing, people talking, and traffic sounds heard through an open window. Dress as you would for an in-person interview, and avoid a light shining on your face that would wash out your features.

   During a camcorder interview you look at the camera, not the screen. Looking at the camera makes it appear that you are looking at the interviewer. It is also important to sit still and not gesture excessively because it can present a distracting picture.

8. **Send a thank-you note.**   The thank-you note, whether by e-mail or handwritten, should briefly mention your interest in the position and perhaps reinforce an important point, such as your confidence in your ability to make a contribution. Because so many managers and human resource professionals are inundated with e-mail messages, a hand-written note stands out better. Sending the note within forty-eight hours is recommended and suggests that you are on top of your game.[18] If necessary, follow up again, but avoid being perceived as desperate or as a pest by making repeated follow-ups.

YOUR ONLINE REPUTATION AND THE JOB SEARCH

A person's online reputation, or online presence, can have a significant impact on the job search. Social media postings can have a powerful impact on an employment decision. "Googling" candidates has become standard practice to uncover both positive and negative information about job applicants. Going one step further, many employers search social websites such as Facebook, Twitter, and Instagram to see if the candidate has engaged in outrageous behavior such as swimming in a public fountain while under the influence of alcohol—and then bragging about the episode on the social media site.

   It is essential to not have embarrassing information about or photographs of you accessible through search engines. Furthermore, unprofessional posts that include many mistakes in grammar and spelling, as well as vulgarities and rants against others, can create a negative image.

   Sometimes this negative information can be hidden by adjusting privacy options. Negative information can sometimes be removed by asking or hiring a service for such purposes. Often, this service consists of pushing down negative information to a lower page on an Internet search. Many social media posts can be readily removed if you have an account with the website. Another aspect of your online reputation is that you might need to distance yourself from others who share your name. It helps to have a clear photo of yourself on the social media sites where you are a member. When you send your résumé, provide a link to your profile.

   To learn about what public information exists about you place your own name in a couple of search engines. Sometimes another person with the same name as yours might have been involved in criminal activity, so be prepared to explain the confusion.

▶ **Learning Objective 14.3** ▶

Career Advancement Strategies and Tactics

As you look to advance your career, it is helpful to divide your approach into developing your personal qualities and developing qualities that focus more on your interaction with the environment.

TAKING CONTROL OF YOURSELF

The unifying theme to the strategies, tactics, and attitudes described in this section is that you must attempt to control your own behavior. You can advance your career by harnessing the forces under your control. Such a perspective is important because individuals have the primary responsibility for managing their own careers. Many large companies have career development programs, but the individual is still responsible for achieving his or her goals.

Develop Expertise, Passion, and Pride

A starting point in getting ahead is to develop a useful job skill. Being skilled at the task performed by the group is also a requirement for being promoted to a supervisory position. After being promoted to a supervisory position or another managerial job, expertise is still important for further advancement. It helps a manager's reputation to be skilled in such things as developing business strategy, social media applications, and preparing a budget.

The subject of expertise has received considerable attention in recent years. Two major conclusions of the relevant studies are that expertise takes a long time to develop and that hard work combined with coaching is more important than raw talent in attaining expertise. *Long time* refers to about ten years in a complex endeavor such as research, writing, music, or charismatic leadership.[19] The hard work should focus on overcoming a specific problem, such as not being able to make presentations.

Although it may take a long time to develop expertise, it does not mean that all people with high levels of expertise are chronologically old. Many people start businesses while in their twenties, or as teenagers, based on expertise. One example is David Karp, who founded the popular blogging site Tumblr, at age twenty-one.

Although expertise is highly recommended, the workplace also demands that a person perform a variety of tasks, such as those required in working on a team. A finance specialist assigned to a product development team would also be expected to know something about marketing, such as how to analyze a marketing survey. A recommended approach is to have depth in your primary field but also have breadth by having several lesser areas of expertise. To illustrate, no matter what your specialty field, you are also expected to have information technology skills.

Passion goes hand in hand with expertise, and it contributes to problem solving. It is difficult to sustain expertise if you are not passionate about your specialty field. The phrase "following your passion" often refers to turning a hobby or intense interest into a career, but corporate employees can also be passionate about work. A work-passionate person, for example, would regularly read information about his or her specialty. Developing expertise and being passionate about your work lead naturally to being proud of what you produce. People who take pride in their work are likely to achieve higher quality and a good reputation. From the standpoint of management, proud workers are major contributors because their pride motivates them to excel.

Develop a Code of Professional Ethics Including Helping Others

An ethical code determines what behavior is right or wrong, good or bad, based on values. The values stem from cultural upbringing, religious teachings, peer influences, and professional or industry standards. A code of professional ethics helps a worker deal with such issues as accepting bribes, backstabbing coworkers, and sexually harassing a work associate.

An aspect of ethics closely related to career advancement is the willingness to help others rather than focus on your own success exclusively. According to the research of Wharton School professor Adam Grant, prosocial behavior (helping others) results in a wide set of relationships and meaningful connections. Studies with campus call-center workers attempting to raise scholarship money found that the workers who understood the positive impact they were making on the lives of others brought in 171 percent more revenue each week.[20]

Perform Well and Become a Star Performer

Good job performance is the bedrock of a person's career. In rare instances, a person is promoted on the basis of favoritism alone. In all other situations, an employee must have received a favorable performance evaluation to be promoted. Before an employee is promoted, the prospective new boss asks, "How well did this person perform for you?" The extreme of good performance is to become a **star performer**, one of a small number of employees who contribute a disproportionate amount of output.[21] An example would be a sales representative who sells four times as much as an average company rep.

Star performer
one of a small number of employees who contribute a disproportionate amount of output

Continue to Hone Your Interpersonal Skills

Interpersonal skills, such as those you have been studying in this book, help propel you forward in most careers. To take an extreme example, most people do not think that morticians need good interpersonal skills. But funeral directors insist that an effective mortician must be able to project empathy and compassion without appearing artificial. Interpersonal skills are potentially important at all job levels. In a recent survey of manufacturing employers in New York State, 48 percent had trouble finding workers with interpersonal skills, including holding a conversation.[22]

Among the many ways in which interpersonal skills help advance your career is to gain you the cooperation of coworkers. A study by Brent A. Scott of Michigan State University and Timothy A. Judge of Notre Dame University found that popular workers (those with good interpersonal skills) drew more coworker support regardless of their place on the organization chart.[23] Getting along well with coworkers, in turn, will often facilitate being promoted. Furthermore, building a strong relationship with your boss is essential for advancing your career.

Develop a Proactive Personality

If you are an active agent in taking control of the forces around you, you have a proactive personality and stand a better chance of capitalizing on opportunities. Also, you will seek out opportunities, such as seeing problems that need fixing. Having a proactive personality was described in Chapter 11 as a leadership characteristic. Stephen Covey classifies proactivity as one of the seven habits of highly successful people because proactive people take responsibility for their own lives, rather than waiting for fate to help them.[24] People who are highly proactive identify opportunities and act on them, showing initiative, and they keep trying until they bring about meaningful change. Instead of relying solely on the manager to figure out what work needs to be accomplished, the proactive employee looks for projects to undertake.

A health and safety specialist with a proactive personality might identify a health hazard others have missed. He or she would identify the nature of the problem and urge management for funding to control the problem, making use of his or her network. Ultimately, his or her efforts in preventing major health problems would be recognized.

It may not be easy to develop a proactive personality, but a person can get started by taking more initiative to fix problems and attempt to be more self-starting. Being proactive clears the path to organizational citizenship behavior.

Human Relations Self-Assessment Quiz 14-3 gives you an opportunity to think about your own tendencies toward having a proactive personality.

Create Good First Impressions and a Favorable Appearance

Each time you interact with a new person inside or outside your company, you create a first impression. Fair or not, these first impressions have a big impact on your career. Your

Human Relations Self-Assessment Quiz   14-3

Tendencies Toward Being a Proactive Personality

Indicate on a 1-to-5 scale the extent of your agreement with the statements below: agree strongly (AS), agree (A), neutral (N), disagree (D), disagree strongly (DS).

Number	Statement	AS	A	N	D	DS
1.	I plan carefully for things that might go wrong.	5	4	3	2	1
2.	I don't worry about problems until after they have taken place.	1	2	3	4	5
3.	If I see something that is broken, I fix it.	5	4	3	2	1
4.	I have been told several times that I am good at taking the initiative.	5	4	3	2	1
5.	I often let things like a computer password expire without making the necessary changes.	1	2	3	4	5
6.	When something important needs doing, I wait for somebody else to take the initiative.	1	2	3	4	5
7.	I think that having a home security system is a good investment of money.	5	4	3	2	1
8.	I look around for good opportunities that would help me in my career or personal life.	5	4	3	2	1
9.	I don't give much thought to the future because there is not much I can do about it.	1	2	3	4	5
10.	It is a good idea to start saving or investing for retirement at the beginning of your career.	5	4	3	2	1

Scoring and Interpretation:

Total the numbers corresponding to your answers, and make these probable interpretations:

40–50 You have strong tendencies toward being a proactive personality. Such proactivity should be (or already is) an asset to you in your career and personal life.

28–39 You have about average tendencies toward being proactive. To enhance your success and have more fun in life, you might attempt to become more proactive.

10–27 You have a problem with proactivity. Both your work and personal life would probably be enhanced if you became more proactive.

Source: Tendencies Toward Being a Proactive Personality by Andrew J. DuBrin.

first impression also creates a halo that may influence perceptions about the quality of your work in the future. If your first impression is negative, you will have to work extra hard to be perceived as competent later on.

Looking Successful. Looking successful contributes to a positive first impression. Your clothing, your desk and cubicle or office, and your speech should project the image of a successful, but not necessarily flamboyant, person. Appearing physically fit is also part of the success image. Your standard of dress should be appropriate to your particular career stage and work environment. The best guideline for dressing successfully is to carefully observe the dress code of your firm. Another guideline to consider is to dress for the job you want next, not the job you have now. Looking successful does not necessarily mean sinking considerable money in clothing and accessories. Many discount stores offer stylish clothing, and physical fitness can be attained without belonging to an athletic club.

Appearing to Be in Control and Intelligent. Projecting a sense of control is another key factor contributing to a positive first impression. Show that you are in control of yourself and the environment and that you can handle job pressures. Avoid letting your body language betray you: Fidgeting or rubbing your face sends negative nonverbal messages. Make your gestures project self-assurance and purpose. A verbal method of appearing in control is to make a positive assertion such as "This is a demanding assignment, and I welcome the challenge."

Part of being in control is to appear as if you are ready to solve difficult problems. Research suggests that among the ways to appear intelligent are looking at others while speaking, standing or sitting up straight, using a middle initial, and wearing glasses.[25]

Tattoos and Body Piercing. Body art in the form of tattoos and piercing often figures into physical appearance. More companies today accept such decorations as a fact of modern culture, and more corporate professionals and managers can be seen with body piercings. Despite this general acceptance of body art, excessive decoration in visible places could be a career deterrent, particularly in more traditional business firms.[26]

Document Your Accomplishments and Be Visible

Keeping an accurate record of your job accomplishments can be valuable when you are being considered for promotion, transfer, or assignment to a team or project. In addition, a record of accomplishments is useful when your performance is being evaluated. You can show your manager what you have done for the company lately. Many professional-level workers maintain a portfolio of their accomplishments, such as samples of work accomplished. The portfolio is much like that used by photographers, artists, and models when applying for a job. Here are two examples of documented accomplishments from different types of jobs:

1. A bank teller suggested that at least one person in the bank should be fluent in American Sign Language to facilitate serving deaf customers. After implementing the idea, the bank attracted many more deaf customers.

2. A maintenance supervisor decreased fuel costs in the office by 27 percent in one year by installing ceiling fans.

After documenting your accomplishments, it pays to advertise and therefore be visible to key people. Let key people know in a tasteful way of your tangible accomplishments, and focus on how these accomplishments helped the organization. You might request an opportunity to make a presentation to your boss to review the status of one of your successful projects. Or you could use e-mail for the same purpose if it would be presumptuous for you to request a special meeting to discuss your accomplishments.

Keep Growing through Continuous Learning and Self-Development

Many employers expect employees to keep learning, either through company-sponsored programs or on their own. It is particularly important to engage in new learning in areas of interest to the company, such as developing proficiency in a second language if the company has customers and employees in other countries. Continuous learning can take many forms, including formal schooling, attending training programs and seminars, and self-study. To engage in continuous learning, it is essential to remain open to new viewpoints on your established beliefs. A belief (or stereotype) that has been true for a long time may no longer hold true. A person might think, for example, that almost all workers older than sixty are simply putting in time until they reach the traditional retirement age of sixty-five. In reality, many workers plan to continue to work well into their seventies and eighties.

Continuous learning and self-development can be used to enhance complementary skills that will enable you to make fuller use of your strengths. A key example is that technical skills can be more effective when communication skills improve, making the person's expertise more apparent and more accessible.[27] With the improved communication skills, the tech whiz might be able to better explain his or her ideas to others, leading to better use of knowledge about technology.

Observe Proper Etiquette

Business etiquette
special code of behavior required in work situations

Proper etiquette is important for career advancement because such behavior is considered part of acting professionally. **Business etiquette** is a special code of behavior required in work situations. Both *etiquette* and *manners* refer to behaving in an acceptable and refined way. The steady decline of civility in the workplace has created a renewed interest in the study and practice of business etiquette.[28]

In the digital era, etiquette is just as important as ever because of the new challenges that high-tech devices bring. For example, should you multitask when on the phone with your boss or a coworker? The globalization of business also creates challenges, such as figuring out when visiting another country whether handshakes are acceptable.

Deciphering what constitutes proper etiquette and business manners requires investigation. One approach is to use successful people as models of behavior and sources of information. Another approach is to consult a current book about business etiquette. The basic rules of etiquette are to make the other person feel comfortable in your presence, to be considerate, and to strive not to embarrass anyone. Also, be cordial to all, remembering that everyone deserves our respect. Specific guidelines for practicing etiquette stem from these basic rules. Figure 14-4 presents examples of good business etiquette and manners.

Develop Your Personal Brand

Personal brand
your distinctive set of strengths, including skills and values

Career advancement includes developing your **personal brand**, or your distinctive set of strengths, including skills and values. (Your expertise usually represents your distinctive set of strengths.) Your brand might also be regarded as your reputation. Although the analogy of each person becoming a recognizable brand name, such as Nike or Tiffany, is far-fetched, the idea of becoming a trusted person of value is sound. Your identity as shown on the Internet, including on social networking sites or your personal blog, is also

**FIGURE 14-4 BUSINESS
ETIQUETTE AND MANNERS**

Five examples of good business etiquette and manners are as follows:

1. Be polite in dealing with work associates. Say "good morning," "good day," or "good evening," and look at the person while delivering the greeting. Get out of your chair when someone wants to shake your hand, give you a high-five, or give you a fist-bump.
2. When dining in a restaurant, the company cafeteria, break room, or even on a bench outside, practice good table manners. Put away your mobile device, and do not talk with your mouth full. If someone else is paying the bill, do not order from the top of the menu.
3. Remember the names of work associates even those who you see only occasionally. If you forget the name it is more polite to ask to be refreshed with the name than not using any name or guessing the name.
4. When another person is opening a door to exit a room or building, do not jump in ahead of him or her. Many people have developed the curious habit of quickly jumping in past another person (moving in the opposite direction) who is exiting. This rude practice can lead to an uncomfortable collision.
5. Women and men should be treated equally but certain common courtesies are still perceived to be positive. Men are no longer expected to hold a chair for a woman in a work setting. Helping a woman pick up a heavy piece of equipment is still welcomed by most women. Men should minimize vulgarities in the presence of women. Helping a woman carrying a large package open a door is good etiquette. A man tipping is hat (even a sports cap) when greeting a woman is regarded as unusually polite behavior.

part of your personal brand. A common practice is to provide a link on a Twitter account that has a one-paragraph summary of your identity.

Your personal brand will be more effective if it is authentic in the sense of accurately reflecting who you are. You might add a little drama to your strengths, but the strengths should still be true. For example, if Mike regularly volunteers to feed people at a mission for the homeless, he might describe himself as having "enduring humanitarian values." Yet it would be a stretch for him to say he is "committed to ending world hunger." Notice that Mike's personal brand would include a deep concern for human welfare.

You begin developing your personal brand by identifying the qualities or characteristics that distinguish you from your coworkers. What have you done recently to make you stand out? What benefits do you offer? Do you deliver high-quality work on time? Are you a creative problem solver? Next, you would make yourself visible so you can cash in on your uniqueness (your brand). Almost all the ideas in this chapter will help you develop your personal brand. Three useful questions to ask in formulating your personal brand are as follows:[29]

■ What am I passionate about—what do I really love?

■ What are my greatest strengths?

■ How can I use my strengths to fuel my passion?

Developing a personal brand statement requires considerable work and might require some professional coaching. Here is the personal brand statement Mike developed:

I am a hard-hitting package of strengths who can be a real asset to an employer. Few people combine superb analytical, information technology, and people skills the way I do. The help I give the homeless shows that I really care about the welfare of others. In school, as well as on the job, I have established a record of high performance and dependability.

Minimize Political Blunders

Political blunder

an insensitive act, also referred to as "putting your foot in your mouth"

An important part of advancing your career is to minimize making mistakes with other people that put you in an unfavorable light. A **political blunder** is an insensitive act, also referred to as "putting your foot in your mouth." With amazing regularity, people get fired for having made an insensitive media post, such as attacking a company executive or making a sexist, racist, or lurid sexual comment. Frequently committed blunders include strong criticism of a boss in a public setting, the boss bypass, and not conforming to the company dress code.

A useful tactic for minimizing blunders is to stop and think before engaging in controversial behavior. For example, a person might think, "I am really enraged with the CEO for blocking salary increases this year. But is it worth blasting her on Twitter just to get revenge?"

▶ **Learning Objective 14.4** ▶

EXERTING CONTROL OVER THE OUTSIDE WORLD

In this section, we emphasize approaches that require you to exert some control over the outside environment. If you do not control it, at least you can try to juggle it to your advantage. For example, the "Find a Mentor" section suggests that you search out a friendly and supportive person in your field who can help you advance in your career.

Establish Career Goals

Planning your career inevitably involves some form of goal setting. Because organizations change so frequently, along with positions, today it may be better to establish general goals that focus on the type of work you want to do in the future. For example, "Within five years I plan to be leading a group of people toward improving the supply-chain management in a business firm".

Careers today have more mobility than in the past. People often move swiftly from job to job and field to field, acquiring new skills along the way. The median number of years a U.S. worker has been in his or her current job is only 4.4, down sharply from the past. Many fewer people stay with the same organization for the last twenty years of their career.[30]

Before establishing career goals, it is helpful to clarify your values, as described in Chapter 5. These are probably the same values that enabled you to choose a career in the first place. While sketching out a career, you should also list your personal goals. They should mesh with your work plans to help prevent major conflicts in your life. Some lifestyles, for example, are incompatible with some career goals. You might find it difficult to develop a stable home life if you aspire to hold a field position in international marketing.

Most career goals should include an approximate time element, which is crucial to sound career management. Your long-range goal might be clearly established in your mind (such as owner and operator of a health spa). At the same time, you must establish short-range goals (get any kind of job in a health spa) and intermediate-range goals. Goals set too far in the future that are not supported with more immediate goals may lose their motivational value.

Achieve Broad Experience

Most people who land high-ranking positions usually have broad experience. You therefore strengthen your credentials by broadening your experience. Achieving breadth early in your career helps because it is easier to transfer when your compensation is not too high. Broadening can come about by performing a variety of jobs or sometimes by performing essentially the same job in different organizations. You can also achieve breadth by working on committees and task forces.

Breadth can also be attained through self-nomination. Have the courage and assertiveness to ask for a promotion or a transfer. Your manager or team leader may not know that you are actually seeking more responsibility. An effective method of convincing him or her is to volunteer for specific job openings or for challenging assignments.

A major benefit of broad experience is that you achieve more career portability, allowing you to move to another employer should the need exist. The employability derives from being a more flexible person with a broader perspective. For example, a person who has worked in both the underwriting (setting rates for risks) and the claims aspects of insurance would be well regarded by insurance companies.

Find a Mentor

The vast majority of successful people have had one or more mentors during their careers. A **mentor** is a more experienced person who guides, teaches, and coaches another individual. In years past, mentors were almost always higher-ranking people. Today, mentors can be peers and even lower-ranking individuals. A lower-ranking individual, for example, can educate you on how other parts of the organization work—something you may need to know to advance. Being mentored by a young person, usually for purposes of learning new technology, is often referred to as *reverse mentoring.*

Many organizations assign a mentor to a company newcomer, yet you might want to supplement company-assigned mentoring with a mentor you find on your own. It is particularly helpful to find a mentor who has the skills or characteristics you would like to develop. For example, if you think that you need to develop your charisma, attempt to find a charismatic mentor. Sometimes you are able to develop a mentor from the contacts you make on the Internet. After the person becomes your mentor, much of the mentoring can take place through e-mail and messaging. E-mentoring will sometimes increase the pool of potential mentors and allow relationships to develop without social bias, such as people being suspicious of the nature of a mentoring relationship between a middle-aged man and a young woman.[31]

A recent development in e-mentoring is to provide frequent, brief feedback to workers being mentored in a Twitter-like format. The brief, frequent electronic feedback fits the preferences of Millennials, who want constant feedback and information on their career progress. Business writer Jeanne Meister explains that today's new mentorship models are more like Twitter conversations than lengthy coaching.[32] A mentor might send a tweet to the person being mentored that says, "Great product demonstration today, but why insult the competition?"

Mentorship is an important development process in many occupations: master–apprentice, physician–intern, teacher–student, and executive–junior executive. An emotional tie exists between the less experienced person (the protégé) and the mentor. The mentor serves as a positive model and a trusted friend. A mentor can also offer candid advice that is not otherwise available.

A variation of traditional one-on-one mentoring is to establish a group of mentors who might help you with different types of problems. Having multiple mentors is often necessary because an individual mentor may not have all the skills, or time, to provide all the guidance you need. One mentor might be quite good at helping you deal with human relations problems, another with communication technology problems, and another with the financial aspects of your job. Having multiple mentors is similar to having a personal board of directors, or a small group of people who serve as your advisers.[33]

Mentor
a more experienced person who
guides, teaches, and coaches
another individual

In return, the person being mentored expresses appreciation, gives positive feedback to the mentor, and shares victories. It is also important to offer a concrete service in return for the mentor's advice. Possibilities include offering to collect information, prepare computer graphics, or run a few errands. Many mentors believe that they have much to learn from their protégés. Finding a mentor involves the same process as networking. You might ask people in your network if they could think of a possible mentor for you. With e-mentoring, geographic distance does not create a substantial barrier. With any prospective mentor, it is best to begin gradually by asking for some advice and then see how the relationship develops.

Deal Constructively with Having a Subordinate Older than You or a Younger Boss

Chronological age no longer governs who is likely to be the subordinate or the boss. Two challenges that must be dealt with effectively to help advance one's career are dealing with a subordinate older than you or having a boss younger than you.

Older Subordinate. A delicate issue is developing a constructive relationship with a subordinate considerably older than you. An effective starting point in building the relationship is to show respect for the subordinate's experience and wisdom. Ask for his or her input based on experience, but avoid phrases such as, "As an old-timer, you must know . . ." Listening carefully to the older subordinate will help you develop a good working relationship.

If the subordinate brings up the problem of age differences, point out that the company appointed you to the position of administrative boss despite the age difference and that you did not create the situation. Working to create teamwork will help break down age barriers because the focus will be on team accomplishment rather than a boss–subordinate rivalry. Include the older subordinate when asking for input about topics often thought to be of more interest to younger workers, such as communication technology.[34]

Younger Boss. Many workers face an ego problem when reporting to a person younger in age, even if the age difference is slight. A starting point in building a constructive relationship is to recognize that having a younger boss is part of the modern world, just like having a doctor or lawyer younger than you. Do not assume that because your boss is younger, he or she is not qualified for the position. Take the initiative to communicate frequently with your boss in an open way that focuses on work issues rather than the age difference. Communicate with your boss as readily as you would with a boss older than you, and you will quickly break down communication barriers.

Look for the learning opportunities that working for a younger boss might bring, such as new ideas based on his or her recent education and fascination with technology. Express your interest in learning new technologies and business processes. Perhaps the younger boss can help you bring other young people into your network, thereby expanding your learning opportunities. Take the opportunity to show that you embrace change, because the negative stereotype about older workers is that they resist change. Unless absolutely necessary, avoid statements such as "We tried that in the past, and it won't work." Show that you are willing to challenge the status quo by making statements such as, "So far our process has worked, but maybe it can work better if we make some changes."

Express enthusiasm for being part of the team, because the majority of younger bosses believe that teamwork is a major contributor to success. However, be willing to express disagreement, but in a diplomatic, collaborative way. A quick way to irritate a younger boss is for you to act in the role of a finger-wagging parent.[35]

Balance Your Life

Balancing your life among the competing demands of work, social life, and personal interests can help you advance your career. Having balance gives you additional energy and vitality that will help you in your career. Having something exciting to look forward to outside of work can sometimes provide a spark that will help you perform well. Also, outside interests, including raising a family, are expensive, giving you another incentive to be an outstanding performer.

Without balance, a career person runs the risk of burnout and feeling that work is not worthwhile. The late Stephen Covey wrote, "Those who work long hours for extended periods are prone to burnout. The trick is to have your priorities clear, honor your commitments, and keep a balance in life."[36]

Developing Your Networking Skills

◀ Learning Objective 14.5 ◀

As a career advancement tactic, networking serves several purposes. The contacts you establish can offer you a promotion, help you find a better position, become a customer, become a valuable supplier, help you solve difficult problems, or find a mentor. People in your network can also offer you emotional support during periods of adversity.

A recommended approach to networking is to keep a list of at least twenty-five people whom you contact at least once a month. The contact can be as extensive as a luncheon meeting or as brief as an e-mail or text message. Many networkers use social media to both develop and maintain contacts. The starting point in networking is to obtain an ample supply of business cards; then introduce yourself to as many potentially valuable network members as feasible. While first developing your network, be inclusive. Later, as your network develops, you can strive to include a greater number of influential and successful people. People in your network can include relatives, classmates, and people you meet while traveling, vacationing, or attending trade shows. Develop both depth and breadth to your network, meaning that some of your network members are truly friends and valuable contacts, whereas others you know less well and may be able to help you only occasionally. At times, you can tap into the networks of your network members, thereby multiplying your own network. However, not everybody wants to give out the names in their network.

Community activities and religious organizations can also be a source of contacts. Golf is still considered the number one sport for networking because of the high-level contacts the sport generates. The range of potential people in your network is much greater over the Internet than if networking is done locally and in person. Some of the people in these groups can become valuable business contacts, although many relationships with your social media "friends" or "followers" are weak associations. Online networking includes newsgroups, mailing lists, chat rooms, and e-mail. Figure 14-5 offers some additional networking suggestions, and Applying Human Relations Exercise 14-1 provides a worksheet for networking.

Networking is obviously beneficial in a field such as direct selling, in which you contact people you know to purchase your goods or services. For example, if you sell products such as financial services, Amway, or Tupperware, you are expected to capitalize on personal contacts. Almost any successful businessperson you meet uses networking, at least to some extent. A study conducted in Germany over a three-year period with over 200 workers in several fields demonstrates that networking really does enhance career success. Networking was shown to enhance current salary as well as growth of salary over time. Furthermore, workers who engaged in more networking had higher job satisfaction. The researchers concluded that networking has a good return on investment.[37]

We caution you again to be selective about your networking. Overreliance on networking, such as contacting people who probably have no interest in hearing from you, can be annoying to the recipient.

FIGURE 14-5

NETWORKING SUGGESTIONS

Source: "Networking Suggestions" by Andrew J. DuBrin.

Some of the additional networking suggestions are as follows:

■ Keep growing and replenishing your network. To maintain a strong network, it helps to add new contacts as well as replace people who have slipped out of your network. Diversify the type of people in your network, as well as the sources of your network member, including new social media websites, and physical locations. Yet keep the number of network members down to a number that you would have time to maintain. Research that about 150 network members is about all most people can manage effectively.

■ Join groups whose mission and members fit your field of interests, such as groups of web developers, accountants, health-care professionals, or real-estate developers.

■ Create good relationships with your peers and fellow students. Some of them may occupy influential positions in the future. ("Look at the paws on them pups.")

■ If you attend a networking event, meet and greet as many people as feasible. Being the first to say "hello" can pay dividends. Deliver a twenty-five-word or so introduction. Explain who you are, what you do professionally, and how you can be helpful.

■ When you ask someone to be part of your network explain how you obtained the person's name, and perhaps why you would like to network with that person. For example, "I have been told you have a sharp entrepreneurial mind, and I have a few innovative ideas I would like to share with you."

Concept Review and Reinforcement

Key Terms

Person–organization fit, 385
Networking, 387
Keywords, 389
Behavioral interview, 394

Star performer, 397
Proactive personality, 397
Business etiquette, 400
Personal brand, 400

Political blunder, 402
Mentor, 403

Summary and Review

Major components of the job search are as follows:

- Target your job search, including a reasonably flexible statement of the type of job you are seeking (your job objective). Knowing what type of organization you would prefer to work for will help focus your job search.
- Launch your search with a positive attitude.
- Be aware of the qualifications employers are seeking.
- Find jobs through networking and the Internet. The most effective method of finding a job is through personal contacts, or networking. Getting someone on the inside to recommend you for a job is the best way to reach the internal job market. Job hunting on the Internet can be done through social networking sites, job boards, job search engines, company websites, and direct entry into a search engine of the job you are seeking. Despite using the Internet, it is important to speak to a person to conduct your job search.
- Prepare an effective job résumé. The major purpose of a résumé is to market yourself to a prospective employer. Effective résumés are straightforward, factual presentations of your experiences, skills, and accomplishments. Avoid making untrue statements on your résumé. There is no one best way to prepare a résumé, but keywords are important, and so is customizing your résumé for a specific position. A résumé should include a section about your job-related skills and accomplishments.
- Accompany your résumé with a cover letter, which should explain who you are and why you are applying for a particular position.
- The successful job interview includes various tactics, including practice and preparation, explaining how you can help the employer, and responding well to a behavioral interview. Also, be prepared to discuss your strengths and weaknesses, ask a few questions, smooth out rough spots in your background, and be ready for a camcorder interview.
- Your online reputation is important for the job search.

One set of strategies and tactics for getting ahead can be classified as taking control of your own behavior. Included are these approaches:

- Develop expertise, passion, and pride.
- Develop a code of professional ethics including helping others.
- Perform well and become a star performer.
- Continue to hone your interpersonal skills.
- Develop a proactive personality.
- Create good first impressions and a favorable appearance.
- Document your accomplishments and be visible.
- Keep growing through continuous learning and self-development.
- Observe proper etiquette.
- Develop your personal brand.
- Minimize political blunders.

Another set of strategies and tactics for career advancement centers on taking control of your environment, or at least adapting it to your advantage. Included are the following:

- Establish career goals.
- Achieve broad experience.
- Find a mentor.

- Deal constructively with having a subordinate older than you or a younger boss.
- Balance your life.

Developing networking skills is a major career advancement tactic that can help you find a new position, become a customer, become a valuable supplier, solve difficult problems, find a mentor, and receive emotional support. Keep a list of at least twenty-five people whom you contact monthly. With mentors, add value while asking for assistance. Social networking sites can be useful in building your network.

Questions for Discussion and Review

14.1 During times when there is a shortage of skilled workers, why is it still important to study how to conduct a job campaign?

14.2 With so much of business-related activities being conducted online or through texting, why leave your home or café to conduct a job search?

14.3 What can you do today to help you develop a contact that could someday lead to a job?

14.4 Make up a behavioral interview question that you might be asked, and develop a good answer.

14.5 Which expertise would you like to have that would probably take ten years to develop?

14.6 What is the most important fact about you that is already in, or should be in, your personal brand?

14.7 If you were a *reverse mentor,* what kind of help do you think you could offer a mentor much older than you chronologically?

14.8 Assume that you wanted to use your human relations course as a way of building your network, how would you decide which other students to invite into your network?

14.9 Explain which social media site you think is, or would be, the best for you in terms of professional networking.

14.10 Which criteria are you using, or will you use, to know if your career is successful?

Web Corner

Personal brand building
www.personalbrandcoaching.com

Career advice, including job search and salaries
www.vault.com

Career advancement suggestions from The Wall Street Journal
www.careerjournal.com

Find a mentor
www.advancementoring.com

INTERNET SKILL BUILDER

Job Finding on the Internet

So many job boards exist on the Internet that conducting an Internet-based job search can be baffling. A direct approach is to enter into a search engine, one at a time, three specific job titles of interest to you. You will be directed to lots of job opportunities closely matching the job titles you entered. You might even be directed to job boards. It may be helpful to enter variations of the same job title, such as both "administrative assistant" and "executive assistant." Your assignment is to identify five jobs for which you appear to be qualified. Even if you have no interest in conducting a job search, it is informative to be aware of job opportunities in your field. Seek answers to the following questions:

1. Do I appear to have the qualifications for the type of job I am seeking?
2. Is there a particular geographic area where the job or jobs I want are available?
3. How good are opportunities in my chosen field?

Developing Your Human Relations Skills

Applying Human Relations Exercise 14-1

Building Your Network

Networking can be regarded as the process of building a team that works with you to achieve success. You can start the following exercise now, but it will probably take your entire career to implement it completely. To start networking or make your present networking more systematic, take the following steps:

Step 1: Jot down your top three goals or objectives for the next three months, such as obtaining a new job or promotion, starting a small business, or doing a field research study.

1. _____
   _____
2. _____
   _____
3. _____
   _____

Step 2: List family members, friends, and acquaintances who could assist you in meeting your goals or objectives. Prepare a contact card or database entry for each person on your list, including as many details as you can about the person and the person's family, friends, employers, and contacts. Include in your contacts members of your online network, assuming they are more than people who do not really know you but simply list you as a "friend" or "favorite."

Step 3: Identify what assistance you will request of your contact or contacts. Be realistic in light of your prior investment in the relationship. Remember, you have to be a friend to have a friend.

Step 4: Identify how you will meet your contact or contacts during the next month. Could it be for lunch or at an athletic field, nightclub, sports club, recreational facility on campus, cafeteria, and so forth? Learn more about your contacts during your face-to-face meetings. In some cases, you may have to use the telephone or e-mail to substitute for an in-person meeting. Look for ways to mutually benefit from the relationship. At the beginning of each week, verify that you have made a small investment in building these relationships.

Step 5: Ask for the help you need. A network must benefit you. Thank the contact for any help given. Jot down on your planner a reminder to make a follow-up call, letter, or e-mail message to your contacts. In this way, you will have less work to do before you make another request for help.

Step 6: For each person in your network, think of a favor, however small, that you can return to him or her. Without reciprocity, a network fades rapidly.

Applying Human Relations Exercise 14-2

Strategies and Action Plans for Career Success

If implemented effectively, the activity described next could bring you enormous career satisfaction and success even if you have already made progress in your career. The activity lists the strategies and tactics presented in this chapter, along with a space for an action plan to accompany the strategy or tactic. Choose about six of the strategies and tactics you think will be the most useful for you, and sketch the basics of the action plan you intend to use to implement the strategy or tactic. Here is an example: Suppose you choose the strategy "Develop a Proactive Personality." Your action plan might be "Will stay on the alert for opportunities to take the initiative. Will look for potential problems and then recommend solutions to my boss."

Number	Career Strategy or Tactic	Action Plan to Implement Strategy or Tactic
1.	Develop expertise, passion, and pride	
2.	Develop a code of professional ethics including helping others	
3.	Perform well and become a star performer	
4.	Continue to hone my interpersonal skills	
5.	Develop a proactive personality	
6.	Create good first impressions and a favorable appearance	
7.	Document my accomplishments and be visible	
8.	Keep growing through continuous learning and self-development	
9.	Observe proper etiquette	
10.	Develop your personal brand	
11.	Minimize political blunders	
12.	Establish career goals	
13.	Achieve broad experience	
14.	Find a mentor	
15.	Deal constructively with having a subordinate older than I or a younger boss	
16.	Balance my life	
17.	Develop my networking skills	

Human Relations Class Activity

Capitalizing on Strengths for Career Success

To assist in achieving your career goals, answer the following questions. Keep in mind, however, that you might want to confine your answers to information that you would be willing to share with fellow students:

1. What are two of my most important assets that will contribute to my career success?
2. How do I capitalize on these assets?

Possible answers to these two questions are almost unlimited, yet here is a sample answer: "Two of my most important assets are my ability to get along well with people and my information technology skills. I could capitalize on these assets by getting a job in industrial sales. You have to get along well with people to sell. You also need to be able search for digitized information such as the trade-in value of the machinery the person is hoping to replace, and to arrive at a fair price for what you are selling."

Each class member, or a group of volunteers, will address the class one by one with answers to the two questions. Perhaps answers to the questions can be distributed electronically to all class members before the day of presentations. After the presentations, hold a brief class discussion about (a) the strengths most commonly cited and (b) the most likely effectiveness of the plans for capitalizing on the assets.

Pamela Develops a Brand Called Pam Peters

Pamela is doing well in her career as a hotel front-office manager. Among her varied duties are greeting hotel guests, handling customer service and complaints, and scheduling housekeeping and the custodial staff. Pamela began working in the hotel field as a high school student when an uncle helped her obtain a position on the wait staff of a local Hilton Hotel. While attending career school, Pamela had worked her way up to an assistant manager at a Holiday Inn Express.

Pamela believes that she has the potential to advance into the executive ranks of a big hotel chain. She is so earnest about advancing in her career that she attended a two-day workshop about building a personal brand. Inspired by what she heard and the written instructions she received, Pamela decided to build a personal brand. The workshop leader, Baxter, told Pamela, "Pam Peters, you are unique, and almost a brand already. Just look at some of your assets. Your education is fine, your work experience is terrific, and as a six-foot-tall woman, you certainly do stand out."

That evening Pamela began working on her brand statement on her laptop and uploaded it to her smartphone so she could tweak it a bit during the day, when so inspired during breaks from her manager position at the hotel. The fifth version of Pamela's brand statement read as follows:

Pam Peters is a total package. She is superskilled, six feet tall, with a winning smile backed up by a warm, engaging personality. Got a hotel problem? Who else are you going to call but the dynamic Pam, who will jump on the problem with wisdom, experience, and outstanding problem-solving ability? She can convert angry customers into loyal customers, and disgruntled hotel employees into superior performers.

Pam can inspire the housekeeping staff into cleaning windows, and she is an expert in Windows. Pam is up-to-date on the latest in communication technology, and she will always be an early user of the next hot technology. Pam Peters is the person to lead your workers to higher levels of teamwork, and your hotel to higher profitability.

Questions:

14.11 What is your evaluation of the effectiveness of Pamela's personal brand statement?

14.12 What suggestions might you offer to Pamela to improve her brand statement?

14.13 To what extent do you think Pamela should even bother having a personal brand?

The HR Manager Reviews "The Brand Called Pam Peters"

Pamela Peters, just described, has an opportunity to meet with the corporate HR (human resources) manager, Luke Watkins, to discuss her career at the hotel. One student plays the role of Pamela, who about five minutes into the interview, requests that the HR manager visit her website to read her brand statement. Another student plays the role of Luke, who, being a bit traditional, is lukewarm toward the idea of a professional person presenting herself as a brand. Pamela is very excited about her personal brand statement, but she quickly learns that she will have to convince Luke of its relevance.

Run the role-play for about seven minutes, and observers will note if Pam is making any progress in using her brand statement to sell her credentials for promotion to Luke Watkins. Observers rate the role-players on two dimensions, using a scale of 1 to 5 from very poor to very good. One dimension is "effective use of human relations techniques." For Pam, focus on how convincing she is in presenting her personal brand. The second dimension is "acting ability." A few observers might voluntarily provide feedback to the role-players in terms of sharing their ratings and observations. The course instructor might also provide feedback.

Human Relations Case Study 14–2

Jay Tries to Climb the Ladder

Jay had been working for Sun Foods since he was fifteen years old. The grocery chain had been a perfect place for his first job. The hours were flexible, and it would put some money in Jay's pocket. After three years, Jay left Sun Foods and went to college for a year, traveled for another, tried a few different jobs. and finally came back to Sun Foods to pursue a career. Jay decided that this work would always be in demand and was not overly dangerous. Furthermore, he enjoyed working with the customers and the other employees.

Jay's goal was to climb the ladder to a position that would provide him a good living. He remembered a meeting with the store manager and a union representative, where it was cited that employee turnover the previous year had been 91 percent, so Jay felt he had a good chance to move up and do well.

Upon being rehired to a new store location to begin his new career, Jay was eager. He picked up all of the extra hours that he could, worked multiple positions, and also engaged with other employees in his off time. Beginning with a part-time position, in a short period of time, Jay was successful in obtaining full-time employment with Sun Foods as a junior supervisor.

As Jay's work at the store moved along, management had attempted to steer his career by indicating to him which positions he should take, and which he should not apply for. Jay was not happy with this and did not follow management's recommendations on more than one occasion. Jay had certain departments that he wanted to work in and was not interested in moving or relocating from his hometown to advance. It was common practice to promote those who were willing to move or relocate for the company, but Jay didn't feel the need to relocate, as there appeared to be more than enough opportunity in his current store location.

Jay began taking evening classes at the local community college to improve his skills, to hopefully apply them one day in a management role at Sun Foods. This plan was not received well by the management team as Jay now had restricted availability, although he would still be able to work his full-time hours. Jay was frustrated but was convinced that if he worked hard and finished his college diploma, he would be sure to find his way up the corporate ladder at Sun Foods.

Jay started to question his career choice when a colleague was promoted to a management position after that position was vacated by a middle manager who was promoted to a senior-level position within the company. With his newfound financial stability, the new manager promptly purchased a new home. Within weeks he was demoted to his old position (and previous rate of pay) because the previous manager returned to his old position, unsatisfied with the job at the senior level. Jay asked himself, "Could this happen to me?"

Jay obtained his college diploma at the time Sun Foods management had recently released an in-house training program that was designed to fast-track employees to management. Jay was sure that by completing the program along with his college degree, and with his years of experience, he would be promoted to a management position.

Jay qualified for and was accepted into the program. He quickly completed the first of the three program courses and wanted to go on to complete the second. The store manager indicated to Jay that he could not complete the next course until the following year. Jay was not pleased and went over the manager's head to the supervisor of training and development at Sun Foods. The latter gave Jay permission to take the second course. The third and final phase of the course was only to be taken with the store manager's approval. Jay was excited about the prospects of completing the final phase.

One day after his shift, Jay saw a sheet of paper with a list of names in the store manager's office. The door was open and no one was around. It was a list of staff to be recommended to the management training program with Jay's name not on it. Not to be discouraged, he again called the supervisor of training and development and was told he would be attending the program. He was pleased until the store manager spoke with Jay and told him that he had spoken with the training supervisor and that Jay would not be attending.

Jay then gave management an ultimatum: He would be looking for jobs elsewhere unless he was accepted into the training program. It took Jay three months to find another position, which had better hours, better pay and benefits, and more support for organizational training and development. During that time he had not been approached to attend the management training program.

14.14 Should Jay take the position? If so, should he inform Sun Foods management beforehand?

14.15 What could Jay have done differently to improve his situation and chances for a promotion at Sun Foods?

14.16 What advice would you give Jay that he could apply to his new position should he decide to accept it? What advice would you give if he turns it down and decides to stay at Sun Foods?

Source: Case provided by Kurt Spady, president and CEO, Avason Consulting Corp.

REFERENCES

1. Amy L. Kristof-Brown, Ryan D. Zimmerman, and Erin C. Johnson, "Consequences of Individuals' Fit at Work: A Meta-Analysis of Person–Job, Person–Organization, Person–Group, and Person–Supervisor Fit," *Personnel Psychology*, Summer 2005, p. 310.

2. Daniel B. Turban, "Be Happy, Don't Wait: The Role of Trait Affect in Job Search," *Personnel Psychology*, No. 2, 2013, pp. 483–514.

3. Cited in Erika Fry, "How to Approach Your Own Career like an Entrepreneur," *Fast Company*, January 1, 2015, p. 86.

4. "Snapshot," *Office Manager Today*, December 2012, p. 5. The data is from a poll at www.theHRSpecialist.com.

5. Alina Tugend, "When Job Hunting, Be Your Own Salesman," *New York Times*, (www.nytimes.com), October 11, 2008, p. 2.

6. Susan Ricker, "Use Twitter to Land Your Next Job," *CareerBuilder*, June 9, 2013.

7. Michelle V. Rafter, "Just Google Him," *Workforce*, April 2015, p. 42.

8. Quoted in Kaitlin Madden, "Job Search Tactics That Still Work: Face-to-Face Networking, Mentors Prove Effective," *CareerBuilder*, December 18, 2011.

9. Toni Vranjes, "Pre-Verified Resumes: How Useful?" *HR Magazine*, January 2014, p. 43.

10. Claire Suddath, "Imaginary Friends," *Bloomberg Businessweek*, January 21–27, 2013, p. 68.

11. Debra Auerbach, "Words That Help or Hurt a Résumé," *CareerBuilder*, August 24, 2014; Diane Stafford, "Take These Buzzwords Off Your '12 Resume," McClatchy Newspapers, December 26, 2011, p. 1.

12. Matt Tarpey, "Hot Résumé Trends for 2015," *CareerBuilder*, December 21, 2014.

13. Cited in Lauren Weber, "Your Résumé vs. Oblivion," *The Wall Street Journal*, January 24, 2012, p. B1.

14. Sara Murray, "Credit Checks on Job Seekers by Employers Attract Scrutiny," *The Wall Street Journal*, October 21, 2010, p. A5.

15. Sam Grobart, "Stay Away from the URL," *Bloomberg Businessweek*, September 9–16, 2013, p. 68.

16. Leslie Kwoh, "When in Doubt, M.B.A.'s Turn to 'Bible,'" *The Wall Street Journal*, November 1, 2012, p. B6.

17. Laslo Bock, *Work Rules!* (New York: Twelve, 2015).

18. "Growing Industries in Need of Workers in 2012," *Forbes*, www.forbes.com, February 14, 2012, pp. 1–4.

19. K. Anders Ericsson, Michael J. Prietula, and Edward T. Cokely, "The Making of an Expert," *Harvard Business Review*, July–August 2007, pp. 114–121.

20. Research reported in Anna Miller, "The 'Science' of Karma," *Monitor on Psychology*, October 2013, pp. 28–30.

21. Herman Aguinis and Ernest O'Boyle Jr., "Star Performers in Twenty-First Century Organizations," *Personnel Psychology*, No. 2, 2014, pp. 313–350.

22. Myles Udland, "Companies Can't Find Workers Who Can Hold a Conversation or Show Up on Time," *Business Insider*, http://finance.yahoo.com, April 17, 2015, pp. 1–6.

23. Brent A. Scott and Timothy A. Judge, "The Popularity Contest at Work: Who Wins, Why, and What Do They Receive?" *Journal of Applied Psychology*, January 2009, pp. 20–33.

24. Stephen R. Covey, *The 7 Habits of Highly Successful People* (New York: HarperCollins, 1989).

25. Research synthesized in Sue Shellenbarger, "You Really Look Smart," *The Wall Street Journal*, January 14, 2015, p. D1.

26. Tim Grant, "Tattoos, Piercings Bad Sign for Job," Scripps Howard News Service, August 19, 2010.

27. John H. Zenger, Joseph R. Folkman, and Scott K. Edinger, "Making Yourself Indispensable," *Harvard Business Review*, October 2011, pp. 84–92.

28. Christine Porath and Christine Pearson, "The Price of Incivility," *Harvard Business Review*, January–February 2013, pp. 114–121.

29. Judy Martin, "Aligning Your Passion with Your Personal Brand," *San Francisco Examiner*, www.examiner.com, March 7, 2009.

30. Anya Kamentz, "The Four-Year Career," *Fast Company*, February 2012, p. 74.

31. Donna M. Owens, "Virtual Mentoring," *HR Magazine*, March 2006, pp. 105–107.

32. Cited in "Etc. Career Counseling," *Bloomberg Businessweek*, March 18–23, 2013, p. 68.

33. Jeanne C. Mesiter and Karie Willyerd, "Mentoring Millennials," *Harvard Business Review*, May 2010, pp. 68–72.

34. "Managing a Staff of Older Employees," *All Business*, www.allbusiness.com, © 1999–2015, accessed April 28, 2015.

35. "Is Your Boss Younger than You? Tricks to Make It Work," www.preretirementlife.com, January 7, 2008; "Dealing with a Younger Boss," www.abclocal.go.com, January 8, 2009.

36. Stephen Covey, "How to Succeed in Today's Workplace," *USA Weekend*, August 29–31, 1997, pp. 4–5.

37. Hans-Georg Wolff and Klaus Moser, "Effects of Networking on Career Success: A Longitudinal Study," *Journal of Applied Psychology*, January 2009, pp. 196–206.

CHAPTER 15

Learning Strategies, Perception, and Life Span Changes

Shutterstock

Outline

A major challenge facing American manufacturing is a shortage of workers qualified to operate and maintain the complex factory machines, which can cost approximately $500,000. Jeff Owens, president of Advanced Technology Services Inc. in Peoria, Illinois, has risen to this challenge. ATS technicians work full-time on the factory floor of manufacturing companies to repair and maintain complex machines. The success of ATS in carrying out its mission depends on recruiting and training its manufacturing specialists, and on also ensuring that these specialists learn what they are taught. The company looks for job candidates with attitudes that would fit into a demanding machine-floor culture. After being hired, they are expected to learn the necessary machine-related skills.

One-fourth of ATS manufacturing technicians were former members of the military. Owens believes that military personnel have great attitudes, combined with technical skill. ATS was named to the list of the 100 most military-friendly companies in America for 2015. Many ATS technicians were trained in the nuclear program of the U.S. Navy and also in advanced avionics or jet engine propulsion. Other useful sources of workers are people raised on a farm and those who enjoy working on cars and trucks.

ATS works closely with high schools, career schools, and community colleges to encourage students to acquire in-demand manufacturing skills, including the ability to navigate the computer controls for factory machines. Continuous improvement is a dominant cultural commitment of ATS. To support the employees' drive to succeed, the company offers up to $5,000 annually in tuition reimbursement for accredited college courses.[1]

This story about a company that provides workers with essential expertise to manufacturers illustrates the importance of employee learning. In this chapter, we deal with a series of issues and topics that enable a person to develop career thrust and stay on track: how people learn, how perception influences their behavior, and the major challenges people face at different stages of their life, including during a career change.

Learning Objectives ▶

After studying the information and doing the exercises in this chapter, you should be able to:

15.1 Understand the basic learning processes, three advanced learning processes, and e-learning.

15.2 Explain the meaning of learning styles, and develop insight into your own style.

15.3 Explain the importance of continuous learning.

15.4 Explain how perception influences behavior.

15.5 Identify the stages of the life cycle.

15.6 Understand the challenges of responding to changes in adolescence, adulthood, and late adulthood.

15.7 Describe the impact of the life span on life and job satisfaction.

15.8 Recognize the realities of dealing with a career change.

15.9 Be better prepared to cope with change.

Major Learning Strategies and Processes

Workers at all levels are expected to learn new job skills and technology continuously. **Learning** is generally considered to be a lasting change in behavior based on practice and experience. Yet it is possible to learn something and store it in your mind without changing your behavior.[2] For example, you read that if you press "F12" in Windows you open the "Save As" function. You keep it in your mind but do not use the command yet. The new knowledge is stored in your upper brain but is not yet put into action. Among the many skills and knowledge employees are expected to learn are as follows:

Learning
generally considered a lasting change in behavior based on practice and experience

- Sales effectiveness
- Customer service
- Surgical technician procedures
- Safety regulation compliance
- Project management certification[3]

Here we describe several different methods of learning, beginning with classical conditioning, the simplest type. Then we describe learning of intermediate complexity, operant conditioning, followed by two ways in which more complicated skills are learned: modeling and informal learning. We conclude with e-learning because of its widespread use in delivering content for learning. Although we describe different methods of learning, most learning depends on several methods. For example, in learning to operate a new vehicle you might need to develop simple reflexes to adjust to getting into the car. You would also use higher-level learning to understand how to use a modern dashboard or follow the driver's manual.

CLASSICAL CONDITIONING: LEARNING SIMPLE HABITS AND REFLEXES

In the late 1890s, Russian physiologist Ivan Pavlov conducted a long series of experiments about digestion. While studying a dog, he noticed that the dog salivated not only with the presence of food in the mouth but also at the sight of the food, the sound of the food trays, and even the footsteps of the experimenter. The principles of **classical conditioning** stemming from his experiments help us to understand the most elementary type of learning: how people acquire uncomplicated habits and reflexes. The basic principles and concepts are included in more complicated forms of learning.

Classical conditioning
principles stemming from Ivan Pavlov's digestion experiments that help people understand the most elementary type of learning: how people acquire uncomplicated habits and reflexes

How Classical Conditioning Takes Place

Classical conditioning works in this manner. Kurt takes an entry-level, unskilled job in a factory. His first day on the job a bell rings in his department at 11:34 a.m. Suddenly, every other worker stops working and opens a lunchbox or heads out to the company cafeteria. Kurt says to himself, "The bell must mean it's time for lunch." By the third day on the job, Kurt develops stomach pangs and begins to salivate as soon as the bell rings. Prior to this job, Kurt was in the habit of eating lunch at 1 p.m. and did not begin to have stomach pangs until that time.

Classical conditioning helps explain such elementary job behavior as how people learn to avoid being conked on the head by cranes and low-hanging pipes. With classical conditioning, people also learn to avoid being burned twice by a hot pipe or to avoid turning off a computer before saving a document.

Habits in Everyday Life

Although habits may appear to be simple mechanisms, they are a major part of everyday life on and off the job. According to several studies, as much as 45 percent of what we do every day is habitual. In this sense, *habitual* refers to performing the same act almost without thinking in the same location or at the same time each day, based on subtle cues.[4] Among these many habits might be locking your car doors as you exit the car, putting one hand on your head each time you are asked a question, and checking your smartphone every time you exit a building. Some reward is usually associated with a habit that encourages a repetition of the behavior. For example, a person might receive many useful messages upon checking the smartphone when exiting a building.

OPERANT CONDITIONING: LEARNING THROUGH THE CONSEQUENCES OF OUR BEHAVIOR

Operant conditioning is learning that takes place as a consequence of behavior. In other words, a person's actions are instrumental in determining whether learning takes place. Operant conditioning is the cornerstone of behaviorism, as reflected first in the work of John B. Watson and then later by B. F. Skinner. The process by which a person learns the correct way to make an overseas phone call illustrates operant conditioning. At first, the instructions may seem confusing, such as whether to first enter 1 or the country code before entering the other numbers. After a few tries, the person chooses the proper sequence of numbers and then has learned how to enter an overseas number.

Operant conditioning
learning that takes place as a consequence of behavior; a person's actions are instrumental in determining whether learning takes place

Reinforcement Strategies

The term *reinforcement* in general refers to the means by which behaviors are selected and retained. It gets at the idea that a response, such as shifting your weight on a snowboard to make a turn, is strengthened. A confusing factor here is that reinforcement strategies apply to both learning and motivation (see Chapter 3). Learning typically precedes motivation because if you have not learned to do something, motivation alone will not get the job done. The four reinforcement strategies are positive reinforcement, negative reinforcement (avoidance learning or motivation), punishment, and extinction.

Positive Reinforcement and Negative Reinforcement. The distinction between positive and negative reinforcement is very important. **Positive reinforcement** adds something rewarding to a situation, such as praise or a gift certificate. Positive reinforcement is thus receiving a reward for making a desired response. **Negative reinforcement** is effective because it removes something unpleasant from a situation. It is a form of avoidance learning or motivation. Negative reinforcement is thus being rewarded by being relieved of discomfort. The international telephone call described above included negative reinforcement. Getting the sequence of numbers correct prevented the unpleasant situation of hearing a voice say, "The number that you entered is incorrect or is no longer in service."

Negative reinforcement is not the same thing as punishment. Negative reinforcement is pleasant and therefore a reward. Punishment, by definition, is something unpleasant, unless the person involved likes to be punished.

Positive reinforcement
increasing the probability that behavior will be repeated by rewarding people for making the desired response; improves learning and motivation

Negative reinforcement
removing something unpleasant from a situation; being rewarded by being relieved of discomfort; form of avoidance learning or motivation

Punishment. Being punished for your mistakes can be an important part of learning. **Punishment** is the introduction of an unpleasant stimulus as a consequence of the learner having done something wrong (in the eyes of the person in control of the situation). Or the threat of punishment can be used instead of actually punishing people for the wrong response in a learning or motivational situation. Punishment assists the operant conditioning process because it weakens the particular response. You tend not to repeat the response because of its negative consequences.

Punishment
the introduction of an unpleasant stimulus as a consequence of the learner having done something wrong

Extinction
the weakening or decreasing of the frequency of undesirable behavior by removing the reward for such behavior

Extinction. The purpose of punishment is to eliminate a response. The same result can often be achieved through the reinforcement strategy of **extinction**. It refers to the weakening or decreasing of the frequency of undesirable behavior by removing the reward for such behavior. It is the absence of reinforcement. One way to stop offensive jokes from a coworker is to neither laugh nor complain. Receiving no reaction, the joke teller stops telling the offensive jokes, and his or her behavior is said to be *extinguished.*

Schedules of Reinforcement

An important issue in operant conditioning (and in motivation) is how frequently to reward people when they make the correct response. Two broad types of schedules of reinforcement are in use: continuous and intermittent.

Under a *continuous schedule,* behavior is reinforced each time it occurs, such as saying "good job" every time a bank teller has exactly the right amount of money in terms of withdrawals and deposits at the end of the day. Continuous schedules usually result in fastest learning, but the desired behavior quickly diminishes when the reinforcement stops. Under an *intermittent schedule,* the learner receives a reward after some instances of engaging in the desired behavior but not after each instance. Intermittent reinforcement is particularly effective in sustaining behavior because the learner stays mentally alert and interested. At any point, the behavior might lead to the desired reward. Lottery tickets that occasionally pay small rewards, such as $10, operate on this principle.

MODELING AND INFORMAL LEARNING: LEARNING COMPLICATED SKILLS

Classical and operant conditioning provide only a partial explanation of how people learn on the job. When you acquire a complicated skill, such as speaking in front of a group, preparing a budget, or designing a store display, you learn much more than simply a single stimulus–response relationship. You learn a large number of these relationships, and you also learn how to put them together in a cohesive, smooth-flowing pattern. Two important processes that help in learning complicated skills are modeling and informal learning. Both are based on processes that are inferred to take place in the brain.

Modeling
learning a skill by observing another person perform the skill; considered a form of social learning because it is learned in the presence of others

Modeling occurs when you learn a skill by observing another person perform the skill. Modeling is considered a form of social learning because it is learned in the presence of others. Many apprentices learn part of their trade by modeling an experienced craftsperson who practices the trade. Modeling is widely used in teaching sports through DVDs that give the viewer an opportunity to observe the skill being performed correctly. Although modeling is an effective way of learning, the learner must also have the proper capabilities and motivation.

Informal learning
planned or unplanned learning that occurs without a formal classroom, lesson plan, instructor, or examination; a way of learning complex skills in the workplace

Informal learning is another way of learning complex skills in the workplace. It is planned or unplanned learning that occurs without a formal classroom, lesson plan, instructor, or examination. The central premise of such learning is that employees acquire important information outside of a formal learning situation. The learning can be spontaneous, such as getting a tip on retrieving information from the intranet while waiting in line at the cafeteria. Or the company might organize the work area to encourage such informal learning, such as having lounges where employees interact. The employees capitalize on a learning situation in an unstructured situation where the rewards stemming from the learning are not explicit.

A key aspect of informal learning in the workplace is knowledge sharing among coworkers. Knowledge-sharing activities include exchanging ideas with coworkers, discussing problems, and seeking advice.[5] Derek, an accountant in one plant of a manufacturing company, might tell Betty, an accountant in a sister factory, "I've found a really efficient low-price contractor for maintenance services based in Gary, Indiana. They are great people, and they hire reliable people who really need a job."

Human learning is a complex field of study, with interesting and useful research emerging regularly. For example, according to one study, when college and high school students were shown two paragraphs in different type fonts, they recalled 14 percent more of the facts printed in the difficult-to-read font.[6] One interpretation of these findings is that if you have to concentrate harder to decipher something, you will remember it better. Which of the following will lead to better recall for you? (a) The original digital camera was invented in the United States. (b) The original digital camera was invented in the United States. Of course, without good enough vision to read the second font, no learning will take place.

E-LEARNING

Important innovations in learning have taken place in both schools and industry through the use of e-learning, or distance learning. Here, the learner studies independently outside of a classroom setting and interacts with a computer in addition to studying course material. **E-learning** is an Internet form of computer-based training. An e-learning course usually is carefully structured, with specific lesson plans for the student. Videos and other graphics are usually incorporated into an e-learning course. E-learning is more of a method of delivering content than a method of learning, yet the process helps us understand more about learning.

A major impetus behind e-learning is that so many employees are geographically dispersed, making it difficult to gather them in one place for learning. Mobile devices facilitate the use of e-learning by employees working in many different locations. For example, 75,000 associates of Keller Williams Reality Inc. use smartphones and tablet computers to view three-minute video lessons that support corporate classroom learning. Lessons are accessed as streaming video or a downloaded podcast.[7]

Another evolution in e-learning has been the business use of massive open online courses, better known as MOOCs. These courses are designed to give hundreds of thousands of students across the world an opportunity to take courses free outside of a university program. When a MOOC is used for business purposes, employees enroll in self-paced digital courses, which include virtual lectures, completing online graded exercises, and also participation in online forums.[8] A MOOC can be chosen that fits the needs of the company, such as training in creativity or data analysis. Another possibility is to design a MOOC for company purposes, such as one designed to transmit information about exceptional customer service.

Although e-learning is technologically different from more traditional forms of learning, it still is based on basic methods of learning. For example, the learner will often need reinforcement to keep going, such as encouragement by the course coordinator or coworker.

E-learning
studying independently outside of a classroom setting and interacting with a computer in addition to studying course material; Internet form of computer-based training

Traits and Attitudes of the Learner

Another relevant aspect of e-learning is that its success depends on self-motivation and self-discipline. Self-motivation is important because an assignment to take an e-learning course by the company often is not motivation enough to work independently. Self-discipline is necessary to create a regular time for performing class work, and it prevents distractions by work or home activities. Data suggests that workers are more likely to apply information acquired in an instructor-led program. One explanation offered is that a commitment will more probably develop between the instructor and the learner than between a computer and a learner.[9]

Strengths and Limitations of E-Learning

E-learning has gained momentum, yet most companies prefer to use blended learning (Internet and classroom) because it combines the personal nature of classroom training with the cost efficiencies of learning via the Internet. The cost efficiencies include decreases in travel and lodging costs and payments to classroom instructors. But classroom training provides the difficult-to-measure benefit of employees spontaneously exchanging ideas that could lead to a creativity breakthrough.

Mark Allen, a professor of education at Pepperdine University, notes that most corporate universities (really training centers) have moved away from strictly online conferences and learning. Information technology is used more effectively to enhance, rather than replace, classroom learning.[10]

In general e-learning is most effective in delivering conceptual subject matter, such as product information, whereas classroom training is more effective for learning interpersonal skills. Furthermore, when an organization wants to build a civil, welcoming workplace, frequent discussions are superior to computer-based lessons.[11] The human touch is important for learning human relations! Frequent e-mail exchanges between students and instructors help bring the human touch into e-learning.

GROUP LEARNING

Group learning
a change in the group's repertoire of potential behavior

Although true learning requires a brain, groups can learn in the sense that members come to adapt their behavior collectively in response to experience. **Group learning** is a change in the group's repertoire of potential behavior. For example, a group of hospital workers might rehearse how to deal with a major health attack such as poisoning of the water supply and then implement the learning should the attack occur. Group learning has three basic features: sharing, storage, and retrieval.[12]

1. *Sharing* is the process by which new knowledge, routines, or behaviors becomes distributed among group members. At the same time, group members must understand that others in the group possess that learning. With our emergency response workers in the hospital, each person shares new insights with the others, such as where to house all the people that might need treatment.

2. *Storage* is the process of storing in memory what has been learned. Similar to learning at the individual level, the change in behavior must be recorded for it to be most useful. The hospital emergency response team should remember what worked and what didn't work in handling one crisis so they can better deal with the next crisis. In addition to memory, a group could store knowledge in a database.

3. *Retrieval* is the ability of group members to find and access the knowledge for subsequent inspection and use. As with individual learning, the group has to be able to access the information when needed. An individual within the group might help the group retrieve the information by stating, "Here's how we dealt with hysterical people during the last emergency."

Social media are used by some companies to facilitate group learning. Group members might access the same Facebook page to quickly and frequently exchange information. For example, the hospital emergency team in question updates each other on what works and what doesn't work in responding to emergencies. A more targeted approach is for a company to use an internal online collaboration network to access relevant information from other employees.[13] For example, a sales representative for a large solar panel company might post the question, "How do we deal with potential customers who worry about what would happen if they needed to replace a roof a couple of years after our panels were installed on their roof?"

▶ **Learning Objective 15.2** ▶

Several Different Learning Styles

Learning style
the idea that different people learn best in different ways

Another important concept in understanding learning is **learning style**, the idea that people learn best in different ways. For example, some people acquire new material best through passive learning. Such people quickly acquire information through studying texts, manuals, magazine articles, and websites. They can juggle images in their mind as they read about abstract concepts such as supply and demand, cultural diversity, or customer service. Others learn best by doing rather than by studying, for example, learning hands-on about customer service by dealing with customers in many situations.

Another key dimension of learning styles is whether a person learns best by working alone or cooperatively, such as in a study group. Learning by oneself allows for more intense concentration, and one can proceed at one's own pace. Learning in groups and through classroom discussion allows people to exchange viewpoints and perspectives. Peer tutoring and cooperative learning are known to be effective for acquiring knowledge.[14] Another advantage of cooperative learning is that it is more likely to lead to changes in behavior. Assume that a manager holds group discussions about the importance of achieving high customer satisfaction. Employees participating in these group discussions are more likely to assertively pursue high customer satisfaction on the job than those who only read about the topic. Learning styles have also been studied more scientifically, and one such approach is described next.

LEARNING STYLES ASSOCIATED WITH PERSONALITY AS MEASURED BY THE GOLDEN PERSONALITY TYPE PROFILER

Another way of understanding learning styles is to recognize that your personality type can influence your learning style. You may have observed, for example, that when an impulsive person needs to learn how to use an electronic device, that person will often grab the device and start hitting the various buttons. A more reflective person will often first read the manual or look over the device carefully before attempting to get it to function.

An accepted method of measuring learning-style types is the Golden Personality Type Profiler.[15] As measured by the Golden instrument, four separate dichotomies direct the typical use of perception and judgment by an individual.

1. **Energy flow: Extraversion versus introversion.** Extraverts direct their energy primarily toward the outer world of people and objects. In contrast, introverts direct their energy primarily toward the inner world of experiences and ideas.

2. **Information gathering: Sensation versus intuition.** People who rely on sensing, focus primarily on what can be perceived by the five primary senses of vision, touch, sight, sound, and smell. People who rely on intuition focus primarily on perceiving patterns and interrelationships.

3. **Decision making: Thinking versus feeling.** People who rely primarily on thinking base conclusions on logical analysis and emphasize objectivity and detachment. People who rely on feelings base conclusions on personal or social values and focus on understanding and harmony.

4. **Lifestyle orientation: Judging versus perceiving.** Individuals who score high on judging tend to orient their lives in a deliberate and planned manner. Individuals who score high on perceiving tend to orient their lives in a spontaneous and open-ended manner.

When the four types are combined with each other, sixteen personality types are formed, such as the ESFP, or The Entertainer. ESFP refers to extraverted/sensing/feeling/perceiving. People of this type are optimistic and are skilled at living joyfully and entertaining others. ESFPs are effective at communicating their good-natured realism to others.

You might want to take the Golden Personality Type Profiler(see Appendix B in this text). Our concern here is with how your personality influences your learning style. Figure 15-1 presents four of the sixteen personality types along with the implications for each one with respect to learning style. You will observe that the learning styles are complex rather than focusing on specific factors, such as preferring observing over reading.

FIGURE 15-1

THE LEARNING STYLES ASSOCIATED WITH FOUR DIFFERENT GOLDEN PERSONALITY TYPES

Personality Type	Highlights of Type	Learning Style Features, Including Preference for Type of Instructor
ENFP (The Proponent) Extraverted/iNtuitive/Feeling/Perceiving	Lives continually in the realm of the possible. When absorbed in his or her latest project, he or she thinks of little else. Filled with energy, he or she is tireless when in pursuit of goals. Has an almost magnetic quality that enables him or her to have fun in almost any setting. The combination of Extraversion, Intuition, and Perceiving is well suited for leadership.	• A preference for lessons that involve adventuresome and creative experiences • A need for time to explore possibilities, ask questions, and use imagination • Learning through a variety of methods: reading, writing, listening, observing, and interacting with others • A dislike of narrow structures or straight lectures • Excelling when the instructor takes a personal interest in him or her
ENFJ (The Communicator) Extraverted/iNtuitive/Feeling/Judging	Chief concern is fostering harmony and cooperation between self and others. Has strong ideals and a potent sense of loyalty, whether to a mate, a school, a hometown, or a favorite cause. Usually good at organizing people to get things done while keeping everyone happy. At work, well-armed to deal with both variety and action. Typically patient and conscientious, he or she makes a concerted effort to stick with a job until finished.	• Performing best in a structured learning environment • Believing interaction with others and discussion of the lesson to be very important • Learning best when he or she understands how the material is connected to helping people • Liking theories and abstractions • Resisting instructors who are not warm and personable
INFP (The Advocate) Introverted/iNtuitive/Feeling/Perceiving	Capable of immense sensitivity and has an enormous emotional capacity, which is guarded closely. Has to know people well before letting down the guard and displaying warmth. Interpersonal relationships are a crucial focus. Has powerful sense of faithfulness, duty, and commitment to the people and causes he or she is attracted to. Able to express emotion and move people through communication. A perfectionist on the job. Prefers a quiet working environment and, despite attraction for human companionship, will often work best alone. Will work at best only in job he or she truly believes in.	• A preference for flexible environments where he or she can use imagination and creativity • Learning best from lectures and written work rather than rote methods • Enjoyment of abstraction and the world of ideas • A preference for instructors who are personally interested in him or her
INFJ (The Foreseer) Introverted/iNtuitive/Feeling/Judging	Imaginative, inspired, tenacious, creative, and inward looking. Also stubborn, easily bored by routine work, and often pays little attention to obstacles. Makes decisions easily. Lives in a world of ideas and will have a unique vision. Pours all own energy into achieving goals. Trusts own intuition. Can express emotion and move people through written communication. Although the companionship of people is cherished, prefers a quiet working environment and working alone. Perfectionist about quality. Creativity is his or her hallmark.	• A value for lifelong learning by interacting with others or through reading and writing • Preference for tools and materials that are organized • Enjoyment of future-oriented concepts, theories, abstractions, and ideas • Avoiding dictatorial educational settings, as well as either/or thinking

Source: "The Learning Styles Associated with Four Different Golden Personality Types" by Andrew J. DuBrin.

Code: E = Extraverted, N = iNtuitive, F = Feeling, P = Perceiving, I = Introverted, J = Judging.

IMPROVING LEARNING AND BRAIN FUNCTIONING THROUGH REST

Interest has escalated for everyday approaches to improving a person's ability to learn and solve problems. We will return to this topic again when we discuss the role of mental and physical activity to enhance learning later in this chapter. Here, we look at the importance of *inactivity* to improve brain functioning and learning. Common wisdom suggests that it is easier to learn when you are rested, and scientific evidence supports this contention. Research synthesized at the University of Rochester Medical Center indicates that the brain needs downtime. Without proper rest, a person does not function as well, mentally or physically.[16] Resting the brain relates to style, because learning when rested is part of one's approach to learning.

The potential benefits of sleep include stronger memory and better attention spans. According to James B. Maas, a psychology professor at Cornell University, good sleep is a necessity rather than a luxury: "Your alertness, energy, performance, thinking, productivity, creativity, safety, and health will be affected by how much you sleep."[17] Besides enhancing alertness, sleep is a way for the brain to store new information in long-term memory. The benefits are most likely to occur from rapid eye movement (REM) sleep, which usually takes place during the sixth and eighth hours of sleep, when people are most likely to dream.

Sleep also improves memory because sleep contributes to a reduction in brain overload. During sleep, the synapses (connections between nerve cells) that were formed during the day's learning can relax a little.[18] A practical implication of this finding is that adequate sleep will do more for your memory than increasing your input of caffeine, because the caffeinated brain might become overcharged with information.

The various approaches to learning, including learning styles, help us understand how people learn. How *much* people learn is another important consideration in understanding learning in the workplace. In general, people with higher mental ability and personality traits that allow them to concentrate better (such as emotional stability and conscientiousness) acquire knowledge and skills more readily.

CONTINUOUS LEARNING DURING YOUR CAREER

◀ Learning Objective 15.3 ◀

For almost all professional, technical, and sales occupations, career success, and even survival, depends on continuous learning (as suggested at several places in this text). Continuous learning relates to learning style because learning throughout one's career is an approach to learning. A commonplace example is that we all have to keep learning how to use new software and hardware just to perform a job. The CEO may need to understand how enterprise-level software helps the different divisions in a firm work together, and the automobile sales rep needs to learn how to estimate trade-in values via the Internet. Acquiring human relations skills, such as working well with coworkers from different cultures, is another area of continuous learning facing many workers.

How Perception Influences Our Interpretation of the World

◀ Learning Objective 15.4 ◀

Understanding learning strategies helps us cope better with the world of work, and understanding how we interpret information we receive is also important. Most of us interpret what is going on in the world outside us as we perceive it, not as it really is. You do not usually experience a mass of colors; instead, you experience a color photograph. You do not experience a thousand different vibrations in the air; instead, you hear a favorite CD. When we answer a question, we answer in terms of our interpretation of what we hear.

An everyday happening, such as a change in air temperature, helps to illustrate the nature of human perception. Assume that you live in Vermont. A temperature of 52°F (11.1°C) would seem warm in January. The same temperature would seem cold in July. Our perception of temperature depends on many things going on inside our mind and body.

Perceptions on the job are very important in such ways as influencing the evaluation of employee performance. A study with working adults in a variety of positions and industries found that employees who have a later start time are perceived to be less conscientious. These perceptions in turn influence supervisors to rate employees as lower performers. In evaluating the data, the researchers took into account total hours worked, objective job performance, and employees' self-ratings of conscientiousness. The results of the study suggest that supervisor ratings of performance are susceptible to stereotypes based on the time of the day when employees start work.[19]

In summary, **perception** deals with the various ways in which people interpret things in the external world and how they act on the basis of these perceptions. The aspects of perception described here are (a) why perceptual problems exist, (b) agreement about perceived events, and (c) how people perceive the causes of behavior. Our discussion focuses on the social rather than the physical aspects of perception, such as taste, sound, and touch.

Perception

the various ways in which people interpret things in the external world and how they act on the basis of these perceptions

WHY PERCEPTUAL PROBLEMS EXIST

Under ideal circumstances, people perceive information as it is intended to be communicated or as it exists in reality. Suppose a company promotes a specialist to a team leader position because he or she is thought to have good potential for advancement. The manager offering the promotion hopes the specialist does not see the promotion as a plot to have the person work extra hours without being paid overtime. (Team leaders usually do not receive overtime pay.) Both characteristics of the stimulus (the idea or thing to be perceived) and the mental processes of people can lead to distorted perceptions. Figure 15-2 outlines why perceptual problems exist.

FIGURE 15-2

CONTRIBUTORS TO PERCEPTUAL PROBLEMS

Source: "CONTRIBUTORS TO PERCEPTUAL PROBLEMS" by Andrew J. DuBrin.

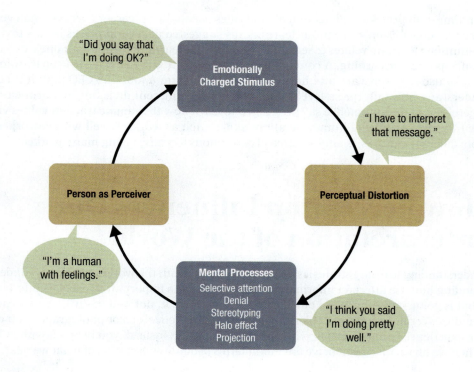

Characteristics of the Stimulus

Perceptual problems are most likely to be encountered when the stimulus or cue to be perceived has an emotional meaning. Assume that Brian, an office supervisor, announces to his staff, "I would like you to meet Brenda. She's a temporary worker here to help us out this week." Announcing the presence of an office temporary could trigger several different perceptions. The specific perceptions would depend on many motives, needs, and the knowledge of department employees. Among the possible interpretations are these:

> "An office temp? I wonder if this means the company is going to cut down the regular workforce and use temps to help us through peak loads."
>
> "This seems to be a sure sign that business has picked up. The front office would never authorize extra help unless business was booming. Things look good for getting a decent raise this year."

To help reduce misperceptions, Brian should provide more complete information on why Brenda is being hired, such as pointing to a surge in orders. Reducing ambiguity helps minimize perceptual errors.

Mental Processes of People

The devices people use to deal with sensory information play a major role in creating perceptual problems. Several of these can also be classified as defensive behavior.

Selective Attention. The major contributor to perceptual distortions is the tendency for us to attend to the stimuli that are most relevant to our needs. Giving exclusive attention to something at the expense of other aspects of the environment is referred to as **selective attention**. If a stimulus fits our needs, desires, or interests, we are likely to give it our attention. At the same time, we are likely to pay only minor attention to the surrounding stimuli. Joe Homeowner hears the wonderful news from the telemarketer that he is eligible to "cash out" on the equity on his home and pay off all those high-interest debts. Only after going forward with the "cashing out" does it sink in for Joe that he now has incurred a new long-term second mortgage on top of his existing mortgage.

Selective attention
giving exclusive attention to something at the expense of other aspects of the environment

Denial. If the sensory information is particularly painful to us—for example, if it hurts our self-esteem—we tend to go one step beyond selective attention. Denial is the process of excluding from awareness an important aspect of reality. This mental process is often found in the workplace, especially when people face such threats as job loss. As part of a downsizing, a woman was told by her manager that she would be terminated in thirty days unless somehow she could find another position in the company. That evening she informed her husband, "Our company is going through a downsizing, so it looks like I will be transferred to a different department in thirty days." By denying the reality of the message, the woman failed to search actively for another job within the company. She finally perceived the message correctly when she was handed her severance check.

Stereotyping. A common method of simplifying perception is to evaluate an individual or thing based on our perception of the group or class to which the person or object belongs. A perceptual disadvantage of stereotyping is that you do not look for the way in which somebody or something might be different from others in the same group. For example, a job seeker might say, "I won't look for a job in the retail field because retailing jobs have such low pay." Such stereotyping might result in the person's neglecting to investigate high-paying opportunities within the retail field based on the rapid promotions possible. Stereotypes can be positive as well as negative.

For example, you might have the stereotype that all accountants are thorough and accurate. As a result, you fail to carefully review the tax return prepared by your accountant.

Halo Effect. We have a tendency to color everything that we know about a person because of one recognizable favorable or unfavorable trait. When a company does not insist on the use of objective measures of performance, it is not uncommon for a supervisor to give a favorable performance rating to people who dress well or smile frequently. The fine appearance or warm smile of these people has created a halo around them. Employees often create a negative halo about a supervisor simply because he or she is gruff or stern in manner or speech.

Projection. Another shortcut in the perceptual process is to project our own faults onto others instead of making an objective appraisal of the situation. Our feelings and thoughts are unacceptable to us, so we attribute them to another person. In this way, we feel less anxious about ourselves. A manager who has a self-discipline problem might respond negatively to an employee's request to work at home one day per week. The manager might say, "Sorry, can't let you work at home. You would probably goof off half the day before you got down to work."

PERCEPTUAL CONGRUENCE

Perceptual congruence
the degree to which people perceive
things the same way

The discussion of perception so far has focused on perceptual errors. At times, most people in the organization perceive an event in the same way. **Perceptual congruence** refers to the degree to which people perceive things the same way. High congruence generally implies valid perception, but people can also agree on a distorted perception. For example, four members of a work team might have the authority to choose a fifth team member. All four might share the same inaccurate perception that a particular candidate is a good fit. After one month, they learn that the individual is a loner who functions poorly in a team environment.

Despite the reservation cited, high congruence generally leads to more positive consequences for the organization than low congruence. A case in point is that it is beneficial for managers and group members to perceive the group members' tasks in the same manner. If store associates and managers at a chain of optician stores agree that their mission is to help people see better—rather than optimizing sales—customers will be better off and the company will stay profitable based on a reputation of being ethical.

ATTRIBUTION THEORY: HOW WE PERCEIVE THE CAUSES OF BEHAVIOR

Attribution theory
the study of the process by which
people ascribe causes to the behaviors
they perceive

An important aspect of perception is our explanation for the causes of behavior. Stated differently, to what do we *attribute* a given behavior? **Attribution theory** is the study of the process by which people ascribe causes to the behavior they perceive. A major finding of attribution theory is that most people give relatively little weight to the circumstances in making judgments about a person's behavior. We are more likely to attribute a person's actions or results to personal characteristics than to outside forces. A supervisor who presses us to finish a project is more likely to be perceived as being impatient than as caught up in a highly competitive environment.

Another finding of attribution theory is that people have a general tendency to attribute their achievements to good inner qualities, whereas they attribute failure to adverse factors within the environment. A manager would thus attribute increased productivity to his or her leadership skills but blame low productivity on poor support from the organization.

How We Respond to Life Span Changes and Challenges

At different stages in life, we face different challenges, beginning with the embryo struggling for enough oxygen and ending with the 100-year-old fretting about physical well-being and passing on his or her estate. (Did you know that sales of birthday cards celebrating a person's 100th birthday have surged in recent years?) Here we overview the stages of the life cycle and the challenges associated with adolescence and beyond.

STAGES OF THE LIFE CYCLE

◀ **Learning Objective 15.5** ◀

Several approaches have been developed over the years to explain the various stages of human development, or the tasks people face at different periods in life. Among the best known is the eight stages of human development formulated by psychiatrist Erik H. Erikson in the 1950s.[20] Figure 15-3 presents an outline of these stages and the associated primary crisis for each one. According to Erikson, the socialization process consists of the "eight stages of man," with each stage representing a psychosocial crisis. The crisis must be resolved at each stage before the next stage can be satisfactorily negotiated.

Satisfactory learning and resolution of each stage is necessary if the child is to manage the next and later stages successfully. The building of a skyscraper is an appropriate metaphor. Each floor, including the foundation and ground level, must be built correctly or the next floor will collapse. An example of this stage-by-stage development is that if the young adult cannot experience intimacy at stage 6, he or she will not be successful at the marriage or parenting that takes place at stage 7.

1. Infancy (0–1 year)
Learning basic trust versus distrust

2. Toddler (1–2 years)
Learning autonomy versus shame (will)

3. Preschool (3–5 years)
Learning initiative versus guilt (purpose)

4. Elementary school (6–12 years)
Learning industry versus inferiority (competence)

5. Adolescence (13–19 years)
Learning identity versus identity diffusion (fidelity)

6. Young adulthood (20–40 years)
Learning intimacy versus isolation (love)

7. Middle adulthood (40–65 years)
Learning generativity (building a generation) versus self-absorption

8. Late adulthood (65 and over)
Learning integrity versus despair (wisdom)

FIGURE 15-3

ERIKSON'S EIGHT STAGES OF DEVELOPMENT AND ASSOCIATED CRISIS

Source: Based on information in Erik H. Erikson *Childhood and Society* (New York: Norton, 1963); Child Development Institute, "Stages of Social Emotional Development in Children and Teenagers," accessed May 10, 2006, www.childdevelopmentinfo.com.

Erikson's stages of human development have prompted later investigation into how humans develop through different phases of their lives. Despite these analyses of life stages, there are huge cultural and individual differences in the successful development of an adult. For example, what about Russian males, whose life expectancy is only about 57 years? (The life expectancy of Russian women is about 77 years. Russian women consume less vodka and smoke less than do their male counterparts.) Do Russian men never deal with stage 8, integrity versus despair? And is it not possible to be a successful, well-adjusted adult even if you are not in a committed relationship and have no children?

Next, we summarize briefly challenges people face in adolescence, adult life, and late life.[21] The first stage, infancy and childhood, is an important building block for later stages but lies outside the purview of our treatment of human relations.

▶ **Learning Objective 15.6** ▶

Adolescence
the period in life from approximately age thirteen to twenty; from a biological standpoint, adolescence begins with puberty

RESPONDING TO CHALLENGES IN ADOLESCENCE

In its technical meaning **adolescence** is the period in life from approximately ages thirteen to twenty. From a biological standpoint, adolescence begins with puberty, the beginning of sexual maturation marked by rising levels of sex hormones and rapid growth. During adolescence, many people start building work-related human skills, such as teamwork, and also engage in career choice and career preparation. Adolescents (or *teenagers*) vary considerably in their accomplishments, with some teenagers being successful entrepreneurs, information technology consultants, professional athletes, and movie stars. Industries such as retailing and food service depend on the adolescent workforce, suggesting that even average teenagers occupy an important work role in society.

Cognitive Challenges

Adolescents headed for a successful career must rise to the challenge of developing logic, abstract thought, and hypothetical reasoning. Many adolescents are studying five different subjects at once and feel compelled to think well enough to perform well in school and on college entrance exams. Adolescents must also deal with the development of moral reasoning, in which they attempt to learn acceptable versus unacceptable codes of conduct. According to Lawrence Kohlberg, former moral education professor at Harvard University, adolescents begin to develop three levels of moral thought:[22]

■ At the *preconventional level*, moral dilemmas are resolved in a self-centered way. An act is moral if it enables someone to avoid punishment or obtain a reward. Obeying safety rules or returning a lost wallet might fit this category of moral development.

■ At the *conventional level*, moral dilemmas are resolved in ways that reflect laws or norms set by parents and other influential adults. Making a complete stop at a stop sign on a country road when no one else is watching would fit the conventional level of moral development.

■ At the *postconventional level*, moral dilemmas are resolved by relating to abstract principles such as equality, justice, and the value of life. An adolescent at this level of moral development might start a food-and-clothing campaign for homeless people in the community.

One reason offered for the unethical behavior of many adults in executive positions in business is that they did not advance to the postconventional level of moral development.

Personality and Social Challenges

As an adolescent struggles to establish a reliable self-concept, or personal identity, he or she faces an **identity crisis**. In a multicultural world, the adolescent may need to establish an ethnic identity. Adolescents often struggle with whether to retain close ties with the family or invest more energy in developing peer relations. Adolescents struggle with sexuality, with some happily engaging in sex and others facing unintended negative consequences such as parenthood, paternity suits, dropping out of school, and sexually transmitted diseases. Another conflict many adolescents face is one of body image, with discontent possibly leading to anorexia and excessive body piercing.

Successfully Managing the Teenage Brain

A cognitive challenge of the adolescent years meriting separate mention is dealing successfully with the **teenage brain**, a stage of brain development in which people are easily influenced by their environment and more prone to impulsive behavior. Based on several research findings, three of the ways the teenage brain differs from the adult brain are as follows:[23]

- The parts of the brain involved in emotional responses are fully engaged, or even more active than in adults. The parts of the brain involved in keeping emotional responses in check are still reaching maturity. As a result, many teenagers have an appetite for novelty and acting on impulse without regard for risk.

- The frontal lobe, responsible for cognitive processes such as reasoning, planning, and judgment, is only about 80 percent developed in teenagers. The frontal lobe finally connects with the rest of the brain between ages 25 and 30.

- The reward centers of adolescent brains lead them to overestimate the value of rewards, more so than children or adults. Teenagers intensely want social rewards, especially respect of their peers.[24] As a result, a teenager might engage in dangerous behavior, such as posting a racy photo of himself or herself on Facebook.

The heavy reliance on parts of the brain involved in impulses (the amygdala) often causes misunderstandings, incendiary language, and faulty decision making despite high cognitive capacity. This helps explain why a teenager might engage in such activity as mastering a complex calculus problem in class or building a robot and then run a red light after class "just for the excitement."

RESPONDING TO ADULT LIFE CHALLENGES

Adulthood is not marked by the same more predictable milestones as childhood and adolescence. Assuming that a person lives until about age eighty, he or she spends more than half of life in the adult stage, so adults face an enormous number of challenges, including managing social life, work, and finances; raising children; keeping a blended family cooperating; staying current with technology; and investing for retirement.

Cognitive Challenges

Adults face the unique challenge of applying the many cognitive skills they have acquired during study. For example, some people who performed well in math exams have no clue how to calculate miles per gallon on a vehicle or balance a checkbook. To prosper in a career, the adult must often learn creative-thinking skills and apply wisdom. For example, the self-employed adult must find a way to convince bankers or venture capitalists on the merits of investing in his or her idea for the launch of a new product or service. An adult

Identity crisis
adolescent struggle to establish a reliable self-concept, or personal identity, including concerns over ethnic identity, the need to keep close ties with the family or develop peer relations, sexuality, and body image

Teenage brain
a stage of brain development in which people are easily influenced by their environment and more prone to impulsive behavior

faces the challenge of learning to think more flexibly rather than finding the "correct" answer to a problem, the essence of creative thinking.

Research about the capacity of the middle-aged adult brain is encouraging. The middle-aged brain not only retains many of the cognitive skills of youth but actually acquires new ones. For many people, the middle-aged brain is calmer, more stable, and better able to sort through social situations. Memorization skills and perceptual speed begin to decline in young adulthood, whereas verbal abilities, spatial reasoning, simple math abilities, and abstract reasoning all improve in middle age.[25] All of these positive results are not surprising when you consider that middle-aged people are at the top of many fields, including business, the sciences, medicine, and the arts.

Personality and Social Challenges

Adults must learn to become less self-centered and refine their interpersonal skills, including developing business etiquette. For some young people, a major adjustment is to learn to take off their sports cap when eating at a restaurant or being interviewed for a job. Many adults in their forties face a **midlife crisis**, when they feel unfulfilled and search for a major shift in career or lifestyle. Adults facing a midlife crisis often wonder whether their choice of career or life partner was the right decision. During the more common **midlife transition**, adults may take stock of their life and formulate new goals, such as an engineer working for IBM deciding to teach high school math. (IBM encourages such transitions to foster math and science knowledge and skills.) Among the dozens of other personality and social challenges facing adults are the loss of a youthful appearance and a decreased reproductive or sexual capacity. Such challenges have spurred the development of plastic surgery, youth-enhancing cosmetics, and lifestyle drugs such as those designed to enhance sexual performance.

The Sandwich Generation Challenge

During the adult stage of life many people face the difficult challenge of being part of the **sandwich generation**, people who take care of both children and aging parents at the same time. The sandwich generation challenge centers on how to care for parents who need assistance in daily living while also providing for their own children.[26]

Taking care of the parent sometimes translates into having an older relative live with the couple or person, along with the children, resulting in an intergenerational household. Such an arrangement was common in the United States in years past and is now common throughout the world. During economic downturns, intergenerational living increases in frequency. The sandwich generation challenge might be faced by a couple or a single parent and is often complicated by the person or couple needing to plan for their own retirement.

Successfully managing the challenge of being a member of the sandwich generation includes such steps as taking the time for oneself or each other to avoid neglecting marriage or personal life. Avoiding emotional, physical, and financial overload is also important. Getting help from community and government resources is another way of coping with the sandwich generation challenge.[27]

RESPONDING TO LATE-LIFE CHALLENGES

The challenges of late life have increased because more people live longer beyond the traditional retirement age, and many remain active and in good health. Yet still other people in late life are infirm, impoverished, and dependent on family and government to maintain their well-being.

Midlife crisis
time that adults in their forties face when they feel unfulfilled and search for a major shift in career or lifestyle

Midlife transition
adults taking stock of their lives and formulating new goals; among dozens of other personality and social challenges facing adults are the loss of a youthful appearance and a decreased reproductive or sexual capacity

Sandwich generation
people who take care of both their children and their aging parents at the same time

Cognitive Challenges

The issue of the cognitive skills of late-life adults has been the subject of much opinion and research in recent years because the life span of people has increased. Furthermore, many old people hold responsible positions, drive cars, and even fly airplanes solo. A major challenge facing people in advanced stages of life is that they experience cognitive decline. One study monitored the daily activities of 698 adults in good physical health from ages seventy-four to eight-four over a ten-year period. The results showed that even everyday cognitive tasks, such as calculating when a prescription refill is needed or tracking down a name in a directory, declined over time. The researchers also found a corresponding decline in reasoning ability, suggesting that a decline in the executive function of the brain might have a bigger impact on daily activities associated with aging than a decline in memory.[28]

Despite the general trend of cognitive decline in late life, some people retain their mental functioning. The ability to learn rapidly and reason abstractly and logically may decline through adulthood, starting as early as age thirty. Part of the problem is that there is a normal slowing down in cognitive functioning starting in the fifties and sixties. Neurotransmitters, the chemicals that enable nerve cells to communicate, diminish.[29] In contrast, wisdom and judgment based on the accumulation of knowledge may increase up into the eighties.

A review of many studies conducted at the University of Victoria examined the effects of physical activity and cognitive training on the brain's executive function. Both interventions were associated with improvements in cognitive function among healthy seniors. The study therefore challenged the idea that aging produces inevitable changes in cognitive ability.[30]

Brain-imaging studies also support the idea that mental workouts help preserve **cognitive fitness**, a state of optimized ability to remember, learn, plan, and adapt to changing circumstances. Acquiring expertise in such diverse areas as playing a cello, juggling, speaking a foreign language, and driving a taxicab expands your neural systems and helps them communicate with one another. This means that learning new skills can alter the physical makeup of the brain even in later life.[31] Workouts help maintain cognitive fitness for an important reason. Better blood flow to the brain takes place, as well as producing chemicals that encourage the growth of connectors between neurons, which are the key to learning and memory.[32]

Cognitive fitness
a state of optimized ability to remember, learn, plan, and adapt to changing circumstances

Personality and Social Challenges

A change noted in late adulthood is that people begin to value the present more because they correctly perceive that they have a shorter future than do younger adults. As a result, late-life adults are less concerned about activities that may have a payoff in the long run, such as networking. Instead, they look to spend time with good friends and family already available. Practical problems for those in the most advanced years are that many friends die and family members move away. Thus, the late-life adult may have to seek out new friends. Retirement communities, including assisted living, provide an opportunity for affluent older people to make new social contacts, to help compensate for the loss of friends and family members.

A challenge for some late-life adults is to engage in fulfilling physical activities to replace favored activities of previous years. For example, a 75-year-old with a hip and knee replacement may not be able to play tennis or golf any longer and may have to find satisfaction in a replacement activity such as light hiking.

An encouraging observation about career people at various life stages is that they often work together cooperatively to blend their talents and knowledge. The Silicon Valley business model has typically paired young tech wizards with older counselors. For example, the head of a tech start-up in his or her twenties might exchange ideas with a big-company technology executive.[33]

▶ **Learning Objective 15.7** ▶

LIFE AND JOB SATISFACTION THROUGHOUT THE LIFE SPAN

People at various stages of their life span often wonder what type of satisfaction and happiness awaits them at later stages. Typical self-questions are these: Will I enjoy my work more in late career? Will I be more (or less) happy in my later years? Although the research evidence about life and job satisfaction throughout the life span is not entirely consistent, some trends are notable.

Life Satisfaction and Age

Life satisfaction tends to increase throughout adulthood, partially because many of the major challenges in life are met as one reaches the fifties and sixties. For example, by middle age most people have completed their formal education, chosen a career, and reared children. According to a study of 2,000 veterans, life satisfaction for men tends to peak at age sixty-five. The life satisfaction and personal traits of the subjects were measured over almost a thirty-year span. Personality factors influenced the happiness and satisfaction curve. Highly extraverted people were more likely to have high levels of life satisfaction and more stability in life satisfaction. (One interpretation of these findings is that extraversion helps a person develop friends, and positive human contact contributes to life satisfaction.)[34]

Recent research suggests that there are geographic and cultural influences on the relationship between job satisfaction and age. In high-income, English-speaking countries, life satisfaction dips around middle age and rises in older age. In the former Soviet Union and Eastern European countries, the findings are different. Older residents reported very low rankings on life satisfaction compared with younger residents in those regions.[35] Another cultural factor influencing the link between life satisfaction and age is that people who grew up in relatively prosperous times have a stronger sense of well-being later life.[36]

Job Satisfaction and Age

Job satisfaction also tends to increase with age, as would be predicted, because work satisfaction is such a major component of life satisfaction. A survey of 62,000 people found that seniors have the highest level of job satisfaction among U.S. workers. Close to 95 percent of seniors reported being satisfied with their jobs, in contrast to 84 percent of workers age eighteen to twenty-nine indicating satisfaction.[37] A later study found that 90 percent of workers age fifty or older reported they were very or somewhat satisfied with their job. The high satisfaction levels were not related to gender, race, educational level, income level, or political beliefs. An explanation of these findings is that older workers have often climbed the career ladder, increased their salaries, and obtained reasonable job security.[38]

▶ **Learning Objective 15.8** ▶

Basic Concepts about Changing Careers

The new type of career emphasizes doing work that fits your major values in life, so many people switch careers to find work that fits their values. And these values could include earning enough money to support a family well and pursue preferred leisure activities. People also switch careers for other factors, such as one's work becoming obsolete. Human Relations Self-Assessment Quiz 15-1 provides you an opportunity to think through why you might need to change careers including changing a field you intended to enter.

Human Relations Self-Assessment Quiz   15-1

Should I Be Thinking about a Career Change?

Listed below are twelve factors or thoughts that prompt many people to change careers or majors.
Check which ones apply to you.

Number	Reason for Career Changing	Yes	No
1.	I hate my field, and I dread going to work.	❑	❑
2.	My job has a negative effect on my physical and mental health.	❑	❑
3.	When I meet people in public or on the Internet, I feel uncomfortable telling them what I do (or will do) for a living.	❑	❑
4.	I need more status than my current field would bring me.	❑	❑
5.	About the only satisfaction I get from my line of work (or would get from my potential line of work) is to pay my living expenses.	❑	❑
6.	My work (or contemplated work) is a poor fit with my personal values.	❑	❑
7.	I envy people who are working in careers they enjoy.	❑	❑
8.	I need much more independence than my career allows (or would allow).	❑	❑
9.	I often calculate how many years there are before I can retire.	❑	❑
10.	I am definitely unsuited for my field (or contemplated field).	❑	❑
11.	My type of work often puts me in such a bad mood that I take it out on family and friends.	❑	❑
12.	I have the energy to do most things in life well other than my job.	❑	❑

Scoring and Interpretation:

If you agreed with eight or more of the above statements, consider seriously speaking to a career counselor about what actions you should take to either find a more satisfying career or make your present career more satisfying. If you agreed with between two and seven of the above statements, give some thought to whether you are in the right career. Also, think through what might be the most unsatisfactory parts of your line of work, with an eye toward making some positive changes. If you agreed with none or one of the above statements, it could mean that you are in the right field in terms of your interests and values. If you also have the right talent and skills, you are headed for (or have already attained) career success.

Source: "Should I Be Thinking about a Career Change?" by Andrew J. DuBrin.

FACTORS INFLUENCING A SUCCESSFUL CAREER CHANGE

A successful career change begins with a clear goal in mind. Clarify what you want to do next and why.[39] An example of a widely expressed vague goal is "I want to change careers so I can help people." A more specific goal with an explanation would be "I want to change careers so I can be a financial planner and help people make better financial decisions"

Many people desiring a career change must confront the reality that they need continuing income to meet their obligations plus finding meaningful work.[40] For example, a person who believes that caring for animals would make a good career switch might not be able to afford working at an entry-level wage as an assistant in a veterinary clinic.

A major principle of career switching is to *be thorough.* Go through the same kind of thinking and planning that is recommended for finding a first career. Obtaining valid career information is essential, such as consulting the online edition of the *Occupational Outlook Handbook.* Conducting informational interviews with people already in the contemplated field is highly recommended. *Finding a mentor* who can help guide you through a career change is also helpful. Facts are also important because so many employees think it is easy to change careers by starting a web-based business from their home, such as selling used clothing or clever T-shirts. Few people engaged in such enterprises earn enough money to pay their living expenses.

One of the first steps in making a career change is to *assess your likes and dislikes.* Many people change careers because they dislike their job, their boss, and their company. Yet you also need to examine your likes and passions, those work-related activities that excite and energize you. Many people learn more about their career preferences by taking a career assessment instrument combined with the guidance of a career counselor.

A new career should be *built gradually.* Few people are able to leave one career abruptly and step into another. For most people who switch careers successfully, the switch is more of a transition than an abrupt change. A constructive approach would be to take on a few minor assignments in the proposed new field and then search for full-time work in that field after building skill. An electronics technician, for example, might request to visit customers with sales representatives to facilitate a switch to industrial selling. To prepare for your new career, you may need to *acquire the necessary education and training,* such as an accountant deciding to become a pharmacist.

Sometimes an interim assignment can offer a person useful ideas for a complete career change or at least a different emphasis. One possibility is filling in for someone who is on family leave because of the birth or adoption of a child. Filling in for the boss can give a person a firsthand sense of managerial work.

Another key factor in many career changes is to *transfer useful skills from the present career to the new career* so you are not starting from zero. Among the skills that transfer well from one career to another are problem solving, interviewing people, persuasive skills, information technology skills, and resolving conflict. Richard Bolles, the author of the famous book about career change, *What Color Is Your Parachute?,* says that transferable skills tend to be immutable: They are things you innately know how to do.[41]

CHANGING CAREERS WITHOUT CHANGING EMPLOYERS

A major concern many people have about changing careers is the loss of job security that they have already established with a large employer. If you stay with the same employer after a career switch, you are able to retain the same benefits, including retirement contribution. Your familiarity with the corporate culture will still be an asset. However, if the employee switches careers into a lower-rated position, a salary cut might occur. Only a select number of large employers offer the opportunity for a career change, yet it can happen. For example, a marketing specialist might obtain a position in the human resources department, and a human resources specialist might become a manufacturing supervisor.

From the employer perspective, programs of internal career changes improve retention rates. From the standpoint of the employee, the same program satisfies his or her need to develop new skills and make a career change.

SELF-EMPLOYMENT AS A CAREER CHANGE

A major reason that many employees consider a new career is that they crave more independence. As a consequence, an increasingly popular path for the career switcher is to move from salaried employment to self-employment. The prospective self-employed person needs to decide on which particular business to enter. For many people, self-employment means continuing to perform similar work, such as the company cafeteria manager entering the food catering business. Other formerly employed workers go into competition with their former employers, such as a restaurant manager opening a restaurant of his or her own. Another approach to self-employment is to choose an enterprise that fits a passion of yours, such as a wine connoisseur opening a wine store or operating a wine store franchise.

A major opportunity for self-employment is to purchase a franchise, thus lowering the risk of a start-up business. Currently, franchises account for about one-third of retail sales in the United States and Canada. Yet franchises require a substantial financial investment, ranging from about $6,000 to over $1 million. Furthermore, some of the big name franchisors, such as Dunkin' Donuts, require that the franchisee purchase multiple stores simply to get started. Another caution is that some franchise operators may work about seventy hours per week to earn about $18,000 per year.

Franchise opportunities continue to grow, with franchises available in many types of businesses and services, including the following:

- Children's enrichment programs, including reading, writing, and physical fitness

- Industrial and residential cleaning services

- Travel agencies for cruises

- Computer troubleshooting

- Senior care and home health aide

Anyone contemplating self-employment of any type should recognize that it offers potentially high rewards as well as risks. Wealth and personal satisfaction are possible. However, if the fledgling enterprise does not do well immediately, the owner may have to live for a couple of years without income.

Tactics for Coping with Change

◀ Learning Objective 15.9 ◀

We have all heard that adapting to change is necessary for career success, and even survival. At the same time, a well-accepted proposition is that change is never easy. Many people need help occasionally when changes at work present challenges. A fitting conclusion to this chapter is therefore to present a few tactics for coping with change. A useful strategy for coping with many changes is to *be proactive, not reactive.*[42] Think through the possible workplace changes that might take place, and get ready as soon as possible. For example, if it appears that your company will be getting rid of as much office space as feasible in the near future, begin preparing yourself for doing more work from remote locations. A few more specific tactics follow.

First, *look for the personal value that could be embedded in a forced change.*[43] If you are downsized, take the opportunity to assume responsibility for your own career rather than being dependent on the organization. Many downsizing victims find a new career for themselves that better fits their interests or try self-employment in search of more job security. Whether or not self-employment is truly more secure than working for a large employer, many people fear that a big company will lay them off during a corporate downsizing.

When faced with a significant change, *ask "What if?" questions,* such as "What if my company is sold tomorrow?" "What if I went back to school for more education?" "What if I did accept that one-year assignment in Germany?" When confronting major change, *force yourself to enjoy at least some small aspect of the change.* Suppose the edict comes through the organization that almost all business travel will be replaced by videoconferencing. This means you will no longer be able to visit friends from other corporate locations. With the time you save, however, you will have spare hours each week for leisure activities.

You are less likely to resist change if you *recognize that change is inevitable*. Dealing with change is an integral part of life, so why fight it? Keep in mind also to *change before you have to, which can lead to a better deal*. If your manager announces a new plan, get on board as a volunteer before you are forced to accept a lesser role. *Stop trying to be in control all the time, because you cannot control everything*. Many changes will occur that you cannot control, so relax and enjoy the ride. Finally, recognize that change has an emotional impact, which will most likely cause some inner turmoil and discomfort. Even if the change is for the better, you might remain emotionally attached to your old system—or neighborhood, car, or desktop computer.

Continuing to acquire useful knowledge is also helpful in dealing with change because you have the new knowledge at hand to get past the change. When digital photography became dominant, the operators of many portrait studios felt threatened and were too slow to offer digital services to their customers. Many of these photographers who waited too long to offer digital services were forced out of business. In contrast, many other portrait photographers were early learners of digital technology and survived the transition well.

Many workers are forced to cope with changes brought about by outsourcing of jobs to lower-wage regions and countries. These workers should search for jobs that cannot be outsourced or that are anchored because they must be done at a specific location, such as calling on an industrial customer. Many personal-service jobs cannot be outsourced or sent offshore, including hairdressers, massage therapists, custodial technicians, and auto mechanics.

Some corporate professional jobs are more difficult to outsource than others. The positions less likely to be outsourced are those requiring the combination of technical (or discipline) skills plus connections with people. A real estate agent with hundreds of personal contacts cannot be replaced by a website. An information systems specialist who performs hands-on work with managers at his or her company cannot be replaced by an information technology specialist working 8,000 miles away in another country. The change management lesson here is that building relationships with work associates helps ward off some of the threats of outsourcing.

Concept Review and Reinforcement

Summary and Review

In this chapter, we have studied additional knowledge that helps a person attain career thrust.

■ Classical conditioning is the most elementary form of learning. It occurs when a previously neutral stimulus is associated with a natural (uncondi-tioned) stimulus. Eventually, the neutral stimulus brings forth the unconditioned response. For example, a factory whistle blown just prior to the lunch break induces employees to salivate and experience hunger pangs.

■ Operant conditioning (or instrumental learning) occurs when a person's spontaneous actions are rewarded or punished, which results in an increase or a decrease in the behavior. Much of human learn-ing occurs through operant conditioning. The four reinforcement strategies involved in such condition-ing are positive reinforcement, negative reinforce-ment, punishment, and extinction. A continuous reinforcement schedule rewards behavior each time it occurs, whereas an intermittent schedule delivers rewards periodically.

■ Two important processes that help in learning com-plicated skills are modeling and informal learning. Modeling occurs when you learn a skill by observing another person perform that skill. Informal learning is unplanned and occurs in a setting without a formal classroom, lesson plan, instructor, or examination. Informal learning can be spontaneous, or the com-pany might organize the work area to encourage

such learning. Knowledge sharing contributes to informal learning.

■ E-learning is an Internet form of computer-based training. The geographic dispersion of employees makes e-learning more important. Self-motivation and self-discipline are essential for the e-learner. Most companies continue to use blended learning (Internet and classroom) to capitalize on the efficiencies of e-learning yet still rely on human contact.

■ Groups can learn in the sense that members come to adapt their behavior collectively in response to expe-rience. Group learning has the three basic features of sharing, storage (in the brain), and retrieval. Social media and collaborative networks are helpful for group learning.

■ People learn best in different ways. For example, some people acquire information best through pas-sive learning. A preference for working alone ver-sus cooperatively is another difference in learning style.

■ According to the Golden Personality Type Profiler, two dimensions of psychological functioning are the basis for the relationship between personality and learning style. We judge through thinking (T) and feeling (F). We perceive through sensing (S) and intu-ition (N). The four mental processes of thinking, feel-ing, sensing, and intuition result in four learning styles, as shown in Figure 15-1.

■ In general, people with higher mental ability and per-sonality traits that allow them to concentrate better (for example, conscientiousness) acquire knowledge and skills more readily.

■ For almost all professional, technical, and sales occupations, career success and survival depend on continuous learning.

■ Perception, the organization of sensory information into meaningful experiences, influences job behavior. Perceptual problems stem from both a stimulus with an emotional meaning and the mental processes of people. These mental processes, or shortcuts, include selective attention, denial, stereotyping, the halo effect, and projection.

■ *Perceptual congruence* refers to the degree to which people perceive things the same way. High congruence generally leads to more positive consequences for the organization than does low congruence.

■ Attribution theory explains how people attribute the causes of behavior. People have a general tendency to attribute their achievements to good inner qualities, whereas they attribute failure to adverse factors within the environment.

■ According to Erickson, the socialization process consists of the "eight stages of man," with each state representing a psychosocial crisis. The crisis must be resolved at each stage before the next stage can be successfully negotiated.

■ The challenges of adolescence include the cognitive challenge of developing logic and abstract thought as well as developing moral reasoning. A key personality and social challenge is the identity crisis. Successfully managing the teenage brain is another challenge, with the brain being quite adept at new learning yet tending toward impulsiveness and faulty decision making.

■ The challenges of adulthood include applying cognitive skills to real-life problems. Adults must also learn to become less self-centered and refine their interpersonal skills. Adults may also face a midlife crisis and a midlife transition, as well as being part of the sandwich generation.

■ The challenges of late adulthood include cognitive decline, even though older people can be trained to learn new, complex tasks. A change facing late-life adults is more of a focus on the present.

■ Life satisfaction tends to increase throughout adulthood but may peak for men at about age sixty-five. Job satisfaction also tends to increase with age, partially because older adults have gravitated into positions for which they have skills and are rewarded.

■ A successful career change begins with a clear goal. A major principle of career switching is to be thorough. Obtain valid career information, and assess your likes and dislikes. A new career should be built gradually, often by phasing into the new career part-time. An increasingly popular path for the career switcher is to move from salaried employment to self-employment.

■ Suggestions for managing change well include being proactive, searching for the personal value that could be embedded in forced change, asking "What if," forcing yourself to enjoy at least some small aspect of the change, recognizing that change is inevitable, and understanding that change has an emotional impact. To help cope with possible changes caused by outsourcing or offshoring of one's job is to incorporate building relationships into one's job.

Questions for Discussion and Review

15.1 What is it about experience working on a farm that would help a person learn how to maintain and repair complex manufacturing machines?

15.2 Distracted driving causes more vehicular accidents than driving under the influence of alcohol, and the punishments for driving while texting have increased substantially. Why, then, do so many people refuse to learn to stop being distracted drivers?

15.3 Provide an example of knowledge that you have acquired without a conscious intention to learn.

15.4 What steps can a company take to encourage informal learning among employees?

15.5 If e-learning is so effective, why haven't most schools of higher education converted completely to distance learning?

15.6 Give an example of where it *is* true that perception is more important than reality.

15.7 What might a person do to increase the probability that work associates will perceive him or her to be intelligent and hard working?

15.8 How does the widespread use of information and communication technology force most workers to be continuous learners?

15.9 What are the reasons that a forty-year-old college president would be regarded as *young* by so many people, yet a forty-year-old professional athlete would be regarded as *old?*

15.10 What is your strategy for dealing with the biggest change you will have to face during the next twelve months?

Web Corner

How to become a more effective learner

www.psychology.about.com (Enter "How to become a more effective learner" into the search box.)

Insight into your learning style based on multiple intelligences

www.edutopia.org (Enter into search box "Learning Styles Quiz Results: Digging Deeper.")

Information about career changing

www.quintcareers.com (Click on "I am a . . . Career-Changer.")

INTERNET SKILL BUILDER

Millennial Life Span Challenges

Although opinions vary as to the precise meaning of a *Millennial,* the term generally refers to the last generation born in the twentieth century. Search the Internet or a database provided by your school or employer to identify about ten life span challenges facing the Millennials, in other words, challenges facing members of this generation attributed to their stage in life. You can probably supplement the list with reading you have done or personal observations.

Developing Your Human Relations Skills

Human Relations Application Exercises

Applying Human Relations Exercise 15-1

Developing Your Brain and Learning Ability

The belief is widespread that the human brain can be developed through mental exercise. We found about 120 million entries using the Bing search engine entry "exercising the brain." Even when a given brain builder may work for many other people, you do not know if the technique will help you specifically. Here is an opportunity to try a brain exercise and see what the positive consequences might be for you. You will need a few minutes a day for at least ten days to determine whether the technique works. First, do one or both of the following exercises for ten to fourteen days:

1. Recite the alphabet backward until you are proficient. Perform the exercise a few times a day until you can do the backward version almost as easily as the forward version.
2. Learn a new word in your native language or your second language every day. Visualize the new words that you have learned during this time span.

After the ten days or two weeks are completed, reflect on your learning ability and memory. Compare your learning on new tasks today with your learning in the past. Is it easier for you to study? Do you grasp the meaning of news stories more quickly? Can you remember phone numbers or e-mail addresses more readily? If other classmates have done this exercise, ask them about their experiences. Have these exercises resulted in more brain power for them?

If these straightforward exercises really improve brain power, what are some of the implications for human relations?

Source: The core idea for the two games is credited to http://me.essortment.com/brainexercises_rcas.htm.

Applying Human Relations Exercise 15-2

Life Span Challenges Facing Seniors

The life span challenges described in this chapter that seniors face are certainly valid. Your role in this exercise is to find out directly what challenges advanced seniors face. We refer to people seventy years old and beyond. The older the people you can find for this study, the better. Do you have access to a person at least 100 years old? Conduct interviews with parents (if they qualify), grandparents, nursing home residents, friends, and neighbors. Obtain a sample of at least four people. Ask your interviewees about the challenges and problems they face now, those in the recent past, and those they anticipate in the future. After you have collected your interview data, answer these questions:

1. What are a few challenges in recalling information and remembering things facing these seniors?
2. What are the physical and health problems facing these seniors?
3. What are the emotional and human relations problems facing these seniors?
4. What could other people do to help these seniors with some of their most pressing concerns?

Human Relations Class Activity

Capitalizing on the Halo Effect

The halo effect can work to a person's advantage or disadvantage in terms of job finding and career advancement, depending on how that person is perceived. The class assignment is to investigate which characteristics or behaviors of a professional or future professional will help or hurt him or her. Each student in the class communicates with an experienced worker in speaking or writing to obtain answers to the following two questions:

1. Give me an example of a characteristic or action of a worker that would make you think he or she either is worthy of hiring or has good potential to advance in his or her career.
2. Give me an example of a characteristic or action of a worker that would make you think he or she either is

not worthy of hiring or has limited potential to advance in his or her career.

Next, individual students enter their survey findings into a shared database or class website or e-mail their findings to all other students. After looking through all the results, reach a conclusion about positive and negative halos held by participants in the survey. For example, two results might be (1) "It looks like having good oral communication skills creates a positive halo" and (2) "It looks like being rude creates a negative halo."

After students have reached their conclusions, a brief class discussion is held about frequent reasons for creating a positive or negative halo and how useful this information might be.

Human Relations Case Study 15–1

Dental Marketing Specialist Brad

Brad, a former marketing and information technology major, at age twenty-one, founded Dental Outreach. The purpose of his small firm was to establish a variety of Internet-based marketing programs for dental practices. His mother and father are both practicing dentists. Being part of a dental family has helped Brad understand the need for dentists to attract new patients, retain current patients, and also expand services, including teeth whitening and restoration. Among the many initiatives taken by his firm was to electronically send birthday cards, reminders about dental appointments, and dental health tips.

Dental Outreach was off to a good start, as Brad sold his marketing program to six dental practices he knew through his family, as well as a couple of referrals. To expand his business, Brad used the phone and an e-mail campaign to line up a few prospects. He thought that as a young entrepreneur with a technology-based company, he should look the role of a tech-savvy young person. So Brad would show up at offices of prospective customers with shaggy hair and stubble on his face, as well as wearing jeans and a T-shirt with Dental Outreach printed on the back.

Brad was successful in a few of these office calls to generate new business, but he encountered some resistance. One office receptionist and manager said to Brad, "Oh, I thought the owner was coming here to discuss Dental Outreach. Are you the tech support person?" One of the dentists who spoke to Brad said, "What you have to offer seems on target. But I am not going to leave the marketing of my practice to a teenager."

After ten sales calls, Brad became a little discouraged. He thought to himself, "Maybe it's too early in my career to operate a dental marketing service."

Questions:

15.11 What does this case have to do with perception, as well as life stages?

15.12 To what extent is Brad being a victim of age discrimination?

15.13 What advice can you offer Brad to help him attain more success in obtaining more customers for Dental Outreach?

Human Relations Case Study 15–2

Amanda Contemplates a Career Change

For twelve years Amanda has been earning a reasonable living as a real estate agent specializing in residential properties in suburban Dallas, Texas. For all her time in real estate she has been affiliated with the same national real estate company. Amanda considers herself to be an independent contractor rather than an employee because all her income is derived from commissions. She also pays for most of the expenses associated with advertising listings on the Internet and in newspapers, and for the use of her car.

Amanda enjoys the independence she feels in her work, but she is also frustrated. She says, "I am getting to hate not knowing whether I am going to make even a dollar in a given week. You would think that after twelve years as a real estate agent, big commissions would just come floating my way. Not true. Every month I have to send out dozens of direct mail flyers and e-mails looking for someone who wants to sell a house. I also make loads of phone calls to people in my network. Having a listing is important because it doubles my commission, should the house be sold. After I am lucky enough to get a listing, I then have to sell the house. Or another agent sells the house, and I get a cut.

"It's great when I make any sale, but the amount of leg work, driving, and expenses is enormous. I show properties mostly during nights and weekends. This creates a lot of conflict with my husband and daughter. I'm getting sick of all this instability in my income and the chaotic scheduling of my personal life.

"My husband, daughter, and parents agree that maybe I should find a new job or a new career. I've looked around a little, but any job I can find pays close to the minimum wage. I'm stuck for an answer as to what to do with my career."

Questions:

15.14 To what extent does Amanda seem to need a career change?

15.15 What advice can you offer Amanda about beginning the process of making a career change?

15.16 Can you think of any other type of work that might fit the skills of a real estate agent?

Human Relations Role-Playing Exercise

Amanda's Friend Listens to Her Problem

One student plays the role of Amanda, who is feeling particularly frustrated today. She hasn't closed a deal in one month, and her expenses have been way above average. She meets with a friend for lunch to talk about her frustration with real estate sales, and to perhaps get some advice about changing careers. Another person plays the role of Amanda's friend, who wants to be helpful but is not a professional career counselor. Run the role-play for about ten minutes. Observers can provide feedback about how effective the friend appears to be in helping Amanda.

REFERENCES

1. Original story created from facts and observations in the following sources: James R. Hagerty, "Factory Niche: Grooming Technically Skilled," *The Wall Street Journal*, May 14, 2014, p. B7; "Development & Training," www.advancedtech.com, © 2014 Advanced Technology Services; "About ATS," www.advancedtech.com.services, accessed May 3, 2015; "Advanced Technology Services Buys Top Technical Training Company," www.advancedtech.com, February 10, 2014, pp. 1–3.

2. John W. Donahoe and David C. Palmer, *Learning and Complex Behavior* (Boston: Allyn & Bacon, 1994), p. 2.

3. Garry Kranz, "Learning Gets a High Degree of Attention at Workplaces," *Workforce*, January 2014, p. 45; Kathryn Tyler, "A New U," *HR Magazine*, April 2012, p. 27.

4. Research reported in Charles Duhigg, "Warning: Habits May Be Good for You," *New York Times*, (www.nytimes.com) July 13, 2008, p. 3.

5. Timothy C. Rednall, Karin Sanders, and Piety Runhaar, "Stimulating Informal Learning Activities through Perceptions of Performance Appraisal Quality and Human Resource Management System Strength: A Two-Wave Study," *Academy of Management Learning & Education*, March 2014, p. 46.

6. "Hard-to-Read Fonts Promote Better Recall," *Harvard Business Review*, March 2012, pp. 32–33.

7. Bill Roberts, "From E-learning to Mobile Learning," *HR Magazine*, August 2012, p. 61.

8. Gary Kranz, "MOOCs: The Next Evolution in E-Learning?" *Workforce*, April 2014, p. 10.

9. "The Business Value of E-Learning," *Elearning!* (www.2elearning.com), December 18, 2007.

10. Cited in Kathryn Tyler, "A New U," *HR Magazine*, April 2012, p. 30.

11. Stephen Paskoff, "The Ethical Workplace," *Workforce Management*, October 2011, p. 49.

12. Jeanne M. Wilson, Paul S. Goodman, and Matthew A. Cronin, "Group Learning," *Academy of Management Review*, October 2007, pp. 1041–1059.

13. Dave Zielnski, "Group Learning: Use Social Media to Engage Employees in Knowledge Sharing," *HR Magazine*, May 2012, p. 49.

14. Wanda L. Stitt-Gohdes, "Teaching and Learning Styles: Implications for Business Teacher Education," in *The Twenty-First Century: Meeting the Challenges to Business Education* (Reston, VA: National Business Education Association, 1999), p. 10.

15. John Patrick Golden, *Golden Personality Type Profiler Technical Manual* (San Antonio, TX: Pearson TalentLens, 2005).

16. "Keep Your Brain Functioning," *University of Rochester Medical Center—Online Medical Encyclopedia*, www.urmc.rochester.edu, pp. 1–3, accessed May 4, 2015.

17. The quote and the content in this section are from Mark Greer, "Strengthen Your Brain by Resting It," *Monitor on Psychology*, July–August 2004, p. 60.

18. Giulio Tononi, "Understanding the Function of Sleep Comes One Step Closer," *Medical News Today*, www.medicalnewstoday.com, May 4, 2007, p. 2.

19. Kai Chi Yam, Ryan Fehr, and Christopher M. Barners, "Morning Employees Are Perceived as Better Employees: Employees' Start Time Influences Supervisor Performance Ratings," *Journal of Applied Psychology*, November 2014, pp. 1288–1299.

20. Erik H. Erikson, *Childhood and Society* (New York: Norton, 1963); Child Development Institute, "Stages of Social-Emotional Development in Children and Teenagers," www.childdevelpmentinfo.com, accessed May 6, 2006.

21. Our discussion of the challenges of adolescence and adulthood follows closely Saul Kassin, *Psychology*, 3rd ed. (Upper Saddle River, NJ: Prentice Hall, 2001), pp. 406–440; and Charles G. Morris and Albert A. Maisto, *Psychology: An Introduction*, 11th ed. (Upper Saddle River, NJ: Prentice Hall, 2002), pp. 418–441.

22. Lawrence Kohlberg, *Essays on Moral Development: Vol. 2. The Psychology of Moral Development* (New York: Harper & Row, 1984).

23. Debra Bradley Ruder, "A Work in Progress: The Teen Brain," *Harvard Magazine*, (http://harvardmagazine.com/2008/09/the-teen-brain.html; "The Teen Brain: Still Under Construction," *The National Institute of Mental Health*, www.nimh.nih.gov.

24. Research reported in Alison Gopnik, "What's Wrong with the Teenage Mind?" *The Wall Street Journal*, January 28–29, 2012, p. C1.

25. Melissa Lee Phillips, "The Mind at Midlife," *Monitor on Psychology*, April 11, 2011, pp. 38–41.

26. Loreen Loonie, "Caregiving—Challenges for The 'Sandwich Generation,'" *Independence Care System*, www.icsny.org, March 7, 2013, pp. 1–4.

27. Sheri Stritof and Bob Stritof, "Sandwich Generation: The Cluttered Nest Syndrome," www.about.com.marriage, accessed April 7, 2009.

28. Stacy Lu, "Our Aging Brains," *Monitor on Psychology*, February 2015, p. 35.

29. Melinda Beck, "The Science behind 'Senior Moments,'" *The Wall Street Journal*, May 27, 2008.

30. Lu, "Our Aging Brains," p. 35.

31. Roderick Gilkey and Clint Kitts, "Cognitive Fitness," *Harvard Business Review*, November 2007, pp. 53–66; Kathleen Smith, "Cognitive Training Slows Cognitive Decline, Major Study Finds," *Monitor on Psychology*, March 2014, p. 10.

32. Research reported in Andrea Bartz, "Watered-Down Thinking," *Psychology Today*, January–February 2011, p. 37.

33. Debra Shigley, "Life's New Timeline," *Psychology Today*, November–December 2011, p. 67.

34. Karen Kersting, "Happiness in Men Usually Drops after Age 65, Study Finds," *Monitor on Psychology*, March 2005, p. 10.

35. "Does Life Satisfaction Increase with Age? Only in Some Places, New Study Finds," http://medicalexpress, November 5, 2014, pp. 1–4.

36. Rick Nauert, "Happiness, Satisfaction with Life Generally Increase with Age," *Psych Central*, February 19, 2013, pp. 1–6.

37. Study cited in Frances Burke, "What Is the Relationship between Job Satisfaction and Age?" www.smallbusiness.chron.com, pp. 1–2, accessed March 26, 2012.

38. Matt Sedensky, "Job Satisfaction, Like Wine, Gets Better with Age," Associated Press, October 28, 2013, pp. 1–4.

39. Cited in Kaitlin Madden, "Plan a Successful Career Change," *CareerBuilder*, March 11, 2012.

40. Robert J. Grossman, "Encore, Encore!" *HR magazine*, July 2014, p. 27.

41. Cited in Gary Kranz, "This 'Parachute's' Color?" *Workforce*, February 2015, p. 43.

42. Tino Toskala, "Coping with Change in Your Workplace—Be Proactive, Not Reactive," Ezine@rticles, www.ezinearticles.com, p. 1, accessed March 26, 2012.

43. This and the next item noted are from Fred Pryor, "What Have You Learned from Change?" *Manager's Edge*, September 1998, p. 2.

CHAPTER 16

Developing Good Work Habits

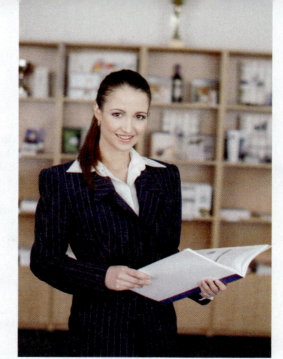

Fotolia

Outline

For many years, Virginia Rometty had been a leader in the technology industry, including holding a position at IBM as the senior vice president and group executive for sales, marketing, and strategy. Effective January 1, 2012, she was elected as president and chief executive officer of IBM. Rometty soon came to be regarded as one of the most powerful women in business.

During Rometty's first several years as CEO of IBM, the company struggled with declining sales and profits. Nevertheless, the company continued to generate annual revenues of over $90 billion and had over 500,000 employees. IBM's technology and services are still used in 70 percent of all enterprises.

"Ginny" Rometty is well-known for being a world-class corporate leader. Less well-known is that she practices everyday productive work habits. She keeps a smartphone at hand to stay connected with business contacts, and occasionally with personal contacts. When on business trips, she also carries in her backpack two of the best personal productivity tools ever invented: school-size notebooks and pencils. In this way, she can immediately record any important business thoughts and also maintain an updated to-do list.

On business trips, Rometty avoids luxury restaurants when possible because they consume so much time and are costly. Instead, Rometty says, "I love Starbucks. And it's convenient and efficient." Also, at Starbucks Rometty gets to see at firsthand young people tapping away on their mobile devices. She can visualize many IBM employees of the future working out of cafés rather than company-based offices.

Rometty began her career at IBM in 1981 as a systems engineer, two years after graduating from Northwestern University with a degree in computer science and electrical engineering. Her first position after college was an internship at General Motors in Detroit.[1]

Learning Objectives ▶

After studying the information and doing the exercises in this chapter, you should be able to:

16.1 Appreciate the importance of good work habits and time management.

16.2 Decrease any tendencies you might have toward procrastination.

16.3 Develop attitudes and values that will help you become more productive.

16.4 Develop skills and techniques that will help you become more productive.

16.5 Overcome time-wasting practices.

An important implication of the story about a major business executive is that being efficient, even in terms of using to-do lists and not squandering time at lunch, is important at all organizational levels. Because good work habits and time management improve productivity, they contribute to success in business.

Work habits refer to a person's characteristic approach to work, including such things as organization, priority setting, and handling of e-mail and intranets. Good work habits and time management are more important than ever because of today's emphasis on **productivity**, which is the amount of useful work accomplished in relation to the resources consumed. Being more productive often translates into eliminating unnecessary steps and finding ways to get more accomplished in less time.

Because so many workers, including telecommuters, are expected to be productive without close supervision, good work habits increase in importance. Furthermore, a person is more likely to be fired from a job or flunk out of school because of poor work habits than because of poor aptitude.

People with good work habits tend to achieve higher career success and have more time to invest in their personal lives. They also enjoy their personal lives more because they are not preoccupied with unfinished tasks. Effective work habits are also beneficial because they eliminate the stressor of feeling you have very little or no control over your life. Being in control also leads to a relaxed, confident approach to work.

◀ **Learning Objective 16.1** ◀

Work habits
a person's characteristic approach to work, including such things as organization, priority setting, and handling of paperwork and e-mail

Productivity
the amount of quality work accomplished in relation to the resources consumed

The goal of this chapter is to help you become a more productive person who is still flexible. Someone who develops good work habits is not someone who becomes so obsessed with time and is so rigid that he or she makes other people feel uncomfortable. Ideally, a person should be well organized yet still flexible.

Information about becoming more productive is organized here into four related categories. First is overcoming procrastination, a problem that plagues almost everybody to some extent. The second is developing attitudes and values that foster productivity. The third category is the lengthiest: developing skills and techniques that lead to personal productivity. The fourth category is overcoming time wasters.

▶ **Learning Objective 16.2** ▶

Procrastination

delaying a task for an invalid or weak reason

Dealing with Procrastination

The leading cause of poor productivity is **procrastination**, delaying a task for an invalid or weak reason. Procrastination is also the gap between intention and action. We want to do something but we delay taking action, often because the immediate reward associated with delay is more important at the moment than the reward that will come later from completing a task.[2] Perhaps Melissa wants to start working on her income tax report because the tax deadline is soon approaching. However, she delays starting the tax project for an hour so she can get the immediate reward of checking the "status" of twenty-five of her Facebook friends. The reward Melissa is delaying is the satisfaction of getting her tax form completed, and perhaps a $2,500 refund.

WHY PEOPLE PROCRASTINATE

People procrastinate for many different reasons, as described in the following list:

1. **Unpleasant task or overwhelming task.** When we perceive the task to be done as unpleasant (such as quitting a job), we tend to procrastinate. Similarly, we tend to procrastinate when we perceive the job facing us to be overwhelming, such as assembling a computer console that arrives in a large box.

2. **Fear of consequences.** Another major cause of procrastination is a fear of the consequences of our actions. One possible negative consequence is a negative evaluation of your work. For example, if you delay preparing a report for your boss or instructor, that person cannot criticize its quality. Bad news is another negative consequence that procrastination can sometimes delay. If you think your smartphone may need to be replaced because it no longer works well, delaying a trip to the electronics store will let you avoid the verdict of "replacement needed."

Fear of success

belief that if one succeeds at an important task, one will be asked to take on more responsibility in the future; a reason some people procrastinate

3. **Fear of success.** Another reason some people procrastinate is the **fear of success**. People sometimes believe that if they succeed at an important task, they will be asked to take on more responsibility in the future. They dread this possibility. A few students procrastinate completing their degree requirements to avoid taking on the responsibility of a full-time position.

4. **Lack of meaningful reward.** People frequently put off tasks that do not appear to offer a meaningful reward. Suppose you decide that your résumé needs a thorough updating, including deleting not-so-relevant information. Even if you know this task should be done, the accomplishment of an updated résumé might not be a meaningful reward, particularly if you are not in the job market.

5. **Rebelling against control.** Many people procrastinate as a way of rebelling against being controlled. Procrastination, used in this way, is a means of defying unwarranted authority.[3] Rather than submit to authority, a person might tell himself,

"Nobody is going to tell me when I should get a physical exam. I'll do it when I'm good and ready." Such people might be referred to as "anti-control freaks."

6. **Enjoying the rush.**   A curious reason for procrastination is to achieve the stimulation and excitement that stems from rushing to meet a deadline. Some people, for example, enjoy fighting their way through traffic or running through an airline terminal so they can make an appointment or airplane flight barely on time. They appear to enjoy the rush of adrenaline, endorphins, and other hormones associated with hurrying.

7. **Perfectionism.**   Finally, some people procrastinate because they are perfectionists. They attempt to perfect a project before being willing to admit the project is completed. As a result, the person procrastinates not about beginning a project but about letting go of it. When asked, "Have you finished that project?" the perfectionist replies, "No, there a few small details that still need to be worked out." Being a perfectionist can also block starting new projects because the perfectionist will often want to keep working on the present project. Perfectionism comes in degrees, with slight perfectionists simply being extremely conscientious and heavy-duty perfectionists almost stalled in their actions.

TECHNIQUES FOR REDUCING PROCRASTINATION

To overcome or at least minimize procrastination, we recommend a number of specific tactics. A general approach, however, is simply to be aware that procrastination is a major drain on productivity. Being aware of the problem will remind you to take corrective action in many situations. When your accomplishment level is low, you might ask yourself, "Am I procrastinating on anything of significance?"

Recognize that your goal is to cross the finish line.   Beth Comstock, a major GE executive, offers sage advice about overcoming procrastination. At one time, she used any excuse she could think of to not finish a project. With coaching from a critical boss, Comstock finally learned that what really counts is crossing the finishing line (getting a project completed).[4]

Calculate the cost of procrastination.   You can reduce procrastination by calculating its cost.[5] One example is that you might lose out on obtaining a high-paying job you really want by not having your résumé and cover letter ready on time. Your cost of procrastination would include the difference in salary between the job you do find and the one you really wanted. Another cost would be the loss of potential job satisfaction. The cost of procrastination directly applies to perfectionism. Because the perfectionist often concentrates on minor tasks such a looking for chipped paint, he or she may miss out on important tasks, such as improving a work process.[6]

Counterattack.   Forcing yourself to do something overwhelming, frightening, or uncomfortable helps to prove that the task was not as bad as initially perceived. Assume that you have accepted a new position but have not yet resigned from your present one because resigning seems so uncomfortable. Set up a specific time to call your manager or send an e-mail to schedule an appointment. Force yourself further to show up for the resignation appointment. After you break the ice with the statement "I have something important to tell you," the task will be much easier.

Jump-start yourself.   You can often get momentum going on a project by giving yourself a tiny assignment simply to get started. One way to get momentum going on an unpleasant or overwhelming task is to set aside a specific time to work on it. If you have to write a report on a subject you dislike, you might set aside Saturday from 3 to 4 p.m. as your time to first attack the project. If your procrastination problem is particularly intense, giving yourself even a five-minute task, such as starting a new file, might help you gain momentum.

Peck away at an overwhelming task. Assume that you have a major project to do that does not have to be accomplished in a hurry. A good way of minimizing procrastination is to peck away at the project in fifteen- to thirty-minute bits of time. Bit by bit, the project will get down to manageable size and therefore not seem so overwhelming. A related way of pecking away at an overwhelming task is to subdivide it into smaller units. For instance, you might break down moving into a series of tasks, such as filing change-of-address notices, locating a mover, and packaging books.

Motivate yourself with rewards and punishments. Give yourself a pleasant reward soon after you accomplish a task about which you would ordinarily procrastinate. You might, for example, jog through the woods after having completed a tough take-home exam. The second part of this tactic is to punish yourself if you have engaged in serious procrastination. How about not visiting your favorite social networking site for one week?

Make a commitment to other people. Put pressure on yourself to get something done on time by making it a commitment to one or more other people. You might announce to coworkers that you are going to get a project of mutual concern completed by a certain date. If you fail to meet this date, you may feel embarrassed.

Express a more positive attitude about your intentions. Expressing a more positive attitude can often lead to changes in behavior. If you choose words that express a serious intention to complete an activity, you are more likely to follow through than if you choose more uncertain words. Imagine that a coworker says, "I *might* get you the information you need by next Friday." You probably will not be surprised if you do not receive the information by Friday. In contrast, if your coworker says, "I *will* get you the information you need by next Friday," there is less likelihood the person will procrastinate.

▶ Learning Objective 16.3 ▶

Effective time management has become an urgent priority for both workplace performance and personal sanity.

—*Fran Finn*

Organizational productivity expert, quoted in *Executive Focus*, February 2009, p. 17

Proper Attitudes and Values to Develop for Productivity

Developing good work habits and time-management practices is often a matter of developing proper attitudes toward work and time. For instance, if you think that your job is important and that time is valuable, you will be on your way toward developing good work habits. In this section, we describe a group of attitudes and values that can help improve your productivity through better use of time and improved work habits.

DEVELOP A MISSION AND GOALS

A mission, or general purpose in life, propels you toward being productive. Assume that a person says, "My mission is to become an outstanding professional in my career and a loving, constructive parent." The mission serves as a compass to direct your activities, such as being well organized in order to attain a favorable performance appraisal.

Goals are more specific than a mission statement. The goals support the mission statement, but the effect is the same. Being committed to a goal also propels you toward good use of time. Imagine how efficient most employees would be if they were told, "Here is five days of work facing you. If you get finished in less than five days without sacrificing quality, you can have that time to yourself." If the saved time fit your mission, such as having more quality time with family members, the impact would be even stronger.

The late Stephen Covey, a popularizer of time-management techniques, expressed the importance of a mission or goals in his phrase, "Begin with the end in mind." List your various roles in life, such as spouse, child, family member, professional, and soccer player. For each role, think of one or two major lifetime goals you have in that area. Then develop a brief mission statement describing your life's purpose that incorporates these goals.[7]

A person might have the mission of becoming an outstanding professional person. Your goals to support that mission might include achieving advanced certification in your field, becoming an officer in a professional organization, and making large donations to charity. When you are deciding how to spend your time each day, give goals related to your mission top priority.

VALUE GOOD ATTENDANCE AND PUNCTUALITY

On the job, in school, or in personal life, good attendance and punctuality are essential for developing a good reputation. Also, you cannot contribute to a team effort unless you are present. Poor attendance and consistent lateness are the most frequent reasons for employee discipline. Furthermore, many managers interpret high absenteeism and lateness as signs of emotional immaturity. An important myth about attendance and punctuality—that a certain number of sick days are owed an employee—should be challenged early in a person's career.

The causes of chronic lateness follow those of the causes of procrastination. Time-management specialist Diane DeLonzor says that the motivations are often unconscious, related to personality characteristics such as lack of self-control and a desire for thrill seeking. Some people are drawn to the adrenaline rush of that last-minute sprint to the meeting (or class), while others receive an ego boost from overscheduling and filling each moment with activity. Trying to get one more thing done before leaving for an appointment will often lead to being late. Keeping a time log (as described later in the chapter) can help control lateness because the result can be a more accurate estimation of the amount of time necessary to complete various activities. For example, if it takes a person forty-five minutes to commute to work, he or she must leave the residence about fifty-five minutes before an important meeting.[8]

VALUE YOUR TIME

People who place a high value on their time are propelled into making good use of time. If a person believes that his or her time is valuable, it will be difficult to engage that person in idle conversation during working hours. Valuing your time can also apply to personal life. The yield from clipping or gathering grocery coupons is an average of $9 per hour—assuming that purchasing national brands is important to you. Would a busy professional person, therefore, be better off clipping and gathering coupons or engaging in self-development for the same amount of time? Being committed to a mission and goals is an automatic way of making good use of time.

VALUE NEATNESS, ORDERLINESS, AND SPEED

Neatness, orderliness, and speed are important contributors to workplace productivity and therefore should be valued. An orderly desk or work area does not inevitably signify an orderly mind. Yet orderliness does help most people become more productive. Less time is wasted and less energy is expended if you do not have to hunt for missing information. Knowing where information is and what information you have available is a way of being in control of your job. When your job gets out of control, you are probably working at less than peak efficiency. Being neat and orderly helps you achieve good performance. Frequently breaking your concentration for such matters as finding an e-mail message you printed a month ago inhibits high performance.

Neatness is linked to working rapidly because clutter and searching for misplaced items consume time. Employers emphasize speed to remain competitive in such matters as serving customers promptly and bringing new products and services to the market. Speed is widely considered a competitive advantage, as in getting a product to market faster than others or delivering takeout lunches on time.

The best approach to maintaining a neat work area and to enhancing speed is to convince yourself that neatness and speed are valuable. You will then search for ways to be neat and fast, such as putting back a reference book immediately after use or making phone conversations brief. The underlying principle is that an attitude leads to a change in behavior.

Clearing your mind of clutter can contribute more to personal productivity than clearing your work space. Time-management consultant Dorothy Madden notes that if there are too many thoughts swirling around in your mind, it is difficult to be organized.[9] Many of the techniques described in this chapter, such as creating to-do lists, are aimed at uncluttering the brain.

Although neatness and orderliness are usually an effective approach to accomplishing work, at times a little disorder can be beneficial, as will be described in the section on time-management techniques.

WORK SMARTER, NOT HARDER

People caught up in trying to accomplish a job often wind up working hard but not in an imaginative way that leads to good results. Much time and energy, therefore, are wasted. A working-smart approach also requires that you spend a few minutes carefully planning how to implement your task. An example of working smarter, not harder, is to invest a few minutes of critical thinking before launching an Internet search. Think through carefully what might be the keywords that will lead you to the information you need. In this way, you will minimize conducting your search with words and phrases that will lead to irrelevant information. For example, suppose you want to conduct research on backstabbing as negative office politics. If you use only the term *backstabbing*, the search engine will direct you to such topics as street crime and medical treatment for wounds. Working smarter is to try "backstabbing in the office" or "backstabbing and office politics."

An advanced approach to working smarter is to avoid doing work that is already being accomplished in another part of the organization by using communication technology designed to foster collaboration. Some programs make it easier to find out what coworkers in other parts of a far-flung company are working on, thus avoiding duplication. Company blogs and intranets can also be helpful in identifying other workers who are engaged in a similar project. For example, you might be mining data attempting to discover which customers are likely to buy a variety of products from your employer.[10] A page on the intranet might tell you that Sally in Madison, Wisconsin, is working on the same project. If you then collaborate, you will save lots of time—and work smarter.

APPRECIATE THE IMPORTANCE OF REST AND RELAXATION

A productive attitude to maintain is that overwork can be counterproductive and lead to negative stress and burnout. Proper physical rest contributes to mental alertness and improved ability to cope with frustration. David Volpi, director of the Manhattan Snoring and Sleep Center, says that insufficient sleep can cause daytime fatigue, poor concentration, irritability, and low energy. Memory and ability to pay attention may also suffer.[11] An optimum amount of sleep for most adults is seven to nine hours per night.[12]

Constant attention to work or study is often inefficient. It is a normal human requirement to take enough breaks to allow you to approach work or study with a fresh perspective. Research suggests that cognitive ability depends on how much sleep a person accumulates during a twenty-four-hour period, not just overnight.[13] It is therefore understandable why napping during the day has gained in popularity as a productivity booster. Workers who have private offices might nap under the desk, while cubicle dwellers often nap with their head on the desk. Each person has to establish the right balance between work and leisure within the bounds of freedom granted by the situation.

Neglecting the normal need for rest and relaxation can lead to **workaholism**, an addiction to work in which *not* working is an uncomfortable experience. (In some cases, therefore, workaholism leads to neglect of rest and relaxation.) Some types of workaholics are perfectionists who are never satisfied with their work and therefore find it difficult to leave work behind. In addition, the workaholic who is a perfectionist may become heavily focused on control, leading to rigid behavior. However, some people who work long and hard are classified as happy workaholics who thrive on hard work and are usually highly productive. As executives, they encourage others to work hard to achieve company goals and also pursue what matters to them in their personal lives.[14]

Workaholism
an addiction to work in which not working is an uncomfortable experience

◀ **Learning Objective 16.4** ◀

Effective Time-Management Techniques

So far, we have discussed improving productivity from the standpoints of dealing with procrastination and developing the right attitudes and values. Skills and techniques also contribute substantially to becoming more productive. Here we describe some well-established methods of work habit improvement along with several new ones. For these techniques to enhance productivity, most of them need to be incorporated into and practiced regularly in our daily lives. This is particularly true because many of these techniques are habits, and habits have to be programmed into the brain through repetition.

CLEAN UP AND GET ORGANIZED

An excellent starting point for improving work habits and time management is to clean up the work area and arrange things neatly. The starting point in the popular system of work habits and time management developed by David Allen is to unclutter your life. You begin by collecting everything that you must do, or hope to do, or that is unfinished or undecided. All of these items are written on sheets of paper, a process referred to as a *mind sweep*.[15] You are likely to find that many of these tasks can be thrown out right away. An example would be throwing out an expired discount coupon from an office supply store. Despite the contribution of a mind sweep, simply jotting down a key task will not remove it completely from your mind, particularly if it is a bothersome task. An example would be an item on a supervisor's to-do list about firing an employee.

Eliminate clutter by throwing out unnecessary paper, and deleting computer files and e-mail messages that will probably never be used again. The idea is to learn to simplify the work area so that there are fewer distractions and the brain can be more focused. In addition, finding important files becomes easier. Personalizing work areas, such as having a collection of knickknacks and mementos, often contributes to clutter. Too much decoration can disrupt productivity because it is distracting.[16]

Getting organized includes sorting out which tasks need doing, including assignments and projects not yet completed. A major cleanup principle is therefore to discard anything that is no longer valuable. A suggestion worth considering is to throw out at least one item every day from the office and home—even if the item thrown out is as humble as an empty ballpoint pen. Because new items come into the office and home almost daily, you will always have possessions left.

One exception to the value of tidiness is that a messy desk is sometimes associated with the ability to think more creatively. For example, an experiment with forty-eight people found that those who worked in a messy room came up with more novel uses for a ping-pong ball.[17] Another consideration is that a major disadvantage of being a *neat freak* is that spending so much time on keeping a desk clutter-free takes time away from dealing with customers or clients.[18]

PLAN YOUR ACTIVITIES

Planning

primary principle of effective time management; deciding what to accomplish and the actions needed to make it happen

The primary principle of effective time management is **planning**, that is, deciding what you want to accomplish and the actions needed to make it happen. The most elementary—and the most important—planning tool is a list of tasks that need doing. Almost every successful person works from a to-do list. These lists are essentially daily goals. Before you can compose a useful list, you need to set aside a few moments each day to sort out the tasks at hand. A good starting point in using to-do lists is to prepare such a list on Sunday for the rest of the week. The list can then be modified on Monday through Saturday. A list used by a working parent is presented in Figure 16-1.

FIGURE 16-1

A SAMPLE TO-DO LIST

Source: "A SAMPLE TO-DO LIST" by Andrew J. DuBrin.

Job

Make 10 calls to prospects for new listings.
Have "For Sale" signs put outside Hanover Blvd. house.
Set up mortgage appointment at 1st Federal for the Calhouns.
Update website listings.
Upgrade antivirus software.
Check for possible sales leads on Facebook, LinkedIn, and Twitter.
Meet with the Guptas at 5 p.m.
Set up time to show house to the Bowens.

Home

Buy running shoes for Todd.
Buy jeans for Linda.
Get icemaker fixed on refrigerator.
Write and send checks for monthly bills.
Clip cat's nails.
Check out problem with hot-water tank.
Make appointment with dentist to have chipped filling replaced.
Check Twitter and send out at least ten tweets this evening.

FIRST REALTY CORPORATION

Jacksonville, Florida

jbartow@firstrealty.com

Where to put your to-do lists.   Many people dislike having small to-do lists stuck in different places. One reason is that these lists are readily lost among other papers. Many people, therefore, put lists on desk calendars or printed forms called *planners,* which are also available for computers. Planners give you an opportunity to record your activities in intervals as small as fifteen minutes. Many people place their to-do list in an appropriate place on their desktop computer or smartphone. Whether you use a paper or digital calendar, it is important to carry it with you so you can refer to it frequently.

Another useful approach for organizing your lists is to use a notebook small enough to be portable. (As described in the chapter opener, the CEO of IBM uses a notebook.) The notebook becomes your master list to keep track of work tasks, errands, social engagements, and shopping items. Anything else requiring action might also be recorded—even a reminder to clean up the work area again. Some people have such clear focus that they register their to-do lists in their brain, thereby skipping paper or a computer.

Many people have observed that accomplishing items on your to-do list is therapeutic, giving you a positive boost in morale. Internet pioneer and founder of several high-technology firms Marc Andreessen compiles a *done list*. Every time he accomplishes something useful during the day, he writes it down on an index card. Andreessen recommends that every time you get something done, write it down and you will get a little rush of endorphins.[19]

No matter where you place your to-do list, its usefulness diminishes if the list is not consulted regularly, perhaps twice per day.

How to set priorities.   Faced with multiple tasks to do at the same time, it is possible to feel overwhelmed and freeze as a result. The time-tested solution is to establish a priority to each item on the to-do list. A typical system is to use A to signify critical or essential items, B to signify important items, and C for the least important ones. Although an item might be regarded as a C (for example, refilling your stapler), it still has a contribution to make to your productivity and sense of well-being. If you are conscientious, small undone items will interfere with your concentration.

To effectively set priorities, you have to recognize which tasks are critical or important. In general, those activities that deal directly with the major purposes of your job are critical, such as dealing with a major customer or completing your portion of a budget. Tasks your manager perceives to be urgent should also be classified as critical tasks. Emergency items, such as dealing with the effects of a tornado or a product recall, are also essential tasks.

How to schedule and follow through.   To be effective, a to-do list must be an action tool. To convert your list into action, prepare a schedule of when you are going to do each of the items on the list. Follow through by doing things according to your schedule, checking them off as you go along. Time-and-activity charts (also referred to as *Gantt charts*) have been used in factories and offices for over a hundred years to keep track of projects. Many people find these basic charts useful in scheduling their own activities and keeping track of progress. Time-and-activity charts also reinforce the reality that much of work is calendar driven. A calendar anticipates all the dates, deadlines, and seasons essential to running a successful business firm. For example, many customers want shipments by a particular date, and bills are due at a specific time. Figure 16-2 presents a time-and-activity chart you might want to use as a personal productivity booster.

A useful principle to keep in mind to implement plans is the planning fallacy. It refers to the idea that many people have a strong tendency to underestimate how long it will take to complete a complex task. As a result, they are frequently late with projects such as completing a report, preparing a budget, or relocating an office. To deal with the planning fallacy, estimating completion time based on past experience is helpful. Another useful

FIGURE 16-2

A TIME-AND-ACTIVITY CHART FOR SCHEDULING ACTIVITIES

Source: "A TIME-AND-ACTIVITY CHART FOR SCHEDULING ACTIVITIES" by Andrew J. DuBrin.

Charting key tasks and their deadlines, along with your performance on the task, can often get you focused and organized.

Deadlines for Task Accomplishment

Task to Be Accomplished	Feb. 1	Feb. 28	Mar. 15	Mar. 31	Apr. 15	Apr. 30
Expense reports	Did it					
Antivirus treatment for PC		Two days late				
Website updated			Blew it			
Plan office party				Did it		
File federal and state tax reports					In the mail at midnight ☺☺	
Provide input to department budget						On time

technique is to break down a task into very detailed steps, such as "How much time will I really need to find a moving company to move the furniture in the office?"[20]

BOOST YOUR ENERGY

Many workers are not as productive as they or the company would like them to be largely because they lack enough energy for the demands of their work. According to Tony Schwartz, the founder of the Energy Project in New York City, increasing your energy is the best way to get more done faster and better. Becoming more energetic leads to more productivity gains than merely working longer hours.

Experience with many companies participating in the Energy Project suggests that workers perform at their peak when they alternate between periods of intense focus and taking appropriate rest pauses. Employees are able to increase their productivity by practicing simple rituals that refuel their energy, such as a brief walk to take a breather, or turning off e-mail at specific times so they can concentrate better.[21] Walks are helpful because physical exercise increases the flow of blood to the brain, resulting in more mental energy. Proper rest, including brief naps, nutrition, and exercise also enhance physical and mental energy.

A study with 214 professional and clerical workers in a software development company provides additional insights into what works and what doesn't work for boosting energy. The participants completed questionnaires about their approaches to energy management as well as their perceived levels of vitality and fatigue (both aspects of energy). Microbreaks unrelated to work, such as making a personal phone call or checking a social media site, were not associated with more energy and less fatigue. These same work pauses were often associated with increased wariness. In contrast, increases in

Human Relations in Practice

Distribution Center Manager Troy Refuels on the Job

Troy is a distribution center manager for a company that makes electronic components used for a wide variety of consumer appliances, including washers and dryers, hair dryers, electronic shopping carts, and electronic scooters for the mobility challenged. In his thirties, Troy has had difficulty managing his anger, which he believes can disrupt his productivity and damage his relationships with subordinates and colleagues.

Troy was one of the first managers in his company to participate in an energy-management program sponsored by his company, and conducted by a consulting firm specializing in workplace energy management. Troy was coached on how to manage his feelings more effectively. He learned to make it a practice to step away from frustrating situations and take walks around the distribution center lot when he felt that his frustration was reaching an uncomfortable level. During his brief walks, Troy would often count to ten and/or breathe deeply.

The walking ritual helped Troy relax, refocus, and then think through more clearly how he should best respond to the frustrating situation or person. As a result of these slight changes, Troy believes that he has more positive energy to invest in his job. He also believes that his job performance has improved.

Question:

In your experience, does dealing better with frustration give you more energy?

Source: The program in question is based on the work of the Energy Project, as described in Tony Schwartz, "The Productivity Paradox: How Sony Pictures Gets More Out of People by Demanding Less," *Harvard Business Review*, June 2010, pp. 64–69.

vitality were associated with short breaks to accomplished work-related tasks such as praising a coworker or preparing a to-do list.[22]

Note that the findings from the Energy Project indicated work pauses as contributing more to energy. It might therefore be useful for you to try both non-work-related, and work-related pauses to see which is most effective for you.

The accompanying Human Relations in Practice illustrates how one worker might boost his energy.

MAKE GOOD USE OF DIGITAL TECHNOLOGY INCLUDING PRODUCTIVITY TOOLS

Used properly, most high-tech devices in the office improve productivity. According to a Pew Research Center report, 46 percent of workers who use online and digital tools say they feel more productive. In descending order, the five electronic and digital technology tools used by these workers were e-mail, the Internet, a landline phone, a cellphone or smartphone, and social media sites. In this report, 30 percent of workers said they were working longer hours because of these tools.[23]

How you use these ever-present devices is the key to increased productivity. Mobile workers, or those who conduct much of their work away from the office, quite often enhance their productivity by accessing intranets and staying in contact with coworkers. Many customer-contact workers are enhancing their productivity by using tablet computers to access vital information about a product or service, such as a pharmaceutical sales rep finding out immediately how a new drug might interact with other drugs.

Making good use of office technology also implies avoiding those aspects of office technology most likely to drain productivity. At the top of the list are those beeps and alerts (or "ghost alerts") that float onto your screen to announce new e-mails or the fact that somebody in your Skype network is now online. An exception is that if your job requires paying immediate attention to incoming e-mail messages, the alerts will enhance your productivity. How about a radiation leak technician being alert to news about radiation leaks?

Productivity tools refer more specifically to information technology devices, including apps aimed directly at enhancing productivity. Among the most popular is Evernote, which gives the opportunity to collect all possibly relevant information in one place, including notes, web pages, file attachments, and invoices. Used selectively and with self-discipline, many of these tools can enhance productivity. In contrast, when these productivity tools are used as an end in themselves and occupy too much of a worker's time, they become a productivity drain. Another problem is that these tools often consume more time than they are worth. Little by little, the information technology enthusiast begins to think that using productivity tools *is* his or her job. Such an individual will often boast about organizing 100 files into one device, communicating with ten people simultaneously, and always being connected. All this activity might not translate into useful work outcomes, such as satisfying customers or improving a business process.

A major consideration is that the time saved using office technology must be invested in productive activity to attain a true productivity advantage. Assume that you save two hours by ordering office equipment over the Internet. If you invest those two hours in activity such as finding ways to save the company money, you are more productive.

A helpful attitude about boosting personal productivity through office technology is to stay alert to new tools that would be useful in your situation. For example, a person who travels frequently for business might be able to use a portable scanner, which scans receipts, business cards, and documents and organizes the information into a database. This information saves time when submitting expense reports. The business owner could use this information for preparing income taxes.

CONCENTRATE ON ONE KEY TASK AT A TIME

Effective people have a well-developed capacity to concentrate on the problem or person they face, however surrounded they are with potential distractions. A key task is one directly related to the purposes of the person's job. The majority of key tasks are actions that earn money, save money, satisfy customers, or build relationships with work associates.

The problems of being distracted by personal e-mail and social media websites are well known. A CareerBuilder survey of more than 3,000 workers found that one in four full-time workers admitted to spending at least one hour each workday on personal phone calls, texts, or e-mails.[24] As discussed in Chapter 6 in relation to creativity, open work spaces are distracting to many workers.

The Flow Experience

The best results from concentration are achieved when you are so absorbed in your work that you are aware of virtually nothing else at the moment—referred to as the *flow experience*. Attaining flow requires uninterrupted concentration. Another useful byproduct of concentration is that it reduces absent-mindedness. If you really concentrate on what you are doing, the chances diminish that you will forget what you intended to do.

The Role of Self-Discipline

Conscious effort and self-discipline can strengthen concentration skills and focus on key tasks. An effective way to sharpen your concentration skills is to set aside ten minutes a day and focus on something repetitive, such as your breathing pattern or a small word. This is the same approach that is used in meditation to relieve stress. After practicing concentration in the manner just described, concentrate on an aspect of your work, such as preparing a report.

An extreme good example of concentration on one task at a time is Jack Dorsey, the cofounder of Twitter and CEO of payments platform Square. On average, he spends eight hours at Twitter and then another eight at Square. "The only way to do this is to be very disciplined," says Dorsey. (You won't find him tweeting away his sixteen-hour workday!) Two examples of his concentration are that he devotes Monday to management meetings and running the company. Tuesday is devoted to product development.[25]

ADHD and Concentration

Some people have difficulty concentrating on important tasks, or almost any task, because they have attention deficit hyperactivity disorder (ADHD). Workers with ADHD may find it difficult to focus on, organize, and finish tasks and often forget to accomplish items on their to-do list. Before workers with ADHD can improve their concentration on important tasks, they may require professional help in terms of medicine, counseling, or cognitive behavior therapy.[26]

STREAMLINE YOUR WORK, AND EMPHASIZE IMPORTANT TASKS

As companies continue to operate with fewer workers than in the past even during good economic times, more nonproductive work must be eliminated. Getting rid of unproductive work is part of improving a business process. Every employee is expected to get rid of work that does not contribute to productivity or help customers. Another purpose of work streamlining is to get rid of work that does not add value for customers. Time-management guru David Allen says that you must constantly recalibrate your resources to attain the best results and must say "not now" to less important tasks.[27]

Here is a sampling of work that typically does not add value:

- Sending receipts and acknowledgments to people who do not need them

- Writing and sending e-mails and reports that nobody reads or needs

- Holding meetings that do not accomplish work, exchange important information, or improve team spirit

- Checking up frequently on the work of competent people

In general, to streamline your work, look for duplication of effort and waste. An example of duplication of effort would be to routinely send people e-mail three times with the same question. An example of waste would be to call a meeting for disseminating information that could easily be communicated by e-mail.

Important (value-contributing) tasks are those in which superior performance could have a large payoff. (*Important tasks* and *key tasks* refer to the same idea.) No matter how quickly you took care of making sure that your store paid its bills on time, for example, this effort would not make your store an outstanding success. If, however, you concentrated your efforts on bringing unique and desirable merchandise into the store, this action could greatly affect your business success.

Many people respond to suggestions about emphasizing important tasks by saying, "I don't think concentrating on important tasks applies to me. My job is so filled with routine that I have no chance to work on the big breakthrough ideas." True, most jobs are filled with routine requirements. What a person *can* do is spend some time, perhaps even one hour a week, concentrating on tasks of potentially major significance.

WORK AT A STEADY PACE

In most jobs, working at a steady clip pays dividends in efficiency. The spurt worker creates many problems for management. Some employees take pride in working rapidly, even when the result is a high error rate. Another advantage of the steady-pace approach is that you accomplish much more than someone who puts out extra effort only once in a while. The completely steady worker would accomplish just as much the day before a holiday as on a given Monday. That extra hour or so of productivity adds up substantially by the end of the year. Despite the advantages of maintaining a steady pace, some peaks and valleys in your work may be inevitable. Tax accounting firms, for example, have busy seasons.

Working at a steady pace throughout the day is difficult because it counters a natural tendency to slow down toward the end of a workday. Ways of dealing with this potential productivity dip are those related to getting an energy boost, such as a quick walk in the fresh air.

CREATE SOME QUIET, UNINTERRUPTED TIME

Many office workers find their days hectic, fragmented, and frustrating. Incessant interruptions make it difficult to get things done. The constant start–stop–restart pattern lengthens the time needed to get jobs done. Quiet time can reduce the type of productivity drain previously described. To achieve quiet time, create an uninterrupted block of time, enabling you to concentrate on your work. This could mean turning off the phone, not accessing your e-mail, and blocking drop-in visitors during certain times of the workday.

Quiet time is used for such essential activities as thinking, planning, getting organized, doing analytical work, writing reports, and doing creative tasks. Interruptions lower productivity more for mental than for physical work. This is true because interruptions break the flow of thought, and it takes time to get back into a train of thought.

Quiet time is difficult to find in some jobs, such as those requiring customer contact. An agreement has to be worked out with the manager about when and where quiet time can be taken. Sometimes the quiet time can be taken at home early in the workday or in a vacated office or conference room.

MAKE USE OF BITS OF TIME, AND USE MULTITASKING FOR ROUTINE WORK

A truly productive person makes good use of miscellaneous bits of time both on and off the job. While waiting in line at a post office, you might update your to-do list; while waiting for an elevator, you might be able to read a brief report; and if you have finished your day's work ten minutes before quitting time, you can use that time to clean out a file. When traveling for business, bring as much work as you can comfortably carry. Many business travelers carry a laptop or tablet computer so they can perform work in transit.

And many professionals use smartphones in place of a larger computer to access company information. Spare time at airports because you arrive early or because of flight delays provides a good opportunity to perform routine work. By the end of the year, your productivity will have increased much more than if you had squandered these bits of time.

Some forms of making use of bits of time, such as reviewing your to-do list as you ride the elevator, are a form of constructive multitasking. Doing two or more routine chores simultaneously can sometimes enhance personal productivity. While exercising on a stationary bike, you might read work-related information; while commuting, listen to the radio for information of potential relevance for your job. Also, while reading e-mail, you might clean the outside of your computer; while waiting for a file to download, you might arrange your work area or read a brief report. Some young people, in particular, are adept at constructive multitasking. A study of 400 adolescents found that most teens perform better while multitasking than when focusing on a single task. However, about 15 percent of those studied (referred to as high media multitaskers) performed better while working with the distractions of e-mail and music than when focusing on one task exclusively.[28]

Despite searching for productivity gains through multitasking, it is important to avoid rude or dangerous acts or a combination of the two. A rude practice is doing paperwork while on the telephone or sitting in class. Dangerous practices include engaging in an intense conversation or sending and receiving text messages while driving. Text messaging is particularly dangerous because the person is forced to lose full eye contact with the road.

STAY IN CONTROL OF PAPERWORK, THE INBOX, AND E-MAIL

Despite the major shift to the use of electronic messages, the workplace is still overflowing with printed messages, including computer printouts. Also, most contracts are usually required to exist in paper form. You will notice your local office supply store has enormous loads of printing paper in stock. Paperwork essentially involves taking care of administrative details, such as correspondence, expense account forms, and surveys. Responding to e-mail messages, instant messages, and text messages has created additional administrative details that require handling, even if they are actually *electronic work* rather than paperwork.

Unless you handle paperwork, e-mail, instant messages, and text messages efficiently, you may lose control of your job or home life, which could lead to substantial negative stress. Ideally, a small amount of time should be invested in paperwork and routine e-mail every day. Non-prime time (when you are at less than peak efficiency but not overly fatigued) is the best time to take care of administrative routine work.

A workable suggestion for most people intent on staying on top of e-mail and instant messages is to set aside some time to respond to every important message that you have not taken care of in the last two days. Move all other messages of potential future value to the archive folder. Whenever you receive a new e-mail or instant message, take action by responding, deleting, forwarding, or storing it. When an e-mail requires a complicated response, you are justified in leaving the e-mail in your inbox until you obtain the information necessary to respond intelligently.[29]

Overcoming Time Wasters

◀ Learning Objective 16.5 ◀

Another basic thrust to improved personal productivity is to minimize wasting time. Workers wasting time is one of the most devastating problems facing work organizations of all types, probably far exceeding the cost from theft and fraud. Time wasting due to electronic distractions has been mentioned or implied several times in this chapter and this book. The Career-Builder survey mentioned above also found that 42 percent of employees were distracted by gossip, and 24 percent by noisy coworkers.[30] Human Relations Self-Assessment Quiz 16-1 gives you an opportunity to think through how you deal with distractions caused by people.

Human Relations Self-Assessment Quiz 16-1

A Checklist of Potential Distractions Stemming from Coworkers to Boss

Coworker or Boss Behavior	Not a Problem	Yes, a Problem
1. Coworker insists I look at a series of his or her photos stored on his or her smartphone.	_____	_____
2. Coworker asks my recommendations for a restaurant or other entertainment venue.	_____	_____
3. While I'm working on an important task, coworker asks me what I think of his or her new outfit.	_____	_____
4. Coworker forwards me an e-mail with a link to a website unrelated to work, such as a PowerPoint presentation of some of the world's most beautiful mountains.	_____	_____
5. Boss stops by to rehash in great detail professional or college sporting event that took place over the weekend.	_____	_____
6. Coworker in adjacent work space talks loudly on his or her phone.	_____	_____
7. Coworker stops by to ask if he or she can bring me back beverage or food from a café or restaurant.	_____	_____
8. Coworker stops by to share a rumor about a major development in the company.	_____	_____
9. Coworker chews gum so loudly that it diverts my attention from what I am doing.	_____	_____
10. Boss stops by to make positive comments about clothing or appearance.	_____	_____
11. Coworker displays pornography on screen of desktop computer and asks me to take a peek.	_____	_____
12. Coworker who wants to engage me in conversation asks, "Do you have a minute?"	_____	_____
13. Coworker drops by and says, "The boss is driving me crazy." Without asking me if I have the time, he or she then explains why the boss is driving him or her crazy.	_____	_____
14. Coworker who looks ill and is coughing and sneezing approaches me to explain that he or she should have stayed home today.	_____	_____
15. With a serious and somber expression, coworker asks me, "Are you worried about us all losing our jobs?"	_____	_____
16. Coworker talks so loudly it is difficult for me to think clearly.	_____	_____
17. Your boss walks over to you with the purpose of micromanaging a task you know how to perform perfectly well.	_____	_____
18. You are working on a key task, and your boss asks for your opinion about how well the department is supporting the company strategy.	_____	_____

Interpretation:

The more of these distractions you checked as being "Yes, a problem," the more you will need to exercise self-discipline to deal with the problem. An effective, general-purpose approach to dealing with a potential interruption is to nip it in the bud by saying, "I am right in the middle of work right now. I will get back to you as soon as feasible."

One caution about interpreting how much time workers waste is that many employees who waste time during the day will speed up their work toward the end of the workday or work at home to catch up on unfinished tasks. Many of the techniques already described in this chapter help save time. The tactics and strategies described next, however, are directly aimed at overcoming the problem of wasted time.

Human Relations Self-Assessment Quiz 16-1 gives you an opportunity to think through how you waste or do not waste work-related time.

MINIMIZE DAYDREAMING

Allowing the mind to drift while on the job is a major productivity drain. Daydreaming is triggered when the individual perceives the task to be boring—such as reviewing another person's work for errors. Unresolved personal problems are an important source of daydreaming, thus blocking your productivity. This is especially true because effective time utilization requires good concentration. When you are preoccupied with a personal or business problem, it is difficult to give your full efforts to a task at hand.

The solution is to do something constructive about whatever problem is sapping your ability to concentrate. Sometimes a relatively minor problem, such as driving with an expired operator's license, can impair your work concentration. At other times, a major problem, such as how best to take care of a parent who has suffered a stroke, interferes with work. In either situation, your concentration will suffer until you take appropriate action.

Human Relations Self-Assessment Quiz 16-2 provides another opportunity to think about time wasting on the job.

PREPARE A TIME LOG TO EVALUATE YOUR USE OF TIME

An advanced tool for becoming a more efficient time manager is to prepare a time log of how you are currently investing your time. For five full workdays or school days, write down everything you do, including such activities as responding to e-mail and taking rest breaks. A daily planner is the tool of choice for a time log. Some people, including many executives, use a spreadsheet for the same purpose. Study your results, and look for patterns of lost time. A hospital administrative worker who used a log discovered that she was spending about twenty minutes at the start of each workday circling around the parking ramp looking for a space. Her conclusion was that by arriving five minutes earlier to the hospital, she could find a space within a few minutes.

One of the most important outputs of a time log is to uncover time leaks. A **time leak** is anything you are doing or not doing that allows time to get away from you. Among them are spending too much time for lunch by collecting people before finally leaving and walking to a coworker's cubicle rather than sending an e-mail. The process of streamlining your work will also identify time leaks.

Time leak
anything you are doing or not doing
that allows time to get away from you

AVOID UNPRODUCTIVE USE OF COMPUTERS

An unproductive use of computers is to tinker with them to the exclusion of useful work. Many people have become intrigued with computers to the point of diversion. They become habituated to creating new reports or exquisite graphics and making endless changes. It is easy to become diverted by the thousands of commands in a program such as Microsoft Word or PowerPoint. Some managers spend so much time with computers that they neglect leadership responsibilities, thus lowering their productivity. Using multiple open tabs on the screen should be done only when absolutely necessary because it invites distractions by jumping from one website to another.[31]

In addition to these problems, Internet surfing for purposes not strictly related to the job has become a major productivity drain. For example, many Internet shopping sites and sports sites have found that their peak number of visits is during traditional working hours. Social networking sites are also visited frequently during typical working hours.

The message is straightforward: To plug one more potential productivity drain, avoid using the computer for nonproductive purposes. Many companies block the use of recreational websites on company equipment so that workers have to resort to authorized sites, such as those selling equipment and supplies!

Human Relations Self-Assessment Quiz   16-2

My Tendencies toward Wasting or Not Wasting Time

Indicate the extent to which you engage in the time-wasting activities listed below on a three-point scale: 1 = never or rarely, 2 = sometimes, 3 = frequently or almost daily. Think of these activities in relation to the job, classroom, or while studying.

Number	Activity or Behavior	Rarely or Never	Sometimes	Frequently or Almost Daily
1.	I access my favorite social media site during the workday.	1	2	3
2.	I daydream about a variety of topics.	1	2	3
3.	I make phone calls related to social life.	1	2	3
4.	I surf the web, such as checking into sports sites, shopping sites, and YouTube.	1	2	3
5.	I run a personal errand.	1	2	3
6.	I look out the window or gaze at the ceiling.	1	2	3
7.	I send and receive text messages unrelated to work.	1	2	3
8.	I go for a brief walk just to relax.	1	2	3
9.	I go to get a beverage or snack.	1	2	3
10.	I engage a coworker in conversation not related to the work or subject under study.	1	2	3

Scoring and Interpretation:

Add the numbers you have circled or checked.

10–15   A score this low suggests that you waste very little time that could contribute to your productivity. However, your productivity might increase slightly if you took an occasional pause from your work to refresh you mind.

16–24   A score within this range suggests that you are about average with respect to wasting time on the job or in relation to study. You might look for ways to waste a little less time, particularly if your score is at the higher end of the average range (20–24).

25–30   A score this high suggests that you are wasting too much time with respect to work or study. As a result, you might be suffering a personal productivity drain. Concentrate more to reduce your time wasting. You might begin by eliminating one of your biggest time wasters and then move on to tackle another.

Source: "My Tendencies Toward Wasting or Not Wasting Time" by Andrew J. DuBrin.

KEEP TRACK OF IMPORTANT NAMES, PLACES, AND THINGS

How much time have you wasted lately searching for such items as a phone number you jotted down somewhere, your keys, or an appointment book? Many managers and professionals store such information in a database, in their cell phones, or even in a word-processing file. Such files are more difficult to misplace than a pocket directory, yet these files should be backed up to prevent lost data.

Two steps are recommended for remembering where you put things. First, have a parking place for everything. Put your keys, appointment book, or smartphone in the same place after each use. (This tactic supports the strategy of being neat and orderly to minimize wasting time.) Second, make visual associations. To have something register in your mind at the moment you are doing it, make up a visual association about that act. Thus, you might say, "Here I am putting my auto insurance policy in the back section of my canvas bag."

SET A TIME LIMIT FOR CERTAIN TASKS AND PROJECTS

Spending too much time on a task or project wastes time. As a person becomes experienced with certain projects, he or she is able to make accurate estimates of how long a project will take to complete. A paralegal might say, "Getting this ready for the lawyer's approval should take two hours." A good work habit to develop is to estimate how long a job should take and then proceed with strong determination to get that job completed within the estimated time period. A productive version of this technique is to decide that some low- and medium-priority items are worth only so much of your time. Invest that much time in the project but no more. Preparing a file on advertisements that come across your desk is one example.

SCHEDULE SIMILAR TASKS TOGETHER (CLUSTERING)

An efficient method of accomplishing small tasks is to group them together and perform them in one block of time. Clustering of this type has several applications. If you are visiting an office supply store, think of whatever you need there to avoid an unnecessary repeat visit. As long as you are visiting a particular search engine, look for some other information you will need soon. A basic way of scheduling similar tasks together is to make most of your phone calls in relation to your job from 11:00 to 11:30 each workday morning. Or you might reserve the last hour of every workday for e-mail and other correspondence. By using this method, you develop the necessary pace and mental set to knock off chores in short order. In contrast, when you flit from one task to another, your efficiency may suffer.

BOUNCE QUICKLY FROM TASK TO TASK

Much time is lost when a person takes a break between tasks. After one task is completed, you might pause for ten minutes to clear your work area and adjust your to-do list. After the brief pause, dive into your next important task. Celebrate your task accomplishment after work, not by taking a break from work during regular working hours.

Incorporating many of the ideas contained in this chapter will help you achieve peak performance or exceptional accomplishment.

Concept Review and Reinforcement

Work habits, 445
Productivity, 445
Procrastination, 446

Fear of success, 446
Workaholism, 451
Planning, 452

Time leak, 461

Summary and Review

People with good work habits tend to be more successful in their careers than poorly organized individuals, and they tend to have more time to spend on personal life. Good work habits are more important than ever because of today's emphasis on productivity.

Procrastination is the leading cause of poor productivity and career self-sabotage and can be viewed as the gap between intention and action. People procrastinate for many reasons, including their perception that a task is unpleasant, is overwhelming, or may lead to negative consequences. Fear of success can also lead to procrastination. Awareness of procrastination can lead to its control.

Seven techniques for reducing procrastination are the following:

- Calculating the cost of procrastination
- Counterattacking the burdensome task
- Jump-starting yourself
- Pecking away at an overwhelming task
- Motivating yourself with rewards and punishments
- Making a commitment to other people
- Expressing a more positive attitude about your intentions

Developing good work habits and time-management practices is often a matter of developing proper attitudes toward work and time. Six such attitudes and values are these:

- Developing a mission and goals
- Valuing good attendance and punctuality
- Valuing your time
- Valuing neatness, orderliness, and speed

- Working smarter, not harder
- Appreciating the importance of rest and relaxation

Eleven skills and techniques to help you become more productive are these:

- Cleaning up and getting organized
- Planning your activities (including the use of time-and-activity charts)
- Boosting your energy
- Getting off to a good start
- Making good use of office technology
- Concentrating on one key task at a time
- Streamlining your work and emphasizing important tasks
- Working at a steady pace
- Creating some quiet, uninterrupted time
- Making use of bits of time and using multitasking for routine work
- Staying in control of paperwork, the inbox, and e-mail

Time wasting is a major problem in the workplace. Seven suggestions for overcoming time wasting are as follows:

- Minimize daydreaming and other distractions.
- Prepare a time log and evaluate your use of time.
- Avoid unproductive use of computers.
- Keep track of important names, places, and things.
- Set a time limit for certain tasks and projects.
- Schedule similar tasks together (clustering).
- Bounce quickly from task to task.

Questions for Discussion and Review

16.1 How would company management know if its workforce were productive?

16.2 What have you observed to be two of the most important areas for improvement in work habits and time management for students?

16.3 Many tidy, well-organized workers never attain much in the way of career success. Which principle of work habits and time management described in this chapter might they be neglecting?

16.4 How can preparing a personal mission statement help a person become better organized?

16.5 Why do so many people need deadlines imposed on them to get their work accomplished?

16.6 How might a person use old shoe boxes or plastic trays to enhance his or her productivity?

16.7 What time-management problems might a person face who works from home or another remote location?

16.8 A study described under the topic of boosting your energy provided negative results for the use of caffeinated beverages as energy boosters. Would this study deter you, or an energy-drink consumer you might know, to cut back energy drinks and instead focus on the meaning of work and relationships?

16.9 In what ways has your use of information technology made you more productive?

16.10 Give an example of how the principles and techniques of good work habits and personal productivity could be applied to a job search.

Web Corner

Procrastination test (must take within forty-eight hours)
www.mindtools.com/ (Enter "Are You a Procrastinator?" into the search box.)

Overcoming perfectionism
www.mindtools.com/ (Enter "Perfectionism" in search box.)

Overcoming Internet addiction
www.helpguide.org/ (Enter "Internet and Computer Addiction" into search box.)

INTERNET SKILL BUILDER

What Are You Doing with Your Time?

Find a basic time-log worksheet on the Internet. You decide on which activities to enter into the time log. After recording how you are using your time after making the analysis on a few different days, ask yourself, "What have I learned that will enhance my personal productivity?" For example, do you see some slipping away of time that is neither enhancing your productivity directly nor providing you a few moments to refresh?

Developing Your Human Relations Skills

Applying Human Relations Exercise 16-1

Squeezing Productivity out of Social Networking Sites

The number of people using social networking sites continues to grow explosively. We all know that these sites can be an enjoyable pastime and a distraction from work. The issue we want you to address in small brainstorming groups is how to use social networking sites to improve your work productivity.

After each group has completed its task of brainstorming ways to improve productivity by being a member of a social networking site, you might hold a class discussion of your major findings. See if the class can reach a consensus on whether social networking sites can be a productivity booster or simply a pleasant diversion.

Applying Human Relations Exercise 16-2

My Personal Procrastination Analysis

The purpose of this exercise is to give you practice in understanding why you might have procrastinated in the past and how you might overcome a similar episode of procrastination in the future. To begin, write a description of some important activity on which you have procrastinated in the past. An *important* activity is one that could have a noticeable impact on your mental or financial well-being. Describe also any negative consequences that might have stemmed from the procrastination. Here is an example from an assistant manager at a health club who lives in the state of New York:

"I knew my vehicle inspection sticker was due in a month. But I was simply so busy with other things, I couldn't get to it. Also, I figured because it was wintertime, I could spread some snow over the dated sticker, and no police office would catch me. Well, it worked out that I was pulled over for the expired sticker. Unfortunately, the officer also found out I had not renewed my driver's license. My total fines were about $500 plus having to spend loads of time at the motor vehicle bureau straightening out the mess."

Use the following table (or copy the form on your computer) to record your procrastination episode and analyze the cause. After you have checked the most likely cause or causes, make a few notes in the third column as to how you might avoid procrastinating about that situation, or a similar situation, in the future.

Procrastination Episode

Reason(s) for Procrastination	Check Each Reason That Applies	Technique I Might Use to Overcome the Procrastination Next Time I Am in That Situation
1. Unpleasant task		
2. Overwhelming task		
3. Possible negative evaluation of my work		
4. Fear of success		
5. Rebelled against being controlled		
6. No meaningful reward		
7. Liked the last-minute rush		
8. I'm a perfectionist		

The assistant manager of the health club admitted that reasons 5 and 6 applied to his situation. He noted that he regards inspection stickers as a form of control over him. He noted also that having the sticker may be important but that he doesn't feel any particular reward for complying with the law. On further reflection, he realizes that some control is necessary in a civilized society. Many uninspected vehicles are a menace on the road. So not getting a sticker has a cost to society as well as to him. He will therefore calculate the personal cost next time. He said, "I know that it is best to tackle a tough task first. It takes a little time and money to get my car inspected, so I should do it first thing on the day set for the inspection."

Human Relations Class Activity

Personal Productivity Checklist

Each class member will use the following checklist to identify the two biggest mistakes per category he or she is making in work habits and time management. The mistakes could apply to work, school, or personal life. In addition to identifying the problems, each student will develop brief action plans about how to overcome them. For instance, "One of my biggest problems is that I tend to start a lot of projects but finish very few of them. Now that I am aware of this problem, I am going to post a sign over my desk that reads, "*No one will give me credit for things I never completed.*"

Students then present their problems and action plans to the class. After each student has made his or her presentation, a class discussion is held to reach conclusions and interpretations about the problems revealed. For instance, it might be that one or two time-management problems are quite frequent.

Overcoming Procrastination

Especially Applicable to Me

1. Increase awareness of the problem. _____
2. Calculate cost of procrastination. _____
3. Counterattack. _____
4. Jump-start myself. _____
5. Peck away at an overwhelming task. _____
6. Motivate myself with rewards and punishments. _____
7. Make a commitment to other people. _____
8. Express a more positive attitude about my intentions. _____

Developing Proper Attitudes and Values

1. Develop a mission, goals, and a strong work ethic. _____
2. Value good attendance and punctuality. _____
3. Value my time. _____
4. Value neatness, orderliness, and speed. _____
5. Work smarter, not harder. _____
6. Appreciate the importance of rest and relaxation. _____

Time-Management Techniques

1. Clean up and get organized. _____
2. Plan my activities (including a to-do list with priority setting). _____
3. Boost my energy. _____
4. Get off to a good start. _____
5. Make good use of office technology. _____
6. Concentrate on one key task at a time. _____
7. Streamline my work and emphasize important tasks. _____
8. Work at a steady pace. _____
9. Create some quiet, uninterrupted time. _____
10. Make use of bits of time, and use multitasking for routine work. _____
11. Stay in control of paperwork, the in-basket, and e-mail. _____

Overcoming Time Wasters

1. Minimize daydreaming. _____
2. Prepare a time log to evaluate my use of time. _____
3. Avoid unproductive use of computers. _____
4. Keep track of important names, places, and things. _____
5. Set a time limit for certain tasks and projects. _____
6. Schedule similar tasks together (clustering). _____
7. Bounce quickly from task to task. _____

Human Relations Case Study 16–1

Chloe Struggles to Get Moving

Chloe is the customer service supervisor at an office supply business located in Portland, Oregon. Her boss, Ron, the director of sales and marketing, asked her to prepare a report as to why the firm has been losing customers. Upon first receiving the assignment, Chloe responded, "Give me a break, Ron. We're losing business because most of our customers are purchasing online directly from manufacturers or from the office supply chains such as Staples and OfficeMax. Amazon.com gets a chunk of our former business also. We offer online sales, but many of our former customers prefer to deal with the big players."

Ron responded harshly, "Chloe, you are oversimplifying the problem. A lot of office supply stores are still around. Most manufacturers don't want to deal with small orders. And the big office-supply chains don't have a monopoly. I want to see your report in ten days."

Chloe said she would try to get the report done on time. Yet she felt she was already overloaded with work, and that the report would not reveal much that she did not already know. She thought, "Maybe I'll get started Sunday afternoon, right after the big football game on TV. That should give me about and hour and a half."

Around 4 p.m. that Sunday, Chloe reflected, "What kind of workaholic am I? Why start working on a report now, when I could take Charlotte (her daughter) and Bo (her dog) for a walk? It's a beautiful fall day.

Chloe decided to begin the report Monday morning, at 11 sharp. "I'll be in my best work mode on Monday."

At 10:45 a.m., one of the distribution specialists sent Chloe an e-mail request that Chloe meet with him ASAP to discuss pricing errors he found on the company website. Chloe thought she should jump on this problem because it was more important than preparing a marketing report.

Chloe then decided to start the customer loss project at 4 p.m. Thursday because her schedule was usually light at that time. When the time came, Chloe felt uneasy: "What should I do to get started? Maybe I'll search the Internet for a few ideas." After inserting the search phrase "Customer loss prevention" into Bing.com, Chloe found more than 34.5 million listings. She reasoned, "Maybe I will read a few dozen of these articles before getting started. Why reinvent the wheel?"

Chloe printed the first ten articles she found and thought she would take them home to read late at night: "Besides, the report is not due for another five days. I have plenty of time." That night Chloe fell asleep on the couch before she took the printed articles from her case.

Questions:

16.11 To what extent does Chloe have a procrastination problem?

16.12 What advice can you offer Chloe to help her get started on writing the report about customer loss?

16.13 What should Ron do to help Chloe get the report completed?

Human Relations Role-Playing Exercise

Dealing with Chloe's Procrastination Problem

One student plays the role of Chloe, who meets briefly with Ron on the day the report was due, but she has not made much progress. She is prepared to offer plausible excuses for not having the assignment completed. Another student plays the role of Ron, who is disappointed and thinks that Chloe is either lazy or has a procrastination problem.

Observers rate the role-players on two dimensions, using a scale of 1 to 5 from very poor to very good. One dimension is "effective use of human relations techniques." For Chloe, observe if she can recognize that she has a procrastination problem. For Ron, focus on how effective he is in helping Chloe be more prompt in getting a work obligation completed. The second dimension is "acting ability." A few observers might voluntarily provide feedback to the role-players in terms of sharing their ratings and observations. The course instructor might also provide feedback.

Human Relations Case Study 16–2

The Busy Office Manager

Mike looked at the kitchen clock and said to Ruth, his wife, "Oh no, it's 7:25, and my turn to drop off Jason and Gloria at the child care center. Once again, I'll start my day late for child care and just barely making it to work on time."

After getting Jason and Gloria settled at the child care center, Mike dashed off to the public accounting firm where he worked as the office manager. Mike found an e-mail from Ann Gabrielli, a partner in the firm: "See you today at 11:30 for the review of overhead expenses. Two other partners will be attending."

According to Mike's calendar, the meeting was one week from today. Mike called Ann immediately and said, "My apologies. My schedule says that the meeting is one week from today, at 11:30. I'm just not ready with the figures for today's meeting"

"My calendar says the meeting is today," responded Ann harshly. "I am ready for the meeting, and so are Craig and Gunther (the other partners). This isn't the first time you've gotten your weeks moved up. The meeting will go on, however poorly you have to perform."

"I'll be there," said Mike. "It's just a question of reviewing some figures that I've already collected." Mike calculated that he had less than three hours to prepare a report on overhead. He then glanced at his calendar to see what else he had scheduled for the morning. All was clear except for the entry: "PA/LC." Mike quickly recalled that the initials stood for "performance appraisal with Lucy Cruthers, the head bookkeeper at the firm." He then sent Lucy an e-mail suggesting that they meet the following week at the same time.

Mike had a difficult time locating the computer file he needed. Mike asked Lois, his administrative assistant, to help him locate the file. She scanned about 100 documents and said, "Here's a possibility, a document labeled PTR. The initials could refer to preparing for partners." Lois proved to be correct, and Mike dug into preparing the report, now only two hours away.

At the meeting, the partners accepted his analysis of overhead expenses and said they would study his findings further. As the meeting ended, a senior partner said to Mike, "If you had gotten your weeks straight, I think you would have presented your analysis in more depth."

Mike returned from lunch at 2 p.m. and decided to finish the report on overhead expenses that he had prepared for the partners. By 4 p.m., Mike was ready to tackle other tasks listed on his daily planner. However, Lois told him that an employment agency representative was in the building and had decided to drop in and talk about their temporary employment services.

"Might as well let her in," said Mike. "We will soon be hiring some temporary bookkeepers. It's getting too late to do much anyway."

On the way home from the child care center, the oldest child, Gloria, asked if the family could eat at a fast-food restaurant this evening. Mike said, "OK, but I'll have to stop at an ATM first. We'll ask Mom if she wants to eat out tonight before her class." Ruth agreed and said to Mike, "By the way, how did your day go?

Mike replied, "I just fell one day further behind schedule. I'll have to do some paperwork after the children are asleep. Maybe we can watch the late news together. We should both be free by then."

Questions:

16.14 What time-management mistakes does Mike appear to be making?

16.15 What does Mike appear to be doing right from the standpoint of managing time?

16.16 What suggestions can you offer Mike to help him get his schedule more under control?

REFERENCES

1. Original story created from facts and observations in the following sources: Gillian Tett, "Lunch with the FT: Ginni Rometty," *Financial Times*, www.ft.com, February 6, 2015, pp. 1–7; Monica Langley, "IBM Chief Searches for Big Blue's Next Act," *The Wall Street Journal*, April 21, 2015, pp. A1, A16; Carol Hymowitz and Sara Frier, "IBM's Rometty Breaks Ground as Company's First Female Leader," *Bloomberg Businessweek*, October 21, 2011, pp. 1–3; Pat Vaughan Tremmel, "Virginia Rometty Chosen for Top Job at IBM," www.northwestern.edu/newscenter, October 26, 2011.

2. Steven Kotler, "Escape," *Psychology Today*, September–October 2009, p. 75.

3. Theodore Kurtz, "Ten Reasons Why People Procrastinate," *Supervisory Management*, April 1990, pp. 1–2.

4. "The Best Advice I Ever Got: Beth Comstock," *Fortune*, November 12, 2012, p. 124.

5. Alan Lakein, *How to Gain Control of Your Time and Your Life* (New York: Wyden Books, 1973), pp. 141–151.

6. "Managing Perfectionism in the Workplace," *Workforce*, March 2013, p. S7.

7. Stephen R. Covey with Elaine Pofeldt, "Why Is This Man Smiling?" *Success*, January 2000, pp. 38–40.

8. Cited in Alfred A. Edmond Jr., "Alone in Your Time Zone," *Black Enterprise*, December 2004, pp. 154–155.

9. Dorothy Madden, "Clear Mind of Clutter to Be More Productive," *Democrat and Chronicle*, March 27, 2012, p. 5B.

10. Michael Mandel, "The Real Reasons You're Working So Hard . . . and What You Can Do about It," *Businessweek*, October 3, 2005, p. 62.

11. Quoted in Dawn Klingensmith, "Shine—and Rise!" www.philly.com, March 19, 2012, p. 2.

12. Siri Carpenter, "Awakening to Sleep," *Monitor on Psychology*, January 2014, p. 42.

13. Research reported in David Wescott, "Etc. Productivity," *Bloomberg Businessweek*, April 23–29, p. 90.

14. Stewart D. Friedman and Sharon Lobel, "The Happy Workaholic: A Role Model for Employees," *Academy of Management Executive*, August 2003, pp. 87–98.

15. Paul Keegan, "The Master of Getting Things Done," *Business 2.0*, July 2007, p. 77.

16. Debra Auerbach, "De-Clutter Your Way to a Productive Day," *CareerBuilder*, February 23, 2014.

17. Lea Winerman, "A Messy Desk Encourages a Creative Mind, Study Finds," *Monitor on Psychology*, October 2013, p. 12.

18. Eric Abrahamson and David H. Freedman, *A Perfect Mess* (Boston: Little Brown, 2007).

19. Janet Choi, "A Productivity Trick That Will Make You Feel Happier about What You Accomplish," www.chicagotribune.com, May 14, 2014, p. 1.

20. Sumathi Reddy, "Why Are You Late?" *The Wall Street Journal*, February 3, 2015, p. D1.

21. Tony Schwartz, "The Productivity Paradox: How Sony Pictures Gets More Out of People by Demanding Less," *Harvard Business Review*, June 2010, pp. 64–69.

22. Charlotte Fritz, Chak Fu Lam, and Gretchen M. Spritzer, "It's the Little Things That Matter," *Academy of Management Perspectives*, August 2011, pp. 28–39; Fritz, "Coffee Breaks Don't Boost Productivity after All," *Harvard Business Review*, May 2012, pp. 24–25.

23. Mike Snider, "Employees' 'Electronic Leash' Getting Tighter," *USA Today*, January 1, 2015, p. 4B.

24. Luke Siuty, "For Workers, There Are Lots of Distractions," *Workforce*, August 2014, p. 12.

25. Stacy Cowley, "A Guide to Jack Dorsey's 80-hour Workweek," *CNN Money*, http://money.cnn.com/2011/11/13/technology/dorsey_techonomy/, November 14, 2011, pp. 1–2.

26. "Attention Deficit Hyperactivity Disorder: What It Is and Who Is Affected," www.health.com, January 12, 2009, Copyright © 2009 Time Inc.

27. David Allen, "When Office Technology Overwhelms, Get Organized," *New York Times*, www.nytimes.com, March 19, 2012, p. 2.

28. Sumathi Reddy, "Study Finds Some Teens Can Excel at Multitasking," *The Wall Street Journal*, October 14, 2014, p. D1.

29. Farhad Manjoo, "An Empty Inbox, or with Just a Few E-mail Messages? Read On," *New York Times*, (www.nytimes.com), March 5, 2009.

30. Siuty, "For Workers, There Are Lots of Distractions," p. 12.

31. Chris Brogran, "The New Attention Deficit," *Entrepreneur*, December 2010, p. 70.

CHAPTER 17

Managing Stress and Personal Problems

Fotolia

Outline

Dylan, age twenty-seven, works as a credit evaluator for a direct mail and online financial services firm that provides working capital to business owners with less than the best credit ratings. Dylan enjoys his job and is pleased that his employer provides a useful service to business owners who need cash but often encounter difficulty when they attempt to secure a low-interest loan from a bank. Dylan's company has favorable ratings from both the Better Business Bureau and online reviews.

Dylan thought he was performing well in his job until he had a recent discussion with his manager, Collin, who downgraded his performance. Collin told Dylan, "I've hinted at this many times before. Your thinking is too superficial for this job. We evaluate credit risk on factors that go beyond simple formulas and credit ratings. We look at the quality and potential of a business. You often function like a simple checklist. Dig deeper in evaluating the potential of a client to pay back a loan, or I will have to replace you."

Dylan was shocked by the negative feedback, but he told Collin he would try to improve. Instead of being angry, Dylan sprang into action. He asked a couple of other people who knew him well about whether or not he dug deeply into problems, or if he was a lightweight thinker. Dylan did receive some gentle feedback that perhaps he was a little too conventional in his thinking.

Dylan began his personal campaign to think more deeply. He asked more questions when evaluating credit applications, and he pondered more deeply over the responses. He read a few articles about critical thinking and attempted to apply the ideas to himself. Dylan also began to question whether he was behaving in stereotyped ways, such as drinking the most popular brand of light beer and getting all his news from the best-known websites. When he read news articles or held conversations with people, Dylan would now often ask "Why?" about opinions expressed.

A couple of months later, Collin offered Dylan a compliment: "Thanks so much for taking my advice seriously, and not quitting. You have been doing a first-rate job of evaluating our customers with second-rate credit."

Learning Objectives ▶

After studying the information and doing the exercises in this chapter, you should be able to:

17.1 Describe the meaning of stress and its physiology.

17.2 Identify several positive and negative consequences of stress.

17.3 Pinpoint potential stressors in personal life.

17.4 Pinpoint potential stressors in the workplace.

17.5 Describe key methods for managing the potential adverse effects of stress.

17.6 Develop insight into dealing with personal problems through understanding self-defeating behavior and the importance of being resilient.

The story about the loan officer being resilient enough to overcome a problem that was threatening his career illustrates one of the topics of this chapter: dealing constructively with personal problems. The major topics of this chapter are the nature and cause of stress and managing personal and work stress.

▶ **Learning Objective 17.1** ▶

Stress
an internal reaction to any force
that threatens to disturb a person's
equilibrium; the internal reaction
usually takes the form of emotional
discomfort

Stressor
the external or internal force that brings
about the stress

Fight-or-flight response
the experience of stress prompts the
adrenal glands to release a flood of
hormones that prepare the body to fight
or run when faced with a challenge

The Physiology and Consequences of Stress

An important part of learning about stress is to understand its meaning, underlying physiology, and consequences to the person. **Stress** is an internal reaction to any force that threatens to disturb a person's equilibrium. The internal reaction usually takes the form of emotional discomfort. A **stressor** is the external or internal force that brings about the stress. Your perception of an event or thought influences whether you find a given event stressful. Your confidence in your ability to handle difficult situations also influences the amount of stress you experience. If you believe you have the resources to conquer the potentially stressful event, you are much less likely to experience stress. A computer whiz, therefore, would not be stressed by the prospect of having to install a new computer operating system.

PHYSIOLOGICAL CHANGES

The stress response begins in the brain, and a number of structures, including the pituitary gland, go on alert. The experience of stress prompts the adrenal glands to release a flood of hormones and chemicals that prepare the body to fight or run when faced with a challenge. This battle against the stressor is referred to as the **fight-or-flight response**. (The "response" is really a conflict, because you are forced to choose between struggling with the stressor or fleeing from the scene.) It helps you deal with emergencies.

The activation of hormones when the body has to cope with a stressor produces a short-term physiological reaction. Among the most familiar reactions are increases in heart rate, blood pressure, and blood glucose as well as blood clotting. Digestion stops during the stress episode. To help you recognize these symptoms, try to recall the internal bodily sensations you felt if you ever were almost in an automobile accident or if you heard some wonderful news. Less familiar changes are a redirection of the blood flow toward the brain and large-muscle groups and a release of stored fluids from places throughout the body into the bloodstream. Cortisol is a key hormone released under stress. Over a prolonged period of time, the cortisol makes people less resilient in coping with additional stress, which leads to difficulty in problem solving and creative thinking.[1]

The physiological changes taking place within the body are similar for both positive and negative stressors. Winning a trophy or being fired, for example, makes you feel about the same inside, at least for the moment. In the long run, however, negative experiences create unpleasant feelings such as anxiety and feeling ill at ease. Anxiety is a feeling of distress or uneasiness caused by fear of an imagined or unidentified problem. For example, you might be anxious about meeting your supervisor today, but you have no specific concern in mind.

▶ **Learning Objective 17.2** ▶

CONSEQUENCES AND SYMPTOMS

If stress is continuous and accompanied by these short-term physiological changes, annoying and life-threatening conditions can occur. A stressful life event usually leads to a high cholesterol level (of the unhealthy type) and high blood pressure. Men who respond most intensely to mental stress run a higher risk of blocked blood vessels. The result is a higher risk of heart attack and stroke. A series of studies indicated that job stressors such as a hostile work environment or excessive working hours can enhance a worker's risk for cardiovascular disease. One explanation of this problem is that mental stress, over time, may injure blood vessels and foster the buildup of arterial plaques.[2] Other conditions associated with stress are migraine headaches, ulcers, allergies, skin disorders, and cancer. Stress often results in memory problems, such as forgetting where you put your keys or not remembering an appointment.

Stress symptoms vary considerably from one person to another. A sampling of common stress symptoms is listed in Figure 17-1.

Challenge versus Hindrance Stressors

A useful framework for understanding work-related stressors is that they can have positive or negative consequences. **Challenge stressors** are stressful events and thoughts that have a positive direct effect on motivation and performance. They include work-related stimuli or forces such as a reasonably high workload, time pressures, and a realistic level of responsibility. Workers perceive these stressors as relatively under their control. Challenge stressors also offer the opportunity for personal growth if they are overcome, such as learning a complex new skill.

Hindrance stressors are those stressful events and thoughts that have a negative effect on motivation and performance. They include work-related stimuli or forces such as negative organization politics, bullying by supervisors and coworkers, confusing regulations, and confusion about responsibilities. Hindrance stressors encompass potentially stressful demands that are usually perceived as beyond the control of the worker and that might block the opportunity for personal growth.[3]

The concept of challenge versus hindrance stressors indicates that stress can play a positive role in our lives. The right amount of stress prepares us for meeting difficult

Challenge stressors
stressful events and thoughts that have a positive direct effect on motivation and performance

Hindrance stressors
stressful events and thoughts that have a negative effect on motivation and performance

FIGURE 17-1

A VARIETY OF STRESS SYMPTOMS

Source: "A VARIETY OF STRESS SYMPTOMS" by Andrew J. DuBrin.

Mostly Physical

Shaking or trembling	Upper- and lower-back pain
Dizziness	Frequent headaches
Heart palpitations	Low energy and stamina
Difficulty breathing	Stomach problems
Chronic fatigue	Constant cravings for sweets
Unexplained chest pains	Increased alcohol or cigarette consumption
Frequent teeth grinding	Frequent need to eliminate
Frequent nausea and dizziness	Skin eruptions and rashes
Premature aging, including a haggard appearance	

Mostly Emotional and Behavioral

Difficulty concentrating	Anxiety
Nervousness	Depression
Crying	Forgetfulness, particularly about things not related to the task at hand
Anorexia	Restlessness
Declining interest in sex and romance	Frequent arguments with others
Feelings of hopelessness, despair, anger, and sadness	Withdrawal from people and listlessness
	Decrease in job performance, including increased tardiness and absenteeism

challenges and spurs us on to peak intellectual and physical performance. (The findings about the immune system, discussed later, support this conclusion.) An optimum amount of stress exists for most people and most tasks. In general, performance tends to be best under moderate amounts of stress. If stress is too great, people become temporarily ineffective because they may freeze or choke. Under too little stress, people may become lethargic and inattentive. Excessive stress can lower job performance because the stressed person makes errors in concentration and judgment.

The Consequences of Negative Stress

Negative stress has enormous consequences to employers as well as individuals. It has been estimated that American companies lose about $300 billion annually taking into account below-standard job performance, turnover, psychological depression, and high medical insurance costs.[4]

A major consequence of stress is that it affects our ability to fight infection. Two major findings emerged from an analysis of 300 studies over a thirty-year span. First, stress does alter immunity, as has been long theorized. Second, short-term stress boosts the immune system, functioning as an adaptive response preparing the body for injury or infection. Giving a public speech or class presentation are examples of short-term stress for most people. Yet long-term chronic stress causes too much wear and tear, breaking down the immune system. An example of a long-term chronic stress would be long-term unemployment.[5]

Another long-term negative consequence to extreme stress is posttraumatic stress disorder (PSTD), an anxiety condition in which the person is disturbed by an intense stressor from the past. Some workplace events that are capable of producing posttraumatic stress disorder include being shot by a robber, witnessing or being part of workplace violence, and observing a coworker being killed in an accident. A tornado or severe snowstorm can also traumatize a subset of employees. PSTD often results in the most negative stress symptoms, including poor concentration, poor sleep, and poor interpersonal relationships. A supervisor and coworkers who communicate an understanding of what the posttraumatic stress disorder sufferer is going through can be helpful.[6]

Overall Relationship between Stress and Job Performance

Figure 17-2 depicts the relationship between stress and performance, as already suggested by the difference between challenge and hindrance stressors. An exception to this

FIGURE 17-2

THE RELATIONSHIP BETWEEN STRESS AND JOB PERFORMANCE

Source: "THE RELATIONSHIP BETWEEN STRESS AND JOB PERFORMANCE" by Andrew J. DuBrin.

relationship is that certain negative forms of stress are likely to lower performance even if the stress is moderate. For example, the stress created by an intimidating boss or worrying about radiation poisoning—even in moderate amounts—will not improve performance.

Moderate stress is placed in the optimal performance zone as it is often created by challenge stressors. In this optimal zone, the body will experience an increase in heartbeat, breathing, and muscle tension, as well as increased physical strength. The mind will experience enhanced alertness and energy, sharper cognitive skills, more optimism and excitement—all leading to higher job productivity.[7] Creativity, an important part of performance in many jobs, tends to be higher under conditions of moderate or low stress.[8]

Burnout as a Consequence of Long-Term Stress

One of the major problems of prolonged stress is that it may lead to **burnout**, a condition of emotional, mental, and physical exhaustion in response to long-term job stressors. The exhaustion aspect of burnout can be triggered by such factors as a heavy physical workload, time pressures, and shift work.[9] Common symptoms of burnout include the following:

- Dreading to go to work in the morning
- Work activities enjoyable in the past that now feeling like drudgery
- Being envious of other people who are happy at work
- Caring less about doing a good job[10]
- Reduced personal accomplishment that is likely to last for years[11]

The burned-out person often becomes cynical. Burnout is most likely to occur among those whose jobs call for frequent and intense interactions with others, such as a social worker, teacher, or customer service representative. Yet people in other occupations also suffer from burnout, especially when not much support from others is present and the rewards are few.

Also, a hostile work environment, such as being harassed by coworkers and managers, is a major contributor to burnout. Students can also experience burnout because studying and preparing reports is hard work. Conscientiousness and perfectionism also contribute to burnout because people with these characteristics feel stressed when they do not accomplish everything they would like. Similarly, being obsessed about what you are doing can trigger burnout.

Burnout can be treated in many ways, just as with the negative effects of stress. Showing gratitude for hard work by employees is particularly helpful in preventing and treating burnout because many cases of burnout are caused by intense feelings of being unappreciated. As with other forms of stress, physical activity can alleviate many burnout symptoms.[12]

Burnout
a condition of emotional, mental, and physical exhaustion in response to long-term job stressors

Sources of Stress in Personal Life

◀ Learning Objective 17.3 ◀

Almost any form of frustration, disappointment, setback, inconvenience, or crisis in your personal life can cause stress. The list is dynamic because new sources of stress emerge continuously. For example, a prolonged downturn in the stock and bond markets can be a stressor for investors who previously paid little attention to how well their investments were performing. Our life stage also helps determine which events are stressors. A person building his or her career is more likely to be more stressed by a limited supply of jobs than a person nearing retirement. Presented next are major categories of stressful events in personal life.

1. Significant life change. A general stressor that encompasses both work and personal life is having to cope with significant change. According the pioneering research of Thomas Holmes and Richard Rahe, the necessity of a significant change in an individual's life pattern creates stress. When a major stressor strikes, such as being fired, you have to readjust. The more significant the change you have to cope with in a short period of time, the greater the probability of experiencing a stress disorder, leading to other medical problems.[13] Two such stressful changes are separation from a partner and personal injury or illness.

2. Low self-esteem. A subtle cause of stress is low self-esteem. People who do not feel good about themselves often find it difficult to feel good about anything. Low self-esteem has several links to stress. One is that being in a bad mood continually functions as a stressor. People with low self-esteem drag themselves down into a funk, which creates stress. Another link between low self-esteem and stress proneness is that people with low self-esteem get hurt more by insults. Instead of questioning the source of the criticism, the person with self-doubt will accept the opinion as valid. An insult accepted as valid acts as a stressor because it is a threat to our well-being.

Low self-esteem is linked to stress in yet another way. People with low self-esteem doubt their ability to work their way out of problems. As a result, minor challenges appear to be major problems. For example, a person with low self-esteem will often doubt he or she will be successful in conducting a job search. As a result, having to conduct a job search will represent a major stressor. A person with high self-esteem might feel better prepared mentally to accept the challenge. (As you will recall, your perception of an event influences whether it is stressful.)

3. Everyday annoyances. Managing everyday annoyances can have a greater impact on your health than major life catastrophes. Among these everyday annoyances are losing keys or a wallet, your hard drive crashing, being stuck in traffic, having your car break down on the way to an important event, and being lost on the way to an important appointment. A major reason everyday annoyances act as stressors is because they are frustrating: They block your path to an important goal, such as getting your work accomplished.

4. Social and family problems. Friends and family are the main sources of love and affection in your life, but they can also be the main source of stress. Most physical acts of violence are committed among friends and family members. One of the many reasons we encounter so much conflict with friends and family is that we are emotionally involved with them.

5. Physical and mental health problems. Prolonged stress produces physical and mental health problems, and the reverse is also true. Physical and mental illness can act as stressors: The fact of being ill is stressful. Furthermore, thinking that you might soon contract a life-threatening illness is stressful. If you receive a serious injury, that, too, can create stress.

6. Financial problems. A major life stressor is financial problems. Although you may not be obsessed with money, not having enough money to take care of what you consider the necessities of life can lead to anxiety and tension. If you do not have enough money to replace or repair a broken or faulty mobile device or automobile, the result can be stressful. A major stressor for recent graduates who move to areas with high costs of living is being unable to afford a comfortable place to live. Figure 17-3 suggests that money problems are the leading stressor, and that two other top stressors are linked to finances: Work and the economy and housing costs are part of the three leading stressors for Americans.

7. School-related problems. The life of a student can be stressful. Among the stressors to cope with are exams in subjects you do not understand well, having to write papers on subjects unfamiliar to you, working your way through the complexities of registration, and having to deal with instructors who do not see things your way. Another source of severe stress for some students is having too many competing demands on their time. On most campuses, you will find someone who works full-time, goes to school full-time, and has a family.

FIGURE 17-3

CAUSES OF STRESS IN AMERICA

Percentage of people who consider the potential stressor to be very or somewhat significant

Rank	Potential Stressor	Percentage
1	Money	64
2	Work	60
3	The economy	49
4	Family responsibilities	47
5	Personal health concerns	46

Source: "Causes of Stress in America". Adapted from "Paying with our Health," www.stressinamerica.org, American Psychological Association, February 4, 2015, p. 10.

PERSONALITY FACTORS CONTRIBUTING TO STRESS

Some people are more stress prone than others because of personality factors. Three key personality factors predisposing people to stress are type A behavior, a belief that external forces control their life, and negative affectivity.

Type A Behavior and Hostility

People with **type A behavior** characteristics have basic personalities that lead them into stressful situations. Type A behavior has two main components. One is a tendency to try to accomplish too many things in too little time. This leads the type A individual to be impatient and demanding. The other component is free-floating hostility. Because of this combined sense of urgency and hostility, trivial things irritate these people. On the job, people with type A behavior are aggressive and hardworking. Off the job, they keep themselves preoccupied with all kinds of errands to run and things to do.

　　Certain features of the type A behavior pattern are related to coronary heart disease. Hostility, anger, cynicism, and suspiciousness lead to heart problems, whereas impatience, ambition, and being work driven are not associated with coronary disease. One study showed that men who received a high score on a personality test about hostility were much more likely to develop coronary heart disease several years later.[14] Many work-driven people who like what they are doing—including many business executives—are remarkably healthy and outlive less competitive people. In reference to heart disease, medical and clinical psychologist David Krantz concluded, "You can be ambitious. You can be time pressured. But if you're not hostile and angry, your risk is lower."[15]

Type A behavior
personality characteristics that lead a person into stressful situations. Type A behavior has two main components: (1) the tendency to try to accomplish too many things in too little time and (2) free-floating hostility

Belief in External Locus of Control

If you believe that your fate is controlled more by external than internal forces, you are probably more susceptible to stress. People with an **external locus of control** believe that external forces control their fate. Conversely, people with an **internal locus of control** believe that fate is pretty much under their control. The link between locus of control and stress works in this manner: If people believe they can control adverse forces, they are less prone to the stressor of worrying about them. For example, if you believe that you can always find a job, you will worry less about unemployment. At the same time, the person who believes in an internal locus of control experiences a higher level of job satisfaction. Work is less stressful and more satisfying when you perceive it to be under your control.

　　The everyday problem of lost computer files illustrates the importance of an internal locus of control. When a hard drive crashes or a valuable file is lost in some other way, the "external" person blames the computer or the software for the stressful event.

External locus of control
individual's belief that external forces control his or her fate

Internal locus of control
individual's belief that fate is pretty much under his or her own control

An "internal," in contrast, would most likely have created backup files along the way. So when a crash occurs, the person is less stressed because relatively little data has been lost.

What about your locus of control? Do you believe it to be internal? Or is it external?

Negative Affectivity

A major contributor to being stress prone is **negative affectivity**, a tendency to experience aversive (intensely disliked) emotional states. Such negative personalities seem to search for discrepancies between what they would like and what exists. Instead of attempting to solve problems, they look for them. Although negative affectivity is a relatively stable personality characteristic, the circumstances a person faces can trigger such behavior.[16] For example, a four-hour wait in an airplane parked on the tarmac might trigger a person's mild tendencies toward negative affectivity.

Negative affectivity
a tendency to experience aversive (intensely disliked) emotional states; predisposition to experience emotional stress that includes feelings of nervousness, tension, and worry

▶ Learning Objective 17.4 ▶

Key Sources of Work Stress

No job is without potential stressors for some people. A survey indicated that work is the major source of stress for Americans, with 74 percent of respondents reporting that work is their top stressor.[17] But when work is lacking stressful elements, it may not have enough challenge to prompt employees to achieve high performance. Figure 17-4 illustrates six major job stressors you might encounter or have already encountered.

FIGURE 17-4

FREQUENT JOB STRESSORS

Source: "FREQUENT JOB STRESSORS" by Andrew J. DuBrin.

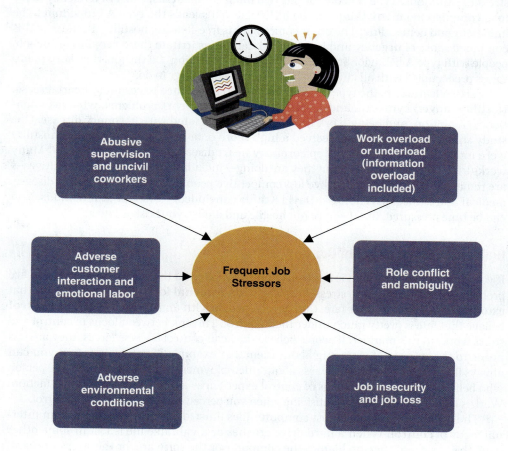

WORK OVERLOAD OR UNDERLOAD

A heavy workload is a widely acknowledged source of job stress. **Role overload**, a burdensome workload, can create stress for a person in two ways. First, the person may become fatigued and thus be less able to tolerate annoyances and irritations. Think of how much easier it is to become provoked over a minor incident when you lack proper rest. Second, a person subject to unreasonable work demands may feel perpetually behind schedule, a situation that itself creates an uncomfortable, stressful feeling. A powerful stressor for knowledge workers is information overload, as described in Chapter 8 about communication in organizations.

A factor contributing to stress is the work-more economy in which many workers take on extra responsibilities and in some cases perform two jobs yet are paid for one. This approach to workforce management usually comes about because a company has suffered from a business downturn and attempts to control costs by maintaining a lean workforce. Many employers give their employees more responsibility to compensate for the void created by laid-off coworkers, hiring freezes, and new business growth. Companies began trimming down their workforces in the 1990s, then demanding more from the survivors, with the trend continuing today.[17]

Another form of work overload is demanding higher and higher speed from workers. Speed is important to companies because delivering goods and services very quickly brings a competitive edge. The most stressful situation occurs when a company downsizes and the remaining workers are expected to carry a heavier workload at a faster pace than previously. The combination of additional responsibility and high speed can be a major stressor. Among the problems are that hurried employees have very little time to ask for help or to carefully study what they are doing.

A disruptive amount of stress can also occur when people experience **role underload**, or too little to do. Some people find role underload frustrating because it is a normal human desire to want to work toward self-fulfillment. Also, making a contribution on the job is one way of gaining self-esteem. Some people, however, find it relaxing not to have much to do on the job. One direct benefit is that it preserves their energy for family and leisure activities.

ROLE CONFLICT AND ROLE AMBIGUITY

Being pulled in two directions is a classic stressor. **Role conflict** refers to having to choose between two competing demands or expectations. Many workers receive conflicting demands from two or more managers. Imagine being told by your manager to give top priority to one project. You then receive an e-mail message from your manager's manager, who tells you to drop everything and work on another project. It's often up to you to resolve such a conflict. If you don't, you will experience stress. Having to choose between taking care of job responsibilities versus personal responsibilities is another potent type of role conflict, such as having to work the night when a good friend is getting married. Do you upset your boss or your good friend?

Not being certain of what they should be doing is a stressor for many people. **Role ambiguity** is a condition in which the job holder receives confusing or poorly defined expectations. A typical complaint is "I'm not really sure I know what I'm supposed to be doing around here." Role ambiguity is related to job control. If you lack a clear picture of what you should be doing, it is difficult to get your job under control.

In addition to creating stress, role conflict and role ambiguity can have a negative impact on organizational citizenship behavior, as suggested by a synthesis of forty-two studies. Apparently the anxiety and discomfort associated with role conflict and role ambiguity distract a person from being a good organizational citizen. The researchers

Role overload
a burdensome workload that creates stress for a person in two ways: (1) The person may become fatigued and less able to tolerate annoyances and irritations, and (2) a person subject to unreasonable work demands may feel perpetually behind schedule, a situation that itself creates an uncomfortable, stressful feeling

Role underload
disruptive amount of stress that can occur when people experience too little to do

Role conflict
having to choose between two competing demands or expectations

Role ambiguity
condition in which the job holder receives confusing or poorly defined expectations

involved in the analysis concluded that employers wishing to encourage more organizational citizenship behavior may want to consider steps to reduce role conflict and ambiguity. Employees should be provided with clearly defined descriptions of job duties and expectations.[18]

JOB INSECURITY AND JOB LOSS

Worrying about losing your job is a major stressor. Even when jobs are plentiful, having to search for another job and facing the prospect of geographic relocation are stressors for many people. Downsizings and corporate mergers—which usually result in downsizing to eliminate duplication in positions—have contributed to job insecurity. The anticipation of layoffs among employees can increase negative stress and lower job performance. In addition, the survivors of a downsizing often experience pressure from the fear of future job cuts, loss of friends, and worry about a sudden increase in workload.

Job loss is a more intense stressor than job insecurity because it is compounded by the stressors of financial problems, decreased status, and blows to the self-esteem. Negative confrontations with creditors might also add to the stress. Furthermore, homelessness might follow job loss, creating a gigantic stressor.

ADVERSE ENVIRONMENTAL CONDITIONS

A variety of adverse organizational conditions are stressors, as identified by the National Institute of Occupational Safety and Health. Several of these adverse conditions are listed below.

1. **Unpleasant or dangerous physical conditions.**   Examples are crowding, noise, air pollution, or ergonomic problems. Steady exposure to *noise pollution* has been associated with high blood pressure and fatal heart attacks.[19] Examples of noise pollution include that created by the constant beeping sound required to be emitted from forklift trucks and construction vehicles, and the beeping noises of electronic devices.

2. **Poor interpersonal relationships.**   Having poor relationships with coworkers and a manager might also contribute to physical problems because of the associated stress. When the poor relationships create conflict, job stress is almost inevitable because conflict leads to stress.

3. **Carpal tunnel syndrome.**   A repetitive-motion disorder most frequently associated with keyboarding and the use of optical scanners is **carpal tunnel syndrome**. The syndrome occurs when repetitive flexing and extension of the wrist causes the tendons to swell, thus trapping and pinching the median nerve. Carpal tunnel syndrome creates stress because of the pain and misery. The thoughts of having to permanently leave a job requiring keyboarding is another potential stressor. Some of the risk factors for carpal tunnel syndrome include pregnancy, obesity, smoking, a previous wrist injury, or arthritis.[20]

Carpal tunnel syndrome
repetitive-motion disorder most frequently associated with keyboarding and the use of optical scanners; occurs when repetitive flexing and extension of the wrist causes the tendons to swell, thus trapping and pinching the median nerve

Repetitive-motion disorders can be prevented somewhat by computer workers taking frequent rest breaks and using a well-designed combination of the worktable, chair, and monitor. Wearing elasticized wrist bands provides enough support to the wrist tendons to prevent many cases of repetitive-motion disorders. Many people who blame their job for having caused carpal tunnel syndrome fail to recognize that they spend perhaps an additional four hours per evening on the keyboard for purposes such as e-mailing friends and visiting websites.

FIGURE 17-5

HOW TO MINIMIZE CUMULATIVE TRAUMA DISORDER

Source: "HOW TO MINIMIZE CUMULATIVE TRAUMA DISORDER" by Andrew J. DuBrin.

An Ergonomic Workstation

- Keep the screen below your eye level.
- Keep your elbows on the same level with home-key row, with your wrists and lower arms parallel to floor.
- Support your back and thighs with a well-constructed chair.
- Position your feet flat on the floor.
- Use lamp to supplement inadequate room lighting.

Being comfortable while working prevents much physical strain. Figure 17-5 presents the basics of a workstation designed on *ergonomic* principles. (Ergonomics has to do with making machines and equipment fit human capabilities and demands.)

ADVERSE CUSTOMER INTERACTION AND EMOTIONAL LABOR

Interactions with customers can be a major stressor. Part of the problem is that the sales associate often feels helpless when placed in conflict with a customer. The sales associate is told that "the customer is always right." Furthermore, the store manager usually sides with the customer in a dispute with the sales associate. Industrial sales representatives might also face adverse customer interaction, such as a customer complaining harshly that a recently purchased machine or software system does not work correctly.

Related to adverse customer interaction is the stressor of having to control the expression of emotion to please or to avoid displeasing a customer. Imagine having to smile at a customer who belittles you or makes unwanted sexual advances. Alicia A. Grandey, associate professor of psychology at Penn State University, defines **emotional labor** as the process of regulating both feelings and expressions to meet organizational goals.[21] The process involves both surface acting and deep acting. Surface acting means faking expressions, such as smiling, whereas deep acting involves changing feelings, such as suppressing anger toward a customer you perceive to be annoying.

Deep acting is often better than surface acting in terms of warding off the potential problems of emotional labor. For example, a study with bus drivers indicated that when they engaged in surface acting to deal with nasty passengers, the emotional state of the drivers worsened. Yet, when the drivers engaged in deep-level acting, they did not experience many problems of emotional withdrawal from work.[22] A later study with seventy-eight bus drivers found that surface acting had negative consequences for home life. The

Emotional labor
process of regulating both feelings and expressions to meet organizational goals

three problems noted were emotional exhaustion, work-to-family conflict, and insomnia.[23]

Sales workers and customer service representatives often experience emotional labor because so often they have to fake facial expressions and feelings to please customers. Nevertheless, according to one study, the top five occupations in terms of emotional labor demands are (1) police and sheriff's patrol officers, (2) social workers, (3) psychiatrists, (4) supervisors of police and detectives, and (5) registered nurses. Bill and account collectors ranked 15![24]

Engaging in emotional labor for prolonged periods of time can lead to job dissatisfaction, stress, and burnout. A contributing cause is that faking expressions and emotions takes a physiological toll, such as the intestines churning. Workers who engage in emotional labor may also develop cardiovascular problems and weakened immune systems.

Workers can avoid many of the problems associated with emotional labor if they have good emotional intelligence in the form of being able to recognize the emotions of a customer, client, or patient. For example, if the industrial sales representative can detect that the complaining customer is frightened about a system failure, the representative can reassure the customer that the problem will soon be under control. A study with nurses and police officers in Germany and Holland demonstrated the importance of recognizing the other person's emotional state. It was found that emotional labor did not always lower a worker's commitment to the organization, providing the police officers and nurses could correctly identify the interaction partner's emotions. (The interaction partner in this case would be the citizen interacting with the police office or the patient interacting with the nurse.)[25]

ABUSIVE SUPERVISION AND UNCIVIL COWORKERS

Being mistreated by a supervisor or coworkers can be a major workplace stressor. Bullying and incivility have already been described in Chapters 9 and 10. Here we mention their stress consequences. What constitutes abusive supervision depends on the perception of subordinates. Supervisors who are abusive are perceived to engage in sustained hostile verbal and nonverbal behaviors, excluding physical contact. Sexual harassment by the supervisor would be considered abusive, as would be insulting a subordinate's appearance. In many cases of supervisors being abusive, the norms of the organization encourage dealing with employees aggressively, including showing very little sympathy.

Recipients of abusive supervision are likely to report high levels of psychological distress. In addition, the recipients of abusive supervision are likely to be irritable, anxious, and depressed, and to experience physical complaints such as chest pains.[26] A woman in her twenties who reported to a supervisor she perceived to be abusive said, "I think Beth (her supervisor) just hates me. She always finds errors in my work. She wrote me up for wearing clothing to the office that others in the group also wear."

The stress resulting from incivility can result in higher absenteeism, increased turnover, less cooperation, and more complaints to management. Studies conducted by incivility researchers Christine Porath and Christine Pearson have shown some of the stress-related negative consequences of coworker incivility. Among those workers who have been on the receiving end of incivility, 80 percent lost time worrying about the incident, and 25 percent admitted to taking their frustration out on customers.[27]

Fortunately, incivility and its negative consequences for stress can sometimes be reduced through training. A study, conducted with 1,173 healthcare workers who underwent a six-month training program to reduce incivility, focused on the healthcare employees working with facilitators on issues related to civil interactions in their work units. The workers who participated in the program reported greater increases in civility and decreases in incivility in their work units, compared to those who were not trained.[28]

Several Effective Approaches to Managing Stress

Because potentially harmful stressors surround us in work and personal life, virtually everybody needs a program of stress management to stay well. Stress management techniques are placed here into four categories: attacking the source of the stress, receiving social support, relaxation techniques, and wellness through proper exercise, diet, and rest. Your challenge is to select those techniques that best fit your circumstances and preferences. You should also be seeking the amount of stress that enables you to capitalize on the benefits of positive stress but not fall prey to the negative symptoms of stress.

DEALING WITH STRESS BY ATTACKING ITS SOURCE

Stress can be dealt with in the short range by indirect techniques such as exercise and relaxation. But to manage stress in the long range and stay well, you must also learn to deal directly with stressors. Many stress management programs ignore this reality. Several of these techniques are described in the next few paragraphs.

Eliminating or Modifying the Stressor

The most potent method of managing stress is to eliminate the stressor giving you trouble. For example, if your job is your primary stressor, your stress level would be reduced if you found a more comfortable job. At other times, modifying the stressful situation can be equally helpful. Using a problem-solving method, you search for an alternative that will change the stressor, such as finding a less congested route to work.

Placing the Stressful Situation in Perspective

Stress comes about because of our perception of the situation. If you can alter your perception of a threatening situation, you are attacking the source. A potentially stressful situation can be put into perspective by asking, "What is the worst thing that could happen to me if I fail in this activity?" The answer to this question is found by asking a series of questions, starting with the grimmest possibility. For instance, you are late with a report that is due this afternoon. Consider the following questions and answers:

- Will my reputation be damaged permanently? (*No*)

- Will I get fired? (*No*)

- Will I get reprimanded? (*Perhaps, but not for sure*)

- Will my boss think less of me? (*Perhaps, but not for sure*)

Only if the answer is yes to either of the first two questions is negative stress truly justified. This thought process allows stressful situations to be properly evaluated and kept in perspective. You therefore avoid the stress that comes from overreacting to a situation.

An analysis of many studies concludes that the most effective approaches to managing workplace stress are **cognitive–behavioral interventions**, essentially a way of thinking constructively about a problem that includes perspective setting. Cognitive–behavioral interventions teach individuals to recognize how their pessimistic and often distorted thoughts of gloom and doom become stressors. Next, they learn to replace their unrealistic and highly pessimistic thinking with more realistic or more optimistic thinking.[29] Visualize an international marketing director who has a fear of flying and consequently suffers

Cognitive–behavioral interventions
a way of thinking constructively about a problem that includes perspective setting

enormous stress each time she has to take a business trip by airplane. She must learn to conquer her pessimistic outlook on flying with more positive thoughts about airline safety.

Gaining Control of the Situation

Feeling that a bothersome situation is out of control is almost a universal stressor. A key method of stress management is therefore to attack the stressor by gaining control of the situation. A multipurpose way of gaining control is to improve your work habits and time management. By being "on top of things," you can make heavy work and school demands less stressful. A trend related to reducing stress by gaining control is to simplify your life by getting rid of unessential activities and possessions. You will gain control of your life situation by having less clutter.

A note of caution is that an oversimplified life can also be an impoverished life, creating stress of its own. Throw out or give to charity those physical possessions that contribute virtually nothing to your life. Yet save the sources of an enriched life. For example, why give up a smartphone, an HD TV, and running shoes if all three are major sources of pleasure and satisfaction?

RECEIVING SOCIAL SUPPORT

Support system

a group of people on whom one can rely for encouragement and comfort

An ideal way to manage stress is one that provides side benefits. Getting close to people falls into this category. You will reduce some stress symptoms and form healthy relationships with others in the process. By getting close to others, you build a **support system**, a group of people on whom you can rely for encouragement and comfort. The trusting relationship you have with these people is critically important. People within your support network include family members, friends, coworkers, and fellow students. In addition, some people in turmoil reach out to strangers to discuss personal problems. According to neuroscientist Steven W. Porges, engaging socially with others triggers neural circuits that calm the heart, relax the intestines, and dampen fear.[30] (Interacting with friendly people is likely to be more beneficial than interacting with hostile individuals.)

A happy marriage is another support system that can help a worker cope with job stress. According to one study with dual-earner couples, happily married women rebounded quicker from daily stress than women with less blissful unions. Stress was measured by saliva samples of the stress-related hormone cortisol.[31]

RECEIVING ORGANIZATIONAL SUPPORT

Receiving organizational support refers here to using the organization as part of your support system when experiencing heavy stress. The support might come from a friendly supervisor who will listen to the problems you are experiencing and perhaps offer some advice. A widely used form of support is an employee assistance program that offers counseling services for a variety of personal problems that could be impairing performance. The five most common employee assistance program services used by companies are job stress, substance abuse, bereavement, work and personal life balance, and relationship counseling.[32] A large employer might have a full-time employee assistance program, whereas small employers use an outside counseling group.

Wellness program

a company-sponsored activity designed to support employees as they learn and sustain behaviors that reduce health risk, improve quality of life, and enhance personal effectiveness

Company-sponsored wellness programs have a variety of offerings useful in combating the adverse effects of stress, including stress management workshops. A **wellness program** is a company-sponsored activity designed to support employees as they learn and sustain behaviors that reduce health risk, improve quality of life, and enhance personal effectiveness. As employees become emotionally and physically healthy, illness-related costs for the employer often decrease.[33] Some companies incorporate an employee assistance program into the wellness program.

Among the components of a wellness program linked to stress management are onsite physical exercise facilities, smoking cessation programs, nondenominational chaplain service, and nutrition classes. Another approach to most of these activities is to place them online, such as a step-by-step physical exercise program. Apps related to wellness have surged in popularity. Many smartphone apps focus on wellness activities, such as tracking steps walked in a day. A growing number of apps, however, are designed to measure chronic diseases including diabetes and high blood pressure.[34]

Closely related to the apps are wearable fitness tracking devices in the form of bracelets that measure physical activity, burned-off calories, and heart rate. Gregory Welk, a professor of kinesiology at Iowa State University, has tested these devices and claims that they are quite often inaccurate.[35]

RELAXATION TECHNIQUES FOR HANDLING STRESS

"Relax" is the advice many people have always offered the stressed individual. Stress experts give us similar advice but also offer specific techniques. Here we describe three techniques that can help you relax and, consequently, help you reduce stress and its symptoms. In addition, Figure 17-6 lists a variety of "stress busters," many of which are relaxation oriented. Recognize that many of these techniques contribute directly to wellness and that stress management is a major component of wellness. Pick and choose among stress management techniques until you find several that effectively reduce your stress.

Relaxation Response

A standard technique for reducing stress is to achieve the relaxation response. The **relaxation response** is a physical state of deep rest in which you experience a slower respiration and heart rate and lowered metabolism. Scientists have shown that the

Relaxation response
a physical state of deep rest in which one experiences a slower respiration and heart rate, lowered blood pressure, and lowered metabolism; a standard technique for reducing stress

FIGURE 17-6

STRESS BUSTERS

Source: "STRESS BUSTERS" by Andrew J. DuBrin.

- Take a nap when facing heavy pressures. Napping is regarded as one of the most effective techniques for reducing and preventing stress.
- Give in to your emotions. If you are angry, disgusted, or confused, admit your feelings. Suppressing your emotions adds to stress.
- Take a brief break from the stressful situation and do something small and constructive, such as washing your car, emptying a wastebasket, or getting a haircut.
- Get a massage, because it can loosen tight muscles, improve your blood circulation, and calm you down.
- Get help with your stressful task from a coworker, boss, or friend.
- Concentrate intensely on reading, surfing the Internet, a sport, or a hobby. Contrary to common sense, concentration is at the heart of stress reduction.
- Take a leisurely day off from your routine, or at least take a brief walk during a particularly stressful day.
- Finish something you have started, however small. Accomplishing almost anything reduces some stress.
- Stop to smell the flowers; make friends with a young child or an elderly person.
- Strive to do a good job but not a perfect job.
- Work with your hands, doing a pleasant task.
- Hug somebody you like and who you think will hug you back.
- Find somebody or something that makes you laugh, and have a good laugh.
- Minimize drinking caffeinated or alcoholic beverages, and drink fruit juice or water instead. Grab a piece of fruit rather than an alcoholic beverage or energy drink.

relaxation response lowers the heart rate, blood pressure, and oxygen consumption. Also, the relaxation response alleviates symptoms associated with many disorders and conditions, including hypertension, arthritis, insomnia, depression, infertility, cancer, anxiety, and even aging. By practicing the relaxation response, you can counteract the fight-or-flight response associated with stress.

According to cardiologist and pioneer in mind–body medicine Herbert Benson, four things are necessary to practice the relaxation response: a quiet environment, an object to focus on, a passive attitude, and a comfortable position. You are supposed to practice the relaxation response for ten to twenty minutes, twice a day. To evoke the relaxation response, Benson advises you to close your eyes. Relax. Concentrate on one word or prayer. If other thoughts come to mind, be passive and return to the repetition.

The relaxation response can be released in many ways besides the ritual just described. Among these methods are participating in repetitive sports such as running, progressive muscular relaxation, practicing yoga, and playing a musical instrument.[36]

Similar to any other relaxation technique, the relaxation response is harmless and works for most people. However, some very impatient people find it annoying to disrupt their busy day to work through the relaxation response. Unfortunately, these may be the people who most urgently need to learn to relax.

Meditation

Meditation
a systematic method of concentration, reflection, or concentrated thinking designed to suppress the activity of the sympathetic nervous system

Perhaps the oldest stress management technique of all, meditation is back in vogue. **Meditation** is a systematic method of concentration, reflection, or concentrated thinking designed to suppress the activity of the sympathetic nervous system. The relaxation response is a meditation technique, and napping provides some of the benefits of meditation. The meditator reaches a deep state of mental and physical calmness and relaxation, driving away accumulated stress. Meditation is also recommended as a way of preventing and slowing down and reducing the pain of chronic diseases such as heart disease, AIDS, and cancer. People who meditate learn to tolerate everyday annoyances better. Meditation has been widely researched, and its key benefits in relation to stress include calming the mind and eliminating anxiety.[37]

A very important benefit of meditation as well as other relaxation techniques is that they enhance mental alertness. It would therefore be beneficial to you to meditate shortly before you need to perform at your best, such as giving a presentation to management about your project. The relaxation response and meditation are quite similar to the more modern approach of *mindfulness,* in which people learn to concentrate on the moment to reduce stress and sharpen their focus. Meditation is now often referred to as *mindfulness meditation.*

The usual approach to meditation involves four simple steps. First, find a quiet place with a minimum of distractions. Second, close your eyes so that you can close yourself off from the outside world. Third, pick a word whose sound is soothing when repeated. Fourth, say the word repeatedly. For most people, one fifteen-minute session daily will accomplish the benefits of meditation. (You will notice the similarity to the relaxation response, which is a form of meditation.) It is also possible to learn to meditate through online podcasts, videos, and mobile apps. An online search will reveal several of these approaches, for example, www.getsomeheadspace.com.

MANAGING STRESS BY STAYING WELL (PROPER EXERCISE, DIET, AND REST)

A far-reaching strategy for managing stress is to both prevent and reduce negative stress by leading a healthy lifestyle, or being well. Three major components to staying well are proper exercise, diet, and rest. The three components are interrelated because each component facilitates the other: For example, if you exercise enough you tend to prefer healthy food; if you diet properly, physical exercise is easier, and so is obtaining rest. Also, if you rest well, you will be in a better frame of mind to exercise, and you will not crave so much caffeine and sugar to stay energized. Proper diet and exercise are also important in helping ward off physical illness that creates stress for the individual.

Exercising Properly, Including Yoga

The right amount and type of physical exercise contributes substantially to wellness. Part of the reason exercise is useful for managing stress is that it contributes to relaxation and being better able to cope with frustration. To achieve wellness, it is important to select an exercise program that is physically challenging but that does not lead to overexertion and muscle injury. Competitive sports, if taken too seriously, can actually increase a person's stress level. The most beneficial exercises are classified as aerobic because they make you breathe faster and raise your heart rate. Most of a person's exercise requirements can be met through everyday techniques such as walking or running up stairs, vigorous housework, yard work, or walking several miles per day. Another potential disadvantage of excessive physical exercise is that it makes you so hungry that you overeat.

A major benefit is the euphoria that often occurs when brain chemicals called *endorphins* are released into the body. The same experience is referred to as "runner's high." Other mental benefits of exercise include increased self-confidence; improved body image and self-esteem; improved mental functioning, alertness, and efficiency; release of accumulated tensions; and relief from mild depression.[38]

Millions of people seek to reduce and prevent stress though yoga, which is both physical exercise and a way of developing mental attitudes that calm the body and the mind. During yoga, blood pressure lowers and your heart works more efficiently. One of yoga's many worthwhile goals is to solder a union between the mind and body, thereby achieving harmony and tranquility. Another benefit of yoga is that it helps people place aside negative thoughts that act as stressors. Yoga can therefore reduce anxiety, with the key being deep, slow breathing, as follows:

> Breathe through your nose, drawing air down into your lungs as you expand your diaphragm. As you relax and exhale, the diaphragm contracts. The process controls the pace of your breathing and creates a natural calmness.[39]

Unlike the relaxation response and mild exercise, yoga has some potentially severe negative consequences to the body. Yoga should be first practiced under the guidance of a certified professional to minimize torn muscles and ruptured blood vessels from extreme bending and twisting.[40]

Resting Sufficiently

Rest offers benefits similar to those of exercise, such as stress reduction, improved concentration, improved energy, and better tolerance for frustration. Achieving proper rest is closely linked to getting proper exercise. The current interest in adult napping reflects the awareness that proper rest makes a person less stress prone and enhances productivity. A growing number of firms have napping facilities for workers, and many workers nap at their desks or in their parked vehicles during lunch breaks. Naps of about twenty minutes taken during the workday are used both as energizers and as stress reducers. To keep the effectiveness of workday napping in perspective, workers who achieve sufficient rest during normal sleeping hours have less need for naps during working hours. But the meditation-like benefits of napping offer an advantage even for the person who sleeps adequately at night.

Maintaining a Healthy Diet

Eating nutritious foods is valuable for mental as well as physical health, making it easier to cope with frustrations that are potential stressors. Many nutritionists and physicians believe that eating fatty foods, such as red meat, contributes to colon cancer. Improper diet, such as consuming less than 1,300 calories per day, can weaken you physically.

FIGURE 17-7

DIETARY GUIDELINES FOR AMERICANS DEVELOPED BY THE U.S. DEPARTMENT OF AGRICULTURE

Source: Dietary Guidelines for Americans Developed by the United States Department of Agriculture.

In turn, you become more susceptible to stress. Some nonnutritious foods, such as those laden with caffeine or sugar, tend to enhance stress levels. According to the Dietary Guidelines of the U.S. Department of Agriculture, a healthy diet is one that

- Emphasizes fruits, vegetables, whole grains, and fat-free or low-fat milk and milk products

- Includes lean meats, poultry, fish, beans, eggs, and nuts

- Is low in saturated fats, trans fats, cholesterol, salt (sodium), and added sugars

These recommendations are for the general public over two years of age and are updated every five years. They are similar to a wealth of scientific research supporting the idea that healthy nutrition depends on a balanced diet consisting of the basic food groups of fruits, vegetables, grains, protein, and dairy. Consult www.ChooseMyPlate.gov, as shown in Figure 17-7.

Alcohol, as in beer, wine, and liquor, consumed in excess is detrimental to physical and mental health. Yet, long-term research at Harvard University and other places as well indicates a key role for the *moderate* use of alcohol. About the amount of two alcoholic beverages daily is associated with reduced risk of many causes of mortality and may help to keep cognitive functioning intact with age.[41] For those opposed to alcohol, the consumption of moderate amounts of dark chocolate apparently provides similar benefits.

▶ **Learning Objective 17.6** ▶

Two Key Perspectives on Understanding and Dealing with Personal Problems

Our approach to understanding and overcoming personal problems will be to first describe self-defeating behavior in general and how to reverse the trend. Personal problems refer to issues people deal with that create trouble for them but are not necessarily emotional illness or personality disorders We then emphasize the importance of resilience in dealing with personal problems.

SELF-DEFEATING BEHAVIOR

Many problems on the job and in personal life arise because of factors beyond our control. Many personal problems, nevertheless, arise because of **self-defeating behavior**. A person with self-defeating tendencies intentionally or unintentionally engages in activities or harbors attitudes that work against his or her best interest.[42] Dropping out of school for no reason other than being bored with studying is one of many possible examples. In short, self-defeating behavior means the same as being your own worst enemy.

On the job, self-defeating behavior typically takes the form of counterproductive work behaviors, or purposeful acts that harm or are intended to harm individuals of the organization.[43] Examples of counterproductive behavior include wasting supplies, being habitually late for meetings, or disrupting a meeting by telling jokes and personal stories

A group of self-defeating behaviors that might escape your attention are **soft addictions**, or ordinary behavior that if done to excess can wreak havoc with your life. Soft addictions often take the form of habits or compulsions that drain your time and money, although they may seem harmless at first.[44] In our complex world, there are extensive opportunities for developing soft addictions. Here are a few examples, and you could probably easily add more to the list:

- Making a purchase from a soft-drink vending machine or carry-out café several times a day

- Watching television or playing video games for so many hours that interaction with people and getting household chores done or studying (or self-improvement) suffers

- Engaging in physical exercise so frequently that you suffer frequent injuries and lack the time to get other things in life accomplished

- Devoting endless hours to being in contact with hundreds of "friends" and "followers" on social networking sites

- Daydreaming excessively

To examine your present tendencies toward self-defeating behavior, take the self-sabotage quiz presented in Human Relations Self-Assessment Quiz 17-1. Taking the quiz will help alert you to many self-imposed behaviors and attitudes that could potentially harm your career and personal life.

Overcoming self-defeating behavior requires hard work and patience. Here we present four widely applicable strategies for overcoming and preventing self-defeating behavior. Pick and choose among them to fit your particular circumstance and personal style.

Solicit Feedback on Your Actions

Feedback is essential for monitoring whether you are sabotaging your career or personal life. A starting point is to listen carefully to any direct or indirect comments from your superiors, subordinates, coworkers, customers, and friends about how you are coming across to them. For example, if three different people comment about you looking bored with the work, perhaps you are not projecting enough energy and enthusiasm.

When someone provides any feedback, respond in this fashion: "Please continue. This is very useful." Do not attack the giver of negative feedback. You asked for it, and the person is truly doing you a favor.

Self-defeating behavior
activities or attitudes that work against one's best interest

Soft addiction
ordinary behavior that if done to excess can wreak havoc with one's life

Human Relations Self-Assessment Quiz   17-1

The Self-Sabotage Questionnaire

Indicate how accurately each of the following statements describes or characterizes you, using a 5-point scale: (0) very inaccurately, (1) inaccurately, (2) midway between inaccurately and accurately, (3) accurately, (4) very accurately. Consider discussing some of the questions with a family member, close friend, or work associate. Another person's feedback may prove helpful in providing accurate answers to some of the questions.

		Answer
1.	Other people have said that I am my own worst enemy.	_____
2.	If I don't do a perfect job, I feel worthless.	_____
3.	I am my own harshest critic.	_____
4.	When engaged in a sport or other competitive activity, I find a way to blow a substantial lead right near the end.	_____
5.	When I make a mistake, I can usually identify another person to blame.	_____
6.	I have a strong tendency to procrastinate.	_____
7.	I have trouble focusing on what is really important to me.	_____
8.	I have trouble taking criticism, even from friends.	_____
9.	My fear of seeming stupid often prevents me from asking questions or offering my opinion.	_____
10.	I tend to expect the worst in most situations.	_____
11.	Many times I have rejected people who treat me well.	_____
12.	When I have an important project to complete, I usually get sidetracked and then miss the deadline.	_____
13.	I choose work assignments that lead to disappointments, even when better options are clearly available.	_____
14.	I frequently misplace things, such as my keys, and then get very angry at myself.	_____
15.	I am concerned that if I take on much more responsibility people will expect too much from me.	_____
16.	I avoid situations, such as competitive sports, where people can find out how good or bad I really am.	_____
17.	People describe me as the "office clown."	_____
18.	I have an insatiable demand for money and power.	_____
19.	When negotiating with others, I hate to grant any concessions.	_____
20.	I seek revenge for even the smallest hurts.	_____
21.	I have an overwhelming ego.	_____
22.	When I receive a compliment or other form of recognition, I usually feel I don't deserve it.	_____
23.	To be honest, I choose to suffer.	_____
24.	I regularly enter into conflict with people who try to help me.	_____
25.	I'm a loser.	_____
	Total Score	_____

Scoring and Interpretation:

Total your answers to all the questions to obtain your score.

0–25 You appear to have very few tendencies toward self-sabotage. If this interpretation is supported by your own positive feelings toward your life and yourself, you are in good shape with respect to self-defeating behavior tendencies. However, stay alert to potential self-sabotaging tendencies that could develop at later stages in your life.

26–50	You may have some mild tendencies toward self-sabotage. It could be that you do things occasionally that defeat your own purposes. Review actions you have taken during the past six months to decide if any of them have been self-sabotaging.
51–75	You show signs of engaging in self-sabotage. You probably have thoughts and carry out actions that could be blocking you from achieving important work and personal goals. If you scored in this range, carefully study the suggestions offered in this chapter.
76–100	You most likely have a strong tendency toward self-sabotage. (Sometimes it is possible to obtain a high score on a test like this because you are going through an unusually stressful period in your life.) Study this section of the chapter carefully and look for useful hints for removing self-imposed barriers to your success. Equally important, you might discuss your tendencies toward undermining your own achievements with a mental health professional.

Source: "The Self-Sabotage Questionnaire" by Andrew J. DuBrin.

Learn to Profit from Criticism

Learning to profit from criticism is necessary to benefit from feedback. Furthermore, to ignore valid criticism can be self-defeating. People who benefit from criticism are able to stand outside themselves while being criticized. It is as if they are watching the criticism from a distance and looking for its possible merits. People who take criticism personally experience anguish when receiving negative feedback. Listening to the criticism without being defensive is equally important. An example of a defensive comment in response to criticism would be "Why are you criticizing me when all the other team members are doing the same thing?" You are less likely to be defensive if you cool down before responding to the criticism.

Ask politely for more details about the negative behavior in question so that you can change if change is warranted. If your boss is criticizing you for being rude with customers, you might respond, "I certainly don't want to be rude. Can you give me a couple of examples of how I was rude? I need your help in working on this problem." After asking questions, you can better determine if the criticism is valid.

Stop Denying the Existence of Problems

Many people sabotage their careers because they deny the existence of a problem and therefore do not take appropriate action. Denial takes place as a defensive maneuver against a painful reality. An example of a self-sabotaging form of denial is to ignore the importance of upgrading one's credentials despite overwhelming evidence that it is necessary. Some people never quite complete a degree program that has become an informal qualification for promotion. Consequently, they sabotage their chances of receiving a promotion for which they are otherwise qualified.

Observe the Discrepancy between Your Ideal Life and What Exists Now

Motivational speaker Kevin Hogan recommends that you write a description of your ideal life. Describe in specific terms what you would like your life to be now or in the future. Use several senses, including touch, taste, and smell. (For example, what would your log cabin or condominium town home smell like?) Next, write a description of your current self and life. You have a reasonably clear idea of what discrepancies have to be closed to attain your goals.[45] It could be that the discrepancies involve some self-defeating behavior, such as having a low credit score.

Visualize Self-Enhancing Behavior

To apply visualization, program yourself to overcome self-defeating actions and thoughts. Imagine yourself engaging in self-enhancing, winning actions and thoughts. Picture yourself achieving peak performance when good results count the most. A starting point is to identify the next job situation you will be facing that is similar to ones you have flubbed in the past. You then imagine yourself mentally and physically projected into that situation. Imagine what the room looks like, who will be there, and the confident expression you will have on your face. Visualization is akin to watching a video of you doing something right.

DEVELOPING RESILIENCE

In Chapter 2, resilience was described in relation to developing self-confidence. Developing resilience is also a master strategy for dealing with personal problems as well as stress. The ability to overcome setbacks is an important characteristic of successful people. **Resilience** is the ability to withstand pressure and emerge stronger because of the experience. The resilient person profits from a setback by learning what to do better next time and thus does not repeat the mistake. The ability to bounce back from a setback, or resilience, is another aspect of emotional intelligence. In the context of emotional intelligence, resilience refers to being persistent and optimistic when faced with setbacks.[46]

Human Relations Self-Assessment Quiz 17-2 gives you an opportunity to examine your tendencies toward being resilient. Here we look at a few more aspects of becoming resilient.

Resilience
the ability to withstand pressure and emerge stronger because of an experience; being challenged and not breaking down

1. **The resilient disposition.** People with a resilient disposition are better able to stay calm and have a healthy level of physical and psychological wellness in the face of challenges.[47] They accept the reality that a problem exists, so they are likely to develop a plan to work their way out of the problem. Assume that Jessica's new boss does not like her because of reasons unrelated to job performance. If Jessica were not resilient, she would become discouraged and think that she is going to experience a setback in her career. If Jessica is resilient, she will develop a few tactics for getting the new boss on her side, such as finding out what tasks her boss thinks should receive the highest priority.

2. **Getting past the emotional turmoil.** An important part of being resilient is to first overcome the emotional turmoil associated with the setback you have encountered, such as losing a job or being left by a spouse or good friend. Discussing your problem with a friend or counselor is a standard approach for overcoming the emotional turmoil that accompanies a setback. Selecting the right person with whom you can vent your problem is an asset in dealing with your problem. Ideally, you should find someone who can help you help yourself by listening carefully and not jumping in with advice immediately.

   After some of the emotional trauma from your problem has been reduced, it is time to use your creative problem-solving skills to find a solution—the skills that you have developed through experience and in your study of other subjects as well as human relations.

Failure is simply the opportunity to begin again, this time more intelligently.

—Henry Ford

3. **Conduct a failure analysis.** After recognizing that a failure has occurred, resilience is enhanced when the person analyzes why the failure took place. For example, if you were passed over for promotion, it would be helpful to learn the truth about why you were not chosen for the position in question.[48] It is best to go beyond the superficial reasons for the failure and to identify root causes, as in problem solving.[49] The root causes get at the true reasons for the failure of a project, task, or interpersonal relationship. Suppose Stacey is bitterly criticized by her boss, the marketing director for the pet food division of her employer, for having produced a Facebook page that had no impact on sales. Stacey might attribute the

Human Relations Self-Assessment Quiz   17-2

The Resiliency Quiz

From 1 to 5, rate how much each of the following applies to you (1 = very little, 5 = very much)

1	2	3	4	5	If I have a bad day at work or school, it does not ruin my day.
1	2	3	4	5	After a vacation, I can usually get right back into work at my regular work pace.
1	2	3	4	5	Every "no" I encounter is one step closer to a "yes."
1	2	3	4	5	The popular saying "Get over it" has a lot of merit in guiding my life.
1	2	3	4	5	The last time I was rejected for a job (or assignment) I wanted, it had no particular impact on me.
1	2	3	4	5	I enjoy being the underdog once in a while.
1	2	3	4	5	I enjoy taking risks because I believe that the biggest rewards stem from risk taking.
1	2	3	4	5	I rarely worry about, or keep thinking about, mistakes I have made in the past.
1	2	3	4	5	If I ran for political office and lost, I would be willing to run again.
1	2	3	4	5	When I encounter a major problem or setback, I will talk over the situation with a friend or confidant.
1	2	3	4	5	I am physically sick much less frequently than most people I know, including friends, coworkers, and other students.
1	2	3	4	5	The last time I lost my keys (or wallet or handbag or cell phone), I took care of the problem within a few days and was not particularly upset.
1	2	3	4	5	I get more than my share of good breaks.

Scoring and Interpretation:

Add the numbers to get your total score.

60–70   You are highly resilient with an ability to bounce back from setbacks.
45–59   You have an average degree of resiliency when faced with problems.
30–44   Setbacks and disappointments are a struggle for you.
1–29   You may need help in dealing with setbacks.

Source: "The Resiliency Quiz" by Andrew J. DuBrin.

failure of the Facebook page to such superficial factors as too much competition, a sluggish economy, and a boss with a tendency to bark at employees. Yet, if Stacey digs further into the root causes of her problem, she might admit that the page she developed lacked creativity and spark.

4. **Resilience training.**   The purpose of much resilience training is to help people steel themselves against difficult situations instead of becoming overly stressed. At the same time, trainees are taught how to learn from the situation.[50] Part of steeling yourself against a highly challenging situation is to think of what skills you have in your repertoire that will help you work your way out of the problem. Suppose that restaurant manager Gary is witnessing a customer go ballistic right in the restaurant. Instead of being overwhelmed by the problem, Gary reflects, "What conflict-resolution technique do I know that will help me conquer this problem? Maybe disarm the opposition will work here." If Gary is able to calm down the customer, he will have learned from the stressful situation.

Concept Review and Reinforcement

Key Terms

Stress, 474
Stressor, 474
Fight-or-flight response, 474
Challenge stressors, 475
Hindrance stressors, 475
Burnout, 477
Type A behavior, 479
External locus of control, 479

Internal locus of control, 479
Negative affectivity, 480
Role overload, 481
Role underload, 481
Role conflict, 481
Role ambiguity, 481
Carpal tunnel syndrome, 482
Emotional labor, 483

Cognitive–behavioral interventions, 485
Support system, 486
Wellness program, 486
Relaxation response, 487
Meditation, 488
Self-defeating behavior, 491
Soft addiction, 491
Resilience, 494

Summary and Review

- The body's battle against a stressor is the fight-or-flight response. Stress always involves physiological changes, such as an increase in heart rate, blood cholesterol, and blood pressure. Men who respond most intensely to mental stress run a higher risk of blocked blood vessels. Stress adversely affects our ability to fight infection. Posttraumatic stress disorder is another consequence of extreme stress.
- Challenge stressors have a positive effect on motivation and performance, whereas hindrance stressors have a negative effect. Negative stress has enormous consequences to individuals and organizations.
- The existence of challenge stressors suggests that the right amount of stress can be beneficial. Performance tends to be best under moderate amounts of stress, yet certain negative forms of stress, such as an intimidating boss, almost always decrease performance.
- Prolonged stress may lead to burnout, a condition of emotional, mental, and physical exhaustion in response to long-term job stressors, such as a heavy workload. Occupations that require frequent and intense interaction with others often lead to burnout.
- Almost any form of frustration, disappointment, setback, inconvenience, or crisis in your personal life can cause stress. The categories of situations that can produce stress include significant life changes, low self-esteem, everyday annoyances, social and family problems, physical and mental health problems, financial problems, and school-related problems.
- Personality factors contribute to stress proneness. People with type A behavior are impatient and demanding

and have free-floating hostility, all of which lead to stress. People with an external locus of control (believing that external forces control their fate) are more susceptible to stress. Negative affectivity (a predisposition to negative mental states) also contributes to stress.
- Sources of job stress are quite varied. Among them are work overload or underload, role conflict and ambiguity, job insecurity and job loss, adverse environmental conditions including unpleasant or dangerous physical conditions, carpal tunnel syndrome, adverse customer interaction, emotional labor (faking expressions and feelings), and abusive supervision and uncivil coworkers.

To successfully manage stress in the long range, you have to deal with the stressors directly. Three direct approaches are to do the following:

- Eliminate or modify the stressor.
- Place the situation in perspective (cognitive–behavioral approaches to managing stress help with perspective setting).
- Gain control of the situation.

Stress can also be reduced through social support and organizational support. Relaxation techniques for handling stress include the relaxation response and meditation. Managing stress by staying well includes proper exercise, diet, and rest. Exercising properly, including yoga, helps reduce and prevent stress. Sufficient rest also helps manage stress. Maintaining a healthy diet makes it easier to cope with frustrations that could be stressful.

Unless personal problems are kept under control, a person's chances of achieving career and personal success diminish. Many personal problems arise out of self-defeating behavior. Soft addictions can be self-defeating. Approaches to overcoming and preventing self-defeating behavior include the following:

- Solicit feedback on your actions.
- Learn to profit from criticism.

- Stop denying the existence of problems.
- Visualize self-enhancing behavior.

Developing resilience is a master strategy for dealing with personal problems as well as stress. To be resilient, it is helpful to have a resilient disposition. Furthermore, get past the emotional turmoil by talking to a confidant and then working to solve the problem, conducting a failure analysis, and getting resilience training if available.

Questions for Discussion and Review

17.1 An office manager in an emergency room, who was also the mother of young triplets, said she knew she was emotionally drained and stressed out because of all her responsibilities. She said she knew that she should manage her stress better, but she simply did not have the time. What advice can you offer this woman?

17.2 Why might attaining the career goals you have established for the next five years or so be stress-reducing?

17.3 What is the reason that so many people who win a fortune in a lottery wind up having more stress than in their previous life? (Some big lottery winners become so depressed they commit suicide.)

17.4 Why do you think having a salaried job and benefits is less stressful for many workers than being self-employed or being paid strictly on commission?

17.5 An eighteen-year-old person says to you, "Whatever career I choose, I want it to last at least fifty years." Which one or two stress management techniques

would you recommend to this person that will facilitate attaining his or her goal?

17.6 How can a person who becomes stressed from having to interact with coworkers several hours a day compete in the modern world?

17.7 Why does a simple act like emptying a wastebasket or cleaning out and washing one's car reduce stress for so many people?

17.8 Self-employed Tony, whose livelihood depends on using his laptop computer, discovers today that his computer is disabled by viruses. Tony is so overwhelmed with stress that he cannot concentrate, and he feels dizzy. Explain what stress management technique you would recommend to Tony for right now.

17.9 Give an example of self-defeating behavior engaged in by a business executive or public-office holder. What appear to be the negative consequences to the person's career stemming from the self-defeating behavior?

17.10 Imagine that a student receives an F in a course. What can he or she do to be resilient?

Web Corner

The nature of stress and stress management
www.stress.org

Burnout self-test
www.mindtools.com (Enter "burnout self-test" into search box.)

Developing resilience
www.psychologytoday.com (Scroll down under "topics" to find "resilience.")

INTERNET SKILL BUILDER

Stress Management Component of Wellness Programs

Use your favorite search engines to learn about how wellness programs help employees directly manage and prevent stress. An exhaustive amount of information exists about wellness programs in general, so you will have to focus your search. See if you can find the extent to which these approaches to stress management and prevention are carried out directly on company time, or if they are to be implemented mostly during nonworking hours.

Developing Your
Human Relations Skills

Applying Human Relations Exercise 17-1

Personal Stress Management Action Plan

Most people face a few powerful stressors in their work and personal life, but few people take the time to clearly identify these stressors or develop an action plan for remedial action. The purpose of this exercise is to make you an exception. Here is an opportunity to inventory your stressors, think through the problems they may be causing you, and develop action plans you might take to remedy the situation. Use the accompanying form or create one with a word-processing table or a spreadsheet program.

Personal Life Stressor	Symptoms This Stressor Is Creating for Me	My Action Plan to Manage This Stressor
1.		
2.		
3.		

Seven days after preparing this worksheet, observe if any of your stress symptoms have diminished. Also, identify those stressors for which only a long-term solution is possible. One student reported that a major work stressor he faced was that he wanted to work in international business that emphasized doing business with Italian fashion companies. Yet he was experiencing stress because he had almost zero knowledge of the Italian language or culture. (By the way, can you offer this man any suggestions?)

Applying Human Relations Exercise 17-2

Overcoming Self-Defeating Behavior

Most people engage in some behavior that could be self-defeating, sometimes to a major degree. For example, hundreds of otherwise rational people are seriously injured every year because they climb on their roof to clean a gutter or replace a shingle. Also, many people walk out into traffic or bump into a lamppost or building while sending or receiving a text message. Another example is that some well-to-do people cannot resist the urge to shoplift occasionally. If you engage in no self-defeating behavior or no behavior that is potentially self-defeating, you are exempt from this exercise. For all others, answer the following four questions:

1. What is my most self-defeating behavior, even if the behavior is infrequent or only has the potential to be self-defeating?
2. If this behavior continues or becomes exaggerated, what are the consequences to my career and personal life?
3. What action steps can I take to overcome this self-defeating behavior?
4. What help can I get to overcome my self-defeating behavior?

The Stress-Buster Survey

Each class member thinks through carefully which techniques he or she uses to reduce work or personal stress. Class members then come to the front of the room individually to make brief presentations of their most effective stress-reduction techniques. After the presentations are completed, class members analyze and interpret what they heard. Among the issues to explore are the following:

1. Which are the most popular stress reduction techniques?
2. How do the stress reduction techniques used by the class compare to those recommended by experts?
3. For each technique mentioned by a class member, indicate whether you think the method of stress busting will be helpful in the long run or is simply a short-term expedient that might even have negative consequences in the long range. Two examples of the latter are (a) "I like to drink a six pack of beer when I'm stressed out" and (b) "If I'm really uptight, I ride my motorcycle about 75 miles per hour in the middle of the night."

4. Send e-mails or text messages to three class members today or tomorrow indicating what you thought of their methods of stress reduction. If everybody in the class sends e-mail messages to three class members, it is most likely that each student will receive some feedback.

Human Relations Case Study 17–1

Rachel Runs the Treadmill

Six thirty Tuesday morning 38-year-old Rachel Mendez hops out of her bed while her husband, Alex Mendez, is still sleeping. Rachel's first stop is to wake up her nine-year-old daughter and encourage her to start getting ready to meet the school bus on time. By 8 a.m., Rachel is in her car and on her way to her job as a business development specialist for a human resource outsourcing company. Her primary responsibility is to entice small- and medium-size companies to turn over most of their human resource functions to her firm.

Just as Rachel begins to manage her e-mail and plan her agenda for the day, she places her right hand about three inches to the right of her heart. Rachel can feel the tightness next to her heart, and in her left arm. She thinks to herself, "This feels like I'm going to have a heart attack, even though it doesn't make sense for a woman my age to be a heart attack victim. But I'm happy that I have an appointment at the cardiology center on Thursday."

At the North Side Cardiology Center, Rachel was first interviewed by Nurse Practitioner Janet Trudeau before her interview with Dr. Harry Ching, the cardiologist. Trudeau first took a brief medical history, followed by an interview. Parts of the interview with Trudeau went as follows:

Trudeau: So tell me in more detail why you came to visit our cardiology center.

Mendez: I have these annoying chest pains next to my heart and in my left arm. The pains usually start when I am extremely aggravated and frustrated. I have the pains about once a day.

Trudeau: Do you ever faint or become light-headed during the pains?

Mendez: No, my problem is just the pains. I keep doing whatever I'm doing when the pain hits.

Trudeau: Tell me about the situations you find so aggravating and frustrating.

Mendez: I'm really stressing out. I have a ton of aggravations and worries. To begin, my nine-year-old daughter, Samantha, has seizures. She is under treatment but the problem remains, and it's worrisome. I worry every day that Samantha will have a seizure and strike her head or get involved in an accident.

My work is also quite worrisome. I work mostly on commission selling human resource services. Our business has grown rapidly in the last few years, but we have kind of dried up the territory. I have to travel more to find new clients. My earnings are taking a turn downward despite the extra travel.

Trudeau: Are you the sole breadwinner in the family?

Mendez: No, my husband Alex is an assistant manager at a Ruby Tuesday restaurant, and he makes a modest living. But talking about aggravation, my husband is a decent guy but he gives me chest pains. I think he cares much more about professional sports, especially the NFL and the NHL, than he does about Samantha and me. If he's watching a game, I can forget about talking about something serious.

And then, of course, Alex works the hours of a restaurant manager, which means that he is often working when I am not working, like on Saturdays and Sundays.

Trudeau: Any other major aggravations in your life?

Mendez: Yes, commuting on busy highways. I can feel my chest pains starting when I think of sitting still for fifteen minutes during rush-hour traffic.

Trudeau: Thank you, Rachel. I will be studying this information before your interview with Dr. Ching. Have a seat in the waiting room. He will be with you in about ten minutes.

Later that day, Mendez had an extensive cardiology exam, including an electrocardiogram. Dr. Ching informed her that despite the muscle tension she was experiencing, her heart was in excellent condition.

Questions:

17.11 What sources of stress does Rachel Mendez appear to be facing?

17.12 What do you recommend Mendez do about the stressors she is facing?

17.13 Given that Mendez does not have a heart problem, should she be concerned about the stressors in her life? Explain your answer.

17.14 How might Mendez organize her work and her life better to feel that her life is less out of control?

Rachel Discusses Her Stress Problem with Alex

One student plays the role of Rachel, who decides to discuss her stress problems with her husband, Alex. She feels that Alex is contributing somewhat to her problems for the reasons described in the case just presented. Another student plays the role of Alex, who has some sympathy for Rachel, yet she does not understand that he leads a stressful life also. He believes firmly that watching professional sports provides him effective stress relief. Run the role-play for about seven minutes. Observers will decide if the couple is on the way to helping each other lead a less stressful life.

Mason Digs a Hole for Himself

Mason enjoys his position as a meat inspector for the state. His job provides him the opportunity to visit meat companies and poultry-processing plants and inspect for any food code irregularities. Mason feels strongly that in his work, he is making good use of his education in physical science as well as human relations skills.

Despite these positive aspects to his career, Mason's boss and a few family members worry that he is creating trouble for himself. A few weeks ago, Mason posted on Facebook, "After my latest meat and poultry plant inspections, I think I'm going to become a vegan." Ten days ago, Mason did not report to work and failed to notify his manager of his absence. When confronted about the problem, Mason replied, "Sorry about that, but I needed to distance myself from the job for a day."

Last week, Mason went shopping in a mall and had a valid credit card with him, along with $175 in cash. Yet he walked out of a store with a men's cashmere sweater.

A member of the security forces stopped Mason on the way out. Instead of referring him to the police for arrest, Mason was charged a $300 security fee on his credit card, and no formal charges were levied against him.

That night, when Mason laughingly told his girlfriend, Lori, about the sweater incident, she responded, "Mason, you are digging a big hole for yourself in many ways. Are you trying to get fired and imprisoned at the same time? I think you need help."

Mason replied, "Lori, chill out. A guy needs to have a little fun."

Questions:

17.15 In your opinion, is Mason just having a little fun, or does he need help?

17.16 If you think that Mason is engaging in self-defeating behavior, what do you recommend he do to deal with the problem?

Dealing with Mason's Self-Defeating Behavior

One student plays the role of Mason's boss, Sandra, who confronts him about some of his questionable behavior, such as the Facebook post about becoming a vegan and being absent for a vague reason. The boss believes that Mason is becoming his own worst enemy. Another student plays the role of Mason, who doesn't think that he is engaging in self-defeating behavior but simply having a little fun.

Observers rate the role-players on two dimensions, using a scale of 1 to 5 from very poor to very good. One dimension is "effective use of human relations techniques." For Sandra, focus in on how well she communicates her message about Mason needing to become a more responsible person. For Mason, see if he begins to understand how his behavior might be self-defeating. The second dimension is "acting ability." A few observers might voluntarily provide feedback to the role-players in terms of sharing their ratings and observations. The course instructor might also provide feedback.

REFERENCES

1. Dona M. Owens, "Stressed Out," *HR Magazine*, March 2014, p. 44.
2. Research reviewed in Mark Greer, "Mental Stress Wreaks Physical Havoc on Workers," *Monitor on Psychology*, May 2005, pp. 28–29.
3. Nathan P. Podaskoff, Jeffrey A. LePine, and Marcie A. LePine, "Differential Challenge Stressor Relationships with Job Attitudes, Turnover Intentions, and Withdrawal Behavior: A Meta-Analysis," *Journal of Applied Psychology*, March 2007, pp. 438–454.
4. "The Financial Burden of Job Stress," *Center for the Promotion of Health in the New England Workplace*, www.uml.edu, 2014, pp. 1–2.
5. Suzanne C. Sergerstrom and Gregory E. Miller, "Psychological Stress and the Human Immune System: A Meta-Analytic Study of 30 Years of Inquiry," *Psychological Bulletin*, No. 4, 2004, pp. 601–630.
6. Rebecca Vesley, "Deal with Post-Traumatic Stress Disorder Post-Haste," *Workforce Management*, June 2013, p. 12.
7. Research synthesized in Sue Shellenbarger, "When Stress Is Good for You," *The Wall Street Journal*, January 24, 2012, p. D1.
8. Kristin Byron, Shalini Khazanchi, and Deborah Nazarian, "The Relationship between Stressors and Creativity: A Meta-Analysis Examining Competing Theoretical Models," *Journal of Applied Psychology*, January 2010, pp. 201–212.
9. Evangelia Demerouti et al., "The Job Demands–Resources Model of Burnout," *Journal of Applied Psychology*, June 2001, p. 502.
10. "Is Your Team Feeling Burned Out?" *Communication Briefings*, December 2010, p. 4. Adapted from Michael Carney and Heather Z. Hutchins, *Tips for Handling Everyday Stress* (London: Global Professional Publishing, 2010).
11. Benjamin B. Dunford et al., "Is Burnout Static or Dynamic? A Career Transition Perspective of Employee Burnout Trajectories," *Journal of Applied Psychology*, May 2012, p. 646.
12. Sharon Toker and Michal Biron, "Burnout and Depression: Unraveling Their Temporal Relationship and Considering the Role of Physical Activity," *Journal of Applied Psychology*, May 2012, pp. 699–710.
13. Rabi S. Bhagat, "Effects of Stressful Life Events on Individual Performance and Work Adjustment Processes within Organizational Settings: A Research Model," *Academy of Management Review*, October 1983, pp. 660–670.
14. Research reported in Etienne Benson, "Hostility Is among Best Predictors of Heart Disease in Men," *Monitor on Psychology*, January 2003, p. 15.
15. Quoted in Nadja Geipert, "Don't Be Mad: More Research Links Hostility to Coronary Risk," *Monitor on Psychology*, January 2007, pp. 50–51.
16. Paul E. Spector, Peter Y. Chen, and Brian J. O'Connell, "A Longitudinal Study of Relations between Job Stressors and Job Strains While Controlling for Prior Negative Affectivity and Strains," *Journal of Applied Psychology*, April 2000, p. 216.
17. Owens, "Stressed Out," p. 44.
18. Erin M. Eatough, Chu-Hsiang Chang, Stephanie A. Miloslavic, and Russell E. Johnson, "Relationships of Role Stressors with Organizational Citizenship Behavior: A Meta-Analysis," *Journal of Applied Psychology*, May 2011, pp. 619–632.
19. Amy Novotney, "Silence, Please," *Monitor on Psychology*, July–August 2011, p. 47.
20. Tedd Mitchell, "'Oh, My Aching Wrist!'," *USA Weekend*, July 3–4, 2010, p. 16.
21. Alicia A. Grandey, "Emotion Regulation in the Workplace: A New Way to Conceptualize Emotional Labor," *Journal of Occupational Health Psychology*, January 2000, pp. 95–110.
22. Brent A. Scott and Christopher M. Barnes, "A Multilevel Field Investigation of Emotional Labor, Affect, Work Withdrawal, and Gender," *Academy of Management Journal*, February 2011, pp. 116–136.
23. David T. Wagner, Christopher M. Barnes, and Brent A. Scott, "Driving It Home: How Workplace Emotional Labor Harms Employee Home Life," *Personnel Psychology*, No. 2, 2014, pp. 487–516.
24. Theresa M. Glomb, John D. Kammeyer-Mueller, and Maria Rotundo, "Emotional Labor Demands and Compensating Wage Differentials," *Journal of Applied Psychology*, August 2004, p. 707.
25. Myriam N. Bechtoldt et al., "The Primacy of Perceiving: Emotional Recognition Buffers Negative Effects of Emotional Labor," *Journal of Applied Psychology*, September 2011, pp. 1087–1094.
26. Simon Lloyd D. Restubog, Kristin L. Scott, and Thomas J. Zagenezyk, "When Distress Hits Home: The Role of Contextual Factors and Psychological Distress in Predicting Employees' Responses to Abusive Supervision," *Journal of Applied Psychology*, July 2011, pp. 713–729.
27. Christine Porath and Christine Pearson, "The Price of Incivility," *Harvard Business Review*, January–February 2013, p. 117.
28. Michael P. Leiter, Heather K. Spence Laschinger, Aria Day, and Debra Gilin Oore, "The Impact of Civility Interventions on Employee Social Behavior, Distress, and Attitudes," *Journal of Applied Psychology*, November 2011, pp. 1258–1274.
29. Katherine. M. Richardson and Hannah. R. Rothstein, "Effects of Occupational Stress Management Intervention Programs: A Meta-Analysis," *Journal of Occupational Health Psychology*, January 2008, pp. 69–93.
30. Cited in Stephanie Gold, "A Higher Road to Relaxation," *Psychology Today*, July–August 2007, p. 57.
31. Amy Novotney, "Marital Bliss May Blunt Office Blues," *Monitor on Psychology*, March 2008, p. 11.
32. Rita Pyrillis, "Devoid of Data," *Workforce*, June 2014, p. 50.
33. Leonard L. Berry, Ann M. Mirabito, and William B. Baun, "What's the Hard Return on Employee Wellness Programs?" *Harvard Business Review*, December 2010, p. 106.
34. Rita Pyrillis, "Wellness Apps for Workers Becoming More Apropos," *Workforce*, January 2014, p. 17.
35. Research cited in Sarah Sipek, "Tough Workout," *Workforce*, May 2015, p. 27.
36. Herbert Benson (with William Proctor), *Beyond the Relaxation Response* (New York: Berkley Books, 1995), pp. 96–97; Sara Martin, "The Power of the Relaxation Response," *Monitor on Psychology*, October 2008, p. 33.

37. Evidence reviewed in Julie Corliss, "Mindfulness Meditation May Ease Anxiety, Mental Stress," *Harvard Health Publications,* www.health.harvard.edu, January 8, 2014, p. 1.

38. Beth Azar, "Another Reason to Break a Sweat," *Monitor on Psychology,* June 2010, pp. 36–38.

39. "Yoga Can Reduce Anxiety," *Personal Best Healthlines,* Special Report, 2007, p. 5.

40. Pamela Paul, "When Yoga Hurts," *Time,* October 15, 2007, p. 71.

41. Stanton Peele, "A Toast to Your Health," *The Wall Street Journal,* February 2, 2011.

42. Mark Goulston, *Get Out of Your Own Way at Work . . . and Help Others Do the Same* (New York: Putnam Adult, 2005); Andrew J. DuBrin, *Your Own Worst Enemy: How to Overcome Career Self-Sabotage* (New York: AMACOM, 1992).

43. Dragos Hiescu et al., "Vocational Fit and Counterproductive Work Behaviors: A Self-Regulation Perspective," *Journal of Applied Psychology,* January 2015, pp. 21–39.

44. Based on the work of Judith Wright, as reported in Julie Deardorff, "Soft Addictions: You Can Get Hooked in So Many Ways," *Chicago Tribune,* March 18, 2007.

45. Kevin Hogan, "Why Everything Goes to Hell . . . How to Stop Self-Sabotage, NOW and Forever!" www.kevinhogan.com/selfsabotage.htm, 2009.

46. Daniel Goleman, "Leadership That Gets Results," *Harvard Business Review,* March–April 2000, p. 80.

47. William Atkinson, "Turning Stress into Strength," *HR Magazine,* January 2011, p. 49.

48. Mitchell Lee Marks, Philip Mirvis, and Ron Ashkenas, "Rebounding from Career Setbacks," *Harvard Business Review,* October 2014, p. 106.

49. Amy C. Edmonson, "Strategies for Learning from Failure," *Harvard Business Review,* April 2011, p. 54.

50. "Resilience Training," www.mayoclinic.org/resilience-training, 1998–2015.

Appendix: Comprehensive Assignment for Applying Human Relations Knowledge

A large number of concepts, facts, and skills have been presented in this textbook. To help you develop a master plan for integrating much of this information and enhancing your human relations skill at the same time, we present the following plan.

First is a large table highlighting the major human relations concepts and skills presented in the text, along with space for you to insert a tentative action plan about how you might use the knowledge or apply the skill under consideration. Usually it will be necessary to refer back to the appropriate chapter to identify the subtopics under a particular topic, such as looking for specific tactics under "Career Advancement Strategies and Tactics."

The topics in the table presented below are often worded in a way that suggests the application of the information. You may not have action plans for every major topic in the text. The action plan might be a few sentences long. For example, next to the outline entry "Techniques for resolving conflict," you might insert "Disarming the opposition should work for me. The next time I am criticized, and I am wrong, I will admit what I did wrong and ask for sympathy." To prepare your action plan, it will usually be necessary to refer back to the discussion of the topic within the text.

Second, after you have made action-plan entries for as many concepts and skills that seem relevant for you at the time, write an essay about how to plan to enhance your human relations effectiveness. The raw data for your essay are the action plans you have developed. In other words, your essay about enhancing your human relations effectiveness is a narrative composite of your action plans.

Chapter Number	Concept or Skill	My Action Plan
1	Human Relations and You	
	Use of human relations knowledge	
	How work and personal life influence each other	
	Development of self-understanding	
	Development of human relations movement	
	Major factors influencing job performance and behavior	
2	Self-Esteem and Self-Confidence	
	Nature of self-esteem	
	Development of self-esteem	
	Consequences of self-esteem	
	Enhancing self-esteem	
	Sources of self-confidence	
	Developing and strengthening self-confidence	
	Avoiding codependency	
3	Self-Motivation and Goal Setting	
	Influence of needs and motives on motivation	
	Contribution of goals to motivation	

	Self-motivation techniques	
	Development of self-discipline	
4	Emotional Intelligence, Attitudes, and Happiness	
	Nature of emotional intelligence	
	Acquiring and changing attitudes	
	Becoming a good organizational citizen	
	Acquiring and enhancing happiness	
5	Values and Ethics	
	Understanding values as part of human relations	
	Importance of business ethics	
	Guidelines for making ethical decisions	
	Guidelines for behaving ethically	
6	Problem Solving and Creativity	
	Characteristics related to problem-solving ability	
	Steps in problem solving and decision making	
	Creativity for decision making	
	Improving my creativity	
	Critical thinking for problem solving	
	Making good use of my multiple intelligences	
7	Personal Communication Effectiveness	
	Steps in communication process	
	Use of nonverbal communication	
	Frequent communication barriers	
	Building bridges to communication	
	Overcoming gender barriers to communication	
	Enhancing listening skills	
8	Communication in the Workplace	
	Use of formal channels of communication	
	Use of informal channels of communication	
	Problems associated with communication technology	
	Performing well in a business meeting	
9	Specialized Tactics for Getting Along with Others in the Workplace	
	Developing a good relationship with my manager or team leader	
	Coping with a problem manager	
	Building better coworker relationships	
	Building better relationships with customers	
10	Managing Conflict	
	Reasons for so much conflict	
	Good and bad side of conflict	
	Techniques for resolving conflict	
	Dealing with difficult people	
	Managing anger	
11	Becoming an Effective Leader	
	Traits and characteristics of effective leaders	

	Behaviors and skills of effective leaders	
	Choosing an effective leadership style	
	Getting along well with subordinates	
	Developing my leadership potential	
	Challenges of being a first-time leader	
12	Motivating Others and Developing Teamwork	
	Diagnosing motivation of others	
	Empowerment, job design, and positive reinforcement for motivating others	
	Building better teamwork	
	Making use of group dynamics	
	Building an effective work group	
13	Diversity and Cross-Cultural Competence	
	Dimensions of differences in cultural values	
	Approaches to improving cross-cultural relations	
	Overcoming cross-cultural communication barriers	
	Using diversity in the company to advantage	
	My legal rights in a culturally diverse organization	
14	Getting Ahead in Your Career	
	Ideas for conducting a job search	
	Constructing an effective job résumé	
	Performing well in a job interview	
	Effective career advancement strategies and tactics	
	Effective networking skills	
15	Learning Strategies, Perception, and Life Span Changes	
	Major learning strategies and processes	
	Choosing a learning style	
	Getting the proper rest for my brain	
	Making my perceptions more accurate	
	Responding to life span changes and challenges	
	Making a career change	
	Coping with change more effectively	
16	Developing Good Work Habits	
	Overcoming procrastination	
	Proper attitudes and values to develop for productivity	
	Effective time-management techniques	
	Overcoming time wasters	
17	Managing Stress and Personal Problems	
	Getting positive consequences from stress	
	Sources of stress in personal life to minimize	
	Sources of work stress to minimize	
	Effective approaches to managing stress	
	Overcoming self-defeating behavior	
	Developing resilience	

Action plan describes how you are going to reach your goal

Active listener person who listens intensely, with the goal of empathizing with the speaker

Adolescence the period in life from approximately age thirteen to twenty; from a biological standpoint, adolescence begins with puberty

Affective component (of attitude) the emotion connected with an object or a task

Affirmative action programs that comply with antidiscrimination laws and attempt to correct past discriminatory practices

Aggressive personalities people who verbally and sometimes physically attack others frequently

Alternative self an understanding of the self, based on what could have been if something in the past had happened differently

Assertive people those who state clearly what they want or how they feel in a given situation without being abusive, abrasive, or obnoxious

Attitude a predisposition to respond that exerts an influence on a person's response to a person, a thing, an idea, or a situation

Attribution theory the study of the process by which people ascribe causes to the behaviors they perceive

Autocratic leader leader who attempts to retain most of the authority granted to the group

Backstabbing an attempt to discredit by underhanded means such as innuendo, accusation, or the like

Barriers to communication (or noise) unwanted interference that can distort or block a message

Behavior modification system of motivation that emphasizes rewarding people for doing the right things and punishing them for doing the wrong things

Behavioral component (of attitude) how a person acts

Behavioral interview a candidate is asked how he or she handled a particular problem in the past

Blind area pane of Johari Window that contains information that others are aware of but we cannot see in ourselves in reference to both positive and negative qualities

Brainstorming technique by which group members think of multiple solutions to a problem

Brainwriting arriving at creative ideas by jotting them down yourself

Bully a cruel and aggressive boss who intimidates and verbally abuses subordinates

Burnout a condition of emotional, mental, and physical exhaustion in response to long-term job stressors

Business etiquette special code of behavior required in work situations

Carpal tunnel syndrome repetitive-motion disorder most frequently associated with keyboarding and the use of optical scanners; occurs when repetitive flexing and extension of the wrist causes the tendons to swell, thus trapping and pinching the median nerve

Challenge stressors stressful events and thoughts that have a positive direct effect on motivation and performance

Chance encounter unscheduled informal contact between managers and employees

Character doing the right things despite outside pressures to do the opposite; includes leaving enduring marks that set one apart from another; being moral

Character trait an enduring characteristic of a person that is related to moral and ethical behavior that shows up consistently

Charisma type of charm and magnetism that inspires others; important quality for leaders at all levels

Classical conditioning principles stemming from Ivan Pavlov's digestion experiments that help people understand the most elementary type of learning: how people acquire uncomplicated habits and reflexes

Codependency a state of being psychologically influenced or controlled by, reliant on, or needing another person who is addicted to substances such as alcohol and drugs, or to behavior such as gambling or Internet use

Cognitive–behavioral interventions a way of thinking constructively about a problem that includes perspective setting

Cognitive component (of attitude) the knowledge or intellectual beliefs an individual might have about an object (an idea, a person, a thing, or a situation)

Cognitive dissonance situation in which the pieces of knowledge, information, attitudes, or beliefs held by an individual are contradictory

Cognitive fitness a state of optimized ability to remember, learn, plan, and adapt to changing circumstances

Cognitive restructuring technique of mentally converting negative aspects into positive ones by looking for the positive elements in a situation

Cognitive skills problem-solving and intellectual skills

Communication the sending and receiving of messages

Communication overload phenomenon that occurs when people are so overloaded with information that they cannot respond effectively to messages

Communities of practice informal employee networks

Conflict condition that exists when two sets of demands, goals, or motives are incompatible

Conflict of interest judgment or objectivity is compromised because of two competing ends that must be satisfied

Confrontation and problem solving the most highly recommended way of resolving conflict; method of identifying the true source of conflict and resolving it systematically

Consensus leader leader who encourages group discussion about an issue and then makes a decision that reflects the consensus of the group members

Consideration the degree to which the leader creates an environment of emotional support, warmth, friendliness, and trust

Consultative leader leader who solicits opinions from the group before making a decision, yet does not feel obliged to accept the group's thinking

Creative self-efficacy the belief that one has the knowledge and skills to produce creative outcomes

Creativity the ability to develop good ideas that can be put into action

Critical thinking solving problems and making decisions through a systematic evaluation of evidence

Cultural intelligence (CQ) an outsider's ability to interpret someone's unfamiliar and ambiguous behavior the same way that person's compatriots would

Cultural mosaic an individual's unique mixture of multiple cultural identities, which yields a complex picture of the cultural influences on that person

Cultural sensitivity an awareness of and a willingness to investigate the reasons why people of another culture act as they do

Cultural training set of learning experiences designed to help employees understand the customs, traditions, and beliefs of another culture

Culture a learned and shared system of knowledge, beliefs, values, attitudes, and norms

Customer service orientation approach of employee whose thoughts and actions are geared toward helping customers

Decision making choosing one alternative from the various alternative solutions that can be pursued

Decoding the process of understanding a message; the receiver interprets the message and translates it into meaningful information

Defensive communication tendency to receive messages in such a way that one's self-esteem is protected

Democratic leader leader who confers final authority on the group; functions as a collector of opinion and takes a vote before making a decision (in extreme sometimes referred to as a *free-rein leader*)

Denial the suppression of information one finds uncomfortable

Developmental opportunity area for growth or a weakness of an individual

Diagonal communication the transmission of messages to higher or lower organizational levels in different departments

Difficult people a coworker is classified as difficult if he or she is uncooperative, disrespectful, touchy, defensive, hostile, or even very unfriendly

Disarming the opposition method of conflict resolution in which you disarm the criticizer by agreeing with his or her criticism

Diversity training program that attempts to bring about workplace harmony by teaching people how to get along with diverse work associates; often aimed at minimizing open expressions of racism and sexism

Downward communication the transmission of messages from higher to lower levels in an organization

E-learning an Internet form of computer-based learning

Emotional contagion the automatic and unconscious transfer of emotions between individuals based on cues that one person observes in another

Emotional effort the work employees invest to express the emotional response customers expect

Emotional intelligence the ability to accurately perceive emotions, to understand the signals that emotions send about relationships, and to manage your own and others' emotions

Emotional labor process of regulating both feelings and expressions to meet organizational goals

Empathy understanding another person's point of view

Employee network (or affinity) groups network group of employees throughout the company who affiliate on the basis of a group characteristic such as race, ethnicity, sex, sexual orientation, or physical ability status

Empowerment process by which a manager shares power with team members, thereby enhancing their feelings of self-efficacy

Encoding the process of organizing ideas into a series of symbols, such as words and gestures, designed to communicate with a receiver

Ethical screening running a contemplated decision or action through an ethics test, particularly when a contemplated action or decision is not clearly ethical or unethical

Ethics the moral choices a person makes

Exit strategy determining in advance how to get out of a bad decision, such as having joined a failing family business

Expectancy theory of motivation people will be motivated if they believe that their efforts will lead to desired outcomes

External locus of control individual's belief that external forces control his or her fate

Extinction the weakening or decreasing of the frequency of undesirable behavior by removing the reward for such behavior

Fear of success belief that if one succeeds at an important task, one will be asked to take on more responsibility in the future

Feedback information that tells one how well he or she has performed

Fight-or-flight response the experience of stress prompts the adrenal glands to release a flood of hormones that prepare the body to fight or run when faced with a challenge

Flow experience total absorption in work; when flow occurs, things seem to go just right

Formal communication channels the official pathways for sending information inside and outside an organization

Frame of reference model, viewpoint, or perspective

Galatea effect a type of self-fulfilling prophecy in which high expectations lead to high performance

Goal an event, circumstance, object, or condition a person strives to attain

Grapevine major informal communication channel in organizations; the grapevine refers to the tangled pathways that can distort information

Grievance procedure formal process of filing a complaint and resolving a dispute within an organization

Group a collection of people who interact with one another and are working toward some common purpose; a team approaches being a supergroup

Group dynamics the forces operating in groups that affect how members work together

Group learning a change in the group's repertoire of potential behavior

Group norms unwritten set of expectations for group members—what people ought to do; basic principle to follow in getting along with coworkers

Groupthink a deterioration of mental efficiency, reality testing, and moral judgment in the interest of group solidarity; extreme form of consensus

Hawthorne effect a phenomenon in a work setting or research in which workers or participants react positively because management or researchers care about them

Hedonic adaptation the tendency to adapt to regard exciting new aspects of life as routine after a while

Hidden area pane of Johari Window that contains information known to us about ourselves but is hidden from others

Hindrance stressors stressful events and thoughts that have a negative effect on motivation and performance

Horizontal communication sending messages among people at the same organization level

Human relations the art of using systematic knowledge about human behavior to improve personal, job, and career effectiveness

Human relations movement movement that began as a concentrated effort by some managers and their advisers

to become more sensitive to the needs of employees or to treat them in a more humanistic manner

Identity crisis adolescent struggle to establish a reliable self-concept or personal identity

Informal communication channels unofficial networks or channels that supplement the formal channels

Informal learning planned or unplanned learning that occurs without a formal classroom, lesson plan, instructor, or examination; a way of learning complex skills in the workplace

Ingratiating an attempt to increase one's attractiveness to others to influence their behavior

Initiating structure organizing and defining relationships in the group by engaging in such activities as assigning specific tasks, specifying procedures to be followed, scheduling work, and making expectations clear

Innovation the commercialization or implementation of creative ideas

Insight an ability to know what information is relevant, to find connections between the old and the new, to combine facts that are unrelated, and to see the "big picture"

Integrity a consistency in the values a person professes, and in the person's behavior

Intermittent rewards sustaining desired behaviors longer and slowing down the process of behaviors fading away when they are not rewarded

Internal locus of control individual's belief that fate is pretty much under his or her own control

Intranet a company version of the Internet with the basic purpose of giving employees a central place to find what they need amidst a sea of digital information

Intrinsic motivation a person's beliefs about the extent to which an activity can satisfy his or her needs for competence and self-determination

Introspection the act of looking within oneself

Intuition an experience-based way of knowing or reasoning in which weighing and balancing of evidence are done automatically

Job enrichment making a job more motivating and satisfying by adding variety and responsibility

Johari Window a grid showing how much information you know about yourself as well as how much other people know about you

Keywords terms for skills, certifications, job activities, and other qualifications sought for a particular job

Leader–member exchange (LMX) model leadership model that focuses on the quality of leader–member relations; recognizes that leaders develop a unique working relationship with each group member

Leader political support political acts and influence techniques used by the leader to provide followers with the resources they need to accomplish individual, group, or organizational objectives

Leadership the process of bringing about positive changes and influencing others to achieve worthwhile goals

Leadership effectiveness situation in which the leader helps the group accomplish its objectives without neglecting satisfaction and morale

Leadership style a leader's characteristic way of behaving in a variety of situations

Learning generally considered a lasting change in behavior based on practice and experience

Learning style the idea that different people learn best in different ways

Management by walking around managers intermingling freely with workers on the shop floor or in the office, as well as with customers

Maslow's hierarchy of needs according to psychologist Abraham H. Maslow, people strive to satisfy the following groups of needs in step-by-step order: physiological needs, safety needs, social needs, esteem needs, and self-actualizing needs

Meditation a systematic method of concentration, reflection, or concentrated thinking designed to suppress the activity of the sympathetic nervous system

Mentor a more experienced person who guides, teaches, and coaches another individual

Micro-inequity small, semiconscious message sent with a powerful impact on the receiver

Micromanagement the close monitoring of most aspects of group member activities by the manager

Midlife crisis time that adults in their forties face when they feel unfulfilled and search for a major shift in career or lifestyle

Midlife transition adults taking stock of their lives and formulating new goals

Mirroring form of nonverbal communication to overcome communication barriers by subtly imitating another; used to improve rapport with another person

Mixed messages a discrepancy between what a person says and how he or she acts

Mixed signals type of message in which the sender might recommend one thing to others yet behave in another way

Modeling learning a skill by observing another person perform the skill; considered a form of social learning because it is learned in the presence of others

Morals an individual's or a society's determination of what is right and wrong

Motivation concept with two widely used meanings: (1) an internal state that leads to effort expended toward objectives and (2) an activity performed by one person to get another to accomplish work

Motive an inner drive that moves a person to do something

Multicultural identities individuals who incorporate the values of two or more cultures because they identify with both their primary culture and another culture or cultures

Multicultural worker one who can work effectively with people of different cultures

Multiple intelligences theory explaining the idea that people know and understand the world in distinctly different ways and learn in different ways and that they possess eight intelligences, or faculties, in varying degrees

Narcissism an extremely positive view of the self, combined with little empathy for others

Need an internal striving or urge to do something, such as a need to drink when thirsty

Need for achievement the desire to accomplish something difficult for its own sake

Negative affectivity a tendency to experience aversive (intensely disliked) emotional states; predisposition to experience emotional stress that includes feelings of nervousness, tension, and worry

Negative reinforcement removing something unpleasant from a situation; being rewarded by being relieved of discomfort; form of avoidance learning or motivation

Negotiating and bargaining situation of conferring with another person to resolve a problem

Networking the process of establishing a group of contacts who can help you in your career

Nonverbal communication using the body, voice, or environment in numerous ways to help get a message across

Open area pane of Johari Window consisting of information that is known to us and others

Open-door policy communication channel that is structured upward and allows an employee to bring a complaint to top management's attention without first checking with the employee's manager

Operant conditioning learning that takes place as a consequence of behavior; a person's actions are instrumental in determining whether learning takes place

Organizational citizenship behavior (OCB) the willingness to go beyond one's job description to help the company, even if such an act does not lead to an immediate reward

Organizational culture values and beliefs of the firm that guide people's actions

Organizational effectiveness the extent to which an organization is productive and satisfies the demands of interested parties, such as employees, customers, and investors

Paraphrase repeating in one's own words what a sender says, feels, and means

Participative leader leader who shares decision-making authority with the group

Passive-aggressive personality a person who appears to enthusiastically and readily respond to another person's request or demand while acting in ways that negatively and passively resist the request

Peak performance exceptional accomplishment in a given task

Peer evaluations system in which teammates contribute to an evaluation of a person's job performance

Perception the various ways in which people interpret things in the external world and how they act on the basis of these perceptions

Perceptual congruence the degree to which people perceive things the same way

Personal brand your distinctive set of strengths, including skills and values

Personal communication style verbal and nonverbal communication style for a unique approach to sending and receiving information

Personal support assisting others in the workplace through the use of interpersonal skills

Personality clash antagonistic relationship between two people based on differences in personal attributes, preferences, interests, values, and styles

Personality disorder a pervasive, persistent, inflexible, maladaptive pattern of behavior that deviates from expected cultural norms

Person–organization fit the compatibility of the individual and the organization

Person–role conflict occurs when the demands made by the organization or a superior clash with the basic values of the individual

Planning deciding what to accomplish and the actions needed to make it happen

Political blunder an insensitive act, also referred to as "putting your foot in your mouth"

Political skill a combination of social astuteness with the capacity to adjust and adapt behavior to the demands of different situations

Positive psychological capital a positive psychological state of development in which you have a storehouse of hope, self-efficacy, optimism, and resilience

Positive reinforcement increasing the probability that behavior will be repeated by rewarding people for making the desired response; improves learning and motivation

Positive self-talk saying positive things about yourself to yourself

Positive visual imagery picturing a positive outcome in your mind

Private self the actual person an individual may be

Proactive personality characteristic of a person who is relatively unconstrained by forces in a situation and who brings about environmental change

Problem gap between what exists and what you want to exist

Procrastination delaying a task for an invalid or weak reason

Productivity the amount of quality work accomplished in relation to the resources consumed

Prosocial motivation the desire to expend effort to help other people

Public self what a person communicates about himself or herself and what others actually perceive about the person

Punishment the introduction of an unpleasant stimulus as a consequence of the learner having done something wrong

Pygmalion effect leader's ability to elevate workers' performance by the simple method of expecting them to perform well; the manager's high expectations become a self-fulfilling prophecy

Recognition need the desire to be acknowledged for one's contributions and efforts and to feel important

Relationship management the interpersonal skills of being able to communicate clearly and convincingly, disarm conflicts, and build strong personal bonds

Relaxation response a physical state of deep rest in which one experiences a slower respiration and heart rate and lowered metabolism; a standard technique for reducing stress

Resilience the ability to withstand pressure and emerge stronger because of an experience

Role tendency to behave, contribute, and relate to others in a particular way

Role ambiguity condition in which the job holder receives confusing or poorly defined expectations

Role conflict having to choose between two competing demands or expectations

Role overload a burdensome workload that creates stress for a person in two ways: (1) the person may become fatigued and less able to tolerate annoyances and irritations and (2) a person subject to unreasonable work demands may feel perpetually behind schedule, a situation that itself creates an uncomfortable, stressful feeling

Role underload disruptive amount of stress that can occur when people experience too little to do

Sandwich generation people who take care of both children and aging parents at the same time

Scientific management approach to work that focuses on the application of scientific methods to increase individual workers' productivity

Selective attention giving exclusive attention to something at the expense of other aspects of the environment

Self a complex idea generally referring to a person's total being or individuality

Self-awareness the ability to understand your own moods, emotions, and needs as well as their impact on others; self-awareness also includes using intuition to make decisions you can live with happily

Self-defeating behavior activities or attitudes that work against one's best interest

Self-determination theory the motivation theory contending that we are most deeply engaged, and do our most creative work, when we feel that we are acting according to our own will and pursuing goals we find meaningful

Self-discipline the ability to work systematically and progressively toward a goal until it is achieved

Self-disclosure the process of revealing one's inner self to others

Self-efficacy confidence in your ability to carry out a specific task in contrast to generalized self-confidence

Self-esteem the experience of feeling competent to cope with the basic challenges in life and of being worthy of happiness

Self-leadership leading oneself; influencing oneself without waiting for an external leader to lead

Self-management the ability to control one's emotions and act with honesty and integrity in a consistent and acceptable manner

Self-respect how you think and feel about yourself

Self-understanding knowledge about oneself, particularly with respect to mental and emotional aspects

Semantics the study of the meaning and changes in the meaning of words or symbols

Servant leader one who serves group members by working on their behalf to help them achieve their goals, not the leader's goals

Sexual equity parity among heterosexual, gay, lesbian, bisexual, and transgender employees

Sexual harassment unwanted sexually oriented behavior in the workplace that results in discomfort or interference with the job

Shadow organizations where much of the real work gets accomplished, the shadow organization is revealed by social network analysis, which traces who talks to whom

Shared leadership the leader granting group members authority to carry out some of the leadership activities

Social awareness having empathy for others and having intuition about work problems

Socialization the process of coming to understand the values, norms, and customs essential for adapting to the organization

Social network analysis the mapping and measuring of relationships and links between and among people, groups, and organizations that reveals the shadow organization

Soft addiction ordinary behavior that if done to excess can wreak havoc with one's life

Star performer one of a small number of employees who contribute a disproportionate amount of output

Stress an internal reaction to any force that threatens to disturb a person's equilibrium; the internal reaction usually takes the form of emotional discomfort

Stressor the external or internal force that brings about the stress

Support system a group of people on whom one can rely for encouragement and comfort

Synergy a product of group effort whereby the output of the group exceeds the output possible if the members worked alone

Team a small number of people who are committed to common goals and approaches to which they hold themselves mutually accountable

Team player one who emphasizes group accomplishment and cooperation rather than individual achievement and not helping others

Teamwork work done with an understanding and commitment to group goals on the part of all team members

Teenage brain a stage of brain development in which people are easily influenced by their environment and more prone to impulsive behavior

Telecommuter employee who works at home or another offsite location full-time or part-time and sends output electronically to a central office

360-degree survey feedback instrument designed to gather information about how a leader can be more effective

Time leak anything you are doing or not doing that allows time to get away from you

Traditional mental set fixed way of thinking about objects and activities

Trust a person's confidence in another individual's intentions and motives and in the sincerity of that individual's words

Two-factor theory of work motivation two different sets of job factors; one set, the motivators, or satisfiers, can motivate and satisfy workers; the other set, dissatisfiers, or hygiene factors, can only prevent dissatisfaction

Type A behavior personality characteristics that lead a person into stressful situations; type A behavior has two main components: (1) the tendency to try to accomplish too many things in too little time and (2) free-floating hostility

Unknown area pane of Johari Window that contains information that you and others do not know about you

Upward communication the transmission of messages from lower to higher levels in an organization

Value the importance a person attaches to something; values are also tied to the enduring belief that one's mode of conduct is better than another mode of conduct

Variable pay incentive plan that intentionally pays good performers more money than poor performers

Webinar a web-based method of holding a seminar

Wellness program a company-sponsored activity designed to support employees as they learn and sustain behaviors that reduce health risk, improve quality of life, and enhance personal effectiveness

Whistle-blower an employee who reports wrongdoing in the organization to parties who can take action

Win–win belief that after conflict has been resolved, both sides should gain something of value

Workaholism neglecting the normal need for rest and relaxation; can lead to an addiction to work in which not working is an uncomfortable experience

Work engagement high levels of personal investment in the work tasks performed in a job

Work ethic a firm belief in the dignity and value of work and, therefore, important for favorably impressing a manager

Work–family conflict conflict that occurs when an individual has to perform multiple roles: worker, spouse or partner, and often parent

Work habits a person's characteristic approach to work, including such things as organization, priority setting, and handling of paperwork, e-mail, and intranets

Workplace bullying hurtful treatment of others in the workplace that is malicious and typically repeated

Worst-case scenario helpful decision-making aid that involves visualizing what you would do if the alternative chosen proved to be dreadful

Company and Organization Index

Name Index

Subject Index